T0135318

Mobile Edge Computing

Anwesha Mukherjee • Debashis De
Soumya K. Ghosh • Rajkumar Buyya

Editors

Mobile Edge Computing

 Springer

Editors
Anwesha Mukherjee
Department of Computer Science
Mahishadal Raj College
Mahishadal, West Bengal, India

Soumya K. Ghosh
Department of Computer Science
and Engineering
Indian Institute of Technology
(IIT) Kharagpur
Kharagpur, West Bengal, India

Debashis De
Centre of Mobile Cloud Computing
Department of Computer Science
and Engineering
Maulana Abul Kalam Azad
University of Technology
Kolkata, West Bengal, India

Rajkumar Buyya
Cloud Computing and Distributed Systems
(CLOUDS) Laboratory, School of
Computing and Information Systems
The University of Melbourne
Melbourne, VIC, Australia

ISBN 978-3-030-69895-9   ISBN 978-3-030-69893-5   (eBook)
https://doi.org/10.1007/978-3-030-69893-5

This Springer imprint is published by the registered company Springer Nature Switzerland AG
The registered company address is: Gewerbestrasse 11, 6330 Cham, Switzerland

Preface

Mobile edge computing (MEC) provides cloud computing services at the edge of mobile network, which facilitates developers, service providers as well as users. For low latency and high bandwidth services, edge computing–assisted IoT has become the pillar for the development of smart homes, smart health, smart traffic management, smart cities, etc. This book will discuss the overview of mobile edge computing along with its real time applications. The book is organized into three parts: Part I, Part II and Part III.

Part I contains seven chapters focusing on the architecture and working model of MEC. In chapter "Introduction to Mobile Edge Computing", an overview of MEC has been given, where the authors have discussed the architecture, applications and challenges of MEC. In chapter "Performance Analysis of Mobile, Edge and Cloud Computing Platforms for Distributed Applications", a comparative analysis of mobile, edge and cloud computing platforms has been provided for distributed applications. Chapter "Performance Analysis of Mobile, Edge and Cloud Computing Platforms for Distributed Applications" provides an experimental work on how to select the best mobile-aware computing environment based on parameters including application type, data size and network bandwidth quality. A comprehensive analysis has been provided that highlights the experiment results and provides recommendations for scheduling the execution of data-intensive applications on mobile-aware computation systems. In chapter "Geospatial Edge-Fog Computing: A Systematic Review, Taxonomy, and Future Directions", geospatial edge-fog computing has been discussed along with future research directions. Chapter "Study of Power Efficient 5G Mobile Edge Computing" has focused on the use of edge computing in the field of fifth generation mobile network. This chapter gives an all-encompassing outline of MEC, its energy-efficient innovation, potentials, needs and applications. Further, the authors have focused on energy-efficient resource allocation and task offloading. The future directions of 5G MEC have been also explored in chapter "Study of Power Efficient 5G Mobile Edge Computing". Sensor mobile edge computing, its architecture and its applications along with future research directions, been demonstrated in chapter "SMEC: Sensor Mobile Edge Computing". The integration of MEC with the Internet of Things (IoT) has been discussed in chapter "IoT Integration with MEC". Chapter "Green-aware Mobile Edge Computing for IoT: Challenges, Solutions and Future Directions" has illustrated a green-aware framework for MEC to address the energy-related challenges and provides a generic model formulation for the green MEC. Few state-of-the-art workloads offloading approaches to achieve green IoT have also been discussed and compared in comprehensive perspectives. Few future research directions related to energy efficiency in MEC have been also explored in this chapter.

Part II contains eight chapters focusing on the systems, platforms, services and issues of MEC. In chapter "Prescriptive Maintenance Using Markov Decision Process and GPU-accelerated Edge Computing", the authors have discussed the GPU-accelerated edge computing for predictive maintenance. A prescriptive maintenance method has been presented in this chapter for a distributed factory environment using the partially observable Markov decision process (POMDP) framework. In chapter "Software-Defined Multi-domain Tactical Networks: Foundations and Future Directions", the authors have discussed the software-defined multi-domain tactical networks. In this chapter, the authors have explicitly analysed the challenges and reviewed the current research initiatives in SDN-enabled tactical networks. Mobility is a vital factor in MEC, which has been the focus of chapters "Mobility Driven Cloud-Fog-Edge Framework for Location-aware Services: A Comprehensive Review" and "Mobility-Based Resource Allocation and Provisioning in Fog and Edge Computing Paradigms: Review, Challenges, and Future Directions". Chapter "Mobility Driven Cloud-Fog-Edge Framework for Location-aware Services: A Comprehensive Review" has discussed the concerns and challenges associated with mobility-driven cloud-fog-edge-based framework to provide several location-aware services to the endusers efficiently. Chapter "Mobility-Based Resource Allocation and Provisioning in Fog and Edge Computing Paradigms: Review, Challenges, and Future Directions" has discussed the current state –of the art of the methods and technologies used to manage the resources to support mobility in fog and edge environments. Chapter "Mobility-Based Resource Allocation and Provisioning in Fog and Edge Computing Paradigms: Review, Challenges, and Future Directions" has also explored future research directions to efficiently deliver smart services in real-time environments. Service migration and security are also important issues in MEC. Optimal migration decisions are challenging because they depend on the cloud environment, or edge nodes belong to different orchestrators, and security issues in the migration process must also be resolved in order to prevent unreliable requests. In chapter "Cross Border Service Continuity with 5G Mobile Edge", different approaches have been discussed to address these challenges by identifying the security implications of migration methods based on the blockchain integration. Chapter "Security in Critical Communication for Mobile Edge Computing based IoE Applications" has discussed the different security protocols in communications for the architectures which can be designed for MEC based Internet of Everything (IoE) applications. In chapter "Blockchain for Mobile Edge Computing: Consensus Mechanisms and Scalability", existing consensus protocols and scalability techniques in both well-established and next-generation blockchain architectures have been discussed, and from that the authors have evaluated the most suitable solutions for managing MEC services and discussed the benefits and drawbacks of the available alternatives. In chapter "Evaluation of Collaborative Intrusion Detection System Architectures in Mobile Edge Computing", the authors have outlined some of the characteristics relevant for evaluating collaborative intrusion detection systems (CIDS) deployment models and surveyed existing CIDS architectures in the context of MEC.

Part III contains seven chapters illustrating various applications of MEC. In chapter "Edge Computing based Conceptual Framework for Smart Health Care Applications Using Z-Wave and Homebased Wireless Sensor Network", the authors have studied the concepts of wireless biomedical image monitoring systems along with their features. The use of MEC in the field of agriculture has been discussed in chapter "Mobile Edge Computing Based Internet of Agricultural Things: A Systematic Review and Future Directions". In chapter "Deep learning in Computer Vision Through Mobile Edge Computing for IoT", the authors have described how deep convolutional neural network (CNN) through MEC can be a potential technique for IoT-based solutions. In chapter "Mobile Edge Computing for Content Distribution and Mobility Support in Smart Cities", the authors have discussed the aspects of distributed multi-tiered mobile edge computing (MEC) architectures, which offer data storage and processing capabilities closer to data sources and data consumers, taking into account how mobility impacts the management of such infrastructure. Chapter "Complex Event Processing in Sensor-Based Environments: Edge Computing Frameworks and Techniques" has focused on an edge computing framework that partitions the processing of sensor data at a mobile node placed at the edge and backend computations at a powerful server. The primary application of the framework is in the area of processing of complex events, each of which may correspond to the simultaneous occurrence of multiple raw events generated by sensors that are monitoring the phenomena of interest. Application of such complex event processing techniques spans smart buildings, smart machinery as well as smart healthcare systems. Chapter "Complex Event Processing in Sensor-Based Environments: Edge Computing Frameworks and Techniques" has focused on using the framework and techniques to a smartphone-based remote patient monitoring system and by using prototyping and measurement presents a rigorous performance analysis of the system. The application design and service provisioning for multi-access edge cloud has been discussed in chapter "Application Design and Service Provisioning for Multi-Access Edge Cloud (MEC)". Finally, in chapter "Simulating Fog Computing Applications Using iFogSim Toolkit" the simulation of fog computing applications has been demonstrated.

Mahishadal, West Bengal, India   Anwesha Mukherjee

Kolkata, West Bengal, India   Debashis De

Kharagpur, West Bengal, India   Soumya K. Ghosh

Melbourne, VIC, Australia   Rajkumar Buyya

Contents

Part I
Foundations and Architectural Elements

Introduction to Mobile Edge Computing

Anwesha Mukherjee, Debashis De, Soumya K. Ghosh, and Rajkumar Buyya

Abstract Fifth generation mobile networks aim to use multi-tier heterogeneous cellular networks integrated with cloud computing to provide users with low latency and energy-aware service. However, for high bandwidth and low latency services, edge/fog computing comes into the scenario. In edge/fog computing, the intermediate devices between end users and cloud participate in processing and storage of data as well as execution of applications. Mobile edge computing provides cloud computing services at the edge of mobile network, which facilitates the developers, service providers as well as the users. Internet of Things (IoT) has become a principle component to design smart technological solutions for our daily life. For low latency and high bandwidth services, edge computing assisted IoT has become the pillar for the development of smart home, smart health etc. This chapter will discuss the overview of mobile edge computing along with its real time applications.

Keywords Mobile edge computing · IoT · Power · Latency

A. Mukherjee (✉)
Department of Computer Science, Mahishadal Raj College, Mahishadal, West Bengal, India
e-mail: anweshamukherjee@ieee.org

D. De (✉)
Centre of Mobile Cloud Computing, Department of Computer Science and Engineering,
Maulana Abul Kalam Azad University of Technology, Kolkata, West Bengal, India
e-mail: dr.debashis.de@ieee.org

S. K. Ghosh
Department of Computer Science and Engineering, Indian Institute of Technology (IIT)
Kharagpur, Kharagpur, West Bengal, India
e-mail: skg@cse.iitkgp.ac.in

R. Buyya
Cloud Computing and Distributed Systems (CLOUDS) Laboratory, School of Computing
and Information Systems, The University of Melbourne, Melbourne, VIC, Australia
e-mail: rbuyya@unimelb.edu.au

© The Author(s), under exclusive license to Springer Nature Switzerland AG 2021
A. Mukherjee et al. (eds.), *Mobile Edge Computing*,
https://doi.org/10.1007/978-3-030-69893-5_1

1 Introduction

Mobile phones have become essential commodity in our daily life. With the advancement in wireless network, the number of mobile phone users have increased drastically. Moreover mobile phone usage is not limited within voice call and SMS service, but also has become a most popular equipment of accessing Internet anytime anywhere. Different mobile apps are nowadays available for online shopping, health monitoring, playing game, watching video etc. Fifth generation mobile network aims to use multi-tier heterogeneous cellular network integrated with cloud computing to provide users latency and energy-aware service [1, 2]. However, for high bandwidth and very low latency services, edge/fog computing comes into the scenario. In edge/fog computing the intermediate devices between end users and cloud participate in processing and storage of data as well as execution of applications [3–8]. Multi-Access Edge Computing which is formerly known as Mobile edge computing (MEC) [3] provides the cloud computing services at the edge of mobile network, which facilitates the developers, service providers as well as the users. In MEC the operators can open their Radio Access Network edge to the authorized third parties in order to provide rapid and flexible deployment of interactive services and applications for the users. Computations are performed usually at the local network edge in edge computing instead of putting it to the remote cloud, that in turn reduces the latency. The network providers meet the customers' demand of good coverage and high bandwidth through the help of MEC. MEC enables Information Technology (IT) and Cloud Computing facilities at the edge of the network. The objective of MEC is to minimize the congestion, reduce latency, and provides better Quality of Service (QoS) by accomplishing the related processing tasks closer to the end user. MEC can be implemented as cellular base stations which in turn can offer rapid application deployment. In [4] the authors have defined MEC as:

> MEC is a new network paradigm that provides information technology services and cloud computing capabilities within the mobile access network of mobile users and has become a technology.

MEC is a principle component for fifth generation (5G) network [4, 9]. As MEC is located close to the mobile users and within the Radio Access Network (RAN), low latency and high bandwidth access can be provided [4]. Hence, the QoS is improved. Moreover, service deployment and caching at the edge of the network helps to efficiently handle user requests and minimize congestion. In mobile edge computing computations are performed at the edge of the network, which helps to minimize the latency.

The MEC can be partitioned into three management systems (MS) [10]: (i) hosting infrastructure, (ii) application platform, and (iii) application. The first one contains a virtualization manager and virtualization layer. The second one offers traffic control, service registry, communication services and RAN information services. The third one serves as a virtualized machine for applications. Before getting deeper into the architecture of MEC, we will discuss few models closely related to MEC.

- Mobile cloud computing: Mobile devices usually have resource limitation, for which they may not be able to store huge volume of data or perform exhaustive computation. To solve the shortcomings, MCC has been developed. Mobile Cloud Computing (MCC) is a paradigm where the computations and storage take place inside the cloud instead of the mobile device [4, 11–15]. The user accesses the data from the cloud whenever required. Similarly when a computation has to be executed, that also is performed inside the cloud and the user gets the result. However, long distant cloud servers may increase the latency and the mobile device's power consumption, which may be crucial for real time application with hard deadline. In such situation it can be fruitful to bring the computation and storage facilities at the edge of the network.
- Fog computing: In case of the fog computing, the intermediate devices between end node and cloud servers, for example switch, router etc. takes part in data processing [8, 16–21]. These devices are known as fog devices. Edge devices in this case serve as a connecting devices with the end nodes. Fog computing is very much related to IoT nowadays. The data collected using IoT devices are preliminarily processed inside the fog device before being forwarded to the cloud. This in turn helps to reduce latency and improve the QoS subsequently.
- Cloudlet: A computer or a cluster of computers which offers the cloud services to the users by acting as an agent, is referred as cloudlet [22–27]. The cloudlet contains cache copies of the data stored inside the cloud. When a user requests to access to the data, the cloudlet meets the requirement. As a result the latency is reduced and the QoS is enhanced. However, cloudlet is mainly popular with wireless access environment.

The concept of MEC is much broader which makes it applicable for Wi-Fi as well as mobile network. Here, we will discuss on the use of cloudlet as well as cellular base station with edge server to depict the scenario of MEC.

2 Architecture of MEC

Mobile edge computing architecture contains the following components [4]:

- Mobile device
- Cellular base station (in case of cellular network)
- Cloudlet (in case of Wi-Fi)
- Edge Server
- Core network
- Cloud

In case of cellular network cellular base station is used along with an edge server. In this case it has to be noted that small cell with storage and computational ability

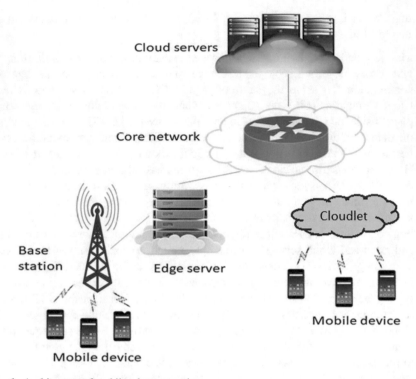

Fig. 1 Architecture of mobile edge computing

has been studied in few existing works [19, 21, 28–32]. In case of Wi-Fi i.e. Wireless Local Area Network (WLAN) or Wireless Metropolitan Area Network (WMAN), cloudlet is used. As cloudlet itself offers the storage and computation facilities, it can act as edge server. The MEC architecture is presented in Fig. 1. As observed from the figure, the mobile devices are connected with the base station (cellular network) or cloudlet (WMAN/WLAN). The base station is connected with edge server. The edge server is connected with the cloud through the core network.

The mobile device users or mobile users and edge server are the key components of MEC, on basis of which two categories of services come [4]:

- Mobile user oriented service
- Edge server oriented service

For the first category, mobile users request for offloading data and/or computation. For the second category, resource management is crucial. Mobile user oriented service mainly deal with offloading. Offloading is of two types [4]:

- Data offloading: User requests for storing data.
- Computation offloading: User requests for execution of a computation.

Edge server oriented service mainly deal with resource allocation and management. Load balancing is a vital issue when multiple users generate request. In such situations, efficient resource management is required.

2.1 Edge Server Placement

For cellular network, it is assumed that the edge servers of MEC are placed in the location of the base station [4]. For WLAN/WMAN, the edge servers are the cloudlets [4]. In WLAN, the number of mobile users is relatively less due to the small network coverage, whereas in WMAN has large number of mobile users due to its large network coverage. Hence, multiple cloudlets are to be placed at different locations. The mobile device access the cloudlet through an access point. If a cloudlet is co-located with an access point, the mobile users under that AP can get minimum cloudlet access delay. Otherwise, the mobile user under that access point if sends some request that will be relayed to nearby cloudlets, which can cause cumulative delay for multi-hop relays. Hence, the cloudlet placement is promising when a number of access points are present. This leads to two optimization problems [4]: cache placement [33] and server placement [34], both of which can be dealt with through a direct reduction to the capacitated K-median problem [35]. Nevertheless, this problem differs; here the assumption is that either there is no limitation in capacity of caches/servers or all the caches/servers have identical capacities though the capacity of each cloudlet may differ and different user requests also may need different resources for computation. This problem has been described as a new capacity cloudlet placement problem in [36]. Here, the objective is to put the cloudlets in such a way that the average access delay between the users and cloudlets can be minimized. To address this issue an effective heuristic solution with good scalability has been proposed in [36]. Another method for cloudlet placement and user allocation under them has been discussed in [24]. The selection of cloudlet while multiple cloudlets are available has been studied in [25, 26]. A location-aware service deployment method has been proposed in [37], where K-means is used. Here, the mobile users are divided into multiple clusters depending on their geographic location and the service instances are deployed to edge servers nearest to the mobile user clusters. The problem of access point ranking has been addressed in [38]. An adaptive integrated access point ordering scheme has been proposed in [38], where the connection features of the access point are analysed.

2.2 Resource Allocation

For the cellular base station based MEC framework, resource allocation and computation offloading both are considered. In MCC, the computation is executed inside the cloud and result is sent back to the mobile device. In MEC the offloading takes place usually inside the edge servers. In [39] the trade-off between latency and reliability in case of task offloading has been studied. A mobile user divides a task into subtasks and offloads those subtasks to multiple edge servers to reduce latency and offloading failure probability. For multi-user environment energy-efficient resource allocation has been discussed in [40], where the authors have considered computation-efficient models for negligible and non-negligible base station execution durations. A total weighting and energy consumption minimization problem has been developed for each model through optimal allocation of communication and computing resources. Computation offloading and interference management have been simultaneously taken into account in [41]. In this work physical resource block allocation, offloading decision and computation resource allocation are considered as optimization problems. Multi-access feature of 5G network has been considered in [42] to develop an energy-efficient computation offloading strategy, which can reduce energy consumption under delay constraint through the integration of radio resource allocation and optimized offloading. In [43] optimal resource allocation has been discussed to reduce the total energy consumption of multi-antenna access point under the respective computation latency constraint. In [44] a wireless network has been considered where each cellular base station is equipped with an edge server, which can assist the mobile user in performing computationally intensive tasks by offloading. The task offloading and resource allocation can be considered jointly in problem formulation to maximize the offloading profit for the user by reducing delay and energy consumption.

In cloudlet based MEC system the allocation of mobile user tasks is a promising issue while multiple cloudlets are present. In [45] a mixed integer linear programming optimization model has been discussed, where two types of cloudlets is used: local and global. When a mobile user asks for a service and the local cloudlets are unable to provide the service, then global cloudlet is used to handle this. In [46] the deployment of server by maintaining QoS and low cost has been highlighted. To solve this problem a low-complexity heuristic algorithm has been proposed. For low-latency and energy-efficiency, a joint optimization method has been proposed in [47]. In this work the bandwidth and resource allocation model are formulated as a Stackelberg game and an iterative algorithm has been used to get Stackelberg equilibrium [47]. Virtual machine (VM) migration is also a prime issue as the user is mobile. In [48] the mobile users get services from a cloudlet as an intermediate node. In [49] the authors have focused on reducing on-grid power consumption of cloudlet using migration. In [50] user mobility based VM migration has been performed between cloudlets. In [51] the VM migration problem has been considered as one-to-one contract game and a learning-based price control scheme has been proposed for better resource management. Two dynamic proxy VM migration schemes have been discussed in [52] to reduce the latency and energy consumption. The problem of dynamic service migration has been considered in [53], where a sequential decision making problem has been formulated based on Markov Decision Process.

3 Latency in MEC

In MEC, the storage and computation execution takes place inside the edge device. To calculate the latency the data transmission, propagation, computation execution and queuing latencies are calculated. During offloading the user device's power consumption is also calculated.

The data transmission latency in MEC is given as [25],

$$L_t = \sum_{i=1}^{h} (1 + U_{fi}) \frac{D_{tui}}{R_{ui}} + \sum_{j=1}^{k} (1 + D_{fj}) \frac{D_{tdj}}{R_{dj}}, \tag{1}$$

where U_{fi} is the failure rate in uplink, D_{tui} is the data amount transmitted in uplink, R_{ui} is the data transmission rate in uplink, between the communicating devices for hop i, D_{fj} is the failure rate in downlink, D_{tdj} is the data amount transmitted in downlink, R_{dj} is the data transmission rate in downlink, between the communicating devices for hop j, h is the number of hops in uplink and k is the number of hops in downlink.

The computation execution latency is given as [25],

$$L_c = \frac{I}{S}, \tag{2}$$

where I is the number of instructions to be executed for the computation and S is the instruction execution speed of the computing device (Edge server/cloudlet).

The propagation latency is given as [25],

$$L_p = \frac{D_p}{S_p}, \tag{3}$$

where D_p is the distance covered between the requesting and serving node, and S_p is the propagation speed.

If the queuing latency is denoted by L_q, the total latency is given as [25],

$$L = L_t + L_c + L_p + L_q. \tag{4}$$

The user device's power consumption during data transmission is given as [25],

$$P_t = P_a \cdot \left((1 + U_{fi}) \frac{D_{tu1}}{R_{u1}} \right) + P_i \cdot \left(\sum_{i=2}^{h} (1 + U_{fi}) \frac{D_{tui}}{R_{ui}} \right)$$
$$+ P_i \cdot \left(\sum_{j=1}^{k-1} (1 + D_{fj}) \frac{D_{tdj}}{R_{dj}} \right) + P_a \cdot \left((1 + D_{fk}) \frac{D_{tdk}}{R_{dk}} \right), \tag{5}$$

where P_a and P_i represents the mobile device's power consumption in active and idle modes respectively. For the first hop the communication takes place from the user to the next node in case of uplink. Hence, in this case the mobile device's power consumption in active mode is considered. Similarly, in case of downlink in case of the last hop (kth hope) the result is received by the mobile device. Thus, in this case the mobile device's power consumption in active mode is considered. In rest cases the mobile device's power consumption in idle mode is considered.

The user device's power consumption during computation is given as [25],

$$P_c = P_i \cdot L_c. \tag{6}$$

As the computation takes place inside the edge device, the power consumption of the mobile device in idle mode is considered.

The user device's power consumption during propagation is given as [25],

$$P_p = P_i \cdot L_p. \tag{7}$$

The user device's power consumption during queuing period is given as [25],

$$P_q = P_i \cdot L_q. \tag{8}$$

The total power consumption of the mobile device i.e. user device is then given as [25],

$$P = P_t + P_c + P_p + P_q. \tag{9}$$

In Fig. 2a and 2b the latency in computation offloading and user device's power consumption during that period, while using MEC and MCC are compared. This is observed that by bringing the computation at the network edge the latency is delivering the result to the mobile user has been reduced by ~45% and power consumption of the user device by ~35% than the mobile cloud computing framework.

In Table 1 three codes have been considered which are offloaded using MEC and MCC. The latency and user device's power consumption during that period are shown. From the experimental results it is observed that MEC reduces the latency by ~40% and user device's power consumption by ~30% with respect to MCC.

From the theoretical and experimental results we observe that MEC reduces the latency and power consumption of the user device than MCC in case of computation offloading.

4   Applications of MEC

There are several applications of MEC discussed as follows.

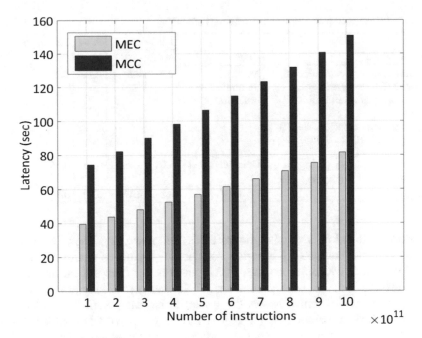

Fig. 2a Latency in MEC and MCC

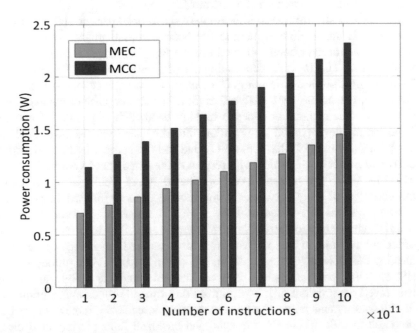

Fig. 2b Power consumption in MEC and MCC

Table 1 Latency and power consumption in code offloading

Device details	Code	Latency (sec)		Power consumption (W)	
		MEC	MCC	MEC	MCC
(i) User device: Asus ZenFone 5, RAM: 2 GB, storage: 16 GB, processor: Intel Atom Z2560 1.6 GHz. (ii) Edge server/cloudlet: Intel(R) Xeon(R) CPU E5-2667 0 @ 2.90GHz (Octa Core).	Matrix multiplication of order 100×100	2.7	4.5	0.15	0.22
(iii) Cloud server: Intel(R) Xeon(R) CPU ES-2667 0 @ 2.90 GHz (Hexa Core)	Creation of text file	5.01	8.35	0.25	0.36
	8-Queens puzzle	2.5	4.17	0.12	0.17

- **MEC in IoT**: IoT is an emerging research field nowadays. Use of MEC in IoT can enhance the QoS by bringing computation resources nearby the network edges [4]. It will offer scalable IoT framework for time critical applications. In IoT-MEC, the data collected using IoT devices get partially processed inside the edge devices, which makes the system faster, energy-efficient and reduces the network operation cost [4, 20]. A mobile edge IoT framework has been proposed in [52], where computing and storage resources are pushed nearby the IoT devices. Another approach EdgeIoT has been proposed in [54], where the data streams has been identified at the mobile edge.

- **MEC in video streaming**: To improve the Quality of Experience (QoE) of video streaming in smart cities a method has been proposed in [55], where users' mobility pattern have been followed and "Follow Me Edge" concept has been implemented. This method reduces the network traffic as well as the delay.

- **MEC in computation offloading**: Computation offloading between the wearable devices and cloud has been analysed in [56]. The convergence of cloud computing and mobile computing depends on high bandwidth edge to edge network. Edge and fog device based computation offloading has been discussed in [19]. It has been shown in [19] that the use of edge and fog computing has reduced the delay and power consumption with respect to the cloud based system.

- **MEC in UAV**: The use of UAV (Unmanned Aerial Vehicle) can strengthen the coverage of relay services for the mobile users in limited infrastructure wireless systems [4]. Based on UAV a MCC framework has been considered in [57], where the mobile UAVs have computing ability to offer computation offloading facilities to the mobile users. This in turn reduces energy consumption meeting the QoS requirements. Here, offloading has been done through uplink and downlink communications between the UAV and the mobile users. This has solved the problem of joint optimization of the bit allocation in uplink and downlink communications. An edge computing based RAN framework has been proposed in [58], where the fronthaul and backhaul links are mounted on the UAVs, which provides faster response time and flexible deployment.

- **MEC in smart healthcare**: In smart health care health sensor devices capture the health status, and the sensor data are stored and processed inside the cloud servers. After processing the data, the health status of the user can be detected. In [59–62], use of fog computing for health care has been discussed. In [20] the use of edge/fog framework in time-critical applications has been shown, where health care has been considered as a case study. By bringing the processing facility closer to the network edge, the delay which is a vital parameter for health care, can be reduced.
- **MEC in smart home**: In [32] the use of fog computing in smart home has been demonstrated. By bringing the computing and storage resources nearby the network edge, the delay, jitter, and energy consumption of the user device can be reduced.
- **MEC in retail**: In [31] a retail application has been discussed based on fog computing, which reduces the delay and energy consumption. The MEC can be used in retail which can improve the energy-efficiency and reduce the delay by pushing the computing and storage resources nearby the network edge.
- **MEC in agriculture**: In [63] the use of edge computing in agriculture has been discussed. The use of MEC in water monitoring system in case of agricultural domain has been explored in [64]. Edge computing can have various **prospects** like safety traceability of products, identification of pest, unmanned agricultural machinery etc. The use of edge computing in agricultural IoT has been demonstrated in [65].

5 Challenges in MEC

Though the use of MEC has provided various advantages like low latency, low power consumption etc., still several challenges remain. The selection of edge device to meet different service requirements of multiple mobile users is a key factor, for which novel strategy is required. Moreover, edge devices have limited resources. Therefore, low-complexity edge device placement and scheduling become vital when large numbers of mobile users are present. Furthermore, the request of mobile user variable, therefore dynamic strategy is required which will deal with user requirements. Instead of these challenges, there are several other issues discussed as follows.

- **Security**: The security threats and challenges in the edge-cloud computing framework has been studied in [66]. In [67] the authors have proposed a fog based storage framework to deal with cyber threat. As a large number of mobile users are present, then privacy is another important issue. Here, the assessment of each mobile node is also very important [68] along with the assessment of invulnerability [69]. In [70] an intrusion detection system has been discussed based on decision tree. A pre-processing algorithm has been designed in [70] to digitize strings in a given dataset and after that the whole data is normalized. Then a decision tree based scheme has been used for the intrusion detection system.

- **Resource management**: Resource allocation and management is another major factor in MEC. Though several schemes have been proposed for deployment of cloudlets for optimal service provisioning, still resource management is a vital challenge in MEC. As multiple users are present and their requirements are also different and most importantly the users have mobility, the resource allocation, release, VM migration, delivery of required service with minimal latency are key challenges.
- **Energy consumption**: In few existing works [19–21] it has been shown that the use of edge/fog based framework has reduced the power consumption of the user device. However, the energy consumption of the overall paradigm is also crucial. Another factor is decision making regarding offloading to edge/fog or cloud; whether partial offloading will be done or multi-level full offloading will be done that is also important to reduce the total energy consumption of the paradigm.
- **Mobility based service provisioning**: The service provisioning becomes a challenge when the customer is mobile. Here the devices have mobility and frequently change their locations in many cases. In such a scenario, tracking the mobility of the user is very important to deliver the required service. The use of artificial intelligence can play a vital role in this case. Several approaches on trajectory analysis exist [71–77]. The integration of these methods with service provisioning can open a new era in MEC.
- **User allocation based edge-cloud placement**: In order to improve the service quality and reduce the cost simultaneously, edge-cloud placement is an important factor. To deal with this challenge, user location can be considered and based on the location mobile users can be allocated to the edge-clouds [78]. This can be treated as a multi-objective optimization problem where the aim is load balancing and reduce the communication delay of the users.
- **Edge-based smart wearable system for maintenance in communication network**: The shortcomings of existing communication system are shortage of real time operation and data interaction maintenance. The decision making and execution process might suffer from inconvenient information interaction and shortage of field links. Use of edge computing can provide a smart wearable maintenance system for communication network [79]. An edge computing based IoT platform can provide real time guidance that can help to enhance the efficacy and quality of on-site maintenance.

Not only the issues discussed above, there are other challenges also like billing, simulation tool designing etc. For cloud computing simulation tools are already available in MATLAB, Python etc. Cloudsim [80, 81] is a popular simulator for cloud computing. EdgeCloudSim [82] has been built on Cloudsim to provide necessary functionalities for edge computing. For fog computing, iFogSim [83, 84] simulator is present. Resource allocation in fog computing considering user mobility has been studied in [85], where MyiFogSim has been built as an extension of iFogSim. To effectively promote MEC development and standardization of experimental design, a simulator is required that will provide the computation, storage and networking facilities at the edge to the mobile users.

6 Summary

This chapter has discussed the architecture and working model of mobile edge computing. The use of edge computing provides lower latency and power consumption of the user device with respect to the cloud only system in case of computation offloading, which we have shown in theoretical and experimental results. The applications and challenges of mobile edge computing are also discussed.

References

1. Zhang, Ke, Yuming Mao, Supeng Leng, Quanxin Zhao, Longjiang Li, Xin Peng, Li Pan, Sabita Maharjan, and Yan Zhang. "Energy-efficient offloading for mobile edge computing in 5G heterogeneous networks." *IEEE access* 4 (2016): 5896–5907.
2. Di Taranto, Rocco, Srikar Muppirisetty, Ronald Raulefs, Dirk Slock, Tommy Svensson, and Henk Wymeersch. "Location-aware communications for 5G networks: How location information can improve scalability, latency, and robustness of 5G." *IEEE Signal Processing Magazine* 31, no. 6 (2014): 102–112.
3. Mao, Yuyi, Changsheng You, Jun Zhang, Kaibin Huang, and Khaled B. Letaief. "A survey on mobile edge computing: The communication perspective." *IEEE Communications Surveys & Tutorials* 19, no. 4 (2017): 2322–2358.
4. Peng, Kai, Victor Leung, Xiaolong Xu, Lixin Zheng, Jiabin Wang, and Qingjia Huang. "A survey on mobile edge computing: focusing on service adoption and provision." *Wireless Communications and Mobile Computing* 2018 (2018).
5. Abbas, Nasir, Yan Zhang, Amir Taherkordi, and Tor Skeie. "Mobile edge computing: A survey." *IEEE Internet of Things Journal* 5, no. 1 (2017): 450–465.
6. Mach, Pavel, and Zdenek Becvar. "Mobile edge computing: A survey on architecture and computation offloading." *IEEE Communications Surveys & Tutorials* 19, no. 3 (2017): 1628–1656.
7. Taleb, Tarik, Konstantinos Samdanis, Badr Mada, Hannu Flinck, Sunny Dutta, and Dario Sabella. "On multi-access edge computing: A survey of the emerging 5G network edge cloud architecture and orchestration." *IEEE Communications Surveys & Tutorials* 19, no. 3 (2017): 1657–1681.
8. Yi, Shanhe, Cheng Li, and Qun Li. "A survey of fog computing: concepts, applications and issues." In *Proceedings of the 2015 workshop on mobile big data*, pp. 37–42. 2015.
9. Hu, Yun Chao, Milan Patel, Dario Sabella, Nurit Sprecher, and Valerie Young. "Mobile edge computing—A key technology towards 5G." *ETSI white paper* 11, no. 11 (2015): 1–16.
10. https://portal.etsi.org/Portals/0/TBpages/MEC/Docs/Mobile-edge_Computing_-_Introductory_Technical_White_Paper_V1%2018-09-14.pdf
11. Fernando, Niroshinie, Seng W. Loke, and Wenny Rahayu. "Mobile cloud computing: A survey." *Future generation computer systems* 29, no. 1 (2013): 84–106.
12. Dinh, Hoang T., Chonho Lee, Dusit Niyato, and Ping Wang. "A survey of mobile cloud computing: architecture, applications, and approaches." *Wireless communications and mobile computing* 13, no. 18 (2013): 1587–1611.

13. Othman, Mazliza, Sajjad Ahmad Madani, and Samee Ullah Khan. "A survey of mobile cloud computing application models." *IEEE communications surveys & tutorials* 16, no. 1 (2013): 393–413.
14. Huang, Dijiang. "Mobile cloud computing." *IEEE COMSOC Multimedia Communications Technical Committee (MMTC) E-Letter* 6, no. 10 (2011): 27–31.
15. De, Debashis. *Mobile cloud computing: architectures, algorithms and applications.* CRC Press, 2016.
16. Bonomi, Flavio, Rodolfo Milito, Jiang Zhu, and Sateesh Addepalli. "Fog computing and its role in the internet of things." In *Proceedings of the first edition of the MCC workshop on Mobile cloud computing*, pp. 13–16. 2012.
17. Vaquero, Luis M., and Luis Rodero-Merino. "Finding your way in the fog: Towards a comprehensive definition of fog computing." *ACM SIGCOMM Computer Communication Review* 44, no. 5 (2014): 27–32.
18. Mahmud, Redowan, Ramamohanarao Kotagiri, and Rajkumar Buyya. "Fog computing: A taxonomy, survey and future directions." In *Internet of everything*, pp. 103–130. Springer, Singapore, 2018.
19. Mukherjee, Anwesha, Priti Deb, Debashis De, and Rajkumar Buyya. "C2OF2N: a low power cooperative code offloading method for femtolet-based fog network." *The Journal of Supercomputing* 74, no. 6 (2018): 2412–2448.
20. Ghosh, Shreya, Anwesha Mukherjee, Soumya K. Ghosh, and Rajkumar Buyya. "Mobi-IoST: mobility-aware cloud-fog-edge-iot collaborative framework for time-critical applications." *IEEE Transactions on Network Science and Engineering* (2019).
21. Mukherjee, Anwesha, Priti Deb, Debashis De, and Rajkumar Buyya. "IoT-F2N: An energy-efficient architectural model for IoT using Femtolet-based fog network." *The Journal of Supercomputing* 75, no. 11 (2019): 7125–7146.
22. Satyanarayanan, Mahadev, Paramvir Bahl, Ramón Caceres, and Nigel Davies. "The case for vm-based cloudlets in mobile computing." *IEEE pervasive Computing* 8, no. 4 (2009): 14–23.
23. Gai, Keke, Meikang Qiu, Hui Zhao, Lixin Tao, and Ziliang Zong. "Dynamic energy-aware cloudlet-based mobile cloud computing model for green computing." *Journal of Network and Computer Applications* 59 (2016): 46–54.
24. Jia, Mike, Jiannong Cao, and Weifa Liang. "Optimal cloudlet placement and user to cloudlet allocation in wireless metropolitan area networks." *IEEE Transactions on Cloud Computing* 5.4 (2015): 725–737.
25. Mukherjee, Anwesha, Debashis De, and Deepsubhra Guha Roy. "A power and latency aware cloudlet selection strategy for multi-cloudlet environment." *IEEE Transactions on Cloud Computing* 7.1 (2016): 141–154.
26. Roy, Deepsubhra Guha, Debashis De, Anwesha Mukherjee, and Rajkumar Buyya. "Application-aware cloudlet selection for computation offloading in multi-cloudlet environment." *The Journal of Supercomputing* 73, no. 4 (2017): 1672–1690.
27. Jararweh, Yaser, Fadi Ababneh Lo'ai Tawalbeh, Fadi Ababneh, Abdallah Khreishah, and Fahd Dosari. "Scalable cloudlet-based mobile computing model." In *FNC/MobiSPC*, pp. 434–441. 2014.
28. Barbarossa, Sergio, Stefania Sardellitti, and Paolo Di Lorenzo. "Joint allocation of computation and communication resources in multiuser mobile cloud computing." 2013 *IEEE 14th workshop on signal processing advances in wireless communications (SPAWC)*. IEEE, 2013.
29. Yu, Shuai, and Rami Langar. "Collaborative Computation Offloading for Multi-access Edge Computing." *2019 IFIP/IEEE Symposium on Integrated Network and Service Management (IM)*. IEEE, 2019.
30. Mukherjee, Anwesha, and Debashis De. "Femtolet: A novel fifth generation network device for green mobile cloud computing." *Simulation Modelling Practice and Theory* 62 (2016): 68–87.
31. Mukherjee, Anwesha, Debashis De, and Rajkumar Buyya. "E2R-F2N: Energy-efficient retailing using a femtolet-based fog network." *Software: Practice and Experience* 49, no. 3 (2019): 498–523.

32. Deb, Priti, Anwesha Mukherjee, and Debashis De. "Design of Green Smart Room Using Fifth Generation Network Device Femtolet." *Wireless Personal Communications* 104, no. 3 (2019): 1037–1064.
33. Qiu, Lili, Venkata N. Padmanabhan, and Geoffrey M. Voelker. "On the placement of web server replicas." *Proceedings IEEE INFOCOM 2001. Conference on Computer Communications. Twentieth Annual Joint Conference of the IEEE Computer and Communications Society (Cat. No. 01CH37213).* Vol. 3. IEEE, 2001.
34. Yin, Hao, Xu Zhang, Tongyu Zhan, Ying Zhang, Geyong Min, and Dapeng Oliver Wu. "NetClust: A framework for scalable and pareto-optimal media server placement." *IEEE Transactions on Multimedia* 15, no. 8 (2013): 2114–2124.
35. Charikar, Moses, Sudipto Guha, Éva Tardos, and David B. Shmoys. "A constant-factor approximation algorithm for the k-median problem." *Journal of Computer and System Sciences* 65, no. 1 (2002): 129–149.
36. Xu, Zichuan, Weifa Liang, Wenzheng Xu, Mike Jia, and Song Guo. "Efficient algorithms for capacitated cloudlet placements." *IEEE Transactions on Parallel and Distributed Systems* 27, no. 10 (2015): 2866–2880.
37. Liang, Tyng-Yeu, and You-Jie Li. "A location-aware service deployment algorithm based on k-means for cloudlets." *Mobile Information Systems* 2017 (2017).
38. Yang, Guoyu, Qibo Sun, Ao Zhou, Shangguang Wang, and Jinglin Li. "Access point ranking for cloudlet placement in edge computing environment." In *2016 IEEE/ACM Symposium on Edge Computing (SEC)*, pp. 85–86. IEEE, 2016.
39. Liu, Jianhui, and Qi Zhang. "Offloading schemes in mobile edge computing for ultra-reliable low latency communications." *IEEE Access* 6 (2018): 12825–12837.
40. Guo, Junfeng, Zhaozhe Song, Ying Cui, Zhi Liu, and Yusheng Ji. "Energy-efficient resource allocation for multi-user mobile edge computing." In *GLOBECOM 2017-2017 IEEE Global Communications Conference*, pp. 1–7. IEEE, 2017.
41. Wang, Chenmeng, F. Richard Yu, Chengchao Liang, Qianbin Chen, and Lun Tang. "Joint computation offloading and interference management in wireless cellular networks with mobile edge computing." *IEEE Transactions on Vehicular Technology* 66, no. 8 (2017): 7432–7445.
42. Zhang, Ke, Yuming Mao, Supeng Leng, Quanxin Zhao, Longjiang Li, Xin Peng, Li Pan, Sabita Maharjan, and Yan Zhang. "Energy-efficient offloading for mobile edge computing in 5G heterogeneous networks." *IEEE access* 4 (2016): 5896-5907.
43. Wang, Feng, Jie Xu, Xin Wang, and Shuguang Cui. "Joint offloading and computing optimization in wireless powered mobile-edge computing systems." *IEEE Transactions on Wireless Communications* 17, no. 3 (2017): 1784–1797.
44. Tran, Tuyen X., and Dario Pompili. "Joint task offloading and resource allocation for multi-server mobile-edge computing networks." *IEEE Transactions on Vehicular Technology* 68.1 (2018): 856–868.
45. Al-Quraan, Muneera, Mahmoud Al-Ayyoub, Yaser Jararweh, Lo'ai Tawalbeh, and Elhadj Benkhelifa. "Power optimization of large scale mobile cloud system using cooperative cloudlets." In *2016 IEEE 4th International Conference on Future Internet of Things and Cloud Workshops (FiCloudW)*, pp. 34–38. IEEE, 2016.
46. Yao, Hong, Changmin Bai, Muzhou Xiong, Deze Zeng, and Zhangjie Fu. "Heterogeneous cloudlet deployment and user-cloudlet association toward cost effective fog computing." *Concurrency and Computation: Practice and Experience* 29, no. 16 (2017): e3975.
47. Meng, Sachula, Ying Wang, Zhongyu Miao, and Kai Sun. "Joint optimization of wireless bandwidth and computing resource in cloudlet-based mobile cloud computing environment." *Peer-to-Peer Networking and Applications* 11, no. 3 (2018): 462–472.
48. Raei, Hassan, Nasser Yazdani, and Reza Shojaee. "Modeling and performance analysis of cloudlet in Mobile Cloud Computing." *Performance Evaluation* 107 (2017): 34–53.
49. Sun, Xiang, and Nirwan Ansari. "Green cloudlet network: A sustainable platform for mobile cloud computing." *IEEE Transactions on Cloud Computing* (2017).
50. Mukherjee, Anwesha, Deepsubhra Guha Roy, and Debashis De. "Mobility-aware task delegation model in mobile cloud computing." *The Journal of Supercomputing* 75, no. 1 (2019): 314–339.

51. Kim, Sungwook. "One-on-one contract game–based dynamic virtual machine migration scheme for Mobile Edge Computing." *Transactions on Emerging Telecommunications Technologies* 29, no. 1 (2018): e3204.
52. Ansari, Nirwan, and Xiang Sun. "Mobile edge computing empowers internet of things." *IEICE Transactions on Communications* 101, no. 3 (2018): 604–619.
53. Wang, Shiqiang, Rahul Urgaonkar, Murtaza Zafer, Ting He, Kevin Chan, and Kin K. Leung. "Dynamic service migration in mobile edge-clouds." In *2015 IFIP Networking Conference (IFIP Networking)*, pp. 1–9. IEEE, 2015.
54. Sun, Xiang, and Nirwan Ansari. "EdgeIoT: Mobile edge computing for the Internet of Things." *IEEE Communications Magazine* 54, no. 12 (2016): 22–29.
55. Taleb, Tarik, Sunny Dutta, Adlen Ksentini, Muddesar Iqbal, and Hannu Flinck. "Mobile edge computing potential in making cities smarter." *IEEE Communications Magazine* 55, no. 3 (2017): 38–43.
56. Ragona, Claudio, Fabrizio Granelli, Claudio Fiandrino, Dzmitry Kliazovich, and Pascal Bouvry. "Energy-efficient computation offloading for wearable devices and smartphones in mobile cloud computing." In *2015 IEEE Global Communications Conference (GLOBECOM)*, pp. 1–6. IEEE, 2015.
57. Jeong, Seongah, Osvaldo Simeone, and Joonhyuk Kang. "Mobile edge computing via a UAV-mounted cloudlet: Optimization of bit allocation and path planning." *IEEE Transactions on Vehicular Technology* 67, no. 3 (2017): 2049–2063.
58. Dong, Yanjie, Md Zoheb Hassan, Julian Cheng, Md Jahangir Hossain, and Victor CM Leung. "An edge computing empowered radio access network with UAV-mounted FSO fronthaul and backhaul: Key challenges and approaches." *IEEE Wireless Communications* 25, no. 3 (2018): 154–160.
59. Mukherjee, Anwesha, Debashis De, and Soumya K. Ghosh. "FogIoHT: A Weighted Majority Game Theory based Energy-Efficient Delay-Sensitive Fog Network for Internet of Health Things." *Internet of Things* (2020): 100181.
60. Ahmad, Mahmood, Muhammad Bilal Amin, Shujaat Hussain, Byeong Ho Kang, Taechoong Cheong, and Sungyoung Lee. "Health fog: a novel framework for health and wellness applications." *The Journal of Supercomputing* 72, no. 10 (2016): 3677–3695.
61. Tuli, Shreshth, Nipam Basumatary, Sukhpal Singh Gill, Mohsen Kahani, Rajesh Chand Arya, Gurpreet Singh Wander, and Rajkumar Buyya. "Healthfog: An ensemble deep learning based smart healthcare system for automatic diagnosis of heart diseases in integrated iot and fog computing environments." *Future Generation Computer Systems* 104 (2020): 187–200.
62. Aazam, Mohammad, Sherali Zeadally, and Khaled A. Harras. "Health Fog for Smart Healthcare." *IEEE Consumer Electronics Magazine* 9, no. 2 (2020): 96–102.
63. O'Grady, M. J., D. Langton, and G. M. P. O'Hare. "Edge computing: A tractable model for smart agriculture?." *Artificial Intelligence in Agriculture* 3 (2019): 42–51.
64. Fan, D. H., and S. Gao. "The application of mobile edge computing in agricultural water monitoring system." In *IOP Conference Series: Earth and Environmental Science, IOP Publishing* 191.1 (2018): 012015.
65. Zhang, Xihai, Zhanyuan Cao, and Wenbin Dong. "Overview of Edge Computing in the Agricultural Internet of Things: Key Technologies, Applications, Challenges." *IEEE Access* 8 (2020): 141748–141761.
66. Roman, Rodrigo, Javier Lopez, and Masahiro Mambo. "Mobile edge computing, fog et al.: A survey and analysis of security threats and challenges." *Future Generation Computer Systems* 78 (2018): 680–698.
67. Wang, Tian, Jiyuan Zhou, Minzhe Huang, MD Zakirul Alam Bhuiyan, Anfeng Liu, Wenzheng Xu, and Mande Xie. "Fog-based storage technology to fight with cyber threat." *Future Generation Computer Systems* 83 (2018): 208–218.
68. Peng, Kai, Rongheng Lin, Binbin Huang, Hua Zou, and Fangchun Yang. "Node importance of data center network based on contribution matrix of information entropy." *Journal of Networks* 8, no. 6 (2013): 1248.

69. Peng, Kai, and Binbin Huang. "The invulnerability studies on data center network." *International Journal of Security and Its Applications* 9, no. 11 (2015): 167–186.
70. Peng, Kai, Victor Leung, Lixin Zheng, Shangguang Wang, Chao Huang, and Tao Lin. "Intrusion detection system based on decision tree over big data in fog environment." *Wireless Communications and Mobile Computing* 2018 (2018).
71. Ghosh, Shreya, and Soumya K. Ghosh. "Thump: Semantic analysis on trajectory traces to explore human movement pattern." *Proceedings of the 25th International Conference Companion on World Wide Web*. 2016.
72. Gabrielli, Lorenzo, Salvatore Rinzivillo, Francesco Ronzano, and Daniel Villatoro. "From tweets to semantic trajectories: mining anomalous urban mobility patterns." In *International Workshop on Citizen in Sensor Networks*, pp. 26–35. Springer, Cham, 2013.
73. Siła-Nowicka, Katarzyna, Jan Vandrol, Taylor Oshan, Jed A. Long, Urška Demšar, and A. Stewart Fotheringham. "Analysis of human mobility patterns from GPS trajectories and contextual information." *International Journal of Geographical Information Science* 30, no. 5 (2016): 881–906.
74. Wagner, Ricardo, José Antonio Fernandes de Macedo, Alessandra Raffaetà, Chiara Renso, Alessandro Roncato, and Roberto Trasarti. "Mob-warehouse: A semantic approach for mobility analysis with a trajectory data warehouse." In *International Conference on Conceptual Modeling*, pp. 127–136. Springer, Cham, 2013.
75. Zheng, Zhong, Soora Rasouli, and Harry Timmermans. "Two-regime Pattern in Human Mobility: Evidence from GPS Taxi Trajectory Data." *Geographical Analysis* 48, no. 2 (2016): 157–175.
76. Li, T., T. Pei, Y. C. Yuan, C. Song, W. Wang, and G. Yang. "A review on the classification, patterns and applied research of human mobility trajectory." *Progress in Geography* 33, no. 7 (2014): 938–948.
77. Ghosh, Shreya, and Soumya K. Ghosh. "Exploring the association between mobility behaviours and academic performances of students: a context-aware traj-graph (CTG) analysis." Progress in Artificial Intelligence 7, no. 4 (2018): 307–326.
78. Guo, Yan, Shangguang Wang, Ao Zhou, Jinliang Xu, Jie Yuan, and Ching-Hsien Hsu. "User allocation-aware edge cloud placement in mobile edge computing." *Software: Practice and Experience* 50, no. 5 (2020): 489–502.
79. Rui, Lanlan, Yabin Qin, Biyao Li, Ying Wang, and Haoqiu Huang. "SEWMS: An edge-based smart wearable maintenance system in communication network." *Software: Practice and Experience* 50, no. 5 (2020): 611–629.
80. Buyya, Rajkumar, Rajiv Ranjan, and Rodrigo N. Calheiros. "Modeling and simulation of scalable Cloud computing environments and the CloudSim toolkit: Challenges and opportunities." *2009 International Conference on High Performance Computing and Simulation*. IEEE, 2009.
81. Calheiros, Rodrigo N., Rajiv Ranjan, Anton Beloglazov, Cesar A. F. De Rose, and Rajkumar Buyya. "CloudSim: a toolkit for modeling and simulation of cloud computing environments and evaluation of resource provisioning algorithms." *Software: Practice and experience* 41, no. 1 (2011): 23–50.
82. Sonmez, Cagatay, Atay Ozgovde, and Cem Ersoy. "Edgecloudsim: An environment for performance evaluation of edge computing systems." *Transactions on Emerging Telecommunications Technologies* 29, no. 11 (2018): e3493.
83. Gupta, Harshit, Amir Vahid Dastjerdi, Soumya K. Ghosh, and Rajkumar Buyya. "iFogSim: A toolkit for modeling and simulation of resource management techniques in the Internet of Things, Edge and Fog computing environments." *Software: Practice and Experience* 47, no. 9 (2017): 1275–1296.
84. Mahmud, Redowan, and Rajkumar Buyya. "Modelling and simulation of fog and edge computing environments using iFogSim toolkit." *Fog and edge computing: Principles and paradigms* (2019): 1–35.
85. Lopes, Márcio Moraes, Wilson A. Higashino, Miriam AM Capretz, and Luiz Fernando Bittencourt. "Myifogsim: A simulator for virtual machine migration in fog computing." In *Companion Proceedings of the 10th International Conference on Utility and Cloud Computing*, pp. 47–52. 2017.

Performance Analysis of Mobile, Edge and Cloud Computing Platforms for Distributed Applications

Mohammad Alkhalaileh, Rodrigo N. Calheiros, Quang Vinh Nguyen, and Bahman Javadi

Abstract Mobile devices and their corresponding services have become ubiquitous and vital components of almost every aspect of social and business life. Mobile services enhance collaboration, communication, monitoring, tracking, streaming, and many other applications. This intense and continuous engagement presents significant challenges due to mobile devices' limited computation power, dependence on batteries, and sensitivity to transmission network capacity and availability. A common technique for resolving mobile shortcomings is to migrate (offload) complex computations to more powerful resources such as edges, clouds, mobile clouds or integration. However, the huge variety in mobile applications complicates alignment of the unique characteristics and user quality of service (QoS) requirements for each application to a convenient offloading plan. The availability of powerful resources at different computing layers is another challenge for offloading techniques. This chapter was designed to generate insights into ways the mobile communications industry could realise cost savings and high-quality data-aware offloading solutions by adopting new technologies such as edge computing and region-based local networks. To demonstrate these insights, this chapter provides an experimental work on how to select the best mobile-aware computing environment based on parameters including application type, data size and network bandwidth quality. Moreover, this chapter provides a comprehensive analysis that highlights the experiment results and provides recommendations for scheduling the execution of data-intensive applications on mobile-aware computation systems.

Keywords Hybrid mobile cloud · Mobile edge-cloud · Data-intensive applications modelling · Computation offloading · Mobile application scheduling · Offloading performance analysis

M. Alkhalaileh · R. N. Calheiros · Q. V. Nguyen · B. Javadi (✉)
School of Computer, Data and Mathematical Sciences, Western Sydney University,
Sydney, NSW, Australia
e-mail: mohammad.nour@westernsydney.edu.au; r.calheiros@westernsydney.edu.au;
q.nguyen@westernsydney.edu.au; b.javadi@westernsydney.edu.au

© The Author(s), under exclusive license to Springer Nature Switzerland AG 2021   21
A. Mukherjee et al. (eds.), *Mobile Edge Computing*,
https://doi.org/10.1007/978-3-030-69893-5_2

1 Introduction

The exponential growth of the mobile telecommunications industry and networking systems has motivated the development of a new generation of mobile applications to provide services for a wide range of industrial and social communication applications, smart systems, and collaboration tools. Mobile computing (MC) has struggled to cope with the huge and growing number of mobile application users, as well as the complexity of some applications, due to limitations on processing capabilities and short battery life [24]. A wide range of computing solutions emerged to overcome these MC challenges by migrating complex workloads to more powerful resources, a process known as mobile offloading [16]. Such resources are located on central clouds and network edges.

Cloud computing offers scalable, reliable and on-demand services which can augment mobile devices to reduce their shortcomings of limited computation and storage. This computing model is known by Mobile cloud computing (MCC) and it's the dominating model employed to run a high percentage of today's mobile applications. However, with the emergence of new application models for Internet of things (IoT) and data streaming, MCC experiences high communication latency while offloading data to remote servers due to large distances between them and the high number of routing devices involved [1]. Thus, researchers have turned their attention towards incorporating approximate resources such as cloudlets [26] and edges [27]. Mobile edge computing (MEC) [20] saves device energy through reducing the time needed to transfer large data files to the cloud. The majority of research work on offloading optimisation with MEC has focused on proposing latency-based workload distribution polices and techniques which consider the capability of edge resources and network performance. However, in data-intensive applications like data analytics, natural language processing and face recognition, computation complexity must also considered to minimise economic cost and energy consumption and achieve the required QoS achievement [21, 36]. The integration between edge and cloud resources provide benefits from the availability access of the edge resources and the high capability of cloud resources. The collaborative computation model between MCC and MEC is referenced to mobile edge cloud computing (MECC) [25].

Cloud-based resource allocation for mobile data-intensive applications is challenging. Simultaneously minimising monetary costs and enhancing customers' QoE requires an efficient cost-optimisation model [11]. Kang et al. [14] proposed a data-centric offloading framework called Neurosurgeon, which differs from a control-centric framework because it produces execution plans or partition decisions according to the structure of data topology and data dependency between application tasks. Zhou et al. [41] proposed a cost-aware offloading middleware on MCC system. Their optimisation model considered the data size parameter at small-scale which is limited to align the challenges of data-intensive tasks scheduling. Patel et al. [23] studied the efficiency of adopting edge-based computing models for data-intensive applications. The work showed a significant reduction on data transfer latency to capture real-time context information. However, multi-user data-intensive applications on edge computing systems bring additional offloading complexity for fair edge resources distribution and computation load balancing. Enzai et al. [10] applied a heuristic algorithm for multi-user offloading scheduling in MECC system. The multi-objective optimisations adopting a weighting model to prioritize scheduling based on heuristics. Vu et al. [33] worked on the multi-user offloading optimisation and adopted a mixed integer nonlinear programming (MINLP) technique on joint MECCC systems. The literature includes many studies of ways to meet the requirements of computation offloading. Some of these focus on techniques to coordinate computing resources, while others pay more attention to offloading optimisation techniques and algorithms. However, few researchers have attempted to map data-intensive offloading challenges and proposed data-centric offloading and scheduling frameworks and techniques.

The size of application data, the quality of the communication network, and the application structure are crucial dimensions of the offloading optimisation process. This chapter presents a comprehensive analysis which culminates in recommendations for offloading data-intensive mobile applications on mobile-aware computation systems. Specifically, this chapter provides a deep analysis of how variables like application data size and network quality affect an application scheduler's selection of a mobile-aware computation environment, i.e., MC, MCC or MECC.

The variation in mobile usage in many application contexts imposes the necessity of handling different types of application models. In this chapter, we consider the features of three models: bag of tasks (BoT), workflows and IoT. These features determine the dependency between application tasks in terms of computation and sharing data. Thus, application complexity and structure need to be considered while planning for offloading to a mobile-aware computing environment.

Each computing model has its own unique characteristics and is appropriate for specific types of mobile applications. For example, MC is reduces computation cost, MEC highly recommended for time-sensitive applications, MCC can support computation-intensive and data-intensive applications with powerful computation capacity, and MECC integrates MEC and MCC to resolve the emergent direction scope of data analytics and IoT-based applications. Furthermore, user QoS requirements are varied, ranging from saving mobile energy, reducing computation cost, and minimising application execution delay. The question is how a user can select a mobile-aware computing paradigm for a specific application such that it satisfies QoS requirements and considers the application structure and contextual execution environment. Moreover, this chapter was designed to generate insights into ways the mobile communications industry could realise cost savings and high-quality data-aware offloading solutions by adopting new technologies such as edge computing and region-based local networks.

This chapter is structured as follows. Section 2 outlines mobile-aware computing environments. Section 3 describes the system architecture. Section 4 describes the system model, offloading technique and cost models, while experimental work is presented in Sect. 5. Results, discussion and recommendations are provided in Sect. 6. Lastly, Sect. 7 illustrates the main findings and provide suggestions for future work.

2 Overview of Cloud, Edge and Mobile Environments

This section describes the adopted MECC architecture. Figure 1 shows three levels of computation environment. At each level, different types of resources are integrated to process mobile application tasks. It is assumed that data can be generated from fixed data storage (local edge or cloud), or from IoT devices like sensors. IoT data are included to study the impact of data transfer on the offloading optimisation decision. Mobile devices are the core computing units for mobile-aware computing models and are assumed for their capability to execute low-intensive application tasks. In MC, all the computation for an application, including task processing and data transfer, is handled by mobile resources, which may encounter deficiencies in delivering high-performance computation for complex functions at the lowest possible energy level. However, mobile device input/output processing and network communications are energy-hungry components, and even though the mobile industry has evolved rapidly, intensive computing remains a major challenge.

Cloud resources are integrated with mobile devices to avoid these shortcomings of computation and storage. Cloud computing is a service-based computing model which delivers computation, storage and communication resources, usually as a

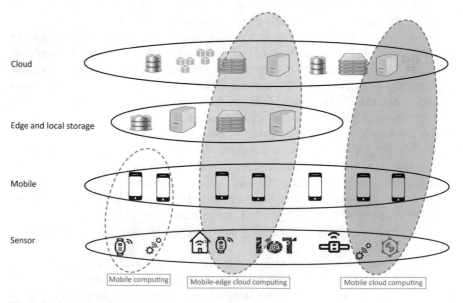

Fig. 1 Mobile edge cloud computing architecture

scalable service and under the "pay-as-you-go" business model [5, 12, 31, 39]. It represents the highest level of computation power in the MCC model. It receives offloading requests, either indirectly forwarded from edges or directly forwarded by mobile devices. Satyanarayanan et al. [26] discussed the cloud computing model and confirmed its preferability as a solution for augmenting the capacities of mobile devices. Integration of cloud computing is promising to mitigate the problems of MC model, for many reasons. First, cloud computing can extend mobile device battery life by migrating complex processing to powerful servers, thus minimising the total execution time on mobile devices. Second, cloud computing providers enable storing and accessing data stores via wireless communication protocols. For instance, cloud computing supports mobile users with image exchange and processing services, which is high considerable for saving energy and storage space. Third, cloud resources can be scaled to meet unpredictable mobile application development demands. Lastly, the availability of multiple cloud service providers makes it feasible to integrate different cloud services to satisfy users' demands.

In MCC architecture, a mobile device can benefit from cloud computation capabilities to reduce the overhead of running heavy workloads locally in the user's mobile device. One limitation of MCC is the high latency of migrating large datasets to a distant data centre. Edge computing can resolve the latency issue by strategic allocation for edge resources closer to users in the access network, which allows high data and service accessibility for network information in real time [34].

Mobile edge computing is not an appropriate computing model for handling large-scale applications, which involve migrating high computation and data workloads. To overcome the physical limitations of edge resources, The collaborative computation model, mobile edge-cloud computing (MECC) is proposed to exploit the availability of huge computation resources in the cloud layer, and moving computation power at the network edge and closer to data sources to reduce the network latency and achieve a cost-efficient execution model [25].

3 System Architecture

Figure 2 presents the MECC offloading framework and corresponding resource layers. The cloud layer provides powerful and scalable resources for computation, storage and networking services. The edge layer includes all computation devices on the path to cloud. Edge devices are accessible via a range of network communication interfaces, including WiFi and cellular networks. The application layer represents the user interaction layer needed to perform local processing and communicate with external resources.

The optimisation engine provides the core services for offloading decision-making; these include context-ware profiling, cost estimation and decision-making. The engine components are explained as follows.

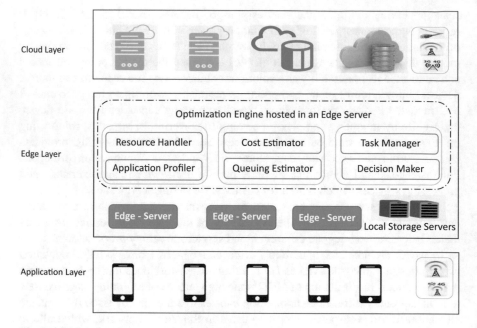

Fig. 2 Mobile-edge cloud computing (MECC) framework

- *Application Profiler*: The profiler records data about the optimisation decision in the context of the current status of the computing environment, and includes energy consumption (for computation and data transfer), network performance (latency and bandwidth) and application execution (offloading decision and, total time and cost).
- *Resource Handler*: Its mission is collecting data about system resources to check their capabilities and availability with regard to computation, storage, energy, and bandwidth. Collected data are sent to the profiling component. Moreover, the resource handler is liable for managing task execution on target computation environment according to the task allocation plan.
- *Queuing Estimator*: Responsible for predicting the task waiting time for execution on cloud and edge servers. The estimate is subject to the distribution of received tasks at the computation server and the capacity of the server itself.
- *Cost Estimator*: The cost estimator calculates the optimisation values of execution time, cost and energy, based on profiling data, to produce an accurate optimisation decision.
- *Task Manager*: The task manager executes the offloading plan by sending application tasks to the resource handler, and then updates profiling data.
- *Decision-Maker*: The decision-maker's mission is to generate and evaluate an alternative application allocation plan. It communicates with the profiler and the queuing estimator to evaluate an offloading plan. The best solution is passed to the resource handler for execution.

The next section describes the proposed system model.

4 System Model

The MECC system is a collaboration between a cloud, M edge devices and N mobiles. Table 1 presents the mathematical symbols used in modelling the application, as well as the cost models. The modelling of a mobile device P_m is represented as follows.

$$P_m = \{\beta, \beta_{cost}, d_m, e_m, w_m\} \tag{1}$$

A mobile device can communicate with remote resources at cloud and edge layers over WiFi and cellular networks. We assumed static provisioning for edge and cloud resources, and that the allocation process is based on heuristics, which are provided by the profiling process. However, with static provisioning, unpredictable workloads can be challenging. To reduce the impact of workload uncertainty, a queuing system is implemented at remote servers to manage the execution of application tasks in case servers become overloaded. The modelling of a remote server P_r is represented as follows:

$$P_r = \{\beta, \beta_{cost}, p, w_r\} \tag{2}$$

4.1 Application Model

An application model represents the internal structure of the application tasks and how they are related in terms of computation and data dependency. In this chapter, we present work on three types of application models: BoT, workflow and IoT.

Table 1 Problem modelling notation

Symbol	Definition
t_i	Application task i
L_i	Data input location
s_i	Data size
I_i	Task complexity in MIPS
∂_i	Task deadline
β	Available network bandwidth
β_{cost}	Data transfer cost with bandwidth β
w_i	Processor speed in MIPS
d_m	Available storage on mobile (MB)
e_m	Available energy (J)
p	Remote processing cost ($/hour)
ω_i	task t_i data sensitivity factor
l	The network latency

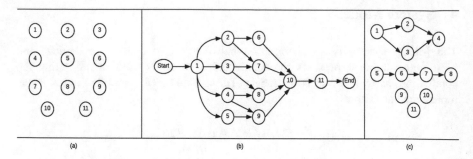

Fig. 3 Application models abstraction. (**a**) BoT. (**b**) Workflow. (**c**) IoT

Figure 3 shows an abstraction of these models. Figure 3a shows the BoT, which is a task-independent application model in which tasks are fully isolated in their input data and computation logic [9]. This model is expected to have additional overheads in terms of data transfer time and cost. The independence of tasks increases the ability to transfer and process large amount of data.

In contrast, in the workflow model, tasks are dependent; they transfer their processing outcomes to corresponding tasks based on the workflow structure. The dependent structure of a workflow model has a significant impact on optimising application execution, because it determines the data flow and the amount of data to be passed between tasks. It is convenient to construct workflow execution schedules that reduce the time and cost overheads of transferring data between dependent tasks. A workflow is a common application model representation for many application domains like scientific domains, stream processing and data analysis [2]. Lastly, IoT applications, in which data is collected from IoT devices (such as sensors) either in online or offline mode, are common in application domains like data analytics and real-time monitoring [8]. This chapter describes an investigation of the contribution of the IoT data collection stage to application offloading optimisation. It is assumed that an IoT application is a combination of BoT and workflow models.

The application modelling includes high-level task modelling to reflect the three applications models (BoT, workflow and IoT). A data-intensive mobile application A represents the execution of a dependent or independent set of tasks, which is modelled as:

$$A = \{t_1, t_2, \ldots, t_n\} \tag{3}$$

where n is the number of tasks. A task t_i is modelled as:

$$t_i = \{L_i, s_i, w_i, \partial_i\} \tag{4}$$

The data size and location are incorporated in the task modelling to reflect the challenges of data-intensive application offloading and demonstrate how it differs from problems like computation-intrusive and latency-sensitive offloading optimisation. To reduce the impact of data distribution over resource layers, we assumed that for an application task, the input data file is centrally allocated in a single file location. Moreover, we assumed that only intermediate data processing is stored at the edge layer, and long-term storage is only available in the cloud system. Intermediate data storage is applied in a range of data-aware applications such as smart homes, autonomous cars, real time monitoring and social sensing. This assumption is highlighted in the resource architecture shown in Fig. 2. In the rest of this section we present and discuss of the cost estimation models used in the offloading optimisation process.

4.2 Task Execution Time Model

The execution time for a task t_i includes the computation time D_i^P, data communication time D_i^C, and average task waiting time D_i^W for execution outside the mobile device. However, task complexity, which is measured by number of instructions I_i, and processing power for the destination machine processor w_{target}, are used in computing the task execution time, as shown in Eq. 6. In the same Equation, the data sensitivity factor ω_i is included to apply the contribution of s_i to the task processing time. A profiling process is conducted to compute the sensitivity factor with consideration of task complexity and estimation stability.

$$D_i = D_i^P + D_i^C + D_i^W \tag{5}$$

$$D_i^P = \frac{I_i}{w_{target}} + (s_i . \omega_i) \tag{6}$$

$$D_i^C = \frac{s_i}{\beta} + l \tag{7}$$

As mentioned earlier, a queuing system is adopted to estimate the task waiting time D_i^W. Each remote server is modelled as a G/G/1 queuing system, in which, the task arrival rate and task service time follow a general distribution [28]. The task waiting time D_i^W is estimated by using Little's rule [19] as follows:

$$D_i^W = \frac{L_q}{\lambda} \tag{8}$$

where L_q is the queue length, and λ is the inter-arrival rate for the incoming tasks at a given server.

4.3 Mobile Device Energy Model

Device energy consumption E_i for running a task t_i expresses the cumulative energy usage for running a task locally E_i^P, sending and receiving data E_i^C, and waiting for remote execution E_i^W. Energy consumption is modelled as follows.

$$E_i = E_i^P + E_i^C + E_i^W \tag{9}$$

$$E_i{}^P = D_i{}^P . \epsilon_i{}^P \tag{10}$$

$$E_i^C = D_i{}^C . \epsilon^C \tag{11}$$

$$E_i^W = D_i{}^W . \epsilon^W \tag{12}$$

Where $\epsilon_i{}^P$, ϵ^W, ϵ^C are energy indicators which measure the energy consumption for task t_i in secondly basis for local task processing, waiting for remote execution, and data transfer, respectively. These energy indicators are profiled through experimental application execution on various data size and network conditions [4].

4.4 Monetary Cost Model

The monetary cost is the total amount of money needed to execute a task t_i in a target computation server P_r. This involves two types of cost: task execution cost C_i^P, which is estimated based on execution time D_i, and the communication cost C_i^C of migrating data, which is estimated based on the data size s_i and communication bandwidth β_{cost} quality.

$$C_i = C_i^P + C_i^C \tag{13}$$

$$C_i{}^P = D_i{}^P . p_i \tag{14}$$

$$C_i^C = s_i . \beta_{cost} \tag{15}$$

4.5 Overview of the Optimisation Technique

The offloading optimising process aims to produce a resource allocation plan to schedule application tasks in the MECC environment in which the minima of execution cost C and time T are achieved. The allocation plan is represented as 2-dimensional array in which each position refers to a task allocation decision in a computing environment (cloud, edge or mobile). Mixed-integer Linear Programming (MILP) is utilised to perform the search for an optimised allocation plan [32]. The application of MILP enforces the linearity in objective functions and model constraints [13]. The Branch and Bound (BB) algorithm is a common approach to solve linear Programming (LP) optimisation problems, and works by relaxing the LP model constraints in integer boundaries [7]. Its iteratively generates optimal value bounds through partitioning the feasible region into convex sets.

The BB algorithm applies a search tree optimisation technique. Each tree node performs the problem (at upper level) partitioning to a subproblem which applies the non-integer constraints and bounds of the original problem [17]. The objective function is formulated as follows.

$$\widetilde{P_0} : min(E * C) \tag{16}$$

subject to R_0 and :

$$(C3) : x_i^l + \sum_{j=1}^{M} x_{ij}^f + x_i^c = 1$$

$$x_i^l, x_{ij}^f, x_i^c \in [0, 1], \forall (i, j) \in N x M$$

where constraints of deadline $D_{t_i} < \partial_i$ and user mobile device energy $E < e$ should be satisfied.

Algorithm 1 describes the BB search optimisation process as follows.

1. The searching process launches with an initial subproblem P_0.
2. $callSolObjectiveValue$ function, Lines 11–12, evaluates the function value of the subproblem at stack top $toCheckSol$. Based on the solution $toCheckSol$, optimisation parameters, that is, execution time D_i, consumed energy E_i and monetary cost C_i, are calculated via $callSolObjectiveValue$. The function provides cost models to evaluate offloading solution values.
3. Branch on $toCheckSol$ to generate new solutions (tree nodes), Line 20. The branching step applies certain rules to partition a problem into subproblems $toAddSubProblems$ through updating one decision variable x_i. Technically, a subproblem represents a candidate offloading decision.
4. The function $checkIntegerConstraints$ is applied to verify each subproblem to match problem constraint boundaries. The process refers to solution bounding, Line 22.

5   Experiment for Data-Intensive Application Offloading

The main motivation for the work outlined in this chapter was to produce insights that would support mobile users to select a cost-efficient offloading plan to run their applications in multiple computing environments. To achieve this, we designed and

---

Algorithm 1: Find optimal application tasks schedule

1: **Inputs:**
2: Application tasks $A = \{t_i, \ldots, t_n\}$
3: Computation resources $R = \{r^l, (r_1^f, \ldots, r_m^f), r_1^c\}$
4: **Output:**
5: initial subproblem P_0
6: **Initialise:**
7: $optVal = \infty$
8: $bestSol = \{\}$
9: $subP = \{P_0\}$
10: **while** $Len(subP > 0)$ **do**
11:    $toChecksol = subP[0]$
12:    $solObjValue = callSolObjectiveValue(A, R, toChecksol)$
13:    **if** $solObjValue > optVal$ **then**
14:        $subP.removeAt(0)$
15:    **else**
16:        **if** $solObjValue < optVal$ **then**
17:            $bestSol = toChecksol$
18:            $optVal = solObjValue$
19:        **else**
20:            $toAddSubProblems = Branch(subP[0])$
21:            **for** $i = 1$ to $Len(toAddSubProblems)$ **do**
22:                **if** $checkIntegerConstraints(toAddSubProblems[i]) == True$ **then**
23:                    $subP.insertAt(0, toAddSubProblems[i])$
24:                **end if**
25:            **end for**
26:        **end if**
27:    **end if**
28: **end while**
29: RETURN $s, optVal$

---

implemented an experiment to provide insights on how an offloading decision can be obtained based on application model, data size, context parameters and computing environment. The experiment examined the optimisation decision with respect to the variation on the aforementioned parameters. In addition, we aimed to evaluate the performance of various types of mobile application models in nominated mobile-aware computing environments. The rest of this section provides details about the evaluation metric, experiment configuration, and the main insights from the experimental results.

5.1 Evaluation Metrics

The optimisation technique aims to construct an offloading plan to map application tasks on environment resources and thereby minimise energy consumption and monetary cost. Both optimisation parameters are affected by the processing time parameter, which includes task processing and data communication. The processing time is an optimisation constraint handled at task level and accordingly at application level.

Conserving energy is a critical aspect of mobile application optimisation where losing device energy is a single point of failure. In this chapter, three energy consumption operations are considered: task processing, data transfer and device waiting (or idle) for remote execution. The contribution of each process is subject to many parameters, including data size, network bandwidth and application complexity.

The second offloading optimisation objective is monetary cost, which involves data transfer and processing cost. For data-intensive applications, data communication cost is not trivial, particularly when a cellular network is utilised. The optimisation algorithm is designed to handle the transfer of large data files to reduce the use of mobile network bandwidth. In addition, this work considers the impact of large data files on the task processing cost. The cost estimation depends on task complexity and how it responds to the change in data size. Here, energy and cost parameters are considered equally in the optimisation decision.

5.2   Experimental Setup

This section outlines the setup used to run data-intensive applications on multiple computing models. To recap, we investigated the role of mobile application structure on offloading optimisation decisions because it defines the computation and data dependency among application tasks. Offloading optimisation is examined for BoT, workflow and IoT. In BoT, tasks are independent on computation and data. The BoT is convenient for studying offloading optimisation for data-intensive applications with data source distribution between local, edge and cloud storage units. The workflow model involves transferring data between tasks. Thus, the task computation target plays the role of data source to dependent tasks. In the IoT model, a combination of BoT and workflow models is assumed, and the impact of collecting data from IoT devices is studied. The data collection can be handled by the mobile device or by edge node.

5.2.1   Computing Resources

The experiment was designed to investigate the efficiency of the computing model on the optimisation decision. Three models were studied: MC, MCC and MECC. Table 2 provides details about the resources configuration. We assumed a small fraction of cost for running a task on a mobile device. We assumed the processing cost on edge was 40% of the cost on cloud.

Table 2 Experiment
resources configuration

Resource name	#Cores	Computation cost ($/hour)
Mobile device	4	0.001
Edge node	16	0.0742
Cloud server	32	0.3712

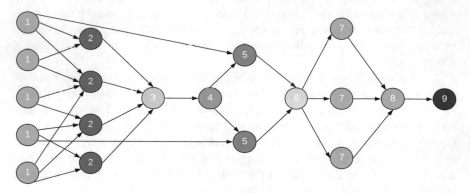

Fig. 4 Montage workflow

5.2.2 Workload Model

We adopted different workload models for BoT, workflow and IOT applications. This section provides the details of workload and data models used in this experiment.

For the workflow model, we employed the Montage workload model provided by Bharathi et al. [6]. A Montage-like workflow is generated to handle sky image processing. The workflow includes a set of tasks to import images, find differences, fit and concatenate, and finally create the mosaic. Figure 4 shows example of Montage workflow structure. In the workflow model, the computation complexity depends on the number of images and the level of overlap between images. For the purpose of offloading optimisation, the attributes of data sensitivity must be set for each application task. The data sensitivity factor relates the data size to the computation time.

The provided profiling data was used to extract the parameters of data sensitivity and generated output sensitivity. Table 3 shows the data and output sensitivity values for workflow task types. Moreover, to have variation in data size for the purpose of studying data change contribution, a uniform distribution for image size and number of input images was adopted. Table 4 provides the details of the data workload model. The data distributions were selected to enable determination of the contribution of data size to the offloading optimisation decision.

For the BoT model, a task workload model considering computation complexity, central processing unit (CPU) load and data sensitivity was developed. The task complexity is determined by the number of million instructions per second (MIPS) and the percentage of CPU usage for processing. The data sensitivity measures

Table 3 Workflow
sensitivity factors

Task	Data sensitivity	Output sensitivity
mProjectPP	0.725	8.955
mDiffFit	0.095	0.054
mConcatFit	2.250	1
mBgModel	1.808	0
mBackground	0.288	1
mImgTbl	0.287	1
mAdd	0.815	0.926
mShrink	0.356	0.020
mJPEG	15.894	0.048

Table 4 Data size
distributions

Number of images [min, max]	Data size [min, max] (MB)
[1, 10]	[5,50]
[10, 20]	[50,100]
[20, 100]	[100,500]
[100, 200]	[500,100]
[200, 400]	[1000,2000]
[400, 600]	[2000, 3000]
[600, 800]	[3000, 4000]
Image size distribution	[3.9, 5.2]

Table 5 Task complexity
models

Task complexity (MIPS)	Low: [20–100] High: [200–700]
CPU load (%)	[0.1–0.9]
Data sensitivity (%)	[0.2–0.8]

the contribution of data change to task complexity or execution time. The data size distribution provided in Table 4 was used. Table 5 shows two task complexity models for low and high-computation applications.

For the IoT model, the workflow and BoT workload models were integrated. An IoT application was designed as mini-batches of workflows and a BoT application.

5.2.3 Network Model

For data-intensive applications, the quality of mobile network has a significant influence on the transfer time. Three types of networks, WiFi, 4G and 3G, were tested. Table 6 presents the network model applied in this experiment. Based on profiling (which provides a distribution of data transfer latency) from our previous work [3, 4], the minimum and maximum bandwidth values of each network were set. Moreover, profiling provides distribution for data transfer latency. The network profiling considered the user mobility which reflects the correspondence between the quality of network bandwidth and user position. Lee et al. [18]

Table 6 Network interface bandwidth

Network type	Bandwidth (MB/s) [Min, Max]	Cost ($/GB)
3G	[2,5]	1.0
4G	[8,12]	1.0
WiFi	[25,30]	0.05
Latency	Min. latency (s)	Max. latency (s)
	0.85	6.5

proposed a mobility-based offloading decision making. Their experimental showed the significant of considering user mobility to reduce response time and energy consumption. In our work, we simulated the user mobility through applying a uniform distribution to express the variation on user mobile network bandwidth and latency.

5.3   Performance Evaluation

In this section we discuss the results of running the offloading optimiser with the experiment setup. For each application model, the impact of variation in data size and bandwidth values is highlighted.

5.3.1   BoT Application Model

A BoT application execution involves running tasks in a separate mode in which tasks are independent in terms of data and computation. In the context of data-intensive applications, this behaviour determines the requirements for transferring large files over the mobile network.

Figure 5 shows the result of running the BoT application over a 4G network. With 4G, the optimiser will try to find an optimised offloading decision to meet the task deadline and reduce the incurred cost of data transfer over the cellular data network. MCC and MECC demonstrate similar behaviour for application execution time along all data size variation intervals. With MECC, the optimiser reduces the consumed energy and cost compared to MCC, particularly with medium and large input files. This is due to the ability to offload data-heavy tasks to nearby edges, and thus reduce the energy consumption for local processing and device waiting.

Moreover, with a 4G network, the optimiser tends to perform more computation using cloud resources to benefit from their high capability, as well as low waiting time compared to edge resources. This opportunity is also applicable in the case of WiFi network availability. Figure 6 provides the result for the WiFi network case. The three computation environments offer convenient BoT cost optimisation and reduce MECC costs with large data files. Even though the results confirm the

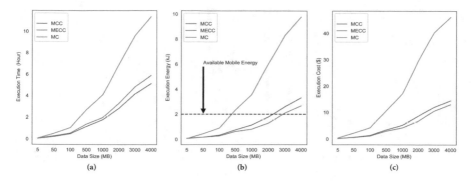

Fig. 5 BoT application model: 4G network. (**a**) Execution time. (**b**) Mobile energy. (**c**) Monetary cost

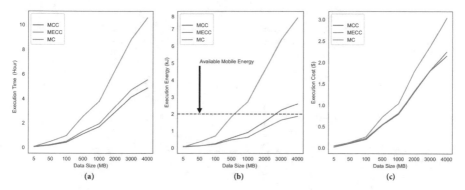

Fig. 6 BoT application model: WiFi network. (**a**) Execution time. (**b**) Mobile energy. (**c**) Monetary cost

limitations of MC due to energy shortage, the adoption of an external mobile energy source would be an effective enabler of local execution for data-intensive mobile applications. Figures 5 and 6 show that the mobile device is capable of running BoT applications even with medium data size on high-bandwidth networks.

5.3.2 Workflow Application Model

A workflow application is a computation model in which application tasks are dependent. In workflow execution, the data location for the first task has a significant impact on the overall optimisation process. Here, the experiment was run with randomisation for the first task to obtain a convenient and stable offloading decision. This section details an analysis of running a workflow application and an investigation of the impact of mobile network and task input data size on evaluation parameters.

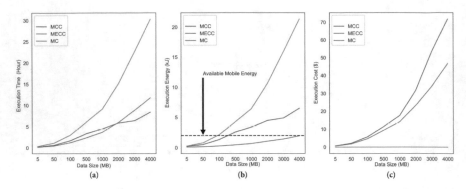

Fig. 7 Workflow application model: 4G network. (**a**) Execution time. (**b**) Mobile energy. (**c**) Monetary cost

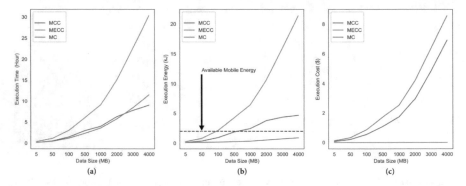

Fig. 8 Workflow application model: WiFi network. (**a**) Execution time. (**b**) Mobile energy. (**c**) Monetary cost

Figures 7 and 8 show the result of running the workflow application with 4G and WiFi networks, respectively. An interesting result is the advantage of MCC over MECC in minimising the workflow execution time, even though the results show that MECC offers a substantial energy saving compared to MCC and MC. With deadline-relaxed workflow applications, the optimiser works effectively to reduce energy and cost by executing tasks with high data dependency at the edge layer. In addition, with the cellular data network 4G in Fig. 7, the incurred cost gap between MECC and MCC reduces as the data sized increases. To overcome the cost overhead of the 4G network for transferring large data sizes, an efficient joint computation between edge and cloud resources is adopted. In the case of the WiFi network, Fig. 8 shows that MCC provides greater savings than MEC. This is due to the efficient usage of the high bandwidth and low-cost Wifi network in mobile-cloud data transfer. This behaviour supports the conclusions on previous section about running the BoT with a WiFi network.

5.3.3 IoT Application Model

As explained earlier, IoT applications are common data analysis applications in which data is collected from IoT devices (such as sensors) either in online or offline mode. An IoT application was modelled as a combination of BoT and workflow sub-applications. In addition, for IoT offloading optimisation, the contribution of data collection stage was studied. Application data is collected by the user's mobile or by a stationary edge device. This section provides an analysis of the execution of an IoT application based on various network bandwidth and data size conditions in the three computing environments.

Figures 9, 10 and 11 present the experimental results of IoT application execution when the user's mobile device is the data collection instrument. Results show that for all network types, the three computing paradigms provide similar results for application execution time. With the 3G network, in Fig. 9, MC demonstrates high

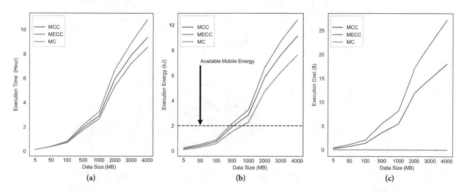

Fig. 9 IoT application with mobile data collection: 3G network. (**a**) Execution time. (**b**) Mobile energy. (**c**) Monetary cost

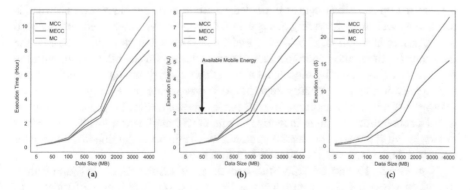

Fig. 10 IoT application with mobile data collection: 4G network. (**a**) Execution time. (**b**) Mobile energy. (**c**) Monetary cost

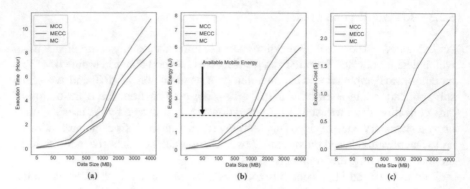

Fig. 11 IoT application with mobile data collection: WiFi network. (**a**) Execution time. (**b**) Mobile energy. (**c**) Monetary cost

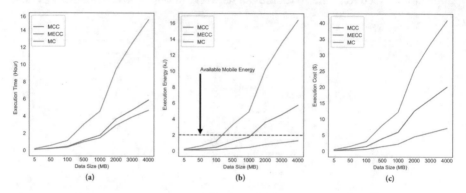

Fig. 12 IoT application with edge data collection: 3G network. (**a**) Execution time. (**b**) Mobile energy. (**c**) Monetary cost

ability to optimise consumed energy and monetary cost. Thus, local processing is a preferred option when data is collected locally and a low-bandwidth network is used. For MC, the processing energy is the only factor considered, because no data transfer is required. For MECC and MCC, the low bandwidth increases the data transfer time, and hence the data transfer energy. On the other hand, with the 4G network (Fig. 10), the high bandwidth allows energy saving by sending some IoT application tasks to nearby edge nodes and reducing the energy consumption overhead of the local execution. In addition, as shown in Fig. 11, the availability of a WiFi connection is a huge incentive to run an IoT application locally in a user's device because the WiFi connection potentially provides a reduction in data transfer energy and cost when data is collected from sensors.

Figures 12, 13 and 14 show the experimental results of an IoT application execution when IoT data is collected at the edge layer. The high performance of running the application in an MECC environment was expected. The optimiser was able to find an optimised solution by running the workflow at the edge layer. This scenario is promising when the mobile network is unstable or unpredictable. In

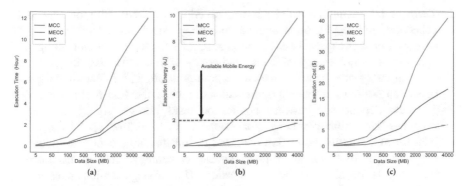

Fig. 13 IoT application with edge data collection: 4G network. (**a**) Execution time. (**b**) Mobile energy. (**c**) Monetary cost

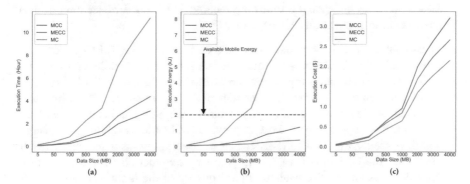

Fig. 14 IoT application with edge data collection: WiFi network. (**a**) Execution time. (**b**) Mobile energy. (**c**) Monetary cost

addition, Figs. 13 and 14 show that the application can be run in MECC and MCC with large data files without violating the energy constraint.

6 Discussion and Recommendations

This section presents the main insights from the experimental results. The results demonstrate the contributions of the studied parameters, namely, application type, network quality and data size, on the offloading optimisation decision. The main insights are represented as follow.

1. Selection of a computing environment to reduce consumed energy and monetary cost is highly dependent on the size of data to be transferred over the communication network. This factor is critical for applications that require heavy data communication with distributed data storage. For example, in BoT applications, edge resources can be effective, particularly with low network quality.

2. There is promising potential for use of edge resources with on-edge data collection. IoT applications involve collecting data from a large number of sensors. For low capability MC, the process of collecting data and acting as a data source is not energy efficient, and costly with cellular data usage. Thus, the availability of edge nodes which can communicate with IoT sensors for data collection is allows offloading optimisation to reduce data transfer time and cost.
3. The data dependency between application tasks plays a significant role in resources allocation planning. For example, in workflow applications, the increase in data communication overhead to transfer large data files motivates the optimiser to adopt an in-place allocation strategy. This means moving the computation close to the data location. This strategy demonstrates viable optimisation results because the allocation targets the closest and highest-capability computation resources.

Based on these insights, the following recommendations for execution of data-intensive mobile applications can be made.

- Data-intensive mobile applications should be handled using MECC. This is the most efficient architecture, particularly for loosely coupled applications, such as BoT, in which data and computation dependencies are low. MECC allows an optimised computation distribution over edge and cloud resources. However, MCC also reduces BoT execution time substantially with high-bandwidth networks.
- For workflow applications, MECC provides valuable capability for energy-sensitive scenarios. As data transfer between workflow tasks increases, results show that the optimal strategy is to perform computation with cloud-only or edge-only resources. The availability and quality of the mobile network are the determinants for strategy selection.
- For IoT applications, the ability of users' devices to collect data from IoT sensors is critical for selecting the best computation environment. With low-bandwidth networks, local processing is the preferred option when data is stored in local devices.

7 Conclusion and Future Work

Rapid and profound advances in the mobile telecommunications industry have created the need for mobile-aware computing models that can benefit from the capabilities of resources at different computation layers, such as the cloud, cloudlet and edge. Moreover, integration between computing models supports the broad engagement of mobile devices in many application domains for academia and industry, which enforces the work with a variety of application models, such as BoT, workflow and IoT.

This chapter describes the variation in computing and application models and how this can impact the offloading decision, that is, how application tasks can be allocated to resources. For data-intensive mobile applications, we included a set of parameters to determine optimisation decision viability for each computing model, including application data size and maximum execution time, network quality and device energy. The results demonstrate the ability to optimise data-intensive application execution while considering the target computing environment and problem constraints such as data size and network bandwidth. Chapter findings highlight the ability to produce potential offloading techniques which can work effectively with cutting-edge technologies to reduce the cost and consumed energy in a variety of application domains. This motivates the direction for localised and region-based mobile computing for more secure, private and cost-efficient mobile applications.

For future work, we suggest the following directions:

- The advancement in mobile research toward workload-based applications in domains like streaming services [30], content delivery applications, social sensing [15] and privacy-awareness enabled applications, motivates the development of sophisticated and intelligent data-intensive offloading mechanisms that depend on application-specific modelling strategies and sophisticated optimisation techniques at large-scale with machine learning and artificial intelligence technologies [29, 37].
- With respect to data-intensive applications, offloading planning is sensitive to context information like network quality and resource availability. For example, in streaming applications, network quality plays a vital role in offloading performance and accordingly application service quality. For such applications, applying dynamic offloading schemes can be more beneficial. Thus, there is considerable scope for research into dynamic offloading with respect to sensitive context aware applications and with the support of cutting-edge technologies like edge computing, 5G and software-defined networking (SDN) [35, 40].
- The vast majority of computation offloading techniques have sought to provide optimisation solutions for latency-sensitive and energy-aware offloading problems. An offloading process is subject to failure for many reasons, including resource unavailability and inadequate network conditions [22]. Therefore, it is critical for offloading systems to guarantee reliable offloading execution, which refers to continuous and successful processing cycles for the desired application. For some applications, reliability is a critical factor. For instance, in Internet of Vehicles (IoV) applications like autonomous driving, interruptions of communication links and processing node failure are inevitable [38].

References

1. Abolfazli, S., Sanaei, Z., Alizadeh, M., Gani, A., Xia, F.: An experimental analysis on cloud-based mobile augmentation in mobile cloud computing. IEEE Transactions on Consumer Electronics **60**(1), 146–154 (2014)
2. Adhikari, M., Amgoth, T., Srirama, S.N.: A survey on scheduling strategies for workflows in cloud environment and emerging trends. ACM Computing Surveys (CSUR) **52**(4), 1–36 (2019)

3. Alkhalaileh, M., Calheiros, R.N., Nguyen, Q.V., Javadi, B.: Dynamic resource allocation in hybrid mobile cloud computing for data-intensive applications. In: International Conference on Green, Pervasive, and Cloud Computing. pp. 176–191. Springer (2019)
4. Alkhalaileh, M., Calheiros, R.N., Nguyen, Q.V., Javadi, B.: Data-intensive application scheduling on mobile edge cloud computing. Journal of Network and Computer Applications p. 102735 (2020)
5. Armbrust, M., Fox, A., Griffith, R., Joseph, A.D., Katz, R., Konwinski, A., Lee, G., Patterson, D., Rabkin, A., Stoica, I., et al.: A view of cloud computing. Communications of the ACM 53(4), 50–58 (2010)
6. Bharathi, S., Chervenak, A., Deelman, E., Mehta, G., Su, M.H., Vahi, K.: Characterization of scientific workflows. In: 2008 third workshop on workflows in support of large-scale science. pp. 1–10. IEEE (2008)
7. Boyd, S., Vandenberghe, L.: Convex optimization. Cambridge university press (2004)
8. Cheng, C.T., Ganganath, N., Fok, K.Y.: Concurrent data collection trees for iot applications. IEEE Transactions on Industrial Informatics 13(2), 793–799 (2016)
9. Cirne, W., Paranhos, D., Costa, L., Santos-Neto, E., Brasileiro, F., Sauve, J., Silva, F.A., Barros, C.O., Silveira, C.: Running bag-of-tasks applications on computational grids: The mygrid approach. In: Parallel Processing, 2003. Proceedings. 2003 International Conference on. pp. 407–416. IEEE (2003)
10. Enzai, N.I.M., Tang, M.: A heuristic algorithm for multi-site computation offloading in mobile cloud computing. Procedia Computer Science 80, 1232–1241 (2016)
11. Feijóo, C., Gómez-Barroso, J.L., Ramos, S.: Implications of data-intensive applications for next generation mobile networks (2014)
12. Foster, I., Zhao, Y., Raicu, I., Lu, S.: Cloud computing and grid computing 360-degree compared. In: 2008 Grid Computing Environments Workshop. pp. 1–10. Ieee (2008)
13. Jain, V., Grossmann, I.E.: Algorithms for hybrid milp/cp models for a class of optimization problems. INFORMS Journal on computing 13(4), 258–276 (2001)
14. Kang, Y., Hauswald, J., Gao, C., Rovinski, A., Mudge, T., Mars, J., Tang, L.: Neurosurgeon: Collaborative intelligence between the cloud and mobile edge. ACM SIGARCH Computer Architecture News 45(1), 615–629 (2017)
15. Kong, P.Y.: Computation and sensor offloading for cloud-based infrastructure-assisted autonomous vehicles. IEEE Systems Journal (2020)
16. Kumar, K., Liu, J., Lu, Y.H., Bhargava, B.: A survey of computation offloading for mobile systems. Mobile Networks and Applications 18(1), 129–140 (2013)
17. Lawler, E.L., Wood, D.E.: Branch-and-bound methods: A survey. Operations research 14(4), 699–719 (1966)
18. Lee, K., Shin, I.: User mobility model based computation offloading decision for mobile cloud. Journal of Computing Science and Engineering 9(3), 155–162 (2015)
19. Little, J.D.: A proof for the queuing formula: L= λ w. Operations research 9(3), 383–387 (1961)
20. Mach, P., Becvar, Z.: Mobile edge computing: A survey on architecture and computation offloading. IEEE Communications Surveys & Tutorials 19(3), 1628–1656 (2017)
21. Nan, X., He, Y., Guan, L.: Optimal resource allocation for multimedia cloud based on queuing model. In: Multimedia signal processing (MMSP), 2011 IEEE 13th international workshop on. pp. 1–6. IEEE (2011)
22. Nguyen, Q.H., Dressler, F.: A smartphone perspective on computation offloading–a survey. Computer Communications (2020)
23. Patel, M., Naughton, B., Chan, C., Sprecher, N., Abeta, S., Neal, A., et al.: Mobile-edge computing introductory technical white paper. White paper, mobile-edge computing (MEC) industry initiative pp. 1089–7801 (2014)
24. Qi, H., Gani, A.: Research on mobile cloud computing: Review, trend and perspectives. In: 2012 Second International Conference on Digital Information and Communication Technology and it's Applications (DICTAP). pp. 195–202. IEEE (2012)
25. Ren, J., Yu, G., He, Y., Li, G.Y.: Collaborative cloud and edge computing for latency minimization. IEEE Transactions on Vehicular Technology 68(5), 5031–5044 (2019)

26. Satyanarayanan, M., Bahl, V., Caceres, R., Davies, N.: The case for vm-based cloudlets in mobile computing. IEEE pervasive Computing (2009)
27. Shi, W., Cao, J., Zhang, Q., Li, Y., Xu, L.: Edge computing: Vision and challenges. IEEE Internet of Things Journal **3**(5), 637–646 (2016)
28. Shore, J.E.: Information theoretic approximations for m/g/1 and g/g/1 queuing systems. Acta Informatica **17**(1), 43–61 (1982)
29. Shuja, J., Bilal, K., Alanazi, E., Alasmary, W., Alashaikh, A.: Applying machine learning techniques for caching in edge networks: A comprehensive survey. arXiv preprint arXiv:2006.16864 (2020)
30. Toma, A., Chen, J.J.: Computation offloading for real-time systems. In: Proceedings of the 28th Annual ACM Symposium on Applied Computing. pp. 1650–1651 (2013)
31. Vaquero, L.M., Rodero-Merino, L., Caceres, J., Lindner, M.: A break in the clouds: towards a cloud definition. ACM New York, NY, USA (2008)
32. Vielma, J.P.: Mixed integer linear programming formulation techniques. Siam Review **57**(1), 3–57 (2015)
33. Vu, T.T., Nguyen, D.N., Hoang, D.T., Dutkiewicz, E.: Optimal task offloading and resource allocation for fog computing. arXiv preprint arXiv:1906.03567 (2019)
34. Wang, P., Yao, C., Zheng, Z., Sun, G., Song, L.: Joint task assignment, transmission, and computing resource allocation in multilayer mobile edge computing systems. IEEE Internet of Things Journal **6**(2), 2872–2884 (2018)
35. Wang, T., Liang, Y., Zhang, Y., Arif, M., Wang, J., Jin, Q., et al.: An intelligent dynamic offloading from cloud to edge for smart iot systems with big data. IEEE Transactions on Network Science and Engineering (2020)
36. Wang, Y., Chen, R., Wang, D.C.: A survey of mobile cloud computing applications: perspectives and challenges. Wireless Personal Communications **80**(4), 1607–1623 (2015)
37. Yang, B., Cao, X., Bassey, J., Li, X., Qian, L.: Computation offloading in multi-access edge computing: A multi-task learning approach. IEEE Transactions on Mobile Computing (2020)
38. Yang, S.: A task offloading solution for internet of vehicles using combination auction matching model based on mobile edge computing. IEEE Access **8**, 53261–53273 (2020)
39. Zhang, Q., Cheng, L., Boutaba, R.: Cloud computing: state-of-the-art and research challenges. Journal of Internet Services and Applications **1**(1), 7–18 (2010)
40. Zhang, Q., Gui, L., Hou, F., Chen, J., Zhu, S., Tian, F.: Dynamic task offloading and resource allocation for mobile-edge computing in dense cloud ran. IEEE Internet of Things Journal **7**(4), 3282–3299 (2020)
41. Zhou, B., Dastjerdi, A.V., Calheiros, R.N., Srirama, S.N., Buyya, R.: mcloud: A context-aware offloading framework for heterogeneous mobile cloud. IEEE Transactions on Services Computing **10**(5), 797–810 (2015)

Geospatial Edge-Fog Computing: A Systematic Review, Taxonomy, and Future Directions

Jaydeep Das, Soumya K. Ghosh, and Rajkumar Buyya

Abstract Real-time geospatial applications are ever-increasing with modern Information and Communication Technology. Latency and Quality of Service-aware these applications are required to process at the edge of the networks, not at the central cloud servers. Edge and fog nodes of the networks are capable enough for caching the frequently accessed small volume geospatial data, processing with lightweight tools and libraries. Finally, display the image of the processed geospatial data at the edge devices according to the user's Point of Interest. Several kinds of research are going on edge and fog computing, especially in the geospatial aspects. Health monitoring, weather prediction, emergency communication, disaster management, disease expansion are examples of geospatial real-time applications. In this chapter, we have investigated the existing work in the edge and fog computing with the geospatial paradigm. We propose a taxonomy on related works. At the end of this chapter, we discuss the limitations and future direction of the geospatial edge and fog computing.

Keywords Edge computing · Fog computing · Geospatial applications · Geographical information system (GIS) · Survey · Taxonomy

J. Das (✉)
Advanced Technology Development Centre, Indian Institute of Technology Kharagpur, Kharagpur, West Bengal, India
e-mail: jaydeep@iitkgp.ac.in

S. K. Ghosh
Department of Computer Science and Engineering, Indian Institute of Technology (IIT) Kharagpur, Kharagpur, West Bengal, India
e-mail: skg@cse.iitkgp.ac.in

R. Buyya
Cloud Computing and Distributed Systems (CLOUDS) Laboratory, School of Computing and Information Systems, The University of Melbourne, Melbourne, VIC, Australia
e-mail: rbuyya@unimelb.edu.au

© The Author(s), under exclusive license to Springer Nature Switzerland AG 2021
A. Mukherjee et al. (eds.), *Mobile Edge Computing*,
https://doi.org/10.1007/978-3-030-69893-5_3

1 Introduction

With the proliferation usage of smartphone and IoT devices, generating, accessing, and analyzing geospatial data becomes a regular activity. To access and analyze these geospatial data, computing and processing resources are required [1]. The provision of resources is varied based on applications. For the large computation, a huge infrastructure is needed for processing a large amount of geospatial data. In such cases, the central cloud computing infrastructure is the only solution. IoT devices have not enough capacity to do so [2]. However, for the small amount of geospatial data processing, analyzing, and decision making, edge, and fog computing is a promising technology [3].

A pictorial view of the cloud, fog, and edge computing with geospatial applications is presented in Fig. 1. Cloud is the core layer where high-end computing servers and databases are present. Users receive virtualized computing instances

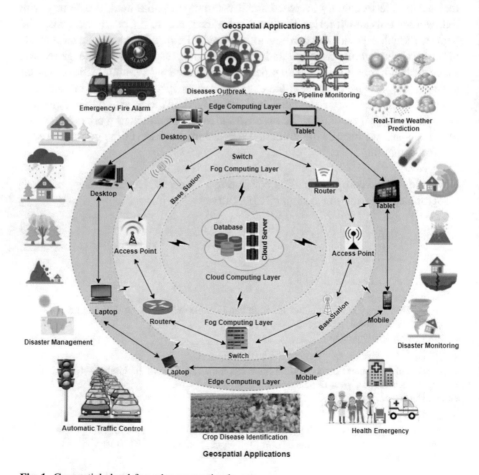

Fig. 1 Geospatial cloud-fog-edge computing layers

with different configurations for their geospatial applications. Moreover, Cloud is present multi-hop distance from geospatial applications.

In fog computing layer, the computation is done in any of the fog nodes i.e., switches, routers, gateways, access points, base stations [4]. These fog nodes are present in between the edge devices, i.e., mobile phone, laptop, tab, and the central cloud server. These fog nodes are capable to compute and analyze the small amount of geospatial data. After processing and analysis of the geospatial data, these fog nodes generate a quick decision to the edge devices. Fog computing is effective in terms of service delay, energy efficiency, network congestion, etc.

Edge computing layer is constructed by the inter-connectivity among nearby edge devices like mobile phones. As edge computing is very near to the edge devices, it facilitates high network bandwidth, ultra-low latency, and real-time response [5, 6] to the geospatial applications like sending alert to the fire station, change the color of traffic signal lights and its timespan, sending a message to the medical person about his/her patient's condition, spread awareness to the fisherman before the tsunami, make attentive to the workers of the gas station about the leakage of methane gas from pipeline [7].

Edge and fog computing (EFC), enriches the computing paradigm for real-time geospatial applications like health monitoring [8–10] systems, sort-term weather prediction, disaster recovery [11, 12], crop diseases monitoring [13]. In all these cases, a quick decision has to be taken depending upon the analysis of captured geospatial data by edge nodes [14]. The response time is a major concern in all of the above situations. Fast decisions can be obtained from a geospatial EFC system than a central geospatial cloud system. Geospatial fog computing helps in the computation of geospatial data, analyzing the data. Return results or alert to the users within a stipulated time duration by the edge nodes. A layered architecture has been proposed in [15]. EFC system has an inner, middle, and outer edge layer. Different edge and fog devices are present in these three layers.

In summary, motivations move towards the Edge-Fog than cloud-centric computing paradigm are low latency or response-time, less network bandwidth utilization, uninterrupted service due to minimum distance from edge devices, resource-constraint at the individual edge devices affects cloud performance, and security of the edge devices is not controllable by cloud from distance [16].

In this chapter, we present a taxonomy based on a survey of Geospatial based Edge-Fog computing. There are many surveys exist in edge and fog computing domain [2, 17–37], but none of them address geospatial aspects. In Sect. 2, we have discussed the geospatial related researches in Cloud, Cloudlet, Mist computing environment. A taxonomy on existing research work in geospatial edge and fog computing has been structured in Sects. 3 and 4 makes a summary of these works in a tabular form for better understanding. Section 5 expresses the limitations in the geospatial edge-fog computing domain. Future scopes of geospatial edge and fog computing is explored in Sect. 6. The conclusion of this chapter has been done in the last section.

2 Existing Computing Paradigms

In this section, we focus on ongoing researches on cloud computing, cloudlet, mist computing with geospatial features.

2.1 Geospatial Cloud Computing

Currently, there are many computing strategies are available. Cloud computing [38] is the core of all these computing, where a large number of servers, databases are available. While huge computing is required for a geospatial application, then cloud is the only option for processing it. As the cloud servers reside multi-hop distance from the geospatial application nodes, it increases the overall communication delay which is sometimes critical for real-time geospatial applications like methane gas leakage monitoring, fire alarming, health monitoring [10]. The characteristics of the Cloud-GIS has been mentioned in [39], which are the extensible geospatial version of the cloud characteristics. These are—(i) elasticity of geospatial resources, (ii) on-demand geospatial services, (iii) measurable and pay-as-you-go for geospatial resources, i.e. geospatial data, geospatial tools, (iv) accessing diversity, (v) transparency, (vi) service based geospatial applications, and (vii) hardware and resource extendable. The geospatial based Infrastructure as a Service (IaaS), Platform as a Service (PaaS) and Software as a Service (SaaS) are discussed in [40]. Along with these geospatial Data as a Service (DaaS) is also a major concern. Some geospatial services on the cloud are also mentioned in [41]. OGC compliant geospatial service orchestrations in the cloud have been done in [42] for geospatial query resolution. Cloud-based GIS architecture models have been discussed in [43–45]. Geospatial data indexing [46, 47] is performed for better data management in the cloud. Geospatial data interpolation [40, 48] is performed in the cloud for determining the missing geospatial data in the public dataset. Geospatial data mining [49, 50] and data processing [51–53] are performed for the getting results of the geospatial data query [54–56]. All these geospatial data mechanisms have been done for getting the results from the geospatial applications running over the cloud computing platform.

2.2 Geospatial Cloudlet

Cloudlet is introduced to improve the latency of the cloud by caching the copies of data while users access the mobile applications [57]. It brings the performance of the cloud closer to mobile users. Cloudlets are computationally less powerful than the central cloud system [58]. Mobile phone, Laptop, an Access point can be used as a cloudlet. If many cloudlets are connected with each other, then the single point of failure can be avoided. Cloudlet supports mobility. The mobile device offloads the codes to the cloudlet and the code is migrated to another nearby cloudlet. While the mobile device reaches under the coverage of the second cloudlet, it starts getting the executed results from the second cloudlet [59]. Location-based service discovery is done by the distributed cloudlets [60] and it generates less traffic in the network than a cloud-based approach. Geospatial query resolution using a cloudlet is performed in [61]. This approach reduces delay and power consumption than remote cloud access for geospatial data analysis.

2.3 Geospatial Mist Computing

According to [62], Mist computing is a computing layer between fog and cloudlets. Sensor and actuator devices are involved in the processing of data, which pushed the computing towards the edge node of the network [63] where edge devices are present. This reduces the communication latency within edge devices in milliseconds. Mist computing enhances the self-awareness among the edge devices in such a way that edge devices perform their operations with unstable Internet connections [15]. A Mist-GIS framework has been developed for clustering and overlying the geospatial data of the Ganga river basin [64] and malaria disease spread in the state of Maharastra, India [65].

2.4 Discussion

The changes of different parameters like distance from applications, computational capacity, cost, energy savings, real-time responses, etc. with respect to computing paradigms are represented in Fig. 2. However, communication delay, computational capacity, the infrastructural cost is more in a cloud environment than the other computing paradigms. Moreover, energy efficiency, closeness to the applications, and real-time response are promising in the edge, fog, and mist computing.

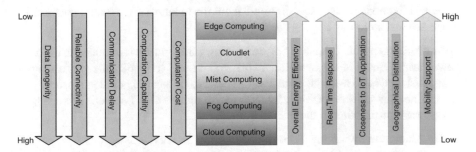

Fig. 2 Different computing layers with parameters

3   Taxonomy

We have represented a taxonomy on geospatial Edge-Fog computing in Fig. 3. This taxonomy is based on the existing works in the geospatial domain where the computation has been done in Edge and Fog computing environment. We have categories the works into four parts. These are-

* *Geospatial Computing:* We focus on service and resource management in edge-fog environments. Resource management is sub-categories in power, delay, cost, and geospatial data management. Whereas, service management is broken into four parts, i.e., network, application, geospatial data service, and quality of service management.
* *Geospatial Data:* The geospatial data which used for the applications running on the Edge-Fog computing are mentioned.
* *Geospatial Analysis Procedures:* The methods or procedures applied to the geospatial data, which help to identify the emergency or severity of the situations through the geospatial applications.
* *Geospatial Applications:* Different types of geospatial applications which run on the edge and fog computing environment.

In the following subsections (Sects. 3.1–3.4), we elaborate existing related works that fall into the four categories mentioned above.

3.1   Geospatial Computing

In this section, we discuss about the overall edge and fog computing management. It includes resource management, and service management.

3.1.1   Resource Management

Resource provisioning has been done depending upon the power, delay, cost by the edge, and fog nodes. Also, keep in mind about the amount of geospatial data can be processed and stored by the edge or fog nodes [19].

Power Management Edge and Fog computing paradigm are introduced to efficient power management of the overall network system. In [3, 66–68], the processing of geospatial data is done at the edge and fog devices of local region. Data processing at local devices reduces the data transfer to the remote cloud server. This leads to low power consumption in the overall system.

Delay Management Delay in communication or in service is crucial for applications. Sometimes, an application loses its relevancy due to the delay. This is one of the major concerns that introduce Edge and Fog computing instead of Cloud

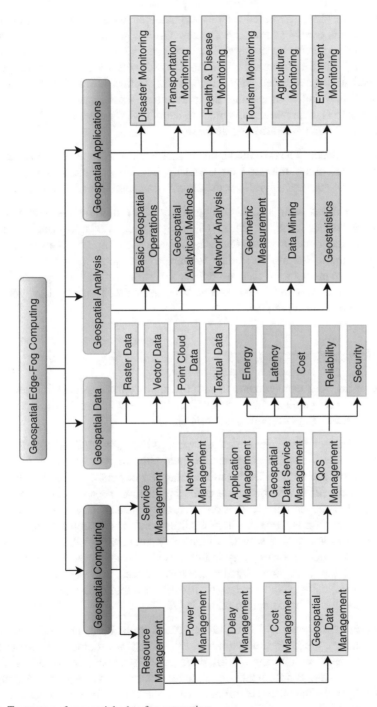

Fig. 3 Taxonomy of geospatial edge-fog computing

computing. In [66], geospatial queries are resolved within nearby Fog devices if concern data is available that fog devices. Otherwise, fog devices communicate to the cloud server for processing. They achieved 47–83% improvement in delay than the only-cloud environment. The shortest path within the critical zone has been determined in case of emergency situation [68] within nearby fog devices. They come by 9–11% better in average delay than the cloud platform. In time-critical applications [67], achieve improvement in delay on user devices as the processing of information done in nearby fog devices.

Cost Management The cost management includes infrastructure deployment cost, networking, or communication cost, and application execution cost [24]. Data offloading cost, process migration cost are also considered for this category.

Geospatial Data Management GIS applications are running based on geospatial data. These data are large in volume [69]. Only pre-processing of data can be done in edge and fog nodes because the infrastructure like memory, processor, storage capacity is small. Pre-processed data forward to the cloud for further processing. Sometimes, frequency used data are only cached in the edge and fog nodes, which helps to reply quickly to the user query. Various methods for matching geospatial vector data are mention in [70].

3.1.2 Service Management

We discuss network management, application management, geospatial data service management, and quality of service(QoS) management as overall service management of the Edge-Fog computing environment.

Network Management Networks are managed in the EFC paradigm through congestion control, seamless connectivity, and network virtualization. Congestion in the network can be avoided by minimizing the communication with the cloud server from the EFC network. Geospatial application requests are coming from any edge devices, and its resolution performed nearby edge or fog nodes. It leads to minimizing network traffic. Seamless connectivity helps to connect edge devices with cloud or fog servers without any latency. Seamless connectivity is possible with handover technology in future vehicular networks [71, 72]. Network virtualization has been done by the software-defined network (SDN). Network function virtualization (NVF) helps to virtualize the traditional network functions. SDN based work in fog computing done in [73, 74].

Application Management Real-time geospatial applications are road traffic monitoring, weather prediction, a spatial query against any point of interest (POI), emergency health monitoring. In all these cases, a cluster of reliable edge-fog nodes, low latency, and dedicated computing resources are required. Augmented reality (AR), real-time video streaming, content caching technique, bigdata analysis discussed in [75]. Using *offloading* technique [76], one nearby edge/fog nodes can forward computational tasks to its adjacent edge/fog node which has better computing resources. *Scaling* is another aspect that helps to run the application smoothly. Always the processing of geospatial data amounts is not the same. When it increases, the computation power needs to increase. This leads to a challenge for edge/fog nodes. In the case of scalability, cloud is still a promising technology.

Geospatial Data Service Geospatial data are integrated from various sources through OGC compliant web services [77]. There are five types of web services available. These are Web Feature Service (WFS), Web Processing Service (WPS), Web Coverage Service (WCS), Web Map Service (WMS), and Catalogue Service for Web (CSW). WFS helps to extract the features according to queries. WPS applies different spatial operations over geospatial data. WMS displays the maps according to user demands. CSW prepares the registry of the available data sources.

QoS Management Best quality of service is achieved in EFC through energy-efficient computation, low latency in communication, overall minimal cost, reliable, and secure connection.

- *Energy:* In the EFC paradigm, energy is consume minimize through energy-aware computation offloading, mobility management federation of constrained devices [35]. In [21], the overall edge computing system will be energy efficient through edge hardware design, computing architecture, operating system, and middleware.
- *Latency:* Computation latency and communication latency are considered for overall service latency management. Computation latency depends upon the configuration (Processor, RAM) of the edge and fog nodes. Whereas, communication latency relies on network bandwidth. It can be considered as within edge nodes, edge node to Fog node, and within fog nodes connectivity.
- *Cost:* It is the summation of the computational cost, deployment cost, and networking cost. Network bandwidth is responsible for the networking cost [78]. Whereas, computing devices like processing unit, RAM, virtual machine cost are considered as computational cost. Deployment of edge-fog nodes and their communication elements expenses come under the deployment cost.
- *Reliability:* It is also the main concern while an application is running on reliable edge or fog nodes. The availability of such computing nodes should be guaranteed. In [35], mentioned to make a fog service reliable the replication of required functions is required, but it may not possible due to the limited computing resources available to the fog devices. So, it is a challenge to make a service reliable and available which is running in edge and fog devices.
- *Security:* Heterogeneous and geographically distributed edge and fog nodes have a major concern about the security. Rogue fog node identification, authentication, strengthen the network, and data storage security are ways to constitute a security in the edge-fog environment [79]. There are various security attacks, like Man-in-the-middle, Distributed Denial-of-Service (DDoS), ripple effects, Injection attacks [33, 80] can be done through unauthorized access of user [81, 82]. Before deployment of any geospatial applications in the EFC system, the four basic security requirements, i.e., availability, authenticity, confidentiality, and data integrity should be verified.

3.2   Geospatial Data

Geospatial data has its geographic location (latitude/longitude) attached to it. These data are captured from different types of sensors. It is also captured by the high-resolution cameras from the satellites. Raster and vector data are primary data format [83], but in [69] types of geospatial data are extended with Point Cloud data and Textual data along with prior two categories.

Raster Data It is made up of a grid of pixels and each pixel has an individual value. All kind of aerial photography and satellite imagery comes into this category. It includes thematic cartographic maps, topographical maps, orthophotos, time series of satellite images.

Vector Data It is made up of the point, polyline, polygon. It has a shape feature, which contains the (x, y) coordinates. The shape contains latitude, polyline longitude information instead of (x,y) while the representation is done on earth surface with 2D view.

Point Cloud Data This kind of data helps to visualize the 3D model of the terrain. Terrestrial Mobile Mapping System (MMS) data [84], LiDAR data are examples of point cloud data [85].

Textual Data Text data are generated from several applications with location-tagged [86]. Social media data like Twitter, Facebook data, online blogs are coming into this category. These help to generate data-driven geospatial semantics.

3.3   Geospatial Analysis Procedures

Geospatial analysis [87, 88] is required for visualization of the geospatial data by using software and tools. The geospatial analysis methods are described below.

Basic Geospatial Operations Buffer creation, nearest neighbor searching, overlay analysis are the basic GIS analysis tools. Overlay of the several geospatial layers has been done based on user queries. It reduces the overload of the computer memory displaying selected data layers instead of all layers. The clip, Intersect, Union are the basic overlay tools. Whereas, the buffering technique is used to identify the affected areas in flood [89], forest fire [90], earthquakes [91], tsunami [92], or disease outbreak like malaria, dengue fever [93], corona etc.

Geospatial Analytical Methods It includes the clustering of the similar point patterns, generation of the heat map, analysis of points density. These methods help to identifying city traffic flow [94], air quality determination [95], monitoring of greenhouse gas emissions from factories, households, livestock agriculture [96].

Network Analysis This type of geospatial analysis is based on graph analysis, where the connection between edges and nodes are defined. Transportation problems can be solved by finding the shortest path between two cities connected by a road network, or rail network, or a combination of both networks. This shortest-path generation helps in healthcare facility [97], tourism facility [98]. Human movement pattern identification after analyzing the trajectories in the road network has been done in [99, 100].

Geometric Measurement Distance and proximity between one point to another point is the basic geometric measurement which is vastly used in the GIS applications. This measurement helps in tourism facility recommendations [101] like nearby hotels, restaurants, visiting places, ATM. It also helps to find nearby hospitals, medical shops in heath-care applications [67, 102]. In disaster management, transfer the victims to the nearby shelters, or reach to the victims with relief [103, 104].

Data Mining A large number of geo-tagged data generate from sensor nodes, drone images, mobile devices, crowdsourcing, etc. Data mining is a technique to generate information after analyzing such unstructured geospatial data. It helps to identify human movement pattern [100], urban growth over a time period [105], smarter traffic light control during time zones [106], wildlife monitoring [107].

Geo-statistics Spatial interpolation is a geo-statistics technique [108] to analyse the surface. This technique estimates the value of an unknown point with the knowledge of nearby known point's value. Kriging [109], Inverse Distance Weighting (IDW), Regression are well known geospatial interpolation techniques. Using these techniques, many geospatial related work like malaria-prone zone identification [110], heavy metal, i.e. zinc, soil contamination [111], recognize area of irrigation water [112] for agriculture had been done.

3.4 Geospatial Applications

Here, we have discussed some geospatial applications which are run on the edge-fog environment or run on the cloud environment with the support of EFC.

Disaster Monitoring Disaster prediction data are stored in telephone central offices (TCOs). These data are important for disaster monitoring. To prevent data loss, a data distribution technique among nearby edge devices has been proposed in [11]. They have used Japan Tsunami prediction data. In [113], identify the missing people in the disaster recognizing by face. To save the energy and network bandwidth only significant facial images are sent to the cloud server. Identifying the disaster-prone area after analyzing geospatial videos and satellite images in fog-cloud environment [12].

Transportation Monitoring A traffic management system [114] is developed where RSU and vehicles (both parked and moving) act as fog nodes according to the queueing theory. They scheduled traffic flow among fog nodes and tried to minimize the response time to make it real-time traffic management.

A mobility pattern of moving agents predicted after applying a machine learning algorithm on spatio-temporal mobility data [67, 115]. It helps to predict the next location of the moving agents, which added advantage for Time-Critical Applications.

A prediction model [94] is generated after analyzing of Bing Maps traffic jam information, and manage traffic flow in the Chicago city.

A smart traffic lighting system is proposed in [106], which is to optimize the management process. The lighting time changes according to the traffic conditions of the roads. It reduces human errors in signaling.

Health and Diseases Monitoring Indoor, outdoor patient's continuous health monitoring is necessary. Mukherjee et al. [116] proposed a cloud-Fog based solution for health monitoring with mobility data of patients while he/she is an outdoor location. Any small health data analysis has been done by fog devices, but any critical data analysis and mobility data analysis has been done in the cloud server.

A heart disease identifying, HealthFog [117], architecture has been developed with deep learning technology. They used FogBus for real-time data analysis by integrating the IoT-Edge-Cloud environment with delay and energy efficiency. Malaria [65, 110], dengue fever [93] prone zone identification with geospatial map and taking action accordingly are some aspects in this category.

Tourism Monitoring Geo-tagged Flickr images are mining to detect the accurate tourist destination in [118]. RHadoop platform helps to organize such big spatial tourism data in the Cloud platform. A mobile-based tourist recommendation system has been developed in [101]. A tourist guide application for Cyprus is discussed in [98].

Agriculture Monitoring Vatsavai et al. [119] synthetically generates images of crop fields. With the anomaly detection, feature extraction, and unsupervised technique, they identified the Weeds and crop diseases. Omran et al. [112] proposed an irrigation water quality evaluation method for agriculture in the Darb El-Arbaein area. They classified water quality depending on the salinity of the water. The computed index value determines the quality of the water. High index (above 70) is good for irrigation, where the lower index (below 40) is bad for irrigation. A livestock agriculture analysis has been done by [96]. They analyze the dataset of biodiversity, climate, water, land, people, farms, and animals using the cloud server.

Environment Monitoring The presence of excessive Carbon Monoxide (CO) gas in the air is a cause of environmental pollution. Monitoring of CO level increment in pollution-prone areas is developed an application of Fog computing [120]. They used krigging methods to identify the distance among CO emission areas, calculated and plotted on Google map using lat/lon information. Air quality also have been checked at low concentration levels in [95] using AirSensEUR.

Various mineral resources of India are determined after data mining of spatial big data and displayed resources using overlay analysis in the QGIS tool [121]. They also have done Ganga river management using mist Computing.

4 Existing Work on Geospatial Edge-Fog Computing: A Glance

We have summarised the existing geospatial applications on the edge and fog computing domain in Table 1. Here, we pointed out the existing papers in the first column. Second column is said about the edge and/or fog nodes used in their work. Other computing paradigm, devices applied in different works are presented in the third column. Fourth column describes the used data in works. In the last column, the geospatial applications had applied in the corresponding research work.

A large number of applications are associated with Geospatial Edge-Fog domain. Methane gas leakage monitoring [7] has been done with collected sensor data by wireless sensor network (WSN) and IoT devices. The data are processed in Raspberry Pi devices and identified the abnormal sensor data from gas leakage areas. In other work on CO gas level monitoring [120], gas sensor data are collected through Mikrokontroller ESP 8266, Access point, MiFi, and data analysis has been done and stored in the Cloud server.

Healthcare applications in EFC has been proposed in [116]. They used health data of various aged group students using Internet of Health Things (IoHT) and stored data in Cloud. Raspberry Pi is used for primary health data analysis. Tuli et al. [117] used patients' heart data for identifying health disease. They used FogBus tool for analysis heart data.

Trajectory data collection for various IoT applications has been elaborated in [122]. They used taxi trajectory data for analysis. The data collection and analysis have been done through edge nodes and fog servers respectively. Real-time traffic management has been proposed by Wang et al. [114]. Road side units(RSU) collects the real-time data of the roads and analysis in nearby cloudlet. The final data are stored in the Cloud.

Time-critical application [67] and mission-critical application [68] has been proposed in EFC domain. Mobility data is analysed to predict the location of the user in a critical time. So that the facility can be provided to the user easily. They used mobile devices for tracking the user location and stored in Cloud. On the other hand, simulated data, and nodes are used for critical mission applications. They used K* heuristic search algorithm for determining the shortest path to reach the critical location for the defense sector.

Different types of image data are analysed in EFC for several applications like disaster situational awareness [12], nanosatellite constellations [123], metropolitan intelligent surveillance [124]. Satellite image data are used for first two applications.

Table 1 Existing work in geospatial edge-fog computing

Work	Edge/fog nodes	Associated computing	Considered data	Applications
Klein et al. [7]	Raspberry Pi	WSN, IoT	Sensor data	Methane gas leaks monitoring
Nugroho et al. [120]	Mikrokontroller ESP 8266, Access point, MiFi	Gas sensor, Cloud server	CO gas sensors data	CO gas level monitoring
Mukherjee et al. [116]	Raspberry Pi	Cloud, IoHT	Student health data	Personalized healthcare
Tuli et al. [117]	FogBus	Cloud, IoT	Heart patient data	Heart diseases monitoring
Cao et al. [122]	Simulated edge nodes	Fog server	Taxi-trajectory data	Trajectory data collection for IoT applications
Wang et al. [114]	RSU	Cloud, Cloudlet	Taxi-trajectory datasets	Traffic management system
Ghosh et al. [67]	Mobile device	Cloud, IoT	Mobility data	Time-critical application
Mishra et al. [68]	Simulation node	WSN, Cloud	Simulated data	Mission critical applications
Chemodanov et al. [12]	Not mentioned	Cloud	Video and satellite image data	Disaster situational awareness
Denby et al. [123]	Jetson TX2	Image sensor	Satellite image data	Nanosatellite constellations
Dautov et al. [124]	Raspberry Pi 3	Cloud	CCTV image data	Metropolitan intelligent surveillance system
Barik et al. [121]	Raspberry Pi	Cloud	Mineral resources data	Mineral resources information management
Vatsavai et al. [119]	Lenovo ThinkStation P320 with GPU	Not mentioned	Synthetically generated image	Weeds and crop diseases identification
Armstrong et al. [125]	Clusters of sensors	IoT sensors, Cloud	Safecast data	Ionizing radiation risk detecting
Richardson et al. [126]	Raspberry Pi-2B, Pi camera	Single board computer	Raster data	Solar forecasting
Tsubaki et al. [11]	Telephone central offices(TCO)	Not mentioned	Japan tsunami prediction data	Data loss prevention in natural disasters.
Barik et al. [127]	Intel Edison	GIS Cloud	Global map data	Different compression techniques over GIS data
Das et al. [66]	Mobile, Laptop	Cloud (GCP)	Road network, rail track, forest data	Geospatial query resolution
Higashino et al. [128]	Cyber physical systems	IoT, Laser range scanner	Not mentioned	Safety management, and vehicle speeds prediction
Liu et al. [113]	Edge server	Cloud, IoT device	Face image data	Missing people search
Liu et al. [129]	Performance oriented edge computing (POEC)	IoT	Not mentioned	Multi-scale 3D scenery processing

Whereas, CCTV image data is used for the intelligent surveillance application. Jetson TX2 and image sensors are used for nanosatellite constellations.

Mineral resources data are captured and analysed in Raspberry Pi and Cloud for providing mineral resources information management [121]. For weeds and crop disease identification [119], Lenovo ThinkStation P320 with GPU has been used to process various high definition synthetic crop images. Safecast data processed for ionizing radiation risk detection [125] and Japan tsunami prediction data analysed for data loss prevention in natural disasters [11]. Solar forecasting [126] has been done with the analysis of raster data in Raspberry Pi-2B and single-board computers. Raster data captured through Pi camera.

Geospatial query processing [66], and different compression techniques [127] over GIS data are done using EFC. Several geospatial queries are done over road network, rail track, forest data. Delay and power consumption has been calculated for different types of geospatial queries. For the compression technique, global map data has been utilized.

5 Limitations in Geospatial Edge-Fog Computing

Every domain has its limitations. We will discuss here the drawbacks of geospatial edge-fog computing.

- Geospatial data are large in volume. It is difficult to store and process it in small computing infrastructure, i.e., EFC. Whereas, the cloud has the advantage of a large data store.
- Large computation is required for geospatial prediction and analysis. Sometimes this cannot be fulfilled by EFC.
- Small number of simulation tool, like iFogSim [130, 131], FogBus [132] for EFC is available.

6 Future Directions

In this section of the chapter, we discuss the future directions of the geospatial EFC research work. Though many explorations have been done in the edge and fog computing, very little progress happened with the geospatial domain. Still, we can think about the following aspects of geospatial Edge-Fog Computing in the future.

- Investigation of pricing policies is required individually for geospatial data providers and Edge-Fog computing service providers.
- Geospatial data management in the EFC environment is a challenge. Keeping a small amount of data within the edge and fog nodes of a distributed manner and synchronize them.

- Geospatial application management, EFC resource provisioning, with artificial intelligence and machine learning technique can be a future trend.
- Every geospatial application, i.e., weather prediction, health-care, crop analysis, etc. has its own requirements that are different from each other. Application relevant policies are required for proper management in the EFC environment.
- Automatic orchestration of different geospatial web services to resolve any geospatial query in the EFC domain can be future aspects.

7 Summary

In this chapter, we have discussed the existing works on the Geospatial Edge-Fog computing domain in detail. We provide a taxonomy over geospatial EFC which considered about the different types of geospatial computing management, geospatial data types, geospatial analysis methods, and geospatial applications. We provide a brief of geospatial EFC existing work in a tabular form. After that, we have discussed the limitations of the geospatial EFC. We ended our discussion with future possibilities of geospatial EFC.

References

1. C. Yang and Q. Huang, *Spatial cloud computing: a practical approach.* CRC Press, 2013.
2. M. Aazam, S. Zeadally, and K. A. Harras, "Offloading in fog computing for iot: Review, enabling technologies, and research opportunities," *Future Generation Computer Systems*, vol. 87, pp. 278–289, 2018.
3. H. Das, R. K. Barik, H. Dubey, and D. S. Roy, *Cloud Computing for Geospatial Big Data Analytics: Intelligent Edge, Fog and Mist Computing.* Springer, 2018, vol. 49.
4. A. V. Dastjerdi, H. Gupta, R. N. Calheiros, S. K. Ghosh, and R. Buyya, "Fog computing: Principles, architectures, and applications," in *Internet of things.* Elsevier, 2016, pp. 61–75.
5. Y. Sahni, J. Cao, and L. Yang, "Data-aware task allocation for achieving low latency in collaborative edge computing," *IEEE Internet of Things Journal*, vol. 6, no. 2, pp. 3512–3524, 2018.
6. W. Z. Khan, E. Ahmed, S. Hakak, I. Yaqoob, and A. Ahmed, "Edge computing: A survey," *Future Generation Computer Systems*, vol. 97, pp. 219–235, 2019.
7. L. Klein, "Geospatial internet of things: Framework for fugitive methane gas leaks monitoring," in *International Conference on GIScience Short Paper Proceedings*, vol. 1, no. 1, 2016.
8. R. Barik, H. Dubey, S. Sasane, C. Misra, N. Constant, and K. Mankodiya, "Fog2fog: augmenting scalability in fog computing for health gis systems," in *2017 IEEE/ACM International Conference on Connected Health: Applications, Systems and Engineering Technologies (CHASE).* IEEE, 2017, pp. 241–242.
9. R. K. Barik, H. Dubey, and K. Mankodiya, "SOA-FOG: secure service-oriented edge computing architecture for smart health big data analytics," in *2017 IEEE Global Conference on Signal and Information Processing (GlobalSIP).* IEEE, 2017, pp. 477–481.
10. T. N. Gia and M. Jiang, "Exploiting fog computing in health monitoring," *Fog and Edge Computing: Principles and Paradigms*, pp. 291–318, 2019.

11. T. Tsubaki, R. Ishibashi, T. Kuwahara, and Y. Okazaki, "Effective disaster recovery for edge computing against large-scale natural disasters," in *2020 IEEE 17th Annual Consumer Communications & Networking Conference (CCNC).* IEEE, 2020, pp. 1–2.
12. D. Chemodanov, P. Calyam, and K. Palaniappan, "Fog computing to enable geospatial video analytics for disaster-incident situational awareness," *Fog Computing: Theory and Practice,* pp. 473–503, 2020.
13. M. A. Zamora-Izquierdo, J. Santa, J. A. Martínez, V. Martínez, and A. F. Skarmeta, "Smart farming iot platform based on edge and cloud computing," *Biosystems engineering,* vol. 177, pp. 4–17, 2019.
14. P. Garcia Lopez, A. Montresor, D. Epema, A. Datta, T. Higashino, A. Iamnitchi, M. Barcellos, P. Felber, and E. Riviere, "Edge-centric computing: Vision and challenges," 2015.
15. C. Chang, S. N. Srirama, and R. Buyya, "Internet of things (iot) and new computing paradigms," *Fog and edge computing: principles and paradigms,* pp. 1–23, 2019.
16. M. Chiang and T. Zhang, "Fog and iot: An overview of research opportunities," *IEEE Internet of Things Journal,* vol. 3, no. 6, pp. 854–864, 2016.
17. E. Baccarelli, P. G. V. Naranjo, M. Scarpiniti, M. Shojafar, and J. H. Abawajy, "Fog of everything: Energy-efficient networked computing architectures, research challenges, and a case study," *IEEE access,* vol. 5, pp. 9882–9910, 2017.
18. M. Ghobaei-Arani, A. Souri, and A. A. Rahmanian, "Resource management approaches in fog computing: a comprehensive review," *Journal of Grid Computing,* pp. 1–42, 2019.
19. C.-H. Hong and B. Varghese, "Resource management in fog/edge computing: a survey on architectures, infrastructure, and algorithms," *ACM Computing Surveys (CSUR),* vol. 52, no. 5, pp. 1–37, 2019.
20. P. Hu, S. Dhelim, H. Ning, and T. Qiu, "Survey on fog computing: architecture, key technologies, applications and open issues," *Journal of network and computer applications,* vol. 98, pp. 27–42, 2017.
21. P. Jiang, T. Fana, H. Gao, W. Shi, L. Liu, C. Cérin, and J. Wan, "Energy aware edge computing: A survey," *Computer Communications,* vol. 151, pp. 556–580, 2020.
22. F. A. Kraemer, A. E. Braten, N. Tamkittikhun, and D. Palma, "Fog computing in healthcare–a review and discussion," *IEEE Access,* vol. 5, pp. 9206–9222, 2017.
23. C. Li, Y. Xue, J. Wang, W. Zhang, and T. Li, "Edge-oriented computing paradigms: A survey on architecture design and system management," *ACM Computing Surveys (CSUR),* vol. 51, no. 2, pp. 1–34, 2018.
24. R. Mahmud, R. Kotagiri, and R. Buyya, "Fog computing: A taxonomy, survey and future directions," in *Internet of everything.* Springer, 2018, pp. 103–130.
25. R. Mahmud, K. Ramamohanarao, and R. Buyya, "Application management in fog computing environments: A taxonomy, review and future directions," *ACM Computing Surveys,* 2020.
26. C. Mouradian, D. Naboulsi, S. Yangui, R. H. Glitho, M. J. Morrow, and P. A. Polakos, "A comprehensive survey on fog computing: State-of-the-art and research challenges," *IEEE Communications Surveys & Tutorials,* vol. 20, no. 1, pp. 416–464, 2017.
27. M. Mukherjee, L. Shu, and D. Wang, "Survey of fog computing: Fundamental, network applications, and research challenges," *IEEE Communications Surveys & Tutorials,* vol. 20, no. 3, pp. 1826–1857, 2018.
28. R. K. Naha, S. Garg, D. Georgakopoulos, P. P. Jayaraman, L. Gao, Y. Xiang, and R. Ranjan, "Fog computing: Survey of trends, architectures, requirements, and research directions," *IEEE access,* vol. 6, pp. 47 980–48 009, 2018.
29. S. B. Nath, H. Gupta, S. Chakraborty, and S. K. Ghosh, "A survey of fog computing and communication: current researches and future directions," *arXiv preprint arXiv:1804.04365,* 2018.
30. O. Osanaiye, S. Chen, Z. Yan, R. Lu, K.-K. R. Choo, and M. Dlodlo, "From cloud to fog computing: A review and a conceptual live vm migration framework," *IEEE Access,* vol. 5, pp. 8284–8300, 2017.
31. C. Puliafito, E. Mingozzi, F. Longo, A. Puliafito, and O. Rana, "Fog computing for the internet of things: A survey," *ACM Transactions on Internet Technology (TOIT),* vol. 19, no. 2, pp. 1–41, 2019.

32. C. Perera, Y. Qin, J. C. Estrella, S. Reiff-Marganiec, and A. V. Vasilakos, "Fog computing for sustainable smart cities: A survey," *ACM Computing Surveys (CSUR)*, vol. 50, no. 3, pp. 1–43, 2017.

33. R. Roman, J. Lopez, and M. Mambo, "Mobile edge computing, fog et al.: A survey and analysis of security threats and challenges," *Future Generation Computer Systems*, vol. 78, pp. 680–698, 2018.

34. S. N. Shirazi, A. Gouglidis, A. Farshad, and D. Hutchison, "The extended cloud: Review and analysis of mobile edge computing and fog from a security and resilience perspective," *IEEE Journal on Selected Areas in Communications*, vol. 35, no. 11, pp. 2586–2595, 2017.

35. A. Yousefpour, C. Fung, T. Nguyen, K. Kadiyala, F. Jalali, A. Niakanlahiji, J. Kong, and J. P. Jue, "All one needs to know about fog computing and related edge computing paradigms: A complete survey," *Journal of Systems Architecture*, vol. 98, pp. 289–330, 2019.

36. W. Shi, J. Cao, Q. Zhang, Y. Li, and L. Xu, "Edge computing: Vision and challenges," *IEEE internet of things journal*, vol. 3, no. 5, pp. 637–646, 2016.

37. P. Zhang, M. Zhou, and G. Fortino, "Security and trust issues in fog computing: A survey," *Future Generation Computer Systems*, vol. 88, pp. 16–27, 2018.

38. R. Buyya, C. S. Yeo, S. Venugopal, J. Broberg, and I. Brandic, "Cloud computing and emerging it platforms: Vision, hype, and reality for delivering computing as the 5th utility," *Future Generation computer systems*, vol. 25, no. 6, pp. 599–616, 2009.

39. Z. Liu, "Typical characteristics of cloud gis and several key issues of cloud spatial decision support system," in *2013 IEEE 4th International Conference on Software Engineering and Service Science*.   IEEE, 2013, pp. 668–671.

40. A. Rezgui, Z. Malik, and C. Yang, "High-resolution spatial interpolation on cloud platforms," in *Proceedings of the 28th Annual ACM Symposium on Applied Computing*, 2013, pp. 377–382.

41. K. Evangelidis, K. Ntouros, S. Makridis, and C. Papatheodorou, "Geospatial services in the cloud," *Computers & Geosciences*, vol. 63, pp. 116–122, 2014.

42. J. Das, A. Dasgupta, S. K. Ghosh, and R. Buyya, "A geospatial orchestration framework on cloud for processing user queries," in *2016 IEEE International Conference on Cloud Computing in Emerging Markets (CCEM)*.   IEEE, 2016, pp. 1–8.

43. Z. Li, C. Yang, Q. Huang, K. Liu, M. Sun, and J. Xia, "Building model as a service to support geosciences," *Computers, Environment and Urban Systems*, vol. 61, pp. 141–152, 2017.

44. T. Xing, S. Zhang, and L. Tao, "Cloud-based spatial information service architecture within lbs," *Positioning*, vol. 2014, 2014.

45. Y. Shi and F. Bian, "The design and application of the gloud gis," in *International Conference on Geo-Informatics in Resource Management and Sustainable Ecosystem*.   Springer, 2014, pp. 56–67.

46. Y. Wang, S. Wang, and D. Zhou, "Retrieving and indexing spatial data in the cloud computing environment," in *IEEE International Conference on Cloud Computing*.   Springer, 2009, pp. 322–331.

47. L.-Y. Wei, Y.-T. Hsu, W.-C. Peng, and W.-C. Lee, "Indexing spatial data in cloud data managements," *Pervasive and Mobile Computing*, vol. 15, pp. 48–61, 2014.

48. V. Siládi, L. Huraj, N. Polčák, and E. Vesel, "A parallel processing of spatial data interpolation on computing cloud," in *Proceedings of the Fifth Balkan Conference in Informatics*, 2012, pp. 193–198.

49. R. C. Mateus, T. L. L. Siqueira, V. C. Times, R. R. Ciferri, and C. D. de Aguiar Ciferri, "Spatial data warehouses and spatial olap come towards the cloud: design and performance," *Distributed and parallel databases*, vol. 34, no. 3, pp. 425–461, 2016.

50. S. J. Park and J. S. Yoo, "Leveraging cloud computing for spatial association mining," in *2014 IEEE International Conference on Systems, Man, and Cybernetics (SMC)*.   IEEE, 2014, pp. 4152–4153.

51. Y. Zhong, J. Han, T. Zhang, and J. Fang, "A distributed geospatial data storage and processing framework for large-scale webgis," in *2012 20th International Conference on Geoinformatics*.   IEEE, 2012, pp. 1–7.

52. R. Sugumaran, J. Burnett, and A. Blinkmann, "Big 3D spatial data processing using cloud computing environment," in *Proceedings of the 1st ACM SIGSPATIAL international workshop on analytics for big geospatial data*, 2012, pp. 20–22.
53. G. Zhang, Q. Huang, A.-X. Zhu, and J. H. Keel, "Enabling point pattern analysis on spatial big data using cloud computing: optimizing and accelerating ripley's k function," *International Journal of Geographical Information Science*, vol. 30, no. 11, pp. 2230–2252, 2016.
54. S. You, J. Zhang, and L. Gruenwald, "Large-scale spatial join query processing in cloud," in *2015 31st IEEE International Conference on Data Engineering Workshops*. IEEE, 2015, pp. 34–41.
55. S. You, J. Zhang, and L. Gruenwald, "Spatial join query processing in cloud: Analyzing design choices and performance comparisons," in *2015 44th International Conference on Parallel Processing Workshops*. IEEE, 2015, pp. 90–97.
56. J. Das, A. Dasgupta, S. K. Ghosh, and R. Buyya, "A learning technique for vm allocation to resolve geospatial queries," in *Recent Findings in Intelligent Computing Techniques*. Springer, 2019, pp. 577–584.
57. V. Prokhorenko and M. A. Babar, "Architectural resilience in cloud, fog and edge systems: A survey," *IEEE Access*, vol. 8, pp. 28 078–28 095, 2020.
58. M. Chen, Y. Hao, Y. Li, C.-F. Lai, and D. Wu, "On the computation offloading at ad hoc cloudlet: architecture and service modes," *IEEE Communications Magazine*, vol. 53, no. 6, pp. 18–24, 2015.
59. A. Mukherjee, D. G. Roy, and D. De, "Mobility-aware task delegation model in mobile cloud computing," *The Journal of Supercomputing*, vol. 75, no. 1, pp. 314–339, 2019.
60. J. Michel and C. Julien, "A cloudlet-based proximal discovery service for machine-to-machine applications," in *International Conference on Mobile Computing, Applications, and Services*. Springer, 2013, pp. 215–232.
61. J. Das, A. Mukherjee, S. K. Ghosh, and R. Buyya, "Geo-cloudlet: Time and power efficient geospatial query resolution using cloudlet," in *2019 11th International Conference on Advanced Computing (ICoAC)*. IEEE, 2019, pp. 180–187.
62. M. Uehara, "Mist computing: Linking cloudlet to fogs," in *International Conference on Computational Science/Intelligence & Applied Informatics*. Springer, 2017, pp. 201–213.
63. J. S. Preden, K. Tammemäe, A. Jantsch, M. Leier, A. Riid, and E. Calis, "The benefits of self-awareness and attention in fog and mist computing," *Computer*, vol. 48, no. 7, pp. 37–45, 2015.
64. R. K. Barik, A. Tripathi, H. Dubey, R. K. Lenka, T. Pratik, S. Sharma, K. Mankodiya, V. Kumar, and H. Das, "MistGIS: Optimizing geospatial data analysis using mist computing," in *Progress in Computing, Analytics and Networking*. Springer, 2018, pp. 733–742.
65. R. K. Barik, A. C. Dubey, A. Tripathi, T. Pratik, S. Sasane, R. K. Lenka, H. Dubey, K. Mankodiya, and V. Kumar, "Mist data: leveraging mist computing for secure and scalable architecture for smart and connected health," *Procedia Computer Science*, vol. 125, pp. 647–653, 2018.
66. J. Das, A. Mukherjee, S. K. Ghosh, and R. Buyya, "Spatio-fog: A green and timeliness-oriented fog computing model for geospatial query resolution," *Simulation Modelling Practice and Theory*, vol. 100, article no. 102043, 2020.
67. S. Ghosh, A. Mukherjee, S. K. Ghosh, and R. Buyya, "Mobi-IoST: mobility-aware cloud-fog-edge-iot collaborative framework for time-critical applications," *IEEE Transactions on Network Science and Engineering*, 2019.
68. M. Mishra, S. K. Roy, A. Mukherjee, D. De, S. K. Ghosh, and R. Buyya, "An energy-aware multi-sensor geo-fog paradigm for mission critical applications," *Journal of Ambient Intelligence and Humanized Computing*, pp. 1–19, 2019.
69. A. Olasz and B. Nguyen Thai, "Geospatial big data processing in an open source distributed computing environment," *PeerJ Preprints*, vol. 4, p. e2226v1, 2016.
70. E. M. Xavier, F. J. Ariza-López, and M. A. Ureña-Cámara, "A survey of measures and methods for matching geospatial vector datasets," *ACM Computing Surveys (CSUR)*, vol. 49, no. 2, pp. 1–34, 2016.

71. M. R. Palattella, R. Soua, A. Khelil, and T. Engel, "Fog computing as the key for seamless connectivity handover in future vehicular networks," in *Proceedings of the 34th ACM/SIGAPP Symposium on Applied Computing*, 2019, pp. 1996–2000.
72. X. Hou, Y. Li, M. Chen, D. Wu, D. Jin, and S. Chen, "Vehicular fog computing: A viewpoint of vehicles as the infrastructures," *IEEE Transactions on Vehicular Technology*, vol. 65, no. 6, pp. 3860–3873, 2016.
73. N. B. Truong, G. M. Lee, and Y. Ghamri-Doudane, "Software defined networking-based vehicular adhoc network with fog computing," in *2015 IFIP/IEEE International Symposium on Integrated Network Management (IM)*. IEEE, 2015, pp. 1202–1207.
74. M. Arif, G. Wang, V. E. Balas, O. Geman, A. Castiglione, and J. Chen, "Sdn based communications privacy-preserving architecture for vanets using fog computing," *Vehicular Communications*, p. 100265, 2020.
75. S. Yi, C. Li, and Q. Li, "A survey of fog computing: concepts, applications and issues," in *Proceedings of the 2015 workshop on mobile big data*, 2015, pp. 37–42.
76. P. Mach and Z. Becvar, "Mobile edge computing: A survey on architecture and computation offloading," *IEEE Communications Surveys & Tutorials*, vol. 19, no. 3, pp. 1628–1656, 2017.
77. B. Wu, X. Wu, and J. Huang, "Geospatial data services within cloud computing environment," in *2010 International Conference on Audio, Language and Image Processing*. IEEE, 2010, pp. 1577–1584.
78. L. Gu, D. Zeng, S. Guo, A. Barnawi, and Y. Xiang, "Cost efficient resource management in fog computing supported medical cyber-physical system," *IEEE Transactions on Emerging Topics in Computing*, vol. 5, no. 1, pp. 108–119, 2015.
79. S. Yi, Z. Qin, and Q. Li, "Security and privacy issues of fog computing: A survey," in *International conference on wireless algorithms, systems, and applications*. Springer, 2015, pp. 685–695.
80. P. Bhattacharya, S. Tanwar, R. Shah, and A. Ladha, "Mobile edge computing-enabled blockchain framework—a survey," in *Proceedings of ICRIC 2019*. Springer, 2020, pp. 797–809.
81. Q. Li, S. Meng, S. Zhang, J. Hou, and L. Qi, "Complex attack linkage decision-making in edge computing networks," *IEEE Access*, vol. 7, pp. 12 058–12 072, 2019.
82. T. Wang, G. Zhang, A. Liu, M. Z. A. Bhuiyan, and Q. Jin, "A secure iot service architecture with an efficient balance dynamics based on cloud and edge computing," *IEEE Internet of Things Journal*, vol. 6, no. 3, pp. 4831–4843, 2018.
83. S. Shekhar and S. Chawla, *A tour of spatial databases*. Prentice Hall Upper Saddle River, 2003.
84. K. Hammoudi, F. Dornaika, B. Soheilian, and N. Paparoditis, "Extracting wire-frame models of street facades from 3d point clouds and the corresponding cadastral map," *IAPRS*, vol. 38, no. Part 3A, pp. 91–96, 2010.
85. P. K. Agarwal, L. Arge, and A. Danner, "From point cloud to grid dem: A scalable approach," in *Progress in Spatial Data Handling*. Springer, 2006, pp. 771–788.
86. Y. Hu, "Geo-text data and data-driven geospatial semantics," *Geography Compass*, vol. 12, no. 11, p. e12404, 2018.
87. M. J. De Smith, M. F. Goodchild, and P. Longley, *Geospatial analysis: a comprehensive guide to principles, techniques and software tools*. Troubador publishing ltd, 2007.
88. A. Kamilaris and F. O. Ostermann, "Geospatial analysis and the internet of things," *ISPRS international journal of geo-information*, vol. 7, no. 7, p. 269, 2018.
89. O. Chakraborty, J. Das, A. Dasgupta, P. Mitra, and S. K. Ghosh, "A geospatial service oriented framework for disaster risk zone identification," in *International Conference on Computational Science and Its Applications*. Springer, 2016, pp. 44–56.
90. K. Puri, G. Areendran, K. Raj, S. Mazumdar, and P. Joshi, "Forest fire risk assessment in parts of northeast india using geospatial tools," *Journal of forestry research*, vol. 22, no. 4, p. 641, 2011.
91. M. Sharifikia, "Vulnerability assessment and earthquake risk mapping in part of north iran using geospatial techniques," *Journal of the Indian Society of Remote Sensing*, pp. 708–716, 2010.

92. N. Wood, J. Jones, J. Schelling, and M. Schmidtlein, "Tsunami vertical-evacuation planning in the us pacific northwest as a geospatial, multi-criteria decision problem," *International journal of disaster risk reduction*, vol. 9, pp. 68–83, 2014.

93. E. M. Delmelle, H. Zhu, W. Tang, and I. Casas, "A web-based geospatial toolkit for the monitoring of dengue fever," *Applied Geography*, vol. 52, pp. 144–152, 2014.

94. A. I. J. Tostes, F. de LP Duarte-Figueiredo, R. Assunção, J. Salles, and A. A. Loureiro, "From data to knowledge: city-wide traffic flows analysis and prediction using bing maps," in *Proceedings of the 2nd ACM SIGKDD International Workshop on Urban Computing*, 2013, pp. 1–8.

95. A. Kotsev, S. Schade, M. Craglia, M. Gerboles, L. Spinelle, and M. Signorini, "Next generation air quality platform: Openness and interoperability for the internet of things," *Sensors*, vol. 16, no. 3, p. 403, 2016.

96. A. Kamilaris, A. Assumpcio, A. B. Blasi, M. Torrellas, and F. X. Prenafeta-Boldú, "Estimating the environmental impact of agriculture by means of geospatial and big data analysis: The case of catalonia," in *From Science to Society*. Springer, 2018, pp. 39–48.

97. I. A. Jalil, A. R. A. Rasam, N. A. Adnan, N. M. Saraf, and A. N. Idris, "Geospatial network analysis for healthcare facilities accessibility in semi-urban areas," in *2018 IEEE 14th International Colloquium on Signal Processing & Its Applications (CSPA)*. IEEE, 2018, pp. 255–260.

98. A. Kamilaris and A. Pitsillides, "A web-based tourist guide mobile application," in *Proceedings of the International Conference on Sustainability, Technology and Education (STE), Kuala Lumpur, Malaysia*, vol. 29, 2013.

99. S. Ghosh, A. Chowdhury, and S. K. Ghosh, "A machine learning approach to find the optimal routes through analysis of gps traces of mobile city traffic," in *Recent Findings in Intelligent Computing Techniques*. Springer, 2018, pp. 59–67.

100. S. Ghosh and S. K. Ghosh, "Thump: Semantic analysis on trajectory traces to explore human movement pattern," in *Proceedings of the 25th International Conference Companion on World Wide Web*, 2016, pp. 35–36.

101. M. Van Setten, S. Pokraev, and J. Koolwaaij, "Context-aware recommendations in the mobile tourist application compass," in *International Conference on Adaptive Hypermedia and Adaptive Web-Based Systems*. Springer, 2004, pp. 235–244.

102. J. S. Brownstein, C. C. Freifeld, B. Y. Reis, and K. D. Mandl, "Surveillance sans frontieres: Internet-based emerging infectious disease intelligence and the healthmap project," *PLoS medicine*, vol. 5, no. 7, 2008.

103. O. Chakraborty, A. Das, A. Dasgupta, P. Mitra, S. K. Ghosh, and T. Mazumder, "A multi-objective framework for analysis of road network vulnerability for relief facility location during flood hazards: A case study of relief location analysis in bankura district, india," *Transactions in GIS*, vol. 22, no. 5, pp. 1064–1082, 2018.

104. A. Dasgupta, S. K. Ghosh, and P. Mitra, "A technique for assessing the quality of volunteered geographic information for disaster decision making," in *International Conference on Computational Science and Its Applications*. Springer, 2018, pp. 589–597.

105. S. Pal and S. K. Ghosh, "Rule based end-to-end learning framework for urban growth prediction," *arXiv preprint arXiv:1711.10801*, 2017.

106. V. Miz and V. Hahanov, "Smart traffic light in terms of the cognitive road traffic management system (ctms) based on the internet of things," in *Proceedings of IEEE East-West Design & Test Symposium (EWDTS 2014)*. IEEE, 2014, pp. 1–5.

107. E. D. Ayele, K. Das, N. Meratnia, and P. J. Havinga, "Leveraging ble and lora in iot network for wildlife monitoring system (wms)," in *2018 IEEE 4th World Forum on Internet of Things (WF-IoT)*. IEEE, 2018, pp. 342–348.

108. N. Cressie, *Statistics for spatial data*. John Wiley & Sons, 2015.

109. S. Bhattacharjee, P. Mitra, and S. K. Ghosh, "Spatial interpolation to predict missing attributes in gis using semantic kriging," *IEEE Transactions on Geoscience and Remote Sensing*, vol. 52, no. 8, pp. 4771–4780, 2013.

110. A. C. Clements, H. L. Reid, G. C. Kelly, and S. I. Hay, "Further shrinking the malaria map: how can geospatial science help to achieve malaria elimination?" *The Lancet infectious diseases*, vol. 13, no. 8, pp. 709–718, 2013.

111. K. Forsythe, K. Paudel, and C. Marvin, "Geospatial analysis of zinc contamination in lake ontario sediments," *Journal of Environmental Informatics*, vol. 16, no. 1, pp. 1–10, 2010.

112. E.-S. E. Omran, "A proposed model to assess and map irrigation water well suitability using geospatial analysis," *Water*, vol. 4, no. 3, pp. 545–567, 2012.

113. F. Liu, Y. Guo, Z. Cai, N. Xiao, and Z. Zhao, "Edge-enabled disaster rescue: a case study of searching for missing people," *ACM Transactions on Intelligent Systems and Technology (TIST)*, vol. 10, no. 6, pp. 1–21, 2019.

114. X. Wang, Z. Ning, and L. Wang, "Offloading in internet of vehicles: A fog-enabled real-time traffic management system," *IEEE Transactions on Industrial Informatics*, vol. 14, no. 10, pp. 4568–4578, 2018.

115. S. Ghosh, J. Das, and S. K. Ghosh, "Locator: A cloud-fog-enabled framework for facilitating efficient location based services," in *2020 International Conference on COMmunication Systems & NETworkS (COMSNETS)*. IEEE, 2020, pp. 87–92.

116. A. Mukherjee, S. Ghosh, A. Behere, S. K. Ghosh, and R. Buyya, "Internet of health things (ioht) for personalized health care using integrated edge-fog-cloud network," *Journal of Ambient Intelligence and Humanized Computing*, 2020.

117. S. Tuli, N. Basumatary, S. S. Gill, M. Kahani, R. C. Arya, G. S. Wander, and R. Buyya, "Healthfog: An ensemble deep learning based smart healthcare system for automatic diagnosis of heart diseases in integrated iot and fog computing environments," *Future Generation Computer Systems*, vol. 104, pp. 187–200, 2020.

118. X. Zhou, C. Xu, and B. Kimmons, "Detecting tourism destinations using scalable geospatial analysis based on cloud computing platform," *Computers, Environment and Urban Systems*, vol. 54, pp. 144–153, 2015.

119. R. R. Vatsavai, B. Ramachandra, Z. Chen, and J. Jernigan, "geoEdge: a real-time analytics framework for geospatial applications," in *Proceedings of the 8th ACM SIGSPATIAL International Workshop on Analytics for Big Geospatial Data*, 2019, pp. 1–4.

120. F. W. Nugroho, S. Suryono, and J. E. Suseno, "Fog computing for monitoring of various area mapping pollution carbon monoxide (co) with ordinary kriging method," in *2019 Fourth International Conference on Informatics and Computing (ICIC)*. IEEE, 2019, pp. 1–6.

121. R. K. Barik, R. K. Lenka, N. Simha, H. Dubey, and K. Mankodiya, "Fog computing based sdi framework for mineral resources information infrastructure management in india," *arXiv preprint arXiv:1712.09282*, 2017.

122. X. Cao and S. Madria, "Efficient geospatial data collection in iot networks for mobile edge computing," in *2019 IEEE 18th International Symposium on Network Computing and Applications (NCA)*. IEEE, 2019, pp. 1–10.

123. B. Denby and B. Lucia, "Orbital edge computing: Nanosatellite constellations as a new class of computer system," in *Proceedings of the Twenty-Fifth International Conference on Architectural Support for Programming Languages and Operating Systems*, 2020, pp. 939–954.

124. R. Dautov, S. Distefano, D. Bruneo, F. Longo, G. Merlino, A. Puliafito, and R. Buyya, "Metropolitan intelligent surveillance systems for urban areas by harnessing iot and edge computing paradigms," *Software: Practice and Experience*, vol. 48, no. 8, pp. 1475–1492, 2018.

125. M. P. Armstrong, S. Wang, and Z. Zhang, "The internet of things and fast data streams: prospects for geospatial data science in emerging information ecosystems," *Cartography and Geographic Information Science*, vol. 46, no. 1, pp. 39–56, 2019.

126. W. Richardson, H. Krishnaswami, R. Vega, and M. Cervantes, "A low cost, edge computing, all-sky imager for cloud tracking and intra-hour irradiance forecasting," *Sustainability*, vol. 9, no. 4, p. 482, 2017.

127. R. K. Barik, H. Dubey, A. B. Samaddar, R. D. Gupta, and P. K. Ray, "FogGIS: Fog computing for geospatial big data analytics," in *2016 IEEE Uttar Pradesh Section International*

Conference on Electrical, Computer and Electronics Engineering (UPCON).   IEEE, 2016, pp. 613–618.

128. T. Higashino, "Edge computing for cooperative real-time controls using geospatial big data," in *Smart Sensors and Systems.*   Springer, 2017, pp. 441–466.

129. S. Liu, X. Chen, B. Qi, and L. Zherr, "Performace oriented edge computing of geospatial information with 3d scenery," in *2018 IEEE 3rd Advanced Information Technology, Electronic and Automation Control Conference (IAEAC).*   IEEE, 2018, pp. 853–858.

130. H. Gupta, A. Vahid Dastjerdi, S. K. Ghosh, and R. Buyya, "ifogsim: A toolkit for modeling and simulation of resource management techniques in the internet of things, edge and fog computing environments," *Software: Practice and Experience*, vol. 47, no. 9, pp. 1275–1296, 2017.

131. R. Mahmud and R. Buyya, "Modelling and simulation of fog and edge computing environments using ifogsim toolkit," *Fog and edge computing: Principles and paradigms*, pp. 1–35, 2019.

132. S. Tuli, R. Mahmud, S. Tuli, and R. Buyya, "Fogbus: A blockchain-based lightweight framework for edge and fog computing," *Journal of Systems and Software*, vol. 154, pp. 22–36, 2019.

Study of Power Efficient 5G Mobile Edge Computing

Priti Deb, Mohammad S. Obaidat, and Debashis De

Abstract Recently, there has been a lot of innovative work on cloud-based mobile networks. While distributed computing gives immense chances, it likewise forces a few difficulties. One of the difficulties that current information system administrators and future Fifth Generation (5G) wireless communication are predicting is a gigantic increment in data traffic. It is anticipated based on the vision of Internet of Things (IoT) that the growing 5G wireless communication will meet an extraordinary increment in congestion of calculating and processing of data as IoT incorporated exaggerated applications. A fundamental innovation in the escalating age of 5G is Mobile Edge Computing (MEC). Before sending the data to the cloud server, MEC can upgrade mobile devices by facilitating inventory intensified applications, process huge information and give the distributed computing platform within the radio access network (RAN). Hence, MEC empowers a wide range of utilizations. Without a doubt, the worldview is moving to the future generation network which could turn into a reality with the coming of new mechanical ideas. The actual response of MEC is still in its early stages and requests for steady endeavors from both scholarly and industry networks. With the ever-developing energy utilization for data and wireless communication innovation, the communication nodes and infrastructure undertake a significant job in worldwide greenhouse substance releases. Thus, the improvement of green 5G has become a significant task for the structure and execution of future remote communication. As MEC is a key segment of 5G, the energy efficiency has become a standard worry for the construction of the MEC component. In this chapter, we initially give an all-encompassing outline of MEC, its energy efficient innovation, potentials, needs,

P. Deb (✉) · D. De
Centre of Mobile Cloud Computing, Department of Computer Science and Engineering, Maulana Abul Kalam Azad University of Technology, Kolkata, West Bengal, India

M. S. Obaidat
College of Computing and Informatics, University of Sharjah, Sharjah, UAE

University of Jordan, Amman, Jordan

University of Science and Technology Beijing, Beijing, China

© The Author(s), under exclusive license to Springer Nature Switzerland AG 2021   71
A. Mukherjee et al. (eds.), *Mobile Edge Computing*,
https://doi.org/10.1007/978-3-030-69893-5_4

and applications. We further sum up exercises gained from energy efficient resource allocation and task offloading. We also talk about difficulties and expected future headings for MEC research.

Keywords 5G · Mobile Edge computing · Power Efficient · Resource Allocation · NOMA

1 Introduction

These days, with the fast improvement of remote innovation and the Internet of things (IoT), an ever-increasing number of smart cell phones, wearable gadgets, have diverse remote systems that get to prerequisites for data transfer capacity and calculation [1, 2]. Later on, cell phones will turn out to be more perceptive, and applications conveyed on them will require broad processing power and tireless information to get to [3]. Be that as it may, the advancement of these new applications and services is restricted by the limited registering force and battery life of these mobile devices [4]. If information eager and computing-intensive jobs can be offloaded to the cloud to execute, it can beat the inadequacies of the absence of processing intensity of the cell phones [5]. Nonetheless, when cell phones are associated with the cloud through a remote system, a moderately long deferral happens, which isn't appropriate for delay-sensitive jobs [6]. In the area of mobile communication, power efficiency [7] and spectral efficiency [8] are leading issues for fifth-generation (5G) wireless networks [9]. 5G mobile network is going through some serious challenges such as the need of one million connections per kilometer square area, and user connectivity in the Gbps data rate to meet the need of the end-users [10]. Due to the limited battery life and dynamic movement of the devices proper network model is very much essential. It is predicted that in 2020 approximately 11.8 billion mobile devices would be connected to the Internet through a 5G wireless network, and more than 8.2% devices will be low power generated smart devices [11]. The communication between mobile devices and edge or cloud system endures with massive transmission power consumption and lack of spectral efficiency problem, especially when using 4G/LTE-A connections are concerned [12, 13]. To reduce the energy consumption, Mobile Edge Computing (MEC) comes into the scenario [14].

MEC provides the Mobile Cloud Computing (MCC) [15, 16] services at the edge of mobile network. MCC is a platform where the computations and storage take place inside the cloud server instead of mobile device. However, long distance cloud server increases the delay and power consumption of the mobile device. Cloudlet is a computer or a cluster of computers. It acts as an agent between cloud servers and users [17]. In case of fog computing [18], the immediate devices between end uses and cloud server take part in data processing. MCC is a combination of mobile computing and cloud computing [19]. It causes problem to the real time applications. To solve this problem, MEC comes into the scenario by processing computation and storage part at the edge of the network. To perform a job given by a mobile device within RAN in the users' close proximity, MEC has a role in this regard [20]. MEC can be called as the complement of Cloud-RAN technology. Requirements of mobile edge computing in the field of wireless communication are as follows [21]:

- Development of high-bandwidth for quick data transfer
- Delay-aware applications
- Aggregating extensiveness of IoT devices
- Energy-efficient networks.

Figure 1 demonstrates the MEC architecture. MEC applications run closure to mobile devices than cloud computing, which reduces delay and power consumption of the network.

Different researches are going on to find the importance and technical characteristics of mobile edge computing in the era of 5G. A MEC survey for the 5G network is performed in [21, 22–24]. In a communication viewpoint, another study is proposed in [25]. A comparative study with cloudlet and fog computing is discussed in [26] while implementing mobile edge computing. Task caching and task offloading models are summarized in [27, 28]. Various resource allocation based on mobile edge computing platforms is illustrated in [29, 30]. In [31–33],

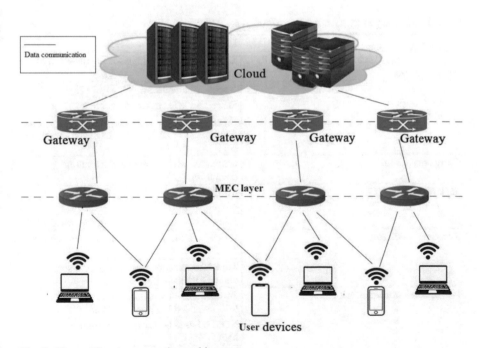

Fig. 1 The mobile edge computing architecture

Energy efficient framework for MEC is conducted. Table 1 summarizes existing research works on mobile edge computing.

As indicated in [34], MEC can be portrayed by certain properties, challenges, use cases, and applications. Figure 2 demonstrates different challenges, properties, and use cases of MEC.

1.1 Properties of MEC

The typical properties of mobile edge computing are discussed as follows:

1.1.1 On-Premises Isolation

Unlike remote cloud servers, Edge is being deployed locally, implying that it can run disengaged from the remainder of the system while approaching nearby assets. This turns out to be especially significant for Machine-to-Machine situations, for instance when managing security or wellbeing frameworks that need high levels of strength.

Table 1 Summary of research works performed on MEC

Subjects	Contributions
Key technologies, architectures, State-of-art, communication	Study of key technologies in the direction of 5G [22]
	Review of architecture for MEC [23]
	Survey on MEC based on communication viewpoint [25]
	State-of-art of multi-access edge computing [21]
Comparative study	Compared MEC with cloudlet and fog computing [26]
Task offloading	MEC based task offloading for ultra-dense mobile network [27]
	Joint task offloading in multi-server MEC [28]
Resource allocation	Resource allocation model for power-efficient MEC [29]
	Time minimization strategy-based resource allocation model [30]
Power-efficient framework	Power-efficient scheduling framework for MEC-enabled Internet of vehicles [31]
	NOMA based power-efficient framework for MEC [32, 33]
	Power-efficient caching for 5G based MEC [34]

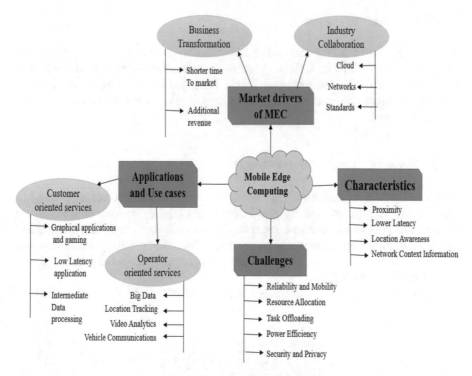

Fig. 2 Summary of MEC: Challenges, properties, and applications

1.1.2 Proximity

In MEC, Edge servers are deployed at the edge of the network close to the IoT devices. It can be used to process the key data generated by the IoT devices with shorter processing time. Being near to the source of data, Edge Computing is especially valuable to catch key data for investigation and big data. Edge computing may likewise have direct access to the IoT devices, which can without much of a stretch be utilized by business explicit applications.

1.1.3 Low-Latency

As Edge computing runs near IoT devices, it extensively lessens delay of the network. This can be used to respond quicker, to improve client experience, or to decrease blockage in other portions of the network. With the help of MEC, it is possible to support real-time IoT applications.

1.1.4 Location-Awareness

At the point when a Network Edge is a piece of a remote system, regardless of whether it is Wi-Fi or Cell, a neighborhood administration can use low-level flagging data to decide the area of each associated gadget. This brings forth a whole group of business-arranged use cases, counting Location-Based Services, Analytics, and some more.

1.1.5 Network Context Information

Constant system information, (for example, radio conditions, arrange insights, and so on.) can be utilized by applications and administrations to offer to set related administrations that can separate the versatile broadband experience and be adapted. New applications can be created (which will profit by this continuous system information) to associate versatile supporters with nearby focal points, organizations, and occasions.

Figure 3 pictorially explains the properties of MEC.

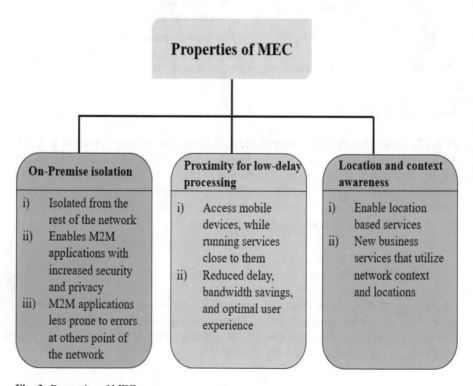

Fig. 3 Properties of MEC

Although a few capabilities and chances, numerous challenges should be concentrated to make a MEC system provides benefits to the end-users. Among the main challenges, we have the ones shown below.

1.2   Challenges of Mobile Edge Computing

1.2.1   Reliability and Mobility

In 5G mobile network, densification management is a crucial feature. The main challenge of MEC is reliability. MEC decreases delay, improves bandwidth in information concentrated applications, and increases responsiveness by handling sensory data locally [35].

1.2.2   Resource Allocation

Wireless channels get bottlenecked with a huge requirement of resources for users. As resources are limited, but mobile traffic increases in an exponential way [36]. Resource scarcity occurs among users. For the effective implementation of MEC proper resource allocation is a great challenge.

1.2.3   Task Offloading

As we have already mentioned that computational resources are limited in edge servers, the distribution of these computing resources for executing task is also challenging. With the small knowledge about wireless communication, clients offload tasks. To control a job offloading, conferring to the remaining battery limit of cell phone and wireless networks is a challenging factor of MEC [37, 38].

1.2.4   Power Efficiency

Power optimization is the most challenging issue. Proper resource allocation and efficient tasks offloading strategies reduce the power consumption of MEC. In 5G wireless communication, NOMA performs a significant role to optimize the power consumption.

1.2.5   Security and Privacy

MEC executes its tasks with the help of different heterogeneous network components, thus security and privacy are a major concern. Though compared to mobile cloud computing MEC has better privacy and security policy, task offloading with proper security is also a challenging issue in MEC.

MEC has several applications and use cases based on customer-oriented services and operator oriented services. They are graphical applications and gaming, low latency applications, big data, location tracking, video analytics, etc.

Business transformation and industry collaboration are the market drivers of MEC.

MEC has been esteemed as a promising innovation for future generation mobile computing for the fast development of wireless technology, because of that it can increase the processing power of clients applications, such as Augmented Reality (AR) [39]. In MEC platform users can offload the applications to the MEC server that are situated at the edge of any network. Coordination with MEC can provide low inertness and low energy utilization [40, 41]. The fundamental thought of MEC is to use the incredible registering offices inside the radio access network, for example, the MEC server synchronized with the nearby mobile base station. Users get advantages from offloading the computationally escalated data to the MEC server. There are two activity modes for MEC, i.e., incomplete and parallel calculation offloading. In the first one, the calculation undertakings can be separated into different parts, where one section is privately performed and the other part is sent to the MEC data center [42, 43]. In twofold calculation offloading, the calculation errands are either privately executed or on the other hand, offloaded to the MEC.

Based on the above challenges, in this chapter different power-efficient network models for mobile edge computing are discussed. To make the network power-efficient we have emphasized on NOMA (Non-Orthogonal Multiple Access) [44] technology for 5G mobile edge computing.

The main contributions of the proposed chapter are:

- The need for energy-efficient MEC framework is discussed
- Different power-efficient models for resource allocations, tasks offloading are illustrated here for mobile edge computing
- NOMA based power efficient model of 5G MEC is explained.
- Future research directions are also elaborated.

Rest of the chapter is organized as follows:

Section 2 explains the factors of the power-efficient mobile edge computing paradigm. Power-efficient models for resource allocation and task offloading are discussed in Sect. 3. Section 3 also includes the discussion of NOMA-enabled MEC. Section 4 gives an overview of the future research directions and Sect. 5 concludes the chapter.

2   Factors of Power Efficient MEC Framework

Power-efficient resource allocation and offloading strategy are most significant to support the usefulness of MEC. While ensuring the delay, it can adequately and efficiently allocate resources. The requirement of power-efficient MEC is as follows:

Heterogeneous edge server: Both the mobile devices and edge servers have a heterogeneous network. The selection of a proper edge server is a crucial issue. Some of the edge servers are suitable for compute-intensive tasks while others are with adequate resources. The selection of offloading strategies depending on the requirement of the user to make the network green is the main factor.

Hierarchical architectures of edge servers: The progressive structure of edge cloud empowers accumulation of the pinnacle loads across various levels of edge server to boost the measure of portable remaining tasks at hand, which are being served [45]. This reduces the power consumption of the network. Figure 4 shows the hierarchical scenario of edge servers.

Communication Cost: The communication and coordination between mobile devices may consume extra energy and incur additional delay. This coordination

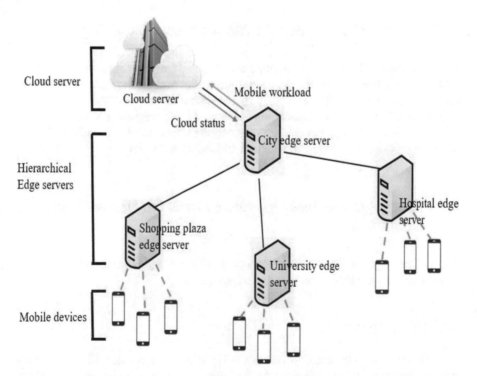

Fig. 4 The Hierarchical architectures of edge servers

Table 2 Summary of research work performed for energy-efficient task offloading

Approach	Environment	Contributions
The mixed-integer non-linear program approach is considered [27]	Heterogeneous network	MEC based task offloading for ultra-dense mobile network
Mixed Integer Linear Program (MILP) approach is considered to get an optimal solution [28]	Multi-cell network	Joint task offloading in multi-server MEC
A location based task offloading approach is considered [48]	Heterogeneous network	Efficient task offloading schemes for vehicular edge computing paradigm
A deep Q-learning approach is considered [49]	Multi-cell network	Energy-efficient task offloading for MEC in an urban area

between devices is a challenging factor to minimize the energy consumption of the network.

3 Power Efficient Models for Mobile Edge Computing

Power-efficient MEC aims to reduce power consumption and communication delay of the network [46]. One of the most significant roles of the 5G mobile network is to reduce energy consumption and delay by incorporating proper resource allocation, task scheduling, and task offloading models. In this regard, different energy-efficient task offloading, and resource allocation models will be discussed. Table 2 summarizes different power-efficient task offloading strategies.

3.1 Power Efficient Task Offloading Model for Mobile Edge Computing

The mobile edge computing paradigm is considered to offload tasks where numerous cell phones are incorporated with an edge cloud.

3.1.1 Tasks Model

In [47] Task Caching and Offloading (TCO) strategy is considered to minimize power consumption. The edge computing paradigm is considered in [48], which comprises various mobile devices and an edge server.

3.1.2   Local Computation Model

For local task computing, assume C_1 as a CPU computing cability of mobile devices N. Local execution time to execute the task $E_{n,k}$. Where, $E_{n,k}$ is the computing task. It has three parameters $E_{n,k} = (P_k, B_k, D_n)$.

P_k is the total number of CPU cycles required to execute the task. B_k defines as the data size of the total executable task and D_n the deadline that is given by mobile user n to complete the task.

The local completion time for the task $E_{n,k}$ is given below.

$$T_{N,k} = P_k / C_N^1$$

Where K is the computation task.

Power consumption in local computing per CPU computing cycle is denoted by σ, where $\sigma = \Omega C^2$, and thus the energy cost of local computation for the computing task can be explained as:

$$Pow_{N,k} = \Omega \left(C_N^1 \right)^2 P_k$$

Where Ω is the energy coefficient.

3.1.3   Edge Computation Model

Compared to the local computing model if task $E_{n,k}$ is offloaded to the nearby edge server, the total duration will be divvied in two segments: (a) time taken to offload the task from the mobile device and it is denoted by $E^{tra}_{n,k}$ and (b) time taken when performing the task on edge server and it is denoted by $E^{pro}_{n,k}$. Hence the total duration is as follows:

$$T^e_{N,k} = E^{tra}_{N,k} + E^{pro}_{N,K} = B_k / r_N + P_k / C_N^1$$

Where r_N is the uplink data rate.

Transmission power cost to offload the task to edge server is represented as:

$$Pow^e_{N,k} = P_{trans} E^{tra}_{N,k} = P_{trans} . B_k / r_N$$

Where P_{trans} is the transmission power of mobile devices.

3.2 Power Efficient Resource Allocation Strategy for MEC

In the MEC paradigm, multiple mobile users at the same time use the same edge server to offload their tasks. In such a scenario, resources have to be shared among mobile devices. Hence, proper resource allocation and reduction of power consumption is very essential for mobile edge computing [29]. Here, we will discuss the Multiple-Access model and NOMA-enabled model for efficient resource allocation.

3.2.1 Multiple-Access Model

Time Division Multiple Access (TDMA) and Orthogonal Frequency-Division Multiple Access (OFDMA) are considered in the multiple-access model for resource allocation.

As the TDMA scheme is considered, time is distributed into equal duration slots. Suppose each slot has a time duration of t seconds. Based on the user-delay requisite slot t is selected. Every time slot t incorporates two consecutive parts: (a) local computing or local offloading and (b) edge computing. Edge computing has a minimum delay. This part consumes a small amount of mobile energy and moreover is much faster than other offloading as reduced size computation is performed. The second part of the above-mentioned scheme is supposed to have an insignificant duration compared to the first part so it is not measured in resource allocation. Total bandwidth is segmented into multiple orthogonal sub-channels in the OFDMA scheme and every sub-channel is allocated to at most one user.

Considering a random slot in TDMA/OFDMA scheme based resource allocation, a base station plans a subset of users for offloading. The offloading can be partial or complete offloading.

3.2.2 NOMA-Enabled Model

Energy consumption in the wireless industry is increasing rapidly [48]. The 5G NOMA is a prime concept in developing an undefined structure of the future network. Non-orthogonal multiple access [50] is an emerging air interface technique of 5G. In comparison with the traditional orthogonal multiple access technologies (OMA), NOMA on a similar spectrum can serve several users [51, 52]. SIC is implemented in NOMA at the receiver's end to retrieve the desired data from the multiplexed signals [53, 54] and Multiuser Superposition Coding (MSC) is adopted in transmitters end. By this technique, 5G NOMA can increase the spectral efficiency of the network. NOMA enabled mobile edge computing meets the QoS of the network by decreasing power consumption.

In a NOMA-enabled MEC network, one base station that is the gateway of an edge server is considered [32, 33]. Here, 2n number of users are divided into n groups with two users in each group.

The set of all groups is denoted as n = {1, 2, · · · n}. In every group, those two users concurrently transfer the data to the base station consuming the same frequency by using NOMA technology. TDMA strategy is considered here for users in various groups. For offloading the task completely or partially, base stations schedule the users accordingly. The users with complete or partial offloading respectively offload a fragment or total task to the mobile base station, however the users with partial or no task to offload compute a portion or total task with the help of local central processing unit. Let the channel be assumed to be recurrently at one level. The mobile base stations have the information of the channels, local computation abilities, and task sizes of different users. With the help of this information, the mobile base station controls the power consumption, the offloaded task, and the segment of offloading time.

4 Research Directions

There are a lot of research works going on, but several research challenges should be further explored to make mobile edge computing more suitable and reliable. This section illustrates some future research outlines for MEC.

Power Supply: To work ideally, the edge server must have the option to work at anyplace. Sadly, every spot on the world might not have a similar kind of intensity gracefully in order to run the servers required for this activity.

Energy Optimization: Recent works emphasize the management of energy consumption from the edge server. Network energy consumption is also important. An efficient optimization technique has to be incorporated for network energy reduction.

Green Energy Usage: The availability of green energy changes with time. How to take advantage of renewable energy to support mobile devices can be further explored. Machine learning can be used to predict the availability of green energy.

Protocol Standardization: Protocol Standardization provides an open platform for researchers to work in a single approved environment. MEC is a latest technology that has not been applied accurately. Thus, a consistent open platform is required to that will permit continuous and competently incorporation of applications through the MEC platforms. This Standardization will also enhance the prompt improvement of mobile edge applications through the industry and academia. Standard protocols are necessary to implement standard features of MEC.

Effective Deployment: Diminishing the delay through best utilization of spectrum may be accomplished with proficient deployment of MEC, while, it is challenging to enhance the bandwidth usage with dependence on complex system modules.

User mobility: In the MEC paradigm organization of continuous services to an often "on-the-move" user is another research issue with straightforward procedure relocation and heterogeneity.

Heterogeneity: Utilization of diverse access in the paradigm of edge devices heterogeneity ought to be provided in the smooth working of MEC activities. This further requires the arrangement of adaptability for various stages with changing the number of clients

Security: The security is the important aspect demanding solutions across the computing and network stack. Providing security to the user data and continuous streaming data are challenging issues. The accessibility of resources is for the most part subordinate upon server limit and remote access mechanism for guaranteeing steady service conveyance. Along with accessibility, the security of information and applications from any gatecrasher ought to be provided with physical measures.

5 Summary and Conclusions

Mobile Edge Computing empowers inventive assistance situations that can guarantee upgraded individual experience and streamlined system activity, just as opening up a new business. Efficient spectrum utilization with optimized power consumption is an emerging criterion for 5G based Mobile network. Delay incurred by task offloading degrades the Quality of Services (QoS) of a network. To reduce energy consumption, delay, and increase spectral efficiency, MEC comes into the scenario. The multimedia applications are the most common mobile application whereas these applications need extensive power consumption and more computing resources. MEC performs the tasks given by the mobile devices within user proximity and sends the results to the device with very low latency. MEC decreases the power consumption of the devices as well as to the network.

In this chapter, we have discussed a power-efficient mobile edge computing framework. Related challenges to achieve the power-efficient MEC is also illustrated here. The energy-efficient tasks model and resource allocation model are explained theoretically and mathematically. NOMA-enabled MEC for power optimization is demonstrated here. Finally, we provide a future research direction to establish more validated research work in the field of power-efficient mobile edge computing.

Acknowledgment The authors are thankful to the Department of Science and Technology (DST) -FIST for SR/FST/ETI-296/2011 and TEQIP-III.

References

1. Schulz, P., Matthe, M., Klessig, H., Simsek, M., Fettweis, G., Ansari, J., and Puschmann, A., 2017. Latency critical IoT applications in 5G: Perspective on the design of radio interface and network architecture. *IEEE Communications Magazine*, 55(2), pp. 70–78.
2. Shit, R. C., Sharma, S., Obaidat, M. S., and Puthal, D., 2020. Adaptive Software Defined Node Deployment for Green Internet of Things. In ICC 2020-2020 IEEE International Conference on Communications (ICC) (pp. 1–6). IEEE.
3. Amtrup, J. W., Ma, J., Thompson, S. M., Shustorovich, A., Thrasher, C. W., and Macciola, A., 2017. U.S. Patent Application No. 15/396,306.
4. Yang, T. J., Chen, Y. H., & Sze, V., 2017, June. Designing energy-efficient convolutional neural networks using energy-aware pruning. In Proceedings of the IEEE Conference on Computer Vision and Pattern Recognition (pp. 5687–5695), IEEE.
5. Gai, K., Qiu, M., & Zhao, H., 2018. Energy-aware task assignment for mobile cyber-enabled applications in heterogeneous cloud computing. *Journal of Parallel and Distributed Computing*, 111, pp. 126–135.
6. Nan, Y., Li, W., Bao, W., Delicato, F. C., Pires, P. F., & Zomaya, A. Y., 2018. A dynamic tradeoff data processing framework for delay-sensitive applications in cloud of things systems. *Journal of Parallel and Distributed Computing*, 112, pp. 53–66.
7. Ghosh, S., De, D., Deb, P., & Mukherjee, A., 2020. 5G-ZOOM-Game: Small cell zooming using weighted majority cooperative game for energy efficient 5G mobile network. *Wireless Networks*, 26(1), pp. 349–372.
8. Jia, M., Yin, Z., Guo, Q., Liu, G., & Gu, X., 2017. Downlink design for spectrum efficient IoT network. *IEEE Internet of Things Journal*, 5(5), pp. 3397–3404.
9. Yu, H., Lee, H., & Jeon, H., 2017. What is 5G? Emerging 5G mobile services and network requirements. *Sustainability*, 9(10), pp. 1848.
10. Shafi, M., Molisch, A. F., Smith, P. J., Haustein, T., Zhu, P., De Silva, P., and Wunder, G., 2017. 5G: A tutorial overview of standards, trials, challenges, deployment, and practice. *IEEE journal on selected areas in communications*, 35(6), pp. 1201–1221.
11. Al-Fuqaha, A., Guizani, M., Mohammadi, M., Aledhari, M., & Ayyash, M., 2015. Internet of things: A survey on enabling technologies, protocols, and applications. *IEEE communications surveys & tutorials*, 17(4), pp. 2347–2376.
12. Sheikh, J. A., Parah, S. A., & Bhat, G. M., 2017. Towards green capacity in massive Mimo based 4G-LTE a cell using beam-forming vector based sectored relay planning. *Wireless Personal Communications*, 97(4), pp. 5767–5781.
13. Mukherjee, A., De, D., & Deb, P., 2016. Interference management in macro-femtocell and micro-femtocell cluster-based long-term evaluation-advanced green mobile network. *IET Communications*, 10(5), pp. 468–478.
14. Abbas, N., Zhang, Y., Taherkordi, A., & Skeie, T., 2017. Mobile edge computing: A survey. *IEEE Internet of Things Journal*, 5(1), pp. 450–465.
15. De, D., 2016. Mobile cloud computing: architectures, algorithms and applications. *CRC Press*.
16. Noor, T. H., Zeadally, S., Alfazi, A., & Sheng, Q. Z., 2018. Mobile cloud computing: Challenges and future research directions. *Journal of Network and Computer Applications*, 115, pp. 70–85.
17. Mukherjee, A., De, D., & Roy, D. G., 2016. A power and latency aware cloudlet selection strategy for multi-cloudlet environment. *IEEE Transactions on Cloud Computing*, 7(1), pp. 141–154.
18. Mukherjee, A., Deb, P., De, D., & Buyya, R., 2019. IoT-F2N: An energy-efficient architectural model for IoT using Femtolet-based fog network. *The Journal of Supercomputing*, 75(11), pp. 7125–7146.
19. Ahmed, E., Gani, A., Khan, M. K., Buyya, R., & Khan, S. U., 2015. Seamless application execution in mobile cloud computing: Motivation, taxonomy, and open challenges. *Journal of Network and Computer Applications*, 52, pp. 154–172.

20. Tran, T. X., Hajisami, A., Pandey, P., & Pompili, D., 2017. Collaborative mobile edge computing in 5G networks: New paradigms, scenarios, and challenges. *IEEE Communications Magazine*, 55(4), pp. 54–61.

21. Pham, Q. V., Fang, F., Ha, V. N., Piran, M. J., Le, M., Le, L. B., and Ding, Z., 2020. A survey of multi-access edge computing in 5G and beyond: Fundamentals, technology integration, and state-of-the-art. *IEEE Access*, 8, pp. 116974–117017.

22. Hu, Y. C., Patel, M., Sabella, D., Sprecher, N., & Young, V., 2015. Mobile edge computing—A key technology towards 5G. *ETSI white paper*, 11(11), pp. 1–16.

23. Mach, P., & Becvar, Z., 2017. Mobile edge computing: A survey on architecture and computation offloading. *IEEE Communications Surveys & Tutorials*, 19(3), pp. 1628–1656.

24. Mao, Y., You, C., Zhang, J., Huang, K., & Letaief, K. B., 2017. A survey on mobile edge computing: The communication perspective. *IEEE Communications Surveys & Tutorials*, 19(4), pp. 2322–2358.

25. Beck, M. T., Werner, M., Feld, S., & Schimper, S., 2014, November. Mobile edge computing: A taxonomy. In Proc. of the Sixth International Conference on Advances in Future Internet (pp. 48–55). Citeseer.

26. Dolui, K., & Datta, S. K., 2017, June. Comparison of edge computing implementations: Fog computing, cloudlet and mobile edge computing. In 2017 Global Internet of Things Summit (GIoTS) (pp. 1–6). IEEE.

27. Chen, M., & Hao, Y., 2018. Task offloading for mobile edge computing in software defined ultra-dense network. *IEEE Journal on Selected Areas in Communications*, 36(3), pp. 587–597.

28. Tran, T. X., & Pompili, D., 2018. Joint task offloading and resource allocation for multi-server mobile-edge computing networks. IEEE Transactions on Vehicular Technology, 68(1), pp. 856–868.

29. You, C., Huang, K., Chae, H., & Kim, B. H., 2016. Energy-efficient resource allocation for mobile-edge computation offloading. *IEEE Transactions on Wireless Communications*, 16(3), pp. 1397–1411.

30. Le, H. Q., Al-Shatri, H., & Klein, A., 2017, June. Efficient resource allocation in mobile-edge computation offloading: Completion time minimization. In 2017 IEEE International Symposium on Information Theory (ISIT) (pp. 2513–2517). IEEE.

31. Ning, Z., Huang, J., Wang, X., Rodrigues, J. J., & Guo, L., 2019. Mobile edge computing-enabled Internet of vehicles: Toward energy-efficient scheduling. *IEEE Network*, 33(5), pp. 198–205.

32. Yang, Z., Hou, J., & Shikh-Bahaei, M., 2018, December. Energy efficient resource allocation for mobile-edge computation networks with NOMA. In 2018 IEEE Globecom Workshops (GC Wkshps) (pp. 1–7). IEEE.

33. Yang, Z., Pan, C., Hou, J., & Shikh-Bahaei, M., 2019. Efficient resource allocation for mobile-edge computing networks with NOMA: Completion time and energy minimization. *IEEE Transactions on Communications*, 67(11), pp. 7771–7784.

34. Patel, M., Naughton, B., Chan, C., Sprecher, N., Abeta, S., & Neal, A., 2014. Mobile-edge computing introductory technical white paper. *White paper, mobile-edge computing (MEC) industry initiative*, pp. 1089–7801.

35. Sung, N. W., Pham, N. T., Huynh, T., & Hwang, W. J., 2013. Predictive association control for frequent handover avoidance in femtocell networks. *IEEE communications letters*, 17(5), pp. 924–927.

36. Pham, Q. V., & Hwang, W. J., 2016. Resource allocation for heterogeneous traffic in complex communication networks. *IEEE Transactions on Circuits and Systems II: Express Briefs*, 63(10), pp. 959–963.

37. Liu, C. F., Bennis, M., & Poor, H. V., 2017, December. Latency and reliability-aware task offloading and resource allocation for mobile edge computing. In 2017 IEEE Globecom Workshops (GC Wkshps) (pp. 1–7). IEEE.

38. Chen, Y., Zhang, N., Zhang, Y., Chen, X., Wu, W., & Shen, X. S., 2019. TOFFEE: Task offloading and frequency scaling for energy efficiency of mobile devices in mobile edge computing. *IEEE Transactions on Cloud Computing*.

39. Ren, J., He, Y., Huang, G., Yu, G., Cai, Y., & Zhang, Z., 2019. An edge-computing based architecture for mobile augmented reality. *IEEE Network*, 33(4), pp. 162–169.

40. Chen, X., Pu, L., Gao, L., Wu, W., & Wu, D., 2017. Exploiting massive D2D collaboration for energy-efficient mobile edge computing. *IEEE Wireless communications*, 24(4), pp. 64–71.

41. Li, M., Yu, F. R., Si, P., Yao, H., Sun, E., & Zhang, Y., 2017, May. Energy-efficient M2M communications with mobile edge computing in virtualized cellular networks. In 2017 IEEE International Conference on Communications (ICC) (pp. 1–6). IEEE.

42. Ning, Z., Dong, P., Kong, X., & Xia, F., 2018. A cooperative partial computation offloading scheme for mobile edge computing enabled Internet of Things. *IEEE Internet of Things Journal*, 6(3), pp. 4804–4814.

43. Dai, Y., Xu, D., Maharjan, S., & Zhang, Y., 2018. Joint computation offloading and user association in multi-task mobile edge computing. *IEEE Transactions on Vehicular Technology*, 67(12), pp. 12313–12325.

44. Kiani, A., & Ansari, N., 2018. Edge computing aware NOMA for 5G networks. *IEEE Internet of Things Journal*, 5(2), pp. 1299–1306.

45. Tong, L., Li, Y., & Gao, W., 2016, April. A hierarchical edge cloud architecture for mobile computing. In IEEE INFOCOM 2016-The 35th Annual IEEE International Conference on Computer Communications (pp. 1–9). IEEE.

46. Ji, L., & Guo, S., 2018. Energy-efficient cooperative resource allocation in wireless powered mobile edge computing. *IEEE Internet of Things Journal*, 6(3), pp. 4744–4754.

47. Hao, Y., Chen, M., Hu, L., Hossain, M. S., & Ghoneim, A., 2018. Energy efficient task caching and offloading for mobile edge computing. *IEEE Access*, 6, pp. 11365–11373.

48. Yang, C., Liu, Y., Chen, X., Zhong, W., & Xie, S., 2019. Efficient mobility-aware task offloading for vehicular edge computing networks. *IEEE Access*, 7, pp. 26652–26664.

49. Zhang, K., Zhu, Y., Leng, S., He, Y., Maharjan, S., & Zhang, Y., 2019. Deep learning empowered task offloading for mobile edge computing in urban informatics. *IEEE Internet of Things Journal*, 6(5), pp. 7635–7647.

50. Mukherjee, A., Deb, P., De, D., & Obaidat, M. S., 2019. WmA-MiFN: A weighted majority and auction game based green ultra-dense micro-femtocell network system. *IEEE Systems Journal*, 14(1), pp. 353–362.

51. Budhiraja, I., Kumar, N., Tyagi, S., Tanwar, S., & Obaidat, M. S., 2020. URJA: Usage Jammer as a Resource Allocation for Secure Transmission in a CR-NOMA-Based 5G Femtocell System. *IEEE Systems Journal*. https://doi.org/10.1109/JSYST.2020.2999474

52. Ha, D. T., Boukhatem, L., Kaneko, M., Nguyen-Thanh, N., & Martin, S., 2019. Adaptive beamforming and user association in heterogeneous cloud radio access networks: A mobility-aware performance-cost trade-off. *Computer Networks*, 160, pp. 130–143.

53. Ding, Z., Liu, Y., Choi, J., Sun, Q., Elkashlan, M., Chih-Lin, I., & Poor, H. V., 2017. Application of non-orthogonal multiple access in LTE and 5G networks. *IEEE Communications Magazine*, 55(2), pp. 185–191.

54. He, S., & Wang, W., 2019. Multimedia upstreaming cournot game in non-orthogonal multiple access Internet of Things. *IEEE Transactions on Network Science and Engineering*, 7(1), pp. 398–408.

SMEC: Sensor Mobile Edge Computing

Anindita Raychaudhuri, Anwesha Mukherjee, and Debashis De

Abstract The development of mobile user equipment progresses cooperatively with the advancement of the latest mobile applications. Still, the limited battery capacity prevents users from running computationally intensive applications on their gadgets. This one stimulated the evolution of Mobile cloud computing (MCC). Instead of its ample data storage and processing capability, MCC suffers from high latency. To deal with the latency problem a novel promising concept known as mobile edge computing has been introduced. Mobile edge computing (MEC) and wireless sensor networks (WSN) are two ever-promising research domains of the wireless network. The integration of MEC with WSN has given birth to Sensor Mobile Edge Computing (SMEC). However, sensor mobile edge computing is an emerging field, and energy-efficiency is one of the major challenges of this field. In MEC, services are provided at the edge of the mobile network for reducing the latency that in turn can improve the quality of user experience. Previously MEC focused on the use of base stations for offloading computations from mobile devices. However, after the arrival of fog computing, the definition of edge devices becomes broader. SMEC is a fusion of mobile edge computing and wireless sensor network. SMEC is an architecture where the sensor nodes capture the status of environmental objects and the collected data are sent to the cloud through the edge devices which participate in data processing also. This chapter discusses sensor mobile edge computing, its architecture, and its applications. The future scopes and challenges of SMEC are also addressed in this chapter.

A. Raychaudhuri (✉)
Department of Computer Science, Sarojini Naidu College for Women, Kolkata,
West Bengal, India
e-mail: anindita.raychaudhuri@sncwgs.ac.in

A. Mukherjee (✉)
Department of Computer Science, Mahishadal Raj College, Mahishadal, West Bengal, India
e-mail: anweshamukherjee@ieee.org

D. De
Centre of Mobile Cloud Computing, Department of Computer Science and Engineering, Maulana
Abul Kalam Azad University of Technology, Kolkata, West Bengal, India

© The Author(s), under exclusive license to Springer Nature Switzerland AG 2021
A. Mukherjee et al. (eds.), *Mobile Edge Computing*,
https://doi.org/10.1007/978-3-030-69893-5_5

Keywords Cloud Computing (CC) · Internet of Things (IoT) · Mobile Edge
Computing (MEC) · Wireless Sensor Network (WSN)

1 Introduction

A Wireless Sensor Network is a group of low powered tiny sensor nodes intended
for monitoring and recording some physical or environmental conditions at different
locations [1]. WSNs can be used in forest fire detection, industrial process monitoring, air pollution measurement, different medical applications, and many more such
different areas. Cloud computing (CC) is the delivery of computation, software,
and storage as service to the users in a virtualized and isolated environment. In the
past decade, Mobile Cloud Computing (MCC) has emerged as a new archetype of
computing due to the popularity of mobile devices and the epidemic rise of mobile
applications [2, 3]. MCC overcomes the computational and storage limitations of
today's smart mobile devices. Although an intrinsic drawback of MCC still exists
that is propagation delay. The growing computing capacities present on smart
devices call for the decentralization of Cloud computing services to avoid latency
issues and fully utilize handy computing abilities at the network edges [4].

Driven by the vision of the Internet of Things (IoT), Mobile Edge Computing
(MEC) is becoming a new trend in computing that addresses the issue of propagation
delay and can provide latency-critical mobile applications [5–11]. For the period of
the last four decades, the development of wireless communication networks took
place based on the requirements of applications and transformed every facet of our
lives [11]. A summary of Wireless Communication evolution is shown in Fig. 1.

Edge computing introduces technologies that allow computation to be performed
at the network edge. Therefore computing is possible near data sources also. Before
going to the discussion on the integration of WSN with MCC and MEC, we define
mobile cloud computing, fog computing, and mobile edge computing.

Definition 1: Mobile Cloud Computing
MCC is a paradigm where the storage as well as the processing of data happens
outside the mobile device. The applications of MCC have moved away from the data
storage and computational power from mobile phones and into the cloud, which in
turn brings mobile computing and applications not just to smartphone users but to a
huge number of mobile subscribers (Mobile Cloud Computing Forum (MCC-forum,
2011)).

Definition 2: Fog Computing
Fog Computing is an infrastructure where the devices present between the end node
and cloud servers take participation in the processing of the data, which in turn
reduces the latency.

Definition 3: Mobile Edge Computing
MEC is a new technology that offers cloud computing capabilities and information
technology services within the mobile access network of mobile users.

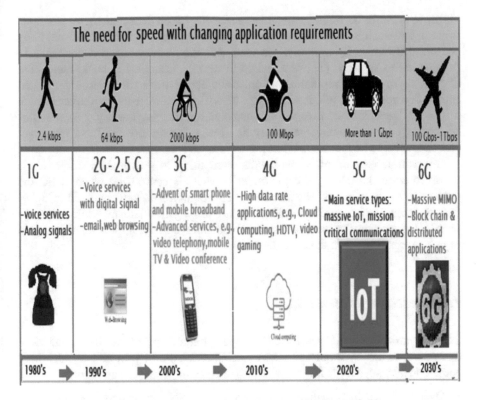

Fig. 1 Evolution of Wireless Communication during the last four decades [11]

1.1 WSN with MCC

Mobile cloud computing is a technology that offers unlimited functionality, mobility, and huge storage capacity through heterogeneous network connectivity. The integration of WSN and MCC draws significant attention from researchers due to its data gathering, storage, and processing capability in a single integrated infrastructure. The main advantage of WSN-MCC integration is the utilization of effective cloud computing infrastructure for storing and processing a huge amount of sensory data and ultimately offering processed data to the end-users [12–17].

1.2 WSN with Mobile Edge Computing (MEC)

Most of the time MEC gets along with cloud computing for supporting and enhancing the end devices' performance. It is possible by pushing cloud resources such as to measure, set of connections, and storage space to the edge of the mobile network. An edge device can be any device that has the computational power and ability to network between data sources and cloud-based data centers, for example, a smartphone can be an edge device which is present between the cloud and body sensors. MEC directly connects the user with the nearest edge network able to provide cloud services [11]. According to recent research, the basic motivation of MEC is to offer computationally intensive applications using resource-limited mobile devices. As a result, it will be able to fulfill the end-users requirements which are latency-sensitive and involve high computation. Among the key characteristics of mobile edge computing proximity and lower latency are the most important characteristics to be mentioned [3–6].

The comparison of MCC with edge computing is provided in Table 1. As observed from the table the deployment in MCC is centralized wherein EC the deployment is distributed. The distance of user equipment from the cloud is higher than the edge device, which results in higher propagation latency while using the cloud. However, in the case of the cloud the storage and computational power is high in comparison with the edge device.

1.3   Research Motivation

The integration of WSN with MCC provides lots of advantages but faced some critical issues which should be taken care of seriously. In [12] authors identified some critical issues regarding WSN-MCC integration which are as follows:

- Over-burdened intermediary sensor node: In WSN sensor nodes are generally equipped with a non-rechargeable battery. It follows multi-hop data communication from source nodes to gateway nodes via intermediary nodes. As a result, intermediary nodes become overburdened. Therefore energy efficiency is a prime concern to make the sensor network operative.

Table 1 Comparison of MCC and Edge Computing [4]

	MCC	EC
Deployment	Centralized	Distributed
Distance to UE	Long	Short
Latency	High	Low
Computational Power	Immense	Limited
Storage capacity	Huge	Limited
Advantages	Resource constraint mobile devices get additional capacity	Reduces latency in computational tasks

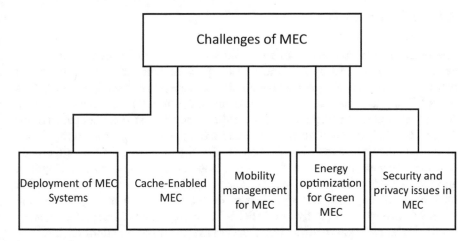

Fig. 2 Challenges of MEC

- The bottleneck of traffic and bandwidth: With the dramatic increase in the number of mobile and cloud users the bandwidth of wireless networks may turn into a bottleneck situation. Besides, high bandwidth is required for multimedia data transmission. Therefore optimization of traffic and bandwidth demand is also an important issue.
- Delay of processing: In WSN the data collected from sensors are offered to end-users based on the need of the applications or users. In that case for some applications, the delay is unavoidable which affects the network performance. Therefore it is desirable to make use of the processing capability of the cloud to empower the WSN for tackling this type of issue.

The primary motivation of MEC is the decentralization of cloud computing services to make it available at the network edges and avoid latency issues. To accomplish this lot of challenges are being faced which are shown in Fig. 2.

As observed from the figure, there are several challenges in MEC such as deployment issue, cache-enabling, mobility management, energy optimization, security, and privacy, etc.

2 Related Work

In this section, we will focus on the existing works in IoT, cloud computing, fog computing, and edge computing applications of the sensor network.

2.1 IoT Applications

The emergence of IoT also termed as Internet of Everything enables the global network of people, processes, data, and things worldwide. WSN is an important part of IoT, and it is mainly accountable for collecting and reporting data. WSNs bring IoT applications more effectiveness and makes it more competence [18, 19]. A large amount of sensory data and its real-time processing is a big challenge for the practical implementation of large scale IoT systems. Edge computing is one of the promising solutions in this respect. But the deployment of an edge node is a fundamental problem. To address this issue authors proposed a deployment approach for edge servers intended for large-scale IoT [20]. They have shown that their proposed approach can significantly reduce the number of edge nodes and improves throughput. Day by day MEC is becoming a key enabler of consumer-centric IoT applications and services that demand real-time operations [21]. As IoT performance mainly depends on the lifetime and coverage area of WSN, designing an efficient method that conserves nodes' energy and reduces the number of dead nodes becomes important issues [22, 23]. Therefore clustering is one of the efficient methods to solve these problems in WSN [24, 25].

With the evolution of IoT, a massive number of sensor-based applications are going to be materialized. Therefore, the deployment of sensors and their mobility is a big concern to fulfill their job competently. In this respect, authors have presented an exhaustive review of existing mobile sinks that support sensors' mobility in the context of IoT applications [26]. The concept of the Green Internet of Things (G-IoT) is considered to play an extremely important role in providing smarter and sustainable cities [27].

2.2 Cloud Computing Applications

In recent days, cloud computing frameworks have become increasingly popular in both academia and industry. At the same time, a significant increase in the usage of smartphone platforms has been noticed worldwide. Therefore Mobile Cloud Computing emerges as a current state of the art technology providing unlimited functionalities in many useful applications [28]. The two closely related emerging technologies IoT and Big Data have matured convincingly to allow smart cities to materialize [29]. Due to the fast increase in the number of smart cities, their sustainability needs to be achieved through transformational urban systems design which may vary from system to system. Big data and Cloud computing play an important role in this perspective [30]. In [31] authors presented a new concept and its technologies that are related to the integration of MCC and context-aware applications. They have introduced CAOS, an android-based framework to illustrate how context-aware apps may be improved with MCC features like data and computing offloading. In [32] authors introduced a new medical big data clustering algorithm in a cloud computing environment. With the help of cloud computing technologies, the need for ubiquitous healthcare services is becoming possible day by day. Besides, big data analysis technologies have shown great possibilities for improving the quality of healthcare services. In [33] authors proposed a medical primary diagnosis framework that is outsourced to the cloud server in an encrypted manner. As a result, it can preserve confidential medical data from an unauthorized user.

2.3   Fog Computing Applications

Traditional cloud computing is facing severe network challenges like network bottlenecks high latency to meet the massive requirements of IoT applications. The circumstances where traditional cloud-based solutions are not appropriate, edge and fog computing is considered the key enabling archetype which brings the cloud resources to the edge of the network [34]. Recently fog computing has emerged as a platform that handles massive data caused by IoT environments and provides networking services between IoT devices and traditional cloud computing [35]. Fog computing has come out as a new paradigm for a large group of applications that are delay-sensitive including smart city, healthcare service, intelligent transportation system, the personalized recommendation of banking products, Block-chain enabled applications, and many more [36–44]. Fog computing provides innovative solutions by bringing resources closer to the user and offer low latency solutions for data processing. Authors proposed a new framework called HealthFog intended for automatic Heart Disease analysis by integrating deep learning concepts with Fog computing [36]. HealthFog delivers healthcare as a fog service using IoT devices and capably manages the health data.

In urban areas, smart cities are already a reality and therefore have attracted the attention of many researchers. In [37] authors presented a hybrid edge-fog-cloud computing architecture for monitoring environmental parameters and traffic flow in a city with very limited infrastructure. In [38] authors presented a comprehensive literature review of the existing work already been done in the area of fog computing applications in smart cities.

2.4   Mobile Edge Computing Applications

According to recent research, the main objective of Mobile Edge Computing is to provide computationally intensive applications using resource-limited mobile devices. MEC servers are small-scale data centers; therefore it is very important to develop innovative approaches for obtaining green MEC. Several approaches are already there for designing green MEC [45–56]. MEC is a furnishing solution to

Table 2 Major contributions of existing publications on MEC

Serial no.	Major contributions	Reference
1	Architecture &Computation offloading	[5–11, 62–64, 67–69, 77–80]
2	Resource allocation	[57–63]
3	Green MEC	[45–56]
4	Mobility management	[26, 65, 85]
5	MEC for IoT applications	[66, 72–77, 81–89]
6	Security & Privacy issues	[75–76, 79, 111–116]
7	MEC with 5G Technologies	[11, 70, 89]

facilitate augmented reality (AR) applications on mobile devices [57, 58], video stream analysis service [59], Cloud-based vehicular networks [60].

For full utilization of the MEC paradigm, few key points should be based on application-oriented which are (1) decision on computation offloading; (2) allocation of computing resources within the MEC, and (3) mobility management. Several researchers have tried to focus on these above mentioned key points along with the other key points like the architecture and model of MEC, its mathematical frameworks, energy efficiency for a better solution [61–69]. MEC facilitates numerous mobile applications like video stream analysis, augmented reality, Vehicular network, gaming and IoT applications [70–89].

The major contributions of existing publications on mobile edge computing are summarized in Table 2. The comparison between Cloud, Fog, and Edge computing concerning processing response is shown in Fig. 3.

3   The Architecture of Sensor Mobile Edge Computing (SMEC)

Sensor Mobile Edge Computing (SMEC) is an integration of a sensor network with mobile edge computing. The four-layer architecture of SMEC is presented in Fig. 4.

SMEC architecture contains the following components:

- Sensor nodes
- Mobile device
- Cellular base station with edge server (in case of the cellular network)
- Cloudlet (in case of Wi-Fi)
- Cloud

The sensor nodes after collecting the object status send the collected data to the mobile device. The mobile device is connected with the base station (cellular network) or cloudlet (WMAN/WLAN). In the case of a cellular network, a cellular base station is used along with an edge server. The edge server is connected with the cloud. In the case of Wi-Fi i.e. Wireless Local Area Network (WLAN) or Wireless

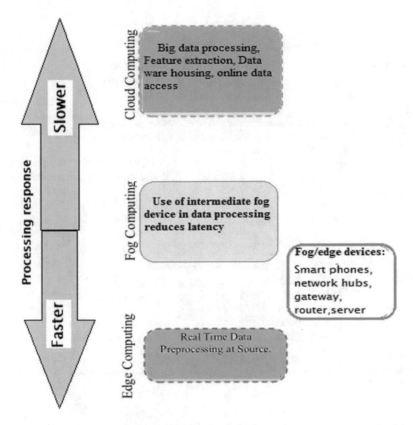

Fig. 3 Comparison between Cloud, Fog and Edge computing

Metropolitan Area Network (WMAN), cloudlet is used. Here, cloudlet offers the storage and computation facilities. The cloudlet is connected with the cloud. In SMEC the mobile device after receiving the sensor data performs preliminary processing on the data and sends them to the edge server through the base station, or to the cloudlet. The data is processed inside the edge server/cloudlet, and then according to the necessity, the data is forwarded to the cloud.

3.1 Advantages of SMEC over SMCC

The advantages of SMEC over SMCC are listed in Table 3.

As observed from the table due to the use of MCC the deployment is centralized in SMCC, where the deployment in SMEC is distributed as edge computing is used. In the case of SMEC, the latency is lower than the SMCC as the distance of the end node from the remote cloud is higher than the edge device. The computational

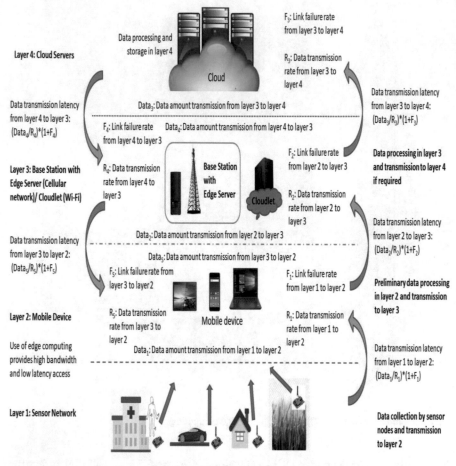

Fig. 4 Four-layer Architecture of SMEC

Table 3 Comparison between SMCC and SMEC

	SMCC	SMEC
Deployment	Centralized	Distributed
Latency	High	Low
Computational Potential	Immense	Restricted
Storage capability	Huge	Limited

power and storage of the cloud are higher than the edge device, the computational power and storage are higher in SMCC than SMEC.

3.1.1 Definition of SMEC

Sensor mobile edge computing is defined as an integrated architecture which is the combination of mobile edge computing and wireless sensor network where the sensor nodes capture the status of environmental objects and the collected data are sent to the cloud through the edge devices. MEC connects the user directly to the nearest cloud service enabled edge network which provides high computation, low latency, and avoid bottleneck situation.

3.2 Latency in SMEC

In SMEC, the storage and computation execution related to the sensor data takes place inside the edge device. To calculate the latency the data transmission, propagation, computation execution, and queuing latencies are calculated.

The data transmission latency in SMEC is given as [78],

$$L_{st} = \sum_{i=1}^{h} \left(1 + U_{fi}\right) \frac{S_{tui}}{R_{ui}} + \sum_{j=1}^{k} \left(1 + D_{fj}\right) \frac{S_{tdj}}{R_{dj}}, \tag{1}$$

Where U_{fi} is the failure rate in the uplink, S_{tui} is the sensor data amount transmitted in the uplink, R_{ui} is the sensor data transmission rate in the uplink, between the communicating devices for hop i, D_{fj} is the failure rate in the downlink, S_{tdj} is the sensor data amount transmitted in the downlink, R_{dj} is the sensor data transmission rate in the downlink, between the communicating devices for hop j, h is the number of hops in uplink and k is the number of hops in the downlink.

The computation execution latency is given as [78],

$$L_{sc} = \frac{I}{I_c}, \tag{2}$$

Where, I is the number of instructions to be executed for the computation and I_c is the instruction execution speed of the computing device.

The propagation latency is given as [78],

$$L_{sp} = \frac{D_p}{S_p}, \tag{3}$$

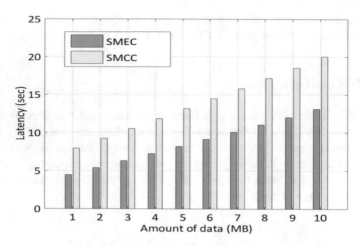

Fig. 5 Latency in SMEC and SMCC

Where, D_{rs} is the distance covered between the requesting and serving node, and D_p is the propagation speed.

If the queuing latency is denoted by L_{sq}, the total latency is given as [78],

$$L_{smec} = L_{st} + L_{sc} + L_{sp} + L_{sq}. \tag{4}$$

In Fig. 5 the latency in SMEC and SMCC are compared. This is observed that by bringing the computation at the network edge the latency has been reduced by ~40% than the cloud-based SMCC framework.

In the next section, we have focused on the applications of SMEC.

4 Application of SMEC

Different applications of SMEC are discussed as follows.

4.1 Vehicular Network

In Vehicular Adhoc Network (VANET) the use of edge computing has been highlighted in [79]. It has been shown that by using edge nodes as an intermediary interface amid vehicle and cloud, the latency has been reduced. A Software Defined Network (SDN) with MEC has been presented in [80] which are intended for establishing the VANET routing path for paired vehicles. In [80] it has been demonstrated that this method provides better throughput.

4.2 Augmented Reality Service

Augmented Reality (AR) presents a virtual environment through which the users observe the real world with virtual objects composited with the real world [81, 82]. With AR a user will be able to work with real 3D objects with their information acknowledged visually from a mobile device. For example, a civil engineer wishes to develop a children's house inside a playground. AR allows him to select the correct place to build the house inside the playground with the help of his mobile device camera. The sensor plays an important role in AR. In SMEC with the help of sensors, virtual reality can be provided to the user to view the real world with virtual objects superimposed with the real world.

4.3 Home Monitoring

A smart room generally contains a computer system with huge storage and processing power to control the activities of the devices within the room. This is expensive as well as introduces overhead to a single device. If SMCC based smart home, the activities can be controlled by the server itself with a cloud environment. In [83] the use of fog computing in the smart home has been demonstrated. In SMEC the computing and storage resources are placed close to the network edge and the delay, jitter, and energy consumption of the user device can be reduced. Recently several researchers have presented IoT based solutions for smart home monitoring [84, 85].

4.4 Healthcare

In smart health care, health sensor devices capture the health status, and the sensor data are stored and processed inside the cloud servers. After processing the data, the health status of the user can be detected [86–89]. In [86], the use of an edge-based framework in time-critical applications has been shown, where health care has been considered as a case study. By bringing the processing facility closer to the network edge, the delay which is a vital parameter for health care can be reduced. In [87], mobility data analytics has been integrated with health care service, for advising users regarding nearby health center.

5 Future Scope

5.1 Bio-inspired SMEC

Bio-inspired computation has started a new era towards the solution of different energy aware, time-critical computational problems in wireless sensor networks. Sensor mobile edge computing is an emerging field that can provide high-quality solutions using resource-limited mobile devices. Mobile edge computing addresses the issues of latency, the limited battery power of mobile devices and security, etc. In recent days Bio-inspired algorithms are getting much attention for providing the best solution in different areas specially WSN, IoT, Fog computing, and Cloud computing [90–107].

In [90] authors presented a hybrid routing algorithm combining ACO and FSOA which addresses one significant issue namely energy consumption of WSN and extends network lifetime. So the concept of applying a hybrid bio-inspired algorithm can also be useful for green SMEC. In [91], a hybrid algorithm has been presented combining improved Bat algorithm and LEACH. In this paper, it was shown that the improved BA has stronger optimization ability that can reduce energy consumption and is able to enhance the lifetime of WSN considerably. In [92] authors presented a cat swarm optimization-based approach which optimizes the energy distribution for the WSNs in real-time. In [93] authors proposed a Chicken Swarm Optimization Algorithm (CSOA) based cluster Size Load Balancing technique for IoT-based sensor networks. In this paper, it has shown significant improvement in terms of network lifetime, overall energy consumption. One GSO-based energy-efficient sensor movement approach is presented in [94] which attempts to optimize both the energy and coverage of mobile WSN at a time. Therefore it will also be effective if it is applied for implanting green SMEC. In [95], the authors presented the MFO based energy-efficient clustering protocol which extends the stability period of the network and optimizes energy consumption. Hence this algorithm can also be useful for green SMEC. Recently bio-inspired algorithms are showing good results in energy optimization in diverse areas specially WSN and IoT which are summarized in Table 4.

5.2 Big Data Analytics in SMEC

Big data analytics in SMEC is another major challenge. SMEC has various application areas like VANET, healthcare, where a large amount of data generation takes place and the analysis of the huge amount of data is required. In [108] big data reinforcement learning method has been proposed along with an integrated paradigm for better performance in smart city applications. In [109] big data analytics in health care has been focused. An edge computing paradigm has been proposed for big data processing and an optimized model for estimating

Table 4 Contributions of bio-inspired algorithms in energy optimization

Bio-inspired Algorithm	Journal name (publication year)	Area
Ant Colony Optimization	Journal of Cleaner Production (2019)	Vehicle routing
	The Journal of Supercomputing (2018)	WSN
Bat Algorithm	Swarm and evolutionary computation (2019)	Vehicle routing
	IEEE Communications Letters (2018)	WSN
Cat Swarm Optimization	International Journal of Distributed Sensor Networks (2015)	WSN
Chicken Swarm optimization Algorithm	Journal of Network and Computer Applications (2019)	IoT
	IEEE Access (2019)	WSN
Fish Swarm Optimization Algorithm	Sensors (2018)	WSN
Glowworm Swarm Optimization	Simulation Modelling Practice and Theory (2016)	WSN
Moth flame Optimization Algorithm	Wireless Personal Communications (2019)	WSN
Particle Swarm Optimization	Wireless Personal Communications (2019)	WSN

epileptogenic network [109]. In [110] a MEC based system has been used alongside a big data-driven scheduling method to achieve communication efficiency.

5.3 Security and Privacy Issues of SMEC

While integrating WSN with MEC then security becomes a major challenge. The security threats in the edge-cloud computing framework have been studied in [111]. In [112] the authors have proposed a fog-based storage framework to deal with the cyber threat. As a large number of mobile users are present, then privacy is another issue. Here, the assessment of each mobile node is also very important [113] along with the assessment of invulnerability [114]. In [115] an intrusion detection system has been discussed based on a decision tree. Security and privacy issues of MEC for heterogeneous IoT are the most promising future research areas [116].

5.4   Dew Computing Based Context-Aware Local Computing

In [117, 118] authors introduced dew computing architecture intended for real-time context-aware service framework. It has been observed that the end-users can get advantage from this framework through data sensing, computing in the IoT environment [118].

5.5   Resource Management

Resource allocation in mobile cloud computing is a major challenge [119]. Similarly, in MEC also resource allocation and management are major factors. In SMEC the deployment of edge servers for optimal service provisioning as well as resource management is a vital challenge. As multiple users are present and their requirements are also different and most importantly the users have mobility, the resource allocation, release, VM migration, delivery of required service with minimal latency are key challenges.

6   Conclusion

This chapter provides a discussion on the architecture and working model of sensor mobile edge computing. The use of edge computing provides lower latency concerning the cloud-only system, which we have shown in theoretical results. The applications of sensor mobile edge computing in health care, smart home management, vehicular network, augmented reality have been discussed. The future research directions of sensor mobile edge computing have been also illustrated where resource management, big data analytics, security, bio-inspired sensor mobile edge computing have been considered.

References

1. Zhu, C., Shu, L., Hara, T., Wang, L., Nishio, S., and Yang, L.T., 2014. A survey on communication and data management issues in mobile sensor networks. *Wireless Communications and Mobile Computing*, *14*(1), pp. 19–36.
2. Gill, S.S., Garraghan, P., Stankovski, V., Casale, G., Thulasiram, R.K., Ghosh, S.K., Ramamohanarao, K. and Buyya, R., 2019. Holistic resource management for sustainable and reliable cloud computing: An innovative solution to global challenge. *Journal of Systems and Software*.
3. Gill, S.S. and Buyya, R., 2019. Sustainable Cloud Computing Realization for Different Applications: A Manifesto. In *Digital Business* (pp. 95–117). Springer, Cham.

4. Ferrer, A.J., Marquès, J.M. and Jorba, J., 2019. Towards the decentralised cloud: Survey on approaches and challenges for mobile, ad hoc, and edge computing. *ACM Computing Surveys (CSUR)*, *51*(6), pp. 1-36.

5. Mao, Y., You, C., Zhang, J., Huang, K. and Letaief, K.B., 2017. A survey on mobile edge computing: The communication perspective. *IEEE Communications Surveys & Tutorials*, *19*(4), pp. 2322–2358.

6. Mach, P. and Becvar, Z., 2017. Mobile edge computing: A survey on architecture and computation offloading. *IEEE Communications Surveys & Tutorials*, *19*(3), pp. 1628–1656.

7. Peng, K., Leung, V., Xu, X., Zheng, L., Wang, J. and Huang, Q., 2018. A survey on mobile edge computing: Focusing on service adoption and provision. *Wireless Communications and Mobile Computing, 2018.*

8. Patel, M., Naughton, B., Chan, C., Sprecher, N., Abeta, S. and Neal, A., 2014. Mobile-edge computing introductory technical white paper. *White paper, mobile-edge computing (MEC) industry initiative*, pp. 1089–7801.

9. Khan, W.Z., Ahmed, E., Hakak, S., Yaqoob, I. and Ahmed, A., 2019. Edge computing: A survey. *Future Generation Computer Systems*, *97*, pp. 219–235.

10. Wang, X., Han, Y., Leung, V.C., Niyato, D., Yan, X. and Chen, X., 2020. Convergence of edge computing and deep learning: A comprehensive survey. IEEE Communications Surveys & Tutorials.

11. Pham, Q.V., Fang, F., Ha, V.N., Piran, M.J., Le, M., Le, L.B., Hwang, W.J. and Ding, Z., 2020. A survey of multi-access edge computing in 5G and beyond: Fundamentals, technology integration, and state-of-the-art. IEEE Access, 8, pp. 116974–117017.

12. Zhu, C., Wang, H., Liu, X., Shu, L., Yang, L.T. and Leung, V.C., 2014. A novel sensory data processing framework to integrate sensor networks with mobile cloud. IEEE Systems Journal, 10(3), pp. 1125–1136.

13. De, D., Mukherjee, A., Ray, A., Roy, D.G. and Mukherjee, S., 2016. Architecture of green sensor mobile cloud computing. *IET Wireless Sensor Systems*, *6*(4), pp. 109–120.

14. Wang, W., Lee, K. and Murray, D., 2012, September. Integrating sensors with the cloud using dynamic proxies. In 2012 IEEE 23rd International Symposium on Personal, Indoor and Mobile Radio Communications-(PIMRC) (pp. 1466–1471). IEEE.

15. Lounis, A., Hadjidj, A., Bouabdallah, A. and Challal, Y., 2016. Healing on the cloud: Secure cloud architecture for medical wireless sensor networks. Future Generation Computer Systems, 55, pp. 266–277.

16. Malik, A. and Om, H., 2018. Cloud computing and internet of things integration: Architecture, applications, issues, and challenges. In Sustainable cloud and energy services (pp. 1–24). Springer, Cham.

17. Dattatraya, P.Y., Agarkhed, J. and Patil, S., 2016, March. Cloud assisted performance enhancement of smart applications in Wireless Sensor Networks. In 2016 International Conference on Wireless Communications, Signal Processing and Networking (WiSPNET) (pp. 347–351). IEEE.

18. Lee, I. and Lee, K., 2015. The Internet of Things (IoT): Applications, investments, and challenges for enterprises. *Business Horizons*, *58*(4), pp. 431–440.

19. Lazarescu, M.T., 2013. Design of a WSN platform for long-term environmental monitoring for IoT applications. *IEEE Journal on emerging and selected topics in circuits and systems*, *3*(1), pp. 45–54.

20. Zhao, Z., Min, G., Gao, W., Wu, Y., Duan, H. and Ni, Q., 2018. Deploying edge computing nodes for large-scale IoT: A diversity aware approach. IEEE Internet of Things Journal, 5(5), pp. 3606–3614.

21. Corcoran, P. and Datta, S.K., 2016. Mobile-edge computing and the Internet of Things for consumers: Extending cloud computing and services to the edge of the network. *IEEE Consumer Electronics Magazine*, *5*(4), pp. 73–74.

22. Alam, S., De, D. and Ray, A., 2015, May. Analysis of energy consumption for IARP, RIP and STAR routing protocols in wireless sensor networks. In 2015 Second International Conference on Advances in Computing and Communication Engineering (pp. 11–16). IEEE.

23. Ray, A. and De, D., 2014. Level wise initial energy assignment in wireless sensor network for better network lifetime. In Advanced Computing, Networking and Informatics-Volume 2 (pp. 67–74). Springer, Cham.
24. Ray, A. and De, D., 2012. P-eechs: Parametric energy efficient cluster head selection protocol for wireless sensor network. International Journal of Advanced Computer Engineering & Architecture, 2(2).
25. Ray, A. and De, D., 2013. Energy efficient clustering algorithm for multi-hop green wireless sensor network using gateway node. Advanced Science, Engineering and Medicine, 5(11), pp. 1199–1204
26. Hamidouche, R., Aliouat, Z., Gueroui, A.M., Ari, A.A.A. and Louail, L., 2018. Classical and bio-inspired mobility in sensor networks for IoT applications. Journal of Network and Computer Applications, 121, pp. 70–88.
27. Maksimovic, M., 2017. The role of green internet of things (G-IoT) and big data in making cities smarter, safer and more sustainable. International Journal of Computing and Digital Systems, 6(04), pp. 175–184.
28. Rahimi, M.R., Ren, J., Liu, C.H., Vasilakos, A.V. and Venkatasubramanian, N., 2014. Mobile cloud computing: A survey, state of art and future directions. Mobile Networks and Applications, 19(2), pp. 133–143.
29. Mohanty, S.P., Choppali, U. and Kougianos, E., 2016. Everything you wanted to know about smart cities: The internet of things is the backbone. IEEE Consumer Electronics Magazine, 5(3), pp. 60–70.
30. Yamagata, Y., Yang, P.P., Chang, S., Tobey, M.B., Binder, R.B., Fourie, P.J., Jittrapirom, P., Kobashi, T., Yoshida, T. and Aleksejeva, J., 2020. Urban systems and the role of big data. In Urban Systems Design (pp. 23–58). Elsevier.
31. Trinta, F., Rego, P.A., Gomes, F., Rocha, L., Viana, W. and de Souza, J.N., 2020. Using Mobile Cloud Computing for Developing Context-Aware Multimedia Applications. In Special Topics in Multimedia, IoT and Web Technologies (pp. 51–89). Springer, Cham.
32. Yu, J., Li, H. and Liu, D., 2020. Modified Immune Evolutionary Algorithm for Medical Data Clustering and Feature Extraction under Cloud Computing Environment. Journal of Healthcare Engineering, 2020.
33. Hua, J., Shi, G., Zhu, H., Wang, F., Liu, X. and Li, H., 2020. CAMPS: Efficient and privacy-preserving medical primary diagnosis over outsourced cloud. Information Sciences, 527, pp. 560–575.
34. Naha, R.K., Garg, S., Georgakopoulos, D., Jayaraman, P.P., Gao, L., Xiang, Y. and Ranjan, R., 2018. Fog Computing: Survey of trends, architectures, requirements, and research directions. IEEE access, 6, pp. 47980–48009.
35. Avasalcai, C., Murturi, I. and Dustdar, S., 2020. Edge and fog: A survey, use cases, and future challenges. Fog Computing: Theory and Practice, pp. 43–65.
36. Tuli, S., Basumatary, N., Gill, S.S., Kahani, M., Arya, R.C., Wander, G.S. and Buyya, R., 2020. HealthFog: An ensemble deep learning based Smart Healthcare System for Automatic Diagnosis of Heart Diseases in integrated IoT and fog computing environments. Future Generation Computer Systems, 104, pp. 187–200.
37. Gia, T.N., Queralta, J.P. and Westerlund, T., 2020. Exploiting LoRa, edge, and fog computing for traffic monitoring in smart cities. In LPWAN Technologies for IoT and M2M Applications (pp. 347–371). Academic Press.
38. Javadzadeh, G. and Rahmani, A.M., 2020. Fog computing applications in smart cities: A systematic survey. Wireless Networks, 26(2), pp. 1433–1457.
39. Giang, N.K., Lea, R. and Leung, V.C., 2020. Developing applications in large scale, dynamic fog computing: A case study. Software: Practice and Experience, 50(5), pp. 519–532.
40. Rehan, M.M. and Rehmani, M., 2020. Blockchain-enabled Fog and Edge Computing: Concepts, Architectures and Applications: Concepts, Architectures and Applications.
41. Hernandez-Nieves, E., Hernández, G., Gil-González, A.B., Rodríguez-González, S. and Corchado, J.M., 2020. Fog computing architecture for personalized recommendation of banking products. Expert Systems with Applications, 140, p. 112900.

42. Shen, X., Zhu, L., Xu, C., Sharif, K. and Lu, R., 2020. A privacy-preserving data aggregation scheme for dynamic groups in fog computing. *Information Sciences*, *514*, pp. 118–130.
43. Kumar, K.V.R., Kumar, K.D., Poluru, R.K., Basha, S.M. and Reddy, M.P.K., 2020. Internet of Things and Fog Computing Applications in Intelligent Transportation Systems. In *Architecture and Security Issues in Fog Computing Applications* (pp. 131–150). IGI Global.
44. Sarkar, S. and Misra, S., 2016. Theoretical modelling of fog computing: a green computing paradigm to support IoT applications. *Iet Networks*, *5*(2), pp. 23–29.
45. Zhang, K., Leng, S., He, Y., Maharjan, S. and Zhang, Y., 2018. Mobile edge computing and networking for green and low-latency Internet of Things. *IEEE Communications Magazine*, *56*(5), pp. 39–45.
46. Jin, X., Zhang, F., Vasilakos, A.V. and Liu, Z., 2016. Green data centers: A survey, perspectives, and future directions. *arXiv preprint arXiv:1608.00687*.
47. Sun, X. and Ansari, N., 2017. Green cloudlet network: A distributed green mobile cloud network. *IEEE Network*, *31*(1), pp. 64–70.
48. Malla, S. and Christensen, K., 2020. The effect of server energy proportionality on data center power oversubscription. *Future Generation Computer Systems*, *104*, pp. 119–130.
49. Lin, M., Wierman, A., Andrew, L.L. and Thereska, E., 2012. Dynamic right-sizing for power-proportional data centers. *IEEE/ACM Transactions on Networking*, *21*(5), pp. 1378–1391.
50. Lin, M., Liu, Z., Wierman, A. and Andrew, L.L., 2012, June. Online algorithms for geographical load balancing. In *2012 international green computing conference (IGCC)* (pp. 1–10). IEEE.
51. Xu, H., Feng, C. and Li, B., 2014. Temperature aware workload managementin geo-distributed data centers. *IEEE Transactions on Parallel and Distributed Systems*, *26*(6), pp. 1743–1753.
52. Toosi, A.N., Qu, C., de Assunção, M.D. and Buyya, R., 2017. Renewable-aware geographical load balancing of web applications for sustainable data centers. *Journal of Network and Computer Applications*, *83*, pp. 155–168.
53. Gong, J., Zhou, S. and Niu, Z., 2013. Optimal power allocation for energy harvesting and power grid coexisting wireless communication systems. *IEEE Transactions on Communications*, *61*(7), pp. 3040–3049.
54. Mao, Y., Zhang, J. and Letaief, K.B., 2016. Grid energy consumption and QoS tradeoff in hybrid energy supply wireless networks. *IEEE Transactions on Wireless Communications*, *15*(5), pp. 3573–3586.
55. Huang, K. and Lau, V.K., 2014. Enabling wireless power transfer in cellular networks: Architecture, modeling and deployment. *IEEE Transactions on Wireless Communications*, *13*(2), pp. 902–912.
56. Ju, H. and Zhang, R., 2013. Throughput maximization in wireless powered communication networks. *IEEE* Transactions on Wireless Communications, 13(1), pp. 418–428.
57. Al-Shuwaili, A. and Simeone, O., 2017. Energy-efficient resource allocation for mobile edge computing-based augmented reality applications. *IEEE Wireless Communications Letters*, *6*(3), pp. 398–401.
58. Schneider, M., Rambach, J. and Stricker, D., 2017, March. Augmented reality based on edge computing using the example of remote live support. In *2017 IEEE International Conference on Industrial Technology (ICIT)* (pp. 1277–1282). IEEE.
59. Anjum, A., Abdullah, T., Tariq, M., Baltaci, Y. and Antonopoulos, N., 2016. Video stream analysis in clouds: An object detection and classification framework for high performance video analytics. *IEEE Transactions on Cloud Computing*.
60. Zhang, K., Mao, Y., Leng, S., He, Y. and Zhang, Y., 2017. Mobile-edge computing for vehicular networks: A promising network paradigm with predictive off-loading. *IEEE Vehicular Technology Magazine*, *12*(2), pp. 36–44.
61. Kabir, M.T. and Masouros, C., 2019. A Scalable Energy vs. Latency Trade-Off in Full-Duplex Mobile Edge Computing Systems. *IEEE Transactions on Communications*, *67*(8), pp. 5848–5861.

62. Dinh, T.Q., La, Q.D., Quek, T.Q. and Shin, H., 2018. Learning for computation offloading in mobile edge computing. *IEEE Transactions on Communications, 66*(12), pp. 6353–6367.
63. Ji, L. and Guo, S., 2018. Energy-efficient cooperative resource allocation in wireless powered mobile edge computing. IEEE Internet of Things Journal, 6(3), pp. 4744–4754.
64. Huang, L., Bi, S. and Zhang, Y.J., 2019. Deep reinforcement learning for online computation offloading in wireless powered mobile-edge computing networks. *IEEE Transactions on Mobile Computing*.
65. Sun, Y., Zhou, S. and Xu, J., 2017. EMM: Energy-aware mobility management for mobile edge computing in ultra dense networks. *IEEE Journal on Selected Areas in Communications, 35*(11), pp. 2637–2646.
66. Sun, X. and Ansari, N., 2016. EdgeIoT: Mobile edge computing for the Internet of Things. *IEEE Communications Magazine, 54*(12), pp. 22–29.
67. Jiang, C., Cheng, X., Gao, H., Zhou, X. and Wan, J., 2019. Toward computation offloading in edge computing: A survey. IEEE Access, 7, pp. 131543–131558.
68. Abbas, N., Zhang, Y., Taherkordi, A. and Skeie, T., 2017. Mobile edge computing: A survey. IEEE Internet of Things Journal, 5(1), pp. 450–465.
69. Liu, H., Eldarrat, F., Alqahtani, H., Reznik, A., De Foy, X. and Zhang, Y., 2017. Mobile edge cloud system: Architectures, challenges, and approaches. IEEE Systems Journal, 12(3), pp. 2495–2508.
70. Taleb, T., Samdanis, K., Mada, B., Flinck, H., Dutta, S. and Sabella, D., 2017. On multi-access edge computing: A survey of the emerging 5G network edge cloud architecture and orchestration. IEEE Communications Surveys & Tutorials, 19(3), pp. 1657–1681.
71. Moura, J. and Hutchison, D., 2018. Game theory for multi-access edge computing: Survey, use cases, and future trends. IEEE Communications Surveys & Tutorials, 21(1), pp. 260–288.
72. Ai, Y., Peng, M. and Zhang, K., 2018. Edge computing technologies for Internet of Things: a primer. Digital Communications and Networks, 4(2), pp. 77–86.
73. Porambage, P., Okwuibe, J., Liyanage, M., Ylianttila, M. and Taleb, T., 2018. Survey on multi-access edge computing for internet of things realization. IEEE Communications Surveys & Tutorials, 20(4), pp. 2961–2991.
74. Premsankar, G., Di Francesco, M. and Taleb, T., 2018. Edge computing for the Internet of Things: A case study. IEEE Internet of Things Journal, 5(2), pp. 1275–1284.
75. Mäkitalo, N., Ometov, A., Kannisto, J., Andreev, S., Koucheryavy, Y. and Mikkonen, T., 2018. Safe and secure execution at the network edge: a framework for coordinating cloud, fog, and edge. IEEE Softw, 35(1), pp. 30–37.
76. Shirazi, S.N., Gouglidis, A., Farshad, A. and Hutchison, D., 2017. The extended cloud: Review and analysis of mobile edge computing and fog from a security and resilience perspective. IEEE Journal on Selected Areas in Communications, 35(11), pp. 2586–2595.
77. Beck, M.T., Werner, M., Feld, S. and Schimper, S., 2014, November. Mobile edge computing: A taxonomy. In Proc. of the Sixth International Conference on Advances in Future Internet (pp. 48–55). Citeseer.
78. *Mukherjee,* A., De, D., and Guha Roy D, 2016. A power and latency aware cloudlet selection strategy for multi-cloudlet environment. *IEEE Transactions on Cloud Computing*, 7(1), pp. 141–154.
79. Garg, S., Singh, A., Kaur, K., Aujla, G. S., Batra, S., Kumar, N., &Obaidat, M. S. (2019). Edge computing-based security framework for big data analytics in VANETs. *IEEE Network, 33*(2), 72–81.
80. Huang, C. M., Chiang, M. S., Dao, D. T., Su, W. L., Xu, S., & Zhou, H. (2018). V2V data offloading for cellular network based on the software defined network (SDN) inside mobile edge computing (MEC) architecture. *IEEE Access, 6,* 17741–17755.
81. Van Krevelen, D. W. F., &Poelman, R. (2010). A survey of augmented reality technologies, applications and limitations. *International journal of virtual reality, 9*(2), 1–20.
82. Chen, D., Xie, L.J., Kim, B., Wang, L., Hong, C.S., Wang, L.C. and Han, Z., 2020, February. Federated Learning Based Mobile Edge Computing for Augmented Reality Applications. In *2020 International Conference on Computing, Networking and Communications (ICNC)* (pp. 767–773). IEEE.

83. Deb, P., Mukherjee, A., & De, D. (2019). Design of Green Smart Room Using Fifth Generation Network Device Femtolet. *Wireless Personal Communications*, *104*(3), 1037–1064.
84. Ray, A. and De, D., 2017. Performance evaluation of tree based data aggregation for real time indoor environment monitoring using wireless sensor network. *Microsystem Technologies*, *23*(9), pp. 4307–4318.
85. Maswadi, K., Ghani, N.B.A. and Hamid, S.B., 2020. Systematic Literature Review of Smart Home Monitoring Technologies Based on IoT for the Elderly. *IEEE Access*, *8*, pp. 92244–92261.
86. Ghosh, S., Mukherjee, A., Ghosh, S. K., &Buyya, R. (2019). Mobi-IoST: mobility-aware cloud-fog-edge-iot collaborative framework for time-critical applications. *IEEE Transactions on Network Science and Engineering*.
87. Greco, L., Percannella, G., Ritrovato, P., Tortorella, F. and Vento, M., 2020. Trends in IoT based solutions for health care: moving AI to the Edge. *Pattern Recognition Letters*.
88. Tamilselvi, V., Sribalaji, S., Vigneshwaran, P., Vinu, P. and GeethaRamani, J., 2020, March. IoT based health monitoring system. In *2020 6th International Conference on Advanced Computing and Communication Systems (ICACCS)* (pp. 386–389). IEEE.
89. Shafique, K., Khawaja, B.A., Sabir, F., Qazi, S. and Mustaqim, M., 2020. Internet of things (IoT) for next-generation smart systems: A review of current challenges, future trends and prospects for emerging 5G-IoT scenarios. *IEEE Access*, *8*, pp. 23022–23040.
90. *Sun, Y.; Dong*, W.; Chen, Y. An improved routing algorithm based on ant colony optimization in wireless sensor networks. IEEE Commun. Lett. 2017, 21, 1317–1320.
91. Cui, Z., Cao, Y., Cai, X., Cai, J. and Chen, J. (2018) Optimal LEACH protocol with modified bat algorithm for big data sensing systems in Internet of Things. Journal of Parallel and Distributed Computing.
92. Chandirasekaran, D. and Jayabarathi, T., 2019. Cat swarm algorithm in wireless sensor networks for optimized cluster head selection: a real time approach. *Cluster Computing*, *22*(5), pp. 11351–11361.
93. Aziz, A., Singh, K., Osamy, W. and Khedr, A.M., 2019. Effective algorithm for optimizing compressive sensing in IoT and periodic monitoring applications. Journal of Network and Computer Applications, 126, pp. 12–28.
94. Ray, A. and De, D., 2016. An energy efficient sensor movement approach using multiparameter reverse glowworm swarm optimization algorithm in mobile wireless sensor network. Simulation Modelling Practice and Theory, 62, pp. 117–136.
95. Mittal, N., 2019. Moth Flame Optimization Based Energy Efficient Stable Clustered Routing Approach for Wireless Sensor Networks. Wireless Personal Communications, 104(2), pp. 677–694.
96. Tabibi, S. and Ghaffari, A., 2019. Energy-efficient routing mechanism for mobile sink in wireless sensor networks using particle swarm optimization algorithm. *Wireless Personal Communications*, *104*(1), pp. 199–216.
97. Li, Y., Soleimani, H. and Zohal, M., 2019. An improved ant colony optimization algorithm for the multi-depot green vehicle routing problem with multiple objectives. Journal of Cleaner Production.
98. Wang, J., Cao, J., Sherratt, R.S. and Park, J.H., 2018. An improved ant colony optimization-based approach with mobile sink for wireless sensor networks. The Journal of Supercomputing, 74(12), pp. 6633–6645.
99. Osaba, E., Yang, X.S., Fister Jr, I., Del Ser, J., Lopez-Garcia, P. and Vazquez-Pardavila, A.J., (2019) A discrete and improved bat algorithm for solving a medical goods distribution problem with pharmacological waste collection. Swarm and evolutionary computation, 44:273–286.
100. Ng, C.K., Wu, C.H., Ip, W.H. and Yung, K.L. (2018) A smart bat algorithm for wireless sensor network deployment in 3-D environment. IEEE Communications Letters, 22(10):2120–2123.
101. Kong, L., Chen, C.M., Shih, H.C., Lin, C.W., He, B.Z. and Pan, J.S., 2014. An energy-aware routing protocol using cat swarm optimization for wireless sensor networks. In Advanced

Technologies, Embedded and Multimedia for Human-Centric Computing (pp. 311–318). Springer, Dordrecht.

102. Kong, L., Pan, J.S., Tsai, P.W., Vaclav, S. and Ho, J.H., 2015. A balanced power consumption algorithm based on enhanced parallel cat swarm optimization for wireless sensor network. International Journal of Distributed Sensor Networks, 11(3), p. 729680.

103. Li, X., Keegan, B. and Mtenzi, F., 2018. Energy Efficient Hybrid Routing Protocol Based on the Artificial Fish Swarm Algorithm and Ant Colony Optimisation for WSNs. Sensors, 18(10), p. 3351.

104. Khan, M.F., Aadil, F., Maqsood, M., Bukhari, S.H.R., Hussain, M. and Nam, Y., 2019. Moth Flame Clustering Algorithm for Internet of Vehicle (MFCA-IoV). IEEE Access, 7, pp. 11613–11629.

105. Ray, A. and De, D., 2016. Energy efficient clustering protocol based on K-means (EECPK-means)-midpoint algorithm for enhanced network lifetime in wireless sensor network. *IET Wireless Sensor Systems*, 6(6), pp. 181–191.

106. Raychaudhuri, A. and De, D., 2020. Bio-inspired Algorithm for Multi-objective Optimization in Wireless Sensor Network. In Nature Inspired Computing for Wireless Sensor Networks (pp. 279–301). Springer, Singapore.

107. Hamrioui, S. and Lorenz, P., 2017. Bio inspired routing algorithm and efficient communications within IoT. IEEE Network, 31(5), pp. 74–79.

108. He, Y., Yu, F. R., Zhao, N., Leung, V. C., & Yin, H. (2017). Software-defined networks with mobile edge computing and caching for smart cities: A big data deep reinforcement learning approach. *IEEE Communications Magazine*, 55(12), 31–37.

109. Hosseini, M. P., Tran, T. X., Pompili, D., Elisevich, K., & Soltanian-Zadeh, H. (2017, July). Deep learning with edge computing for localization of epileptogenicity using multimodal rs-fMRI and EEG big data. In *2017 IEEE International Conference on Autonomic Computing (ICAC)* (pp. 83–92). IEEE.

110. Cao, Y., Song, H., Kaiwartya, O., Zhou, B., Zhuang, Y., Cao, Y., & Zhang, X. (2018). Mobile edge computing for big-data-enabled electric vehicle charging. *IEEE Communications Magazine*, 56(3), 150–156.

111. Roman, R., Lopez, J., & Mambo, M. (2018). Mobile edge computing, fog et al.: A survey and analysis of security threats and challenges. *Future Generation Computer Systems*, 78, 680–698.

112. Wang, T., Zhou, J., Huang, M., Bhuiyan, M. Z. A., Liu, A., Xu, W., &Xie, M. (2018). Fog-based storage technology to fight with cyber threat. *Future Generation Computer Systems*, 83, 208–218.

113. Peng, K., Lin, R., Huang, B., Zou, H., & Yang, F. (2013). Node importance of data center network based on contribution matrix of information entropy. *Journal of Networks*, 8(6), 1248.

114. Peng, K., & Huang, B. (2015). The invulnerability studies on data center network. *International Journal of Security and Its Applications*, 9(11), 167–186.

115. Peng, K., Leung, V., Zheng, L., Wang, S., Huang, C., & Lin, T. (2018). Intrusion detection system based on decision tree over big data in fog environment. *Wireless Communications and Mobile Computing*, 2018.

116. Du, M., Wang, K., Chen, Y., Wang, X. and Sun, Y., 2018. Big data privacy preserving in multi-access edge computing for heterogeneous Internet of Things. *IEEE Communications Magazine*, 56(8), pp. 62–67.

117. Ray, P.P., Dash, D. and De, D., 2019. Internet of things-based real-time model study on e-healthcare: Device, message service and dew computing. *Computer Networks*, 149, pp. 226–239.

118. Roy, S., Sarkar, D. and De, D., 2020. DewMusic: crowdsourcing-based internet of music things in dew computing paradigm. *Journal of Ambient Intelligence and Humanized Computing*, pp. 1–17.

119. De, Debashis. Mobile cloud computing: architectures, algorithms and applications. CRC Press, 2016.

IoT Integration with MEC

AmirHossein Jafari Pozveh and Hadi Shahriar Shahhoseini

Abstract Internet of Things (IoT) as a backbone of future customer value enables ubiquitously available digital services. However, providing smart digital services in an IoT ecosystem that billions of devices are connected to the network, needs high processing power and high capacity as well as low latency communications. In this regard, the emergence of MultiAccess Edge Computing (MEC) technology offers cloud computing capabilities to the network edge to meet IoT-based application requirements by providing real-time, high-bandwidth, low-latency access to the network resources. In this chapter, the most important topics related to IoT integrated with MEC have been presented. After introduction, the role of MEC in providing IoT services by using real-time analysis, caching and computing mechanisms are explained. By considering the importance of the integration in service delivery and platform in the next-generation networks (e.g. 5G), the MEC API section is presented. It discusses about the interaction of devices, third-parties and service providers with MEC platform through API as a common language. Then, the mobility management in IoT ecosystem related to service delivery and QoS using MEC has been studied. Finally, after presenting a benchmark for deployed IoT use cases by famous operators, challenges and future direction have been surveyed.

Keywords MEC platform · IoT · Offloading · Local caching · Mobility management

1 Introduction

Emerging new communication technologies and developing next-generation networks like 5G, have enabled billions of devices to connect to the network from different domains and provide various advanced services. This massive connection

A. J. Pozveh (✉) · H. S. Shahhoseini
School of Electrical Engineering, Iran University of science and Technology (IUST), Tehran, Iran
e-mail: amirafari@iust.ac.ir; shahhoseini@iust.ac.ir

of things to the Internet has led to a new concept called Internet of Things (IoT). The basic concept of IoT is that anything can be connected to the network at any time through the communication infrastructure [1]. IoT plays an important role in addressing the challenges facing the world and enhances the quality of life in terms of healthcare, productivity, and entertainment. The IoT has great potential for developing smart applications and as a key provider activates new business models emerged due to using IoT based services such as any of the smart home, smart healthcare, smart transportation. The deployed IoT applications can be classified into four groups. These 4 types are monitoring (control devices, environmental status, notifications, alerts), control (control of device functions), optimization (device performance, diagnostics, repair, etc.), and autonomy (autonomous operations). Of course, in the implementation and development of IoT applications the key issues of availability, management, reliability, interoperability, scalability (large-scale expansion and integration), security, and privacy should be considered [2].

Potential IoT applications can be provided regarding service category defined by the International Telecommunication Union (ITU) in 5G era in terms of ultra-reliable low latency communications (URLLC), enhanced Mobile Broadband (eMBB), massive machine-type communications (mMTC) [3] as shown in Table 1.

In Table 2, recent research works regarding URLLC, eMBB, and mMTC service types for IoT use cases have been presented. As seen, in eMBB service category, there are three types of IoT applications, including Media/Entertainment, Content Sharing/Caching and High bit rate Video Streaming.

The most important examples in the Media/Entertainment are gaming, Virtual reality (VR)/Augmented Reality (AR)/Mixed reality (MR), and distance education. It should say that gaming, mobile VR, MR, and AR applications are use case-specific, and sit at the crossroads between eMBB and URLLC. Content Sharing/Caching applications in eMBB service category such as Local Office data sharing are related to cases that a high bite rate is required. The last one in eMBB service category is the video Streaming use cases that need a High bit rate e.g., the Ultra-high-definition (3D/UHD) video service is a clear example of this IoT application.

Table 1 Based features for the service category [3]

Category	Basic features	Application
eMBB	Higher data rate (large payload, massive internet connectivity)	Cloud office/gaming, virtual/augmented reality (VR/AR) and ultra-high-definition (3D/UHD) video.
URLLC	Ultra-responsive connection with ultra-low latency. Not very high data rate	Industrial automation, autonomous driving, mission-critical applications, and remote medical assistance
mMTC	Massive connectivity of IoT devices	Low power devices in a massive quantity

Table 2 Recent studies for IoT applications in ITU's Service category

Service category	IoT application	Example	Research works
eMBB	Media/Entertainment	Gaming, VR/AR, distance education	[4–6]
	Content Sharing/ Caching	Local Office data sharing	[7, 8]
	High bit rate Video Streaming	Ultra-high-definition (3D/UHD) video	[9, 10]
URLLC	Manufacturing	Industrial and Automation	[11–13]
	Healthcare	Remote medical assistance	[14–16]
	Transport sectors	Automation, autonomous driving	[17–20]
	Entertainment	Gaming, VR/AR	[21–23]
mMTC	Manufacturing and industry	Monitoring for manufacturing equipment, e.g., machine tools, robotic arms, feeding machine)	[24, 25]
	Healthcare	Monitoring (Smart Watches, Fitness Trackers, Wearables and "Hearables")	[26–28]
	Smart Cities, Energy, and Logistics	Smart home, smart parking, smart transport system	[29–35]
	Farming and agriculture	Smart agriculture	[36–39]

In URLLC service category, manufacturing (e.g., Industrial and Automation), healthcare (e.g., Remote medical assistance), transport sectors (e.g., V2X and autonomous driving), and Entertainment use cases (e.g., gaming, VR/AR) are the most important IoT applications.

mMTC service category embraces Manufacturing and Industry (e.g., monitoring for manufacturing equipment such as machine tools, robotic arms, feeding machine), Healthcare Monitoring (e.g., Smart Watches, Fitness Trackers, Wearables and "Hearables"), Smart Cities, Energy, and Logistics (e.g., Smart home, smart parking, smart transport system) and Farming and Agriculture IoT applications (e.g., Smart agriculture). All the applications require a massive number of devices such as sensors that typically transmit and receive an only small amount of data sporadically.

Basic three-layer architecture for IoT has been proposed in Fig. 1a [40]. It includes perception, network and application layers. In the first layer, i.e., the perception layer, the sensors collect information from the physical environment. Each device has a specific identity (e.g., ID, IP) and may use various technologies, including cellular and non-cellular networks such as NB-IoT, LTE-M, Lora, Sigfox.

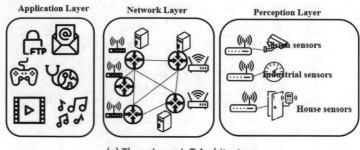

(a) Three Layer IoT Architecture

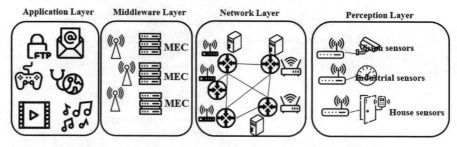

(b) Three Layer IoT Architecture with MEC as Middleware Layer

Fig. 1 Three-layer IoT architecture with MEC as Middle layer

The second layer, i.e. the network layer, transmits the gathered raw data to the application layer (IoT platform) for processing and analysis. The third layer, i.e. the application layer, manages and analyzes the raw collected data from layer 1.

This layer provides a high-level intelligent solution for IoT based services. To clarify further, consider the healthcare application. The information collected from the perception layer is transmitted to the health platform in layer 3 through the network layer to be analyzed and monitored on the healthcare platform and in a critical situation, alarms will sent to the medical center.

IoT-based services have different service requirements. To meet these service requirements in IoT environment, the service delivery's limitations should be addressed. For example, in remote surgery via a remote robot, low latency and reliability are important. If the operation information is transferred with latency, the cancer operation by the robot may be corrupted. For this purpose, the Middleware layer as Multiple Access Edge Computing (MEC) is placed between the network layer 2 and application layer 3 in IoT architecture as shown in Fig. 1b.

MEC is a good solution technology that sits between layers 1 and 3 and provides specific distributed computing for faster data processing and response time. Unlike traditional computing methods such as cluster computing [41], MEC can be deployed in a distributed manner and various scheduling algorithms [42] can be used for resource management. Meanwhile, MEC is an enabler for 5G. It facilitates the data processing and analysis of the massive connection of a large number of things for new services that emerged in 5G environment. MEC, in the IoT ecosystem, acts as a gateway that in addition to collecting data from heterogeneous sources with different protocols and sensors equipped by different technologies, also provides special edge functions. In this regard, ETSI [43] mentioned in the technical reports that MEC can have an important role in IoT ecosystem in providing service. MEC started in 2014 with a group of 6 vendors and operators (Huawei, IBM, Intel, Huawei, NTT, Vodafone) that presented a vision for MEC in the form of a technical white paper and studied a particular group at ETSI. ETSI MEC industry specification group that now has more than 60 members and participants.

In this regard, MEC-based solutions can be implemented in different tiers in the network architecture such as eNB/gNB, Multi-RAT aggregate point and local data centers according to applications and according to service providers' (SPs) and the operators' network architecture [44]. For example, for stadiums, shopping malls, airports or car factories, the MEC platform can be placed at the customer's location. SPs and operators can build edge computing "cloudlet" by utilizing MEC and run various ecosystems of applications within their network. In other words, by using MEC solution, a golden opportunity is obtained for SPs to make the most of the services they create in the IoT environment and gain more market share. In addition, by utilizing network function virtualization (NFV) and software defined network (SDN) technologies combined with the low latency of 5G network, operators will be able to provide flexible, scalable, with agility advanced services and deliver various contents and applications, and services that could not be provided before.

Edge Cloud can be implemented as public/private/hybrid based on service type and operator requirements and link communication. Table 3 shows edge cloud implementation types based on the network used [45].

In private edge cloud/private network case, the edge service provider has a completely isolated edge infrastructure whose inputs, outputs, data processing and even data storage are private due to private edge and the QoS of the communication is provided according to the dedicated network. In the private edge cloud/public network case, the edge service provider uses a completely private isolated edge infrastructure. So, data input and output, processing and even data storage are isolated. Moreover, the cloud resources are controlled completely locally, which is costly. In this case, the communication network is public and the service provider has no dedicated communication link and uses the public network.

In public edge cloud/public network case, public edge agents and infrastructure are used to support computing on shared/dedicated resources provided by the public network operator and data can be stored and accessed publicly. In public edge cloud/private network case, the service provider has a dedicated communication network meeting QoS provisioning and uses the shared edge cloud. For Hybrid cases, a hybrid model is created for edge cloud and/or network that allows flexibility dedicated network/edge cloud resources when they are required and data control and access are focused.

Table 3 Edge Cloud Type vs Network Type

Edge Cloud Network	Private	Public	Hybrid
Private	Isolated edge resources with data privacy, Local control, QoS support for Communication Costly	Using shared resources for Data processing and storage, QoS support for Communication	Local and isolated/shared cloud resources (computing, storage), QoS support for Communication
Public	Isolated edge resources with data privacy, Local control Private Network is not feasible or costly	Using shared resources for Data processing and storage, Private Network is not feasible or costly	Local and isolated/shared cloud resources (computing, storage), Private Network is not feasible or costly
Hybrid	Isolated system with data privacy, Local control Private communication according to requirements, Trade off between cost, feasibility and use case	Using shared resources for Data processing and storage, Private communication according to requirements, Trade off between cost, feasibility and use case	Local and isolated/shared cloud resources (computing, storage), Private communication according to requirements, Trade off between cost, feasibility and use case, Flexible and least costly

Table 4 Recent studies in field of IoT integration with MEC

Focus area	Sub-topic	Research works
Framework and architecture	End to end	[46–48]
	Use case	[49, 50]
	Service optimization	[51–54]
Survey	Deployment and integration	[55, 56]
	Use case	[57–59]
	Trend	[60–62]
Resource management	Slicing	[63, 64]
	Resource utilization/Computational cost	[65–68]
	Service quality	[69–72]
	Energy management	[73, 74]
Security	Security framework and architecture	[75–77]
	Survey and trend	[78–82]
	Privacy and data integrity	[83–86]
	Attacks & threats & defense solution	[87–91]
Orchestration	Service orchestration	[92, 93]
	Network orchestration	[94, 95]
Functionality	Real time data analysis	[96–98]
	Local content/caching	[99, 96, 100–102]
	Computing	[103–107]
Mobility management	Service quality	[108, 109]
	Security	[110]
	Trend and analysis	[111, 112]

In the recent years, various works have been studied in area of integration of IoT with MEC to increase performance, energy efficiency, new use case and ease of implementation. Integration means various IoT applications can be run on the MEC platform by combining computing resources to create integrated services. In Table 4, recent studies have been presented regarding framework and Architecture, survey, resource Management, security, orchestration, functionality and mobility Management. In each topic, based on the research works, the most important sub topics have been presented.

2 Chapter Organization

This chapter discusses the most important topics related to IoT integrated with MEC. In this regard, in part 1, MEC functionalities that can help in provisioning of IoT applications are discussed for various use cases. After that MEC API is examined for the cases that third-parties as an owner of the IoT applications can use from MEC platform. The next section addresses mobility issues of IoT devices related to service delivery and QoS in the MEC based network architecture. After that, the famous operators that during recent years they have deployed IoT use cases based on MEC architecture have been presented. Finally, challenges and future direction have been given.

3 MEC Functionalities for IoT Services

In the digital transformation of vertical industries, a massive amount of data is generated in a massive IoT ecosystem, which requires edge computing services close to devices to achieve the reliable local offload and backend cloud integration for real-time data processing and content localization. MEC edge computing as a platform can have an important role in this environment. In this regard, three main functionalities that MEC can provide are.

- Real-time analysis and low latency
- Local content/caching
- Computing

This section studies these functionalities from the viewpoint of IoT-based services. A discussion is provided for each function in terms of architecture, service scenarios, and applications.

3.1 Real-Time Analysis and Low Latency Functionality

The main question to be answered in this section is how MEC can help provide Real-Time Data (RTD) analysis services for the IoT ecosystem. RTD services fall into the URLLC service category presented in Table 1. In the traditional cellular networks, which are deployed in a centralized manner, data from IoT devices is transferred for analysis to the IoT application located in the core network or Internet through the RAN section as well as Backhaul network (as shown in Fig. 2). In this case, Round Trip Time (RTT) from IoT devices to IoT platform used for processing is too high. This latency is not proper for URLLC services.

However, thanks to MEC, it makes possible delivering the required resources for IoT applications close to the edge of the network. MEC provides an effective solution to minimize response time for ultra-responsive connection with ultra-low latency and not very large data. as shown in Fig.3, MEC is placed between the access network and core network [43] and the IoT gateway application (IoT GWApp) is placed on MEC servers. Data from things is sent to MEC servers for local analysis at the edge in the IoT GWApp. So, RTD processing as well as actuators triggering can be performed within a fraction of seconds. The architecture allows the cloud provider, IoT gateways and end devices to be integrated and support end-to-end mission-critical services [55].

Application Case
By using MEC-enabled architecture, low latency and reliable required services fall under the URLLC category and many applications in this category can be deployed. The service types are classified into four groups, including medical and health care,

Fig. 2 Architecture of the traditional Cellular Networks

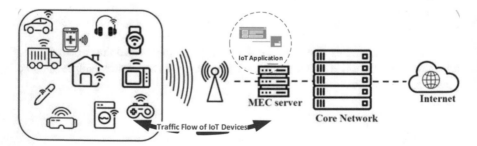

Fig. 3 MEC-enabled architecture for real-time analysis

Table 5 URLLC service categories and industrial/user requirements

Application field	Application
Medical and Health Care	Remote surgery or remote patient's diagnosis
Media/Entertainment/Business	Live reporting of an event, live sports events, online gaming, cloud-based entertainment (VR/AR).
Transport	Drone-based delivery, remote driving, self-driven cars, traffic management, sub-station management (system synchronization, traffic management)
Industrial	Automation Control systems, automated assembly lines with robots, machine status reports, process surveillance, power grid management.

media/entertainment/business, transportation and industrial applications as shown in Table 5 [113]. Here, for each service category, the role of MEC in the service is presented.

In *medical and healthcare applications,* remote surgery is a use case that requires a reliable and a low latency connection. Robot-based operations using tactile Internet makes better quality care alongside experienced doctors in terms of high-precision diagnosis and treatment. Using the MEC system can increase data transfer reliability and reduce delay to 1–10 milliseconds so that the instructions given to the robot by the therapist will be very reliable with a slight delay. This is not a case with current technologies, as losing packets and delays of 100 milliseconds can significantly reduce reliability.

For *Media/Entertainment/Business* applications, VR/AR and gaming are the most general application cases. In the VR service, the user needs to experience the "touch-sensitive virtual environment". However, it requires a low latency connectivity of about a few milliseconds to give users a real sense for their actions. Today's networks have a long delay in establishing stable communication for highly sensitive interactions. The MEC system supports a real-time visualized environment in interaction with users in order of milliseconds. For the AR case (e.g. engineering, museum guides and assistance systems), additional information is added to the user's vision by utilizing IoT devices such as glasses. In this case, real time connectivity is required to avoid latency while interacting with real world. However, the current networks are limited and, therefore, unable to support these requirements. MEC can address this issue in terms of providing a real-time connection. In the *gaming application cases,* since the next generation games deal with not only entertainment but also education and problem solving, the low latency interaction between the players and game processors is an important challenge that can affect the verisimilitude of the game. They can be addressed by placing game servers near the edge on the MEC platform.

In *transportation applications,* e.g., self-driving cars, drone-based delivery, remote driving, and traffic management, providing the service requires a quick response to the controllers and actuators in milliseconds. The MEC solution supports sending alarms and commands in a real-time manner by bringing computation

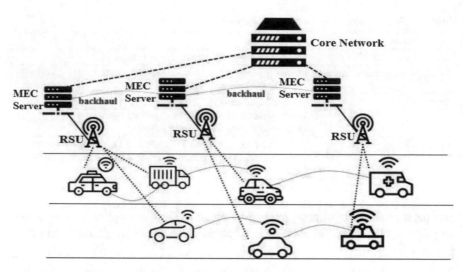

Fig. 4 MEC-enabled real-time V2V analysis application case

at the network edge close to the device. One example of the V2V application has been shown in Fig. 4. As presented in the figure, it is necessary for the vehicle to exchange the messages (e.g. location, speed update) through the road-side units (RSU) along the road. In the case of high-speed mobility, a low latency packet delay communication is required. It cannot be expected that the required latency is provided by running a V2V application on the cloud core far from the edge since its response time from the core to the vehicle may suffer from a large latency.

In the *industrial application*, (e.g., automation control systems, automated assembly lines with robot and power grid management), humans are replaced by robots or algorithms in the control process such as car assembly process. This architecture requires RTD analysis with minimum latency. Because if any delay is occurred in the system, e.g. during the assembly process, it may cause damage to the production line. However, MEC supports RTD analysis for automation control that meets the strict requirements of latency for industrial applications.

3.2 Local Content/Caching Functionality

In a IoT ecosystem, delivering services in eMBB and mMTC categories, require high bandwidth such as such as video streaming, broadcasting and tourist guide. This traffic is divided into two types, namely: *large/multimedia data* (e.g., such as video/audio files in Ultra-HD video service) and *IoT data* (e.g., sensors' data in metering case). Generally, the same interesting videos may be requested in many times by users and on the other hand huge IoT data are generated by low-rate monitoring and measurement applications running on billions of devices. In the

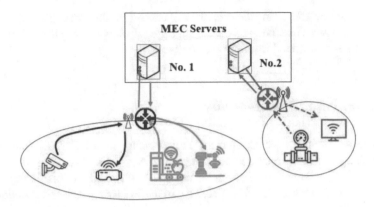

Fig. 5 MEC role for caching data in eMBB

5G network, the required resources can be supported for both data types in access networks. Supporting high data rate in radio access network (RAN) is provided by using various techniques such as mmWave spectrum, multi input multi output (MIMO) and dual connectivity (DC). However, there are limitations in providing the required capacity for transmission networks (XHaul) as well as supporting latency requirements to transfer the generated data to the core of the mobile operator.

Caching the content/data locally as a functionality of MEC system is a proper solution to address this issue by decreasing required bandwidth in the backhaul up to 35% [114]. So, the users' quality of experience (QoE) would be improved and less bandwidth is required in backhaul infrastructure.

In Fig. 5, the general MEC caching system has been shown. As seen, an MEC server has been placed near the user in access edge and BSs regarding to geographical area to cache the data based on predefined strategies such as the probability of reuse in the future. Here, two popular concepts are discussed. The first concept is the fact that caching saves a huge amount of data generated by things (e.g. cameras) on the MEC server. In this case, when a user/customer/system (e.g. automation system) requests the saved data, the requested data are provided by MEC server without transmitting through the entire network (i.e. backhaul and core). The second concept is sharing the popular/interested contents (e.g. video streams) with a group of users. In this regard, the content data have been saved in MEC server and delivered when they are requested. As a result, content delivery would be improved and bandwidth is effectively utilized.

The caching process is managed by an authorized caching application placed on the MEC platform. As an example, consider the video-broadcasting services utilizing caching mechanism. The video-broadcasting based caching application uses a transcoder function run in the MEC server to send users the different video qualities with various bit-rates according to device capabilities [115]. In the tourist guide example, tourists want to visit a historic place or museum and use complementary technologies such as AR to experience a better feeling. Information about the historic site or museum is already cached on the MEC platform close to the visitor and gives him/her a real-time, high-quality service with the ability to omit communication overhead from the core network.

3.3 Computing Functionality

This section discusses the Computing Functionality of MEC. This functionality helps reduce the radio resource consumption (i.e., 12%), shortening the reaction time (i.e. 10%), lessening the system latency (i.e., 14%), and diminishing the overall energy consumption (i.e.,12.35%) [31, 116] in the IoT ecosystem and is divided into two categories:

- Offloading
- Data analysis

The goal of offline processing is the reduction of computational operation from IoT devices to increase energy efficiency and QoE. However, data analysis function in MEC is used for analyzing or pre-process aggregated data in the IoT ecosystem to improve the quality of service delivery.

3.3.1 Offloading

Offloading is appealing to emerging IoT cloud-based applications. Because, the computing capabilities of end devices, such as mobile devices, sensors and actuators, are still constrained for executing smart and autonomic tasks such as many services related to the smart city by the fundamental challenges, such as memory size, battery life, and computation power. For delivering many of smart services, MEC as a extra entity is a good platform to perform tasks on behalf of the user's device and return the outcome. In other words, offloading is a procedure that migrates resource-intensive computations from a device to the resource-rich nearby infrastructure [117]. If the offloading is performed near the user's device at the edge of the network, computational requirements of an IoT application, load balancing, energy management and latency management would be provided more effectively.

MEC solution architecture for offloading at the edge of networks has been presented in Fig. 6 [118]. As shown, the compute intensive functions of IoT applications are executed on the MEC platform sit on the RAN (e.g., eNB, RNC) with the high computation power instead of execution on the device. In [119], a MEC solution offloading has been proposed by providing computing services at the edge of network to minimize energy consumption by considering the device's limitations and latency constraints. Authors in [120] have presented an offloading algorithm in which the memory objects delivered by various IoT devices to edge cloud are placed on the LTE nodes. It decreases latency and offloading cost. For communication services, such as video call, MEC solution also can be used. In

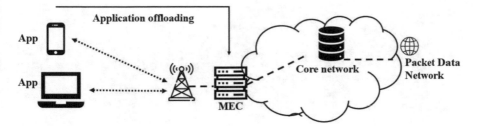

Fig. 6 Application computation offloading using MEC

[121], the video encoding process for a video call has been proposed to be offloaded to the MEC edge server. It used a communication protocol for negotiating the offloading strategy, which reduces energy consumption of mobile devices during video call service.

The decision about what to offload and how to offload it depends on three factors [122]. The first factor is whether the process can be offloaded or not? The second factor is how much data should be processed. This is specifically important because when the network can't estimate the number of input data (such as stream data), it is difficult to determine the amount of processes to be offloaded. The third factor is data dependency and what parts have to be offloaded. In this regard, various optimization schemes in the MEC area for computation offloading in 5G heterogeneous networks have been studied to minimize energy consumption in both the network and the device as well as optimizing allocated resources. Their goals are to provide an optimal solution to minimize energy consumption in the connected things, taking the acceptable delay and computation performance. Moreover, there are limited computing resources in an MEC platform located in the base station and edge data centers in comparison with the cloud core and not all application types with different computing requirements can be processed on the MEC platform for the IoT based service. Therefore, an interplay for joint resource management for running the IoT application and meeting service requirements is needed between the MEC platform at the edge and cloud core tier [123]. Various researches have been presented for orchestration mechanisms and resource allocation in a MEC-enabled network with cloud core for IoT applications, referred to the references [124].

Offloading Levels
Offloading can be done at different levels, as shown in Fig. 7. Authors in [125] have classified these levels into three categories: full computation, task/component, and method/thread offloading.

- Full computation offloading
  If offloading is full, all computation is performed by the IoT application on MEC platform, and the device (sensor, actuator or mobile phone) is only responsible for UI, input/output and data gathering. A common example is web-app [126], in which thin clients only get user input and browse the results.
- Task/Component offloading

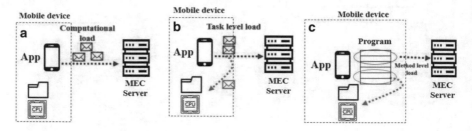

Fig. 7 Computation offloading types

Offloading at this level is based on dividing the application into separate tasks and components and placing high-processing components at the edge of the network for processing. To do this, first, the workflow execution should be specified. Then the task with high computation requirement is partitioned for offloading. Different methods for partitioning the applications have been proposed in the researches [127–129]. AR service is an example that can clear the concept. To provide AR service, it is required to be divided into four tasks including capturing photo/video, object tracking, rendering and display. Since object tracking and rendering are the tasks with high processing requirements, these parts are offloaded in the MEC platform and others are run on the device.

- Method offloading

  In general, an application is composed of many methods that can be partitioned and the selected methods are offloaded based on computation limitation. In the recent years, many methods have been proposed for partitioning in the method level presented in [130]. Methods of OCR in an AR application are an example related to IoT integration with MEC. They can be offloaded on MEC platform and then the other parts of AR service are run on the device.

3.3.2 Data Analytics

In the IoT ecosystem, a massive amount of raw data is generated by billions of IoT devices. Authors in [43] mentioned that 15 petabytes would be generated by IoT devices in a month that should be transferred from devices through core network to the cloud servers and the IoT platform. It results in high latency and increases backhaul traffic.

Data analytics as a computing function of MEC in the IoT ecosystem discusses the analysis gathered raw data at the network edge that is received from of a large number of various IoT devices, embedded with sensors and actuators, connected with various technologies such as LTE, GSM, Wi-Fi using different protocols, packet sizes and encryption algorithms.

Processing near the edge results in avoiding transmission of large amounts of data from end devices through backhaul and core network [43]. Deploying MEC solution

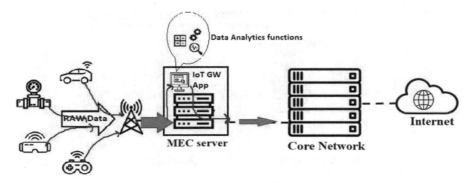

Fig. 8 Data analysis functionality of MEC for IoT based services

as a good candidate to perform all the analytic tasks, decreases the traffic of the core network, optimizes bandwidth utilization, reduces the demand of computational resources in the central data centers [55, 131], and therefore addresses the main challenges in IoT ecosystem management of the large-scale data collected over a time period at a IoT platform located beyond the core network. So, MEC has a critical role in service provision by operators in smart city applications and rollout 5G [132].

In Fig. 8, a high-level architecture for *Data analysis functionality* in MEC has been shown. An IoT GW application is located on the MEC platform, in the middle layer between the IoT device and the network core. It collects, integrates and analyzes the raw packets received from the IoT devices and performs analytic functions before sending data to the core or delivering to the IoT platform. To clearly understand the data analysis at the network edge, two service scenarios which are video analysis and metering are discussed. In video analytics, two application cases of intelligent video acceleration and video stream analysis service are popular [43].

In intelligent video acceleration use case, a radio analytic program is placed at ME Host near users between the radio and the core network to analyze the user's information and radio link status. The use case has been shown in Fig. 9. The result of analysis is sent to the video server as a signal. Video server uses this information to select the suitable video coding method and adjust the data rate for the users. Moreover, in the cases that video content server uses the TCP protocol, the radio link information, that obtained from RAN analytic application on the MEC server, helps TCP protocol distinguish congestion or low-quality wireless link and so the TCP congestion window based on the appropriate condition is adjusted.

Another application in the context of smart city is video based monitoring system, [117] which consists of many cameras in a region. The captured pictures from cameras are analyzed by video analytics applications placed on MEC platform as shown in Fig. 10. The MEC provides more resources for analyzing the received camera data (e.g. Video rendering). After analysis, if required (an anomaly is detected), the application sends some information (such as trigger alerts for different events) to video service platform in the core network. In fact, the use of MEC and

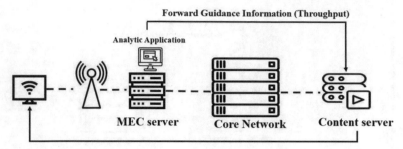

Fig. 9 Video Acceleration using radio information status

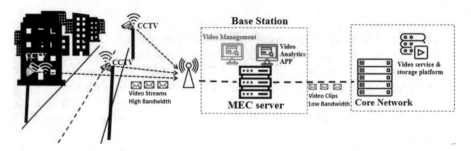

Fig. 10 Video stream analysis

the application placed on it, increases the flexibility of the analysis and decreases the volume of data that should be sent to the core [133].

In the metering example, as a general application of IoT in smart city, the information is received via sensors and gathered in a gateway. The received data are analyzed and appropriate action is performed. For example, consider smart agriculture, in which sensors gather humidity, temperature and minerals. After the analysis, decision making is done about water, humidity and fertilizers management through actuators.

In the cases where the received data from sensors act as big data and a high-power computation resource is required, the best way to analyze the data can be placing an intelligent or smart agricultural application on MEC platform near the sensor location. This leads to a reduction in the volume of raw data transmitted through the backhaul and core and analysis is performed quickly at the edge.

Data analytics can be performed in a hieratical manner according to resource requirements and application type. In the cases that low capacity resources are required, analysis is performed in the MEC platform. If the MEC platform has no resource to perform data processing, other resources in the network (e.g. core resources) are allocated.

For example, consider authentication-based face recognition used to identify the employees of an organization. The purpose of this application is to identify

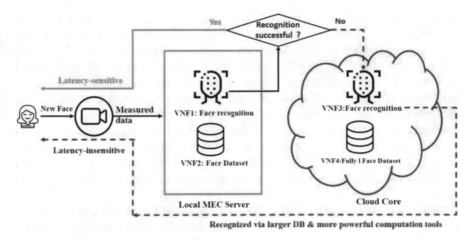

Fig. 11 Authentication based Face recognition

the person who enters the organization. Identification is based on the analysis of people's faces and the comparison with the pre-created database. To get employees' information quickly, the light data base (DB VNF) and face recognition application (Face recognition VNF) are placed at the edge of the network. Figure 11 demonstrates this service. If the employee is identified through the company's data center, the authentication process ends. Otherwise, the face recognition request will be sent to the cloud core to perform heavier calculations on the larger database.

4 MEC API

MEC API helps third parties interact their executed applications on the MEC platform by using application programming interface (API) and so they can provide customized IoT services. In this regard, ETSI Group has provided a set of standards related to open MEC and the use of API to provide various services in an open environment. This helps integrate different services in IoT ecosystem for a variety of verticals and applications. In this case authorized developers and content providers can deploy versatile and uninterrupted applications.

IoT applications implemented on the MEC platform intract with different service providers, third parties and devices (e.g. sensors and actuators), for sending configuration sets and receiving the gathered data for analysis. In legacy, each vendor or service provider has its protocol to communicate with IoT applications. Operators can open the edge devices of RANs to third-party partners by utilizing open API architecture. It allows operators to rapidly deploy innovative applications and content toward mobile subscribers, enterprises, and other vertical segments [134, 135]. Meanwhile, in recent years, by introducing the integration in service delivery and open platforms, the API has been proposed as a common language for the MEC system. Therefore, third parties, things and service providers can use the API to interact with the IoT application run on the MEC platform. It enables the IoT application to communicate with things without knowing how to they implemented it. For better clarification, consider the auto-config robot example. In this case, commands are sent to the robot from the IoT application, and after completing assigned tasks, the robot sends the result to the application and receives the new configuration via the API. Here, API has been used to read environmental data from sensors inside the robot and write to the actuators (e.g. motor movement). In this case, an agent is installed on the robot and uses API to communicate with the IoT application for registration, authentication, data analysis, and management functions.

Regarding API usage in MEC, ETSI have presented four API types including Bandwidth manager service (BWMS) API, Radio network information (RNI) API, UE identity API and Location API. IoT applications can use these APIs to obtain user information, required resources to provide services, and get radio information for better service delivery. The UE identity API has been defined to allow UEs to use specific traffic rules in the ME system. Based on this API, the MEC platform handles traffic rules and applies them to the UE's service. Moreover, UE uses the API to access the list of Applications registered on the MEC platform. IoT application also uses this API to manage access control and the integrity of user content.

The second API is the Bandwidth manager (BWM) API on the MEC platform which allows a fair distribution of bandwidth resources shared between various IoT applications. It is useful in the cases that a set of IoT applications run on the MEC platform and compete to get at least the required throughput and priority.

The third API on the MEC platform is Location API that is related to the user information. This API provides location information for the authorized IoT application. The most important information that can be obtained from Location API is: Location information of all UEs that are connected in a specific region, list of services that are located in a particular region and the information of all radio nodes that are connected to the MEC platform.

The last API, the RNI API, is used in cases that IoT applications need knowledge about the radio network conditions to improve service delivery. IoT applications use RNI API to get the low-level information in accordance with 3GPP. Figure 12 shows an example of employing this API for a video streaming application. As shown in the figure, the Video application sends UE the requested video with the appropriate bitrate and throughput according to the received radio information.

5 Mobility Management

In a MEC-based architecture where connected devices have mobility, there are significant challenges regarding to service quality. For IoT applications, seamless service provisioning is required. Recent research works have been proposed as listed

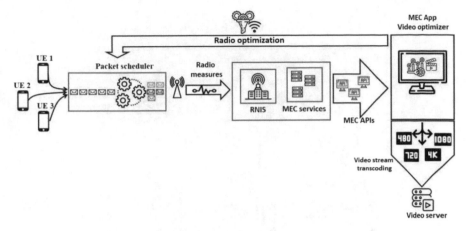

Fig. 12 Video optimization aware of using RNI API [28]

in Table 4. However, in a MEC-based architecture where connected devices have mobility, there are significant challenges regarding to service quality.

In MEC system that IoT applications services to the mobile customers, two scenarios can occur. In the first cases, if the device is receiving a service and moves to the coverage of another radio access networks in the same MEC domain, the new connection to new access point (AP) may have lower quality. This issue can cause an interruption in receiving URLLC or eMBB services due to the limitation in providing real-time, reliability or bandwidth requirements. This scenario has been shown in Fig. 13a. In another case, if the device hands over to another AP and MEC domain is changed, the new MEC domain may not be able to meet the service requirements (Bandwidth, processing power, reliability, etc.) as well as the old one. So the devices may be disconnected completely from the MEC system with a sharp drop in service quality. This case has been shown in Fig. 13b. Therefore, in the IoT ecosystem with mobile devices integrated with MEC, the following topics should be considered for designing the service relocation policies to have continuous service provisioning

- Location management: it is important because providing service requires knowledge about location of the device for resource allocation and traffic routing
- Connectivity and quality: by moving devices to a new location, access technologies providing service may be changed (e.g. from WiFi to cellular network). In this case, connection quality and connectivity status may change and quality of service experience may decrease. So, in mobility management context, connection management and successful handover between different access technologies as a hot topic should be studied.
- Load balancing for MEC domains: In the MEC based architecture, device mobility may cause service migration between MEC domains. In the case, the

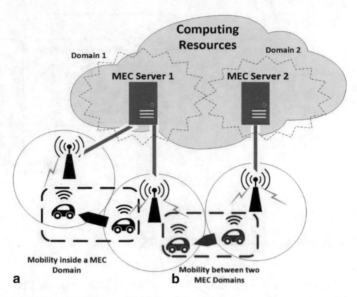

Fig. 13 Mobility Scenario between MEC Domains

application run on MEC to provide IoT based service, may not be supported in New MEC domain.

On the other hand, due device mobility, load of MEC servers in different locations are changing. So, resource management methods should be considered for VNF migration, offloading to cloud core, and task scheduling.

6 Benchmark

Besides theoretical research studies, many vendors and companies have launched MEC solution for IoT service scenarios. In 2014, Nokia Networks introduced a real-world MEC platform using VM hypervisor to deploy virtual [136]. In [137], an adaptive operation platform (AOP) has been proposed for a fog computing environment by considering the operational requirements of industrial IoT. The authors in [138] deployed the M2M fog platform and evaluated the legacy architecture, Device-to-Device (D2D) and small cell-based deployment. However, the most famous operators that implement MEC based services are going to commercialize IoT based MEC. Therefore, in this study the proposed and implemented MEC platforms from most famous operators/institutes are discussed including China Mobile, AT&T, SKT, Deutsche Telekom and 5GPPP.

6.1   China Mobile

China Mobile tested the cloud game on the edge with the help of ZTE and cloud game provider Tencent on a 5G pilot network in Guangzhou in 2019 [139]. The architecture includes 5G Core UPF (User Plane Function) in the local MEC for cloud gaming traffic loading, MEP (Multi-access Edge Platform) for cloud-based gaming exposure, and RAN-aware capability exposure, including RNIS (Radio Network Information) Service, TCPO service (TCP optimization) and VO (video optimization) service.

In this architecture, cloud-based game providers offer gaming services at the edge of the network by using the Edge Cloud Game Connector in MEP PaaS for seamless cloud service. It results in a cloud game service with faster image rendering speed for users with higher rate. Because directly rendered media stream as an offloading computation is performed in the local MEC and delivered to the user at a faster speed. It saves network bandwidth and reduces the delay in providing game service to users.

6.2   AT&T

AT&T provides an enterprise grade solution for the next generation of opportunities. AT&T MEC provides edge-based services for stadiums, retail, manufacturing and healthcare [140]. In stadiums, as an area with massive interconnected devices during events, the solution speeds up customer transactions. It provides some data for visitors such as seat locations, queue times, and customized promotions through smartphones. In retail, AT&T MEC decreases the required bandwidth for inventory robot used in remote operation of today's retail leaders. Inventory robot sends data, high-resolution images, as a real-time data to the small cell. The small cell relays data to the aggregation point where AT&T MEC is installed. The data is processed as AT&T MEC and saved in the local data center. When an end-point retail leader requests the inventory data, AT&T MEC service can route cellular processed data through the small cell from local data center. This solution is also used in manufacturing by offloading the analysis of high-resolution video from camera for decision, production process, advanced detection and error identification. AT&T MEC helps businesses to improve the processing of the traffic for low-latency and in a secure manner.

6.3   SKT

SK Telecom (SKT) designed a scalable, visualized and reliable 5G MEC platform based on the ETSI reference architecture [141]. The MEC architecture for 5G

SK Telecom, is based on 3GPP and ETSI MEC standards. This platform helps provide a variety of 5G services with low latency requirements and security features. It is designed based on network functions (NFV) to have flexibility in resource management and service delivery. The implemented SK Telecom MEC platform includes an edge routing function, a MEC service enabler consisting of an API port, and the MEC service and MEC platform management (MECPM) system. The role of the Edge Routing Function is to categorize user's traffic and send it to the relevant application running on the MEC platform. MEC Service Enabler is also a key element of SK Telecom's MEC platform that can be used in the development of MEC applications. Its main functions are MEC service discovery, routing, authentication, licensing, and MEC service level agreement (SLA) management. The MEC Platform Manager (MEPM), hosted by the MEC, enables MEC Platform software and MEC applications to work on the MEC host. MEPM features include MEC Orchestrator, MEC Platform Manager, and key elements of the infrastructure manager Virtualization is defined in the ETSI MEC standard. SKT MEC minimized the transport latency and enabling the 5G network by bringing the cloud server closer to the user to provide ultra-low latency services and provide 5G network with very low latency.

6.4 Deutsche Telekom

Deutsche telekom completes World's First Public Mobile Edge Network, Powered By MobiledgeX Edge-Cloud R1.0 to deploy the backend applications close to mobile users on the Telekom Deutschland network in Germany in a live test for augmented reality (AR) and mixed reality (MR) applications [142]. The platform helps make edge infrastructure available to third parties. Moreover, for developers, MobiledgeX Edge-Cloud R1.0 enables application containers to be deployed with the same simplicity as over-the-top datacenter-based cloud providers. In this solution, by using cloud containers near end devices, the service requirements could be met in the next generation networks regarding the following cases:

- Automatic applications deployment based on verified location and identities near users for the purpose of serving massive multi-user tasks such as multiplayer games, robotics and AR.
- Support low latency connection and processing
- Guarantees Local Privacy Regulations for video and Image Processing

6.5 5GPPP

5GCITY [143] was introduced as one of the 5GPPP projects with the aim of maximizing return of investment in digital market chain (user, service provider, cloud provider, telecom provider and infrastructure provider). It was planned to design an open platform with multi-tenant support that transfers cloud-based application from core datacenter to the edge of the network in such a way that the caching and computing is performed in an integrated MEC.

5GCity architecture is based on "neutral hosting" that helps media service providers to collaboratively implement innovative applications offloaded on a neutral host platform and improve the user service experience. It is composed of 3 Tiers based on geographical area. The first tier includes far-edge area (small cell, WiFi) with macro computing resources, the second tier, i.e. edge area, includes street cabinets with constrained computing resources and in the third level at Central/Core of network, powerful computing resources are included.

In 5GCITY architecture from a vertical viewpoint, three main layers including application layer, orchestration layer and infrastructure layer have been designed. The application layer provides the tools for service implementation by operators and third parties. The orchestration layer as the service entry point is responsible for managing the platform and infrastructure resources (WAN, VIM, SDN Controller). The third layer is the infrastructure layer that provides the necessary resources in virtual computing and radio infrastructure.

7   Challenges and Issues

Despite development in MEC, there are still bottlenecks in implementation and commercialization. These challenges are discussed in five categories including security, technology maturity, resource management, openness, service continuity and interoperability.

Security
Security issues are topics that may often cause cost to communication networks [144]. In this regard, different algorithms have been proposed to defend attacks in different network layers and various network protocols [145, 42]. Meanwhile, MEC-enabled IoT systems that use network resources have security challenges that have been discussed from different aspects [117]. The first one is privacy. MEC platform is placed between two layers of perception (1) and application in an IoT reference architecture. Therefore, the information received from devices, things and sensors is transmitted through it. If unauthorized applications on the MEC platform have access to this information, privacy can be compromised. For example, for various services in the IoT ecosystem, information such as employment, family service status, user location, and intelligent data are passed to the MEC platform for data mining and data integration. If this information leaks for any reason, it can cause financial and non-financial losses due to revealing important and classified business secrets and users' data. The next issue is the security challenges related to new technologies.

MEC-enabled IoT ecosystem uses new multiple technologies such as SDN, NFV simultaneously to provide IoT based services in different protocol layers [146, 147]. These technologies are new and so they have potential multi-layer security concerns that are not yet known. Moreover, security challenges can be originated from openness in MEC platform. In recent years, the issue of openness has moved towards open platform and programmability for MEC, which allows a number of third parties and hardware and software vendors to participate in its development. Risk management is this open system including multi-vendor developed system must be considered. On the other hand, different IoT applications are running on the same MEC platform. If the shared traffic and data access aren't isolated, data and gathered information might be leaked. The last security issue is related to MEC architecture. Legacy network architecture is centralized, and these authentication protocols may not be compatible with next generation systems i.e. distributed MEC systems. Therefore, availability of new distributed authorization and authentication algorithms for distributed MEC systems is a challenge that should be addressed.

Resource Management/Placement

Resource management of different domains distributed at the edge as well as orchestration plays an important role in the success of the MEC as a platform for implementing IoT applications in the IoT ecosystem and the related challenges should be addressed [63, 148, 74, 149]. The first challenge is fair resource sharing and load balancing for edge resources shared between IoT applications. To prevent computation offloading congestion, optimal, practical and simple models should be used to build, design and implement appropriate resource management algorithms. Another challenge is determining the appropriate location for deploying cloud infrastructure. It is an open question in which eNB, central office or local data centers are optimal to implement the MEC Platform. It depends on different factors. For example, for VR or autonomous cars, the latency is very critical, and the proximity of VR/autonomous-driving applications to devices is an important requirement. For VR, the base station is a good place to deploy MEC platform. However, for autonomous driving, the MEC node may be inside the Vehicle [150]. For cases where latency is not important, e.g. caching, the MEC platform can be located at the aggregation point or central office.

Openness

Lack of openness is a challenge that can increase market monopolies and reduce the possibility of various services growing. The main reason for lack of openness is that large companies tend to define customized protocols to lock the market with their products. In this environment, costumers are forced to use specific infrastructure, and changing the operator or service provider can cause a high cost for them. If the edge computing architecture is not built based on the concept of openness, various implementation scenarios for IoT based services will be created and so integration of these services is an issue that should be addressed. This is a bold challenge since stakeholders have no incentive to cooperate and do not provide open and clear interface software and hardware.

Integration
Currently, the IoT ecosystem has not yet matured in terms of technology and application. It is in the early stages of deployment and different applications for different services have been developed. Moreover, devices and things use heterogeneous technologies such as LTE, NR-IoT, NB-IoT, and different encrypted messages. The variety causes a challenge for integration of IoT applications from different vendors.

Service Continuity
IoT devices (i.e. user equipment, sensors) have limited computing power. Edge computing is used to compensate this limitation and offload required computation for service delivery. The challenge appears in the cases that provision of continuous service is required for the things that have movement and periodic connection (e.g. devices in V2X and drones) because load balancing and/or resource migration (VNF migration), in which IoT applications are run on the MEC platform as the VNFs, may be required due to device movement. This may result in an interruption in the service during migration and therefore the service suffers from latency.

8   Future Research Direction

By developing new communication technologies, business models and customer requirements, many improvements would be performed in deployment and integration of IoT with MEC. In this regard, future direction section discusses about resource management and orchestration, mobility management, slicing, optimization algorithms and business models.

The first topic that can be interested is resource management for IoT-based services. Because with the development of the network and communications and the maturity of the IoT ecosystem, a large number of things in a specific geographical area are connected to the network, and to handle this volume of traffic and data processing a lot of resources are required on the edge. In this regard, resource sharing (like tower sharing) is an interesting topic that can be effective in reducing the costs of CAPEX and OPEX. Because the nature of MEC is its distribution, if an operator wants to provide the necessary resources for all services in all areas, it needs high investment. The most important issues that can be researched are: the level of operator investment for computing power at the edge, interoperability and security for different domains that operators have invested, how to handle the high computing volume for a collaboration between the nodes distributed in the network, and finally, how much computing is done at the edge and in the cloud core if different cloud tiers are used?

Another interesting topic is resource orchestration. Orchestration is defined as the method used to provide end-to-end service by managing cloud resources in different domains and in association with other technologies, such as software defined network and virtualized technologies. Here, to provide IoT based services in an enabled MEC network, it is necessary to orchestrate resources from various technologies, including NFV and SDN, which are simultaneously used in a network. Current orchestration deployments for edge cloud IoT applications, whether open source or commercial, are simple and rule based. With the development of networks and more complexity in the use of MEC based service in IoT ecosystem, dynamic and automated orchestration methods are needed for routing traffic to specific network parts, load balancing, resource optimizing and service provisioning.

Moreover, artificial intelligence and machine learning algorithms are hot topics that have been used for different applications [151]. AL/ML can also be applied for processing data collected from the IoT environment as well as load balancing and performance optimization of edge computing resources. Applying the artificial intelligence in the MEC enabled IoT ecosystem helps provide smart services based on the optimal use of existing network edge resources and the capabilities of things.

In the 5G network, which the service should be provided for mobile users/devices, a mobility management system is needed to support service migration and operates based on application relocation policies. The system should manage edge resource resources, device mobility and applications run on MEC platform by taking into account the service requirement, network conditions and device connection technology (e.g. WiFi, Bluetooth, cellular, etc.). In this regard, the most important research works that can be performed are 1) management of the resources for the moving device hand over to another MEC domain according to the service application on new MEC domain, (2) coordination between the two MEC platforms in the two different domains to provide a continuous service for executing service application, (3) using AI bases methods to provide the cached content placed in the old MEC domain for the user in the new MEC domain, and finally providing solution for the cases that new device connection has not met required QoS for the inter domain mobility between different MEC domains.

Providing different logical networks with dedicated resources for each IoT application can be obtained by network slicing techniques. It allows to allocate specific resources to predefined users or applications over a shared physical infrastructure. Slicing can be deployed in a end to end manner including core, transport and radio access network. In the Context of MEC, different slicing frameworks is presented for IoT services in 5G era by considering the flexible and dynamic placement of edge resources, guarantee Quality of Service (QoS), and make available great scalability in terms of number of connected end-devices and application services.

In addition to technical aspects in of MEC, business models in providing MEC based services should be taken according to the costs of deployment and value added obtained from service delivery. For example consider two IoT use cases, the first one such as V2X need a real-time infrastructure with high coverage in geographical area of the service delivery. On the other hand, some others such as metering applications (energy, water metering) only need an infrastructure supports a huge number of devices. The infrastructure requirements of each use case is different to another, and based on business model of the operator, investment as well as economic aspect of delivered services should be planned. For example when a mobile operator is new, an initial step for providing the edge based service is the local use cases that only specified areas are equipped for edge based services (e.g. local airport).

9 Summary

Connecting millions of things from different domains opened up a new concept called the Internet of Things (IoT). This massive connection needs high capacity transport network as well as low latency communication and high processing power. MEC as a middleware layer can be placed between the network layer and application layer of IoT architecture to address the service requirements in terms of processing power and low latency response for different service categories (eMBB, URLLC and mMTC). MEC plays an important role through the main functionalities, as host of application execution of the IoT based services, including Real-time data Analysis, local caching and computing. Meanwhile, in recent years, by introducing the integration in service delivery and platform, the API has been proposed as a common language for the MEC system in a way that third parties, things and service providers can use the API to interact with the IoT application. Despite development in MEC, there are still challenges such as cost modeling, commercialization, and technology maturity that need to be considered.

Acknowledgments The authors would like to thank Ahmad Mosayyebi and Shakiba Shahbandegan for their careful reading and editing the text of the manuscript.

References

1. Kafle VP, Fukushima Y, Harai H (2016) Internet of things standardization in ITU and prospective networking technologies. IEEE Communications Magazine 54 (9):43–49
2. Čolaković A, Hadžialić M (2018) Internet of Things (IoT): A review of enabling technologies, challenges, and open research issues. Computer Networks 144:17–39
3. Popovski P, Trillingsgaard KF, Simeone O, Durisi G (2018) 5G wireless network slicing for eMBB, URLLC, and mMTC: A communication-theoretic view. Ieee Access 6:55765–55779
4. Qiao X, Ren P, Dustdar S, Chen J (2018) A new era for web AR with mobile edge computing. IEEE Internet Computing 22 (4):46–55
5. Tun YK, Alsenwi M, Tran NH, Han Z, Hong CS (2020) Energy Efficient Communication and Computation Resource Slicing for eMBB and URLLC Coexistence in 5G and Beyond. IEEE Access 8:136024–136035
6. Tang J, Shim B, Quek TQ (2019) Service multiplexing and revenue maximization in sliced C-RAN incorporated with URLLC and multicast eMBB. IEEE Journal on Selected Areas in Communications 37 (4):881–895
7. Wang K, Ji W, Li J, Wang H, Cao T Wireless Content Caching in Sliced Cellular Networks with Multicast Beamforming. In: 2019 11th International Conference on Wireless Communications and Signal Processing (WCSP), 2019. IEEE, pp 1–6
8. Chen W-E, Fan X-Y, Chen L-X A CNN-based Packet Classification of eMBB, mMTC and URLLC Applications for 5G. In: 2019 International Conference on Intelligent Computing and its Emerging Applications (ICEA). IEEE, pp 140–145

9. Comşa I-S, Muntean G-M, Trestian R (2020) An Innovative Machine-Learning-Based Scheduling Solution for Improving Live UHD Video Streaming Quality in Highly Dynamic Network Environments. IEEE Transactions on Broadcasting

10. Gomez-Barquero D, Li W, Fuentes M, Xiong J, Araniti G, Akamine C, Wang J (2019) IEEE Transactions on Broadcasting special issue on: 5G for broadband multimedia systems and broadcasting. IEEE Transactions on Broadcasting 65 (2):351–355

11. Cheng J, Chen W, Tao F, Lin C-L (2018) Industrial IoT in 5G environment towards smart manufacturing. Journal of Industrial Information Integration 10:10–19

12. Khoshnevisan M, Joseph V, Gupta P, Meshkati F, Prakash R, Tinnakornsrisuphap P (2019) 5G industrial networks with CoMP for URLLC and time sensitive network architecture. IEEE Journal on Selected Areas in Communications 37 (4):947–959

13. Fitzgerald E, Pióro M Efficient pilot allocation for urllc traffic in 5g industrial iot networks. In: 2019 11th International Workshop on Resilient Networks Design and Modeling (RNDM), 2019. IEEE, pp 1–7

14. Gupta R, Tanwar S, Tyagi S, Kumar N (2019) Tactile-internet-based telesurgery system for healthcare 4.0: An architecture, research challenges, and future directions. IEEE Network 33 (6):22–29

15. Alliance N (2019) Verticals URLLC Use Cases and Requirements. NGMN Alliance

16. Vergutz A, Noubir G, Nogueira M (2020) Reliability for Smart Healthcare: A Network Slicing Perspective. IEEE Network 34 (4):91–97

17. Feng L, Li W, Lin Y, Zhu L, Guo S, Zhen Z (2020) Joint Computation Offloading and URLLC Resource Allocation for Collaborative MEC Assisted Cellular-V2X Networks. IEEE Access 8:24914–24926

18. van Dam J-F, Bißmeyer N, Zimmermann C, Eckert K (2019) Security in hybrid vehicular communication based on its g5, lte-v, and mobile edge computing. In: Fahrerassistenzsysteme 2018. Springer, pp 80–91

19. Hochstetler J, Padidela R, Chen Q, Yang Q, Fu S Embedded deep learning for vehicular edge computing. In: 2018 IEEE/ACM Symposium on Edge Computing (SEC), 2018. IEEE, pp 341–343

20. Zhao J, Wang L, Wong K-K, Tao M, Mahmoodi T (2018) Energy and latency control for edge computing in dense V2X networks. arXiv preprint arXiv:180702311

21. Liu Y, Ling J, Shou G, Seah HS, Hu Y Augmented reality based on the integration of mobile edge computing and fiber-wireless access networks. In: International Workshop on Advanced Image Technology (IWAIT) 2019, 2019. International Society for Optics and Photonics, p 110490M

22. Draxinger W, Miura Y, Grill C, Pfeiffer T, Huber R A real-time video-rate 4D MHz-OCT microscope with high definition and low latency virtual reality display. In: European Conference on Biomedical Optics, 2019. Optical Society of America, p 11078_11071

23. Chakareski J, Gupta S Multi-Connectivity and Edge Computing for Ultra-Low-Latency Lifelike Virtual Reality. In: 2020 IEEE International Conference on Multimedia and Expo (ICME), 2020. IEEE, pp 1–6

24. Varga P, Peto J, Franko A, Balla D, Haja D, Janky F, Soos G, Ficzere D, Maliosz M, Toka L (2020) 5g support for industrial iot applications–challenges, solutions, and research gaps. Sensors 20 (3):828

25. Horsmanheimo S, Säe J, Jokela T, Tuomimäki L, Nigussie E, Hjelt A, Huilla S, Dönmez T, Le Bail N, Valkama M Remote Monitoring of IoT Sensors and Communication Link Quality in Multisite mMTC Testbed. In: 2019 IEEE 30th Annual International Symposium on Personal, Indoor and Mobile Radio Communications (PIMRC), 2019. IEEE, pp 1–7

26. Ananth S, Sathya P, Mohan PM Smart Health Monitoring System through IOT. In: 2019 International Conference on Communication and Signal Processing (ICCSP), 2019. IEEE, pp 0968–0970

27. De Michele R, Furini M Iot healthcare: Benefits, issues and challenges. In: Proceedings of the 5th EAI International Conference on Smart Objects and Technologies for Social Good, 2019. pp 160–164

28. Alam MM, Malik H, Khan MI, Pardy T, Kuusik A, Le Moullec Y (2018) A survey on the roles of communication technologies in IoT-based personalized healthcare applications. IEEE Access 6:36611–36631

29. Ahmed S, Rahman MS, Rahaman MS A blockchain-based architecture for integrated smart parking systems. In: 2019 IEEE International Conference on Pervasive Computing and Communications Workshops (PerCom Workshops), 2019. IEEE, pp 177–182

30. Sicari S, Rizzardi A, Coen-Porisini A (2019) Smart transport and logistics: A Node-RED implementation. Internet Technology Letters 2 (2):e88

31. Gill SS, Garraghan P, Buyya R (2019) ROUTER: Fog enabled cloud based intelligent resource management approach for smart home IoT devices. Journal of Systems and Software 154:125–138

32. Yassine A, Singh S, Hossain MS, Muhammad G (2019) IoT big data analytics for smart homes with fog and cloud computing. Future Generation Computer Systems 91:563–573

33. Liu Y, Yang C, Jiang L, Xie S, Zhang Y (2019) Intelligent edge computing for IoT-based energy management in smart cities. IEEE Network 33 (2):111–117

34. Mochamad Rifki Ulil A, Sukaridhoto S, Tjahjono A, Kurnia Basuki D (2019) The vehicle as a mobile sensor network base iot and big data for pothole detection caused by flood disaster. E&ES 239 (1):012034

35. Rahman MA, Rashid MM, Hossain MS, Hassanain E, Alhamid MF, Guizani M (2019) Blockchain and IoT-based cognitive edge framework for sharing economy services in a smart city. IEEE Access 7:18611–18621

36. Fan D, Gao S The application of mobile edge computing in agricultural water monitoring system. In: IOP Conference Series: Earth and Environmental Science, 2018. vol 1. IOP Publishing, p 012015

37. Trilles S, Torres-Sospedra J, Belmonte Ó, Zarazaga-Soria FJ, González-Pérez A, Huerta J (2019) Development of an open sensorized platform in a smart agriculture context: A vineyard support system for monitoring mildew disease. Sustainable Computing: Informatics and Systems

38. Miles B, Bourennane E-B, Boucherkha S, Chikhi S (2020) A study of LoRaWAN protocol performance for IoT applications in smart agriculture. Computer Communications

39. Awan SH, Ahmed S, Nawaz A, Sulaiman S, Zaman K, Ali M, Najam Z, Imran S (2020) BlockChain with IoT, an emergent routing scheme for smart agriculture. Int J Adv Comput Sci Appl 11:420–429

40. Lin J, Yu W, Zhang N, Yang X, Zhang H, Zhao W (2017) A survey on internet of things: Architecture, enabling technologies, security and privacy, and applications. IEEE Internet of Things Journal 4 (5):1125–1142

41. Shahhoseini H, Naderi M, Buyya R Shared memory multistage clustering structure, an efficient structure for massively parallel processing systems. In: Proceedings Fourth International Conference/Exhibition on High Performance Computing in the Asia-Pacific Region, 2000. IEEE, pp 22–27

42. Saeed M, Shahhoseini HS APPMA-An anti-phishing protocol with mutual authentication. In: The IEEE symposium on Computers and Communications, 2010. IEEE, pp 308–313

43. Hu YC, Patel M, Sabella D, Sprecher N, Young V (2015) Mobile edge computing—A key technology towards 5G. ETSI white paper 11 (11):1–16

44. Roman R, Lopez J, Mambo M (2018) Mobile edge computing, fog et al.: A survey and analysis of security threats and challenges. Future Generation Computer Systems 78:680–698

45. GSMA (October 2020) 5G IoT Private & Dedicated Networks for Industry 4.0.

46. Zanzi L, Cirillo F, Sciancalepore V, Giust F, Costa-Perez X, Mangiante S, Klas G (2019) Evolving Multi-Access Edge Computing to Support Enhanced IoT Deployments. IEEE Communications Standards Magazine 3 (2):26–34

47. Rahimi H, Zibaeenejad A, Safavi AA A novel IoT architecture based on 5G-IoT and next generation technologies. In: 2018 IEEE 9th Annual Information Technology, Electronics and Mobile Communication Conference (IEMCON), 2018. IEEE, pp 81–88

48. Qiu T, Chi J, Zhou X, Ning Z, Atiquzzaman M, Wu DO (2020) Edge Computing in Industrial Internet of Things: Architecture, Advances and Challenges. IEEE Communications Surveys & Tutorials
49. Shah VS (2018) Multi-agent cognitive architecture-enabled IoT applications of mobile edge computing. Annals of Telecommunications 73 (7–8):487–497
50. Balasubramanian V, Kouvelas N, Chandra K, Prasad RV, Voyiatzis AG, Liu W A unified architecture for integrating energy harvesting IoT devices with the mobile edge cloud. In: 2018 IEEE 4th World Forum on Internet of Things (WF-IoT), 2018. IEEE, pp 13–18
51. Deng S, Xiang Z, Yin J, Taheri J, Zomaya AY (2018) Composition-driven IoT service provisioning in distributed edges. IEEE Access 6:54258–54269
52. Redondi AE, Arcia-Moret A, Manzoni P Towards a scaled IoT pub/sub architecture for 5G networks: The case of multiaccess edge computing. In: 2019 IEEE 5th World Forum on Internet of Things (WF-IoT), 2019. IEEE, pp 436–441
53. Marjanović M, Antonić A, Žarko IP (2018) Edge computing architecture for mobile crowdsensing. IEEE Access 6:10662–10674
54. Ejaz M, Kumar T, Ylianttila M, Harjula E Performance and Efficiency Optimization of Multi-layer IoT Edge Architecture. In: 2020 2nd 6G Wireless Summit (6G SUMMIT), 2020. IEEE, pp 1–5
55. Porambage P, Okwuibe J, Liyanage M, Ylianttila M, Taleb T (2018) Survey on multi-access edge computing for internet of things realization. IEEE Communications Surveys & Tutorials 20 (4):2961–2991
56. Guardo EL (2018) Edge Computing: challenges, solutions and architectures arising from the integration of Cloud Computing with Internet of Things.
57. Ksentini A, Frangoudis PA (2020) On extending ETSI MEC to support LoRa for efficient IoT application deployment at the edge. IEEE Communications Standards Magazine 4 (2):57–63
58. Trakadas P, Nomikos N, Michailidis ET, Zahariadis T, Facca FM, Breitgand D, Rizou S, Masip X, Gkonis P (2019) Hybrid clouds for data-Intensive, 5G-Enabled IoT applications: an overview, key issues and relevant architecture. Sensors 19 (16):3591
59. Khan UY, Soomro TR Applications of IoT: Mobile Edge Computing Perspectives. In: 2018 12th International Conference on Mathematics, Actuarial Science, Computer Science and Statistics (MACS), 2018. IEEE, pp 1–7
60. Liu Y, Peng M, Shou G, Chen Y, Chen S (2020) Toward Edge Intelligence: Multiaccess Edge Computing for 5G and Internet of Things. IEEE Internet of Things Journal 7 (8):6722–6747
61. Sekaran R, Patan R, Raveendran A, Al-Turjman F, Ramachandran M, Mostarda L (2020) Survival Study on Blockchain Based 6G-Enabled Mobile Edge Computation for IoT Automation. IEEE Access 8:143453–143463
62. Zhu R, Liu L, Song H, Ma M (2020) Multi-access edge computing enabled internet of things: advances and novel applications. Springer,
63. Husain S, Kunz A, Prasad A, Samdanis K, Song J Mobile edge computing with network resource slicing for Internet-of-Things. In: 2018 IEEE 4th World Forum on Internet of Things (WF-IoT), 2018. IEEE, pp 1–6
64. Dighriri M, Otebolaku A, Alfoudi A, Lee GM (2020) Slice Allocation Management Model in 5G Networks for IoT Services with Reliable Low Latency.
65. Pham T-M (2020) Optimization of Resource Management for NFV-Enabled IoT Systems in Edge Cloud Computing. IEEE Access 8:178217–178229
66. Zhou Z, Yu S, Chen W, Chen X (2020) CE-IoT: Cost-Effective Cloud-Edge Resource Provisioning for Heterogeneous IoT Applications. IEEE Internet of Things Journal
67. Xiong X, Zheng K, Lei L, Hou L (2020) Resource Allocation Based on Deep Reinforcement Learning in IoT Edge Computing. IEEE Journal on Selected Areas in Communications 38 (6):1133–1146
68. Zhang Y, Liu J-H, Wang C-Y, Wei H-Y (2020) Decomposable Intelligence on Cloud-Edge IoT Framework for Live Video Analytics. IEEE Internet of Things Journal
69. Lei L, Xu H, Xiong X, Zheng K, Xiang W (2019) Joint computation offloading and multiuser scheduling using approximate dynamic programming in NB-IoT edge computing system. IEEE Internet of Things Journal 6 (3):5345–5362

70. Huang J, Li S, Chen Y (2020) Revenue-optimal task scheduling and resource management for IoT batch jobs in mobile edge computing. Peer-to-Peer Networking and Applications:1–12
71. Lee J, Kim DJ, Niyato D (2020) Market Analysis of Distributed Learning Resource Management for Internet of Things: A Game Theoretic Approach. IEEE Internet of Things Journal
72. Qian LP, Feng A, Huang Y, Wu Y, Ji B, Shi Z (2018) Optimal SIC ordering and computation resource allocation in MEC-aware NOMA NB-IoT networks. IEEE Internet of Things Journal 6 (2):2806–2816
73. Du Y, Wang K, Yang K, Zhang G Energy-efficient resource allocation in UAV based MEC system for IoT devices. In: 2018 IEEE Global Communications Conference (GLOBECOM), 2018. IEEE, pp 1–6
74. Liu B, Liu C, Peng M (2020) Resource Allocation for Energy-Efficient MEC in NOMA-Enabled Massive IoT Networks. IEEE Journal on Selected Areas in Communications
75. Zarca AM, Bernabe JB, Trapero R, Rivera D, Villalobos J, Skarmeta A, Bianchi S, Zafeiropoulos A, Gouvas P (2019) Security management architecture for NFV/SDN-aware IoT systems. IEEE Internet of Things Journal 6 (5):8005–8020
76. Almajali S, Salameh HB, Ayyash M, Elgala H A framework for efficient and secured mobility of IoT devices in mobile edge computing. In: 2018 third international conference on fog and mobile edge computing (FMEC), 2018. IEEE, pp 58–62
77. Li C-Y, Lin Y-D, Lai Y-C, Chien H-T, Huang Y-S, Huang P-H, Liu H-Y (2020) Transparent AAA Security Design for Low-Latency MEC-Integrated Cellular Networks. IEEE Transactions on Vehicular Technology 69 (3):3231–3243
78. Ding AY (2019) MEC and Cloud Security. Wiley 5G Ref: The Essential 5G Reference Online:1–16
79. Durresi M, Subashi A, Durresi A, Barolli L, Uchida K (2019) Secure communication architecture for internet of things using smartphones and multi-access edge computing in environment monitoring. Journal of Ambient Intelligence and Humanized Computing 10 (4):1631–1640
80. He D, Chan S, Guizani M (2018) Security in the Internet of Things supported by mobile edge computing. IEEE Communications Magazine 56 (8):56–61
81. Ranaweera P, Jurcut AD, Liyanage M Realizing multi-access edge computing feasibility: Security perspective. In: 2019 IEEE Conference on Standards for Communications and Networking (CSCN), 2019. IEEE, pp 1–7
82. Ni J, Lin X, Shen XS (2019) Toward edge-assisted Internet of Things: From security and efficiency perspectives. IEEE Network 33 (2):50–57
83. Hewa T, Braeken A, Ylianttila M, Liyanage M Multi-Access Edge Computing and Blockchain-based Secure Telehealth System Connected with 5G and IoT.
84. Du M, Wang K, Chen Y, Wang X, Sun Y (2018) Big data privacy preserving in multi-access edge computing for heterogeneous Internet of Things. IEEE Communications Magazine 56 (8):62–67
85. Li X, Liu S, Wu F, Kumari S, Rodrigues JJ (2018) Privacy preserving data aggregation scheme for mobile edge computing assisted IoT applications. IEEE Internet of Things Journal 6 (3):4755–4763
86. He X, Jin R, Dai H (2018) Deep PDS-learning for privacy-aware offloading in MEC-enabled IoT. IEEE Internet of Things Journal 6 (3):4547–4555
87. Tan X, Li H, Wang L, Xu Z Global Orchestration of Cooperative Defense against DDoS Attacks for MEC. In: 2019 IEEE Wireless Communications and Networking Conference (WCNC), 2019. IEEE, pp 1–6
88. Ge S, Lu B, Xiao L, Gong J, Chen X, Liu Y (2020) Mobile Edge Computing Against Smart Attacks with Deep Reinforcement Learning in Cognitive MIMO IoT Systems. Mobile Networks and Applications 25 (5):1851–1862
89. Singh J, Bello Y, Refaey A, Erbad A, Mohamed A (2020) Hierarchical Security Paradigm for IoT Multi-access Edge Computing. IEEE Internet of Things Journal

90. Krishnan P, Duttagupta S, Achuthan K (2019) SDNFV Based Threat Monitoring and Security Framework for Multi-Access Edge Computing Infrastructure. Mobile Networks and Applications 24 (6):1896–1923
91. ALshukri D, Sumesh E, Krishnan P Intelligent Border Security Intrusion Detection using IoT and Embedded systems. In: 2019 4th MEC International Conference on Big Data and Smart City (ICBDSC), 2019. IEEE, pp 1–3
92. Huang M, Liu W, Wang T, Liu A, Zhang S (2019) A cloud-MEC collaborative task offloading scheme with service orchestration. IEEE Internet of Things Journal
93. Wu Y (2020) Cloud-Edge Orchestration for the Internet-of-Things: Architecture and AI-Powered Data Processing. IEEE Internet of Things Journal
94. He W, Guo S, Liang Y, Qiu X (2019) Markov approximation method for optimal service orchestration in IoT network. IEEE Access 7:49538–49548
95. Muñoz R, Vilalta R, Casellas R, Martínez R, Yoshikane N, Tsuritani T, Morita I Orchestration of Optical Networks and Cloud/Edge Computing for IoT Services. In: 2019 24th Opto-Electronics and Communications Conference (OECC) and 2019 International Conference on Photonics in Switching and Computing (PSC), 2019. IEEE, pp 1–3
96. Nguyen T-D, Huh E-N, Jo M (2018) Decentralized and revised content-centric networking-based service deployment and discovery platform in mobile edge computing for IoT devices. IEEE Internet of Things Journal 6 (3):4162–4175
97. Alameddine HA, Sharafeddine S, Sebbah S, Ayoubi S, Assi C (2019) Dynamic task offloading and scheduling for low-latency IoT services in multi-access edge computing. IEEE Journal on Selected Areas in Communications 37 (3):668–682
98. Liu J, Zhang Q (2020) Using Imperfect Transmission in MEC Offloading to Improve Service Reliability of Time-Critical Computer Vision Applications. Ieee Access 8:107364–107372
99. Zahed MIA, Ahmad I, Habibi D, Phung QV (2020) Green and Secure Computation Offloading for Cache-Enabled IoT Networks. IEEE Access 8:63840–63855
100. Chen M, Wang L, Chen J, Wei X, Lei L (2019) A computing and content delivery network in the smart city: Scenario, framework, and analysis. IEEE Network 33 (2):89–95
101. Yuan Q, Zhou H, Li J, Liu Z, Yang F, Shen XS (2018) Toward efficient content delivery for automated driving services: An edge computing solution. IEEE Network 32 (1):80–86
102. Prerna D, Tekchandani R, Kumar N, Tanwar S (2020) An Energy-Efficient Cache Localization Technique for D2D Communication in IoT Environment. IEEE Internet of Things Journal
103. Almajali S, Dhiah el Diehn I, Salameh HB, Ayyash M, Elgala H (2019) A distributed multi-layer MEC-cloud architecture for processing large scale IoT-based multimedia applications. Multimedia Tools and Applications 78 (17):24617–24638
104. Elgendy IA, Zhang W-Z, Zeng Y, He H, Tian Y-C, Yang Y (2020) Efficient and Secure Multi-User Multi-Task Computation Offloading for Mobile-Edge Computing in Mobile IoT Networks. IEEE Transactions on Network and Service Management
105. Papathanail G, Fotoglou I, Demertzis C, Pentelas A, Sgouromitis K, Papadimitriou P, Spatharakis D, Dimolitsas I, Dechouniotis D, Papavassiliou S COSMOS: An Orchestration Framework for Smart Computation Offloading in Edge Clouds. In: NOMS 2020-2020 IEEE/IFIP Network Operations and Management Symposium, 2020. IEEE, pp 1–6
106. Min M, Xiao L, Chen Y, Cheng P, Wu D, Zhuang W (2019) Learning-based computation offloading for IoT devices with energy harvesting. IEEE Transactions on Vehicular Technology 68 (2):1930–1941
107. Hsu C-W, Hsu Y-L, Wei H-Y Energy-Efficient and Reliable MEC Offloading for Heterogeneous Industrial IoT Networks. In: 2019 European Conference on Networks and Communications (EuCNC), 2019. IEEE, pp 384–388
108. Wang D, Tian X, Cui H, Liu Z (2020) Reinforcement learning-based joint task offloading and migration schemes optimization in mobility-aware MEC network. China Communications 17 (8):31–44
109. Shah SDA, Gregory MA, Li S, Fontes RDR (2020) SDN Enhanced Multi-Access Edge Computing (MEC) for E2E Mobility and QoS Management. IEEE Access 8:77459–77469

110. Dhanvijay MM, Patil SC (2020) Optimized mobility management protocol for the IoT based WBAN with an enhanced security. Wireless Networks:1–19

111. Aljeri N, Boukerche A (2020) Mobility Management in 5G-enabled Vehicular Networks: Models, Protocols, and Classification. ACM Computing Surveys (CSUR) 53 (5):1–35

112. Leppanen T, Savaglio C, Lovén L, Jarvenpaa T, Ehsani R, Peltonen E, Fortino G, Riekki J Edge-based Microservices Architecture for Internet of Things: Mobility Analysis Case Study. In: 2019 IEEE Global Communications Conference (GLOBECOM), 2019. IEEE, pp 1–7

113. Pantović V Enabling Technology in Three Primary 5G Services. In: Sinteza 2019-International Scientific Conference on Information Technology and Data Related Research, 2019. Singidunum University, pp 301–306

114. Patel M, Naughton B, Chan C, Sprecher N, Abeta S, Neal A (2014) Mobile-edge computing introductory technical white paper. White paper, mobile-edge computing (MEC) industry initiative:1089–7801

115. Tran TX, Hajisami A, Pandey P, Pompili D (2017) Collaborative mobile edge computing in 5G networks: New paradigms, scenarios, and challenges. IEEE Communications Magazine 55 (4):54–61

116. Pham Q-V, Fang F, Ha VN, Piran MJ, Le M, Le LB, Hwang W-J, Ding Z (2020) A survey of multi-access edge computing in 5G and beyond: Fundamentals, technology integration, and state-of-the-art. IEEE Access 8:116974–117017

117. Ai Y, Peng M, Zhang K (2018) Edge computing technologies for Internet of Things: a primer. Digital Communications and Networks 4 (2):77–86

118. Mao Y, You C, Zhang J, Huang K, Letaief KB (2017) A survey on mobile edge computing: The communication perspective. IEEE Communications Surveys & Tutorials 19 (4):2322–2358

119. Zhang K, Mao Y, Leng S, Zhao Q, Li L, Peng X, Pan L, Maharjan S, Zhang Y (2016) Energy-efficient offloading for mobile edge computing in 5G heterogeneous networks. IEEE access 4:5896–5907

120. Ding Z, Xu J, Dobre OA, Poor HV (2019) Joint power and time allocation for NOMA–MEC offloading. IEEE Transactions on Vehicular Technology 68 (6):6207–6211

121. Beck MT, Feld S, Fichtner A, Linnhoff-Popien C, Schimper T ME-VoLTE: Network functions for energy-efficient video transcoding at the mobile edge. In: 2015 18th International Conference on Intelligence in Next Generation Networks, 2015. IEEE, pp 38–44

122. Mach P, Becvar Z (2017) Mobile edge computing: A survey on architecture and computation offloading. IEEE Communications Surveys & Tutorials 19 (3):1628–1656

123. Sarrigiannis I, Ramantas K, Kartsakli E, Mekikis P-V, Antonopoulos A, Verikoukis C (2019) Online VNF Lifecycle Management in an MEC-Enabled 5G IoT Architecture. IEEE Internet of Things Journal 7 (5):4183–4194

124. Toosi AN, Mahmud R, Chi Q, Buyya R (2019) Management and Orchestration of Network Slices in 5G, Fog, Edge and Clouds. Fog and Edge Computing 10

125. Lin L, Liao X, Jin H, Li P (2019) Computation offloading toward edge computing. Proceedings of the IEEE 107 (8):1584–1607

126. Yang F, Gupta N, Gerner N, Qi X, Demers A, Gehrke J, Shanmugasundaram J A unified platform for data driven web applications with automatic client-server partitioning. In: Proceedings of the 16th international conference on World Wide Web, 2007. pp 341–350

127. Wu H, Knottenbelt WJ, Wolter K (2019) An efficient application partitioning algorithm in mobile environments. IEEE Transactions on Parallel and Distributed Systems 30 (7):1464–1480

128. Mohtavipour SM, Shahhoseini HS A Low-Cost Distributed Mapping for Large-Scale Applications of Reconfigurable Computing Systems. In: 2020 25th International Computer Conference, Computer Society of Iran (CSICC), 2020. IEEE, pp 1–6

129. Aali SN, Shahhosseini HS, Bagherzadeh N Divisible load scheduling of image processing applications on the heterogeneous star network using a new genetic algorithm. In: 2018 26th Euromicro International Conference on Parallel, Distributed and Network-based Processing (PDP), 2018. IEEE, pp 77–84

130. Liu J, Zhang Q (2019) Code-partitioning offloading schemes in mobile edge computing for augmented reality. IEEE Access 7:11222–11236
131. Tu Y, Ruan Y, Wang S, Wagle S, Brinton CG, Joe-Wang C (2020) Network-Aware Optimization of Distributed Learning for Fog Computing. arXiv preprint arXiv:200408488
132. Taheribakhsh M, Jafari A, Peiro MM, Kazemifard N 5G Implementation: Major Issues and Challenges. In: 2020 25th International Computer Conference, Computer Society of Iran (CSICC), 2020. IEEE, pp 1–5
133. ETSI G 004, Mobile Edge Computing (MEC) Service Scenarios V1. 1.1,(2015).
134. Reznik A, Arora R, Cannon M, Cominardi L, Featherstone W, Frazao R, Giust F, Kekki S, Li A, Sabella D (2017) Developing software for multi-access edge computing. ETSI White Paper 20
135. Datta SK, Bonnet C MEC and IoT Based Automatic Agent Reconfiguration in Industry 4.0. In: 2018 IEEE International Conference on Advanced Networks and Telecommunications Systems (ANTS), 2018. IEEE, pp 1–5
136. Nokia I (2013) Increasing Mobile Operators Value Proposition With Edge Computing. Technical Brief
137. Gazis V, Leonardi A, Mathioudakis K, Sasloglou K, Kikiras P, Sudhaakar R Components of fog computing in an industrial internet of things context. In: 2015 12th Annual IEEE International Conference on Sensing, Communication, and Networking-Workshops (SECON Workshops), 2015. IEEE, pp 1–6
138. Vallati C, Virdis A, Mingozzi E, Stea G Exploiting LTE D2D communications in M2M Fog platforms: Deployment and practical issues. In: 2015 IEEE 2nd World Forum on Internet of Things (WF-IoT), 2015. IEEE, pp 585–590
139. Mobile C (2020) 5G MEC-Based Cloud Game Innovation Practice
140. AT&T AT&T Multi-Access Edge Computing https://www.business.att.com/products/multi-access-edge-computing.html.
141. Dongkee L, SK Telecom, et al. (2019) Case Study of Scaled-Up SKT* 5G MEC Reference Architecture.
142. Deutsche Telekom Completes World's First Public Mobile Edge Network. (2019).
143. Kaloxylos A, Gavras, Anastasius, & De Peppe, Raffaele (2020) Empowering Vertical Industries through 5G Networks - Current Status and Future Trends. Zenodo,
144. Shahhoseini HS, Jafari AH, Afhamisisi K (2015) An MDP Approach for Defending Against Fraud Attack in Cognitive Radio Networks. IETE Journal of Research 61 (5):492–499
145. Saeed M, Shahhoseini HS, Mackvandi A An improved two-party Password Authenticated Key Exchange protocol without server's public key. In: 2011 IEEE 3rd International Conference on Communication Software and Networks, 2011. IEEE, pp 90–95
146. Naderi H, Shahhoseini H, Jafari A Availability-Based Routing Algorithm Using AHP Method in IP/MPLS Networks. In: 2012 International Conference on Computer Science and Service System, 2012. IEEE, pp 605–609
147. Monge AS, Szarkowicz KG (2015) MPLS in the SDN Era: Interoperable Scenarios to Make Networks Scale to New Services. " O'Reilly Media, Inc.",
148. SHAHHOSEİNİ HS, JAFARİ AH (2015) Reputation Based Cooperation Between Network Operators in the Heterogeneous Wireless Environments. Cumhuriyet Üniversitesi Fen-Edebiyat Fakültesi Fen Bilimleri Dergisi 36 (3):1326–1331
149. Mohammadkhani S, Pozveh AHJ, Karagiannidis GK (2020) Robust Tomlinson-Harashima Precoding for Two-Way Relaying. Wireless Personal Communications:1–13
150. Zamzam M, Elshabrawy T, Ashour M Resource Management using Machine Learning in Mobile Edge Computing: A Survey. In: 2019 Ninth International Conference on Intelligent Computing and Information Systems (ICICIS), 2019. IEEE, pp 112–117
151. Jafari AH, Shahhoseini HS (2015) A Reinforcement Routing Algorithm with Access Selection in the Multi–Hop Multi–Interface Networks. Journal of Electrical Engineering 66 (2):70–78

Green-Aware Mobile Edge Computing for IoT: Challenges, Solutions and Future Directions

Minxian Xu, Chengxi Gao, Shashikant Ilager, Huaming Wu, Chengzhong Xu, and Rajkumar Buyya

Abstract The development of Internet of Things (IoT) technology enables the rapid growth of connected smart devices and mobile applications. However, due to the constrained resources and limited battery capacity, there are bottlenecks when utilizing the smart devices. Mobile edge computing (MEC) offers an attractive paradigm to handle this challenge. In this work, we concentrate on the MEC application for IoT and deal with the energy saving objective via offloading workloads between cloud and edge. In this regard, we firstly identify the energy-related challenges in MEC. Then we present a green-aware framework for MEC to address the energy-related challenges, and provide a generic model formulation for the green MEC. We also discuss some state-of-the-art workloads offloading approaches to achieve green IoT and compare them in comprehensive perspectives. Finally, some future research directions related to energy efficiency in MEC are given.

Keywords Mobile edge computing · Smart devices · Energy efficiency · Low latency · Workloads offloading

M. Xu (✉) · C. Gao
Shenzhen Institutes of Advanced Technology, Chinese Academy of Sciences, Shenzhen, China
e-mail: mx.xu@siat.ac.cn; chengxi.gao@siat.ac.cn

S. Ilager · R. Buyya
Cloud Computing and Distributed Systems (CLOUDS) Laboratory, School of Computing and Information Systems, The University of Melbourne, Melbourne, VIC, Australia
e-mail: silager@student.unimelb.edu.au; rbuyya@unimelb.edu.au

H. Wu
Center for applied mathematics, Tianjin University, Tianjin, China
e-mail: whming@tju.edu.cn

C. Xu
State Key Lab of IOTSC, University of Macau, China
e-mail: czxu@um.edu.mo

1 Introduction

The concept of the IoT has evolved remarkably based on the evolution of wireless communication and mobile technologies [1]. IoT has been regarded as a global network consisting of connected smart devices, which contributes to the arising and evolving of various novel mobile applications. Furthermore, with fast development, IoT has the potential to promote many more possible applications and scenarios, such as smart cities, smart home, smart health-care, smart agriculture, and so on. However, since IoT devices have the inherent features, including constrained power capacity, low computation capacity, and storage, provisioning limited resources for a great amount of computation-intensive applications on devices is a significant challenge [2–5].

To handle the fast increase of mobile applications and ensure the performance of applications on IoT devices, application tasks are offloaded to cloud that gathers adequate computation resources from remote servers [6]. This motivates the paradigm named mobile cloud computing (MCC) [7]. In MCC, mobile devices can utilize the computing and storage resources from remote clouds, which can be accessed via a core network. The MCC paradigm can extend battery life, enhance mobile devices' capacity to handle complex tasks, provide larger storage space. However, communication cost and service delay are two significant issues that can undermine the user experience, due to increased load on the core network.

To address the above limitation of MCC, Mobile Edge Computing (MEC) paradigm was proposed that enables efficient execution of applications requiring low latency with constrained energy [8]. MEC is a type of computing paradigm that enables capabilities of cloud computing to be extended at the edge of network [9]. However, ensuring low latency as required is still quite challenging, especially when "Internet of Everything" has evolved as a reality based on the recent IoT technologies, and amidst IoT devices are more diverse in their capabilities and requirements. Moreover, energy efficiency has become an extremely important factor in designing MEC solutions as IoT devices have limited energy and battery life. Therefore, without proper coordination among the resource constrained smart IoT devices and offloading necessary tasks to MEC may lead to higher energy costs and latency.

Another way to relieve the energy constraint of MEC enabled IoT system is by utilizing green energy (e.g. solar, wind, etc.) [10]. Using green energy as the energy sources rather than coal-based brown energy alone can reduce the carbon emission efficiently. Besides, the outdoor IoT devices powered by green energy can also extend their battery life. Enabling the edge servers and IoT devices to be supported by green energy reduces the dependency on coal-based energy sources. There have been some proposed green-aware approaches for MEC enabled IoTs [11, 12]. To some extent, the availability of green energy is intermittent and unpredictable, therefore, it is required to design a hybrid power supply of both green energy and brown energy to fully assure the stability and availability of services.

1.1 MEC Characteristics

To support the sustainable development of IoT technology, MEC has been applied to many IoT scenarios. The MEC provides the following useful characteristics:

Proximity Unlike remote clouds, in MEC, edge servers are deployed at the network edge close to the IoT devices. It can be used to process the key data generated by the IoT devices with shorter processing time as edge servers are generally more powerful than IoT devices.

Low Delay Offloading data from IoT devices to edge servers can achieve low delay (e.g. data transmission time, task processing time), improve user experience, and reduce potential core-network congestion. It is also possible to support real-time applications for time-critical emergency IoT applications.

High Bandwidth The communications between IoT devices and MEC servers can fully utilize the available bandwidth and gain high transmission rate, which can improve the system performance of MEC-enabled IoT.

Location and Mobility Awareness With real-time location data received from IoT devices, the application can estimate the status of the whole system. In addition, in case of mobile devices that move dynamically, tasks can be offloaded to a set of proximal MEC servers. There is a requirement for continuous task offloading service that is seamlessly integrated with platforms.

Flexible Deployment MEC is able to host critical missions with IoT applications. These applications can be deployed by the network managers or third-party developers rather than only from cloud service providers.

Heterogeneous Resource Collaboration To handle the large number of computing workloads, the services require to utilize resources both from cloud computing and edge computing together. Furthermore, coordinating heterogeneous resources is also required to meet the different requirements of various applications.

Figure 1 shows the MEC enabled IoT scenario. Based on the above features, MEC has been applied to many areas and consists of different types of IoT applications, e.g. transportation, smart grid, agriculture, and healthcare. These IoT applications along with their IoT devices can be placed at the edge of the network. To be more specific, the edge devices can be deployed at the network gateway, base stations, or local area network, which can connect the IoT devices via 5G or WiFi. As for the cloud resources they work as a central manager and monitor the status of edge devices. They can also act as remote repositories to store the data and perform off-line batch processing tasks.

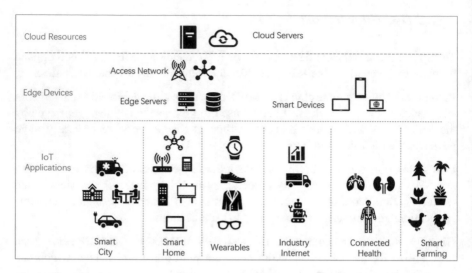

Fig. 1 MEC for typical IoT applications

1.2 Need for Sustainable IoT Application Management in MEC

According to the above discussions, an efficient offloading policy is quite important to support the effectiveness of MEC for IoT, as it can adequately allocate resources in an energy-efficient manner while satisfying the latency requirements. To develop efficient offloading policies of MEC enabled IoT, the following challenges should be addressed:

Heterogeneity of Edge Servers and IoT Devices Both the mobile devices and edge servers have heterogeneous network, computing and storage resources, which makes the selection of offloading devices a challenge. For instance, some of the edge servers are suitable for processing compute-intensive tasks while some others are with adequate storage resources. When designing offloading policies, the heterogeneity of resources should be considered to take full advantage of resources.

Offloading Trigger When to trigger the offloading process should be carefully investigated. Always offloading tasks without context-awareness to edge servers can lead to higher delay, if the communication cost is much higher than the processing cost on edge servers in some particular situations, e.g. network congestion, can lead to degraded performance. Therefore, an efficient trigger mechanism is essential.

Coordination Costs The communication cost exists among devices to coordinate tasks, e.g. mobile games. Thus, coordination among devices may consume extra energy and incurs additional latency because of communication overhead. Furthermore, the costs grow exponentially with the increased amount of devices, thus the bottleneck exists when scaling the number of IoT devices to a large scale.

Partial Task Offloading Apart from full task offloading, tasks can be partitioned into different parts. Thus, how to select the appropriate parts to offload to ensure the latency and energy requirement is another challenge, especially for the cases when there is a data dependency between different parts.

Security Guarantee In the IoT network, MEC servers can encounter security attacks like the masquerade attacks. Privacy information can also be revealed in the offloading process. Protecting privacy information while maintaining operational efficiency is a critical challenge.

In summary, when designing efficient workloads offloading policy in MEC enabled IoT, and to address the above challenges, some key research questions should be considered, including:

- When to offload the task to edge servers?
- Partial offloading or full offloading of application tasks?
- Which edge server should be selected to process the offloaded tasks?

In this work, to address the aforementioned challenges, we present a green-aware framework for MEC. We focus on the problem modeling for the workloads offloading in MEC for IoT. In addition, we review some state-of-the-art green-aware offloading approaches.

The main **contributions** of this work are as follows:

- We propose a green-aware framework to support the MEC enabled IoT by taking advantage of green energy to reduce the power consumption and service latency.
- We model the task offloading approach in a general way by considering the local processing model and edge processing model to achieve an energy-efficient and QoS-aware objective.
- We review state-of-the-art green-aware workloads offloading approaches of MEC-enabled IoT to identify the advantages and limitations of current solutions.
- We outline the future research directions in the related area to help the researchers to investigate the future possible trends.

To help the readers to follow the contents easily, the abbreviation notations used in this work are summarized in Table 1.

The rest of this paper is organized as follows: we start by presenting the general green-aware framework for MEC enabled IoT in Sect. 2, where we highlight the latest advances and trends in green-aware MEC. In Sect. 3, we formulate the general problem modeling and the offloading approaches in green-aware MEC enabled IoT. Then we discuss state-of-the-art green-aware approaches for MEC enabled IoT by identifying their merits and limitations in Sect. 4. Afterward, we present a number of future research directions in Sect. 5. And final, we conclude the work in Sect. 6.

Table 1 Summary of abbreviation notations used in this work

Abbreviations	Meaning
MEC	Mobile Edge Computing
IoT	Internet of Things
MCC	Mobile Cloud Computing
GS-MEC	Green and Sustainable Mobile Edge Computing approach
LSTM	Long Short-Term Memory
LSDQN	Long Short-Term Memory enhanced Deep Q-Network approach
DQN	Deep Q-Network
LETOC	Lyapunov-based algorithm for online optimization
GOLL	Green Offloading with Low Latency
SOMEC	A Selective Offloading in Mobile Edge Computing approach
GreenEdge	Approach leveraging device-to-device communication and energy harvesting

2 Green-Aware Framework for MEC

Green-aware MEC for IoT aims at reducing energy consumption and communication delay, which plays a crucial role in the IoT paradigm by taking advantage of green energy. In the IoT scenario, it is more important to consider the limited energy capacity of IoT devices. Extending the active time of IoT devices can enhance the lifetime, which makes the task offloading necessary to save the power consumption of IoT devices. The battery status of IoT devices can be obtained in a real-time manner and then reserved in an energy buffer when the IoT devices interact with surroundings. However, it is challenging to achieve the energy efficiency goal via task offloading. In this regard, we propose a framework of green-aware MEC enabled IoT. Figure 2 shows our proposed framework and detailed components are introduced as follows:

The major components in the framework can be divided into two parts including IoT devices and edge servers. The main components in the IoT devices part are: Energy Manager, QoS Manager, Offloading Scheduler, and Synchronizer.

Energy Manager It is responsible for managing the energy usage of IoT devices. Based on energy usage, it can also trigger the offloading operations.

QoS Manager It monitors the QoS information of IoT devices and applications, such as communication latency. It also determines the service requirements and anticipated latency for executing the tasks.

Offloading Scheduler It decides whether to offload the tasks or not as well as which part of tasks should be offloaded. It also partitions the tasks and selects the target edge server to send the offloaded task.

Synchronizer It is responsible for handling the communications and synchronizing the data when offloading the tasks, e.g. full or partial offloading. For instance, some data should be processed locally and the processed data in edge servers

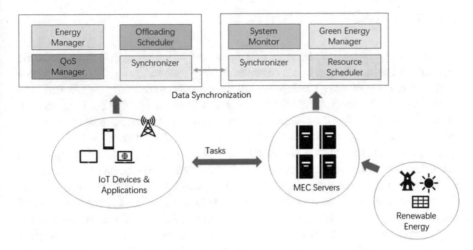

Fig. 2 Framework of Green-aware MEC for IoT

should be synchronized when data are sent back. It interacts with the corresponding Synchronizer component in the edge server part, and it also ensures data integrity.

In our proposed framework, the edge servers can be powered by both brown energy and green energy. The green energy is produced via renewable sources, like solar and wind. The major components in edge servers part include System Monitor, Green Energy Manager, Resource Scheduler, and Synchronizer.

System Monitor It monitors the status of edge servers, including CPU usage and storage usage. It can also alert the anomaly of the system.

Green Energy Manager It controls the green energy usage for edge servers in terms of the availability of green energy to maximize the utilization of green energy. It can also include the green energy prediction module.

Resource Scheduler It manages the resources in MEC devices to support the process of offloaded tasks to reduce the processing time by allocating resources to corresponding tasks.

Synchronizer it is responsible for synchronizing the data with IoT devices. It receives the tasks and sends the data back to IoT devices and ensures them to be consistent.

3   Problem Modelling: Green-Aware Offloading

Based on our proposed framework, our target problem of MEC for IoT can be modeled in the following way, which contains the task model, green energy model, local processing model, and edge processing model.

3.1 Task Model

In the whole system, we assume that there are M edge severs, the processing capacity of the servers can be represented as f_k^{max}, where $k = 1, 2, \ldots, M$. These edge servers are deployed independently in M base stations located in different areas. Considering there are N IoT devices and $N(t)$ active IoT devices in the system at time interval t among the whole scheduling period T. Each device has a compute-intensive task, while can be denoted as $T_i = \{s_i, c_i, d_i\}$, where $i = 1, 2, \ldots, N$, s_i is denoted as the data amount of the input task, c_i is the required computation resources, e.g. millions of instructions. d_i is the deadline constraint of this task. For T_i, it can be consist of three parts: $x_i^l(t)$, $x_i^e(t)$, and $x_i^d(t)$. The $x_i^l(t)$, $x_i^e(t)$ denote the percentage (should be a real value between 0 and 1) of tasks processed on IoT devices locally or tasks executed on edge servers respectively. The $x_i^d(t)$ denotes the admission control by dropping tasks, which is either 0 or 1, representing whether the task is dropped or not. These three parameters should conform to the following constraint:

$$x_i^l(t) + x_i^e(t) + x_i^d(t) = 1, \forall t \in T, \forall i \in N \tag{1}$$

$$x_i^l(t), x_i^e(t) \in [0, 1], x_i^d(t) \in \{0, 1\}, \forall t \in T, \forall i \in N \tag{2}$$

3.2 Green Energy Provisioning Model

The availability of green energy can vary significantly in different locations with varied weather conditions [13]. For example, in some locations with the summer time, the solar power is adequate, while in some other places with the winter time, the wind can be the main green energy sources. In addition, the availability is heavily dependent on the weather conditions, therefore, can vary significantly in different time zones. In our model, the green energy has a higher priority to be used, which means the green energy will be used firstly until it lasts and the coal-based brown energy will be used as the complementary.

We consider that the edge servers are powered by both brown energy and green energy. At time interval t, the amount of green energy is $R_k(t)$, which is tightly coupled with the available amount of renewable energy, for instance, the solar power is 0 at night while it can reach the peak at noontime in a sunny day. And k denotes the location that offers green energy. To make the system extensible, we also consider that there is a set of cloud servers behind edge servers as backups.

3.3 Local Processing Model

In the local processing model, the tasks are processed locally, thus $x_i^l(t) = 1$, $x_i^e(t) = 0$ and $x_i^d(t) = 0$. Assuming the local IoT device processing capacity is

$f_i(t)$ at time interval t, which is constrained by the maximum processing capacity f_i^{max} as $f_i(t) \leq f_i^{max}$. Then the task processing delay D_i for executing T_i is as follows:

$$D_i = \frac{c_i}{f_i(t)}, \quad \forall t \in T, \forall i \in N \tag{3}$$

Let $P_i^l(t)$ represent the energy consumption of processing the tasks locally. Derived from [14], the energy consumed for the task by local processing can be expressed as:

$$P_i^l(t) = k \bullet (f_i(t))^2 \bullet D_i, \quad \forall t \in T \tag{4}$$

where k is the energy factor depends on the hardware architecture.

3.4   Edge Processing Model

In contrast to the local processing choice if the task T_i is offloaded to edge server k, the total processing time will be constituted with 3 parts, including the running time for device to access edge server k, the task communication time and the processing time. In this way, $x_i^l(t) = 0$, $x_i^e(t) = 1$ and $x_i^d(t) = 0$. Therefore, the time delay $D_{i,k}$ of processing the task T_i on the edge server k can be represented as:

$$D_{i,k} = \frac{d_i}{r_k} + \frac{c_j}{f_{i,k}(t)} + C_k \tag{5}$$

where r_k is the device transmission rate to access base station k, based on Shannon-Hartley formula, the transmission rate from the IoT device to edge server can be calculated as $r_k = wlog_2\left(1 + \frac{s \bullet p(t)}{\sigma}\right)$, where w and σ are the channel bandwidth and noise power, s is the transmission power of IoT device, and $p(t)$ is the channel gain from the device to the server. $f_{i,k}(t)$ is amount of the communication resources allocated by MEC server k at time interval t for offloading T_i. C_k is the running time for device to connect the MEC server k, which can be a value in a range, e.g. 5–50 ms.

Let $P_i^e(t)$ denote the power consumption of executing the tasks on the edge servers. Therefore, the energy used for processing the tasks on the edge servers can be represented as:

$$P_i^e(t) = p_i \bullet D_{i,k}, \quad \forall t \in T \tag{6}$$

where p_i is the transmission power scheduled for IoT device i.

3.5 Optimal Green-Aware Offloading

Let us denote R_i as the reward of device i gains by offloading the task T_i to the MEC server k. The R_i is correlated with the delay reduction and energy consumption improvement. We assume that the scheduler in IoT devices can make efficient decisions, thus the system can maximize their reward by selecting the offloading choices.

$$\max_{T_{i,k}, f_{i,k}} R_i = \sum_{k=1}^{M} T_{i,k} \left(\lambda \left(D_{i,0} - D_{i,k} \right) + \epsilon \left(P_{i,0} - P_{i,k} \right) \right) \tag{7}$$

$$s.t. \sum_{k=1}^{M} T_{i,k} \bullet D_{i,k} \leq d_i \tag{8}$$

$$\sum_{k=1}^{M} T_{i,k} f_{i,k} \leq f_k + f_k^b \tag{9}$$

$$constraints \ (1), (2) \tag{10}$$

where $D_{i,0}$ and $P_{i,0}$ are the time and energy consumption to locally process the task on IoT devices. $P_{i,k}$ is the energy cost for offloading task T_i to MEC server k. The λ and ϵ are coefficients. The f_k^b represents the computing resource used from the backup server MEC server k. Some system constraints should also comply like the maximum green energy usage should be more than the capacity of green equipment. The offloaded tasks should not surpass the maximum allowed tasks. The choices are two-folded: offloaded or not. The CPU utilization of offloaded tasks should not be more than the maximum resource utilization.

Once the tasks are offloaded, MEC servers optimize their resource usage by taking advantage of green energy. Since renewable energy availability heavily dependent on the many factors related to weather, using green energy is one of the motivated policies of the MEC servers. Therefore, for the offloading process, in the non-cooperative game between the MEC servers, the possible decisions of server k can be denoted as $\left(x_k, f_k^b \right)$. For edge server k, then the optimization problem is formulated as:

$$\max_{x_i, f_k^b} R_k^s = x_k \sum_{i=1}^{N} f_{i,k} - \beta_k \bullet \min \left(\sum_{i=1}^{N} f_{i,k}, f_k^{max} \right) - y \bullet f_k^b \tag{11}$$

$$s.t. \ x_k, f_k^b \geq 0 \tag{12}$$

where β_k is the changing rate/transformation rate of green energy at location k that can be computed based on the green energy model in Sect. 3.2, and y is the ratio of resources bought from backup servers.

Since the computation capacity of each MEC server is limited, there is competition among offloaded tasks to utilize the resources, which makes the decisions to be a non-cooperative game. The task offloading process among devices is a concave multiple-player game, thus a Nash equilibrium can exist [15]. As the reward function R_k^s continues in terms of x_k and f_k^b, it can be easily solved by integer programming, Lyapunov optimization, game theory, or other approaches.

Scalability Discussion The scalability of the proposed work depends on the methods that solve the above problem. For example, Lyapunov optimization based algorithms can be more time-consuming than heuristic algorithms when the number of devices in the system increases largely, while Lyapunov optimization based algorithms can achieve better optimized results. Therefore, there are trade-offs between the performance and scalability that can be determined by the service providers according to their focus.

4 State-of-the-Art Offloading Approaches

In the following, we provide an overview of existing approaches to green-aware MEC enabled IoT to identify their advantages and limitations. We also present a comparison among the investigated approaches from multiple perspectives. Although there are numerous research works addressing offloading in MEC, we focus on essential works that directly address the green-aware offloading problem.

4.1 GS-MEC

Green and Sustainable Mobile Edge Computing (GS-MEC) [11] is a framework to support IoT devices to be self-powered by taking advantage of green energy for the IoT scenario. Its optimization objective is to improve energy efficiency and system sustainability. Compare with the traditional communication framework for the Cloud enabled IoT environment, GS-MEC adopts a parallel offloading strategy in MEC. GS-MEC considers packet losses to ensure the reliability of the framework. Energy Harvesting Technologies are applied to take full usage of green energy supporting the IoT system in a smart home, which is equipped with a set of IoT devices. To power the devices with green energy, the IoT devices are consist of energy-harvesting components that can convert green energy into electrical energy. Based on the models including computing model, energy model, task cost, the optimization problem is formulated as a minimization problem of latency and maximization task admission rate under the constraint of energy. An offloading algorithm based on Lyapunov optimization [16] is also proposed in GS-MEC to solve the optimization problem. Lyapunov optimization is used to decompose the formulated problem into subproblems that can be solved easier and apply the variable substitution optimization technique to decompose variables. In the proposed algorithm, the energy consumption of IoT devices, transmission power, CPU frequency of IoT devices, and the offloading decision would be obtained in each time interval. And it can offer sufficient power for IoT devices by controlling both the CPU frequencies and transmission power by managing energy.

Both theoretic analysis and simulation results have demonstrated the proposed approach can reduce latency efficiently. The advantage of the framework is that it considers the parallel offloading. However, the proposed algorithm is only compared with some simple baselines.

4.2 LSDQN

LSDQN [12] is an approach based on Long Short-Term Memory (LSTM) enhanced Deep Q-Network for dynamic task management problem in MEC. Its objective is to improve the average uplink transmission rate while reducing the power consumption of the IoT network. LSDQN considers that IoT devices can be supported by the power from a rechargeable battery via harvesting energy from the nearby environment. In the proposed approach, LSTM is applied to estimate the battery status to provide information for IoT devices to make access control based on Deep Q-Network (DQN). LSTM is a widely used network structure of recurrent neural networks to solve the gradient disappearance problem via storing historical information in memory, and DQN is a machine learning method that can learn the optimal policy as per optimization function. To achieve the objective, the uplink rate and energy optimization problem is modelled as a Markov decision process without the knowledge of system dynamics. A MEC access control management policy is also proposed. In the policy, the dynamics of energy and network status are considered to support the decision for the tasks about which MEC server to offload the tasks to. The proposed approach can be applied to the scenario with limited information about future energy supply by taking advantage of LSTM to reduce the prediction loss. In each time interval, the IoT device chooses the most suitable MEC server to transfer data based on the device state and battery status. A software-defined network manager is also applied to capture all the system status. Experiments based on simulations have demonstrated the effectiveness of the proposed approach.

4.3 LETOC

LETOC [17] is a Lyapunov-based algorithm for online optimization on energy cost and time to address the energy-aware computation offloading in MEC for IoT. The objective of LETOC is to minimize the long-term cost of system while ensuring the user experience in terms of quality of service. LETOC is a near-optimal policy for deciding control actions on application offloading by balancing the trade-offs between cost and response time. It also considers taking advantage of green energy, thus reducing the usage of brown energy. LETOC incorporates green energy sources to ensure the IoT devices are running well and manages energy-efficient data offloading. The optimization problem is converted into a constrained stochastic optimization problem and then solved based on Lyapunov optimization. LETOC can distribute incoming tasks to the corresponding servers without prior knowledge of user and system status. LETOC also takes into account the cost related to fees paid for grid power. A discrete time-model is considered in the scheduling process. Optimality analysis is also provided for LETOC, which proves the proposed approach can achieve the average response to be close to the theoretical optimum. Simulation evaluations have validated the performance of the proposed approach, which achieves better performance than the baselines.

4.4 GreenEdge

GreenEdge [18] is an approach leveraging device-to-device communication and energy harvesting techniques to support task execution in a sustainable and collaborative manner. Device to device communication is defined as the direct communication between two wireless devices in proximity by passing information through the base station. GreenEdge aims to reduce the power demand of IoT devices via offloading more workloads to devices that support energy harvesting, especially for the situation when IoT devices have insufficient energy supply. Tasks in GreenEdge can be executed in three ways: local execution, device to device offloaded execution, and edge offloaded execution. The discrete time-slotted model is adopted to capture the system dynamics like in Sect. 4.3. According to current task characteristics and renewable energy availability, in each time interval, the resource scheduler in GreenEdge dynamically optimizes the execution mode for each task to optimize the energy efficiency of edge devices. The optimization problem is formulated as a minimizing problem of the long-term brown energy usage by managing the rechargeable battery usage at each time interval. Then the optimization problem is solved by the Lyapunov-based online optimization framework. The optimization can also make trade-offs between brown energy and battery energy usage. The proposed approach has shown the possibility to be applied to some IoT applications, e.g. smart street lighting and smart bike-sharing.

4.5 GOLL

Green Offloading with Low Latency (GOLL) [19] is a mobility-aware and layered MEC framework to support low-latency and green IoT. It aims to exploit MEC for mobile devices to support multiple layer computing resources to be shared among edge servers. During the task offloading process, the task offloading policy selected by the smart devices is determined based on the computing price of edge servers. GOLL considers that edge servers can be indirectly connected according to their offered resource prices during the service bidding process, in which the edge server with the lowest resource price can be offloaded with tasks. Therefore, the price is considered as the link to two non-cooperative games among the smart devices and MEC servers. In this work, a Stackelberg game [20] is also applied to handle the offloading problem in the proposed framework, which is a solution for the optimal offloading problem. In the proposed framework, the utilization of MEC servers can be improved while the energy consumption and service latency can be reduced. An iterative-based heuristic algorithm is utilized to achieve the corresponding results. In each iteration, the smart device can respond as per the prices announced by edge servers, and the edge servers can make the optimal decision according to the obtained response of the devices. When the strategy is not updating anymore, the iteration process stops. The efficiency of the proposed schemes is validated through numerical results, which shows better performance than baselines.

4.6 SOMEC

A selective offloading in mobile edge computing (SOMEC) is proposed in [21] for green Internet of Things, which is included in a lightweight framework to deal with the scalability problem. The approach does not need the coordination among devices and can operate at the IoT device and edge servers separately by integrating latency constraints in requests. The objective of the SOMEC is minimizing the power consumption of devices. The communication overheads can also be reduced by device self-nomination for tasks processing or self-denial for tasks. The proposed framework is lightweight concerning communication overheads. The devices can independently send offloading requests and the servers can make decisions on whether to admit requests or not. The working process of the proposed framework mainly contains three steps. Firstly, each mobile device will dispatch an offloading request to the selected edge server including the resource and QoS requirements. Thereafter, servers receive the offloading requests, and they would only admit some of the selected users or workloads for offloading. In this step, the corresponding resources should be allocated to meet the requirements. Finally, the mobile devices can offload the tasks based on the admission results.

4.7 Discussions of the Investigated Work

To compare the differences among the investigated papers, we compare these works from multiple perspectives as shown in Table 2. The different perspectives include:

Table 2 Comparison of state-of-the-art approaches

Approach	Environment	Optimization Objective	Energy-saving Component	Green Energy Sources	Workloads	Experiments Platform	Merits	Demerits
GS-MEC [11]	Heterogeneous	To minimize response time and packet loss under energy limitation	IoT devices	Energy harvester	Images compression application	Simulation	Reduced completion time, task cost, and ratio of dropped task	Performance under heterogeneous environment can be further investigated
LSDQN [12]	Heterogeneous	To improve uplink transmission rate while minimizing transmission energy	IoT network	Rechargeable battery	Synthetic	Simulation	Improved uplink rate and reduced energy consumption	To evaluate the scalability of the proposed framework
LETOC [17]	Homogeneous	To balance response time and energy cost	IoT devices	Solar energy	Poisson distribution service rate	Simulation	Near optimal solution for balancing response time and energy cost	Weather forecasting approach can be improved
GreenEdge [18]	Heterogeneous	To minimize fossil energy consumption while ensuring task performance	Edge data centers	Energy harvester	Commercial IoT applications	Theoretical analysis	Device to device communication is considered	Performance evaluations should be conducted
GOLL [19]	Heterogeneous	To maximize service provider utilities while reducing device energy consumption	IoT devices	Solar, wind	Synthetic	Numerical analysis	Reduced latency and energy	More parameters can be evaluated in experiments, e.g. varied vehicle speed
SOMEC [21]	Heterogeneous	To minimize energy consumption and reduce communication overheads	IoT devices	Solar, wind	Face recognition application	Numerical analysis	Improved system scalability	Green usage can be added into the decision engine component

Environment It represents the environment that the proposed approach can be applied, including a heterogeneous or homogeneous environment, which manages heterogeneous or homogeneous resources and devices. In the investigated approaches, most of them are targeting for the heterogeneous environment except for LETOC, which is applied for the homogeneous environment.

Optimization Objective It is the primary objective that the investigated paper aims to achieve. As green-aware scheduling is one of the focus of these works, energy-related optimization is the objective shared by all investigated papers. However, these papers have some differences in other optimization objectives. For instance, GS-MEC focuses on minimizing response time and packet loss, while LSDQN pays more attention to transmission rate optimization. LETOC aims to balance the response time and energy cost, and GreenEdge targets to minimize fossil energy usage while ensuring task performance. GOLL focuses on maximizing service provider utilities, while SOMEC spends more effort on reducing communication overheads.

Energy-Saving Component It represents the component that will optimize energy by the investigated approaches. The energy consumption optimization of IoT devices is managed by GS-MEC, LETOC, GOLL, and SOMEC. As for GreenEdge, it provides a holistic energy optimization for edge data centers. LSDQN focuses on optimizing the energy of the IoT network.

Green Energy Sources It is the energy sources that provide green energy to support the green-aware scheduling of the system. GS-MEC and GreenEdge utilize energy harvester, LSDQN uses a rechargeable battery, LETOC considers solar energy, GOLL and SOMEC consider green energy from both solar and wind.

Workloads It compares the workloads used in different approaches for performance evaluations. Synthetic workloads are used in LSDQN, LETOC, and GOLL. GS-MEC evaluates performance with image compression application, and SOMEC analyzes with face recognition applications. As for GreenEdge, it applies commercial IoT application workloads.

Experiments Platform It represents the experimental approach for evaluating the performance as well as the platform for conducting experiments. GS-MEC, LSDQN, and LETOC are using simulations, GreenEdge applies theoretic analysis, GOLL and SOMEC conduct numerical analysis.

Merits and Demerits It summarizes the advantages and disadvantages of investigated papers. For example, MS-MEC can reduce completion time, task cost, and the ratio of the dropped task, however, the performance under a heterogeneous environment should be further investigated.

5   Future Research Directions

As discussed in the previous sections, the green-aware offloading for MEC enabled IoT has attracted attention and achieved significant progress in recent years benefiting from its ability to reduce energy while ensuring system performance. However, there are some research challenges that should be further explored to make MEC more efficient and reliable. This section discusses several future research directions outlining the different avenues.

Energy Consumption Optimization Current works mostly focus on the management of the energy consumption from edge servers. More energy consuming parts, e.g. network energy consumption can be further explored.

Evaluations with Real Testbed The experiments of current research are mostly based on simulations or numerical analysis. There is a lack of a real testbed or prototype system that can evaluate the performance of proposed approaches.

Benchmarks Presently, no standard benchmarks for performance evaluation of green-aware offloading approaches are provided. A benchmark is demanded to evaluate the energy efficiency performance of novel algorithms and compare them with other approaches aiming for similar objectives.

Collaboration with MCC MEC has been validated as an effective way to reduce the latency of services and improve user experiences. However, it is still promising to take the heterogeneity of both mobile cloud computing and mobile edge computing together to build a hybrid environment for selecting task offloading destinations. Furthermore, considering distributed cloud data centers can also improve the usage of green energy.

Green Energy Usage Maximization The availability of green energy keeps changing along with time. How to take advantage of green energy to support IoT devices can be further investigated, e.g. machine learning or deep learning approaches to predict the availability of green energy and resource usage.

Varied QoS Satisfactory Some of the current research has considered the trade-offs between energy consumption and quality of service. This can be further investigated by considering the optimal way to physically allocate the resources according to expected users with varied QoS requirements rather than a single QoS requirement.

Managing the Mobility of IoT Devices Most of the research propose the offloading decision that assumes strictly static scenarios rather than dynamic scenarios, i.e. the IoT devices do not move during the offloading time. However, the transmission rate can be significantly influenced if channel quality drops during the movement. This can lead to more energy consumption or higher delay. Therefore, a more advanced model considering the movement of IoT devices should be proposed. Predictions techniques for movement can be explored.

Joint Data Management Current research focuses on offloaded data while neglecting the conventional data that is not offloaded to the MEC, e.g. HTTP, FTP that has to be transmitted over backhaul links and radio in parallel to the offloaded data. Therefore, it is required to schedule communication resources for the management of conventional data (e.g. the data not exploiting MEC). Therefore, the joint data management approach for both offloading and conventional data is required.

Multi-tenancy Management The MEC computing infrastructure is shared environment and different user's applications will be hosted on MEC servers. Hence, solving the inference issues and providing the performance isolation for applications to guarantee the required SLAs is crucial.

Security Management The security is an important aspect requiring solutions across the computing and network stack. In specific to MEC, it is more challenging to provide the privacy for user data due to shared resources and continuous streaming data that flows between IoTs and MEC servers [22]. Considering the resource capabilities in IoTs and MECs, light weight security solutions need to be incorporated to manage the privacy and confidentiality of the user's or application's data.

6 Summary and Conclusions

In this work, we present a discussion on green-aware mobile edge computing for IoT. Specially, we discuss the related challenges about how to apply MEC for IoT to achieve the energy efficiency objective. Moreover, we propose a general framework including the necessary entities to support the green-aware resource scheduling in the MEC scenario. Thereafter, we present a green-aware model for offloading tasks from IoT devices to edge servers to achieve the efficient management of energy and latency. Then we investigate several state-of-the-art approaches in the related area and compare them from comprehensive perspectives. Finally, we provide a set of future research directions, where we hope to attract researchers' attention to establish more validated research in the green-aware MEC enabled IoT area, e.g. collaborating the MEC with MCC together to take advantage of the heterogeneity of them for task offloading.

Acknowledgements This work is supported by Key-Area Research and Development Program of Guangdong Province (NO. 2020B010164003), and SIAT Innovation Program for Excellent Young Researchers, National Natural Science Foundation of China (NO. 62102408).

References

1. Redowan Mahmud, Ramamohanarao Kotagiri, and Rajkumar Buyya. Fog Computing: A Taxonomy, Survey and Future Directions, pages 103–130. Springer Singapore, Singapore, 2018.
2. Nirwan Ansari and Xiang Sun. Mobile edge computing empowers internet of things. IEICE Transactions on Communications, 101(3):604–619, 2018.
3. Yi Liu, Chao Yang, Li Jiang, Shengli Xie, and Yan Zhang. Intelligent edge computing for iot-based energy management in smart cities. IEEE Network, 33(2):111–117, 2019.
4. Pavel Mach and Zdenek Becvar. Mobile edge computing: A survey on architecture and computation offloading. IEEE Communications Surveys & Tutorials, 19(3):1628–1656, 2017.
5. Luigi Atzori, Antonio Iera, and Giacomo Morabito. The internet of things: A survey. Computer Networks, 54(15):2787–2805, 2010.
6. Minxian Xu, Rajkumar Buyya. BrownoutCon: A software system based on brownout and containers for energy-efficient cloud computing. Journal of Systems and Software, 155:91–103, 2019.
7. Niroshinie Fernando, Seng W Loke, and Wenny Rahayu. Mobile cloud computing: A survey. Future generation computer systems, 29(1):84–106, 2013.
8. H. Wu, W. J. Knottenbelt, and K. Wolter. An efficient application partitioning algorithm in mobile environments. IEEE Transactions on Parallel and Distributed Systems, 30(7):1464–1480, July 2019.
9. Shinan Song Zhanyang Zhang Chengxi Gao Shuhui Chu, Zhiyi Fang and Chengzhong Xu. Efficient Multi-Channel Computation Offloading for Mobile Edge Computing: A Game-Theoretic Approach. IEEE Transactions on Cloud Computing, pages 1–12, 2020.
10. Minxian Xu, Adel N. Toosi, Behrooz Bahrani, Reza Razzaghi, and Martin Singh. Optimized renewable energy use in green cloud data centers. In Sami Yangui, Ismael Bouassida Rodriguez, Khalil Drira, and Zahir Tari, editors, Service-Oriented Computing, pages 314–330, Cham, 2019. Springer International Publishing.
11. Yiqin Deng, Zhigang Chen, Xin Yao, Shahzad Hassan, and Ali MA Ibrahim. Parallel offloading in green and sustainable mobile edge computing for delay-constrained iot system. IEEE Transactions on Vehicular Technology, 68(12):12202–12214, 2019.
12. Lijuan Xu, Meng Qin, Qinghai Yang, and KyungSup Kwak. Deep reinforcement learning for dynamic access control with battery prediction for mobile-edge computing in green iot networks. In 2019 11th International Conference on Wireless Communications and Signal Processing (WCSP), pages 1–6. IEEE, 2019.
13. Minxian Xu and Rajkumar Buyya. Managing renewable energy and carbon footprint in multi-cloud computing environments. Journal of Parallel and Distributed Computing, 135:191–202, 2020.
14. Nikzad Babaii Rizvandi, Javid Taheri, and Albert Y. Zomaya. Some observations on optimal frequency selection in dvfs-based energy consumption minimization. Journal of Parallel and Distributed Computing, 71(8):1154–1164, 2011.
15. Robert Aumann and Adam Brandenburger. Epistemic conditions for nash equilibrium. Econometrica, 63(5):1161–1180, 1995.
16. Lei Zheng and Lin Cai. A distributed demand response control strategy using Lyapunov optimization. IEEE Transactions on Smart Grid, 5(4):2075–2083, 2014.
17. Yucen Nan, Wei Li, Wei Bao, Flavia C Delicato, Paulo F Pires, Yong Dou, and Albert Y Zomaya. Adaptive energy-aware computation offloading for cloud of things systems. IEEE Access, 5:23947–23957, 2017.
18. Zhi Zhou. Greenedge: Greening edge datacenters with energy-harvesting iot devices. In 2019 IEEE 27th International Conference on Network Protocols (ICNP), pages 1–6. IEEE, 2019.
19. Ke Zhang, Supeng Leng, Yejun He, Sabita Maharjan, and Yan Zhang. Mobile edge computing and networking for green and low-latency internet of things. IEEE Communications Magazine, 56(5):39–45, 2018.

20. Jin Zhang and Qian Zhang. Stackelberg game for utility-based cooperative cognitive radio networks. In Proceedings of the tenth ACM international symposium on Mobile ad hoc networking and computing, pages 23–32, 2009.
21. Xinchen Lyu, Hui Tian, Li Jiang, Alexey Vinel, Sabita Maharjan, Stein Gjessing, and Yan Zhang. Selective offloading in mobile edge computing for the green internet of things. IEEE Network, 32(1):54–60, 2018.
22. Pardis Emami Naeini, Sruti Bhagavatula, Hana Habib, Martin Degeling, Lujo Bauer, Lorrie Faith Cranor, and Norman Sadeh. Privacy expectations and preferences in an iot world. In Thirteenth Symposium on Usable Privacy and Security (SOUPS 2017), pages 399–412, 2017.

Part II
Systems, Platforms and Services

Prescriptive Maintenance Using Markov Decision Process and GPU-Accelerated Edge Computing

Chen-Khong Tham and Naman Sharma

Abstract Developments in the Industrial Internet of Things (IIoT) have enabled large-scale sensing and data collection, leading to predictive maintenance and the Industry 4.0 revolution. Predictive maintenance minimizes machine maintenance downtime, while simultaneously minimizing the risk of failures. Prescriptive maintenance aims to improve on that by directly optimizing the maintenance decisions. We present a prescriptive maintenance method for a distributed factory environment using the Partially Observable Markov Decision Process (POMDP) framework. To allow for continual learning, a particle filter algorithm enables online estimation of POMDP models, allowing unique adaptation to each machine. Performance evaluations of the POMDP model with respect to several other models show significant improvements in revenue and reduced downtime. The POMDP and particle filter computations are implemented on GPU-accelerated edge computing devices which achieve speed-ups of 4 to 20 times compared to the CPU-only versions.

Keywords Prescriptive maintenance · Industrial IoT · Partially observable MDP · Particle filter · GPU

1 Introduction

Over the past decade, there have been significant efforts to enable better maintenance scheduling using the power of big data analytics. This area has evolved into three primary types of analytics: descriptive, predictive and prescriptive.

Descriptive maintenance only aims to provide insights into the past operating conditions of the machine, enabling us to understand what happened and why. Predictive maintenance goes a step further and uses machine health data collected

C.-K. Tham (✉) · N. Sharma
Department of ECE, National University of Singapore, Singapore, Singapore
e-mail: eletck@nus.edu.sg; naman.sharma@u.nus.edu

© The Author(s), under exclusive license to Springer Nature Switzerland AG 2021
A. Mukherjee et al. (eds.), *Mobile Edge Computing*,
https://doi.org/10.1007/978-3-030-69893-5_8

for each machine individually to predict its health. Finally, prescriptive maintenance not only aims to predict the health of a machine, but also suggest how we can respond to future events. The aim of prescriptive maintenance is to provide "Just-in-Time" maintenance: the ideal trade-off between performing maintenance too frequently, which is inefficient and uneconomical, vs. too rarely which risks equipment failure and downtime costs.

Predictive maintenance often involves the estimation of metrics such as the Health Index (HI) or the Time-to-Failure for a given machine. Based on these estimated metrics, decisions can then be made by either humans or rule-based systems to improve the usage and efficiency of a machine. A McKinsey report [1] predicts that in 2025, a predictive maintenance manufacturers' savings could be between \$240 and \$630 billion. Prescriptive maintenance (RxM) is considered to be superior to predictive maintenance (PdM) because it leverages the power of big data to optimize this decision-making process.

Further aiding the development of data analytics for machine maintenance are advancements in the area of *edge computing*. Edge computing is the paradigm in which computation-capable devices are used in conjunction with data-gathering devices. In the case of manufacturing, edge computing corresponds to having compute-capable devices near the manufacturing machines from which data is being continuously collected. A typical factory floor setup is shown in Fig. 1, consisting of several Industrial Edge Analytics Hubs (IEAHs) connected to several machines. These IEAHs collaborate through a common server which also connects the cluster to the cloud.

In this chapter, we present four areas of work:

1. development of a framework that can be used to perform prescriptive maintenance in a distributed scenario as depicted in Fig. 1,
2. use of the Partially Observable Markov Decision Process (POMDP) method for maintenance decision-making,
3. continual learning by using a methodology to adapt the model for each machine individually in an online manner, and

Fig. 1 Schematic of a factory floor equipped with edge computing nodes for predictive and prescriptive maintenance

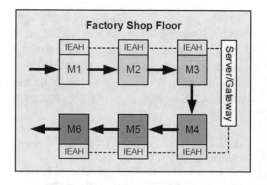

4. analysis of resource utilization when using GPU-enabled edge devices to allow for a highly parallelized solving of the POMDP.

This chapter is organized as follows: Sect. 2 describes earlier work that have been done in the area of predictive and prescriptive maintenance. In Sect. 3, we present the POMDP model used in this work, as well as the complete framework. Performance evaluations with different edge computing nodes are described in Sect. 4, and detailed results are presented in Sect. 5.

2 Related Work

2.1 Predictive Maintenance

A number of previous works have focused on using predictive maintenance to create Machine Health Monitoring Systems (MHMS). Utilizing Markov models for optimizing maintenance is not new: Dawid et al. [2] perform a survey of Markov models used in maintenance in the context of offshore wind. They provide a thorough review on the various Markov models commonly used: Markov chain, Markov Decision Process (MDP), Hidden Markov Model (HMM) and Partially Observable MDP (POMDP) [3].

Markov processes have been used to simulate the deterioration of electrical substation components [4]. Similarly, Besnard and Bertling [5] applied Markov chains to model the deterioration of wind turbines, where they compared the condition monitoring approach to that of inspection and concluded that the former was more effective. In both approaches, the Markov chain model was only used to predict the availability of the machines in the future. The decision to perform maintenance is then taken based on these availability measures.

Hidden Markov Models (HMMs) have also been used in literature to monitor the health of machines [6, 7]. HMMs were shown to provide better performance for machine health monitoring than other methods. Although HMMs allow the state of the machine to be inferred from observations, the model does not allow any decision making, requiring a separate model.

Yao et al. [8] proposed a two layer model to perform maintenance scheduling. The MDP model acts as the higher-level model and provides "maintenance windows" in which maintenance tasks should be performed, by looking at the failure dynamics of the tool and the long-term demand pattern. The lower-level decision is taken by a linear programming model that considers current demands and decides exactly when to perform the maintenance task inside the window provided by the MDP model. This approach allows them to solve the PdM problem faster, since solving a large MDP can take time and quickly become intractable due to the "curse of dimensionality".

Chan and Asgarpoor [9] provide a Markov process model that can be used to model the deterioration of a machine over different stages. This model allows the machine to go into maintenance states or failure states. We extend this model in two ways. First, we incorporate 'maintenance' and 'no maintenance' actions and convert it into an MDP. Second, we extend the model to allow for sensor values to be used as observations, which is more realistic, but introduces uncertainty in the states. In order to model these aspects, a POMDP is required. However, solving a POMDP is more computationally expensive than solving an MDP. In this paper, we propose schemes to speed-up the computation for solving POMDPs.

2.2 Prescriptive Maintenance

Despite having a definite advantage over predictive maintenance, there are few works on building prescriptive maintenance decision making models. The broader category of prescriptive maintenance, i.e., prescriptive analytics, has seen a rise in academic interest over the past years. Lepenioti et al. [10] provide a comprehensive review of works on prescriptive analytics.

Most works done in the area of prescriptive maintenance have been conceptual. A generalized prescriptive maintenance system was proposed in PriMa [11], describing how a predictive analytics toolbox works with the data warehouse using semantic based learning to provide recommendations and decision support to a human maintenance manager. Building on the work on PriMa, [12] conceptualizes how a Dynamic Bayesian Network (DBN) can be used to reduce the complexity of multi-modal data and integrate temporal distribution of events to perform the semantic-based learning and reasoning aspect of PriMa.

The challenges which prevent the adoption of prescriptive maintenance include the difficulty in quantifying their benefits over their predictive maintenance counterparts. A RxM model requires decisions to be made and followed by the machine. This requires either a real-life machine to show improvement or a very well-implemented simulation that responds to the decisions made by the model. The latter is becoming increasing common with the advent of the 'digital twin' made possible by IoT.

Most prescriptive maintenance models have the following common aspects [13]:

1. Information extraction: automating the collection of machine data to be fed into the model.
2. Data-driven module: anomaly detection analysis to allow for knowledge extraction from the machine data.
3. Integration module: acts as the connector between the output of the data-driven module and the input to the decision making optimization module.
4. Optimization module: prioritizes asset management interventions, to allow for maximum efficiency.

Until now, knowledge extraction and decision optimization have been two distinct stages. Therefore, an integration module is required to connect the two.

In this work, we implement a prescriptive maintenance model that does not require such an integration module, but combines the data-driven module and the optimization module to learn the optimal decisions directly from historical and real-time data collected at the machines.

3 System Design and Modelling

3.1 POMDP Model

The health of a machine with maintenance decisions can be modelled using a MDP. We extend the model proposed in [9] and the complete model is depicted in Fig. 2. The model differentiates between failures due to deterioration, state F_1, and random unforeseen failure, state F_0. The deterioration of the machine is split into k discrete states D_k, where a higher k refers to a larger degree of deterioration. The time spent in state D_k is exponentially distributed with a mean of $1/\lambda_1$. Maintenance tasks occur as a Poisson process with parameter λ_m. The duration of these maintenance tasks is exponentially distributed with a mean of $1/\mu_m$. It is assumed that a maintenance task at state D_k improves the state of the machine only partially, bringing it back to state D_{k-1}. The random failures that occur are distributed as a Poisson process with parameter λ_0. The transitions between the

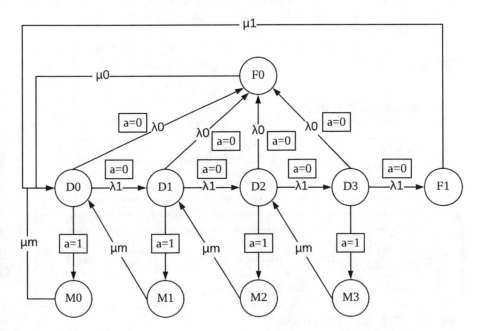

Fig. 2 MDP model of the health of a machine, with maintenance decisions indicated in rectangles

different states are dependent on the actions performed by the machine at any given time. The decisions available to the agent are: $a = 0$ (do nothing), and $a = 1$ (do maintenance).

Subsequently, under the POMDP framework, the state of the machine is not known to the agent. Therefore, it can only infer the state of the machine from observations such as the sensor measurements coming from the machine.

3.2 Model Estimation and Decision Algorithm

Model estimation comprises two stages: offline model estimation and online model re-estimation, depicted in Fig. 3. The offline model estimation uses available historical sensor data from the machine to define the deterioration states D_k. This is done by training a Support Vector Machine (SVM) to predict failure based on the sensor information available from the machines. Once these states have been defined based on offline data, the parameters $\theta = \{\lambda_0, \lambda_1, \mu_0, \mu_1, \mu_m\}$ of the machine can be calculated using the Maximum Likelihood Estimate (MLE) equations for Poisson parameters.

This offline estimate of the model can be utilized for the second stage of online model re-estimation. The aim of this second stage is to make good decisions about scheduling maintenance while adjusting the model to the current machine in a continual manner. This involves re-estimating the parameter θ for the machine. A particle filter based approach is incorporated for this purpose. The particle filter is a recursive algorithm based on the Monte Carlo method of solving the filtering problem [14].

The high level algorithm followed at every time step is shown in Algorithm 1. The updateParameters() function implements the particle filter, which

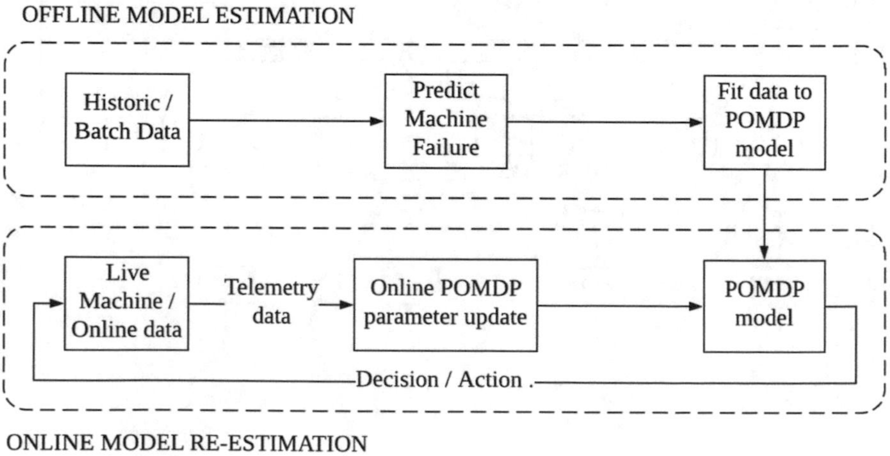

OFFLINE MODEL ESTIMATION

ONLINE MODEL RE-ESTIMATION

Fig. 3 Model estimation process

Algorithm 1: Prescriptive maintenance using POMDP

Global: Action performed at previous time step, a
Global: Current belief estimate, $\hat{B}(s)$
Global: Current POMDP model, $\hat{\Theta}$
Global: Current optimal policy, $\hat{\pi}(s)$
Global: Convergence threshold, τ

Input: Observation z_{t+1}
Output: Action a_{t+1}

1: **Procedure** decisionStep(z_{t+1}):
2:     # Estimate current state
3:     $\hat{B}(s) \leftarrow$ updateBelief(z_{t+1}, a)
4:     # Update POMDP parameters
5:     $\Theta' \leftarrow$ updateParameters(z_{t+1}, a)
6:
7:     # Selection next action
8:     **if** !Converged($\hat{\Theta}, \Theta'$) **then**
9:         $\hat{\Theta} \leftarrow \Theta'$
10:        $\hat{\pi}(s) \leftarrow$ solvePOMDP($\hat{\Theta}$)
11:     $a \leftarrow \hat{\pi}(\hat{B}(s))$
12:     **return** a

Input: Previous parameter estimates Θ_{old}
Input: New parameter estimates Θ_{new}
Output: Boolean indicating if parameters have converged.

13: **Function** Converged($\Theta_{old}, \Theta_{new}$):
14:     **for** $\theta_{old} \in \Theta_{old}, \theta_{new} \in \Theta_{new}$ **do**
15:        **if** $\frac{|\theta_{old} - \theta_{new}|}{\theta_{old}} > \tau$ **then**
16:           **return** false
17:     **return** true

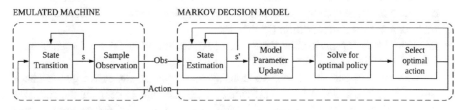

Fig. 4 Model estimation and prescriptive maintenance (RxM) framework

is in between the updateBelief() and solvePOMDP() functions. The updateBelief() function takes the previous belief vector as input and updates it based on the previous action and the current observation. At every iteration, the action selected by the algorithm is based on the optimal policy achieved after solving the POMDP using the solvePOMDP() function.

The complete model estimation and prescriptive maintenance framework is shown in Fig. 4.

4 Performance Evaluations

The offline model obtained in the first stage described in Sect. 3.2 will be created using the machine telemetry data available from the Microsoft machine dataset [15]. Once the offline model has been created, a machine can be emulated as an agent following the MDP process in Fig. 2. Using the Microsoft machine dataset, a separate Gaussian Mixture Model (GMM) is then trained to estimate the distribution of the sensor values in different deterioration states. The observations can then be extracted based on the state of the machine from the corresponding GMM model. The framework involves using the sensor values to estimate the state of the machine, adjusting its estimates of the machine parameters and then providing the user with the decision to perform maintenance or not.

We evaluate the system performance on two different edge computing systems:

- EPC: An embedded PC with an Intel i7-6700 CPU @ 3.40 GHz with 4 cores. It also includes a NVIDIA GTX 1060 6 GB GDDR5 graphics card with 1280 CUDA cores.
- TX2: A NVIDIA Jetson TX2 which is a GPU-enabled edge device. It includes a hexa-core ARMv8 64-bit CPU. The TX2 has an integrated NVIDIA Pascal GPU with 256 CUDA cores.

The EPC represents the computational capabilities of a powerful edge node with a GPU, whereas the low-power TX2 acts as a lower-end edge device with GPU capabilities.

Another aspect that can affect the run time is T_u, the period at which the POMDP is solved by the decision maker using the updated machine parameters. Consequently, our results will focus on the comparison between:

- POMDP vs. POMDP-PF: comparison of the POMDP with particle filter approach to online parameter estimation (POMDP-PF) with a POMDP approach that does not do re-estimation (POMDP).
- EPC vs. TX2: comparing the time taken to solve the POMDP on the embedded PC and the TX2.
- Convergence check (CC) vs. No convergence check: the convergence check only solves the POMDP if a sufficiently large change is seen in the machine parameters from the last time the POMDP was solved. In the absence of this check, the POMDP is solved at every $T_u = 100$ iterations.
- CPU vs. GPU: comparing the benefits of using a GPU implementation of the POMDP solving algorithm with a CPU-only implementation.

5 Evaluation Results

In this section, we will look at performance evaluation results from two key aspects: application performance and system performance. Application performance will focus on the cumulative reward and downtime of the emulated machines. System performance will look at the time complexity when the algorithms are executed on different edge computing platforms.

5.1 Application Performance

The performance of the PdM application will be analyzed on three characteristics: the cumulative reward and downtime, the accuracy of state estimation and the accuracy of parameter estimation. Machine uptime enable useful production with positive rewards, whereas downtime due to maintenance and failures incur costs. Figure 5 shows the cumulative reward that the three algorithms were able to achieve over 10,000 iterations. The 95% confidence intervals of the results are also shown. The particle filter based POMDP-PF algorithm is able to outperform the vanilla POMDP algorithm that does not use particle filters. The POMDP algorithm is seen to provide increasingly negative rewards. This behavior can be analyzed using Fig. 6 which shows the online estimates of the machine parameters over time. We see that the POMDP-PF algorithm is better able to track the real parameter values of the machine. The negative gradient of the cumulative reward for the POMDP algorithm is caused because it overestimates the value of λ_1, which is the rate of deterioration of the machine. The POMDP algorithm believes that the machine deteriorates faster than it actually does, and hence it decides to perform maintenance more frequently. This maintenance action carries with it a negative reward, leading to the downward curve.

Using the convergence check with the POMDP-PF (POMDP-PF-CC) allows the POMDP to be solved less often. Here, we see that the decision maker performs worse at the beginning. This is because the POMDP is not being solved as frequently as before and may lead to some non-optimal decisions being taken at the beginning.

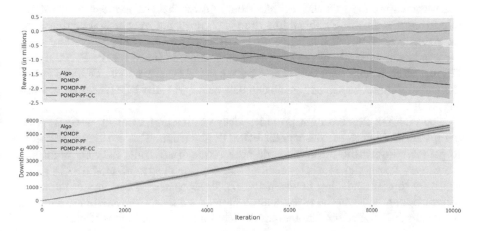

Fig. 5 Cumulative reward and downtime over 10,000 iterations

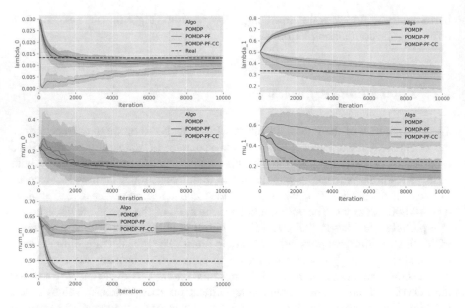

Fig. 6 Machine parameter estimates over 10,000 iterations

However, as the POMDP solution becomes closer to the optimal, the POMDP-PF-CC algorithm is able to achieve a performance level closer to that of the POMDP-PF algorithm. The POMDP-PF-CC graph then becomes a horizontally displaced version of the POMDP-PF graph due to the negative rewards collected at the start of the emulations. This is confirmed when we observe the movement of the Mean Absolute Percentage Error (MAPE) of the estimated parameters in Fig. 7. The MAPE for the POMDP-PF-CC algorithm is initially much higher with a higher variation between executions. Over time, it then achieves a MAPE as good as or even better than the POMDP-PF algorithm. Given that the number of POMDPs solved reduces drastically, this initial drop in performance may be potentially worth the reduction in time taken to solve the POMDPs. An interesting observation is that the confidence intervals of the estimated parameters in Fig. 6 for the POMDP-PF-CC algorithm is larger than the others for the first 4,000 iterations. This shows that the variation in the expected results can also be larger if the POMDP is solved less frequently.

The POMDP-PF algorithm provides a state estimation accuracy of 64.26%, as compared to 44.96% for the vanilla POMDP algorithm. This is due to its ability to get more information from a single observation. The vanilla POMDP algorithm is not very successful in distinguishing between the deterioration states D_k. This difficulty in distinguishing between the D_k states translates into the difficulty of differentiating between the maintenance states. As a result, the machine following the vanilla POMDP algorithm undergoes deterioration failure more often.

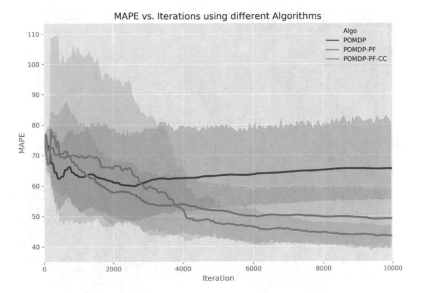

Fig. 7 MAPE over 10,000 iterations

5.2 System Performance

Performing a convergence check before executing the POMDP-PF algorithm with the updated parameters can affect the application performance of the machine. However, the relative trade-off between quality of solution and the run time of the algorithm can be controlled by a threshold parameter. It is important to find a threshold which allows us to solve a smaller number of POMDPs without compromising too much on the performance of the machine. Solving the machine POMDP model can be expensive depending on the size of the action space and the observation space. The emulated machine has 257 possible observations. Reducing the number of times the POMDP is solved in this case can be very beneficial. Figure 8 shows the average number of POMDPs solved over 10,000 iterations for each algorithm. For algorithms not performing the convergence check, this number is equal to $\lfloor \frac{10000}{T_u} \rfloor$. However, the use of a convergence check can reduce this number by 20%–70%.

For such large POMDPs, solving them on the CPU quickly becomes impractical. A powerful GPU may be required if this problem is to be solved within an acceptable time limit. Figure 9 compares the run time for different algorithms. As the POMDP becomes large, the speed-up achieved by using a GPU accelerated implementation can be quite significant. Table 1 tabulates this speed-up by comparing the run time of each algorithm to the run time of the CPU implementation. A speed-up of 21.75 time for the EPC-GPU case implies that the EPC-CPU run time was 21.75 times

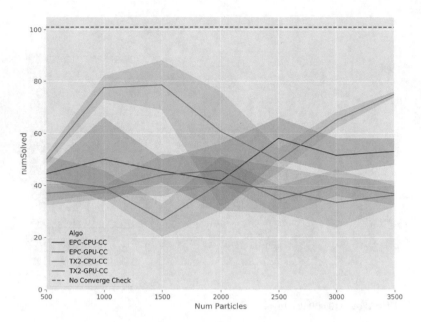

Fig. 8 Number of POMDPs solved vs. number of particles

larger than the EPC-GPU run time. In time sensitive cases, where some decrease in the quality of the solution is acceptable, this run time can be further reduced by more than half by using the convergence check. We observe that even for the fastest 'GPU-CC' case, the proportion of time spent on the particle filter computation is minimal. This can also be seen from the fact that the total run time does not show a trend based on the number of particles used. In such cases, parallelizing the particle filter algorithm will not be very useful to reduce the overall run time. However, in cases where the POMDP model used is less complex, the time taken to solve the POMDP to obtain the optimal solution may become comparable to the time taken for the particle filter update. In such case, parallelizing the particle filter on a GPU may be beneficial.

Comparing the two results in Figs. 9a and b, we observe that the EPC is much more powerful than the TX2, which is expected. However, the run time results on the TX2 show that the framework can be applied on an edge device located near the machines, provided that the edge device is GPU-capable. The TX2-GPU-C run time is within 2,000 seconds for 10,000 iterations. Given that each iteration corresponds to an equivalent of 6 hours in the Microsoft machine dataset, the TX2 is able to provide near real-time solutions allowing optimal decisions to be made without sending the sensor data to be processed at a more powerful server.

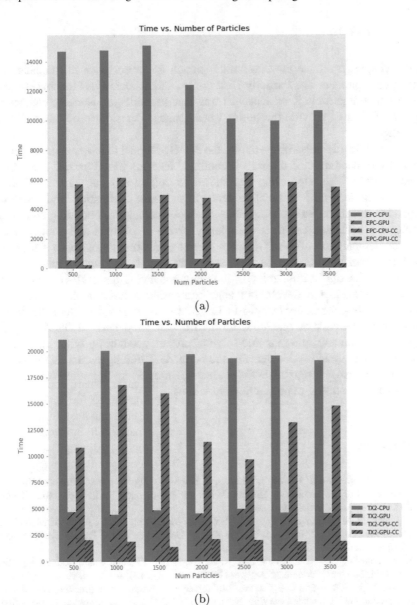

Fig. 9 Run time results for each algorithm vs. number of particles on the different edge computing platforms. (**a**) EPC. (**b**) TX2

Table 1 Speed-up of POMDP solve time on the different platforms

	CPU	CPU-CC	GPU	GPU-CC
EPC	1	2.27	21.75	55.85
TX2	1	1.51	4.34	11.63

6 Conclusion

In this chapter, we have presented an approach for prescriptive maintenance in a factory environment. The Partially Observable Markov Decision Process (POMDP) combined with particle filter approach was used to model the machine characteristics over time and provide the optimal maintenance decision to be taken at every time step.

The particle filter algorithm enables the POMDP model to re-estimate the parameters of the machine, and allows for continual learning based on real-time sensor measurements. This algorithm was shown to outperform the standard POMDP algorithm in terms of cumulative reward, and state estimation and parameter estimation accuracy, while being able to adapt to changing operating conditions. Finally, we evaluated the time complexity of the algorithms and showed that a GPU implementation of the POMDP solver at edge computing nodes can achieve significant speed-up and reduce the overall time taken by the algorithm.

Our future work in this area will look into enhancing the POMDP model used in the framework and developing edge computing nodes which are connected wirelessly using, for example, Wi-Fi 6 or 5G. This more advanced model considers a connected network of machines on a particular shop floor of the factory and requires the status of one machine to be taken into account by other machines in order for better system-wide decisions to be made. Building such a model is more complex as it also needs to be flexible to handle different configurations of machines to accommodate different production workflows.

References

1. J. Manyika, M. Chui, P. Bisson, J. Woetzel, R. Dobbs, J. Bughin, and D. Aharon, "Unlocking the potential of the Internet of Things," McKinsey & Company, Tech. Rep., 2015. [Online]. Available: https://www.mckinsey.com/
2. R. Dawid, D. McMillan, and M. Revie, "Review of Markov models for maintenance optimization in the context of offshore wind," in *Annual Conference of the Prognostics and Health Management Society 2015*, 2015, pp. 1–11.
3. L. P. Kaelbling, M. L. Littman, and A. R. Cassandra, "Planning and acting in partially observable stochastic domains," *Artificial Intelligence*, vol. 101, no. 4, pp. 99–134, 1998.
4. F. Yang, C. M. Kwan, and C. S. Chang, "Multiobjective evolutionary optimization of substation maintenance using decision-varying Markov model," *IEEE Transactions on Power Systems*, vol. 23, no. 3, pp. 1328–1335, 2008.
5. F. Besnard and L. Bertling, "An approach for condition-based maintenance optimization applied to wind turbine blades," *IEEE Transactions on Sustainable Energy*, vol. 1, no. 2, pp. 77–83, 2010.
6. O. Geramifard, J. X. Xu, T. Sicong, J. H. Zhou, and X. Li, "A multi-modal hidden Markov model based approach for continuous health assessment in machinery systems," in *IEEE IECON (Industrial Electronics Conference) Proceedings*, 2011.
7. O. Geramifard, J. X. Xu, J. H. Zhou, and X. Li, "A physically segmented hidden Markov model approach for continuous tool condition monitoring: diagnostics and prognostics," *IEEE Transactions on Industrial Informatics*, vol. 8, no. 4, pp. 964–973, 2012.

8. X. Yao, M. Fu, S. I. Marcus, and E. Fernandez-Gaucherand, "Optimization of preventive maintenance scheduling for semiconductor manufacturing systems: Models and implementation," in *IEEE Conference on Control Applications*, 2001, pp. 407–411.
9. G. K. Chan and S. Asgarpoor, "Optimum maintenance policy with Markov processes," *Electric Power Systems Research*, vol. 76, no. 6–7, pp. 452–456, 2006.
10. K. Lepenioti, A. Bousdekis, D. Apostolou, and G. Mentzas, "Prescriptive analytics: literature review and research challenges," 2020.
11. F. Ansari, R. Glawar, and T. Nemeth, "PriMa: a prescriptive maintenance model for cyber-physical production systems," *International Journal of Computer Integrated Manufacturing*, vol. 32, pp. 482–503, 2019.
12. F. Ansari, R. Glawar, and W. Sihn, "Prescriptive Maintenance of CPPS by Integrating Multimodal Data with Dynamic Bayesian Networks," in *Machine Learning for Cyber Physical Systems*. Springer Verlag, 2020, vol. 11, pp. 1–8.
13. A. Consilvio, P. Sanetti, D. Anguita, C. Crovetto, C. Dambra, L. Oneto, F. Papa, and N. Sacco, "Prescriptive maintenance of railway infrastructure: from data analytics to decision support," in *MT-ITS 2019 - 6th International Conference on Models and Technologies for Intelligent Transportation Systems*, 2019.
14. M. S. Arulampalam, S. Maskell, N. Gordon, and T. Clapp, "A tutorial on particle filters for online nonlinear/non-Gaussian Bayesian tracking," *IEEE Transactions on Signal Processing*, vol. 50, no. 2, pp. 174–188, 2002.
15. Microsoft, "Predictive maintenance dataset," 2016. [Online]. Available: https://github.com/Microsoft/SQL-Server-R-Services-Samples/

Software-Defined Multi-domain Tactical Networks: Foundations and Future Directions

Redowan Mahmud, Adel N. Toosi, Maria Alejandra Rodriguez,
Sharat Chandra Madanapalli, Vijay Sivaraman, Len Sciacca,
Christos Sioutis, and Rajkumar Buyya

Abstract Software Defined Networking (SDN) has emerged as a programmable approach for provisioning and managing network resources by defining a clear separation between the control and data forwarding planes. Nowadays SDN has gained significant attention in the military domain. Its use in the battlefield communication facilitates the end-to-end interactions and assists the exploitation of edge computing resources for processing data in the proximity. However, there are still various challenges related to the security and interoperability among several heterogeneous, dynamic, intermittent, and data packet technologies like multi-bearer network (MBN) that need to be addressed to leverage the benefits of SDN in tactical environments. In this chapter, we explicitly analyse these challenges and review the current research initiatives in SDN-enabled tactical networks. We also present a taxonomy on SDN-based tactical network orchestration according to the identified challenges and map the existing works to the taxonomy aiming at determining the research gaps and suggesting future directions.

R. Mahmud (✉) · M. A. Rodriguez · L. Sciacca · R. Buyya
School of Computing and Information Systems, The University of Melbourne,
Melbourne, VIC, Australia
e-mail: mahmudm@student.unimelb.edu.au; maria.rodriguez@unimelb.edu.au;
len.sciacca@unimelb.edu.au; rbuyya@unimelb.edu.au

A. N. Toosi
Faculty of Information Technology, Monash University, Melbourne, VIC, Australia
e-mail: adel.n.toosi@monash.edu

S. C. Madanapalli · V. Sivaraman
School of Electrical Engineering and Telecommunications, The University of New South Wales,
Sydney, NSW, Australia
e-mail: sharat.madanapalli@unsw.edu.au; vijay@unsw.edu.au

C. Sioutis
Department of Defence, Defence Science and Technology, Melbourne, VIC, Australia
e-mail: Christos.Sioutis@dst.defence.gov.au

© The Author(s), under exclusive license to Springer Nature Switzerland AG 2021   183
A. Mukherjee et al. (eds.), *Mobile Edge Computing*,
https://doi.org/10.1007/978-3-030-69893-5_9

Keywords Software defined networking · Tactical environment · Battlefield communication · Multi-bearer network

1 Introduction

Networking and communication technologies, especially for competitive and resource constrained environments like battlefields, are continuously evolving [1]. Similarly, the sensitivity to latency varies significantly between different military applications. For example, the data packet delivery deadline for an application assisting unmanned aerial vehicle (UAV) navigation is quite stringent compared to that of a slow speed on-ground military vehicle. On the other hand, the lifetime and the amount of data handled by a sense-process-actuate cycle-based application is quite shorter than an application broadcasting wartime video stream [2]. Moreover, military applications require a variety of networking support such as narrowband, broadband, and mobile services to operate. For example, the applications serving tactical wallet Radio Frequency Identification (RFID) and military vehicle Remote Keyless Entry (RKE) harness narrowband services to meet their instantaneous demands. Conversely, the application sharing satellite images need broadband services for higher transmission capacity. If the underlying network is unable to satisfy such diverse requirements of a military application, its QoS (e.g., throughput, response time, and packet loss rate) is expected to degrade and the consequences of QoS degradation for any military application can be devastating during military operations [3]. Therefore, the satisfaction of QoS for military applications is crucial in tactical environments. It also urges the network infrastructure to be adaptive so that any change in the application's QoS requirements can be handled [4].

Existing data packet technologies, for example multi-bearer network (MBN)can address these requirements to some extent [5]. MBN possesses the capability of carrying data packets via alternative bearer channels as per their QoS requirements. It is complemented by Differentiated Services (DiffServ) that classifies and manages different types of IP traffic (e.g. voice, video, text) flowing over a given network (Fig. 1). Nevertheless, communication among multiple nodes within and beyond the battlefields are no longer simply point-to-point. It can be point-to-multipoint and multipoint-to-multipoint as well. In such cases, the realization of MBN incurs additional operational expenses. Moreover, the lack of fair distribution of network resources among the bearer channels can result in severe resource underutilization which is unacceptable for both network operators and military application users [6]. Additionally, the sole advancement of the underlying network is not sufficient to ensure robustness within the multi-domain military operations. It also requires systematic and unified coordination with the computing systems such as fog, mobile edge and cloud infrastructure [7]. Therefore, to address these issues and limitations, it is preferable to extend the concept of SDN in tactical networks. Figure 2 depicts a prospective structure of SDN in military communications.

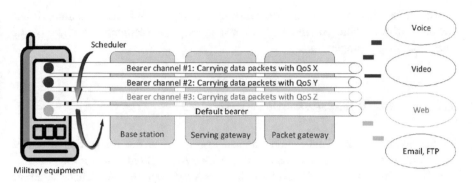

Fig. 1 Multi-bearer network with differentiated services

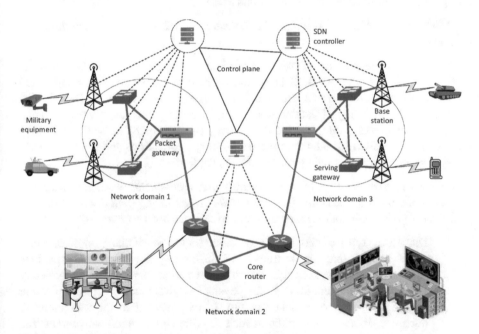

Fig. 2 A prospective SDN-enabled multi bearer network

SDN promotes dynamic provisioning and reconfiguration of network resources by separating the control plane from the data plane [8]. The control plane consists of a logically centralized entity called the SDN controller, which has a global view of the network and makes decisions about how the data packets should flow through the network. Conversely, the data plane consists of network nodes such as routers/switches that actually move packets from one place to another. SDN facilitates virtualization on top of the physical network so that users can implement end-to-end overlays and segment the network traffic. Such logical partitioning also assists the service providers and network operators to provision a separate virtual network with specific policies which consequently complements the objective of MBN and edge computation.

1.1 Research Questions and Challenges

In the context of battlefields and tactical applications, the integration of SDN and MBN is subjected to various heterogeneous, intermittent, and ad-hoc communications with diverse traffic patterns and security requirements. These inherent constraints trigger the following research questions that should be addressed to exploit the combined benefits of SDN and MBN.

1. *How can SDN-based solutions be extended to MBN, including wireless networks?*

   Most of the existing SDN-based solutions are applicable to wired networks [9]. On the other hand, SDN operations in wireless networks is complicated due to the presence of a large number of unsettled access points. There is also a high possibility of data packet collisions sent by the mutually out-of-range access points. Moreover, the dependency on centralized network controllers is not feasible for latency-sensitive military applications and can expose the whole system to single point of failure problem.

2. *How can SDN be employed for securely and dynamically managing traffic of multiple security classifications, to handle traffic of different sensitivities and access policies, in an environment that includes legacy applications?*

   There are 5 types of classified information including official, protected, secret and top secret that can be transferred during any military communications [10]. However, the security class of information can change dynamically according to the context of the physical environment. For example, the mobilization plan of a fleet can turn from protected to top secret during wartimes. To handle the traffic of such classified information with compatible security features and access flexibility, a consistent inspection of the data packets and environmental context is required. Nevertheless, this approach can expose sensitive traffic data to various untrusted SDN controllers. On the other hand, there exist numerous legacy military applications that still follow the traditional monolithic architecture and provide limited scope to implement SDN-based approaches and resist the secured traffic management and packet inspection.

3. *How can time-sensitive traffic be managed by a multi-bearer SDN, particularly when the on-demand time-sensitive channels are required?*

   Sensitivity to latency varies between military applications. In such cases, the proactive quantification of QoS requirements and their efficient allocation to the network resources without allowing over and under provisioning are very important [11]. However, due to less reaction time and variations of resource demands, such SDN-assisted support is difficult to ensure in the battlefields.

4. *How might distributed applications be enhanced with network awareness and control, potentially through coupling to SDN, to make warfighting functions more resilient to degraded network conditions or resource limitations?*

Unlike single-process applications, the components of distributed applications run on multiple hosts simultaneously and process a given task in a collaborative manner [12]. This consequently helps in attaining scalability and fault tolerance. However, the physical distribution of the components makes the use of networking resources essential in enabling communication and coordination between components. This communication overhead can greatly hinder real-time, latency-sensitive interactions [13]. The ability to have fine-grained control that facilitates the dynamic reconfiguration of network resources to suit distributed applications' needs can greatly improve their resilience and performance. The distributed management of applications is also complex as it requires a fine-grained control over the execution of application components deployed in heterogeneous computing and networking domains [14].

5. *What middleware technologies are suitable for the interoperability of services (distributed application software) in this environment, and why?*

SDN middleware encapsulates third-party services including databases and application programming interfaces (APIs) that help bridging multiple SDN-enabled systems by going beyond their communication and architectural heterogeneity. Middleware also assists the control plane in interacting with the data plane to perceive the traffic and topology information in a compatible format [15]. However, in the battlefield context, the attainment of interoperability through middleware is complicated because of the involvement a large number of entities seeking consistent protocol translation and resource discovery support from the middleware. They also increase the management overhead of middleware. Therefore, it is important to select appropriate interoperable technology based on the application requirements and underlying protocols so that the responsiveness and performance of the middleware do not degrade.

In literature, there exists a notable number of works that focus on addressing these challenges through efficient SDN orchestration. This paper aims at categorizing and reviewing them in a systematic manner. It also exploits the detailed scope for further research in this direction by exploiting the current research gaps. The major contributions of this paper are listed below.

- Proposes a system model and a taxonomy for SDN orchestration, especially from the perspective of tactical networks.
- Reviews the existing literature on SDN-enabled tactical networks and identifies their pros and cons.

- Investigates the current research gaps in augmenting SDN with tactical networks and offers future directions for further improvement in this domain.

The rest of the paper is organized as follows: Sect. 2 highlights the proposed taxonomy. The literature review is presented in Sects. 3 to 7. Section 8 discusses the research gaps and future directions. Finally, Sect. 9 concludes the paper.

2 System Model and Taxonomy

To simplify the synthesis of different military devices, tactical network and applications, we propose a layered SDN framework as depicted in Fig. 3. The framework is composed of four planes: application, control, forwarding, and orchestration. Applications with varying QoS and security requirements lie in the application plane. These can be SDN-aware applications communicating directly with an SDN

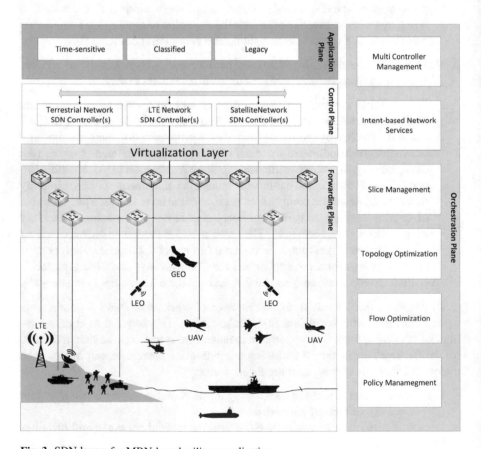

Fig. 3 SDN layers for MBN-based military applications

controller, or legacy applications simply sending data through the network. The control plane is composed of multiple, specialized SDN controllers that have the ability to communicate, either in a peer-to-peer fashion or through an orchestrating controller with a global, multi-network view. The forwarding plane consists of networking nodes that have the ability of forwarding packets based on the routing policies implemented by the SDN controllers. Finally, the orchestration plane spans across all layers and is responsible for monitoring and aggregating data to be used in a meaningful way to support efficient network orchestration in terms of controller management, service resiliency, interoperability, and policy enforcement.

According to the proposed system model, the policy-driven management of orchestration plane is very essential to enhance the competency of SDN-enabled tactical networks in supporting diverse physical and logical networking components and military applications. In existing literature, accrediting this necessity various SDN orchestration policies has been developed. Figure 4 depicts a taxonomy on different aspects of SDN orchestration, especially from the perspective of tactical network. In the following Sects. 3–7, the detailed description of the taxonomy and its mapping to the existing literature are provided.

3 Multi-controller Management

The implementation of SDN with single controller is unsuitable to deal with the increasing rate of traffic transmission in the battlefields. Moreover, in the tactical context, two military devices such as a submarine and a drone interacting with each other may not be located at the same network domain. In such cases, the implementation of SDN with multiple controllers can play a vital role. The coexistence and collaboration of multi-controllers solve the problems encountered by a single controller and help in cross-domain interactions. However, the operations of multiple SDN controllers in military oriented MBN is subjected to consistency and load balancing-related issues. Three types of controller management approaches (as shown in Fig. 5) are widely used to deal with these issues in SDN.

3.1 Bootstrapping

In bootstrapping, a rendezvous node deploys multiple SDN controllers between the application and the data plane. The bootstrapping node notifies the network configuration information to the controllers, sets their initial topology, and determines the coordination mechanism. To build the topology model for the SDN controllers, the bootstrapping node transmits Link Layer Discovery Protocol (LLDP) packets to various networking nodes including switches and gateways, and substrates the network based on their responses. The bootstrapping node also installs default flow-rules for the data plane so that the network can remain functional even after

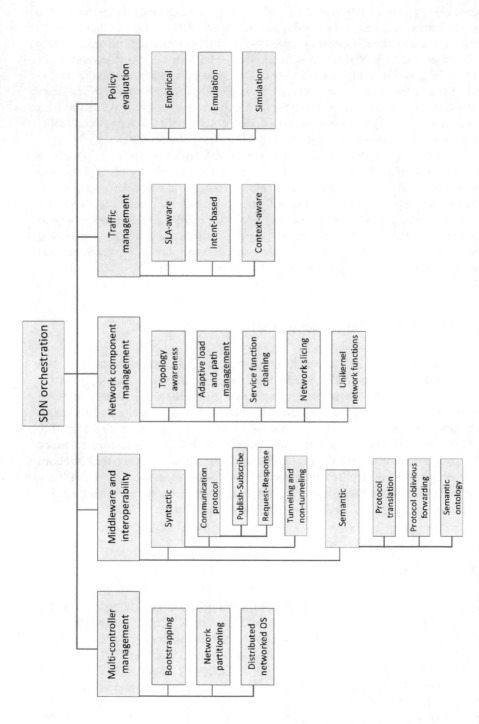

Fig. 4 A taxonomy on SDN orchestration

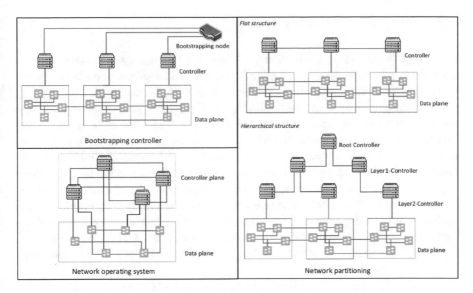

Fig. 5 Different controller management approaches

the failure of the controllers. Moreover, it is capable of increasing or decreasing the number of controllers dynamically according to the requirements of SDN operations.

To simplify the initialization phase of the SDN network, a bootstrapping approach named InitSDN is proposed in [16]. InitSDN helps in modularizing the network applications and facilitates controller migration by only updating their topology. In [17], another bootstrapping approach is proposed that assists tactical networks to transmit the control commands and the data traffic using the same underlay network. It enables a data plane node to *(i)* identify and register with any of the available SDN controllers, *(ii)* parse the corresponding data flow rules through intermediate switches, *(iii)* initiate a secure control channel with the controller, and *(iv)* interact with the topology database.

Bootstrapping is supportive for dynamic network extension and legacy routing, and can effectively handle uncertain failures within the control and data plane [18]. A bootstrapping networking device can also serve the purpose of a edge computing node. However, for bootstrapping, the controllers and data plane nodes are required to be explicitly accessible, which is not recommended for military use cases. Moreover, bootstrapping a wireless SDN is a challenging task as the controllers and data plane nodes only share local connectivity information and resist the attainment of global bootstrapping convergence instantly.

3.2 Network Partitioning

In network partitioning, the data plane is divided into multiple domains, and for each domain a local SDN controller is assigned. The interactions between the controllers are made through either a hierarchical or a flat structure. In a hierarchical structure, a group of controllers residing at the upper layer explicitly manage the controllers in the immediate underneath layer. The number of these logical layers is set by the network operator based on the network topology size, the traffic load, and the network resource availability. Moreover, in this setup, the controllers in the same layer do not communicate with each other directly. Their internal communication happens via the upper layer controllers. Conversely, in the flat structure, the controllers of various data plane domains spontaneously interact with each other using east and west bound APIs to maintain a global view of the underlying network. Among the celebrated SDN controllers, ONIX, HyperFlow and OpenDayLight use the flat structure whereas, Kandoo, Orion and D-SDN follow the hierarchical structure [19].

Nevertheless, network partitioning becomes vigorous when the traffic load is evenly distributed among the controller. By exploiting the k-means clustering algorithm and the cooperative game theory, a load management policy for multi-controllers is proposed in [20]. The policy enables a data plane node to form coalitions with other nodes and balance the topology size for each controller in partitioned SDN. Internet 2 OS3E and Internet Topology Zoo is used to evaluate the performance of the policy. On the other hand, in [21], a Louvain heuristic algorithm is developed to limit the number of data plane nodes managed by a controller so that the controllers do not get overloaded.

Network partitioning is supportive to wireless networking because of its localized characteristics and inherently complements the realization of edge computing. However, the interaction of two controllers in partitioned networks is time consuming as it requires the assistance of multiple intermediate controllers. The impact of such delays in tactical scenarios is evaluated in [22]. Moreover, in partitioned networks, a significant amount of resources is consumed only to synchronize controllers, which is not suitable for resource constrained environments like battlefields.

3.3 Networked Operating System (NOS)

In this approach, a physically distributed but logically centralized network operating system runs across multiple controllers. The network applications within the operating system support the controllers to handle the traffic flow and maintain a global view of the network [23]. Additionally, these applications can enable any data plane node to connect with different controllers but allow only one controller to manage that node at a time. If the controller fails, another controller is set as the node manager based on a consensus-based leader selection algorithm. Moreover, the operating system supports the dynamic updates of the applications without interrupting the traffic flow. SDN frameworks including Open Network Operating System (ONOS), Switch Light, Open Network Linux (ONL), DENT and Coriant predominantly follow the concepts of a networked operating system in their control plane implementation [24].

Apart from the benchmarks, there exist several customized implementation of network operating system for SDN controllers. For example, in [25], a network operating system named MNOS is developed that augments the cyberspace to mimic defence technique and protects the controllers from data alteration. It also creates the functional equivalent variants of the controllers using dissimilar redundancy design principles to overcome their device-level heterogeneity. In [26], another network operating system named NOSArmor is proposed that augments security blocks to the controllers. The blocks are responsible for role-based authorization, location tracking, link verification, rule-based negotiation, protocol verification, system call checking and resource management. Moreover, there are some extensions of network operating system that either protect the control plane from the compromised controllers by exploiting the packet trajectory information [27] or apply lightweight virtualization techniques such as containers for resource constrained controllers [28].

Network operating systems are modular and fault tolerant. Additionally, the expansion and consolidation of network operating system-based control planes are comparatively easier and less time consuming. However, such control planes are required to be deployed locally for synchronization, which may not be feasible for military use cases requiring cross-network domain communications. They also lack support for channel-level management of MBN [5].

4 Middleware and Interoperability

To ensure efficient tactical interactions, SDN middleware requires to support interoperability between the control and the data plane nodes. The overall interoperability of any system can be discussed from two perspectives, syntactic and semantic. Table 1 illustrates the differences between syntactic and semantic interoperability. In the literature, there are different techniques that help in enabling syntactic and semantic interoperability in SDN. However, these interoperability techniques have their own pros and cons in dealing with the dynamics of battlefield communications and diverse traffic priorities.

Table 1 Differences between syntactic and semantic interoperability

Facts	Syntactic interoperability	Semantic interoperability
Targets	Data exchange	Data interpretation
Deals with	Format of data	Contents and attributes of data
Enablers	Communication protocol	Information model

4.1   Syntactic

Syntactic interoperability is responsible for the synergies of the data packets and their formats transmitted and packaged by the heterogeneous control and data plane nodes. It is also regarded as the prerequisite for attaining semantic interoperability in SDN. Syntactic interoperability explicitly depends on the communication protocols offered by the middleware and the characteristics of the overlays that logically connects the nodes with the middleware. Different communication protocols and overlay mechanisms associated with the syntactic interoperability are discussed below.

4.1.1   Communication Protocols

Most of the existing SDN middleware systems have a message-oriented architecture that allows them to handle uncertain communication delays during interactions with different control and data plane nodes. Additionally, the functionalities of a message-oriented middleware are highly scalable compared to that of a remote procedure call-based middleware [29]. Two types of communication protocols such as Publish-Subscribe (PubSub) and Request-Response (RR) are widely used in message-oriented systems.

i. **Publish-Subscribe**: PubSub communication protocols assist the control plane node in publishing the commands to the middleware and enable data plane nodes to get the respective commands from the middleware. The opposite happens when data is transferred from the data plane to the control plane. PubSub protocols support event-driven interactions between the communicating entities. Message Queuing Telemetry Transport (MQTT), Data Distribution Service (DDS) and Advanced Message Queuing Protocol (AMPQ) are among the most used PubSub communication protocols.

   • *Message Queuing Telemetry Transport (MQTT)*: MQTT protocol defines a MQTT broker at the middleware and a set of logical clients over the control and data plane to publish and subscribe information. MQTT sorts information in topics and allow nodes to subscribe multiple topics and receive all information published under each topic. For example, in [30], an MQTT enabled SDN framework for UAV swarms is proposed that creates different MQTT information topics for exchanging network conditions, security policies, QoS requirements, electronic state and controller commands.

      Usually MQTT depends on TCP for data transmission. There is a variant of MQTT for sensor networks, named MQTT-SN that uses either UDP or Bluetooth for transmitting data. MQTT is also used to create multicast trees between the publishers and the subscribers for minimizing data transfer delay [31]. In another work, MQTT has been exploited in multi layers to offer network interoperability for the controllers deployed in hierarchical structure [32].

MQTT is considered highly feasible for Internet of Things-driven interactions because of its lightweight structure and minimized data packets [33]. Nevertheless, MQTT often experiences serious traffic congestion problem at the broker side and requires Transport Layer Security (TLS) support. Moreover, MQTT is less resilient to the mobility of subscribing and publishing nodes, and prone to single point failure. These limitations can resist the real timeliness of the system and increase overhead of the middleware [34].

- *Data Distribution Service (DDS)*: DDS allows asynchronous data exchange among communicating entities without implementing any logical broker. Unlike MQTT, DDS incorporates a built-in discovery mechanism that assists subscribers in finding the available publishers for interactions. The default transport layer protocol for DDS is UDP, although it can be easily integrated with TCP. The header length of DDS is 16 bytes which is 8 times higher than that of MQTT and possesses 20 more QoS levels for controlling volatility, resource utilization, availability, delivery, reliability, ownership, duplication, and latency tolerance of the data. Therefore, a DDS middleware requires to extract the data-centric information of the packets for their QoS-satisfied distribution to the subscribers [35].

  In SDN, the concept of DDS middleware has been widely used to manage the distributed control plane. For example, in [36], a DDS-based hierarchical controller plane structure is modelled that distributes time-critical synchronization and system breakdown information among the controllers by publishing their type in proactive manner to achieve better performance. Another SDN control mechanism is developed in [37] for dynamically configuring network based on the importance of shared data among the digital twins. The mechanism set this data importance in terms of the latency sensitivity attribute of the packets defined by the DDS QoS level. Moreover, in [38], a DDS-based SDN middleware is considered that supports on-demand access to UAV-aided services from authorized entities at the ground. It also facilitates distributed DDS orchestration to enhance interoperation and meet mobility constraints of UAVs.

  DDS supports security plugin models and offers vendor level interoperability using RTPS (Real Time Publish Subscribe) protocol. Due to built-in QoS maintenance mechanism, DDS also performs better in low latency communication. However, DSS is heavyweight for resource constrained battlefield networking nodes and consumes more bandwidth than MQTT.

- *Advanced Message Queuing Protocol (AMQP)*: In AMQP broker, the published messages received by the exchange component are organized in multiple queues based on a set of certain rules called bindings. The published messages contain various meta-data that help the broker to retrieve context and priority of the packets without exploiting the payload directly. Similar to MQTT, AMQP exploits TCP for data transmission and provides three QoS levels namely, i. at most once, ii. exactly once and iii. at least once. However, the header length of AMQP is 8 bytes higher than that of MQTT.

AMQP-based SDN middleware systems are often used to build distributed control plane. In [40], such a middleware has been considered that augments RabbitMQ and ActiveMQ with AMQP for supporting reliable message communication among the controllers. Similarly, in [41], another AMQP middleware is modelled to exchange information regarding network bandwidth, network topologies and inter-connected nodes among the distributed controllers.

Nevertheless, AMQP helps in enhancing communication flexibility by providing a scope to dynamically integrate different network standards and protocols. Additionally, the AMQP packet size is negotiable that makes it suitable for transferring large number of payloads. On the contrary, AMQP does not facilitate automatic resource discovery like DDS and lacks explicit support to enable Last-Value-Queues update. AMQP can also create a large backlog of messages when there is a poor availability of network resources and resists real-time battlefield communications by increasing the network delay [42]. Additionally, Fig. 6 illustrates the differences of MQTT, DDS and AMQP from the perspective of CPU, memory and latency-driven performances.

ii. **Request-Response**: In RR communication protocols, when a data plane node needs any command from the control plane, it sends a request to the corresponding controller through middleware. In response, the controllers transfer necessary instructions to the data plane node. The opposite happens when the control plane seeks state information from the data plane. RR issues both request and response packets in a synchronous manner. In Table 2, a summary comparison between PubSub and RR has been illustrated. Constrained Application Protocol (CoAP) is one of the most celebrated RR protocols that deals with IoT communications in resource constrained networking environments [43].

- **Constrained Application Protocol (CoAP)**: CoAP relies on both UDP and RESTful protocol that makes it more compatible for resource constrained IoT devices. Moreover, CoAP offers reduced implementation and communication complexities compared to other RR protocols like HTTP. As a means of reliability. CoAP also incorporates an exponential back-off feature-based retransmission mechanism. CoAP supports two different levels of QoS functionalities, namely (1) Confirmable, (2) Non-Confirmable. Its header length is 4 bytes and can be easily augmented with cellular networks.

  In the literature, there exist several researches studies where CoAP has been used to model communications among distributed control plane entities. For example, in [44], a control plane structure for software defined wireless network is developed that exploits CoAP for exchanging topology discovery and flow control information among the controllers. In another work [45], CoAP has been used to allow controllers for managing flow tables, modifying node routing characteristics, and obtaining data plane information with respect to link quality, geographical location and energy level. Moreover, in [46], a real-world SDN middleware named Ride has been developed that

Fig. 6 Comparison between MQTT, DSS and AMQP [39]. (**a**) CPU usage. (**b**) Memory usage. (**c**) Latency

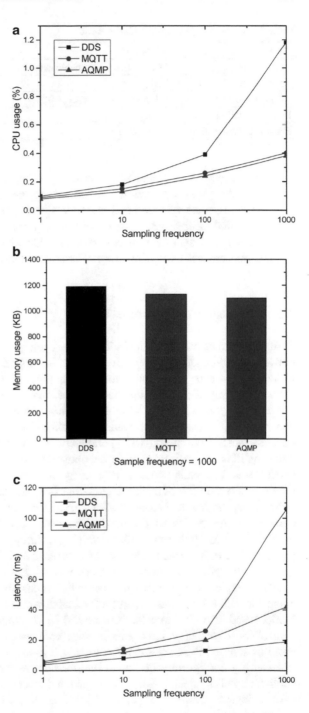

Table 2 Comparison between PubSub and RR

Facts	PubSub	RR
Suitable for	Competitive, unreliable network	Robust, reliable network
Traffic load	High	Low
Interaction driver	Report-by-exception (RBE)	Polling at regular interval
Dynamic scaling	Adaptive	Inflexible
Security augmentation	Complicated	Easy

exchanges CoAP packets for managing a workflow consisting various tasks including host registration, network configuration, on-demand network state analysis, fault detection and recovery. CoAP offers faster wake up times and extended sleepy states that consequently improves energy consumptions of control and data plane nodes. However, CoAP has limitations in communicating devices using Network Address Translation (NAT) technique.

4.1.2 Tunneling and Non-tunneling

Tunneling allows private communications to exchange data packets across a public network using encapsulation. By default, it supports encryption and helps in establishing secure and remote connections among the networks. These features make tunneling highly feasible to use in virtual networks. There exist different tunneling protocols such as Virtual Extensible LAN (VXLAN), GPRS Tunneling Protocol (GTP), Network Virtualization using Generic Encapsulation (NVGRE), stateless transport tunneling (STT) and Network Virtualization Overlays 3 (NVO3) that simplifies the realization of virtual networks [47]. Moreover, in SDN, tunneling is often used to manage connection among the data plane nodes, especially during the uncertain mobility of packet destinations [48]. In such cases, tunnels are created dynamically to handover data packets from the previous serving switch to the current serving switch of the destination node. On the other hand, in [49], an SDN-enabled dynamic multipath forwarding technique has been developed that can merge traffics of multiple tunnels at any data plane node based on source-destination address with a view to minimizing the number of flow entries within the system.

Moreover, there exist other initiatives that focus on improving tunneling mechanisms in SDN. For example, in [50] a Match-Action Table (MAT) programming model-based IP tunnel mechanism, named MAT tunnel is developed that allows controllers to set flow table entries with both encapsulation and decapsulation specifications of the corresponding tunnel. It consequently reduces the overhead of manually configuring the tunnel interface at the data plane. Similarly, in [51], another tunneling mechanism is developed that detects multiple shorter repair paths when a single link failure happens in SDN. This feature helps in faster fault recovery.

However, the packet drop rate in tunneling increases unevenly when mixed traffic (voice and video) are transferred. Forward error correction in this case incurs additional bandwidth overhead and wastes network capacity. The repackaging feature of tunneling reduces the effective size of data packets and affects the transfer delay. It consequently increases packet fragmentation that consumes additional memory and processing power at the destination node for merging. Because of these limitations, tunneling is often discouraged while transferring large amounts of data to resource constrained destinations. Therefore, non-tunneling communications for virtual networking is gradually getting attention in both research and industry. In [52], a non-tunneling protocol named FlowLAN is developed that adopts Network Prefix Translation technique to augment both the physical and logical addresses of packet destination nodes and tags them in the flow field of the packet header with respect to the corresponding network identifier. It helps realizing the virtual networks as a distributed system that can communicate without encapsulation or decapsulation. To support the movement of cells in LTE network, another non-tunneling approach named MocLis is developed in [53]. MocLis adopts Locator/ID split approach while dealing with the mobility of cells and their nested user equipment. Nevertheless, non-tunneling approaches lack standardization that makes them less compatible to apply in highly heterogeneous communication environments like battlefield.

4.2 Semantic

In SDN, a middleware needs to support semantic interoperability to ensure the unambiguous interpretation of command and status information that is exchanged between the controllers and data plane nodes. It simplifies the knowledge discovery between these two planes. Semantic interoperability acts as a function of semantic interoperability and fails drastically if the data packets are distorted during transmission from source to destination. There exist different techniques including protocol translation, protocol oblivious forwarding and semantic ontology that enable semantic interoperability in SDN.

4.2.1 Protocol Translation

Protocol translation converts the data, commands and time synchronization information issued by the control plane into the compatible format of the data plane nodes in which they are navigating. It also enables the data plane nodes to interact with controllers despite of the differences in their native protocol stacks. To perform this operation, a Protocol Converter software installed on the middleware removes the protocol headers of the sender completely and wrap the payload with the target protocol header [54]. There are different technical companies like Cisco and Valin corporation that develop software solutions for protocol translation. Figure 7 depicts the internal architecture of a conceptual protocol converter software.

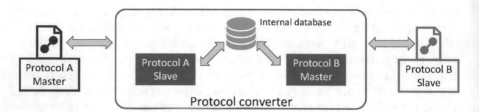

Fig. 7 Architecture of a protocol converter

In [55], the operations of a protocol translating middleware named TableVisor is discussed. TableVisor uses the match-action architecture to match the intents of the exchanged data packets to the existing flow table entries, action space and target header fields. The expressiveness of TableVisor is translating protocols is defined by the intersections of possible command attributes from both source and target protocol. The protocol translation mechanism discussed in [56] shows almost the similar functionalities like TableVisor. However, for [56], the translation rules are defined by the controllers, not by the middleware. Conversely, in [57], the middleware translates the source data and protocol commands into multiple segments as per the primitive network requirements with respect to latency, packet collision and packet delivery rate so that the destination nodes can easily parse the segments with their default protocol stack and set the rank for each requirement.

Although protocol translation helps in alleviating protocol and data format-wise heterogeneity of control and data plane nodes, it limits the scope of simultaneous interactions. It requires an in-depth understanding of the packets that urge to deploy trusted middleware systems across the network. However, such facilities are not often possible to ensure in constrained communication environments like battlefield.

4.2.2 Protocol Oblivious Forwarding

Protocol oblivious forwarding makes the format of a packet transparent to the data plane nodes. In this case, the data plane nodes extract and assemble key features from the packet header to conduct flow table lookups based on the controller instructions. It enables data plane to support any new protocols and forwarding requirements in a flexible manner. To perform this operation, packet meta-data are augmented with generic information including flow logic and life span. The difference between protocol translation and oblivious forwarding is illustrated in Table 3.

A protocol-oblivious forwarding-based routing mechanism is proposed in [58] that can redirect a packet to multiple destination addresses in a multi-homing scenario. It completements the SDN ability of switching transmission path dynamically and enables the destinations to adjust packet receiving rate as per the status of network resources. Moreover, to assist protocol oblivious forwarding in perceiving device-level context, a State Parameter Field is augmented to its generic structure

Table 3 Differences between protocol translation and oblivious forwarding

Protocol translation	Protocol oblivious forwarding
Requires protocol specific knowledge	Protocol specific knowledge is oblivious
Parsing packet data for target protocol is difficult in real-time	Extraction of meta data from packet is easier
Conversion or translation support for user-defined or newly introduced protocols are not always available	Data plane can adopt any protocols

in [59]. It also incorporates a direct entry matching policy for flow table lookup that enables protocol oblivious forwarding to check device status in time optimized manner. Moreover, in [60], the concept of protocol oblivious forwarding has been extended to offer protocol independent interactions among the controllers arranged in a hierarchical structure. It enhances the flexibility in distributed controller operations.

Despite having certain advantages over protocol translation, protocol oblivious forwarding is considered infeasible to sensitive communications as it lacks explicit security measures. Therefore, to protect the protocol oblivious forwarding operations from diverse attacks, a proactive security framework for SDN is proposed in [61]. Moreover, protocol oblivious forwarding depends on a set of stateful information which makes it less resilient to failure or alteration of the networking system.

4.2.3   Semantic Ontology

A significant amount of control data is exchanged between control and data plane nodes while transferring network packets from a place to another. The existing Network Operating System (NOS)-based control data modelling techniques such as type checking and code templating perform well when the flow rules are static. To parse the non-deterministic behaviors of applications and networks in the flow rules and modelling the control data accordingly, semantic ontology is often used. Semantic ontology incorporates various reasoning rules and integrity constraints that helps in automating state inference across the SDN layers. Additionally, it simplifies the remote configurations of data plane nodes and allow controllers to define complex data relationships [62]. An illustration of semantic ontology-based operations in SDN domain is depicted in Fig. 8.

Based on the concept of semantic ontology, an autonomous fault management agent for SDN is developed in [63]. It compares network status with semantic models using Bayesian reasoning as inference method for determining the category of a fault. In another work [64], sematic ontology has been applied to automate the creation of virtual network functions (VNFs). It also fosters the synthesis of VNFs with user requirements and enabled controllers to recommend similar services based on network service description (NSD). Moreover, in [65], another semantic-based

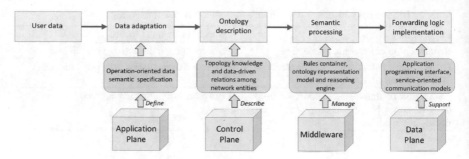

Fig. 8 Semantic ontology-based operations in SDN layers [66]

framework for distributed control plane is proposed that incorporates local ontology from each controller and forwards them to the master controller for ensuring overall semantic interoperability within the network.

However, the scope of applying semantic ontology is constrained as it depends on specific format of data and all entities within the network should have in-depth understanding of that format. Moreover, semantic ontology can expose data to security threats for the sake of reasoning which is not acceptable during battlefield communications.

5 Network Component Management

Conceptually, network components are classified into two categories, network infrastructure and network services. Network infrastructure incorporates the topology and the data forwarding paths. From the perspective of SDN, network slices can also be considered as a virtualized infrastructure for the network. Conversely, network services provide support for caching, network address translation, encryption, and intrusion detection. Recently network services are set to be decoupled from proprietary hardware to virtualized software platforms using Network Function Virtualization (NFV) techniques. Although it is not a must to implement SDN and NFV together, both technologies can complement each other in enhancing network automation. For example, the implementation of SDN without virtualizing network functions results in hardware dependency which is conflicting with the instinct of SDN that focuses on performing network control through software. In this part of the report, existing approaches to manage network components are discussed in an integrated manner. Sections 5.1–5.3 discuss the approaches from the perspective of network infrastructure whereas Sects. 5.4–5.5 focus on the approaches based on network service.

5.1 Topology Awareness

As noted, tactical operations often take place in inaccessible locations where the arrangement of infrastructure network is difficult. In such cases, on-demand network services can be offered by creating MANET. MANET enables the participating nodes to interact with each other with the goal of completing their assigned tasks. Moreover, MANET provides a scope to integrate the concept of SDN for efficiently coordinating the communicating nodes in pursuing their collective goal. An SDN-enabled MANET structure for battlefield communication is depicted in Fig. 9. However, the network topology in MANET embraces complex configurations and can change very frequently. Therefore, from the perspective of tactical operations relying on Mobile Ad-hoc Network (MANET), topology awareness is very important. Topology awareness refers to the complete understanding of various dynamics related to the communicating entities and their underlying network while making any network management decision. It consequently helps in optimizing the packet routing path, consolidating the number of redundant networking nodes, scaling-up the network, and deploying edge computing nodes.

In literature, there exists a notable number of works that address the topology awareness in SDN-enabled MANET. For example, a distributed SDN controller placement problem for MANET is formulated in [68]. This work explicitly considers the topology of the network in terms of controller's accessibility from the data plane nodes and minimizes the cost of circulating synchronization messages among the controllers within the topology. In another work [69], the communication and topology-driven incompatibility between SDN (inherently centralized and structured) and MANET (inherently distributed and dynamic) is discussed. It also develops a protocol for localized data plane nodes that dynamically adapts the packet routing path according to the changes in network topology without solely relying on the centralized SDN controllers. The performance of the developed

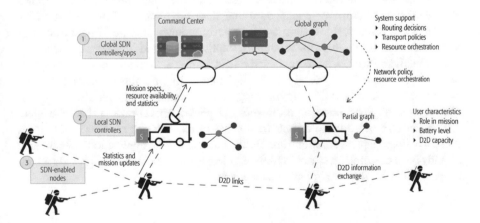

Fig. 9 SDN-enabled MANET for battlefield communication [67]

protocol is validated using a real-world dataset mentioned in [70]. Furthermore, a multi-path transmission control protocol for decreasing network handover delay and improving transmission throughput in SDN-enabled naval battlefield network is proposed in [71]. The ad-hoc network model also incorporates a connectable relay point to maintain the communications during uncertain topology changes. On the other hand, to ensure security in SDN-enabled MANET during topology alteration, a distributed firewall system is developed in [72]. It relies on ONOS control platform and control the access of unreliable ad-hoc nodes by distributing filter rules across the network. Similarly, in [73], a flow-based framework for tactical mobile ad-hoc network is proposed that exploits both machine learning-based classification and SDN concepts for anomaly detection within the network topology. However, these topology-aware solutions are very less-adaptive and scalable to deal unpredictable growth of packets in different bearer channels of tactical ad-hoc network.

5.2   Adaptive Load and Path Management

Battlefield communication network requires consistent adjustment of loads and routing paths while transferring video streams or performing surveillance operations using limited bandwidth of uneven availability. For example, in [74], the dynamic optimization of end-to-end paths between the source and the destination is exploited for adaptive video streaming in the battlefield network. The path selection algorithm applied adopted in [74] is depicted in Fig. 10. Additionally, in [75], an adaptive link sensing approach for an aerial battlefield network is proposed that exploits back-up routing path in case of sudden network congestion. The implications of adaptive routing for mobile military devices are also discussed in [76]. It aims at virtualizing the network functions at the granular level to enhance network survivability.

Apart from them, in [77], an adaptive tactical data collection system is developed that selects the data sourcing node according to the link availability and traffic characteristics in terms of packet rate and flow distribution. When the network resources are limited, the system autonomously reduces the rate of data transmission. It also helps to reduce the amount of duplicate data and improves the accuracy of data analysis. Moreover, to balance the load among distributed controllers, a self-adaptive technique is proposed in [78]. It dynamically migrates switches from one controller to another considering the geographical boundary and variation of loads. The scheme triggers based on a threshold of packet arrival rate to the controllers which can also be adjusted as per the context of the network resources. However, these existing adaptive solutions are highly suitable for the applications which have already been customized to run in SDN. For legacy applications, they provide a very narrow scope for further service enhancement.

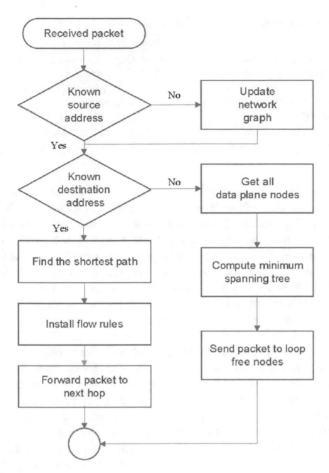

Fig. 10 Path selection algorithm [74]

5.3 Network Slicing

Through network slicing, operators can create unique but logical partitions of a physical network infrastructure and simplify their multiplexing for end-to-end communications. Network slices can be expanded across different network domains such as access, core, and transport, and can be exploited to meet diverse requirements of a particular application [79]. It harnesses both SDN and NFV concepts to increase service flexibility within the network. Since network slices are isolated, they inherently avoid the control plane congestion of one slice to affect the other slices. Moreover, every network slice maintains a set of resource and network function management policies to address speed, capacity, connectivity, and coverage-driven issues. Unlike virtual private network (VPN), network slicing does not solely rely on tunneling. It also differs from Differentiated Services (DiffServ) as noted in Table 4.

Table 4 Differences between network slicing and differentiated service

Network slicing	Differentiated service
Allows multiple logical networks to run on top of a shared physical network	Controls and classifies network traffic to set their flow precedence
Simultaneously deals with the networking, computation, and storage aspects of the underlying resources	Only deals with the networking aspect of the underlying resources
Can isolate traffic of one tenant from others and supports optimum grouping of the traffic	Cannot discriminate the same type of traffic coming from different tenants

Different SDN-enabled frameworks harness the concept of network slicing for offering better services. For example, in [80], an end-to-end network slicing framework incorporating a virtual resource manager is proposed that places network slices over physical resources based on the data traffic pattern, user connectivity demands and channel bandwidth. The resource manager can also deal with the sudden surges in resource demand and offers scope for integrating real-time decision-making policies. In another work [81], a data-driven resource management framework for network slices is proposed. The resource cognitive engine of the framework collects the resource usage data and incorporate a machine learning technique for their uniform scheduling. Conversely, the service cognitive engine analyses the user's requirements and interact with the global cognitive engine for improving the resource utilization and user's quality of experience. Similarly, in [82], a machine learning-based network slicing framework is proposed that divides each logical slice into a set of virtualized sub-slices and orchestrate them with different prioritized resources as per the application requirements. The framework also engages separate sub-slices to handle spectral efficiency, low latency service delivery, and power consumption, and uses the Support Vector Machine (SVM) algorithm to extract the features of assigned applications. Nevertheless, in literature, very few research initiatives have been found that focus on augmenting network slicing with military applications. To address this gap, a set of military services including push-to-talk, cellular convergence, prioritized on-demand access, satellite backhaul for redundancy and signal jamming are identified in [6] where network slicing can be easily adopted for improved performance, security and availability. However, the explicit isolation of network slices makes the coordination of security policies difficult and can lead to a breach of confidentiality in battlefield communication [83].

5.4   Service Function Chaining (SFC)

Service function chaining refers to a complete suite of connected virtual network services such as firewalls, VoIP, directory service, deep packet inspection, load balancer and time service that allows traffic to use any combination of them as per the requirements in terms of security, lower latency and enhanced service quality. It

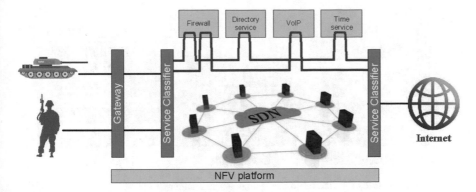

Fig. 11 Service function chaining in battlefield communication

also enables SDN controllers to customize a chain and apply them to different traffic flows depending on the source, destination, or type of traffic. Figure 11 provides an abstract representation of service function chaining for battlefield communication.

In the literature, there has been notable initiatives that focus on improving virtual network function placement in SFC. For example, a Mixed Integer Linear Programming (MILP) model to minimize the intra-communication delay between different network function instances is proposed in [84]. It meets diverse carrier-grade requirements such as latency and resource availability for an application requesting to access the service chain. In [85], another MILP model for optimizing energy consumption across multiple network domains is proposed. It considers the order of accessing the chain as a constraint and sets a domain-level function graph to orchestrate the incoming network service requests. The SDN-based resource management architecture developed in [86] also aims at optimizing energy usage while placing different network functions over the computing instances and defining their routing path. As supplements, some other works are developing SFC-constrained shortest path service access mechanisms for SDN. In [87], such a mechanism is proposed that transforms the basic network graph to an SFC-constrained network graph. Moreover, it applies a pruning algorithm based on service dependency for reducing the size of newly generated network graph so that the shortest path can be calculated in timely manner. In another work [88], simple breadth-first search algorithm has been adopted to determine the shortest path. There also exists a performance evaluation framework named SFCPerf [89] to check the compatibility of these approaches in real-world test bed. However, the existing solutions have significant configuration complexity that make them infeasible to deal with the instant demands of battlefield communications.

5.5 *Unikernel Network Functions*

Besides virtual machines and containers, unikernels are also increasing in popularity as a virtualized software platform for implementing NFV. Unikernels refer to single-

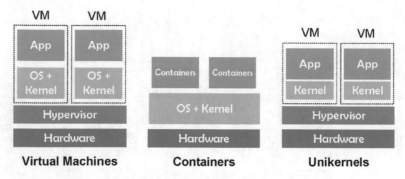

Fig. 12 Architecture of virtual machines, containers and unikernels

address-space machine images that can run on standard hypervisors by exploiting only kernel space libraries. The structure of unikernels is considerably lightweight compared to that of VMs, and containers, thus they can boot faster. Moreover, a unikernel can execute a single process at a time, which consequently results in less management and processing overhead. Figure 12 illustrates the architectural differences between VMs, containers and unikernels. Because of the low memory footprint and initiation time, unikernels are considered more well-suited for network function virtualization than VMs and containers, especially when they are used to complement any SDN-enabled system.

The concept of unikernel is relatively new and its standards are still evolving. In [90], an SDN-enabled framework is developed that can create unikernels dynamically. It enhances system reliability with respect to anomaly or security attacks and helps in recovering the system functionalities within minimal time. Similarly, in [91], the Topology and Orchestration Specification for Cloud Applications (TOSCA)-language has been extended to support the creation and orchestration of unikernels with security constraints. It also enables the unikernels to offer on-demand network services to the users. In another work [92], the initiation time of different unikernel-based network services is optimized by consistently modifying their schedulers according to the service requirements. Although unikernels outperform VMs and containers in various aspects, the packet loss rate with unikernels is higher than others. This limitation of unikernels can affect any battlefield communication requiring high throughput.

6 Traffic Management

Quality-of-Service (QoS) and Quality-of-Experience (QoE) related traffic management has been studied for many years, and a significant amount of research has been devoted to understanding, measuring, and modelling QoS/QoE for a variety of network services [93]. Considering different network segments, disparate application needs, and multiple transmission bearers involved in the end-to-end service delivery chain, it is challenging to identify the root causes of service quality impairments. It also increases the complexities in finding effective solutions for meeting the end users' requirements and expectations in terms of service quality. We briefly survey state-of-the-art findings and present emerging concepts and challenges related to managing service quality for networked services, especially in the context of the move towards softwarised networks, the exploitation of big data analytics and machine learning, and the steady rise of new application services (e.g. multimedia, augmented and virtual reality). We address the implications of such paradigm shifts in terms of new approaches in QoS modelling and the need for novel monitoring and management infrastructures.

Traditionally, QoS-driven application management has primarily addressed control and adaptation on the end-user and application host/cloud level, often studied from an application provider perspective in the context of optimizing the quality of Over-The-Top (OTT) applications and services. As an example, applications such as HTTP-based adaptive video streaming dynamically adapt to varying network conditions to maintain a high level of QoS. Such a mechanism represents an application control loop that is often independent of network management mechanisms. On the other hand, network providers generally rely on performance and traffic monitoring solutions deployed within their access/core network to obtain insight into impairments perceived by end users. QoS-driven network management mechanisms have thus focused on the network provider point of view and considered control mechanisms, such as optimized network resource allocation, admission control, QoS-driven routing, and so on. Such control thus aims to facilitate efficient network operations and maintain high QoS, without directly managing the applications.

SDN serves as a technology for decoupling hardware resources from software and functionality, enabling programmability of the networking infrastructure. The programmable and flexible resource allocation, coupled with softwarisation, enable the network and application to engage in a "conversation" using software APIs. While this explicit negotiation approach offers clear opportunities, there are many challenges that need to be addressed (as shown in Fig. 13), including encryption of traffic, virtualization of resources, contextualization of application data, measurement of service quality, fairness, business arrangements, and federation across networks. In what follows we briefly review the evolution of QoS traffic management and recent directions enabled by SDN.

6.1 Service Level Agreement (SLA)-Aware Traffic Management

The notion of using service level agreements (SLAs) for QoS dates back to the IETF IntServ and DiffServ frameworks [95], whereby the application specifies its requirements in the form of a FlowSpec, which includes both its traffic profile

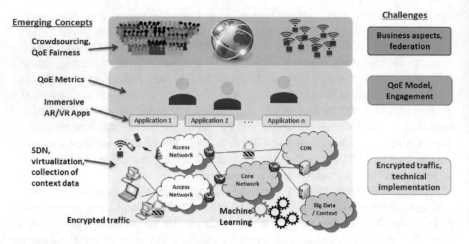

Fig. 13 Emerging concepts and challenges in QoS management [94]

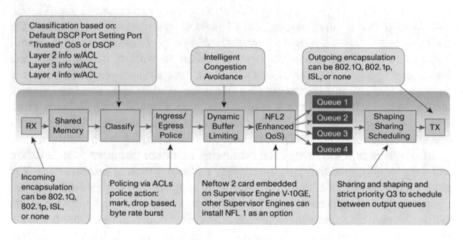

Fig. 14 Mechanisms for implementing SLA-based QoS [95]

(rate and burstiness) and requirements profile (in terms of guaranteed bandwidth and latency)—once accepted by the network (via some form of admission control), this forms an agreement (SLA) that then needs to be respected by both parties. The realization of this framework (as shown in Fig. 14) requires admission control (often via a bandwidth broker), traffic classification (using packet header fields), packet marking (typically as a DiffServ Code Point or DSCP), traffic policing (via a token bucket), and priority or weighted fair scheduling to ensure network resources are shared in order to meet the pre-negotiated SLAs.

While conceptually elegant, the major challenges with this approach relate to the large amount of state information along with the complex policing/scheduling mechanisms needed for managing the per-flow SLA, as well as limitations in being able to map application-level QoE to network-level QoS parameters—these aspects are explored in depth in [96], which also develops a new method called SFQP (SLA-aware Fine-grained QoS Provisioning) to perform the mapping and bandwidth enforcement using SDN principles. Other works including [3] have also explored the application of QoS methods enabled by SDN protocols (OpenFlow in particular) to support the classification, prioritization, and shaping of application flows with a view towards enabling dynamic QoS control.

In networks where the applications are not enabled with capabilities to explicitly negotiate SLAs, the application behavior as well as requirements may need to be inferred. The work in [97] develops an application-aware traffic engineering system that cooperates with deep packet inspection (DPI) services to apply SDN based prioritization and route selection to application flows. A specific application of this concept to VoIP and M2M communication in developed and demonstrated in [98], whereby it is shown that SDN can be used to proactively manage UDP/RTP media streams to enhance their service quality.

6.2 Intent-Based Traffic Management

Intent-based networking (IBN) is a relatively new concept in SDN for managing a network, end-to-end, through the use of DevOps and high-level "intents". The term IBN was first coined by Gartner in 2017, though components of intent-based networking began well before and continue to be developed by networking enterprises. Traditional networking relied on command line interface (CLI) to manually set up policies for all vendors' networking devices individually. The intent-based networking approach changes this to operate it as a Network-as-a-Service (NaaS), meaning it is end-to-end networking that seamlessly manages all devices on one interface. While similar to the principles of SDN, IBN differs by integrating DevOps into the process. This makes networking management a lifecycle process that, according to Cisco, "bridges the gap between business and IT."

As a simple example of IBN, consider an Intent whereby the network operator wants to ensure that the command and control (C&C) communications in the region receive uninterrupted service levels during combat (as shown in Fig. 15). The Translation of this would build a policy which guarantees that C&C users and applications are placed on a secure segment that receives the highest priority service. The Activation of this intent may apply priority-service levels between all users and applications on the C&C bearer segment across all network elements. The Assurance module will use telemetry to monitor and analyze the network against this desired outcome, to remediate, optimize, and correct as appropriate. In order for intent-based networking to achieve its full potential, these functions are applied across all networking domains and build on a programmable network infrastructure.

Intent-based networking is being incorporated into many of the emerging SDN platforms. Both the Open Networking Operating System (ONOS) and the Open-

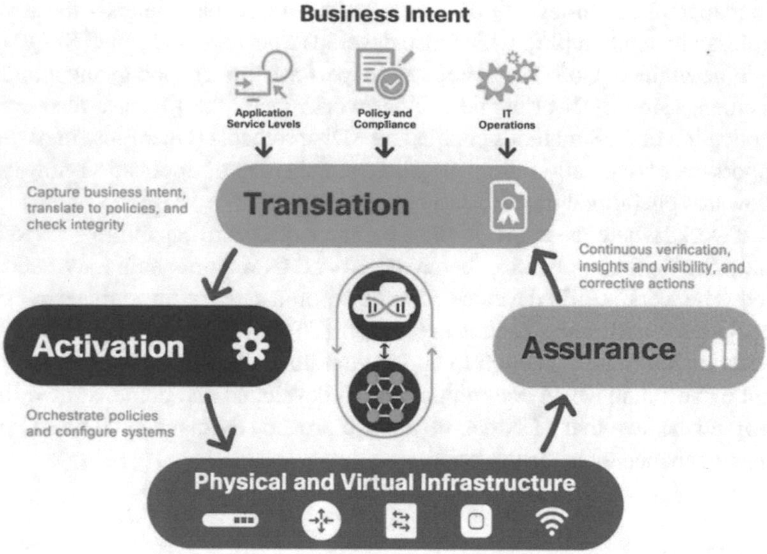

Business Intent

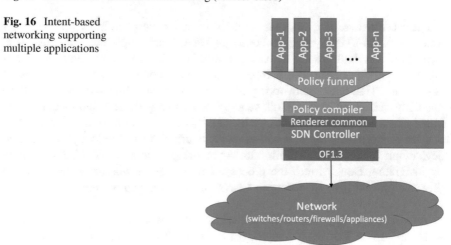

Fig. 15 Elements of intent-based networking (source: Cisco)

Fig. 16 Intent-based
networking supporting
multiple applications

DayLight (ODL) SDN controllers incorporate "intents". An example framework for intents is specified by Group Based policy (GBP), which has the concept of end-point groups (EPGs) so that policies can be applied to groups of entities based on their labels, and the policies themselves are contracts with "qualities" and "clauses".

One of the significant benefits of using high-level intents rather than low-level network configuration is that human errors are reduced. The high-level intents are automatically "compiled" by a policy compiler that translates the intents into network device configuration, which is pushed down to each network element. Further, multiple applications can co-exist without conflict; as shown in Fig. 16, application policies are taken through a policy funnel into a compiler that flags, and potentially automatically resolves, any conflicts in their policies. Apstra reports in [99] that IBN can be applied in a vendor- and technology-independent way, yielding a saving of seven cents per dollar revenue.

6.3 Context-Aware Traffic Management

Context-aware traffic management is emerging as an approach to address some of the gaps in SLA and intent-based methods. The SLA-aware method requires applications to specify their requirements, which can be very challenging especially when they are adaptive themselves. The intent-based methods also need to be aware of context, such as whether the network is operating in a friendly or hostile environment. The context-aware approach considers the "experience" of the application, couples that with the context, and takes reactive actions to rectify the problem.

This thinking is leading to the concept of a "self-driving network" [100] as depicted in Fig. 17, whereby the network is continually monitored using fine-grained telemetry, the collected data is analyzed in real-time, and appropriate intervention is done via programmable network interfaces to take an appropriate control action. Research work in [101] develops a framework for adjusting network behavior dynamically to adapt to application behavior and validates it via implementation on multiple SDN switches in [102]. Conceptually, both Self-driving networking and Intent-based networking aims at autonomic management of the network. However, intent-based networking consistently tunes the networking environment as per the user's feedback whereas, self-driving networking monitors the differences of the current and the desired network state and tunes the networking environment accordingly.

Google has demonstrated that it is able to adapt its traffic management across data centres [103], within a data centre [104, 105], and throughout its peering

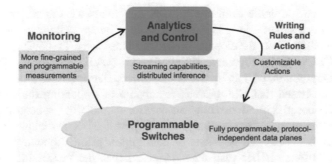

Fig. 17 Self-driving network with monitor-analyse-control loop [100]

locations [106] using dynamic application level measurements and fine-grained SDN control. Network operators are stymied in this effort due to lack of visibility into application performance, compounded by the increasing encryption of packets by application – however, new methods are being developed by a research team that use machine learning-based methods to identify applications [107] and infer experience [108], and further take corrective action reactively when application experience shows symptoms of degradation [109]. Moreover, QoS-aware traffic management is progressing towards this virtuous cycle of a self-aware network that constantly monitors application experience, makes inferences based on operator-supplied intents combines with contextual information, and then enforces control into the programmable network substrate in an automated manner.

7 Policy Evaluation

There are different ways to evaluate the efficiency of SDN-based policies such as empirical, emulation and simulation. Empirical analysis refers to an evidence-based approach that relies on real-world implementation and results. From the perspective of SDN, empirical analysis is an essential. However, since an SDN environment incorporates numerous entities interacting with each other across control, data and application plane, the real-world implementation of SDN for research is costly. Moreover, modification of any entity in real-world implementation is tedious. In this case, emulation or simulation can be adopted for approximate imitation of SDN-based operations. Emulation duplicates the behavior of the real system whereas simulation mimics the behavior but does not offer the exact matching. In the following subsections, the recent practices on empirical, emulation and simulation-based analysis of SDN operations are discussed.

7.1 *Empirical*

There has been a notable initiative in SDN that focuses on empirical evaluation of policies. For example, in [110], a small-scale software defined cloud datacenter named CLOUDS-Pi is developed. To enable Raspberry Pi devices as network switches, CLOUDS-Pi augments Open vSwitch (OVS) with each of them and uses OpenDaylight (ODL) as the SDN controllers. Through use case study, it has also been illustrated that CLOUDS-Pi is capable of evaluating the performances of any SDN-based virtual machine management and flow scheduling policies. In another work [111], the performance of seven SDN switches (as noted in Table 5) are benchmarked in terms of throughput, priority queuing, flow tables and packet buffers. It has also been observed that the processing time of the switches is predictable and is aligned with the line rate. Moreover, in [112], a publicly available bug repository for OpenDaylight SDN controller is mined

Table 5 Specifications of the investigated switches [111]

Switch	ASIC	CPU	Firmware (release date)
HP E3800	HPE ProVision	Freescale P2020	KA.16.04.0016 (2018-06-22)
HP 2920	HPE ProVision	Tri Core ARM1176	WB.16.08.0001 (2018-11-28)
Dell S3048-ON	Broadcom StrataXGS	undisclosed	DellOS 9.14 (2018-07-13)
Dell S4048-ON	undisclosed	undisclosed	DellOS 9.14 (2018-07-13)
Pica8 P3290	Broadcom Firebolt 3	Freescale MPC8541CDS	PicOS 2.10.2 (2018-01-19)
Pica8 P3297	Broadcom Triumph 2	Freescale P2020	PicOS 2.11.19 (2019-02-27)
NEC PF5240	Undisclosed	Undisclosed	OS-F3PA6.0.0.0 (2014-06)

to localize the most problematic software components and model the stochastic behavior of bug manifestation. Later, the information is applied to improve the dependability of different components such as core controller functions, embedded applications, plug-ins, and drivers in the control plane. Furthermore, the effect of strong and eventual consistency constraints on scalability and correctness of control plane is investigated in [113]. It has also evaluated an adaptive consistency model that improves the request handling throughput and response time of controllers. However, because of large-scale and sophisticated deployment of SDN components, the arrangement of empirical analysis in battlefield communication is often regarded as infeasible.

7.2 Emulation

As noted, military tactical networks require to support mission-critical operations in the austere environment by going beyond the mobility, intermittent link state, and variable bandwidth-related issues. In real-world SDN environments, the manifestation of such dynamic configurations for research purpose is extremely challenging. Therefore, it is widely adopted to imitate military tactical networks using different emulation tools such as Emane [114], Mininet [115] and Core [116]. An emulator simultaneously captures the characteristics of tactical communications and integrates SDN methodologies to assess different control and management policies over an imitated military tactical network [117]. Figure 18 depicts how emulators can be augmented in node-to-node communications.

Among the SDN emulators, Mininet is the most popular. In the literature, Mininet has been adopted to evaluate policies for deploying SDN controllers [68], enhancing controller's adaptivity [69], automating distributed firewalls [72], managing data flow [73], augmenting Named Data Networking (NDN) [118] and creating inte-

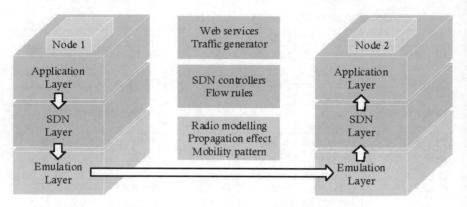

Fig. 18 Node to node communication within an emulated tactical SDN [117]

grated SDN environments [119] in tactical networks. Mininet is lightweight, boots faster and offers higher scalability. However, it is difficult to employ Mininet for dealing with non-Linux-compatible OpenFlow switches or applications.

Extendable Mobile Ad-hoc Network Emulator (Emane) is another celebrated emulator for tactical networks which has been used in [120–122] and [123] to evaluate various policies for group-based communications, latency-aware queuing control, situation-aware publish subscribe model and mission-centric content sharing respectively. Emane incorporates more detailed radio models that simplify the emulation of MANET, although it lacks an accurate interference model based on Signal-to-Interference-and-Noise-Ratio (SINR) and extensive libraries for imitating complex scenarios in SDN environments.

There exists another emulator named Common Open Research Emulator (CORE) that has been used in evaluating policies for delay tolerant routing [124], data and control plane security management [125], and disruption-tolerant networking [126]. CORE offers highly customizable programming interfaces that simplifies its augmentation with other emulators including Emane. However, it lacks facilities for distributed emulation. Apart from Emane, Mininet and Core, there exists another emulator named Containernet which has been used in [127] for hybrid service function chaining.

7.3 Simulation

The existing emulators for SDN mainly focus on network resources management and provide a very limited scope to apply application and computing resource-level management techniques such as service placement and resource consolidation. To address this issue, different simulators such as OPNET, NetSim and CloudSim-SDN are used in SDN-based policy evaluation. Among them, OPNET is used in [128] for simulating data distribution in a tactical network. In [129] and [130], OPNET is also

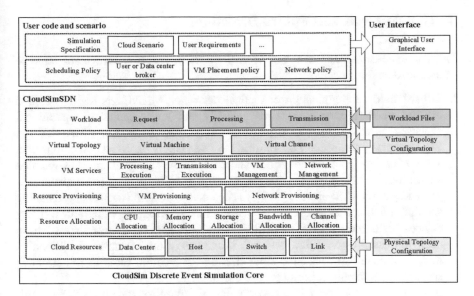

Fig. 19 Overview of CloudSim-SDN

adopted to evaluate a cooperative trust scheme and QoS-aware routing policy for military communications respectively. Although OPNET provides a set of extensive libraries for detailed networking models, it lacks support for customization.

Like OPNET, NetSim is used in simulating different network and application management scenarios. For example, in [131], a hybrid routing policy for MANET and in [132], an intrusion detection framework for military communication is evaluated through NetSim. One of the main advantages of NetSim is that it can simulate the functions of a wide range of networking devices. On the other hand, the operations of NetSim are handled by a single event queue that often resists the modeling of complex scenarios. Similar to NetSim, CloudSim-SDN is another discrete event simulator [8]. It has been developed by the Cloud Computing and Distributed Systems (CLOUDS) Laboratory, University of Melbourne. As noted in Fig. 19, CloudSim-SDN runs on top the basic CloudSim simulator [133] that allows users to model both physical and virtual topology, and application scenarios [134]. Using this feature of CloudSim, different simulators for other computing paradigms for example iFogSim [135] and MR-CloudSim [136] have also been developed. However, using CloudSim-SDN, a user can either utilize built-in resource management and scheduling policies or can develop their own by extending the abstract interfaces. As a means of policy evaluator, CloudSim-SDN has been used in [137] that focuses on latency-aware network function provisioning. It has also been adopted for simulating elastic service function chaining [138] and energy-efficient network optimization [139] policies. However, the current version of CloudSim-SDN lacks supports for handling the dynamics of tactical network but there is always a potential scope to augment them in CloudSim-SDN.

8   Gap Analysis and Future Directions

The lessons learned and the gaps identified from the literature study can be summarized as follows:

1. In battlefield communication or tactical networks, MANET is highly adopted because of its flexibility, ease of mobility and lower capital or operational expenses. However, the convergence of multi-bearer networking, MANET and SDN, specially for military operations, has been barely explored in the literature.

2. The device-level interactions and connectivity at the data plane of SDN-enabled tactical networks is unpredictable and unreliable. Military devices also have limited energy supply to operate [140]. In such cases, dynamic network partitioning and fault tolerance techniques can be useful in supporting the vulnerable military devices losing connections with the controllers. However, these aspects have been addressed by very few research initiatives in the literature. Additionally, there is a significant lack for emulation and simulation tools to imitate such scenarios specifically for military use cases.

3. Inherently, the controller is a single point of failure for the entire SDN architecture. To deal with this issue, the concept of multi controllers in SDN has been developed. However, the existing East–West communication mechanisms between the controllers still follow the traditional centralized architecture and cannot ensure robust spanning of network through flat controller orientation. Moreover, the Northbound and Southbound interfaces for multi-controller SDN architectures are currently poorly defined and hinder the real-time integration of the management systems and the peer-level networks. These constraints affect the multi-domain communications, slice management and intent-based networking in tactical environments, especially when one ground military device sends information to an aerial or submerged military device. To address such scenarios, efficient multi-controller orchestration policies must be developed according to the requirements of battlefield communications.

4. The subordinates of a tactical network are hierarchically arranged. At lower levels, line-of-sight connectivity is operated by distributed wireless mesh (MANETs). Multiple MANETs can also coexist at this level with thin Inter-MANET connectivity. At the mid hierarchical levels, satellite communication techniques are harnessed, whereas a mix of terrestrial wireless, SATCOM and wireline connectivity is exploited at the higher levels of the tactical network. Most of the mechanisms are well suited for legacy network and provide a narrow scope to integrate SDN functionalities. In the literature, there is also a significant lack in building interoperability among MANET, terrestrial wireless, and satellite communication techniques, especially through SDN middleware.

5. A wide range of traffic from real-time (e.g. situation and location-aware dissemination) to elastic (e.g. audio or video files) is generated during battlefield communication. This traffic can be both unidirectional and bidirectional between mobile (e.g. tanks and submarine) and fixed entities (e.g. ground stations). To meet QoS requirements under such diverse circumstances, different sophisticated

and adaptive traffic management schemes are required for tactical networks. These schemes should also support the analysis of ingress/egress packets and the appropriate selection of differentiated services and network slices. On the other hand, the efficiency of these schemes is highly subjected to the QoS requirements of the SDN-enabled applications and the security concerns of the battlefield communications. However, in the literature, the quantification of QoS parameters and security classifications with respect to tactical networks and the management of traffic in accordance are narrowly explored.

6. As noted, intent-based networking allows users and operators to define their service expectations from the network and simultaneously creates the desired networking state for meeting those expectations. The ultimate goal of intent-based networking is to reduce the complexities of enforcing various network management policies. However, the augmentation of intent-based networking with traditional SDN architecture requires a comprehensive synthesis of artificial intelligence (AI), network automation and machine learning (ML). On the other hand, autonomic network management depends on four different aspects: (*i*) Self-configuration: configures the network components (e.g. nodes and bandwidth), (*ii*) Self-healing: treats the faults and adapts with the dynamics, (*iii*) Self-optimization: enhances performance of the networking components, (*iv*) Self-protection: protects from the security attack. Nevertheless, in the literature, these essential aspects of intent-based networking have not been fully investigated with respect to tactical networks.

9 Summary

The concept of SDN is gradually attracting attention in military use cases. However, the adoption of SDN in tactical network is subjected to diverse challenges with respect to interoperability, distributed application, unpredictable service demand, security constraints and edge computation. Although there exist a notable number of works on the literature aiming at addressing these challenges, they have certain limitations and compatibility issues with existing tactical communication standards such as MBN and MANET. In this work, we reviewed such research initiatives that primarily focus on the SDN-based network orchestration problem in the tactical environments. We proposed a taxonomy to categorize the existing solutions systematically and determined the research gaps for further improvement in this domain.

Acknowledgments This work was supported by the Next Generation Technologies Fund, managed by the Defence Science and Technology Group, the Department of Defence, Australian Government. The authors would also like to thank Shashikant Ilager and Muhammed Tawfiqul Islam for discussions and comments on improving the paper.

References

1. Afrin, M., Razzaque, M., Anjum, I., Hassan, M.M., Alamri, A., et al.: Tradeoff between user quality-of-experience and service provider profit in 5g cloud radio access network. Sustainability **9**(11) (2017) 2127
2. Mahmud, R., Ramamohanarao, K., Buyya, R.: Edge affinity-based management of applications in fog computing environments. In: Proceedings of the 12th IEEF/ACM International Conference on Utility and Cloud Computing. UCC '19, New York, NY, USA, ACM (2019) 1–10
3. Adedayo, A.O., Twala, B.: Qos functionality in software defined network. In: 2017 International Conference on Information and Communication Technology Convergence (ICTC), IEEE (2017) 693–699
4. Mahmud, R., Ramamohanarao, K., Buyya, R.: Latency-aware application module management for fog computing environments. ACM Trans. Internet Technol. **19**(1) (November 2018) 9:1–9:21
5. Thottan, M., Di Martino, C., Kim, Y.J., Atkinson, G., Choi, N., Mohanasamy, N., Jagadeesan, L., Mendiratta, V., Simsarian, J.E., Kozicki, B.: The network os: Carrier-grade sdn control of multi-domain, multi-layer networks. Bell Labs Technical Journal **24** (2019) 1–26
6. Grønsund, P., Gonzalez, A., Mahmood, K., Nomeland, K., Pitter, J., Dimitriadis, A., Berg, T.K., Gelardi, S.: 5g service and slice implementation for a military use case. In: 2020 IEEE International Conference on Communications Workshops (ICC Workshops), IEEE (2020) 1–6
7. Mahmud, R., Srirama, S.N., Ramamohanarao, K., Buyya, R.: Profit-aware application placement for integrated fog–cloud computing environments. Journal of Parallel and Distributed Computing **135** (2020) 177–190
8. Son, J., Dastjerdi, A.V., Calheiros, R.N., Ji, X., Yoon, Y., Buyya, R.: Cloudsimsdn: Modeling and simulation of software-defined cloud data centers. In: 2015 15th IEEE/ACM International Symposium on Cluster, Cloud and Grid Computing, IEEE (2015) 475–484
9. Afrin, M., Mahmud, R.: Software defined network-based scalable resource discovery for internet of things. EAI Endorsed Transactions on Scalable Information Systems **4**(14) (2017)
10. Gkioulos, V., Gunleifsen, H., Weldehawaryat, G.K.: A systematic literature review on military software defined networks. Future Internet **10**(9) (2018) 88
11. Mahmud, R., Toosi, A.N., Ramamohanarao, K., Buyya, R.: Context-aware placement of industry 4.0 applications in fog computing environments. IEEE Transactions on Industrial Informatics **16**(11) (2020) 7004–7013
12. Mahmud, R., Ramamohanarao, K., Buyya, R.: Application management in fog computing environments: A taxonomy, review and future directions. ACM Comput. Surv. **53**(4) (July 2020)
13. Afrin, M., Mahmud, M.R., Razzaque, M.A.: Real time detection of speed breakers and warning system for on-road drivers. In: 2015 IEEE International WIE Conference on Electrical and Computer Engineering (WIECON-ECE). (Dec 2015) 495–498
14. Afrin, M., Jin, J., Rahman, A., Tian, Y.C., Kulkarni, A.: Multi-objective resource allocation for edge cloud based robotic workflow in smart factory. Future Generation Computer Systems **97** (2019) 119–130
15. Mahmud, R., Koch, F.L., Buyya, R.: Cloud-fog interoperability in iot-enabled healthcare solutions. In: Proceedings of the 19th International Conference on Distributed Computing and Networking. ICDCN '18, New York, NY, USA, ACM (2018) 32:1–32:10
16. Patil, P., Gokhale, A., Hakiri, A.: Bootstrapping software defined network for flexible and dynamic control plane management. In: Proceedings of the 2015 1st IEEE Conference on Network Softwarization (NetSoft), IEEE (2015) 1–5
17. Bentstuen, O.I., Flathagen, J.: On bootstrapping in-band control channels in software defined networks. In: 2018 IEEE International Conference on Communications Workshops (ICC Workshops), IEEE (2018) 1–6

18. Sakic, E., Avdic, M., Van Bemten, A., Kellerer, W.: Automated bootstrapping of a fault-resilient in-band control plane. In: Proceedings of the Symposium on SDN Research. (2020) 1–13
19. Bannour, F., Souihi, S., Mellouk, A.: Distributed sdn control: Survey, taxonomy, and challenges. IEEE Communications Surveys & Tutorials **20**(1) (2018) 333–354
20. Killi, B.P.R., Reddy, E.A., Rao, S.V.: Cooperative game theory based network partitioning for controller placement in sdn. In: 2018 10th International Conference on Communication Systems & Networks (COMSNETS), IEEE (2018) 105–112
21. Chen, W., Chen, C., Jiang, X., Liu, L.: Multi-controller placement towards sdn based on louvain heuristic algorithm. IEEE Access **6** (2018) 49486–49497
22. Tran, J.A., Ramachandran, G.S., Danilov, C.B., Krishnamachari, B.: An evaluation of consensus latency in partitioning networks. In: MILCOM 2019-2019 IEEE Military Communications Conference (MILCOM), IEEE (2019) 853–858
23. Anadiotis, A.C.G., Milardo, S., Morabito, G., Palazzo, S.: Toward unified control of networks of switches and sensors through a network operating system. IEEE Internet of Things Journal **5**(2) (2018) 895–904
24. Giorgetti, A., Sgambelluri, A., Casellas, R., Morro, R., Campanella, A., Castoldi, P.: Control of open and disaggregated transport networks using the open network operating system (onos). IEEE/OSA Journal of Optical Communications and Networking **12**(2) (2019) A171–A181
25. Hu, H., Wang, Z., Cheng, G., Wu, J.: Mnos: a mimic network operating system for software defined networks. IET Information Security **11**(6) (2017) 345–355
26. Jo, H., Nam, J., Shin, S.: Nosarmor: Building a secure network operating system. Security and Communication Networks **2018** (2018)
27. Shaghaghi, A., Kanhere, S.S., Kaafar, M.A., Jha, S.: Gwardar: Towards protecting a software-defined network from malicious network operating systems. In: 2018 IEEE 17th International Symposium on Network Computing and Applications (NCA), IEEE (2018) 1–5
28. Riggio, R., Khan, S.N., Subramanya, T., Yahia, I.G.B., Lopez, D.: Lightmano: Converging nfv and sdn at the edges of the network. In: NOMS 2018-2018 IEEE/IFIP Network Operations and Management Symposium, IEEE (2018) 1–9
29. Sunyaev, A.: Middleware. In: Internet Computing. Springer (2020) 125–154
30. Xiong, F., Li, A., Wang, H., Tang, L.: An sdn-mqtt based communication system for battlefield uav swarms. IEEE Communications Magazine **57**(8) (2019) 41–47
31. Park, J.H., Kim, H.S., Kim, W.T.: Dm-mqtt: An efficient mqtt based on sdn multicast for massive iot communications. Sensors **18**(9) (2018) 3071
32. Tamri, R., Rakrak, S.: The efficient network interoperability in iot through distributed software-defined network with mqtt. In: International Conference Europe Middle East & North Africa Information Systems and Technologies to Support Learning, Springer (2019) 286–291
33. Shieh, C.S., Yan, J.Y., Gu, H.X.: Sdn-based management framework for iot. International Journal of Computer Theory and Engineering **11**(1) (2019)
34. Dinculeană, D., Cheng, X.: Vulnerabilities and limitations of mqtt protocol used between iot devices. Applied Sciences **9**(5) (2019) 848
35. Dizdarević, J., Carpio, F., Jukan, A., Masip-Bruin, X.: A survey of communication protocols for internet of things and related challenges of fog and cloud computing integration. ACM Computing Surveys (CSUR) **51**(6) (2019) 1–29
36. Llorens-Carrodeguas, A., Cervello-Pastor, C., Leyva-Pupo, I.: A data distribution service in a hierarchical sdn architecture: Implementation and evaluation. In: 2019 28th International Conference on Computer Communication and Networks (ICCCN), IEEE (2019) 1–9
37. Yun, S., Park, J.h., Kim, H.s., Kim, W.T.: Importance-aware sdn control mechanism for real-time data distribution services. In: 2018 International Conference on Information and Communication Technology Convergence (ICTC), IEEE (2018) 1113–1118

38. Vidal, I., Bellavista, P., Sanchez-Aguero, V., Garcia-Reinoso, J., Valera, F., Nogales, B., Azcorra, A.: Enabling multi-mission interoperable uas using data-centric communications. Sensors 18(10) (2018) 3421

39. Talaminos-Barroso, A., Estudillo-Valderrama, M.A., Roa, L.M., Reina-Tosina, J., Ortega-Ruiz, F.: A machine-to-machine protocol benchmark for ehealth applications–use case: Respiratory rehabilitation. Computer methods and programs in biomedicine 129 (2016) 1–11

40. Moon, J.H., Shine, Y.T.: A study of distributed sdn controller based on apache kafka. In: 2020 IEEE International Conference on Big Data and Smart Computing (BigComp), IEEE (2020) 44–47

41. Al Awadi, A.H.R.: Dual-layer sdn model for deploying and securing network forensic in distributed data center. Current Journal of Applied Science and Technology (2017) 1–11

42. Bloebaum, T.H., Johnsen, F.T.: Evaluating publish/subscribe approaches for use in tactical broadband networks. In: MILCOM 2015-2015 IEEE Military Communications Conference, IEEE (2015) 605–610

43. Yánez, W., Mahmud, R., Bahsoon, R., Zhang, Y., Buyya, R.: Data allocation mechanism for internet-of-things systems with blockchain. IEEE Internet of Things Journal 7(4) (2020) 3509–3522

44. Miguel, M.L., Penna, M.C., Jamhour, E., Pellenz, M.E.: A coap based control plane for software defined wireless sensor networks. Journal of Communications and Networks 19(6) (2017) 555–562

45. Miguel, M.L., Jamhour, E., Pellenz, M.E., Penna, M.C.: Sdn architecture for 6lowpan wireless sensor networks. Sensors 18(11) (2018) 3738

46. Benson, K.E., Wang, G., Venkatasubramanian, N., Kim, Y.J.: Ride: A resilient iot data exchange middleware leveraging sdn and edge cloud resources. In: 2018 IEEE/ACM Third International Conference on Internet-of-Things Design and Implementation (IoTDI), IEEE (2018) 72–83

47. Jahan, S., Rahman, M.S., Saha, S.: Application specific tunneling protocol selection for virtual private networks. In: 2017 International Conference on Networking, Systems and Security (NSysS), IEEE (2017) 39–44

48. Nguyen, T.T., Bonnet, C., Harri, J.: Sdn-based distributed mobility management for 5g networks. In: 2016 IEEE Wireless Communications and Networking Conference, IEEE (2016) 1–7

49. Wang, Y.C., Lin, Y.D., Chang, G.Y.: Sdn-based dynamic multipath forwarding for inter–data center networking. International Journal of Communication Systems 32(1) (2019) e3843

50. Zhang, K., Bi, J., Wang, Y., Zhou, J., Liu, Z.: Tunneling over ip based on match-action table in software defined networks. In: Proceedings of the 13th International Conference on Future Internet Technologies. (2018) 1–4

51. Yang, Z., Yeung, K.L.: Sdn candidate selection in hybrid ip/sdn networks for single link failure protection. IEEE/ACM Transactions on Networking 28(1) (2020) 312–321

52. Yi, B., Congxiao, B., Xing, L.: Flowlan: A non-tunneling distributed virtual network based on ipv6. In: 2016 IEEE Information Technology, Networking, Electronic and Automation Control Conference, IEEE (2016) 229–234

53. Ochiai, T., Matsueda, K., Kondo, T., Takano, H., Kimura, R., Sawai, R., Teraoka, F.: Moclis: A non-tunneling moving cell support protocol based on locator/id split for 5g system. In: 2018 IEEE International Conference on Communications (ICC), IEEE (2018) 1–7

54. Chen, J., Ye, Q., Quan, W., Yan, S., Do, P.T., Zhuang, W., Shen, X.S., Li, X., Rao, J.: Sdatp: An sdn-based adaptive transmission protocol for time-critical services. IEEE Network 34(3) (2019) 154–162

55. Geissler, S., Herrnleben, S., Bauer, R., Grigorjew, A., Zinner, T., Jarschel, M.: The power of composition: Abstracting a multi-device sdn data path through a single api. IEEE Transactions on Network and Service Management 17(2) (2019) 722–735

56. Conti, M., Kaliyar, P., Lal, C.: Censor: Cloud-enabled secure iot architecture over sdn paradigm. Concurrency and Computation: Practice and Experience 31(8) (2019) e4978

57. Municio, E., Balemans, N., Latré, S., Marquez-Barjal, J.: Leveraging distributed protocols for full end-to-end softwarization in iot networks. In: 2020 IEEE 17th Annual Consumer Communications & Networking Conference (CCNC), IEEE (2020) 1–6

58. Ma, P., You, J., Wang, J.: An efficient multipath routing schema in multi-homing scenario based on protocol-oblivious forwarding. Frontiers of Computer Science 14(4) (2020) 1–12

59. Jia, Z., Wang, J., Chen, X., Kang, L.: Enable device-aware flow control with enhanced protocol-oblivious forwarding (pof). In: 2019 IEEE 9th International Conference on Electronics Information and Emergency Communication (ICEIEC), IEEE (2019) 5–8

60. Li, M., Wang, X., Tong, H., Liu, T., Tian, Y.: Sparc: Towards a scalable distributed control plane architecture for protocol-oblivious sdn networks. In: 2019 28th International Conference on Computer Communication and Networks (ICCCN), IEEE (2019) 1–9

61. Mei, L., Tong, H., Liu, T., Tian, Y.: Psa: An architecture for proactively securing protocol-oblivious sdn networks. In: 2019 IEEE 9th International Conference on Electronics Information and Emergency Communication (ICEIEC), IEEE (2019) 1–6

62. Rotsos, C., Farshad, A., King, D., Hutchison, D., Zhou, Q., Gray, A.J., Wang, C.X., McLaughlin, S.: Reasonet: Inferring network policies using ontologies. In: 2018 4th IEEE Conference on Network Softwarization and Workshops (NetSoft), IEEE (2018) 159–167

63. Benayas, F., Carrera, Á., García-Amado, M., Iglesias, C.A.: A semantic data lake framework for autonomous fault management in sdn environments. Transactions on Emerging Telecommunications Technologies 30(9) (2019) e3629

64. Kim, S.I., Kim, H.S.: Semantic ontology-based nfv service modeling. In: 2018 Tenth International Conference on Ubiquitous and Future Networks (ICUFN), IEEE (2018) 674–678

65. Atoui, W.S., Yahia, I.G.B., Gaaloul, W.: Semantic-based global network view construction in software defined networks with multiple controllers. In: 2018 4th IEEE Conference on Network Softwarization and Workshops (NetSoft), IEEE (2018) 252–256

66. Tao, M., Ota, K., Dong, M.: Ontology-based data semantic management and application in iot-and cloud-enabled smart homes. Future generation computer systems 76 (2017) 528–539

67. Poularakis, K., Iosifidis, G., Tassiulas, L.: Sdn-enabled tactical ad hoc networks: Extending programmable control to the edge. IEEE Communications Magazine 56(7) (2018) 132–138

68. Liu, W., Hu, X., Yan, X.: Controller deployments based on qos guarantees in sdn-enabled tactical ad hoc networks. In: 2020 12th International Conference on Communication Software and Networks (ICCSN), IEEE (2020) 73–78

69. Poularakis, K., Qin, Q., Nahum, E.M., Rio, M., Tassiulas, L.: Flexible sdn control in tactical ad hoc networks. Ad Hoc Networks 85 (2019) 71–80

70. Suri, N., Hansson, A., Nilsson, J., Lubkowski, P., Marcus, K., Hauge, M., Lee, K., Buchin, B., Mısırhoğlu, L., Peuhkuri, M.: A realistic military scenario and emulation environment for experimenting with tactical communications and heterogeneous networks. In: 2016 International Conference on Military Communications and Information Systems (ICMCIS), IEEE (2016) 1–8

71. Zhao, Q., Du, P., Gerla, M., Brown, A.J., Kim, J.H.: Software defined multi-path tcp solution for mobile wireless tactical networks. In: MILCOM 2018-2018 IEEE Military Communications Conference (MILCOM), IEEE (2018) 1–9

72. Logan, B.E., Xie, G.G.: Automating distributed firewalls: A case for software defined tactical networks. In: MILCOM 2019-2019 IEEE Military Communications Conference (MILCOM), IEEE (2019) 1–6

73. Zwane, S., Tarwireyi, P., Adigun, M.: A flow-based ids for sdn-enabled tactical networks. In: 2019 International Multidisciplinary Information Technology and Engineering Conference (IMITEC), IEEE (2019) 1–6

74. Zacarias, I., Schwarzrock, J., Gaspary, L.P., Kohl, A., Fernandes, R.Q., Stocchero, J.M., de Freitas, E.P.: Enhancing mobile military surveillance based on video streaming by employing software defined networks. Wireless Communications and Mobile Computing 2018 (2018)

75. Chen, K., Lv, N., Zhao, S., Wang, X., Zhao, J.: A scheme for improving the communications efficiency between the control plane and data plane of the sdn-enabled airborne tactical network. IEEE Access **6** (2018) 37286–37301

76. Śliwa, J.: Sdn and nvf in support for making military networks more survivable. In: 2019 International Conference on Military Communications and Information Systems (ICMCIS), IEEE (2019) 1–6

77. Zhou, D., Yan, Z., Liu, G., Atiquzzaman, M.: An adaptive network data collection system in sdn. IEEE Transactions on Cognitive Communications and Networking **6**(2) (2019) 562–574

78. Priyadarsini, M., Mukherjee, J.C., Bera, P., Kumar, S., Jakaria, A., Rahman, M.A.: An adaptive load balancing scheme for software-defined network controllers. Computer Networks **164** (2019) 106918

79. Toosi, A.N., Mahmud, R., Chi, Q., Buyya, R.: 4. In: Management and Orchestration of Network Slices in 5G, Fog, Edge, and Clouds. John Wiley & Sons, Ltd (2019) 79–101

80. Marinova, S., Rakovic, V., Denkovski, D., Lin, T., Atanasovski, V., Bannazadeh, H., Gavrilovska, L., Leon-Garcia, A.: End-to-end network slicing for flash crowds. IEEE Communications Magazine **58**(4) (2020) 31–37

81. Hao, Y., Jiang, Y., Hossain, M.S., Ghoneim, A., Yang, J., Humar, I.: Data-driven resource management in a 5g wearable network using network slicing technology. IEEE Sensors Journal **19**(19) (2018) 8379–8386

82. Singh, S.K., Salim, M.M., Cha, J., Pan, Y., Park, J.H.: Machine learning-based network sub-slicing framework in a sustainable 5g environment. Sustainability **12**(15) (2020) 6250

83. Cunha, V.A., da Silva, E., de Carvalho, M.B., Corujo, D., Barraca, J.P., Gomes, D., Granville, L.Z., Aguiar, R.L.: Network slicing security: Challenges and directions. Internet Technology Letters **2**(5) (2019) e125

84. Hawilo, H., Jammal, M., Shami, A.: Network function virtualization-aware orchestrator for service function chaining placement in the cloud. IEEE Journal on Selected Areas in Communications **37**(3) (2019) 643–655

85. Sun, G., Li, Y., Yu, H., Vasilakos, A.V., Du, X., Guizani, M.: Energy-efficient and traffic-aware service function chaining orchestration in multi-domain networks. Future Generation Computer Systems **91** (2019) 347–360

86. Tajiki, M.M., Salsano, S., Chiaraviglio, L., Shojafar, M., Akbari, B.: Joint energy efficient and qos-aware path allocation and vnf placement for service function chaining. IEEE Transactions on Network and Service Management **16**(1) (2018) 374–388

87. Sallam, G., Gupta, G.R., Li, B., Ji, B.: Shortest path and maximum flow problems under service function chaining constraints. In: IEEE INFOCOM 2018-IEEE Conference on Computer Communications, IEEE (2018) 2132–2140

88. Sun, G., Xu, Z., Yu, H., Chen, X., Chang, V., Vasilakos, A.V.: Low-latency and resource-efficient service function chaining orchestration in network function virtualization. IEEE Internet of Things Journal (2019)

89. Sanz, I.J., Mattos, D.M.F., Duarte, O.C.M.B.: Sfcperf: An automatic performance evaluation framework for service function chaining. In: NOMS 2018-2018 IEEE/IFIP Network Operations and Management Symposium, IEEE (2018) 1–9

90. Compastié, M., Badonnel, R., Festor, O., He, R., Kassi-Lahlou, M.: Unikernel-based approach for software-defined security in cloud infrastructures. In: NOMS 2018-2018 IEEE/IFIP Network Operations and Management Symposium, IEEE (2018) 1–7

91. Compastié, M., Badonnel, R., Festor, O., He, R.: A tosca-oriented software-defined security approach for unikernel-based protected clouds. In: 2019 IEEE Conference on Network Softwarization (NetSoft), IEEE (2019) 151–159

92. Ventre, P.L., Lungaroni, P., Siracusano, G., Pisa, C., Schmidt, F., Lombardo, F., Salsano, S.: On the fly orchestration of unikernels: Tuning and performance evaluation of virtual infrastructure managers. IEEE Transactions on Cloud Computing (2018)

93. Mahmud, R., Srirama, S.N., Ramamohanarao, K., Buyya, R.: Quality of experience (qoe)-aware placement of applications in fog computing environments. Journal of Parallel and Distributed Computing **132** (2019) 190 – 203

94. Skorin-Kapov, L., Varela, M., Hoßfeld, T., Chen, K.T.: A survey of emerging concepts and challenges for qoe management of multimedia services. ACM Transactions on Multimedia Computing, Communications, and Applications (TOMM) **14**(2s) (2018) 1–29

95. Mirashe, S.P., Kalyankar, N.: Quality of service with bandwidth. arXiv preprint arXiv:1003.4073 (2010)

96. Li, G., Wu, J., Li, J., Zhou, Z., Guo, L.: Sla-aware fine-grained qos provisioning for multi-tenant software-defined networks. IEEE access **6** (2017) 159–170

97. Jeong, S., Lee, D., Hyun, J., Li, J., Hong, J.W.K.: Application-aware traffic engineering in software-defined network. In: 2017 19th Asia-Pacific Network Operations and Management Symposium (APNOMS), IEEE (2017) 315–318

98. Ohms, J., Gebauer, O., Kotelnikova, N., Wermser, D.: Qos in software-defined networking-concepts and experiences. Mobilkommunikation: Technologien und Anwendungen

99. Ratkovic, A.L., Thambidurai, J., Kulkin, M.: Intent-based analytics (August 25 2020) US Patent 10,756,983.

100. Feamster, N., Gupta, A., Rexford, J., Willinger, W.: Nsf workshop on measurements for self-driving networks. In: Workshop on Measurements for Self-Driving Networks was held at Princeton University on April. Volume 4. (2019) 5

101. Zinner, T., Jarschel, M., Blenk, A., Wamser, F., Kellerer, W.: Dynamic application-aware resource management using software-defined networking: Implementation prospects and challenges. In: 2014 IEEE Network Operations and Management Symposium (NOMS), IEEE (2014) 1–6

102. Durner, R., Blenk, A., Kellerer, W.: Performance study of dynamic qos management for openflow-enabled sdn switches. In: 2015 IEEE 23rd International Symposium on Quality of Service (IWQoS), IEEE (2015) 177–182

103. Jain, S., Kumar, A., Mandal, S., Ong, J., Poutievski, L., Singh, A., Venkata, S., Wanderer, J., Zhou, J., Zhu, M., et al.: B4: Experience with a globally-deployed software defined wan. ACM SIGCOMM Computer Communication Review **43**(4) (2013) 3–14

104. Moshref, M., Yu, M., Govindan, R., Vahdat, A.: Dream: dynamic resource allocation for software-defined measurement. In: Proceedings of the 2014 ACM conference on SIGCOMM. (2014) 419–430

105. Kumar, A., Jain, S., Naik, U., Raghuraman, A., Kasinadhuni, N., Zermeno, E.C., Gunn, C.S., Ai, J., Carlin, B., Amarandei-Stavila, M., et al.: Bwe: Flexible, hierarchical bandwidth allocation for wan distributed computing. In: Proceedings of the 2015 ACM Conference on Special Interest Group on Data Communication. (2015) 1–14

106. Yap, K.K., Motiwala, M., Rahe, J., Padgett, S., Holliman, M., Baldus, G., Hines, M., Kim, T., Narayanan, A., Jain, A., et al.: Taking the edge off with espresso: Scale, reliability and programmability for global internet peering. In: Proceedings of the Conference of the ACM Special Interest Group on Data Communication. (2017) 432–445

107. Gharakheili, H.H., Lyu, M., Wang, Y., Kumar, H., Sivaraman, V.: itelescope: Softwarized network middle-box for real-time video telemetry and classification. IEEE Transactions on Network and Service Management **16**(3) (2019) 1071–1085

108. Madanapalli, S.C., Gharakheili, H.H., Sivaraman, V.: Inferring netflix user experience from broadband network measurement. In: 2019 Network Traffic Measurement and Analysis Conference (TMA), IEEE (2019) 41–48

109. Madanapalli, S.C., Gharakheili, H.H., Sivaraman, V.: Assisting delay and bandwidth sensitive applications in a self-driving network. In: Proceedings of the 2019 Workshop on Network Meets AI & ML. (2019) 64–69

110. Toosi, A.N., Son, J., Buyya, R.: Clouds-pi: A low-cost raspberry-pi based micro data center for software-defined cloud computing. IEEE Cloud Computing **5**(5) (2018) 81–91

111. Van Bemten, A., Đerić, N., Varasteh, A., Blenk, A., Schmid, S., Kellerer, W.: Empirical predictability study of sdn switches. In: 2019 ACM/IEEE Symposium on Architectures for Networking and Communications Systems (ANCS), IEEE (2019) 1–13

112. Vizarreta, P., Sakic, E., Kellerer, W., Machuca, C.M.: Mining software repositories for predictive modelling of defects in sdn controller. In: 2019 IFIP/IEEE Symposium on Integrated Network and Service Management (IM), IEEE (2019) 80–88

113. Sakic, E., Kellerer, W.: Impact of adaptive consistency on distributed sdn applications: An empirical study. IEEE Journal on Selected Areas in Communications **36**(12) (2018) 2702–2715

114. United States Naval Research Laboratory: Extendable mobile ad-hoc network emulator (emane) (https://www.nrl.navy.mil/itd/ncs/products/emane (accessed October 6, 2020))

115. Foundation, O.N.: Mininet (https://www.opennetworking.org/mininet/ (accessed October 6, 2020))

116. United States Naval Research Laboratory: Common open research emulator (core) (https://www.nrl.navy.mil/itd/ncs/products/core (accessed October 6, 2020))

117. Marcus, K.M., Chan, K.S., Hardy, R.L., Paul, L.Y.: An environment for tactical sdn experimentation. In: MILCOM 2018-2018 IEEE Military Communications Conference (MILCOM), IEEE (2018) 1–9

118. Campioni, L., Hauge, M., Landmark, L., Suri, N., Tortonesi, M.: Considerations on the adoption of named data networking (ndn) in tactical environments. In: 2019 International Conference on Military Communications and Information Systems (ICMCIS), IEEE (2019) 1–8

119. Zhao, Q., Brown, A.J., Kim, J.H., Gerla, M.: An integrated software-defined battlefield network testbed for tactical scenario emulation. In: MILCOM 2019-2019 IEEE Military Communications Conference (MILCOM), IEEE (2019) 373–378

120. Suri, N., Breedy, M.R., Marcus, K.M., Fronteddu, R., Cramer, E., Morelli, A., Campioni, L., Provosty, M., Enders, C., Tortonesi, M., et al.: Experimental evaluation of group communications protocols for data dissemination at the tactical edge. In: 2019 International Conference on Military Communications and Information Systems (ICMCIS), IEEE (2019) 1–8

121. Li, S.: Low latency queuing control in extendable mobile ad-hoc network emulator (emane). Master's Thesis (2019)

122. Johnsen, F.T., Bloebaum, T.H., Jansen, N., Bovet, G., Manso, M., Toth, A., Chan, K.: Evaluating publish/subscribe standards for situational awareness using realistic radio models and emulated testbed. International Command and Control Research and Technology Symposium (ICCRTS) proceedings (2019)

123. Strayer, T., Ramanathan, R., Coffin, D., Nelson, S., Atighetchi, M., Adler, A., Blais, S., Thapa, B., Tetteh, W., Shurbanov, V., et al.: Mission-centric content sharing across heterogeneous networks. In: 2019 International Conference on Computing, Networking and Communications (ICNC), IEEE (2019) 1034–1038

124. Dudukovich, R., Clark, G., Papachristou, C.: Evaluation of classifier complexity for delay tolerant network routing. In: 2019 IEEE Cognitive Communications for Aerospace Applications Workshop (CCAAW), IEEE (2019) 1–7

125. Singh, P.K., Kar, K.: Countering data and control plane attack on olsr using passive neighbor policing and inconsistency identification. In: Proceedings of the 15th ACM International Symposium on QoS and Security for Wireless and Mobile Networks. (2019) 19–28

126. Penning, A., Baumgärtner, L., Höchst, J., Sterz, A., Mezini, M., Freisleben, B.: Dtn7: An open-source disruption-tolerant networking implementation of bundle protocol 7. In: International Conference on Ad-Hoc Networks and Wireless, Springer (2019) 196–209

127. Peuster, M., Kampmeyer, J., Karl, H.: Containernet 2.0: A rapid prototyping platform for hybrid service function chains. In: 2018 4th IEEE Conference on Network Softwarization and Workshops (NetSoft), IEEE (2018) 335–337

128. Miletić, S., Đorđević, B., Ranđić, S., Vasić, A.: Impact hardware raid solutions at the data distribution on tactical integrated telecommunication and computer network. In: 2019 27th Telecommunications Forum (TELFOR), IEEE (2019) 1–4

129. Lim, J., Keum, D., Ko, Y.B.: A cooperative trust evaluation scheme for tactical wireless sensor networks. In: Proceedings of the 3rd International Conference on Software Engineering and Information Management. (2020) 183–187
130. Keum, D., Lim, J., Ko, Y.B.: Trust based multipath qos routing protocol for mission-critical data transmission in tactical ad-hoc networks. Sensors **20**(11) (2020) 3330
131. Bodra, S.P., et al.: Performance analysis of hybrid routing in manet with group mobility for search and rescue applications. In: Proceedings of International Conference on Wireless Communication, Springer (2020) 353–361
132. Rath, M., Pattanayak, B.K.: Prevention of replay attack using intrusion detection system framework. In: Progress in Advanced Computing and Intelligent Engineering. Springer (2019) 349–357
133. Calheiros, R.N., Ranjan, R., Beloglazov, A., De Rose, C.A., Buyya, R.: Cloudsim: a toolkit for modeling and simulation of cloud computing environments and evaluation of resource provisioning algorithms. Software: Practice and experience **41**(1) (2011) 23–50
134. Mahmud, M.R., Afrin, M., Razzaque, M.A., Hassan, M.M., Alelaiwi, A., Alrubaian, M.: Maximizing quality of experience through context-aware mobile application scheduling in cloudlet infrastructure. Software: Practice and Experience **46**(11) (2016) 1525–1545
135. Mahmud, R., Buyya, R.: 17. In: Modeling and Simulation of Fog and Edge Computing Environments Using iFogSim Toolkit. John Wiley & Sons, Ltd (2019) 433–465
136. Jung, J., Kim, H.: Mr-cloudsim: Designing and implementing mapreduce computing model on cloudsim. In: 2012 International Conference on ICT Convergence (ICTC), IEEE (2012) 504–509
137. Son, J., Buyya, R.: Latency-aware virtualized network function provisioning for distributed edge clouds. Journal of Systems and Software **152** (2019) 24–31
138. Toosi, A.N., Son, J., Chi, Q., Buyya, R.: Elasticsfc: Auto-scaling techniques for elastic service function chaining in network functions virtualization-based clouds. Journal of Systems and Software **152** (2019) 108–119
139. Jayanetti, A., Buyya, R.: J-opt: A joint host and network optimization algorithm for energy-efficient workflow scheduling in cloud data centers. In: Proceedings of the 12th IEEE/ACM International Conference on Utility and Cloud Computing. (2019) 199–208
140. Afrin, M., Jin, J., Rahman, A.: Energy-delay co-optimization of resource allocation for robotic services in cloudlet infrastructure. In: International Conference on Service-Oriented Computing, Springer (2018) 295–303

Mobility driven Cloud-Fog-Edge Framework for Location-Aware Services: A Comprehensive Review

Shreya Ghosh and Soumya K. Ghosh

Abstract With the pervasiveness of IoT devices, smart-phones and improvement of location-tracking technologies, huge volume of heterogeneous geo-tagged (location specific) data is generated facilitating several location-aware services. The analytics with this spatio-temporal (having location and time dimensions) datasets provide varied important services such as, smart transportation, emergency services (health-care, national defence or urban planning). While cloud paradigm is suitable for the capability of storage and computation, the major bottleneck is network connectivity loss. In time-critical application, where real-time response is required for emergency service-provisioning, such connectivity issues increases the latency and thus affects the overall quality of system (QoS). To overcome the issue, fog/edge topology is emerged, where partial computation is carried out in the edge of the network to reduce the delay in communication. Such fog/edge based system complements the cloud technology and extends the features of the system. This chapter discusses cloud-fog-edge based hierarchical collaborative framework, where several components are deployed to improve the QoS. On the other side mobility is another critical factor to enhance the efficacy of such location-aware service provisioning. Therefore, this chapter discusses the concerns and challenges associated with mobility-driven cloud-fog-edge based framework to provide several location-aware services to the end-users efficiently.

Keywords Mobility · Location-aware service · Cloud computing · Edge computing · Trajectory data analytics

S. Ghosh (✉) · S. K. Ghosh
Department of Computer Science and Engineering, Indian Institute of Technology (IIT) Kharagpur, Kharagpur, West Bengal, India
e-mail: shreya.cst@gmail.com; skg@cse.iitkgp.ac.in

1 Introduction

With the rapid development of sensor and communication technologies, GPS equipped devices and Internet of Things (IoT), varied objects such as people, resources, vehicles are interconnected and intertwined in anywhere at any time. Alongside, with the proliferation of mobile phone users and deployment of GPS enabled smart-devices, a huge amount of GPS traces of different geographical regions are easily available. This massive amount of GPS traces has fostered various research directions namely human movement behavior or activity learning [1–3] traffic analysis, improved route planning [4, 5] and resource allocation [6]— which subsequently lead to smart-living of people. While IoT provides seamless connectivity to correlate people and objects, cloud paradigm offers distributed platform to efficiently carry out the compute-intensive tasks. Furthermore, with the latest technology, smart mobile devices are emerging as varied application enablers for customized users' recommendation systems, e-health apps and intelligent route planner. Mobile cloud computing (MCC) promotes innovative solutions and approaches to leverage the computational and storage power of cloud computing and extend the applications and services to mobile phone users on demand basis. In recent times, IoST (Internet of Spatial Things) [7] has been emerged, which integrates IoT and spatio-temporal data. The analysis of spatio-temporal traces such as movement information, traffic data, weather information, help to incorporate context, and thus adds more intelligence in the processing.

In this direction, this chapter focuses on several aspects of mobility-aware cloud-fog-edge computing and we put forward the future research avenues and open challenges in this research domain. Figure 1 illustrates the overall architecture of the mobility-aware cloud-fog-edge network. As depicted, there are several applications, namely smart transportation system, smart mobility services, smart home etc. It

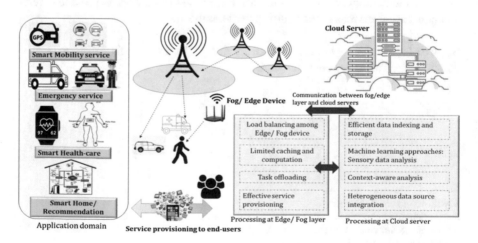

Fig. 1 Overall architecture of the mobility-aware cloud-fog-edge network

may be noted that when the user is in move, the seamless connectivity becomes a challenging issue which in turn increases the delay/service-provisioning time and affects the QoS. The subsequent increase in delay of delivering result may be fatal in case of emergency services such as ambulance or fire extinguisher car. On the other hand, mobility related information plays an important role [8]. If the optimal route (less congestion and distance) can be extracted a priori, then the service provisioning time can be reduced further. In this direction, the framework has three layers. In the bottom layer, the end-users are present. In the top-most layer, the compute-intensive tasks such as mobility-analysis, sensor-data mining and health-data analysis are carried out in distant cloud servers. The intermediate layers (Fog and edge layer) are used to cache processed information and communicate with the agents for fast delivery of the service. This chapter aims to provide a systematic survey focusing on different research aspects and existing works in all these layers (cloud-fog-edge). Furthermore, the chapter also highlights the challenging and interesting applications using this cloud/fog/edge networks. The major contributions of this chapter are summarized as follows:

1. A novel taxonomy based on the existing approaches and algorithms to provide mobility-aware services in the cloud-fog-edge hierarchical network is presented.
2. The data processing and machine learning techniques at fog/edge and cloud servers are systemically discussed.
3. A topology of varied applications and services provisioned by the hierarchical network is presented.
4. The open research challenges and issues are discussed to provision intelligent and efficient location-based services.

This survey will be beneficial for researchers, policymakers and can act as the foundation of mobility-driven cloud-fog-edge network.

2 Motivations and Related Computing Paradigms

In this section, we explain the motivation or utility of mobility-aware cloud-fog-edge framework, and briefly describe the definitions of cloud, fog, edge nodes and mobility-modelling. We also refer few use-cases where mobility-driven framework is necessary.

Owing to the huge amount of data generated from varied IoT devices, it is crucial to store, manage and analyse for extracting meaningful information from the datasets. Few examples of the datasets are movement data from vehicles, people; climatology parameters from the sensor nodes; or data collected from smart-home system. Cloud computing is the on-demand availability of computer system resources, and facilitates services over the Internet. It may be noted that most of the tech giants host cloud services and provides public cloud platforms, such as, Google Cloud Platform (GCP), Amazon EC2, Microsoft Azure, IBM Bluemix etc. In summary, this technology is beneficial for its flexibility, efficiency and on-demand service. The cloud servers or data-centers help to store this huge amount of historical records to analyse and find patterns. This in turn helps to facilitate applications such as smart and effective transportation, intelligent defence techniques or weather prediction. In addition, most of the times the accumulated data from the IoT or sensors are unstructured, and partial computation is required near the source of the data. Again, the IoT devices or sensors span a large geographical area, and sending data to distant cloud servers frequently affects the efficacy of the system as a whole. This gap is managed by the fog/edge computing. The fog/edge computing brings down the computing closer to the end-user or the devices where data has been collected, unlike carrying out all computations in the cloud data-centers. The users can get the storage or computing services at the edge of the network using this cloud-fog-edge collaborative framework.

Any network device with the capability of storage, computing, and connectivity can be used as fog/edge nodes. For instance, the routers, switches, video surveillance cameras etc. deployed at any location with a network connection. These nodes accumulate data and can partially compute, if required. The data processing is performed at the edge network [9], which consists of end devices, such as, mobile phone, border routers, bridges, set-top boxes, base stations, wireless access points etc. It may be noted that these must have necessary capabilities for supporting edge computation. In summary, edge computing provides faster responses, and also reduces the need of sending bulk data to the cloud datacenters. Integrating the edge and cloud paradigms, several new research topics have been emerged. Mobile Edge computing (MEC) and Mobile Cloud computing (MCC) are two prominent research areas in this domain. MEC is one of the key enablers of smart cellular base stations. It combines the capability of edge servers along with the cellular base stations [10]. The connection with the distant cloud server is optional in MEC. Moreover, researchers are working such that MEC can support 5G communication. In short, mobile edge computing aims to provide faster cellular services for the customers and thus, enhances network efficiency. On the other hand, now-a-days people tend to execute necessary tasks/application in their handheld devices. But these handheld devices are resource-hungry and have limited storage and computation capability. Hence, it is better to perform or offload compute intensive tasks outside the handheld devices. In such scenarios, mobile cloud computing plays an important role. The light-weight cloud servers *cloudlet* [11] are placed at the edge network. Like MEC, MCC combines the capability and features of cloud computing, mobile computing and wireless communication for better Quality of Experience (QoE) of the end-users.

However, there are few challenges in this collaborative framework. Firstly, how we can manage the fog/edge computing infrastructure and what resource allocation scheme can be adapted. Since, these fog/edge nodes have limited resources, proper resource management should be adapted when large number of service-requests are made at a particular instance. Moreover, several factors such as service availability, power or energy consumption [12], latency or delay should be considered while developing such framework. Therefore, the mapping of cloud/fog/edge nodes to several applications remains a challenging issue. Another critical part is security and privacy issues such as, trust management, access control etc. A proper security model based on the sensitivity of the datasets and requirements of the application is much needed in such cloud/fog/edge infrastructure.

There are several use-cases which utilize such cloud-fog-edge collaborative framework [13, 14]. The work *Mobi-IoST* (Mobility-aware Internet of Spatial Things) [8] illustrates an example of time-critical application, where latency or delay is very important and can be fatal. For instance, in an ambulance, continuous monitoring of patient's vital health parameters such as blood-pressure, pulse-rate, body-temperature etc. is required. These data are collected by IoT devices and the accumulated health data is sent to the nearby fog device through a client application. In this work, authors have used Road Side Units (RSU) as fog device, while the moving agent is the edge device. The preliminary checking of the health data is carried out in RSUs and in case any abnormality is detected, the data is sent to the cloud server. The cloud datacenter extracts the location of the ambulance, and redirects it towards the nearest health center. In the paper, authors have also emphasized the present state of the traffic is important, since the ambulance or any vehicle with patient needs to travel the roads with minimum congestion. Another work, named *Locator* [15], develops a hierarchical framework with cloud, edge, fog nodes to provide food delivery services in minimum delay. There are also several sub-domains of IoT, such as, Internet of Multimedia Things (IoMT), Internet of Health Things (IoHT) [16], Internet of Vehicles (IoV) etc. [7]. The work focusing on Internet of Health Thing using delay-aware fog network is mentioned in [17]. It may be noted that mobility or continuous change of locations of users or agents is a challenging, since connectivity may be lost. Therefore, analysing the movement patterns of users is important to enhance the quality of service. Mobility analytics is an integral part of developing an effective and delay-aware solution for any mission-critical or time-critical application.

In brief, after analysing the features of cloud-fog-edge computing, the challenges in this domain can be listed as follows.

- **Resource Management**: Since the fog and edge nodes have limited resources, it is difficult to assign large scale analytics in resource constrained nodes. Therefore, proper resource management modules should be developed to avoid this bottleneck. One aspect is adapting distributed fog/edge environment to cope up with the growing data amount. Also there must be specific policies to assign computational tasks and services among edge, fog and cloud nodes. Data visualization through web-interfaces are also not easy task through edge or fog nodes.
- **Mobility Sensitive**: Seamless connectivity due to the mobility of IoT devices is a critical concern for time-critical applications. The connection interruption and consequently the increase in delay affects the QoS. With the rapid use of mobile (smart) devices, the framework must be able to accommodate mobility data. How to analyse the huge amount of movement information and extract useful patterns are challenging tasks. Moreover, predicting next location-sequences of agents is also crucial, since it may help to take decision or offload task in the nearby

fog nodes. However, there are several factors such as, present traffic condition, users' own preferences and time of the movement etc. These external contexts make the location prediction task more difficult. On the other hand, mobility data is sensitive, and proper measures must be taken to secure the whereabouts of the users.

- **Security Aspect**: Fog or edge nodes are highly vulnerable to security attacks. Since these nodes handle and manage sensitive data (health related or mission critical, like Defence application), proper security measurements are must. Access control schemes, including, authenticated access to services and nodes, security algorithms are required in distributed paradigm like edge/Fog computing are hard to ensure. Again, strict implementation or methods of security mechanisms affect the quality of service of edge and fog computing.
- **Infrastructure or Organizational structure**: As mentioned, the framework has different types of components, like cloud servers, edge and fog nodes. Several objects like routers, access points can act as potential edge and fog computing infrastructure. Therefore, the processors of these components are quite different. Implement an end-to-end framework using different components is a really difficult task. It is absolutely necessary to select suitable devices based on operational requirements and execution environment. The resource configuration and location of the deployment are also two major factors to provide better service.

In the next part, we will discuss the taxonomy in varied aspects and briefly describe the existing literature in each of the aspects systematically.

3 Taxonomy: Cloud-Fog-Edge System

In this section, we discuss the taxonomy of Cloud-fog-edge collaborative system. For this taxonomy, we explore the system aspect and the associated challenges in this domain. Figure 2 shows the cloud-fog-edge system taxonomy, where we observe four broad aspects, such as, *infrastructure protocol*, *seamless connectivity*, *security issues* and *resource provisioning*.

3.1 Infrastructure Protocol

The cloud-fog-edge collaborative system has different challenges. Amongst them, few challenges are identified and discussed here.

As mentioned earlier, varied devices based on the requirement of the system can act as fog/edge nodes. In general, the fog/edge nodes are geographically-distributed. These are deployed at varied places, such as, shopping malls, roads, airport-terminals etc. These nodes are virtualized and have network connectivity

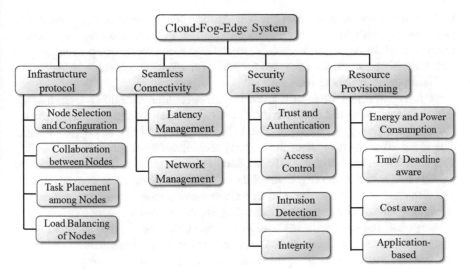

Fig. 2 Taxonomy of cloud-fog-edge system

along with storage and computation capabilities. Some of the works classify the nodes as micro/macro/nano-servers based on their physical size [18]. Zeng et al. [19] utilize fog server as computational and storage servers in a software-defined embedded system. In [8], authors use RSU as fog-device to communicate between end-user and cloud-data center, since the user is in move. Cloud-based services are extended using cloudlets [11, 20]. The authors present a methodology for user-cloudlet association to reduce the cost in fog computing [20]. The conventional base stations are used for data signal processing and connectivity [21]. Small cell base stations are also used as fog nodes.

The communication or collaboration among the nodes is an important aspect as well. Fog nodes can form a cluster and collaborate among them for execution of a task [22, 23]. These clusters are formed either the types of the nodes (homogeneity) or the location of the deployed nodes. Computational load balancing and functional sub-system development have the higher priority while forming the cluster. Although, this cluster based technique is effective for some cases, the static clusters become the bottleneck in scalability of the system. In summary, based on the requirement (computation, storage and cost) of the application, proper node selection is very important. Peer to Peer (P2P) collaboration among the nodes is another technique, which can be either hierarchical or flat order [24]. There are several types based on proximity, such as home, local, non-local. Anyway, reliability and access control are the issues associated with P2P. Master-slave is another technique in this node-collaboration [25].

Load balancing amongst these nodes are a challenging issue to prevent overloading of any particular node. A novel load balancing technique for edge data centers is presented in [26]. The authors in [27] propose dynamic edge selection to balance the loading of the nodes. Another work [28] explores the dynamic resource allocation and come up with an adaptive resource allocation scheme. The proposed method integrates utilization of bandwidth, computation resources by using dynamic load balancing. Oueis et al. [23] propose another dynamic load balancing technique by analysing the data flow in real-time.

In task-placement there is a trade-off between high capability infrastructure (cloud data centers) and connectivity issues. Several researchers have explored the cloud-edge topology [29], fog-to-cloud [30] or combined fog-cloud [31] system. The cloud-edge hybrid system for learning techniques has been proposed in [32]. The authors claim that the load variations in a neural network also should be considered for better efficacy. Each of the integrated system has its own advantages and disadvantages. It may be note that cloud servers have more computation and storage capabilities however, they are vulnerable to network connectivity lost issue. In such case, fog/edge nodes exhibit less network communication cost and better latency. Therefore, the time-critical applications such as, emergency services or defence applications should adapt such system, where real-time response can be made.

3.2 Connectivity

Seamless connectivity is a critical issue in enhancing the quality of service (QoS). Latency management consists of managing the service delivery time by an accepted temporal threshold. The temporal threshold is measured by the maximum latency of a service request or the requirement regarding QoS. Some researchers have emphasized on efficient collaboration technique such that execution can be made faster [23]. Zeng et al. [19] minimizes the computation and communication latency by task distribution. A low-latency Fog network has been presented in [33] for better latency management. The aim of all these works to select the node capable to provide service in minimum delay.

3.3 Security Issues

Security is a major concern as there are several communication between underlying network and cloud data-centers [34, 35].

Users authentication is one of the major aspect in fog/edge based systems. Here, the components follow "pay as you go" model, therefore, there is restricted access. There are various methods, like, *user authentication*, *device authentication*, *data migration authentication and instance authentication* [36]. Since the data are collected from end-users in most of the cases, proper privacy assurance is required [22].

The encryption in the fog/edge nodes is also required, since the data is send to cloud datacenters from fog/edge devices. Aazam et al. [37] has appended a data encryption layer in their system architecture for encryption. As fog/edge nodes have limited resources, it is difficult to manage large concurrent service-requests. Here, *Denial-of-Service (DoS)* is critical since it affects the system throughput at a large margin. Intrusion detection method is required to prevent such DoS attack. A work [38] propose a cloudlet mesh based security framework to detect such intrusion on cloud and any intermediate communication. Access control is a reliable method to preserve the security and privacy of user. A fine-grained data access control scheme on attribute-based encryption (ABE) is presented in [39]. Another Work [40] proposes a policy-based resource access control in fog computing for secure interoperability.

Integrity is another important part of privacy. A Lightweight Privacy-preserving Data Aggregation (LPDA) scheme is proposed in [41] where it can aggregate the data of hybrid IoT devices, and prevent any false data injection. It has also outperformed other existing approaches in terms of computational costs and communication overhead. A differential privacy-based query model is presented in [42] for sustainable fog computing, where *Laplacian mechanism* is utilized. This method has better efficiency and reduced energy consumption compared to existing methods. Huo et al. [43] present a location difference-based proximity detection (LoDPD) protocol, where *Paillier encryption algorithm and decision-tree theory* is used.

Authentication is not sufficient because the devices itself are vulnerable to malicious attacks. Trust is important factor here, where fog nodes verify the requests from the end-users or IoT devices, as well as, the end-users verify the services received from trusted fog/edge nodes [44]. In other words, system needs to confirm whether the fog/edge nodes are secured, thus, a robust trust model is required. There are several issues like how to measure trust in the fog/edge nodes and which attributes should be included in the trust model. The conventional trust models in cloud computing are not useful due to lack of centralized management and mobility issues.

However, there are unsolved challenges like how to implement intrusion detection in geo-distributed, large-scale, high-mobility fog computing system to satisfy latency requirement. Further studies need to investigate how fog computing can be beneficial for intrusion detection on both client side and the centralized cloud side.

3.4 *Resource Provisioning*

Another challenge is to efficiently allocate cloud/fog/edge computing infrastructure to different services. At each time-instance, IoT device or end-users can request huge number of service-request, but each fog/edge device is resource-constraint. Therefore, the components (edge and fog device/node) should be efficiently managed. The resource management among fog/edge nodes is another aspect here. This should be considered based on service-requirements and service-availability, energy consumption. In summary, the mapping of the resources to fog/edge service nodes is compelling issue.

Since the fog/edge nodes have limited computing and storing resources, it is not possible always to satisfy all service-requests. To resolve this, *satisfaction function* is formulated to measure the allocated resources to execute the service-request. The satisfaction function is defined as [45]:

$$f(res) = \begin{cases} \log(res + 1) & 0 \leq res \leq res_{min} \\ \log(res_{max} + 1) & res \geq res_{max} \end{cases} \tag{1}$$

where f is the satisfaction function, the allocated resource and maximum resource are denoted by res and res_{max} respectively. The objective is to maximize the overall $f(res)$ for all end-users is defined as:

$$\textbf{Objective} \quad \max f_{All} \tag{2}$$

$$\textbf{s.t.} \begin{cases} f_{All} = \sum_{u=1}^{U} \{pr_u \times f_u(res_u)\} \\ res_1 + res_2 + \cdots + res_u \leq RES \\ pr_1 + pr_2 + \cdots + pr_u = 1 \\ res_1, res_2, \ldots, res_u \geq 0 \end{cases} \tag{3}$$

where the priority value, user and total resource are defined as pr, u and RES respectively [45].

A simulation toolkit for measuring the efficacy of any fog-based framework is presented in [46]. A *LP-based two-phase heuristic algorithm* resource management framework is proposed in [47] in fog-based medical cyber-physical system.

4 Taxonomy: Mobility Management

With the advancement of Global Position Systems (GPS) and location acquisition technology, there is a growing need to analyse the huge amount of accumulated GPS log. The time-stamp location traces (latitude, longitude) is defined as *trajectory*. Several researches have been carried out in this domain. After carefully studying the existing literature, we come up with the taxonomy (refer Fig. 3) of mobility-aware system where *mobility data storage, pattern mining, mobility knowledge extraction* and *privacy issues* are highlighted.

Trajectory database size is huge due to its dynamic nature. There are several works on efficient trajectory data storage technique. This includes mobility data segmentation, mobility data indexing and trajectory data optimization.

There are varied trajectory indexing techniques. In [48], a multi-version structure, named *HR+*, is proposed, where a node can store different time-stamp entries.

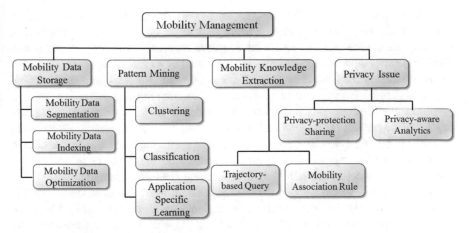

Fig. 3 Taxonomy of mobility-aware system

Thus it reduces the space complexity. A two-level index structure is proposed in [49], where the index of spatial and temporal information is decoupled. Ghosh et al. propose a *k-level temporal hash-based scheme* [50], where a hash function is used to store the movement data efficiently. Another work, named *Trajstore* [51] dynamically co-locates and compresses data on same disk by creating an optimal index. Zhou et al. [52] presents a grid-based index. Here, the study area/region is segregated into different rectangular cells of fixed size. In each such segment, the information of the mobility information is stored separately. Another work *Mobi-IoST* [8] presents an unique grid-based trajectory information segmentation, where in each segment a fog node is present and the fog node stores such information.

Pattern mining is another major aspect of trajectory data analysis. The objective is to *find the intent behind any move* [1], and making sense of the trajectory log [53]. In this context, *semantic trajectory* is defined, where raw trajectory log is complemented with additional information such as, point-of-interests (POI) of the path followed, stay-points and duration, speed, transportation mode etc. The process of appending such semantic information is defined as *semantic enrichment*. Different works have proposed several methods to semantically enrich the movement log based on the requirements of the application. In *Traj-cloud* [54], the authors describe the process of geo-tagging the trajectory points using reverse geo-coding. Google place API is used to extract the POI-information. Another work, named *STMaker* [55] presents a system, where raw GPS log is segmented based on the behavioral features of the moving agent. Then, each such segment is identified by a short textual description. Furthermore, short textual messages from social networking sites also append semantic information about the movement. Based on this idea, TOPTRAC [56] detects latent topic in trajectory dataset. It also extracts mobility patterns among different semantically connected regions. A clustering-based approach to find out the semantic regions is proposed in [57].

Clustering and classification are another important aspects of mobility pattern mining. Trajectory data is presented as sequences of *stop* and *move* along with a temporal scale. Clustering is beneficial for grouping the similar type of movements. Thus, trajectory clustering techniques are presented by a number of works. Amongst varied distance-based clustering, EDR (Edit Distance on Real sequence), DTW (Dynamic Time Warping) and LCSS (Longest Common Subsequences) are popular. A partition-and-group based method is presented in [58] to extract common trajectory segments. This TRACLUS framework use the minimum description length (MDL) and a density-based line-segment clustering method. Representative Trajectory Tree is proposed in [59] for temporal-constrained sub-trajectory clustering. A novel trajectory clustering approach using deep representation learning is presented in [60], where a sequence to sequence auto-encoder is utilized. TULER presents a RNN based model to extract the dependency of checking [61]. The work *MovCloud* [62] proposed a mobility-clustering algorithm based on the semantic behaviour of the users and the clustering algorithm is deployed in the cloud servers for fast execution. Classification of trajectories aim to train the model and use it for prediction. A work [63] augments duration information to enhance the prediction accuracy, along with spatial distribution and shape of the trajectories as features of the classification algorithm. Another work by Ghosh et al. [64] categorizes users based on their regular movement pattern. The study has been carried out in an academic campus, and the algorithm can classify users as *professor, student, staff* categories effectively.

To retrieve information from a dataset, query processing is important. There are varied types of queries, namely, *point query, range query, trajectory query* etc. The range or R-query ($RangeQ(S, T)$) finds all trajectory segments which intersects the given spatial (S) and temporal (T) extent.

$$RangeQ(S, T) \rightarrow Traj$$

where $Traj$ is the set of trajectory segments within S spatial and T temporal extent. The T-Query or trajectory-based query finds all trajectory segments of a moving agent (a) within the temporal interval (T).

$$TrajectoryQ(a, T) \rightarrow Traj$$

Here, $Traj$ is the output trajectory of the query. Several researchers have deployed novel methods to resolve queries effectively. A location based searching is proposed in [65], where different locations are assigned different importance or priority. For instance, location with geo-tagged information (such as, photograph) is more important than others. It finds the k-most important connected trajectories. Range queries are studied in [66, 67]. Vieira et al. [68] defines *pattern query* where trajectory segments with specific movement features are extracted. Aggregated queries [69] produces an aggregate measure. There are also other context-based or application-based queries [70, 71]. Mobility association rule defines the interrelation of two or more mobility events in temporal scale [50, 72, 73].

5 Taxonomy: Location-Aware Services

Location-aware services utilize the geographical location information to provide services to the end-users. Figure 4 illustrates different types of location-based services, namely, *personalized service, urban planning, time-critical applications* and *defence applications.*

Personalized service includes the notification or recommendation sent to the user based on her location. For instance, user's location is nearest to a new shopping mall, which is providing discounts on specific items. The system can provide alert to the user regarding this. Again, the system can predict probable congestion on a road-segment and notifies the user a priori to avoid the road-segment. Urban planning consists of sustainable solution in terms of energy and power consumption and smart transportation. Location-based services can also benefit to time-critical applications, where real-time response is required. Defence application can also get support from location-data analytics.

There are huge number of works where several challenging applications are mentioned and mobility analytics or location-based data mining supports these applications. Table 1 depicts few of these applications and the approaches followed in those works. The work by Han Su et al. [74] explores how to make the route description more customized and intuitive depending on the user. The authors present the problem of extracting optimal partition of a given route that maximizes the familiarity of user and generates proper sequence. The visited POI-assignment task is carried out in [75] where authors formulate the problem using 0-1 ILP formulation. It may be noted that characteristics and attributes of geographical locations are important for location recommendation. Zhao et al. [76] proposes a novel method of personalized location recommendation by sentimental–spatial POI mining (SPM). The incomplete or sparse data is a major problem in predicting next location sequences efficiently. The authors in [77] propose a novel layered and

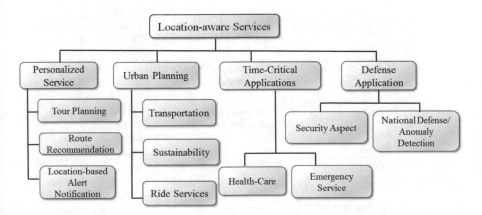

Fig. 4 Taxonomy of location-aware services

Table 1 Classification of location-based applications and approaches

Type of service	Author and year	Application	Approach
Personalized service	Han Su et al. [74]	Personalized route description system	User knowledge measurement and route summarization
	Jun Suzuki et al. [75]	Assign personalized visited points	Visited POI selection based and 0-1 ILP formulation
	Zhao et al. [76]	Personalized location recommendation	Sentimental-spatial POI mining
	Ghosh et al. [77]	Location prediction from sparse trajectory data	Hierarchical and layered Hidden Markov model (HMM) construction
	Tarik Taleb et al. [78]	Network slicing for personalized 5G mobile telecommunication	Mobile network personalization service orchestrator (MNP-SO) and the mobile service personalization service
	Ghosh et al. [3]	Activity-based user profiling	Allens' temporal calculus based activity data analysis
	Han Zou et al. [79]	Inferring user identity and mobility	WiFi-enabled nonintrusive device and user association scheme
	Fei Wu et al. [80]	Personalized annotation of mobility records	Markov random field to maximize the consistency
Urban planning	Kong X et al. [81]	Recommendation of services to taxi drivers	TLR model based on Gaussian process regression and statistical approaches
	Boting Qu et al. [82]	Profitable taxi travel route recommendation	Probabilistic network model and Kalman filtering
	Gang Pan et al. [83]	land-use classification from taxi trajectory data	Support Vector Machine (SVM) classifier with features extracted
	Hua Cai et al. [84]	Environmental benefits of taxi ride-sharing	Quantifies the environmental benefits of taxi ride sharing
	Tingting Li et al. [85]	Emission pattern mining for pollution detection	Spatial and temporal dynamic emission patterns in varied traffic zones
	Gong et al. [86]	Inferring trip-purposes from taxi trajectory data	Spatio-temporal analysis and probability modelling by Bayes' rules
	M Ota et al. [87]	Simulation of taxi ride-sharing	Linear optimization algorithm and efficient indexing scheme

(continued)

Table 1 (continued)

Type of service	Author and year	Application	Approach
	SP Chuah et al. [88]	Designing and optimization bus-routes	Clustering of taxi-rides and optimization problem to design bus-routes
Time-critical applications	Ghosh et al. [8]	Recommending optimal path for and actuating signals for emergency services (say, health-care)	Probabilistic graphical model and k-order Markov chain
	Mukherjee et al. [89]	IoHT for personalized health monitoring and recommendation	Generative adversarial networks based analysis
Defence applications	Du Bowen et al. [90, 91]	Identifying pickpocket suspects from check-in data	Two-step framework of regular passenger filtering and suspect detection from movement traces

hierarchical HMM with other contextual data. The authors in [80] aim to annotate the mobility records by their semantics (what the user is doing at that location). The work does not assume the availability of training data. Similarly there are works on sustainable polices like reducing carbon footprint by ride-sharing system [84, 85]. Another interesting application is presented in [91] and [90], where the authors find out pickpocket suspects from large scale transit data.

6 Conclusions and Future Research Directions

With the proliferation of GPS-enabled devices and smart hand-held devices, huge volume of data is generated. This huge amount of data can be beneficial for mining behavioural patterns of users and thus fostering challenging applications in our daily life. However, analysing such big amount of data is not possible for resource-constraint devices. Therefore, cloud technology is important. But, communication with distant cloud servers may affect the latency of the service-response and reduces the QoS. Therefore, partial computation must be carried out at the edge of the network, and thus, fog/edge nodes are incorporated. In this book chapter, we provide a brief summarization of issues and challenges in a mobility-driven cloud-fog-edge based framework for facilitating location-based services. We have presented three taxonomies of existing works in system aspect, mobility management and several types of location-based services. Further, a tabular representation of few prominent applications have been highlighted. Although there are huge amount of works in this domain, we have identified few challenges and opportunities which can be explored in the future.

- **Heterogeneity of the layers:** There is a big challenge in the heterogeneous nature of the components at fog/edge layers. The system should be able to orchestrate several different types of devices with heterogeneous cores. Significant architectural advancements should be made both from hardware and deployment of such system.
- **Security:** Although there are few works in security mechanism, but the cross-layer security or privacy policies are still un-explored and a big threat to both system and end-users.
- **Sustainable mobility:** Increasing power and energy consumption and thus increasing carbon footprint are big issues in present times. Although there are few works on ride-sharing to reduce the carbon footprints, considering budget and deadline [92], in reality this is still a big issue. The proper mechanism to deploy such initiatives is yet to be done. There is also concern of user-security while sharing rides with unknown people.
- **Sharing data with people:** Sharing data (transportation, urban planning, health-care facilities etc.) with citizen is absolutely necessary. This not only brings transparency, people can make proper decision if they know the available resources. While few developed countries have systematic data sharing policies, developing countries like India, is still far behind. A significant progress can be made if the research community can come up with appropriate data sharing policies and modules for such cases.

We believe that the book-chapter will provide a brief but comprehensive review of cloud-fog-edge collaborative framework to the readers.

Acknowledgment This work is partially supported by TCS PhD (https://www.tcs.com/research-scholarship-program-computer-science-phds-india) research fellowship.

References

1. Shreya Ghosh and Soumya K Ghosh. Thump: Semantic analysis on trajectory traces to explore human movement pattern. In *Proceedings of the 25th International Conference on World Wide Web*, pages 35–36, 2016.
2. Shreya Ghosh and Soumya K Ghosh. Exploring the association between mobility behaviours and academic performances of students: a context-aware traj-graph (CTG) analysis. *Progress in Artificial Intelligence*, 7(4):307–326, 2018.
3. Shreya Ghosh, Soumya K Ghosh, Rahul Deb Das, and Stephan Winter. Activity-based mobility profiling: A purely temporal modeling approach. In *Proceedings of the Web Conference 2018*, pages 409–416, 2018.
4. Shreya Ghosh, Abhisek Chowdhury, and Soumya K Ghosh. A machine learning approach to find the optimal routes through analysis of GPS traces of mobile city traffic. In *Recent Findings in Intelligent Computing Techniques*, pages 59–67. Springer, 2018.

5. Sayan Sinha, Mehul Kumar Nirala, Shreya Ghosh, and Soumya K Ghosh. Hybrid path planner for efficient navigation in urban road networks through analysis of trajectory traces. In *2018 24th International Conference on Pattern Recognition (ICPR)*, pages 3250–3255. IEEE, 2018.

6. Yu Zheng. Trajectory data mining: an overview. *ACM Transactions on Intelligent Systems and Technology (TIST)*, 6(3):1–41, 2015.

7. Khalid A Eldrandaly, Mohamed Abdel-Basset, and Laila A Shawky. Internet of spatial things: A new reference model with insight analysis. *IEEE Access*, 7:19653–19669, 2019.

8. Shreya Ghosh, Anwesha Mukherjee, Soumya K Ghosh, and Rajkumar Buyya. Mobi-IoST: mobility-aware cloud-fog-edge-IoT collaborative framework for time-critical applications. *IEEE Transactions on Network Science and Engineering*, 2019.

9. Blesson Varghese, Nan Wang, Sakil Barbhuiya, Peter Kilpatrick, and Dimitrios S Nikolopoulos. Challenges and opportunities in edge computing. In *2016 IEEE International Conference on Smart Cloud (SmartCloud)*, pages 20–26. IEEE, 2016.

10. Zohreh Sanaei, Saeid Abolfazli, Abdullah Gani, and Rajkumar Buyya. Heterogeneity in mobile cloud computing: taxonomy and open challenges. *IEEE Communications Surveys & Tutorials*, 16(1):369–392, 2013.

11. Mahadev Satyanarayanan, Grace Lewis, Edwin Morris, Soumya Simanta, Jeff Boleng, and Kiryong Ha. The role of cloudlets in hostile environments. *IEEE Pervasive Computing*, 12(4):40–49, 2013.

12. JAYDEEP DAS, SHREYA GHOSH, SOUMYA K GHOSH, and RAJKUMAR BUYYA. Rescue: Green healthcare services using integrated IoT-edge-fog-cloud computing environments. 2018.

13. Shreya Ghosh and Soumya K Ghosh. Exploring mobility behaviours of moving agents from trajectory traces in cloud-fog-edge collaborative framework. In *2020 20th IEEE/ACM International Symposium on Cluster, Cloud and Internet Computing (CCGRID)*, pages 893–897. IEEE, 2020.

14. Shreya Ghosh, Jaydeep Das, Soumya K Ghosh, and Rajkumar Buyya. Clawer: Context-aware cloud-fog based workflow management framework for health emergency services. In *2020 20th IEEE/ACM International Symposium on Cluster, Cloud and Internet Computing (CCGRID)*, pages 810–817. IEEE, 2020.

15. Shreya Ghosh, Jaydeep Das, and Soumya K Ghosh. Locator: A cloud-fog-enabled framework for facilitating efficient location based services. In *2020 International Conference on COMmunication Systems & NETworkS (COMSNETS)*, pages 87–92. IEEE, 2020.

16. Randa M Abdelmoneem, Abderrahim Benslimane, and Eman Shaaban. Mobility-aware task scheduling in cloud-fog IoT-based healthcare architectures. *Computer Networks*, page 107348, 2020.

17. Anwesha Mukherjee, Debashis De, and Soumya K Ghosh. FogIoHT: A weighted majority game theory based energy-efficient delay-sensitive fog network for internet of health things. *Internet of Things*, page 100181, 2020.

18. Fatemeh Jalali, Kerry Hinton, Robert Ayre, Tansu Alpcan, and Rodney S Tucker. Fog computing may help to save energy in cloud computing. *IEEE Journal on Selected Areas in Communications*, 34(5):1728–1739, 2016.

19. Deze Zeng, Lin Gu, Song Guo, Zixue Cheng, and Shui Yu. Joint optimization of task scheduling and image placement in fog computing supported software-defined embedded system. *IEEE Transactions on Computers*, 65(12):3702–3712, 2016.

20. Hong Yao, Changmin Bai, Muzhou Xiong, Deze Zeng, and Zhangjie Fu. Heterogeneous cloudlet deployment and user-cloudlet association toward cost effective fog computing. *Concurrency and Computation: Practice and Experience*, 29(16):e3975, 2017.

21. Lin Gu, Deze Zeng, Song Guo, Ahmed Barnawi, and Yong Xiang. Cost efficient resource management in fog computing supported medical cyber-physical system. *IEEE Transactions on Emerging Topics in Computing*, 5(1):108–119, 2015.

22. Xueshi Hou, Yong Li, Min Chen, Di Wu, Depeng Jin, and Sheng Chen. Vehicular fog computing: A viewpoint of vehicles as the infrastructures. *IEEE Transactions on Vehicular Technology*, 65(6):3860–3873, 2016.

23. Jessica Oueis, Emilio Calvanese Strinati, and Sergio Barbarossa. The fog balancing: Load distribution for small cell cloud computing. In *2015 IEEE 81st vehicular technology conference (VTC spring)*, pages 1–6. IEEE, 2015.
24. Kirak Hong, David Lillethun, Umakishore Ramachandran, Beate Ottenwälder, and Boris Koldehofe. Mobile fog: A programming model for large-scale applications on the internet of things. In *Proceedings of the second ACM SIGCOMM workshop on Mobile cloud computing*, pages 15–20, 2013.
25. Wangbong Lee, Kidong Nam, Hak-Gyun Roh, and Sang-Ha Kim. A gateway based fog computing architecture for wireless sensors and actuator networks. In *2016 18th International Conference on Advanced Communication Technology (ICACT)*, pages 210–213. IEEE, 2016.
26. Deepak Puthal, Mohammad S Obaidat, Priyadarsi Nanda, Mukesh Prasad, Saraju P Mohanty, and Albert Y Zomaya. Secure and sustainable load balancing of edge data centers in fog computing. *IEEE Communications Magazine*, 56(5):60–65, 2018.
27. Chin-Feng Lai, Dong-Yu Song, Ren-Hung Hwang, and Ying-Xun Lai. A QoS-aware streaming service over fog computing infrastructures. In *2016 Digital Media Industry & Academic Forum (DMIAF)*, pages 94–98. IEEE, 2016.
28. Apostolos Destounis, Georgios S Paschos, and Iordanis Koutsopoulos. Streaming big data meets backpressure in distributed network computation. In *IEEE INFOCOM 2016-The 35th Annual IEEE International Conference on Computer Communications*, pages 1–9. IEEE, 2016.
29. Badrish Chandramouli, Joris Claessens, Suman Nath, Ivo Santos, and Wenchao Zhou. Race: Real-time applications over cloud-edge. In *Proceedings of the 2012 ACM SIGMOD International Conference on Management of Data*, pages 625–628, 2012.
30. Vitor Barbosa C Souza, Wilson Ramírez, Xavier Masip-Bruin, Eva Marín-Tordera, G Ren, and Ghazal Tashakor. Handling service allocation in combined fog-cloud scenarios. In *2016 IEEE international conference on communications (ICC)*, pages 1–5. IEEE, 2016.
31. Vitor Barbosa C Souza, Wilson Ramírez, Xavier Masip-Bruin, Eva Marín-Tordera, G Ren, and Ghazal Tashakor. Handling service allocation in combined fog-cloud scenarios. In *2016 IEEE international conference on communications (ICC)*, pages 1–5. IEEE, 2016.
32. Yiping Kang, Johann Hauswald, Cao Gao, Austin Rovinski, Trevor Mudge, Jason Mars, and Lingjia Tang. Neurosurgeon: Collaborative intelligence between the cloud and mobile edge. *ACM SIGARCH Computer Architecture News*, 45(1):615–629, 2017.
33. Krittin Intharawijitr, Katsuyoshi Iida, and Hiroyuki Koga. Analysis of fog model considering computing and communication latency in 5g cellular networks. In *2016 IEEE International Conference on Pervasive Computing and Communication Workshops (PerCom Workshops)*, pages 1–4. IEEE, 2016.
34. Mithun Mukherjee, Rakesh Matam, Lei Shu, Leandros Maglaras, Mohamed Amine Ferrag, Nikumani Choudhury, and Vikas Kumar. Security and privacy in fog computing: Challenges. *IEEE Access*, 5:19293–19304, 2017.
35. Shanhe Yi, Zhengrui Qin, and Qun Li. Security and privacy issues of fog computing: A survey. In *International conference on wireless algorithms, systems, and applications*, pages 685–695. Springer, 2015.
36. Clinton Dsouza, Gail-Joon Ahn, and Marthony Taguinod. Policy-driven security management for fog computing: Preliminary framework and a case study. In *Proceedings of the 2014 IEEE 15th international conference on information reuse and integration (IEEE IRI 2014)*, pages 16–23. IEEE, 2014.
37. Mohammad Aazam and Eui-Nam Huh. Fog computing and smart gateway based communication for cloud of things. In *2014 International Conference on Future Internet of Things and Cloud*, pages 464–470. IEEE, 2014.
38. Yue Shi, Sampatoor Abhilash, and Kai Hwang. Cloudlet mesh for securing mobile clouds from intrusions and network attacks. In *2015 3rd IEEE International Conference on Mobile Cloud Computing, Services, and Engineering*, pages 109–118. IEEE, 2015.
39. Shucheng Yu, Cong Wang, Kui Ren, and Wenjing Lou. Achieving secure, scalable, and fine-grained data access control in cloud computing. In *2010 Proceedings IEEE INFOCOM*, pages 1–9. IEEE, 2010.

40. Clinton Dsouza, Gail-Joon Ahn, and Marthony Taguinod. Policy-driven security management for fog computing: Preliminary framework and a case study. In *Proceedings of the 2014 IEEE 15th international conference on information reuse and integration (IEEE IRI 2014)*, pages 16–23. IEEE, 2014.

41. Rongxing Lu, Kevin Heung, Arash Habibi Lashkari, and Ali A Ghorbani. A lightweight privacy-preserving data aggregation scheme for fog computing-enhanced IoT. *IEEE Access*, 5:3302–3312, 2017.

42. Tian Wang, Jiandian Zeng, Md Zakirul Alam Bhuiyan, Hui Tian, Yiqiao Cai, Yonghong Chen, and Bineng Zhong. Trajectory privacy preservation based on a fog structure for cloud location services. *IEEE Access*, 5:7692–7701, 2017.

43. Yan Huo, Chunqiang Hu, Xiaowei Qi, and Tao Jing. LoDPD: a location difference-based proximity detection protocol for fog computing. *IEEE Internet of Things Journal*, 4(5):1117–1124, 2017.

44. Ryan KL Ko, Peter Jagadpramana, Miranda Mowbray, Siani Pearson, Markus Kirchberg, Qianhui Liang, and Bu Sung Lee. Trustcloud: A framework for accountability and trust in cloud computing. In *2011 IEEE World Congress on Services*, pages 584–588. IEEE, 2011.

45. Jie Lin, Wei Yu, Nan Zhang, Xinyu Yang, Hanlin Zhang, and Wei Zhao. A survey on internet of things: Architecture, enabling technologies, security and privacy, and applications. *IEEE Internet of Things Journal*, 4(5):1125–1142, 2017.

46. Harshit Gupta, Amir Vahid Dastjerdi, Soumya K Ghosh, and Rajkumar Buyya. ifogsim: A toolkit for modeling and simulation of resource management techniques in the internet of things, edge and fog computing environments. *Software: Practice and Experience*, 47(9):1275–1296, 2017.

47. Lin Gu, Deze Zeng, Song Guo, Ahmed Barnawi, and Yong Xiang. Cost efficient resource management in fog computing supported medical cyber-physical system. *IEEE Transactions on Emerging Topics in Computing*, 5(1):108–119, 2015.

48. Ke Deng, Kexin Xie, Kevin Zheng, and Xiaofang Zhou. Trajectory indexing and retrieval. In *Computing with spatial trajectories*, pages 35–60. Springer, 2011.

49. V Prasad Chakka, Adam Everspaugh, Jignesh M Patel, et al. Indexing large trajectory data sets with SETI. In *CIDR*, volume 75, page 76. Citeseer, 2003.

50. Shreya Ghosh, Soumya K Ghosh, and Rajkumar Buyya. Mario: A spatio-temporal data mining framework on google cloud to explore mobility dynamics from taxi trajectories. *Journal of Network and Computer Applications*, page 102692, 2020.

51. Philippe Cudre-Mauroux, Eugene Wu, and Samuel Madden. Trajstore: An adaptive storage system for very large trajectory data sets. In *Proceedings of the 26th International Conference on Data Engineering (ICDE 2010)*, pages 109–120. IEEE, 2010.

52. Jingbo Zhou, Anthony KH Tung, Wei Wu, and Wee Siong Ng. R2-d2: a system to support probabilistic path prediction in dynamic environments via semi-lazy learning. *Proceedings of the VLDB Endowment*, 6(12):1366–1369, 2013.

53. Han Su, Kai Zheng, Kai Zeng, Jiamin Huang, Shazia Sadiq, Nicholas Jing Yuan, and Xiaofang Zhou. Making sense of trajectory data: A partition-and-summarization approach. In *2015 IEEE 31st International Conference on Data Engineering*, pages 963–974. IEEE, 2015.

54. Shreya Ghosh and Soumya K Ghosh. Traj-cloud: a trajectory cloud for enabling efficient mobility services. In *2019 11th International Conference on Communication Systems & Networks (COMSNETS)*, pages 765–770. IEEE, 2019.

55. Han Su, Kai Zheng, Kai Zeng, Jiamin Huang, and Xiaofang Zhou. Stmaker: a system to make sense of trajectory data. *Proceedings of the VLDB Endowment*, 7(13):1701–1704, 2014.

56. Younghoon Kim, Jiawei Han, and Cangzhou Yuan. Toptrac: Topical trajectory pattern mining. In *Proceedings of the 21th ACM SIGKDD International Conference on Knowledge Discovery and Data Mining*, pages 587–596, 2015.

57. Mingqi Lv, Ling Chen, and Gencai Chen. Discovering personally semantic places from gps trajectories. In *Proceedings of the 21st ACM international conference on Information and knowledge management*, pages 1552–1556, 2012.

58. Jae-Gil Lee, Jiawei Han, and Kyu-Young Whang. Trajectory clustering: a partition-and-group framework. In *Proceedings of the 2007 ACM SIGMOD international conference on Management of data*, pages 593–604, 2007.
59. Nikos Pelekis, Panagiotis Tampakis, Marios Vodas, Christos Doulkeridis, and Yannis Theodoridis. On temporal-constrained sub-trajectory cluster analysis. *Data Mining and Knowledge Discovery*, 31(5):1294–1330, 2017.
60. Di Yao, Chao Zhang, Zhihua Zhu, Jianhui Huang, and Jingping Bi. Trajectory clustering via deep representation learning. In *2017 international joint conference on neural networks (IJCNN)*, pages 3880–3887. IEEE, 2017.
61. Qiang Gao, Fan Zhou, Kunpeng Zhang, Goce Trajcevski, Xucheng Luo, and Fengli Zhang. Identifying human mobility via trajectory embeddings. In *IJCAI*, volume 17, pages 1689–1695, 2017.
62. Shreya Ghosh, Soumya K Ghosh, and Rajkumar Buyya. Movcloud: A cloud-enabled framework to analyse movement behaviors. In *CloudCom*, pages 239–246, 2019.
63. Dhaval Patel, Chang Sheng, Wynne Hsu, and Mong Li Lee. Incorporating duration information for trajectory classification. In *2012 IEEE 28th International Conference on Data Engineering*, pages 1132–1143. IEEE, 2012.
64. Shreya Ghosh and Soumya K Ghosh. Modeling of human movement behavioral knowledge from gps traces for categorizing mobile users. In *Proceedings of the 26th International Conference on World Wide Web*, pages 51–58, 2017.
65. Da Yan, James Cheng, Zhou Zhao, and Wilfred Ng. Efficient location-based search of trajectories with location importance. *Knowledge and Information Systems*, 45(1):215–245, 2015.
66. Kai Zheng, Goce Trajcevski, Xiaofang Zhou, and Peter Scheuermann. Probabilistic range queries for uncertain trajectories on road networks. In *Proceedings of the 14th International Conference on Extending Database Technology*, pages 283–294, 2011.
67. Liming Zhan, Ying Zhang, Wenjie Zhang, Xiaoyang Wang, and Xuemin Lin. Range search on uncertain trajectories. In *Proceedings of the 24th ACM International on Conference on Information and Knowledge Management*, pages 921–930, 2015.
68. Marcos R Vieira, Petko Bakalov, and Vassilis J Tsotras. Querying trajectories using flexible patterns. In *Proceedings of the 13th International Conference on Extending Database Technology*, pages 406–417, 2010.
69. Yanhua Li, Chi-Yin Chow, Ke Deng, Mingxuan Yuan, Jia Zeng, Jia-Dong Zhang, Qiang Yang, and Zhi-Li Zhang. Sampling big trajectory data. In *Proceedings of the 24th ACM International on Conference on Information and Knowledge Management*, pages 941–950, 2015.
70. Bolong Zheng, Nicholas Jing Yuan, Kai Zheng, Xing Xie, Shazia Sadiq, and Xiaofang Zhou. Approximate keyword search in semantic trajectory database. In *2015 IEEE 31st International Conference on Data Engineering*, pages 975–986. IEEE, 2015.
71. Kai Zheng, Shuo Shang, Nicholas Jing Yuan, and Yi Yang. Towards efficient search for activity trajectories. In *2013 IEEE 29Th international conference on data engineering (ICDE)*, pages 230–241. IEEE, 2013.
72. Shreya Ghosh and Soumya K Ghosh. Exploring human movement behaviour based on mobility association rule mining of trajectory traces. In *International Conference on Intelligent Systems Design and Applications*, pages 451–463. Springer, 2017.
73. Shreya Ghosh and Soumya K Ghosh. Exploring human movement behaviour based on mobility association rule mining of trajectory traces. In *International Conference on Intelligent Systems Design and Applications*, pages 451–463. Springer, 2017.
74. Han Su, Guanglin Cong, Wei Chen, Bolong Zheng, and Kai Zheng. Personalized route description based on historical trajectories. In *Proceedings of the 28th ACM International Conference on Information and Knowledge Management*, pages 79–88, 2019.
75. Jun Suzuki, Yoshihiko Suhara, Hiroyuki Toda, and Kyosuke Nishida. Personalized visited-poi assignment to individual raw gps trajectories. *ACM Transactions on Spatial Algorithms and Systems (TSAS)*, 5(3):1–28, 2019.

76. Guoshuai Zhao, Peiliang Lou, Xueming Qian, and Xingsong Hou. Personalized location recommendation by fusing sentimental and spatial context. *Knowledge-Based Systems*, page 105849, 2020.
77. Soumya K Ghosh and Shreya Ghosh. Modeling individual's movement patterns to infer next location from sparse trajectory traces. In *2018 IEEE International Conference on Systems, Man, and Cybernetics (SMC)*, pages 693–698. IEEE, 2018.
78. Tarik Taleb, Badr Mada, Marius-Iulian Corici, Akihiro Nakao, and Hannu Flinck. Permit: Network slicing for personalized 5g mobile telecommunications. *IEEE Communications Magazine*, 55(5):88–93, 2017.
79. Han Zou, Yuxun Zhou, Jianfei Yang, and Costas J Spanos. Unsupervised WiFi-enabled IoT device-user association for personalized location-based service. *IEEE Internet of Things Journal*, 6(1):1238–1245, 2018.
80. Fei Wu and Zhenhui Li. Where did you go: Personalized annotation of mobility records. In *Proceedings of the 25th ACM International on Conference on Information and Knowledge Management*, pages 589–598, 2016.
81. Xiangjie Kong, Feng Xia, Jinzhong Wang, Azizur Rahim, and Sajal K Das. Time-location-relationship combined service recommendation based on taxi trajectory data. *IEEE Transactions on Industrial Informatics*, 13(3):1202–1212, 2017.
82. Boting Qu, Wenxin Yang, Ge Cui, and Xin Wang. Profitable taxi travel route recommendation based on big taxi trajectory data. *IEEE Transactions on Intelligent Transportation Systems*, 21(2):653–668, 2019.
83. Gang Pan, Guande Qi, Zhaohui Wu, Daqing Zhang, and Shijian Li. Land-use classification using taxi gps traces. *IEEE Transactions on Intelligent Transportation Systems*, 14(1):113–123, 2012.
84. Hua Cai, Xi Wang, Peter Adriaens, and Ming Xu. Environmental benefits of taxi ride sharing in Beijing. *Energy*, 174:503–508, 2019.
85. Tingting Li, Jianping Wu, Anrong Dang, Lyuchao Liao, and Ming Xu. Emission pattern mining based on taxi trajectory data in Beijing. *Journal of Cleaner Production*, 206:688–700, 2019.
86. Li Gong, Xi Liu, Lun Wu, and Yu Liu. Inferring trip purposes and uncovering travel patterns from taxi trajectory data. *Cartography and Geographic Information Science*, 43(2):103–114, 2016.
87. Masayo Ota, Huy Vo, Claudio Silva, and Juliana Freire. Stars: Simulating taxi ride sharing at scale. *IEEE Transactions on Big Data*, 3(3):349–361, 2016.
88. Seong Ping Chuah, Huayu Wu, Yu Lu, Liang Yu, and Stephane Bressan. Bus routes design and optimization via taxi data analytics. In *Proceedings of the 25th ACM International on Conference on Information and Knowledge Management*, pages 2417–2420, 2016.
89. Anwesha Mukherjee, Shreya Ghosh, Aabhash Behere, Soumya K Ghosh, and Rajkumar Buyya. Internet of health things (ioht) for personalized health care using integrated edge-fog-cloud network. *Journal of Ambient Intelligence and Humanized Computing*.
90. Bowen Du, Chuanren Liu, Wenjun Zhou, Zhenshan Hou, and Hui Xiong. Catch me if you can: Detecting pickpocket suspects from large-scale transit records. In *Proceedings of the 22nd ACM SIGKDD International Conference on Knowledge Discovery and Data Mining*, pages 87–96. ACM, 2016.
91. Bowen Du, Chuanren Liu, Wenjun Zhou, Zhenshan Hou, and Hui Xiong. Catch me if you can: Detecting pickpocket suspects from large-scale transit records. In *Proceedings of the 22nd ACM SIGKDD International Conference on Knowledge Discovery and Data Mining*, pages 87–96. ACM, 2016.
92. Jaydeep Das, Shreya Ghosh, Soumya K. Ghosh, and Rajkumar Buyya. LYRIC: Deadline and budget aware spatio-temporal query processing in cloud. *IEEE Transactions on Services Computing* (2021). https://doi.org/10.1109/TSC.2021.3073006

Mobility-Based Resource Allocation and Provisioning in Fog and Edge Computing Paradigms: Review, Challenges, and Future Directions

Sudheer Kumar Battula, Ranesh Kumar Naha, Ujjwal KC, Khizar Hameed, Saurabh Garg, and Muhammad Bilal Amin

Abstract Fog and Edge related computing paradigms promise to deliver exciting services in the Internet of Things (IoT) networks. The devices in such paradigms are highly dynamic and mobile, which presents several challenges to ensure service delivery with the utmost level of quality and guarantee. Achieving effective resource allocation and provisioning in such computing environments is a difficult task. Resource allocation and provisioning are one of the well-studied domains in the Cloud and other distributed paradigms. Lately, there have been several studies that have tried to explore the mobility of end devices in-depth and address the associated challenges in Fog and Edge related computing paradigms. But, the research domain is yet to be explored in detail. As such, this chapter reflects the current state-of-the-art of the methods and technologies used to manage the resources to support mobility in Fog and Edge environments. The chapter also highlights future research directions to efficiently deliver smart services in real-time environments.

Keywords Internet of things · Mobility · Resource allocation · Fog computing and Edge computing

1 Introduction

In recent years, there has been a rapid rise in the Internet of Things (IoT) devices and applications, and the range of the services offered by them. The services include smart transportation [1], disaster-related services [2], smart cities [3] and so on. These devices and applications provide services in a Cloud-like manner

S. K. Battula (✉) · R. K. Naha · U. KC · K. Hameed · S. Garg · M. B. Amin
School of Information and Communication Technology, College of Sciences and Engineering, University of Tasmania, Hobart, TAS, Australia
e-mail: sudheerkumar.battula@utas.edu.au; raneshkumar.naha@utas.edu.au; ujjwal.kc@utas.edu.au; hameed.khizar@utas.edu.au; saurabh.garg@utas.edu.au; bilal.amin@utas.edu.au

© The Author(s), under exclusive license to Springer Nature Switzerland AG 2021
A. Mukherjee et al. (eds.), *Mobile Edge Computing*,
https://doi.org/10.1007/978-3-030-69893-5_11

close to users with the help of end devices [4, 5]. Accordingly, new computing paradigms, such as Fog and Edge have evolved. Fog computing provides users with a decentralized environment where computational resources are brought to the Edge of the network so that they can perform real-time computational work on data without compromising bandwidth and latency issues in Cloud networks. In Fog computing, computational resources, including applications, services, and data, are placed between data and the Cloud. In Edge Computing, several endpoints (powerful IoT devices) are placed near the edges of the network to perform computations on data sources where data is generated, without having to be transferred elsewhere [6, 7].

In paradigms like Edge and Fog, not only the end devices but the users also, are mobile. The allocation and provisioning of the resources should be done in real-time within strict time constraints, even without any prior knowledge on future dynamics of the user mobility to offer and deliver seamless services without any interruption [8]. Additionally, such real-time capabilities also require resources (or a pool of resources) that are capable of completing the task or the application within a given time window. Consequently, Mobile Computing (MC) environments need to choose and provision adequate resources in an optimal manner, which can be non-trivial. For both requirements of effective resource allocation and provisioning, the mobile nature of the Fog, Edge, and end devices invites a number of challenges that can interrupt the execution of the tasks. On top of the mobility, various hardware and OS capabilities of the devices add more complexities to resource management [9]. For example, due to Fog device versatility, hardware and software of a new Fog device that is meant to replace a failed one, may not be compatible or match with the failed device while attempting to migrate the application to a nearby device in a Fog environment and consequently, the execution of the application fails. Due to different operating systems installed on each Fog device and frequent updates to the operating system, the devices can be vulnerable to several kinds of attacks and errors arising from incompatible versions of the devices [10].

In Mobile Edge Computing (MEC) paradigms, it is desirable to have an effective resource management mechanism that achieves efficiency and high performance for both systems and networks, while ensuring the fast and efficient distribution and delivery of resources to users and their processes. To ensure efficiency and high performance, some essential factors such as cost-efficient computation, bandwidth utilization, minimum delays, and energy consumption of the mobile devices are important milestones that have drawn researchers' attention to suggesting key resource management techniques in the MC environment [11]. In cost-efficient computation, Mobile Edge devices first meet user process requirements and then define appropriate procedures for managing available and allocated resources to maximize overall system profitability. The quality of services is also an important factor to consider while providing and allocating mobile resources, which necessitates a dynamic need for the resources available to the process to improve the overall quality of service within the network. Moreover, processing IoT applications intermediate computing devices often leads to several other difficulties in device managing systems [12]. For example, inadequate security protocols and frequent joining and leaving devices can lead to various security attacks and, in some cases, can cause data leakage. On the other hand, due to the limited energy and power of Fog, Edge, or end devices, the framework needs to be designed with a view to energy-saving capabilities as well [13]. Additionally, most of the applications are time-sensitive, and executing the applications within strict deadlines can be difficult [14].

On the other hand, the mobility of the end devices is entirely different from other computing paradigms as it does not follow any single random distribution. The mobility of the devices is direction-oriented as well as it depends on the source and destination of the devices. As a result, modeling the real environment is also a challenging task. Nonetheless, it is undeniable that when it comes down to effective resource allocation and provisioning in MC paradigms, such as Fog and Edge, the mobility of the end devices should be considered along with different other requirements. Several works [15, 16] have already conducted comprehensive sweeps of existing techniques in resource management in Fog and Edge computing paradigms. But, given the fact that the mobility of the end devices in such paradigms are now being explored in depth in several dimensions, a survey that reflects the current state-of-the-art of all the existing techniques, primarily centered around the mobility, is still missing. As such, with all these aspects in hindsight, this chapter first discusses in detail the different requirements and challenges in each layer of Fog, Edge, or other intermediate computing devices to achieving an effective MEC environment. The chapter then provides a comprehensive picture of the current works carried out to handle mobility in the Fog and Edge environment to put light on the future directions where future works can be directed to deliver high-quality IoT services in a computer paradigm characterized by mobility and dynamicity. The specific contributions of the chapter are as follows.

1. A summary of the requirements and challenges in each layer of MC paradigms to effective resource management
2. A comprehensive sketch of existing resource allocation and provisioning mechanisms in Fog and Edge computing centered around the mobility of the end devices
3. A reflection of the techniques used to model the mobility in MC paradigms
4. A summary of the existing mathematical models used for resource allocation in Fog and Edge computing
5. An overview of how future research works should address the challenges, including the mobility-related ones to ensure effective resource allocation in MEC

The work is organized as follows. Section 2 sheds light on the existing mobile-based resource provisioning and allocation mechanisms in Edge computing, while Sect. 3 follows the same summary for Fog computing. Section 4 explains in detail the existing modeling techniques used to add/support mobility in Fog and Edge computing environment. Section 5 briefly discusses several mathematical models considered in mobility-based resource allocation, while Sect. 6 presents various case studies with applications and use cases. Section 7 highlights the future direction for the research on mobility-based resource allocation and provisioning in MC paradigms, while Sect. 8 concludes the work.

2 Existing Mobile Based Resource Provisioning and Allocation Mechanisms in Edge

Through the age of IoT, Fog/Edge computing is the exciting option to meet the latency requirements of IoT applications by shifting the service delivery from the Cloud to the Edges. This also allows lightweight IoT devices to improve their scalability and energy consumption, provides contextual information processing, and mitigates the backbone network traffic burden [17]. Computation offloading is an important feature for Edge level processing where application offloads to the mobile devices that are resource-constrained to meet process requirements with moderate computation demands. The mobility feature of such an environment makes resource allocation and provisioning a challenging task. This section discusses resource allocation and provisioning in Mobile Edge related computing environments.

Zhang et al. [18] implemented a network-slicing 5G system conceptual architecture and proposed convergence management mechanisms between separate access networks and shared power/subchannel allocation schemes in two-tier network slicing-based spectrum sharing structures. In their proposed method, conflict with the co-interference, and cross-tier interference are taken into account. The core network is developed into a historically distributed architecture to decrease monitoring and data transfer delays by control plane separation from the user plane. The core Cloud offers some essential control features such as virtualized resource management, mobility management, and intrusion management. In the Edge Cloud, which is a centralized body of virtualized services, we can find servers and other applications in the radio access network. The Edge Cloud conducts data transfer primarily, and control functions including the encoding of the basebands. To optimize uplink efficiency on each subchannel, research modeled the uplink resource assignment issue for small cells considering the four limitations. First and foremost, each small cell consumer transmits its full power. Secondly, each user of ultra-Reliable and Low Latency Communication (uRLLC) is required to have the minimum data rate requirement. Thirdly, the minimum interference level is obtained from small cell users by the macrocell. Finally, in one transmission cycle, a subchannel can be assigned to a maximum of one consumer in each small cells. Computer simulations were used to show the promising performance of network-based 5G networks.

Ren et al. [17] explored the implementation of Edge computing to construct transparent IoT systems by implementing an IoT architecture focused on computing in transparency. Edge Computing architecture attempts to solve two big IoT applications issues—the first being how to manage data processing requests in real-time and context, and the second being how can IoT tools, the core component of transparent calculation, be distributed on-demand applications/services dynamically. The work also identified benefits and related challenges for the architecture. The architecture provides a scalable IoT platform to deliver intended services for lightweight IoT devices on time, to respond to changing user needs. The IoT architecture, based on transparent computing, can also offer several advantages: (1) reduced response delay (2) enhanced functional scalability (3) centralized resource management (4) on-demand and cross-platform service provisioning and (5) context-aware service support. The projects still face several challenges to their execution, which remarkably hamper the development of associated applications even though the architecture could utilize the advantage of transparent computing for the construction of IoT platforms with scalability. These challenges are: (1) unified resource management platform for heterogeneous IoT devices (2) provision service dynamically on lightweight IoT devices and (3) allocation of computation between the Edge and end devices.

In the Edge network Tasiopoulos et al. [19] built an auction-based allocation and resource provision which maps the application instances known as Edge-MAP. Edge-MAP takes account of the versatility and restricted computing resources available in the Edge micro clouds for the allocation of resources for device bidding applications. The provision of geo-distributed cloudlet services to low latency applications differs in that the allocation of resources must bear in mind the effect of network conditions, such as latency between end-users and Cloud presence points, on the QoS applications. Besides, for the mobile users, as users switch the connectivity to another base station, the latency to an assigned VM changes. Even ideal VM allocations for user requests are thus redundant over time, i.e. user mobility/handoffs are accompanied by VM reassignments if necessary. When a fixed number of VM's are allocated for a long time to an application, VM handoffs lead to available VM's that can be utilized by the users of other apps instead. In this context, to prevent the misuse of VMs, we argue about the need to include low-latency on-demand applications, in which a VM would be instanced on application request for the period of the engagement of the end-user. The provision of VMs takes place through periodical/discrete operation of the auction mechanisms, where the minimum length of the auction and VM configuration for each length/time slice is limited by the added overhead. However, the work did not demonstrate how the provisioning method will work in a complex heterogeneous IoT and edge/Fog environment.

Liu et al. [20] proposed a blockchain platform for MEC video sharing with the adaptive block size. First of all, they developed an incentive system for the partnership between producers of content, video transcoders, and consumers. Besides, the work revealed a block-size video-streaming adjustment system. Also, the work considered two offload modes to avoid the risk of overloading MEC nodes. These modes are—transfer to neighboring MEC nodes and transfer to a device-to-device (D2D) user group. The work then formulated the concerns of resource assignment, download schedule, and adaptive block size as an optimization problem. The problem distribution of the work was done using a low complexity alternating direction method in the algorithm based on multipliers. They showed that the optimum policy for maximum average transcoding profit is not uniform amongst different small cells or transcoders. They did not take account of a variety of factors such as the holding interest, communication, reputation value, and computation ability. The work also failed to demonstrate the intelligent contract as the Alternating Direction Method of Multipliers (ADMM) coordinator, a means of efficiently facilitating distributed optimization among non-trusting nodes.

Naha et al. [14] suggested the allocation and provisioning of resources through the use of hybrid and hierarchical resource rankings and provisioning algorithms for the Fog-Cloud computing paradigm. The resource allocation method assigns Fog-Cloud resources by rating the resources based on the number of resource constraints within Fog devices. The resource provisioning approach offers a hierarchical and flexible mechanism to meet the complex requirements of the users. The work achieves resource distribution and scheduling in the Fog-Cloud environment with three separate measures to reach the deadline by considering complex user requirements. In the first phase, Fog resources are identified to comply with the deadline requirements from the available devices in the Fog environment. The algorithm allocates jobs in Fog devices because the Cloud response time is high relative to the Fog. The second step is to try to accomplish this task using Fog servers and Cloud resources if available resources are not adequate in the Fog. Here it considers computing response time, bandwidth, and power for these resources when selecting Cloud resources. Thirdly, it investigates whether or not services in the Fog environment are unavailable. In such a case, the system would attempt to complete the work with Cloud resources before the resource unavailability message is generated. Dynamic changes of resources and failure to handling, such as resource and communication failures in a Fog computing paradigm, were not considered. The work also did not consider designing a simulation of a complex Fog environment with a bigdata IoT application.

A low-complex heuristic algorithm was introduced by Liao et al. [21] by providing a near-optimal low-time solution. The goal is to maximize the number of battery charged UE tasks successfully offloaded while maintaining a reasonable level of network efficiency. A low complexity heuristic algorithm was developed to resolve the formulated nonlinear mixed-integer programming problem. The work looked at the interference between all of the EU and used hyper graphic approaches in the pre-allocation of channels. Task offload was then evaluated following the estimation and allocation of contact resources. The work assumes the duality uplink and downlink to be accomplished with optimum transmitting capacity. UEs adjust to the discharge assignments upon receiving the feedback from MEC to increase the network performance, and bandwidth will be reassigned. A detailed investigation was carried out to find the relationship between the number of tasks successfully discharged and the number of UEs under different MEC computing tools. However, the research did not concentrate much on the latest communication framework for joint optimization, smart coded caching, and computation in the MEC networks and their unprecedented applications. The use of large-scale enhancement learning for the competitive pricing policy, which can equalize mobile operator cost and UEs' economic impact, has not been considered.

Table 1 provides a detailed comparison of existing techniques for mobile-based resource provisioning and allocation mechanism in Fog/Edge computing

Table 1 Comparison of existing mobile based resource provisioning and allocation mechanisms to support mobility nature edge

Ref	Problem addressed	Techniques used	Performance challenges	Use cases	Experimental setup	Evaluation criteria	Dataset used
[18]	Handover and network slicing issues in 5G networks	Joint power and sub channel allocation scheme	Quality of service	Not defined	Not defined	Capacity of slice, Transmit power, Latency	Not defined
[17]	Transparent and service provisioning issues	Not defined	Lightweight computing, Transparency, Scalability	Transparent computing based wearables	TCwatch and Smart watch	App size, Latency, Energy consumption	Smart Wearable data
[19]	Edge resource provisioning and latency	Auction based resource allocation and provisioning mechanism	Mobility, Quality of service	Vehicle as a mobile users in cellular areas	Cellular infrastructure (1 km radius)	Requests Generation, Execution time, Iterations comparison, Price, Quality of service	Mobility dataset5 (TAPASCologne project)
[20]	Resource allocation, and scheduling issues	Incentive mechanism, Low-complexity alternating direction method	Quality of service, Efficiency, Video Quality	Not defined	Network coverage radius of the MBS as 1000 m	Transcoding revenue, Bandwidth consumption, tolerance	Not defined
[14]	Dynamic changes in the parameters of user requirements	Hybrid and hierarchical based resource ranking and provisioning algorithms	Quality of service	Not defined	CloudSim toolkit	Processing time, Instance cost, Network delay	Not defined
[21]	Network resource scheduling issue in user equipment's	Centralized decision and resource allocation algorithm,	Energy consumption, Quality of service	Not defined	Matlab	Optimal transmission power, computation, Distance	Not defined

environments. Following parameters such as problem addressed, techniques used, performance challenges, use cases, experimental setup, evaluation criteria, and data set, are used for comparison purposes.

3 Existing Mobile Based Resource Provisioning and Allocation Mechanisms in Fog

Fog environment offers a wide range of interesting services with its highly mobile end devices. With mobility comes several factors that have to be considered while managing the resources during provisioning and allocation. In this section, we describe the existing works to reflect the current state-of-the-art of resource management in mobility management in the Fog environment.

Waqas et al. [22] pointed mobility as an inseparable entity of Fog computing that enables a wide range of interesting services to improve the user experience. In a mobility-aware Fog environment, the user information is constantly updated at Fog servers and nodes to increase the effectiveness of the services on offer. Such constant information updates can invite several challenges, such as prediction of user behaviors, resource constraints, geographical limitations, and so on. Developed as an extension to Cloud computing, Fog computing is agile, highly mobile, and has low latency. While offering different computing services, Fog servers and devices can be mobile and such mobility should be handled properly to ensure low latency for the services offered. Mobility management should consider not just mobile devices, but also resource management including allocation and scheduling mechanisms. In this section, we present the works that have introduced innovative measures to tackle mobility while provisioning and allocating resources in the Fog environment.

Gosh et al. [23] proposed a mobility and delay-aware framework called LOCA-TOR that offers efficient location-based resource provisioning in an intelligent transportation system. The framework uses an optimal matching algorithm of the MapReduce paradigm to minimize the time required for service-provisioning and service waiting. LOCATOR was implemented on Google Cloud Platform using different realistic datasets that characterize mobility and shown to offer less execution time than that of the baseline methods.

Babu et al. [24] proposed architecture for Fog-based node-to-node communication in 5G network. The node-to-node communication is enabled by Fog servers and data analytics unit. In the proposed architecture, the authors proposed a robust mobility management scheme for mobile users to make such communication possible. Mobility management comprises location management and calls delivery procedures. The location management procedure updates the most recent location information, while the call delivery procedure delivers the call to the target node to enable node-to-node communication. The work offers several advantages of low overhead database update cost, data loss, signal exchange, easier update, and high security compared to similar networks. The authors also highlighted costly real-time implementation, poor results with a 3G network, limited privacy, and data replication as the major limitations of the proposed work.

Xie et al. [25] proposed a method for offloading tasks in vehicular Fog computing based on the mobility of vehicle nodes to minimize the service time. The mechanism used vehicle-to-vehicle (V2V) links to offload a task decomposed into subtasks in any proportion from user to service-vehicle in parallel. The mechanism used a hidden Markov model to predict V2V links state based on the mobility information of the vehicles collected. A rule was then set to choose the target service-vehicles and the proportion of decomposition of a task into subtasks, based on the predicted results. The mechanism was shown to have a better performance on service time and total finished tasks when compared to single-point and random task offloading.

The authors in [26] proposed URMILA (Ubiquitous Resource Management for Interference and Latency-Aware services) to switch between Fog and Edge resources for IoT services ensuring the latency of those services are met. The authors proposed a novel algorithm to find and choose the most suitable Fog node to serve IoT applications remotely when the application could be served with the Fog resource. The devised method considers the interference caused due to co-located and competing IoT services on multiple Fog nodes and controls the application executions such that the SLOs are met with low latency. The capabilities of the algorithm were tested with the real-world context on an emulated yet realistic IoT testbed.

Wang et al. [27] considered architecture for three-layered Fog computing networks (FCN) and characterized the user equipment mobility with sojourn time in each coverage of FCN. The user formulated the reduction of the probability of migration as a mixed non-linear programming problem that would maximize the revenue of user equipment. In the mixed-integer problem, the first part is task off-loading, while the second part is resource allocation. The task-offloading problem was solved by using Gini coefficient-based FCNs selection algorithm (GCFSA) that gave a sub-optimal strategy. The resource allocation problem was solved by a genetic algorithm based distributed resource optimization algorithm (ROAGA). In the proposed approach, the probability of migration was significantly reduced even when the mobility of the user equipment was well-handled. Simulation results proved the supremacy of the approach over baseline algorithms in terms of quasi-optimal revenue.

Starting with an argument that presents the migration of user application modules among Fog nodes as one of the solutions to mitigate the mobility issue in the Fog environment, Martin et al. [28] proposed an autonomic framework called MAMF that handles the container migration while adhering to QoS requirements. The proposed framework borrows the concepts of MAPE loop and Genetic algorithm to suitably decide the container migration in Fog within the deadlines for each application. Under this approach, a predetermined value of use location is used for the next time instant to initiate the migration of containers. The re-allocation problem was modeled as an Integer Linear Programming problem within the framework. The experiments were conducted in iFogSim toolkit, which showed improvement in execution cost, network usage, and request execution delay with the framework when compared to other methods.

Two different analytical models are proposed in [29] to address the issue arisen when the communication with the remote Cloud fails due to mobile devices in the Fog environment and the user does not get the requested service outputs. In the first model, remote Cloud servers were used to execute the task and the results were delivered to the mobile devices through push notification when the mobile was reconnected with the network after the mobile device lost the connection with the Cloud instance in the first place because of the mobility. In the second model, the virtual machine live migration was proposed whenever the mobile device changed the location. The present state of the instance was transferred to a new Cloudlet where the execution was resumed after the offloading. The experimental results showed a decrease in power consumption by 30–78% with the proposed models when compared to existing approaches.

Gosh et al. [30] proposed a collaborative real-time framework named Mobi-IoST that includes Cloud, Fog, Edge, and IoT layers to handle the mobility dynamics of any agent within the framework. In the framework, the spatiotemporal GPS logs along with other situational information are analyzed and fed into a machine learning algorithm that ultimately predicts the location of the moving agents in real-time. A probabilistic graphical model was used to model the mobility of the agent. The model enabled the prediction of the next location of the agent where the processed information was to be delivered. The tasks were delegated among the service nodes based on the mobility model. The framework was proven to provide better QoS in real-time applications and minimize delay and power consumption.

To fulfill the strictest requirements of enormous traffic demands and low latency, Santos et al. [31] proposed Kubernetes-based Fog architecture, which is an open-source orchestration platform on container-level. The authors implemented a network and mobility-aware scheduling approach in a smart city deployment scenario as an extension to existing scheduling mechanisms in Kubernetes. The authors validated the formulation of optimization of IoT services problem using the same approach to prove the applicability of such theoretical approaches in real-life practical deployments. The experimental results highlighted the reduction in network latency by 70% when compared to existing default scheduling mechanisms.

The authors in [32] highlighted the mobility of devices in Fog computing as one of the key factors to influence the application performance. The work then emphasizes the consideration of not just the mobility but the combination of distributed capacity and types of user application also for resource management in Fog computing to deal with the issues created by the mobile devices. The authors compared three different scheduling policies—delay priority, concurrent, and first come first serve (FCFS) and to understand the influence of mobility in resource management and improve the application execution based on their characteristics.

The authors in [27] integrated the Fog architecture with information-centric Internet of Vehicles (IoV) to provide support for the mobility of vehicle nodes through different schemas that consider data characteristics. In the proposed mechanism, the authors also considered the computation, storage, and location information of

Fog nodes for the exchange of information. The feature of IoV was also taken into consideration for communication in a mobile environment.

In a nutshell, various methods such as task offloading, live migration, and task delegation have been well-studied and implemented with demonstrated improvements when it comes to managing mobility in a computing environment regarding resource allocation and provisioning. Fast forward to the future, where all the end devices would offer seamless services to the users without any interruptions and guaranteed quality of service, the novel resource provisioning, and allocation algorithms should combine all those methods to handle the trade-offs within resource management in better ways.

4   Modelling Techniques to Support Mobility to Enhance the QoS of the Applications

Fog computing and its associated Edge-computing paradigms have been introduced to meet the demands of those complex nature applications that need efficiency, performance, reliability, mobility, and scalability at their top priority. The Fog computing approach provides the user with access through local data processing and data output rather than storing and maintaining information in extensively extracted Cloud storage facilities. Compared to Cloud computing that is often based on centralized architectures and provides the computation and storage service at fixed locations, Fog computing, and Edge computing are decentralized, distributed, and hierarchical, and their service locations are close to the end-user [7, 33].

Mobility of Fog computing is a critical challenge for most Fog computing-based real-time IoT applications because mobility requires keeping a network connection alive between sensor nodes and gateways, which are often referred to as Fog nodes. After all, network disruption often leads to unavailability of system services and, in some cases, high latency between network components. Moreover, the rapid advancements in the mobile communication technologies such as 5G wireless, it allows mobile users to off-load their computational processes to nearby deployed servers to reduce the consumption of resource-constrained devices with limited battery, memory, and processing power [34, 35].

To facilitate the application mobility function across Fog nodes, Martin et al. [28] proposed the mobility architecture to address the issue of moving containers corresponding to the user application modules. The transfer of containers is carried out in an automated mobile manner employing an automatic control loop called the Monitor–Analyze–Plan–Execute (MAPE) loop and Genetic Algorithm. The proposed structure incorporates agents who are responsible for gathering information on the environmental context to describe the implementation plan in a well-defined manner. To measure the movement of user devices to the Fog environment to which they are currently attached, the Monitoring mechanism senses a change between the user device and the distributed Fog nodes. The approach uses the pre-defined value of the user location to launch the migration process to improve service quality for Fog nodes.

QoS management consists of various methods used to delegate essentially distributed resources to Fog-user applications, selecting an acceptable way to allocate virtual resources to the physical resource. Therefore, a Fog-based resource allocation model was introduced in [36], with the main goal of addressing the issues of the mobility of nodes, assigning tasks, and also presenting virtual machine problems in a single Fog computing context. The purpose of the proposed approach is also defined by efficient resource allocation and mobility algorithm, which focuses primarily on optimizing the distribution of resources and reducing the number of users interacting with Fog nodes for different tasks.

To resolve the problem of mobility and increased latency in the vehicle Cloud computing environment, a directional model of vehicle mobility has been proposed [37] to achieve a guaranteed level of road vehicle service. In the proposed model, the entire network is divided into three sub-models based on their movement and rotation around the network. Within each model, vehicles are responsible for communicating with others via roadside units. The purpose of the proposed model is to reduce the latency and response time of the vehicle tasks. Also, various algorithms, such as greedy search algorithms, bipartite matching algorithms are used to solve optimization and cost flow issues.

Chen et al. [38] presented the Edge cognitive computing architecture to enable dynamic service migration based on the behavioral patterns of mobile users. Advanced cognitive services based on various artificial intelligence methods are used at the Edge of the network in the proposed architecture. The benefit of inducing these services to the Edge computing model is that it can achieve higher energy efficiency and service quality relative to current Edge computing paradigms. Besides, the simulation analysis highlights the importance of the proposed architecture in terms of low latency, dynamic user interface, high system resource usage that eventually achieves overall service quality at both user and system level.

The locality of Fog computing has made it a challenge to maintain consistency as mobile users are moving through different access networks. To deal with the locality problem of Fog users, Bi et al. [39] suggested the software-defined networking (SDN) architecture that divides system features into two modules. One module is responsible for managing the mobility of users across the network, while the other module serves as a router and only handles data routing functions. Besides, to demonstrate the flexibility of the proposed model, an effective route optimization algorithm is also proposed that overcomes the problems of network performance overhead as well as delays in data communication. Efficient signaling operations are also advocated to provide mobile users with transparency and usability assistance in Fog computing. The simulation results of the proposed model illustrate the assurance of service continuity for mobile users and increased the efficiency of data transmission when re-registering users on other access networks.

Providing seamless connectivity to mobile users in Fog computing-mobile networks is a major challenge since it requires adequate load balancing mechanisms to offload computing to mobile users and a consistent channel to communicate with others. To take this concept into account, Ghosh et al. [30] suggested Mobi-IoST—a collaborative system consisting of multiple components offering efficient delivery of various types of services to consumers, regardless of their mobile locations. Also, the proposed system is capable of providing users with an appropriate decision-making process on the knowledge and data they provide. The Cloud portion is responsible for analyzing the location data of IoT devices obtained from Fog nodes based on their mobility patterns. The mobility prediction module predominantly stores the model information and location logs of mobile users in different settings and utilizes the Markov model to make decisions on location logs to detect their locations efficiently.

High latency is also a major challenge in the Fog computing world, where mobile devices are faced with issues of proper access and control of Cloud resources by moving users around the network. To fix this problem, Zhang et al. [40] introduced an effective mobility-based method to transfer virtual machines between Edge Cloud data centers to mitigate network overhead. To meet the migration criteria of virtual machines, two algorithms (M-Edge and M-All) are used to identify machines based on mobile users in the network. Further, weight-based and predictive-based algorithms are used to support user mobility. The strength of the proposed approach is that it greatly decreases the network overhead and latency of the migration of virtual machines in the MEC environment.

Lee et al. [41] presented a Mobility Management System based on the Multi-Access Edge Computing (MEC) model that incorporates the idea of a protected access region called zones where mobile users can access server resources efficiently and monitor contents when traveling. The benefit of having the zone is that mobile users are still able to link and communicate with other mobile users within the specified boundary. In specified zones, mobile users must first register with the nearest zone and transmit their information and then access the network resources identified by the access control list.

Another mobility management issue in a high-density Fog computing environment is discussed by Rejiba et al. [42] where a user-centric mechanism is used to select Fog nodes to perform various tasks. The objective of the proposed work is to allow mobile users to learn and connect to a Fog node using a multi-armed bandit algorithm. In the learning method, an epoch model is used where the total number of Fog nodes is almost equal to the number of specifications (processes) to be completed. As a consequence, the quality of service is achieved by using a limited number of Fog nodes to execute the operation with the best possible capacity. Real-time user data and location patterns are used for simulation purposes.

In MEC environments, users with a mobility orientation frequently change their positions at various periods, so it is very hard to switch between different servers to provide them with the resources they need to maintain the quality of service. To overcome this issue, Peng et al. [43] proposed mobility intelligence and migration enables an online decision-making framework called MobMig to solve the Edge user allocation problem in an efficient and real-time manner. The proposed system completely automates current static location-aware systems that have resulted in system inefficiency and time delay invariant. Proper service selection and allocation to the right users in the MC system is a major challenge due to resource constraints and the restricted functionality of mobile devices. To overcome these challenges, Wu et al. [44] suggested a heuristic approach by integrating genetic and annealing algorithms to accommodate multiple service requests from mobile users. The benefit of the proposed approach is that it can substantially reduce the response time in the selection and delivery of the service over the MEC network.

A user-centric mobility approach in the Fog computing environment, with the cooperation of user interface and resource allocation scenarios, is introduced by Tong et al. [47] to resolve issues of inappropriate resource allocation and lack of user experience in the context of unpredictable Fog scenarios. In the proposed approach, mix-integer non-linear programming is resolved using a novel algorithm called UCAA—low complexity two-step interactive optimal algorithm. For user experience, two decision-based algorithms, such as semi-definite programming and Kuhn-Munkres are proposed and used in the proposed scenario. Also, to fix the problem of resource allocation, the overall scenario is divided into two phases: transmission power selection and resource allocation, and each phase is individually addressed. The analysis of the proposed approach achieves substantial overall performance in the allocation of server resources and enhanced user experience in Fog computing environments.

With end-user mobility, the migration of services between different mobile users is a challenging task to ensure the quality of service and operating costs of the overall network. To resolve these challenges, Ouyang et al. [48] introduced a dynamic mobility-aware service model to balance the efficiency and cost of the computing infrastructure for end-users. To overcome the unpredictable mobility of users, the Lyapunov optimization technique is used to divide the long-term optimization problem into a set of real-time optimization problems solely based on the NP-hard problem. Also, the proposed method uses the Markov approximation algorithm to find the optimization of such real-time problems. The advantage of the proposed system is that it can substantially reduce the time complexity for large-scale end-user applications.

Optimal task scheduling and off-loading tasks in MEC are both critical challenges due to vehicle mobility, moving patterns, and varying traffic loads. To resolve these problems, the energy-efficient dynamic decision-based approach is introduced by Huang et al. [49] where a transmission system called uplink is implemented to allow traffic from vehicles to roadside units. A dynamic process (or task) offloading mechanism is used to reduce latency, energy consumption, and packet rate. Moreover, a resource allocation method is also proposed to tackle the different complexity of each vehicle and its waiting pattern for resource accessibility. For dynamic task offloading and efficient allocation of resources, a Lyapunov mechanism is proposed to ensure the efficiency of the system.

Table 2 provides a detailed comparison of existing techniques for modeling the mobility used to improve the quality of service (QoS) of the applications. Following parameters such as problem addressed, techniques used, performance challenges, use cases, experimental setup, evaluation criteria, and data set, are used for comparison purposes.

Table 2 Comparison of existing techniques for modelling the mobility used to improve the Quality of Service (QoS) of the applications

Ref	Problem addressed	Techniques used	Performance challenges	Use cases	Experimental setup	Evaluation criteria	Dataset used
[28]	Migrations of containers or applications	MAPE loop and genetic algorithm	Quality of service	Not defined	iFogSim Toolkit	Network usage, delay (Execution and Request) Monetary cost	Vehicular dataset, (General Departmental Council of Val de Marne)
[36]	Migration of applications, Resource allocation issues	Not defined	Quality of service	Not defined	CloudSim tool kit	Processing time	Not defined
[38]	Service migration issue	Edge cognitive computing	Energy efficiency, Quality of service	Not defined	Android application program	Latency, Service resolution, User Experience	Not defined
[39]	Mobility support to mobile users	An efficient route optimization algorithm	Quality of experience	Not defined	Mininet-WiFi package	System cost, Handover latency	Not defined
[30]	Mobility dynamics of the moving agent	Machine learning approaches, probabilistic graphical model	Energy efficiency Quality of service	Not defined	Matlab	Delay, Power consumption, Accuracy, Recall F-measure	Mobility dataset generated from 100 smart phones
[45]	Communication inefficiency and security of data	Not defined	Security Reliability Efficiency	Smart grid	IoT platform ThingSpeak, Matlab, IEEE 13-bus test grid	Different Simulation Times (Initialization, execution, termination), energy computation	Not defined

(continued)

Table 2 (continued)

Ref	Problem addressed	Techniques used	Performance challenges	Use cases	Experimental setup	Evaluation criteria	Dataset used
[40]	Network overhead issue because of migration of virtual machines	Naïve migration algorithms (M-All and M-Edge)	Quality of service	Not defined	Not defined	Trajectory, Overhead analysis, Performance analysis	Microsoft Geolife Trajectories 1.3
[41]	Access to MEC Architecture, Unnecessary delays in request processing	Zone based access	Quality of service	Not defined	CloudSim and Edge CloudSim	User mobility model, Number of mobile users, average task size, WLAN bandwidth, VM processor speed,	Not defined
[42]	Mobility issue in user patterns	Bandit learning model	Quality of service	Not defined	Not defined	Medium and high Fog nodes density	Android mobile data collected at downtown street in Vilanova I La Geltru
[43]	Edge user resource allocation issue	Random way point (RWP) mobility model OPT, FFP, and Greedy Approach	Quality of service	Central business district in Melbourne, Australia	Not defined	User coverage rate and capacity	Google map
[46]	Reliability of smart mobility applications	Not defined	Quality of service	Vehicular network	Python based modules	High density vs low density	Real VANET called BusNet

Ref	Issue	Algorithm	Service of Quality	Application	Simulation tool	Parameters	Data
[44]	Service composition in mobile users and communities	Krill-Herd algorithm		Mobile web service	Build on simulation tool using .Net platform	Population size, maximum iterations, searching constant	Not defined
[47]	Lack of mobility support and high delay	semi-definite programming based algorithm, Kuhn-Munkres algorithm	user experience, system performance	IIoT Healthcare smart grid smart traffic	Matlab	User-centric utility	Not defined
[48]	Service migration across mobile users	Lyapunov optimization, Markov approximation	Performance Time complexity	Not defined	ONE simulator	Average perceived latency, long term cost	Video streaming data
[49]	optimal task offloading decisions	Lyapunov optimization	Energy consumption, Quality of Experience	Vehicular Networks	Not defined	Transmission power, Noise power, Channel bandwidth, CPU frequency, Packet drop rate, Energy consumption	Not defined
[50]	Mobility-Aware Task Offloading issue in vehicular networks	Not defined	Performance Service Quality	Not defined	Vehicular network	System cost, Latency threshold,	Not defined
[51]	Delay and energy consumption during sending and receiving request from server	Weighted majority game theory	Latency Energy efficiency	Health care	Test bed is created to gather heart rate, Raspberry Pi	Data transmission, delay, energy	Real-time patient data (heart rate)

5   Mathematical Models for Mobility Based Resource Allocation

This section discusses various existing mathematical models that have been used to solve the mobility challenges in dynamic resource allocations.

Aazam et al. [52] proposed a mathematical model for the dynamic allocation of resources in fog computing and, in particular, in the industrial internet, to achieve both qualities of experience and quality of services. The net promoter score is used in the proposed model to calculate the user's input from a given scale with total scores of 0–10, divided into three parts, i.e. negative (0–6), neutral (7–8), and positive (9–10). By calculating these scores from the user's historic net promoter score, the user is assigned dynamic resources with different cases ranging from the default, smaller, and higher scores. Lu et al. [53] proposed an efficient mechanism to achieve a dynamic allocation of resources in the Fog-based high-speed train setup and to improve communication performance in the mobility environment. Also, to maximize the energy efficiency of the proposed mechanism, a mathematical model is proposed to solve the problem of rapid convergence using iterative algorithms. In the mathematical model, the following scenarios related to resource allocation problems are considered, such as subcarrier allocation, transmitting power, and antenna allocation. Also, each scenario is then resolved by decoupling the cases from the others in iterative ways.

Lee et al. [54] presented a mathematical model to solve resource problems in the Fog computing-based industrial internet of things. The purpose of presenting the mathematical model is to explain the relationship between computing cost and service popularity to solve the problem of constructing utilities for shared dynamic resources used in Fog computing. Babu and Biswash [55] presented a mathematical model for a mobility-based management technique designed to achieve node-to-node communication in Fog computing-based 5G networks. The following scenarios, including energy consumption, communication latency, robustness, signaling costs, delay, and latency, are considered in this model. Hui et al. [56] proposed an idea to build a resource allocation mechanism for the Edge-computing environment based on mobility to achieve better stability and secure system data operations. To formulate their proposed idea, a differential mathematical model is presented to define the relationship between the resources allocated to the intrusion detection system (IDS) and the users. To enhance the applicability of their model, the quantitative analysis is also combined with the proposed differential model. By having this integrated model, the system is better able to maintain scalability and security.

Xiang et al. [57] presented a mathematical model called JSNC for efficient slicing of mobile and Edge computing resources in the Fog-based Cloud computing environment. This mathematical modeling aims to analyze the problems for minimizing the latency or delay between the transmission of resources, performing operations on user traffic gather from multiple traffic classes, and applying the constraints on different capacities network. The proposed mathematical model is integrated with a mixed-integer nonlinear spatial modulation to effectively evaluate the two heuristic approaches, including sequential fixing and greedy approaches. Oueida et al. [58] presented mathematical modeling using the Petri net framework for the validation of non-consumable resources in Cloud computing and Edge computing. This mathematical framework provides for the validation of the known framework used in the medical field called the Emergency Department (ED). For validation of the proposed model, the following parameters, such as patient length of stay, patient waiting time, and resource utilization rate, are used as basic performance measurement criteria. Zhang et al. [59] presented a mathematical model for the Joint Optimization Framework to optimize the content cache and resource allocation issues in MEC. The presented model is integrated with the policy gradient and value integration methods for determining the performance of communication links with two scenarios such as vehicle to infrastructure and vehicle to vehicle. At the top of that, the mathematical model is also given for the content of the cache scenario in MEC.

Huang et al. [60] proposed an energy-efficient, enhanced learning algorithm for task offloading and resource allocation in a Fog-based vehicular network. To validate the proposed algorithm, a mathematical model is then presented covering the different delay aspects, for instance, delay of task execution. Lin et al. [61] proposed a task offloading and resource allocation model based on a new multi-objective resource constraint mechanism for smart devices in a Fog-based Cloud environment. The proposed model is enhanced by a regression algorithm to make user requests without repeating the sequence. To validate their proof, a mathematical model is presented for the resolution of tasks related to offloading and resource allocation issues, taking into account different evaluation parameters, including processing time of virtual machines, tasks, completion time, and energy consumption.

The comparison of these models are presented in Table 3.

6 Application Use Cases

Fog computing is fully accessible to a wide variety of potential IoT applications, covering a significant proportion of many industries and businesses. It offers various advantages to those applications where real-time connectivity, streaming, fast processing, delay less communication, and low latency are the most and the top priority requirements. Figure 1 illustrates the taxonomy of mobility-based use cases and applications in the Fog/Edge environments.

6.1 Vehicular Networks

As part of the innovative IoT technologies, Vehicular Ad-hoc Networks (VANETs) offers an opportunity for the modern world by introducing new ways of linking

Table 3 Comparison of mobility-based resource allocation mathematical models

Ref	Application domain	Problems formulated	Model/technique used	Evaluation parameters considered
[52]	Industrial Internet of Things	Dynamic resource allocation	Net promoter score	Quality of service, Quality of experience
[53]	High-speed trains	Dynamic resource allocation, Communication performance	Mixed integer programming	Subcarrier allocation Transmit power Antenna allocation
[54]	Industrial Internet of Things	Resource portioning	Not defined	Quality of service, Quality of experience
[55]	5G networks	Mobility management	Net promoter score	Energy consumption, Communication delay, Robustness, Signalling cost, Delay, Latency
[56]	Intrusion detection system	Resource allocation	Differential Equation Model	Scalability
[57]	5G networks	Efficient slicing of resources	Not defined	Scalability
[58]	Smart Healthcare	Resource allocation	Petri net framework	Patient length stay, Patient waiting time, Resource utilization rate
[59]	Internet of Vehicles	Content cache and resource allocation	Markov decision process model	Scalability
[60]	Vehicular Networks	Task offloading and resource allocation	Deep Reinforcement Learning	Task execution delay, Energy consumption, Offloading execution time, Local execution time
[61]	Smart Healthcare	Task offloading and resource allocation	Fruit Fly Optimization	Processing time of virtual machines, Completion time, Energy consumption, Data center cost

on-road vehicles and passengers and offering new driving paradigms such as intelligent auxiliary driving and automatic driving [46]. Further, it enhance the existing transportation system with the new intelligent features including navigation, city traffic anomaly detection, bus stop arrival time estimation, and path finding along with the planning as well [62]. It also can detect and respond in real-time

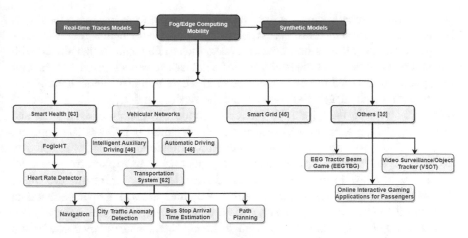

Fig. 1 Taxonomy of fog/edge mobility supported applications

to unforeseen incidents where traditional concepts such as Cloud computing are unable to perform immediate actions. Fog Computing considers VANETs to be a further prerequisite for the technological challenge, bringing computer tools, applications, and services closer to their users and enabling mobile applications and services to be delivered with a minimum of delay. To address the mobility challenges of smart applications in the VANET context, Pereira et al. [46] proposed a simplified architecture that uses proof-of-concept technologies to provide Fog computing mobility services across VANET safely and efficiently. The architecture tested on a smaller traffic dataset where the achieved results show the reliability and quality of the information broadcast over a short period.

In another study, Yang et al. [50] suggested a mobility-aware task offloading scheme to tackle the issues of computing, time selection, communication, high latency, and efficient resource allocation in VANETs. The proposed scheme uses the concept of MEC where each MEC server works independently or in conjunction with access points to efficiently perform mobility aware off-loading tasks. Besides, MEC servers also use the location-based off-loading system to unload tasks to adjacent mobility access points by moving vehicles. The benefit of the proposed scheme is that mobility vehicles based on initial locations may either select a local computing access point or reload their processing tasks to the next access points to achieve the quality of service and balance latency and network computation costs at an optimal stage.

6.2 Smart Healthcare

Smart healthcare is one of the most ambitious applications that combines current computing paradigms such as IoT, Fog, and Cloud to provide patients with an enhanced and futuristic range of services. In smart healthcare, patient-related data is collected by different sensors, such as smartwatches, wrist bands, thermometers, and processed by different intermediate nodes, such as Fog, and further shared with Cloud servers, to take specific health-related actions. The network used for this form of application is called the body area network, where users (patients, doctors) can access their health data using various mobile devices and have separate control over data stored in the Cloud. To reduce the impact of energy consumption and processing delays of various Cloud servers in the smart healthcare environment, Fog computing has been proposed where various intermediate nodes called Fog nodes serve the processing and storage of patient data. To explain this scenario, Mukherjee et al. [63] suggested a Fog-based smart healthcare infrastructure where different indoor and outdoor sensors in the body area network gather patient data and send it to Fog nodes. Each Fog node used the concept of game theory called weighted majority to minimize the average latency, jitters, and energy consumption of the overall Fog computing-based health-care system.

6.3 Smart Grid

Smart grid is also a potential application of Fog-based IoT that combines the benefits of various ICT technologies to provide reliable, secure, and high-quality power services to consumers in an effective and specified manner. Smart grids are designed to monitor the power consumption of each household and to build a secure communication channel between users and different energy providers. Current solutions used by smart grid networks are solely focused on single or consolidated Cloud paradigms where Cloud providers are responsible for collecting and storing energy usage data and maintaining the profile of each household user. However, with an increasing number of smart devices connected to smart grid architectures, Cloud-based approaches often fail to provide real-time services on user data measurement and sometimes cause more delays in the network. In order to overcome these issues, Fog-based smart grid frameworks are introduced where Fog nodes are able to perform different computing services on user data rather than sending and storing Cloud parties [45].

6.4 Others

The scope of Fog and Edge computing paradigms is not limited to a few applications but provides a wide range of applications used in human daily life. For example, vision and hearing for mobility-impaired users, video surveillance, augmented reality, and mostly for gaming frameworks. One advantage of these Fog-based applications is that they require very low latency for communication between stations and Clouds [32].

7 Future Direction of Mobility-Based Resource Allocation and Provisioning in Fog and Edge related Computing Paradigms

This section concludes several future directions from the potential challenges of existing mobility-based resource allocation and provisioning frameworks for Fog and Edge-related computing paradigms. These challenges provide guidelines for researchers to develop efficient solutions for mobility-based resource allocation in Fog/Edge computing.

7.1 Mobility-Based Resource Allocation and Provisioning

Achieving the efficiency of Fog resources using different security enhancement policies is a difficult challenge, as each policy has its limitations, and therefore a multi-dimensional enhancement platform to support a variety of policies should be proposed to maximize profit and efficiency. In a mobility-based Fog computing environment, the energy consumption of mobile IoT devices is a challenging problem as most devices spend their energy and execution time connecting to different Fog devices in different regions, and therefore energy-efficient solutions for the placement and location of devices need to be considered as part of future work. The distribution of computational tasks on different Fog nodes in a resource-restricted environment is a difficult task, as Fog nodes must be aware of the computational capabilities of the IoT nodes deployed and their remaining use capacity. Also, the migration of services or applications from the Cloud to Fog nodes is a challenging issue that needs to be considered for efficient delivery and proper use to achieve QoS. Moreover, the available resources of Fog/Edge nodes should be properly managed through virtualization and efficiently allocate the resources because of limited resource nodes. To this end, efficient allocation, provisioning of resources, and scheduling algorithms should be developed to improve QoS in the Fog and Edge-based environment.

7.2 Security and Privacy

Despite offering a large number of benefits to users in terms of distributed processing, minimizes latency, mobility support, and position awareness, etc., the security and privacy of users and their data stored and exchanged by various Fog computing nodes is becoming a critical challenge. While a range of security solutions have been put forward to ensure the authentication, authorization, access control, and availability of Fog services, as well as the confidentiality, integrity, and reliability of data stored on Cloud servers. Nevertheless, due to a significant increase in data volume and processing nodes, more robust and secure solutions based on quantum cryptography and blockchain could also be used to build a trustworthy relationship between Fog computing nodes.

7.3 Power Utilization and Management

Fog nodes have to manage a large number of concurrent requests from computers, users, and other Fog nodes simultaneously. Researchers have suggested various approaches to solve this situation, such as adding more Fog nodes and increase the resource vector that will ultimately accommodate multiple requests to some extent. However, on the other hand, these approaches contribute to the extra power usage of the overall network, which greatly reduces the energy and efficiency of restricted mobile devices. For the power utilization and management of both Fog and Edge nodes, this problem must be tackled to achieve the QoS of the underlying network and to maximize the efficiency of Fog nodes during the migration of services and tasks among other nodes.

7.4 Fault Tolerance

Fault tolerance is an essential challenge in the Fog computing environment that ensures the continuous delivery of services and operations to mobile nodes regardless of location and network processing efforts. This also ensures that every node completes their task in an event of breakdown with little to no human interference. To achieve fault tolerance of MC nodes, a range of failover and redundancy solutions such as RAID models, backup of user data, upgrade of security patches, constant power supply, etc. However, these solutions require extra hardware but instead provide Fog nodes services at fixed locations, so there is a need to improve capabilities and design low power fault tolerance techniques for the mobile nature of Fog nodes.

7.5 Support For Application Placements Strategies

Application placement strategies in Fog and Edge computing offer a way to meet the challenging needs of complex resources for an increasing number of IoT devices in time-critical scenarios. Since IoT devices operate constantly in the deployed environments for the sensing and computation of data, many Cloud/Fog resources are required to perform tasks in time. Current application placement approaches often fail to satisfy the resource needs of a growing number of devices and only applicable to IoT applications that do not always change their locations, such as parking sensors. It is, therefore, a challenging task to develop an application placement strategy that needs support for the mobility and heterogeneous design of IoT devices and takes less time to perform parallel tasks.

7.6 Support Interoperability

The design model of Fog and Edge-based computing environments consists of heterogeneous nature of devices distributed at remote locations, connected via various data centers, and using a wide variety of protocols such as wireless, Bluetooth, 4G, and 5G. With the abundance of various types of technical components with specific design models and capacities, it is also difficult to work seamlessly and share resources among others. A proper interoperability framework is thus required that can manage the dynamic nature of devices and protocols, as well as fulfill the need for a common remote resource sharing platform to improve efficiency and transparency at a significant level.

7.7 Unified and Dynamic Resource Management and Provisioning

A crucial and difficult issue is to develop a single resource management framework, which is similar to personal computer Meta OS, to provide on-demand and cross-domain services for heterogeneous IoT devices. The platform should be a centralized IoT-based management framework that distinguishes hardware and software logically from devices and ensures that all software and hardware resources, including commodity OSes and their applications, are managed uniformly and that versatile services are provided via heterogeneous IoT devices. Required services can be configured on the IoT devices and performed dynamically according to the request. If the instance OS on the IoT device cannot support the requested service, the server-side will load a compatible instance OS for the service. So it is a crucial challenge in this regard to get dynamic OS boots and service loading on lightweight IoT devices from the Edge servers. While using the computing resources of Edge servers, IoT-based computing infrastructure will be capable of using a more powerful computing paradigm. The main challenge is how machine tasks are distributed between terminals and Edge servers. The development of various techniques for partitioning a task has been accelerated by evolving distributed computing environments to allow for simultaneous partitioned tasks at several geographic locations [17, 64].

8 Conclusion

Near-to-the-Edge services have now started delivering exciting services in every field with the help of nodes and devices in paradigms such as Fog and Edge. These nodes are highly dynamic and mobile, which pose several challenges in resource management including provisioning and allocation while serving the users for different applications. As such, in this chapter, we presented a comprehensive list of challenges for a MEC paradigm that can deliver seamless services, irrespective of its highly mobile nodes and devices. We also presented a true reflection of the current-state-of-the-art of the works done, centered around the mobility of the end devices, to address the challenges while managing the resource. Based on our analyses, we also highlighted the need for such a mobile environment to be integrated with emerging technologies like 5G and SDN along with other future research directions for MEC.

References

1. Sneha Tammishetty, T Ragunathan, Sudheer Kumar Battula, B Varsha Rani, P RaviBabu, RaghuRamReddy Nagireddy, Vedika Jorika, and V Maheshwar Reddy. Iot-based traffic signal control technique for helping emergency vehicles. In *Proceedings of the First International Conference on Computational Intelligence and Informatics*, pages 433–440. Springer, 2017.
2. KC Ujjwal, Saurabh Garg, James Hilton, Jagannath Aryal, and Nicholas Forbes-Smith. Cloud computing in natural hazard modeling systems: Current research trends and future directions. *International Journal of Disaster Risk Reduction*, page 101188, 2019.
3. Hamidreza Arasteh, Vahid Hosseinnezhad, Vincenzo Loia, Aurelio Tommasetti, Orlando Troisi, Miadreza Shafie-khah, and Pierluigi Siano. Iot-based smart cities: a survey. In *2016 IEEE 16th International Conference on Environment and Electrical Engineering (EEEIC)*, pages 1–6. IEEE, 2016.
4. Flavio Bonomi, Rodolfo Milito, Jiang Zhu, and Sateesh Addepalli. Fog computing and its role in the internet of things. In *Proceedings of the first edition of the MCC workshop on Mobile cloud computing*, pages 13–16, 2012.
5. Sudheer Kumar Battula, Saurabh Garg, James Montgomery, and Byeong Ho Kang. An efficient resource monitoring service for fog computing environments. *IEEE Transactions on Services Computing*, 2019.
6. Jürgo S Preden, Kalle Tammemäe, Axel Jantsch, Mairo Leier, Andri Riid, and Emine Calis. The benefits of self-awareness and attention in fog and mist computing. *Computer*, 48(7):37–45, 2015.
7. Ranesh Kumar Naha, Saurabh Garg, Dimitrios Georgakopoulos, Prem Prakash Jayaraman, Longxiang Gao, Yong Xiang, and Rajiv Ranjan. Fog computing: Survey of trends, architectures, requirements, and research directions. *IEEE access*, 6:47980–48009, 2018.
8. Sonia Shahzadi, Muddesar Iqbal, Tasos Dagiuklas, and Zia Ul Qayyum. Multi-access edge computing: open issues, challenges and future perspectives. *Journal of Cloud Computing*, 6(1):30, 2017.
9. Minh-Quang Tran, Duy Tai Nguyen, Van An Le, Duc Hai Nguyen, and Tran Vu Pham. Task placement on fog computing made efficient for iot application provision. *Wireless Communications and Mobile Computing*, 2019, 2019.
10. Maurizio Capra, Riccardo Peloso, Guido Masera, Massimo Ruo Roch, and Maurizio Martina. Edge computing: A survey on the hardware requirements in the internet of things world. *Future Internet*, 11(4):100, 2019.

11. Hasan Ali Khattak, Hafsa Arshad, Saif ul Islam, Ghufran Ahmed, Sohail Jabbar, Abdullahi Mohamud Sharif, and Shehzad Khalid. Utilization and load balancing in fog servers for health applications. *EURASIP Journal on Wireless Communications and Networking*, 2019(1):91, 2019.
12. Pavel Mach and Zdenek Becvar. Mobile edge computing: A survey on architecture and computation offloading. *IEEE Communications Surveys & Tutorials*, 19(3):1628–1656, 2017.
13. Yonal Kirsal, Glenford Mapp, and Fragkiskos Sardis. Using advanced handover and localization techniques for maintaining quality-of-service of mobile users in heterogeneous cloud-based environment. *Journal of Network and Systems Management*, 27(4):972–997, 2019.
14. Ranesh Kumar Naha, Saurabh Garg, Andrew Chan, and Sudheer Kumar Battula. Deadline-based dynamic resource allocation and provisioning algorithms in fog-cloud environment. *Future Generation Computer Systems*, 104:131–141, 2020.
15. Cheol-Ho Hong and Blesson Varghese. Resource management in fog/edge computing: a survey on architectures, infrastructure, and algorithms. *ACM Computing Surveys (CSUR)*, 52(5):1–37, 2019.
16. Mostafa Ghobaei-Arani, Alireza Souri, and Ali A Rahmanian. Resource management approaches in fog computing: A comprehensive review. *Journal of Grid Computing*, pages 1–42, 2019.
17. Ju Ren, Hui Guo, Chugui Xu, and Yaoxue Zhang. Serving at the edge: A scalable iot architecture based on transparent computing. *IEEE Network*, 31(5):96–105, 2017.
18. Haijun Zhang, Na Liu, Xiaoli Chu, Keping Long, Abdol-Hamid Aghvami, and Victor CM Leung. Network slicing based 5g and future mobile networks: mobility, resource management, and challenges. *IEEE communications magazine*, 55(8):138–145, 2017.
19. Argyrios G Tasiopoulos, Onur Ascigil, Ioannis Psaras, and George Pavlou. Edge-map: Auction markets for edge resource provisioning. In *2018 IEEE 19th International Symposium on" A World of Wireless, Mobile and Multimedia Networks"(WoWMoM)*, pages 14–22. IEEE, 2018.
20. Mengting Liu, F Richard Yu, Yinglei Teng, Victor CM Leung, and Mei Song. Distributed resource allocation in blockchain-based video streaming systems with mobile edge computing. *IEEE Transactions on Wireless Communications*, 18(1):695–708, 2018.
21. Yangzhe Liao, Liqing Shou, Quan Yu, Qingsong Ai, and Quan Liu. Joint offloading decision and resource allocation for mobile edge computing enabled networks. *Computer Communications*, 2020.
22. Muhammad Waqas, Yong Niu, Manzoor Ahmed, Yong Li, Depeng Jin, and Zhu Han. Mobility-aware fog computing in dynamic environments: Understandings and implementation. *IEEE Access*, 7:38867–38879, 2018.
23. Shreya Ghosh, Jaydeep Das, and Soumya K Ghosh. Locator: A cloud-fog-enabled framework for facilitating efficient location based services. In *2020 International Conference on COMmunication Systems & NETworkS (COMSNETS)*, pages 87–92. IEEE, 2020.
24. S Babu and Sanjay Kumar Biswash. Fog computing–based node-to-node communication and mobility management technique for 5g networks. *Transactions on Emerging Telecommunications Technologies*, 30(10):e3738, 2019.
25. Jindou Xie, Yunjian Jia, Zhengchuan Chen, and Liang Liang. Mobility-aware task parallel offloading for vehicle fog computing. In *International Conference on Artificial Intelligence for Communications and Networks*, pages 367–379. Springer, 2019.
26. Shashank Shekhar, Ajay Chhokra, Hongyang Sun, Aniruddha Gokhale, Abhishek Dubey, Xenofon Koutsoukos, and Gabor Karsai. Urmila: Dynamically trading-off fog and edge resources for performance and mobility-aware iot services. *Journal of Systems Architecture*, page 101710, 2020.
27. Dongyu Wang, Zhaolin Liu, Xiaoxiang Wang, and Yanwen Lan. Mobility-aware task offloading and migration schemes in fog computing networks. *IEEE Access*, 7:43356–43368, 2019.
28. John Paul Martin, A Kandasamy, and K Chandrasekaran. Mobility aware autonomic approach for the migration of application modules in fog computing environment. *Journal of Ambient Intelligence and Humanized Computing*, pages 1–20, 2020.

29. Anwesha Mukherjee, Deepsubhra Guha Roy, and Debashis De. Mobility-aware task delegation model in mobile cloud computing. *The Journal of Supercomputing*, 75(1):314–339, 2019.
30. Shreya Ghosh, Anwesha Mukherjee, Soumya K Ghosh, and Rajkumar Buyya. Mobiiost: mobility-aware cloud-fog-edge-iot collaborative framework for time-critical applications. *IEEE Transactions on Network Science and Engineering*, 2019.
31. José Santos, Tim Wauters, Bruno Volckaert, and Filip De Turck. Resource provisioning in fog computing: From theory to practice. *Sensors*, 19(10):2238, 2019.
32. Luiz F Bittencourt, Javier Diaz-Montes, Rajkumar Buyya, Omer F Rana, and Manish Parashar. Mobility-aware application scheduling in fog computing. *IEEE Cloud Computing*, 4(2):26–35, 2017.
33. Tarik Taleb, Konstantinos Samdanis, Badr Mada, Hannu Flinck, Sunny Dutta, and Dario Sabella. On multi-access edge computing: A survey of the emerging 5g network edge cloud architecture and orchestration. *IEEE Communications Surveys & Tutorials*, 19(3):1657–1681, 2017.
34. Jianbing Ni, Kuan Zhang, Xiaodong Lin, and Xuemin Sherman Shen. Securing fog computing for internet of things applications: Challenges and solutions. *IEEE Communications Surveys & Tutorials*, 20(1):601–628, 2017.
35. Rodrigo Roman, Javier Lopez, and Masahiro Mambo. Mobile edge computing, fog et al.: A survey and analysis of security threats and challenges. *Future Generation Computer Systems*, 78:680–698, 2018.
36. Sathish Kumar Mani and Iyapparaja Meenakshisundaram. Improving quality-of-service in fog computing through efficient resource allocation. *Computational Intelligence*, 2020.
37. Yalan Wu, Jigang Wu, Long Chen, Gangqiang Zhou, and Jiaquan Yan. Fog computing model and efficient algorithms for directional vehicle mobility in vehicular network. *IEEE Transactions on Intelligent Transportation Systems*, 2020.
38. Min Chen, Wei Li, Giancarlo Fortino, Yixue Hao, Long Hu, and Iztok Humar. A dynamic service migration mechanism in edge cognitive computing. *ACM Transactions on Internet Technology (TOIT)*, 19(2):1–15, 2019.
39. Yuanguo Bi, Guangjie Han, Chuan Lin, Qingxu Deng, Lei Guo, and Fuliang Li. Mobility support for fog computing: An sdn approach. *IEEE Communications Magazine*, 56(5):53–59, 2018.
40. Fei Zhang, Guangming Liu, Bo Zhao, Xiaoming Fu, and Ramin Yahyapour. Reducing the network overhead of user mobility–induced virtual machine migration in mobile edge computing. *Software: Practice and Experience*, 49(4):673–693, 2019.
41. Juyong Lee, Daeyoub Kim, and Jihoon Lee. Zone-based multi-access edge computing scheme for user device mobility management. *Applied Sciences*, 9(11):2308, 2019.
42. Zeineb Rejiba, Xavier Masip-Bruin, and Eva Marin-Tordera. A user-centric mobility management scheme for high-density fog computing deployments. In *2019 28th International Conference on Computer Communication and Networks (ICCCN)*, pages 1–8. IEEE, 2019.
43. Qinglan Peng, Yunni Xia, Zeng Feng, Jia Lee, Chunrong Wu, Xin Luo, Wanbo Zheng, Hui Liu, Yidan Qin, and Peng Chen. Mobility-aware and migration-enabled online edge user allocation in mobile edge computing. In *2019 IEEE International Conference on Web Services (ICWS)*, pages 91–98. IEEE, 2019.
44. Hongyue Wu, Shuiguang Deng, Wei Li, Jianwei Yin, Xiaohong Li, Zhiyong Feng, and Albert Y Zomaya. Mobility-aware service selection in mobile edge computing systems. In *2019 IEEE International Conference on Web Services (ICWS)*, pages 201–208. IEEE, 2019.
45. Miodrag Forcan and Mirjana Maksimović. Cloud-fog-based approach for smart grid monitoring. *Simulation Modelling Practice and Theory*, 101:101988, 2020.
46. Jorge Pereira, Leandro Ricardo, Miguel Luís, Carlos Senna, and Susana Sargento. Assessing the reliability of fog computing for smart mobility applications in vanets. *Future Generation Computer Systems*, 94:317–332, 2019.
47. Shiyuan Tong, Yun Liu, Mohamed Cheriet, Michel Kadoch, and Bo Shen. Ucaa: User-centric user association and resource allocation in fog computing networks. *IEEE Access*, 8:10671–10685, 2020.

48. Tao Ouyang, Zhi Zhou, and Xu Chen. Follow me at the edge: Mobility-aware dynamic service placement for mobile edge computing. *IEEE Journal on Selected Areas in Communications*, 36(10):2333–2345, 2018.

49. Xiaoge Huang, Ke Xu, Chenbin Lai, Qianbin Chen, and Jie Zhang. Energy-efficient offloading decision-making for mobile edge computing in vehicular networks. *EURASIP Journal on Wireless Communications and Networking*, 2020(1):35, 2020.

50. Chao Yang, Yi Liu, Xin Chen, Weifeng Zhong, and Shengli Xie. Efficient mobility-aware task offloading for vehicular edge computing networks. *IEEE Access*, 7:26652–26664, 2019.

51. Anwesha Mukherjee, Debashis De, and Soumya K Ghosh. Fogioht: A weighted majority game theory based energy-efficient delay-sensitive fog network for internet of health things. *Internet of Things*, page 100181, 2020.

52. Mohammad Aazam, Khaled A Harras, and Sherali Zeadally. Fog computing for 5g tactile industrial internet of things: Qoe-aware resource allocation model. *IEEE Transactions on Industrial Informatics*, 15(5):3085–3092, 2019.

53. Lingyun Lu, Tian Wang, Wei Ni, Kai Li, and Bo Gao. Fog computing-assisted energy-efficient resource allocation for high-mobility mimo-ofdma networks. *Wireless Communications and Mobile Computing*, 2018, 2018.

54. Gaolei Li, Jun Wu, Jianhua Li, Kuan Wang, and Tianpeng Ye. Service popularity-based smart resources partitioning for fog computing-enabled industrial internet of things. *IEEE Transactions on Industrial Informatics*, 14(10):4702–4711, 2018.

55. S Babu and Sanjay Kumar Biswash. Fog computing–based node-to-node communication and mobility management technique for 5g networks. *Transactions on Emerging Telecommunications Technologies*, 30(10):e3738, 2019.

56. Hongwen Hui, Chengcheng Zhou, Xingshuo An, and Fuhong Lin. A new resource allocation mechanism for security of mobile edge computing system. *IEEE Access*, 7:116886–116899, 2019.

57. Bin Xiang, Jocelyne Elias, Fabio Martignon, and Elisabetta Di Nitto. Joint network slicing and mobile edge computing in 5g networks. In *ICC 2019-2019 IEEE International Conference on Communications (ICC)*, pages 1–7. IEEE, 2019.

58. Soraia Oueida, Yehia Kotb, Moayad Aloqaily, Yaser Jararweh, and Thar Baker. An edge computing based smart healthcare framework for resource management. *Sensors*, 18(12):4307, 2018.

59. Mu Zhang, Song Wang, and Qing Gao. A joint optimization scheme of content caching and resource allocation for internet of vehicles in mobile edge computing. *Journal of Cloud Computing*, 9(1):1–12, 2020.

60. Xinyu Huang, Lijun He, and Wanyue Zhang. Vehicle speed aware computing task offloading and resource allocation based on multi-agent reinforcement learning in a vehicular edge computing network. *arXiv preprint arXiv:2008.06641*, 2020.

61. Kai Lin, Sameer Pankaj, and Di Wang. Task offloading and resource allocation for edge-of-things computing on smart healthcare systems. *Computers & Electrical Engineering*, 72:348–360, 2018.

62. Quan Yuan, Haibo Zhou, Jinglin Li, Zhihan Liu, Fangchun Yang, and Xuemin Sherman Shen. Toward efficient content delivery for automated driving services: An edge computing solution. *IEEE Network*, 32(1):80–86, 2018.

63. Anwesha Mukherjee, Debashis De, and Soumya K Ghosh. Fogioht: A weighted majority game theory based energy-efficient delay-sensitive fog network for internet of health things. *Internet of Things*, page 100181, 2020.

64. Yaoxue Zhang, Ju Ren, Jiagang Liu, Chugui Xu, Hui Guo, and Yaping Liu. A survey on emerging computing paradigms for big data. *Chinese Journal of Electronics*, 26(1):1–12, 2017.

Cross Border Service Continuity with 5G Mobile Edge

Hamid R. Barzegar, Nabil El Ioini, Van Thanh Le, and Claus Pahl

Abstract One of the core elements for the upcoming generation of wireless cellular networks is the availability of network service access continuity in addition to high-speed internet and low latency. The forthcoming fifth generation (5G) greatly improves users' demand in terms of faster download rates, exceptional system availability, superb end to end coverage with exceptionally low latency and ultra reliability. One of the solutions to provide end to end low latency is the utilization of Mobile Edge Computing (MEC) in the network. MEC provides cloud advantages to users by setting up a small cloud server in the edge node (i.e. close to the end-user), which decreases the amount of latency in network connections, in this regard, service migration has required as users migrate to the new location. Optimal migration decisions are challenging because they depend on the cloud environment, or edge nodes belong to different orchestrators, and security issues in the migration process must also be resolved in order to prevent unreliable requests. This study provides different approaches to address these challenges by identifying the security implications of migration methods based on the blockchain integration.

Keywords Service continuity · Edge computing · Mobile edge · Video streaming · 5G

1 Introduction

Mobile Edge Computing (MEC) has cloud benefits to network consumers by setting up a small computing node very close to the end-user which, respectively, reducing latency in user connections and required bandwidth. However, as services and network infrastructures are deployed at the edge of the network, every time that users change location, services need to move as well to guarantee seamless

H. R. Barzegar (✉) · N. El Ioini · V. T. Le · C. Pahl
Faculty of Computer Science, Free University of Bolzano/Bozen, Bolzano, Italy
e-mail: hamidreza.barzegar@unibz.it; Nabil.ElIoini@unibz.it; VanThanh.Le@unibz.it;
Claus.Pahl@unibz.it

service continuity. In cross border scenarios, service continuity becomes even more challenging since it adds the burden to the network re-selection between two adjacent Mobile Network Operators (MNO) with different network configuration in terms of cloud-settings, or edge nodes belong to separate orchestrators and various policies. Additionally, security issues in the migration process also needed to be addressed to protect the network from cyber-attacks. MEC in combination with the expected high-performance New Radio (NR)/5G has a great potential to push back many limitations of the previous wireless cellular networks. Since the utilization of various types of smart equipment in vehicles has become so common, therefore, vehicles are already considered as connected devices. Nonetheless, very shortly, they will also communicate directly with each other (Vehicle to Vehicle (V2V) communication) and communicate with the road infrastructure (Vehicle to Infrastructure (V2I)) or in general, Vehicle to everything (V2X). This interaction requires a Cooperative, Connected, Automated and Autonomous Mobility (CCAM)[1] platform. The European Union (EU) supports projects in this context such as 5G-CARMEN[2] [1], 5G-CROCO,[3] and 5G-MOBIX[4] which aim to develop a new MEC-centric platform that encourages greener, safer, and more intelligent transport infrastructure through European countries.

The goal of these projects is to ensure Service Continuity (SC) in the cross border scenarios [2]. However, providing a seamless link/connection while users cross boundaries is a major challenge that goes beyond basic techniques such as network re-selection between various MNOs. It requires MEC-coordinated support as well. The main goal is to provide large scale SC for cross organizational boundaries to maximize the level of service availability and reliability with the highest level of transparency to the user. Recent developments in cloud and edge computing in tandem with 5G will bring about a dramatic shift by having the proper infrastructure to provide the required SC structures. In this chapter, we will present the current status of 5G-enabled MEC and our proposed solution for SC. It also highlights the key transparent problems that need to be resolved in the coming years. We show that in order to provide a solution, an ultra-Reliability and Low Latency Communication (uRLLC) MEC is a suitable platform direction. The architecture is based on the European Telecommunications Standards Institute (ETSI) MEC standards, which enables applications through a distributed multi-edge platform built from a range of nodes close to the next generation NodeB (gNB). This study investigates the advantages and disadvantages of migration strategies based on measuring metrics for both views of end-users and service providers, and evaluates our implementation with benchmark running to review blockchain overhead in the verification process.

This chapter book organized as following; Sect. 2 reviews background technologies and literature review of 5G service continuity. Section 3 introduces and

---

[1] https://ec.europa.eu/transport/themes/its/c-its_en.

[2] https://5gcarmen.eu/.

[3] https://5gcroco.eu/.

[4] https://www.5g-mobix.com/.

discuss security management for service continuity. 5G-CARMEN architecture and different use-cases of that describes in Sect. 4. Video streaming as a selected use-case of 5G-CARMEN for development and implementation describes in Sect. 5. Section 6 provides our future research directions. Finally, Sect. 7 presents our conclusion.

2 Background and Related Work

This section reviews the background techniques, technologies which provides service continuity for cellular networks and literature review.

2.1 Cloud Computing

Cloud computing has been one of the hottest key technical subjects in the last decade. This phenomena has had many wide-ranging implications across digital engineering, data storage, and information technology (IT) [3]. Cloud computing is a sharing of computational power, storage, server and other IT services over the Internet on the basis of users' demand, which has the ability to be easily created and released with limited management intervention or participation of service providers [4]. In other words, cloud computing is a kind of technique that provides resources with higher efficiency to the end-user through the virtualization techniques. The key features of cloud computing are availability, scalability remote manageability. The main elements in this technique are the services and data that are spread across the network. As a result, it increases availability and reliability, but it is also not close enough to the end-user to minimize the delay. Cloud infrastructure and IoT merging allows a vast range of technology scenarios [5] as one of the potential solutions.

2.2 Edge Computing

The concept of edge computing is primarily to drive services to the edge of the network. In this regard, computation as well as the required storage cloud has located really next to the end user as close as possible. Multi-Access Edge Networking is one of the core cornerstones of 5G broadband networks [6]. The edge cloud is a distributed virtualized services architecture [7, 8]. This offers infrastructure as services in a layered way to create a complete technology stack, including digital systems or software, hardware platforms and applications [9, 10]. With the MEC, all data generated by IoT devices will be stored, analyzed and processed one stage before being moved to the cloud. In certain instances of use such as autonomous driving, vehicle to vehicle communication which they need to have low latency, this may be significantly Improving the efficiency of facilities such as the lightweight edge [11] a lightweight virtualization platform for cooperative, connected and integrated mobility focused on industry-standard innovations such as Message Queuing Telemetry Transport (MQTT) protocol for communication, Prometheus for tracking and Docker swarm for the application of containerized services in combination with openFaas [12].

Aforementioned a MEC is a form of distributed computing that moves computations and data storage away from the centralized cloud center and get closer to users [13]. The main benefit for this architecture from the user point of view is to receive the same service but in the lowest latency and context-aware services which, should be listed as one of the key uses of the 5G network. In the event of a lack of the MEC architecture, the mobile Internet of Things (IoT) devices should send all captured data to the cloud-side for analysis and processing. However, these edge devices are suffering from low computing performance, therefore in the MEC architecture scenario, first of all, the data can be pre-processed and then passed to the cloud side. Another advantage is the collected data can be used for local decision-making or retained for future use. This is the way, MEC provides many advantages and generates situations that optimize interaction among consumer devices and the network, as like as; reducing the use of bandwidth through allowing local decisions.

In the traditional cloud network, to access services, applications have to request to a static host from anywhere, it puts a burden on the main cloud to address several thousand requests per second, and users have to suffer the high response time, so MEC could contribute in the scope by setting up a small server to process user requests with low latency. The MEC node can cover a wide range of mobile network, in order to keep user's applications always online, we need to cover all possible geographic areas for user activities.

2.3   Service Continuity

Service continuity (SC) should be defined as a continuous service delivery from the end-users point of view while they are moving [14] from one point to another point. The SC process can be addressed at different layers such as network, devices and domains [15], from the network view, SC is called handover or handoff which transfers user sessions to the next Road Site Unit (RSU). In terms of devices, MECs have to communicate to exchange user service data, and the domain layer is related to internet service providers, telecom operators and other parties that participate into the SC process. Figure 1 illustrates the SC concept when users moves from edge node in one country to another edge node in adjacent country. SC is a challenging activity, subject to various variables and over several dimensions. The heterogeneity of the supporting edge cloud, communications infrastructures and the variability in the different cross-domain scenarios call for a reliable architecture.

Service migration is a part of the SC concept that presents for the movements in the application layer of MEC, which facilitate the migration of responding services

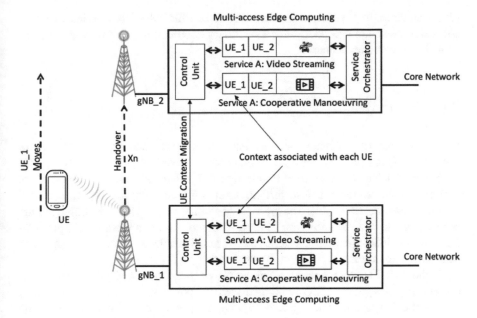

Fig. 1 Illustration of service continuity

from the current connected MEC to the next one. The two main techniques in this regard are live migration and cold migration [16]. While live migration presents a process of transferring a running service to another host transparently, cold migration has to pause the service and then resume it after this movement. Three cutting-edge researches on service migration are Follow-Me Cloud (FMC) [17], Markov Decision Process (MDP) [18] also Time Window [19]. These three-studies support the migration process by tracking user behaviors to estimate the service movement. FMC optimizes the migration based on geographical distance, workload or operator policies. MDP calculates the next reaching node probability based on Markov model, the solution is genetic to cover any direction of UE moving, other related attributes as distance, migration cost and duration are also obtained. Time Window searches the optimal service placement to reduce the total service down time, the searching problem can be turned to a concern with the shortest path, it is more dynamic for MDP and can be applied in other scenarios.

As the handover process is the key concern in the radio component of the wireless cellular networks, it draws the attention of many researchers. SC for the optimization of the handover has been investigated in [20, 21]. In [22] SC has been deployed as the primary driver of 5G in heterogeneous environments. Seamless SC by moving facilities closer to the user equipment (UE), i.e. near to eNodeB as a potential alternative [2] and studied precisely in [23]. Various traditional and non-conventional methods, as well as protocols for the sake of full SC through in-advance bandwidth reservations, have also been presented in [24], to avoid dropping calls during the active session. The follow-me edge-cloud has been proposed in

[25]. The concept is based on the architecture of MEC Mobility Services. End-to-end delay has been defended which considers computations and applied into the changing edge nodes scenario.

2.4 SC for MEC

It is valid that MEC decreases network loads dramatically and improves Quality of service (QoS) for mobile users by deploying services as close as possible to the edge of the network but, The downside to this approach is the constraint of resources and network coverage, and it is also difficult to stabilize SC with the appropriate QoS for given specifications [26]. Today, most of the networking services deployed are built on top of the Transmission Control Protocol (TCP) protocol, that provides reliable and inter-operable services over a non reliable and non cross platform communication transport connectivity mediums.

Authors in [27] come up with a Follow Me edge cloud (FMEC) definition based on mobility design for MEC, which in their proposed model end-to-end latency computations specified and applied to what they were called it as an evolving edge nodes scenario. Their study has demonstrated detailed migration strategies and is similar to our mobility simulation. Nevertheless, their research focuses only on improvements to the access point without any concrete implementation, which contributes to the security problem as discussed above, and our analysis may show possible scenarios when new systems have introduced.

Authors in [28] discussion of a container oriented model for the MEC framework, model which has been proposed is included of two proactive and reactive migration approaches for stateless applications. In this scenario when the user begins moving out of the node field, the first method is to deploy a new container to the next node and transfer all the volume data before switching the user traffic and turn off the original server. The second one demands all neighbor nodes to create replica services in advance, so when the handover event begins, the user just has to pick the nearest one and we can skip all migration time since the service has already begun. However, the second case leads to a resource problem since the replicated services are not used for a long time until they are used, so it is not easy to scale up the models because we have multiple users of different services, these problems are overcome in [29] of optimization techniques for both migration scenarios.

Considering the orchestrator strategy for control containers in [30] the container orchestrator model for auto scaling telecommunications services have been tested. Docker Swarm, Marathon and Kubernetes are selected, only Kubernetes has an incorporated self-scaling mechanism called Horizontal Pod Autoscaling, combined with a Kube-controller. However, the authors argued that such orchestrators often generate inadequate outcomes and that the solutions are not sufficient for real-time telecommunications services. Their research is based on auto-scaling with the already deployed container, but we have to pull the necessary image before we use it in our simulation, so it takes more time to ask the neighbor to pull the images in advance has provided a boost to the migration process, particularly with the orchestrator, when we do not have to test the car ID when the services are restarted.

2.5   Emerging 5G as an Enabling Technology

The coming generation of the cellular network (5G) projects to significantly boost consumer appetite in terms of excellent user coverage, superb end to end connection with low latency, ultra reliability, and higher data rates. While current methods, such as handover and roaming procedures, have already been adopted as potential alternatives in previous generations, mobile users also experience delays during network switching in cross-border scenarios.

In fact, cellular mobile communications have undergone four generations of evolution. The first generation (1G) roll-out has introduced the first version of a wireless service, which has transformed the way mobile phones are used. Almost 10 years later, the second generation (2G) was introduced to meet and resolve the demands of faster and more stable networking. The third generation (3G) arrived to further boost connectivity speed and efficiency by adding broadband connectivity. Often trying to increase the connectivity rates, the fourth generation (4G) came up with a new challenge related to network bandwidth. Alongside the speed of connection, a variety of other characteristics have been researched and developed from generation to generation [31].

Based on the formal definition of 3GPP, 5G is based on New Radio (NR). NR is expected to improve performance to LTE in terms of connection density (mMTC), spectral efficiency (eMBB), latency and reliability of the network (uRLLC), terminal/network energy consumption, data rate, for various application scenarios [32]. Figure 2 depicted three major 5G use cases with descriptions of based services and applications. According to the third Generation Partnership Project (3GPP) plan, future wireless cellular networks are required to handle at least 10 times more traffic while maintaining ultra-low latency and high reliability. Compared with 4G network, coming 5G utilize virtualization techniques that provide system scaling and fast deployment. Figure 3 illustrates architecture of 5G System Service-based.

Requirements of the 5G have been finalized in International Telecommunication Union (ITU) [33] and 3GPP [32]. The technology must be assisted by the 5G in the three major use cases. The key use case of the 5G is as follows:

- enhanced Mobile BroadBand (eMBB): refers to extensible reliance on the Conventional Mobile BroadBand (MBB) via enhanced peak/average/cell-edge data, power and coverage. 10 to 100 times improvement over 4G.
- ultra-Reliable Low Latency Communications (URLLC): focuses on critical technologies in terms of Round-Trip Time (RTT) safety and reliability, such as tactical wireless communication, autonomous driving, and tele surgery around 1 ms end to end latency.

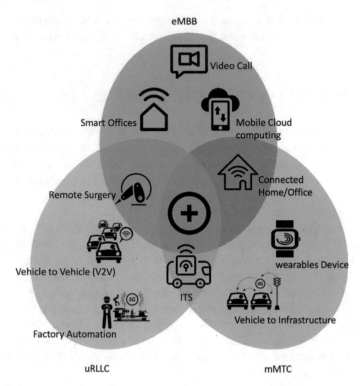

Fig. 2 Three key scenarios of 5G use with examples of related applications

- massive Machine Type Communications (mMTC): Requirements for evolving 5G IoT contexts with a very large range of embedded devices, such as individual sensors which they can be connected to 5G network via various network access to provides about thousands x bandwidth per area per device [33].

The 5G 3GPP system consists primarily of three components; firstly User Equipment (UE) secondly Access Network(AN), and thirdly Core Network(CN). In addition to these three divisions of network, Data Network (DN) or the Internet is the most important element of current networks either cellular or non-cellular wireless as well as fixed networks. Figure 3 illustrates this network division.

As universal access and pervasive communication across large scale areas has already been provided to smartphone users by the previous generation of cellular networks, connectivity with high speed and movement across roads, highways, rail and so on in vehicular network with a stationary access-point is also difficult to provide a smooth SC.

In this regards several techniques related to network management have been considered for 5G-CARMEN. Authors in [34] come with the possibility of MANagement and Orchestration (MANO) system of physical and virtualized resources. Utilization of MEC very close to the RSU to improves the reliability and low-

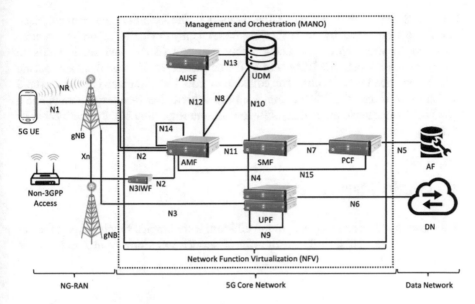

Fig. 3 5G system service-based network architecture

latency-aware results a management platform for Virtual Network Function (VNF) placement and service migration [35]. In the [36] assessment of V2V networks and 5G when the network cannot reach the whole path then should boost network signalling has been analyzed. Authors in [37] have introduced a controlling design that provides both physical and virtual infrastructure to track the network location and current state of remote and virtualized service functions. New architecture for the 5G network integrating the MEC and the network slicing for autonomous and connected vehicles discussed in [38]. Studies on various groups of genome processing services result in a new approach that leverages network replacements caching and thus makes service implementation scalable for all optimization techniques [39]. Sciancalepore et al. in [40] proposed a network management and orchestration architecture supporting network slicing for services and tenants. By providing multi-domain provider collaboration, the framework enables the service deployment over multiple domains and an efficient sharing of resources across network slices. The main corresponding two components in the framework are an inter-slice resource broker which allocates resources over the network based on policies, user demands and service level agreement (SLA), an orchestrator receives requests from tenants to decide the network slice resource.

Considering service controller in 5G-CARMEN, Gand et al. in [11] designed an architecture for server-less container cluster which could be setup in light weight edge node as Raspberry Pi (RPi). OpenFaas deploys on the top of Docker Swarm, If a service is requested, openFaas will distribute it among the available worker RPi. All metric services as CPU or energy controls by Prometheus which triggers auto-scaling and load balancing in the cluster. The paper [41] proposed a MEC-based collision-avoidance system that is used in the mobility environment. Each vehicle has equipped by an OBU (On-Board Unit) device to report the vehicle status as location, speed via basic safety message (BSM) and sends alerts in emergency situations. All BSM sent to the connected MEC to analyse and decide whether we need a notification for collision or not. The main idea is to understand which brute force all received data from the vehicle, but their experiments show good performances in preventing collision without impacting MEC effectiveness or network latency.

3 Security Management for SC

This section has the aim to explain the different technologies which put on together to provide trust and security on the top of service migration from one MNO to adjacent MNO.

3.1 Underlying Technologies

Within this section, we provide an overview of the technologies underpinning our design, these techniques will be combined to create our trust migration framework.

3.1.1 Distributed Ledger Technologies

Distributed Ledger Technologies (DLTs) is a repository for storing transactions, managed in a decentralized peer-to-peer network, without any centralized control. Since the launch of the blockchain, which is considered to be the first implementation of the DLT, numerous other implementations have been introduced. Each of them focuses on specific features or addresses previous limitations. El Ioini et al. compare three major DLT implementations in [42]. The three DTLs mentioned are blockchain, tangle, and hash-graph. The main aim of these DLTs is to create a secure environment without a trusted third party. In our context, we have chosen to explore blockchain because it is more advanced and offers a lot more functionality than others (e.g. smart contracts).

3.1.2 Blockchain

Blockchain is indeed an array of records, called blocks, that are connected and secured by cryptography, where each block header contains a hash pointer to the previous block. Also, consensus between maintaining nodes enhances blockchain and prevents tampering. Generally, blockchain platform has divided in to three different kinds of blockchain networks which are; permission-less, permissioned and last one private platform. Although private blockchain is operated by one organization, the permissioned blockchain is managed by multiple organizations along with the level of controls. Permission-less blockchain instead, operates as a transparent and open network, where anyone can send transactions and is managed by miners. In addition, there are mechanisms within the blockchain that make it secure [43].

The proposed scenario in this study explains authentication and trust activities between various parties and can come from different nations, for instance of Europe, making use of the security system as Hyperledger is a viable solution.

4 5G-CARMEN

The 5G-CARMEN stands for "5G for Connected and Automated Road Mobility in the European unioN". The project is a part of Horizon 2020 that is the biggest EU Research and Innovation program. 5G-CARMEN's objective is to develop a 5G network from Bologna, Italy to Munich, Germany to incorporate various scenarios that improve the use of 5G in cross-border mobility, such as situation awareness, cooperative maneuvering, video streaming, and green driving. 5G gives a boost to the entire telecommunication network with low latency for applications and services that keeps their connections with cloud servers.

4.1 Architecture

SC is a challenging operation, susceptible to different variables and over several dimensions. The heterogeneity of support infrastructures and the uncertainty of the various handover situations call for a simplified and more stable architecture. The launch of the 5G certainly has an important part to play. However, questions still need to be adequately resolved in order to have a consistent ending to final solutions. The first issue involves the awareness of placement services, that is, the ability to deliver services in the best places to ensure a high degree of coverage. Here, we are discussing situations in which services literally pursue moving vehicles by deploying them to the nearest MEC nodes. This field needs to be more explored, in particular in connection with the launch of 5G. The second concern involves cross organizational boundary awareness, that is, the ability to deliver facilities separately from the underlying provider or technologies used. Conversely, the idea of rooming service continuity has to be decoupled from the mobile operator or the telecommunications operator. The aim is to establish an abstract model that isolates the services rendered by all the parties concerned. Figure 4 depicts the system migration architecture of mobile edge computing in cross boarder scenario as users are faced with network re-selection. For edge clouds, application and

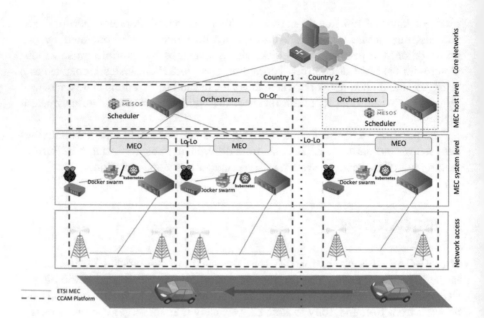

Fig. 4 The system architecture of service migration in MEC between two countries

service orchestration may help control and orchestrate systems via containers [13] determine requirements, review technologies and architecture of MEC in 5G-enabled CCAM platforms.

Figure 4 demonstrates the migration of networks in MEC as connected wireless users use ongoing call and/or data contact with a cellular network within the borders of two adjacent countries. In the presence of international roaming (network reselection), the problem is the migration of session/service between two separate MNOs/networks, that are regulated by two distinct authorities.

4.2   SC in 5G-CARMEN

The proposed architecture is made up of a collection of edge and cloud computing services deployed at the top of the 5G network. This facilitates the creation of a distributed network of non federated large scale MEC networks, able to satisfy the demands of various situations. In this system every MEC node could support a car inside its radius. MEC nodes function independently or cooperation can be formed between MEC nodes belonging to separate providers (clusters). When cars are on the move, the services required will be accompanied by the transfer of resources from one MEC node to the next one. Migration management can vary based on a variety of parameters. Figure 5 presents this message flow for 5G-

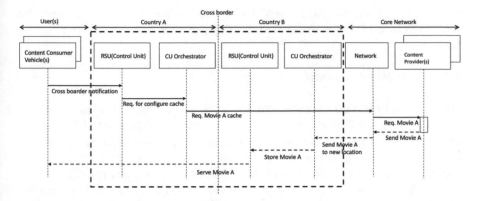

Fig. 5 5G-CARMEN message flow through Lo-Lo interface

CARMEN through Lo-Lo interface while the vehicle is moving from country A to the adjacent country (B). In this scenario, the orchestrator is in charge of data migration among different MEC nodes. When the vehicle reaches the border, the country B orchestrator will be aware of the operating services of this specific vehicle in advance and will set up its services to provide smooth operation. Therefore, instead of passing the whole flow of migration to the core of the system and making a network re-selection (local breakout) process that takes more time, this approach to service conversion can be implemented with less time and very close to the end user. In this project (5G-CARMEN) several techniques have been considered such as a MANagement and Orchestration (MANO) system for physical and virtualized resources [34], utilization of mobile (also called multi-access) edge clouds close to the roadside [35], evaluation of V2V infrastructure [36], and blockchain based SC in MEC [44, 45] to reduce latency.

4.3 5G-CARMEN Use Cases

For the intent of investigating MEC-oriented SC from different perspectives, four major use-cases shall be considered (which we derive from the 5G-CARMEN project) as following:

4.3.1 Cooperative Maneuvering

Intelligent tactics in circumstances such as shifting directions, overtaking, entering/exiting highways, maximizing traffic movement and minimizing traffic congestion, must be used to ensure secure and effective navigation between various automobiles. Therefore, if this action could take place on the basis of vehicle data gained, decision-making would be very secure and successful. Cooperative maneuvering, except cooperative lane merging, for V2V connectivity [46].

4.3.2 Situation Awareness

Both cases of human drivers and autonomous vehicles are constrained in their ability to ensure safe and effective travel by their understanding of the road traffic situation. In this respect, the use of local sensors for human drives and autonomous vehicles is very essential, e.g. cameras, accelerators, radars, etc. Unfortunately, in most situations, such points of risk remain concealed until the very last second, like road objects, traffic queues, other cars or vulnerable road users, such as motorcyclists or pedestrians. In addition, any other abrupt changes in road conditions or weather conditions such as heavy fog, snow, rain will raise the likelihood of an accident if the driver or Artificial Intelligence (AI) behind the autonomous vehicle has not been aware of all these kinds of details. This project would also present the alternatives for this usage in the event that the vehicles are presented with the above-mentioned condition. The two main circumstances for situations awareness are; (1) Vehicle sensors and state sharing (2) Back situation awareness of an emergency vehicle arrival. Back situation awareness, with special emphasis on emergency situations in which an emergency car is entering to the road, and all drivers are advised to leave the lane for Vehicle to Network (V2N) communication.

4.3.3 Green Driving

In addition to safety and traffic performance, European road operators and authorities have applied their control skills to air quality and air pollution, which may use signalling to limit speed in highly polluted areas. However, 5G-CARMEN has options to facilitate greener driving.

4.3.4 Video Streaming

On-demand broadcasting of content, live streams and high definition (HD) videos is one of the passenger's requirements for an autonomous vehicle that improves the quality of experience (QoE) anywhere it might be. The two most critical considerations, on the one hand, are the estimation of the predicted QoS network and on the other hand, the constructive adaptation of streaming software in order to prevent interruptions in the infrastructure wherever possible. It is essential to ensure high quality delivery of service, including in cross country border circumstances and inter operator circumstances. This use case aims to provide consumers with a seamless presentation of video content even in difficult situations, such as cross-border and network re-selections.

5   Video Streaming SC Use Case Deployment

In order to demonstrate the accomplishment of 5G-CARMEN we have chosen video streaming use case to present seamless SC. In this regard we have developed a new simulator environment based on two different environments which provide the roaming scenario. As a first try, we have implemented video streaming SC based on Omnet++ simulator,[5] and the second approach is the implementation of the same requirements on the top of the NS3 simulator. Deployment of SC simulator based on Omnet++ has its advantages but, the main drawback is the SimuLTE[6] since the developers of this project do not release any update, therefore, the system is not compatible with the new version of Omnte++ and Operating System (OS) respectively. Furthermore, after we investigate more issues based on Omnet++ we have considered to model SC on the top of the NS3.[7]

The second contribution is, propose a new method for prediction algorithm which consequence on the latency reduction with minimum delay or without any delay but just has an impact on the QoS. The third contribution is about exploiting data protection for SC which here possibility of blockchain has been kept to account. The fourth contribution in this stage of the project is, investigate and setup a laboratory environment sandbox based on the Raspberry Pi[8] IV to indicate new methods and proposed algorithms.

5.1   Software Deployment

In this section mainly we describe how is the software architecture could be applied to support video streaming SC use cases. We have investigated different architecture to find the most adaptable solution. To be specific, Omnet++ and NS3 based solutions are our target since they enable mobility simulator for network communication use cases. Simulator environment is essential to boost the experiment result of building on-top modules.

5.1.1   Omnet++ Software Architecture

Figure 6 illustrates service management architecture, on-car service makes a request for video streaming, the request should be forwarded from eNodeB, PGW and then to service provider cloud. The provider has to verify the user validity before offering

---

[5]https://omnetpp.org/.

[6]https://simulte.com/.

[7]https://www.nsnam.org/.

[8]https://www.raspberrypi.org/.

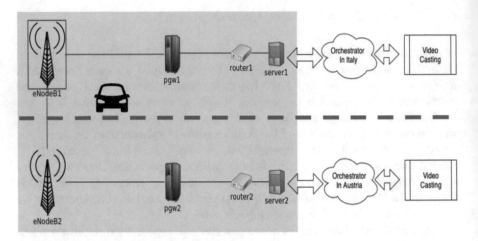

Fig. 6 Video streaming management system architecture

a streaming server, in case of acceptance, the nearest physical MEC will be chosen to deploy a server and response the video casting link to the user application. When the user vehicle gets far from the current connected MEC, the application and mobile user will disconnect with the MEC and reconnect with the next nearest one, a new streaming server will be deployed and continued data streaming.

Figure 7 shows in detail our architecture components, orchestrator is built in Nodejs[9] to control Docker container which is used to simulate servers in MEC. Omnet++ takes a responsibility to build a simulation environment, SIMULTE provides LTE components as eNodeB and Packet Data Network Gateway (PGW), it connects with SUMO simulator[10] for mobility via Veins.[11] Requests and signals are forwarded and propagated by protocols in INET framework.[12] We used curl requests and Restful service to make communications between the Omnet++ components and the orchestrator.

Implementation of Omnetpp++ Based Simulator

In this implementation car/UE in Fig. 6, gathers radio messages from the current connected eNodeB, then convert them to understandable messages applications at high level in term of data processing, for example, in-car multi-media applications. In this simulator, a python-based reader has been developed to receive requests from

---

[9]https://nodejs.org.

[10]https://www.eclipse.org/sumo/.

[11]https://veins.car2x.org/.

[12]https://inet.omnetpp.org/.

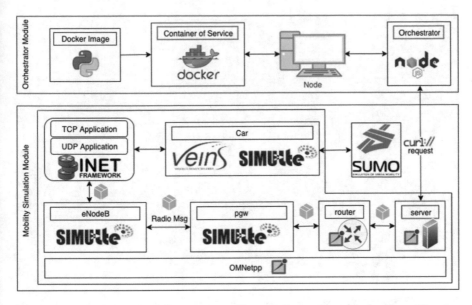

Fig. 7 Video streaming simulation system architecture for service migration in mobile edge computing

the car and responses from servers to show into the car screen. To simplify the model, we only set up a simple server to response its current time stamp and then send it to the UEs. For the handover event, the UE will compute the signal power received from eNodeB to activate the migration procedure to the next eNodeB when the UE get far from the current one.

Figure 7 is about the component design, the simulator is composed by many sub-modules to communicate with others, and also communicate with the orchestrator to control real applications, all parts here is built on Ubuntu 16.04 LTS.

5.1.2   NS3 Software Architecture

The second implementation is based on NS3 simulator which is an architecture for crossing domain scenario, the simulator has been published in [47], in the scope of this paper, we only present general concepts and initial results. The main idea of the simulator is to build two LTE networks and facilitate them to communicate via the roaming channel (with interfaces $S6d$ and $S8$) as the general design in Fig. 8.

Originally, NS3 only provides a single LTE-EPC (Long Term Evolution-Evolved Packet Core) which also means that we only have a single LTE network to work with, besides this, all IP configuration in the LTE network is fixed and not flexible. Figure 9 illustrates additional modules. Therefore, we will try to re-configure the model, build more components to fit our design with two LTEs as following:

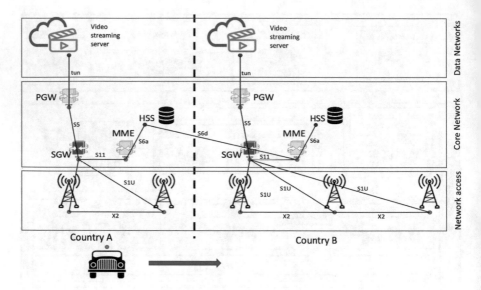

Fig. 8 NS3 simulator general design

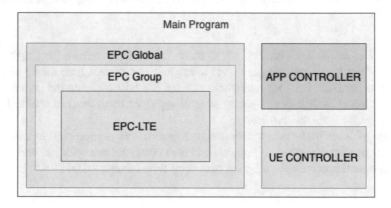

Fig. 9 Additional modules

- EPC Group: Server, PGW, SGW and eNodeB will be separated from the original LTE-EPC code pack, each region will keep an EPC group and it could configure its IP address range independently.
- EPC Global: has and control many EPC group along with the right to control the roaming procedure and assign IP address for that. We also configure the tap devices here to make the system consistency even when the UE leaves the current LTE, it is still in the EPC Global.
- APP Controller: only used for simulated application in NS3 like ping, TCP and UDP messages or even video streaming.
- UE Controller: control all UE behaviors as moving velocity and direction, it also supports triggering the migration process by listening the signal changes.

Implementation of NS3 Based Simulator

To enable the flexibility of the host machine, we packed the entire simulator environment (only NS3 work) in a single Docker container, other parts as MEC servers also packed in its Docker container respectively. Based on the configuration, we could deploy the simulator in different host environment to check the efficiency. Our NS3 simulator is stored in the Docker Registry.[13] Based on the architecture of the simulator based environments, we would build other modules on top of it and show preliminary results.

5.2 Security Mechanisms

Security and integrity are important since in multiple parties could join into the process as LTE providers, infrastructure providers, and they will do verification in each step so we need an adaptable system to boost the process while still maintains the provider agreements. MEC is setup in constraint devices with limited resources, MECs are independent, and migrating services to the unknown MEC could lead to security issues in user data, so we need a mechanism to verify incoming requests from UE, check the next MEC status and protect user data in running services. Details of this implementation are explained in [44].

The MEC trust migration, mainly focused on MEC and describes migratory techniques and manages security issues when vehicles change access points within MEC. The architecture proposed in this study provides on-road vehicles to support online connections to servers by maintaining the advantages of operating services close to users when the car starts to keeps distance from the edge node, while the next closest node will trigger a new connection and service to continue the current on-car application. The migration time must be extremely low, especially for real-time services such as mapping, video streaming, but it leads to a security issue that a node can handle unknown requests instead of a re-connecting one from a trusted vehicle. This study also analyzes the overhead of verification in the migration process, to be specific, we evaluate the application of blockchain in checking untrusted behaviors.

5.3 Proposed Prediction Algorithm Methods for SC

Crossing national borders could take place in a tunnel or in a poor GPS signal covered area, therefore, we go for different approaches; in this study, we use the UE's received radio signals to determine the movement. The radio signal is in our

---

[13]https://hub.docker.com/repository/docker/levanthanh3005/ns3.

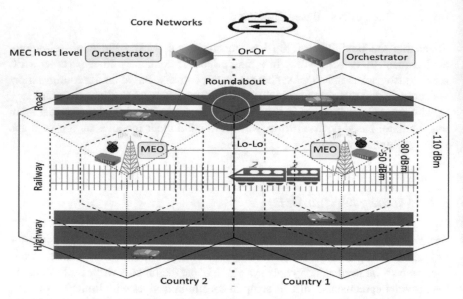

Fig. 10 Prediction method based on the base-station signal level and 120° cell sectoring

opinion the only reliable way to determine whether a UE is covered or not. The radio signal threshold determines the exact network migration [48] instant, while the position can change depending on many other factors such as UE's sensitivity, gain, weather conditions and many others [49]. In this review, two types of methods were suggested with different upsides and downsides based on two different technologies. The first is based on the frequency of the eNodeB signal and cell sectoring. The second approach is the based on GPS utilization for the prediction algorithm to reduce the time of migration and improve the QoE.

gNB/eNodeB Based Prediction Method

This solution is based on the signal strength of UE and signal strength plus correct cell sectoring of gNB/eNodeB. This algorithm relies on allocated resources of base station [50] i.e. in addition to measure the signal level we should detect the location of mobile users. Two thresholds have been considered in this approach. Figure 10 shows this process. When the vehicle/UE reaches the first threshold, migration of apps, running service or resources will be activated and notification will send to the system. Depending on the location of the user (i.e. road way, highway or rail way) we define the user sector used in conjunction with the relevant region (e.g., −80 dBm) to be known until the first and second thresholds are met. Once the second threshold has been passed, a transition phase to migration of services or apps is started to deploy the operation on the adjacent network.

GPS Based Prediction Method

Because at the beginning of the journey the majority of drivers use the built-in GPS of the car to find the optimum route in terms of traffic, road maintenance, and so on,

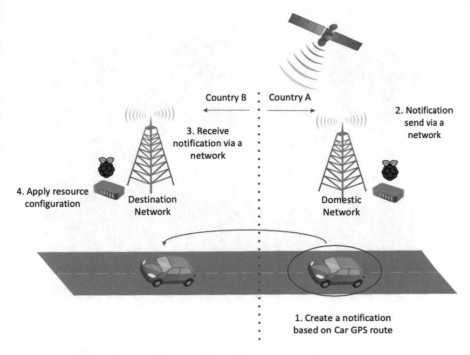

Fig. 11 Prediction method based on the GPS and network information

therefore, from the beginning of the journey system can use this information and has a rough approximation of the cross-border moment. The network is then in a position to calculate when the car reaches the border and the network has enough time to assess the requirement for the other side of the border. Figure 11 illustrates this prediction method. At the first point after the distance has been chosen, the car's GPS warning will be sent to the home network and the visiting network will be informed by the orchestrator.

5.4 Develop and Setup a Lab Environment

To test the proposed algorithm, we setup a cluster of Raspberry Pi as a testbed. Figure 12 presents the current design of cluster of raspberry pi III.

The new design is under developing and proposed architecture is represented in Fig. 13. This version of edge development is including of 60 raspberry Pi *IV* which Table 1 presents the main specifications of this new single board computer.

Fig. 12 The cluster of 8 Raspberry Pis III

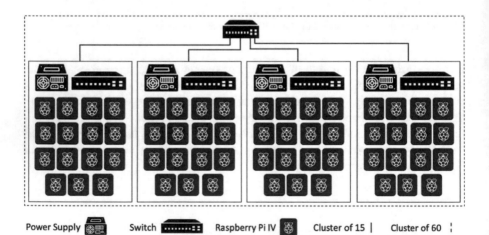

Fig. 13 Cluster of 60 Raspberry Pis IV

Table 1 Specification of the Raspberry Pi IV

Parameter	Value
Architecture	Cortex-A72 quad-core (ARM v8)
SoC	BCM2711 64-bit
CPU	1.5 GHz
Memory	4G RAM LPDDR4-2400 SDRAM
Storage	16G SD card
WiFi	2.4 GHz and 5.0 GHz IEEE 802.11ac wireless
Ethernet	Gigabit

5.5 Assessment

This study has been experimentally tested the efficiency and overhead of the usage of blockchain in the Hyperledger fabric system in terms of blockchain security based. Tables 2 and 3 present the configuration of this experiment. In order to make a reliable test result with Docker images, we set up two separate Ubuntu machines to make sure that pulling Docker images does not have any advantage over the previously drawn Docker packs, for example, if we need to pull a python-based image and our machine already has a python-based image, the pulling time will be faster than the one that does not have python. The testing strategy which considers in this study includes the analysis of migration processes and blockchain. The blockchain application will be applied for both simulators, since it is outside of the scope of simulator environment so in the study just we present the result of evaluating timing aspects effected to total migration time.

5.5.1 Omnet++ Simulation Evaluation

The environment settings for Omnet++ are described with Fig. 6 (video streaming). Only the two eNodeBs connect the others to activate the handover/network re-selection requests. Each time the car receives signals from eNodeB and then calculates the strongest signal to choose the next closer eNodeB when it gets far away from the current connection. Omnet++ offers three simulation times of normal, fast and express. In the normal mode, it runs slowly, and we can debug and see all logs, the signal streams are clearly previewed in the mode. Fast mode speeds up the

Table 2 Configuration for mobility simulator

Parameter	Value
eNB TxPower	6
Frequency	$2.1GHz$
eNB Antenna Gain	$18dBm$
VUE Antenna Gain	$0dBm$
Handover Latency	$0.05sdBm$
Path Loss Scenario	URBAN MACROCELL
Number of eNBs	2

Table 3 Configuration for Omnet++ Edge node environment

Parameter	Value
Number of machines	2
Operation System	Ubuntu 16.04.1 LTS
Graphic card	NVIDIA
Memory	8GB
Network	53 Mbps in download and upload
Docker version	18.09.3
Docker Image Weight	355MB

normal mode but with lower time waiting and the express mode skips all logs and runs extremely fast. Omnet++ runs based on simulation time (simTime) and this is a discreet event simulator, so running events don't function at a normal time but have an event list and run events one by one. We activate simulators to communicate with REST servers, so these timelines are different, and in Omnet++ they are too slow compared to real time stamps on REST servers. Therefore, we select the fast mode to drive the simulation process that is closest to the real-time flow. In our experiment, for three cases, we only consider the handover case, and it takes around 3000 ms to adjust the eNodeB. The simulator will become the basic module for our next evaluation.

Performance of Resource Allocation

The Omnet++ based environment has showed the execution time during the migration process with stateless applications, the migration procedure starts with the blockchain authentification, and then pull the Docker images from Docker registry after deploying the required service at MEC. Testing was carried out on two computer systems or machine which introduced for two MEC devices, depending on MEC models, we have different configurations, for example, in case of MEC-Swarm, another machine will join and work on behalf of an orchestrator. There are several time metrics during the handover process [26].

Communication channels and mobility simulator configuration are defined in Tables 2 and 3. In order to test the Docker images, we prepared a simple web service packed in an Docker image based Python core and response the current time-stamp via port 3000. It only takes 354 MB in size disk and in deployment, the pulling time is 47,080 ms (PIT). Obviously, a heavier image takes more time in pulling, for instance, a 5.3 Gb Docker image (Jupiter notebook) could take up to 5 min only to download from Docker Hub while a super light image as NodeJs with 55 MB just takes 3 s. The network stability and connection will affect to the PIT value so the revolution of 5G could support here to boost that.

Considering Orchestrator Arrangement Time (OAT), it is always zero for all cases, in Single-MEC, nodes are orchestrated by themselves, as the conventional model, for MEC-Cluster, as nodes already knew others, and find the next node at the first request time, the last technique is also identical, so we can save OAT time in that case.

For the blockchain verification part, smart contract based on the Hyperledger with different functions has been developed, we also have a log function to track all service deployment and user activities why using the services at MEC.

Figure 14 demonstrates the execution time changes for the three selected simulation scenarios i.e. Migration overhead, the key issue is the drawing of the model, while in this scenario, our designed image should be taken into account to be a standard size model, the time investment is around 46,980 ms. It worth to mention that observed the launch time of the container would be shorter if we could have a time interval after pulling, in Single-MEC, it recommended to starts the service right

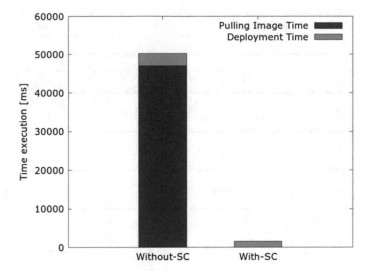

Fig. 14 Migration overhead

after pulling all sub-parts of images that could take more around 3.1 s, however, with MEC-Cluster and MEC-Swarm, the Deployment Time (DT) is only 1.6 s (a half of that). Besides that, in MEC-Swarm, the verification process of blockchain is already underway in the previous node, so it can save a huge amount of time, for next-step users could be interrupted for about 2 or 3 s in the other strategies. High-security and user-experiment is the trade-off of the network because though the chain is getting longer, we can spend more time on it.

5.5.2 NS3 Simulation Evaluation

In NS3 simulator setup, we first defined the experiment settings and then deploy it before evaluate the real applications.

Experiment Setting

Figure 8 presented the topology design of our simulator and Fig. 15 illustrates roaming and service migration flow. We have two LTE-EPCs and they connects with others via roaming procedure. In order to run the real applications via the simulator, we applied tap device of NS3 and built bridges to the real world. The tap device will connect with Docker containers and then forward requests through it.

The experiment setting of the simulator only is showed in Table 4, the UE speed here is 10.8 m/s corresponding with 39 km/h as the normal car speed in the road which is reported by the survey [51].

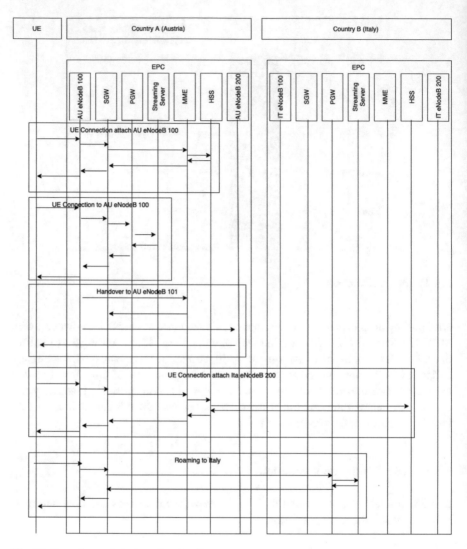

Fig. 15 Roaming and service migration flow

The edge node configuration is demonstrated in Table 5, as we investigated from,[14] the average distance among eNodeBs is around 200 m so in our simulator environment, all eNodeBs will be in the same road with the same distances among each pair of them. Followed by the technical document[15] with the LTE delay as

---

[14]www.cellmapper.net.

[15]https://www.cisco.com/c/dam/global/en_ae/assets/expo2011/saudiarabia/pdfs/lte-design-and-deployment-strategies-zeljko-savic.pdf.

Table 4 Configuration for NS3 mobility simulator

Metrics	Values
Number of LTE-EPC network	2
Distance between eNodeBs	200 m
Number of eNodeB	5
eNodeB Tranmission Power	43 dBm
UE Tranmission Power	23 dBm
UE speed	10.8 m/s

Table 5 Configuration for NS3 host environment

OS	macOS Mojave
Processor	2.3 GHz Intel Core i5
Memory	8 GB
Docker version	18.09.2

smaller than 100 ms, so all LTE socket delay will be set as 100 ms while the roaming socket (S8) is configured by the propagation delay that is reflected by the distance between the two LTE networks. The roaming and service migration flow are presented in Fig. 15.

Measurement

Concerning SC downtime, we also experiment the similar results as Omnet++ in Fig. 14. Besides that, the total latency during the migration process and response time in both roaming and non-roaming situations will be examined with two applications as ping and video streaming, they both run in real Docker services.

Ping

The two Figs. 16 and 17 presented the signal and latency changes in cases of domain changes. The current time-stamp is in the X axis while the Y2 axis is for the current distance and Y2 axis is about RSRP values and the latency. For the first case in Fig. 16, the average time of response in ping is 18 ms while the maximum one is 24 ms, video streaming service and gaming can run without any issues in this network capacity. In contrast, the ping response average is more than 30 ms in the roaming case and the maximum one is 54 ms, that makes a bit lag for some heavy games and live video streaming. In addition, if we increase the distance between the two LTEs, the S8 delay will be escalated dramatically. Besides that, in case of local server, changing LTE also means modifying the IP address of the user which makes the video streaming of user get a bit pause while updating the IP and make it inconvenient as non-continuous service.

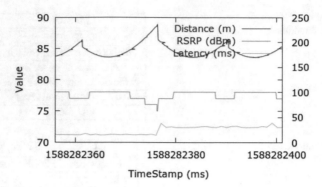

Fig. 16 Roaming server requests

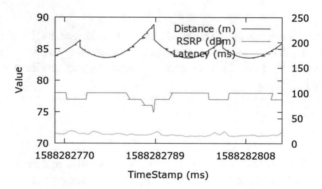

Fig. 17 Local server requests

Video Streaming Result

The video streaming application will show clearly how the migration process affects user experiment by checking the video frames. We pulled a Firefox browser based on Docker Image to work as a UE screen while a Mist server[16] will run on other Docker containers and stream video frames. The Mist server takes only 310 MB in size disk that is really light weight but support many different types of streaming protocols.

However, in term of statistic, the Mist server does not have many options to check the quality of service, the memory usage, CPU and network bandwidth are the only metrics we could get as Fig. 18. In the graph, the connection becomes unstable, especially in the handover event, at the same time, the CPU is released a bit because it does not have to do streaming.

---

[16]https://www.mistserver.org.

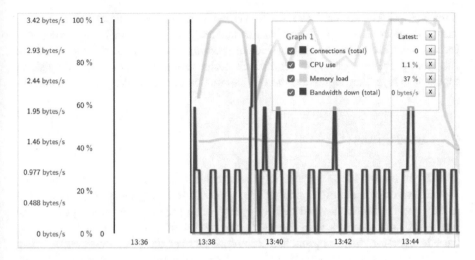

Fig. 18 Metric statistic in Mist server

5.5.3 Simulator Evaluation Overview

Generally, the both simulator enable a comprehensive environment, nevertheless, from telecommunication networking perspective and reference scenarios, NS3 has more advantages by supporting roaming procedure, while Omnet++ only perform a normal handover. Besides that, based on NS3, we could get a better result in real time service and signal changes during user moving with the graph 16 and 17 that we cannot collect the data in Omnet++. Therefore, NS3 will be our choice for further researches.

6 Future Research Directions

SC is a challenging undertaking, susceptible to different variables and over several dimensions. The heterogeneity of the supporting infrastructures especially in 5G which is based on different technology to deliver high speed and more reliable network connection on the other hand the variability of the various handover situations among these different technologies calls for a simplified and more robust architecture. The launch of 5G certainly plays an important part, but problems do need to be adequately handled in order to provide a stable end to end-to-end solutions. The first issue involves the awareness of placement programs, that is, the ability to deliver services in the best places to ensure a high degree of network coverage. Here we are discussing scenarios like the one outlined in [52], which services basically pursue moving vehicles by installing them at the nearest MEC nodes. This field needs to be more explored, in particular in connection with the launch of 5G. The second issue involves cross-organizational boundary recognition, that is, the necessary to produce facilities separately from the underlying provider or technologies used. Conversely, the idea of rooming SC has to be kept separate from the mobile operator or the telecommunications sector. The aim is to establish an abstraction layer that segregates the services rendered from all the parties concerned.

7 Conclusions

In order to allow broad scale SC to cross organizational and cross-border borders, a combination of technology and techniques needs to be implemented and tuned to satisfy precise functional and quality criteria. The primary aim is to optimize the availability of resources with the maximum degree of transparency for the client. Mobile operators have approached this problem over the past few decades using various methods, most of which have been thwarted by the underlying technologies. However, recent developments in cloud and edge computing in tandem with 5G could bring about a dramatic transition by having the proper networks to provide the channels required for seamless continuity of service.

Acknowledgments The study was carried out within the scope of the EU Horizon 2020 initiative 5G-CARMEN co-funded by the EU under grant agreement No. 825012. The viewpoints expressed are those of the authors and do not necessarily represent the project. The Commission shall not be responsible for any usage that may be made of any of the information contained therein.

References

1. Hamid R Barzegar, Nabil El Ioini, Van Thanh Le, and Claus Pahl. 5g-carmen: Service continuity in 5g-enabled edge clouds. In *8th European Conference On Service-Oriented And Cloud Computing*, 2020.
2. H. Assasa, S. V. Yadhav, and L. Westberg. Service mobility in mobile networks. In *2015 IEEE 8th International Conference on Cloud Computing*, pages 397–404, 2015.
3. Raheleh Kooshesh, Mahdi Mollahasani, and Hamid Reza Barzegar. Implement e-government based approach on cloud computing. *Journal of Basic and Applied Scientific Research*, 3(11):488–493, 2013.
4. Peter Mell, Tim Grance, et al. The nist definition of cloud computing. 2011.
5. Alessio Botta, Walter De Donato, Valerio Persico, and Antonio Pescapé. Integration of cloud computing and internet of things: a survey. *Future generation computer systems*, 56:684–700, 2016.
6. Jude Okwuibe, Juuso Haavisto, Erkki Harjula, Ijaz Ahmad, and Mika Ylianttila. Orchestrating service migration for low power mec-enabled iot devices. *arXiv preprint arXiv:1905.12959*, 2019.
7. Remo Scolati, Ilenia Fronza, Nabil El Ioini, Areeg Samir, and Claus Pahl. A containerized big data streaming architecture for edge cloud computing on clustered single-board devices. 05 2019.
8. Remo Scolati, Ilenia Fronza, Nabil El Ioini, Areeg Samir, Hamid R. Barzegar, and Claus Pahl. *A Containerized Edge Cloud Architecture for Data Stream Processing*. 05 2020.

9. Claus Pahl, Ilenia Fronza, Nabil El Ioini, and Hamid R. Barzegar. A review of architectural principles and patterns for distributed mobile information systems. In *15th International Conference on Web Information Systems and Technologies - WEBIST*, 09 2019.
10. C. Mouradian, D. Naboulsi, S. Yangui, R. H. Glitho, M. J. Morrow, and P. A. Polakos. A comprehensive survey on fog computing: State-of-the-art and research challenges. *IEEE Communications Surveys Tutorials*, 20(1):416–464, 2018.
11. Fabian Gand, Ilenia Fronza, Nabil El Ioini, Hamid R. Barzegar, and Claus Pahl. Serverless container cluster management for lightweight edge clouds. In *The 10th International Conference on Cloud Computing and Services Science, CLOSER 2020*, 02 2020.
12. Fabian Gand, Ilenia Fronza, Nabil El Ioini, Hamid R. Barzegar, and Claus Pahl. A lightweight virtualisation platform for cooperative, connected and automated mobility. In *6th International Conference on Vehicle Technology and Intelligent Transport Systems (VEHITS)*, 02 2020.
13. Claus Pahl and Brian Lee. Containers and clusters for edge cloud architectures–a technology review. In *2015 3rd international conference on future internet of things and cloud*, pages 379–386. IEEE, 2015.
14. Florin Sultan, Kiran Srinivasan, Deepa Iyer, and Liviu Iftode. Migratory tcp: Connection migration for service continuity in the internet. pages 469–470, 01 2002.
15. I. Jorstad, Do Van Thanh, and S. Dustdar. An analysis of service continuity in mobile services. In *13th IEEE International Workshops on Enabling Technologies: Infrastructure for Collaborative Enterprises*, pages 121–126, 2004.
16. H. Abdah, J. P. Barraca, and R. L. Aguiar. Qos-aware service continuity in the virtualized edge. *IEEE Access*, 7:51570–51588, 2019.
17. T. Taleb, P. Hasselmeyer, and F. G. Mir. Follow-me cloud: An openflow-based implementation. In *2013 IEEE International Conference on Green Computing and Communications and IEEE Internet of Things and IEEE Cyber, Physical and Social Computing*, pages 240–245, 2013.
18. A. Ksentini, T. Taleb, and M. Chen. A Markov decision process-based service migration procedure for follow me cloud. In *2014 IEEE International Conference on Communications (ICC)*, pages 1350–1354, 2014.
19. Shiqiang Wang, Rahul Urgaonkar, Ting He, Kevin Chan, Murtaza Zafer, and Kin K. Leung. Dynamic Service Placement for Mobile Micro-Clouds with Predicted Future Costs. *IEEE Transactions on Parallel and Distributed Systems*, 28(4):1002–1016, 2017.
20. Peppino Fazio, Mauro Tropea, Floriano De Rango, and Miroslav Voznak. Pattern prediction and passive bandwidth management for hand-over optimization in qos cellular networks with vehicular mobility. *IEEE Transactions on Mobile Computing*, 15(11):2809–2824, 2016.
21. Xiaorong Zhu, Mengrong Li, Wenchao Xia, and Hongbo Zhu. A novel handoff algorithm for hierarchical cellular networks. *China Communications*, 13(8):136–147, 2016.
22. Josef Noll and Mohammad MR Chowdhury. 5g: Service continuity in heterogeneous environments. *Wireless Personal Communications*, 57(3):413–429, 2011.
23. Y. Mao, C. You, J. Zhang, K. Huang, and K. B. Letaief. A survey on mobile edge computing: The communication perspective. *IEEE Communications Surveys Tutorials*, 19(4):2322–2358, 2017.
24. Peppino Fazio, Floriano De Rango, and Mauro Tropea. Prediction and qos enhancement in new generation cellular networks with mobile hosts: A survey on different protocols and conventional/unconventional approaches. *IEEE Communications Surveys & Tutorials*, 19(3):1822–1841, 2017.
25. Tarik Taleb, Adlen Ksentini, and Pantelis Frangoudis. Follow-me cloud: When cloud services follow mobile users. *IEEE Transactions on Cloud Computing*, 2016.
26. S. Wang, J. Xu, N. Zhang, and Y. Liu. A survey on service migration in mobile edge computing. *IEEE Access*, 6:23511–23528, 2018.
27. Abdelkader Aissioui, Adlen Ksentini, Abdelhak Mourad Gueroui, and Tarik Taleb. On enabling 5g automotive systems using follow me edge-cloud concept. *IEEE Transactions on Vehicular Technology*, 67(6):5302–5316, 2018.

28. Ivan Farris, Tarik Taleb, Antonio Iera, and Hannu Flinck. Lightweight service replication for ultra-short latency applications in mobile edge networks. In *2017 IEEE International Conference on Communications (ICC)*, pages 1–6. IEEE, 2017.
29. Ivan Farris, Tarik Taleb, Miloud Bagaa, and Hannu Flick. Optimizing service replication for mobile delay-sensitive applications in 5g edge network. In *2017 IEEE International Conference on Communications (ICC)*, pages 1–6. IEEE, 2017.
30. D. Luong, H. Thieu, A. Outtagarts, and Y. Ghamri-Doudane. Cloudification and autoscaling orchestration for container-based mobile networks toward 5g: Experimentation, challenges and perspectives. In *2018 IEEE 87th Vehicular Technology Conference (VTC Spring)*, pages 1–7, 2018.
31. H.R. Barzegar, V.T. Le, C. Pahl, and N. E. Ioini. Wireless network evolution towards service continuity in 5g enabled mobile edge computing. In *International Conference on Fog and Mobile Edge Computing (FMEC)*, 2020.
32. 3GPP_TR_38.913. Study on scenarios and requirements for next generation access technologies. 2016.
33. Oumer Teyeb, Gustav Wikstrom, Magnus Stattin, Thomas Cheng, Sebastian Faxer, and Hieu Do. Evolving lte to fit the 5g future, ericsson technology review, 2017.
34. F. Z. Yousaf, V. Sciancalepore, M. Liebsch, and X. Costa-Perez. Manoaas: A multi-tenant nfv mano for 5g network slices. *IEEE Communications Magazine*, 57(5):103–109, 2019.
35. N. Slamnik, H. C. Carvalho, C. Donato, S. Latré, R. Riggio, and J. Marquez. Leveraging mobile edge computing to improve vehicular communications. In *2020 IEEE 17th Annual Consumer Communications Networking Conference (CCNC)*, pages 1–4, 2020.
36. G. Elia, M. Bargis, M. P. Galante, N. P. Magnani, L. Santilli, G. Romano, and G. Zaffiro. Connected transports, v2x and 5g: Standard, services and the tim - telecom Italia experiences. In *2019 AEIT International Conference of Electrical and Electronic Technologies for Automotive (AEIT AUTOMOTIVE)*, pages 1–6, 2019.
37. Mauro Femminella and Gianluca Reali. Gossip-based monitoring of virtualized resources in 5g networks. In *IEEE INFOCOM 2019-IEEE Conference on Computer Communications Workshops (INFOCOM WKSHPS)*, pages 378–384. IEEE, 2019.
38. Estefanía Coronado, Gabriel Cebrián-Márquez, Giovanni Baggio, and Roberto Riggio. Addressing bitrate and latency requirements for connected and autonomous vehicles. In *IEEE INFOCOM 2019-IEEE Conference on Computer Communications Workshops (INFOCOM WKSHPS)*, pages 961–962. IEEE, 2019.
39. Gianluca Reali, Mauro Femminella, Luca Felicetti, and Matteo Pergolesi. Orchestration of cloud genomic services. In *2019 Eleventh International Conference on Ubiquitous and Future Networks (ICUFN)*, pages 494–499. IEEE, 2019.
40. Christian Sciancalepore, Vincenzo and, Faqir Zarrar Yousaf, Pablo Serrano, Marco Gramaglia, Julie Bradford, and Ignacio Labrador Pavón. A future-proof architecture for management and orchestration of multi-domain nextgen networks. *IEEE Access*, 7:79216–79232, 2019.
41. Marco Malinverno, Giuseppe Avino, Claudio Casetti, Carla Fabiana Chiasserini, Francesco Malandrino, and Salvatore Scarpina. Mec-based collision avoidance for vehicles and vulnerable users. *arXiv preprint arXiv:1911.05299*, 2019.
42. Nabil El Ioini and Claus Pahl. A review of distributed ledger technologies. In *OTM 2018 Conferences - Cloud and Trusted Computing (C&TC 2018)*, 10 2018.
43. Arvind Narayanan, Joseph Bonneau, Edward Felten, Andrew Miller, and Steven Goldfeder. *Bitcoin and cryptocurrency technologies: a comprehensive introduction*. Princeton University Press, 2016.
44. V.T. Le, C. Pahl, and N. E. Ioini. Blockchain based service continuity in mobile edge computing. In *2019 Sixth International Conference on Internet of Things: Systems, Management and Security (IOTSMS)*, pages 136–141, 2019.
45. H.R. Barzegar, V.T. Le, C. Pahl, and N. E. Ioini. Service continuity for ccam platform in 5g-carmen,. In *16th international wireless communications and mobile computing conference (iwcmc 2020)*, 2020.

46. Patrick Pirri, Claus Pahl, Nabil El Ioini, and Hamid R. Barzegar. Towards cooperative maneuvering simulation: Tools and architecture. In *IEEE Consumer Communications & Networking Conference (CCNC)*, 2021.
47. Van Thanh Le, Nabil El Ioini, Hamid R. Barzegar, and Claus Pahl. A multi-domain network simulator based on ns-3. In *10th International Conference on Simulation and Modeling Methodologies, Technologies and Applications*, 2020.
48. Marco Pomalo, Van Thanh Le, Nabil El Ioini, Claus Pahl, and Hamid R. Barzegar. A data generator for cloud-edge vehicle communication in multi domain cellular networks. In *7th International Conference on Internet of Things: Systems, Management and Security (IOTSMS)*, 2020.
49. Marco Pomalo, Van Thanh Le, Nabil El Ioini, Claus Pahl, and Hamid R. Barzegar. Service migration in multi-domain cellular networks based on machine learning approaches. In *7th International Conference on Internet of Things: Systems, Management and Security (IOTSMS)*, 2020.
50. Marco Schito, Hamid R Barzegar, and Luca Reggiani. Resource allocation with interference information sharing in multi-carrier networks. In *2016 IEEE 27th Annual International Symposium on Personal, Indoor, and Mobile Radio Communications (PIMRC)*, pages 1–6. IEEE, 2016.
51. Research department. Free speed survey, 2012. URL: https://www.rsa.ie/Documents/Road%20Safety/Speed/Speed_survey_2011.pdf [accessed: 2020-25-04].
52. T. Ouyang, Z. Zhou, and X. Chen. Follow me at the edge: Mobility-aware dynamic service placement for mobile edge computing. *IEEE Journal on Selected Areas in Communications*, 36(10):2333–2345, 2018.

Security in Critical Communication for Mobile Edge Computing Based IoE Applications

Tanmoy Maitra, Debasis Giri, and Arup Sarkar

Abstract The new era of the Internet of Everything (IoE) applications demands low latency along with security into the networks. The cloud-based architecture alone cannot provide low response time to the users or mobile devices (like phone, laptop, sensors device, etc.). Therefore between mobile devices and cloud, edge devices (known as Fog device) are introduced as middleware device. From the edge devices, users can get information from local devices without interacting with the cloud via the Internet or radio. In such complicated networks, security preservation in communications becomes a challenging task. The security protocols for critical communication in such applications (e-medical, e-banking) are based on the architecture of the networks which can be centralized or distributed or hybrid (a mixture of centralized and distributed). This book chapter discusses the different security protocols in communications for the aforementioned architectures which can be designed for Mobile Edge Computing (MEC) based IoE applications. Moreover, this chapter covers (a) architectures and their security threats, (b) necessity of security model in such applications, (c) different secure communication protocols for those applications, (d) challenges to design security protocols to reduce response time, and latency (e) the future direction of this research domain which can be explored more.

Keywords Internet of Everything (IoE) · Edge device · Security · Communication protocol · Privacy

T. Maitra (✉) · A. Sarkar
School of Computer Engineering, KIIT Deemed to be University, Bhubaneswar, Odisha, India
e-mail: tanmoy.maitrafcs@kiit.ac.in; arup.sarkarfcs@kiit.ac.in

D. Giri
Department of Information Technology, Maulana Abul Kalam Azad University of Technology, Nadia, West Bengal, India

1 Introduction

According to Gartner [1], in 2015, the Internet of Everything (IoE) was recorded as one of the lid trends. IoE can be defined as it *"is bringing together people, process, data, and things to make networked connections more relevant and valuable than ever before-turning information into actions that create new capabilities, richer experiences, and unprecedented economic opportunity for businesses, individuals, and countries"* (Cisco, 2013).

The Internet of Everything (IoE) expresses a world where billions of objects along with sensors to determine and evaluate their location; connected to public or private networks using all standard and proprietary protocols. Edge computing is changing the way we manage, process, and distribute data from millions of devices worldwide. The tremendous growth of Internet-connected devices in IoE, along with new applications that need simultaneous computing power, continues to drive edge-computing systems. Accelerated networking technologies, such as 5G wireless, artificial intelligence, auto-driving cars, allow video processing and analytics, and robotics to accelerate the design or hold up of real-time applications to edge and computing systems, to name a few. Due to the growth of IoE-generated data, the initial aim of edge computing was to address bandwidth costs for long-distance travel data, with the emergence of real-time applications advancing the need for processing technology [2].

Edge computing defined by Gartner as "data processing as part of a distributed computing topology located near the edge – where things and people produce or receive that information" [2]. In its early stages, edge computing did not depend on any central location thousands of miles away but rather brings computing and data storage closer to assembling devices. This is done in such a way that data, especially real-time data, does not suffer from delayed issues that can affect the performance of an application. Besides, companies can preserve money by completing processing locally, reducing the amount of processing required either centrally or in cloud-based locations.

Edge computing was created because of the significant extension of IoE devices, which are wirelessly connected through the Internet to fetch data from the cloud or return data to the cloud. Many IoE devices produce large amounts of data during their activities. Also, edge computing may provide new functionality that was not previously available. For example, an organization can use an edge computer to analyze their data on the edge, which makes it possible in real-time. Typically, the major benefits of edge computing are low latency, low bandwidth usage and low associated costs, and low use of resources in the server.

A drawback of edge computing is that it can increase attack vectors. As the devices are connected to each other wirelessly, authentication is the key factor in communication for such cloud-edge infrastructure. In [3], it has been reported that edge computing has increased dramatically in recent years which is targeting aging. Among all the security attacks, the most remarkable attacks occurring in the practical world is the Mirai virus [3]. Mirai virus captures more than 65000 IoE devices within the first 20 h after its deliverance in August 2016. A few days later, these compromised devices shut down over 178 000 domains and turned to Botnet to run Distribution Denial Services (DDoS) attacks against edge servers. Within a short period, a variety of Mirai, such as the IORPitter and Hazim, were captured, and they are believed to infect 3 million IoE devices in 2017 [4]. Since the discovery of the first Mirai botnet in 2016, the IoE botnet attacks were disclosed to have caused more than $100 million in damage as of September 2018 [4]. It is noted that these numbers only indicate attacks and property damage that were officially pointed out and enlisted, but the total amount of unauthorized attacks/damage may be very high.

The arrangement of this chapter is maintained as follows. Section 2 discusses some mobile edge computing-based IoE based applications and their security. Section 3 demonstrates the different architecture used in MEC. Section 4 discusses possible attacks on communication in MEC and list out the cryptographic solution. Section 5 illustrates a secure communication protocol in an edge-cloud environment that can be applied to the healthcare system. The brief discussion on some other related existing secure communication protocols is given in Sect. 6. In Sect. 7, the security challenges of MEC discuss. At the end, the conclusion is given.

2 Applications and Security

Edge computing applications, data, and services can be used to push the logical end of a network away from central computing. This enables additional data sources to be in the age of analysis and data. Edge encompasses a wide range of computing technologies, such as remote sensing systems, filling traditional data stocks, and augmented reality.

It is easy to search clarifications for what edge computing is and how it works. Most companies need to know how it can affect their business. Internet of Everything (IoE) gadgets is now available on the market in large numbers. Thus, agencies require seeing how new evolutions in edge computing practice can be made more convenient for them. Figure 1 shows some mobile edge computing-based IoE applications.

Here, some of the most novel applications in the mobile edge computing are addressed:

Manufacturing: By putting data storage and registering in industrial equipment, manufacturers can collect data that will consider better perception and adequacy of redundancy, while reducing costs and requirements while maintaining better stability and remunerative time. Common manufacturing frameworks guided by consistent data diversity and will help more companies make changes to the order created to meet prospects for operational requirements.

Smart Cities: The edge computing architecture responds to real-time changes on behalf of devices that control utilities and other public administrations. With the increasing number of autonomous e-devices and the ever-increasing IoE, smart

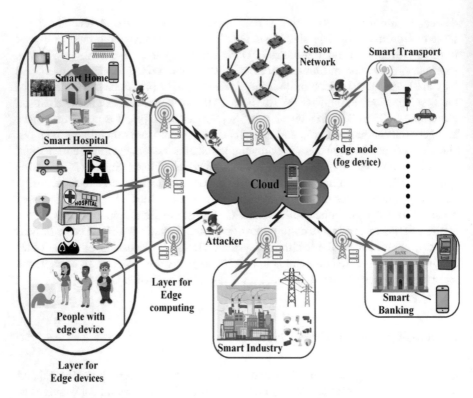

Fig. 1 The layered architecture of mobile edge computing-based IoE

cities [5] can change how people survive and benefit from urban environments.
Since all end computing applications rely on gadgets to collect data to perform
basic processing tasks, they will have the ability to react rapidly with the
changing circumstances occurring in the future city.

Healthcare: IoE gadgets are perfect for providing a vast array of patient-borne
health information (PGHD) [6, 7], allowing healthcare providers to access
essential data about their patients rather than interface with intermediate and fragmented databases. Treatment devices can be similarly determined to determine
and collect information about the entire treatment. Regulatory requirements for
the exchange and risk of medical data make it challenging to implement any edge
solution.

Augmented Reality: Wearable augmented reality (AR) gadgets such as smart eye-
glasses and headsets are sometimes used to create this effect; however, most
customers have run into AR via their mobile displays. Anyone who has made
a noise like Pokémon Go or used a channel on Snapchat or Instagram has
used AR. The innovation behind AR is that devices expect to process visual
information and are incorporated into pre-rendered visual elements. Without an
edge computing design, this visual information will be distributed back to a

centralized cloud server where digital components can be added before being sent back to the gadget. This course of sequence inevitably leads to significant delays.

AI Virtual Assistant: By incorporating edge systematization into the systems, organizations can completely improve performance and reduce inactivity. Instead of sending AI virtual assistants to a focused server and sending data requests, they can locally spread weights between edge data centers playing some processing capabilities. It can be said that the multiplication of localized data servers for both cloud and edge computing has made it easier than ever for the association to be in a position to expand its network and maximize the benefits of its data resources.

Smart Transport: Smart transport [8] is the future of the world transportation system. With comparison to before, today we have more and better transportation options, and we have new ideas to enhance, invest, and consume transportation services. To reduce traffic congestion and improve living standards, the city government aims to promote green, efficient transportation systems. With the help of IoE, cloud and edge computing makes it easier.

Smart Building: Adaptability is crucial in smart building [9] because, it interacts with the systems, people, and exterior elements around them with the help of IoE devices then stores in the cloud. Data are collected through Edge computing devices. Edge devices have learned from past experience and real-time input. It enhances comfort, efficiency, flexibility, and security to facilitate the needs of people and trade between them. Here is the use of Edge Computing.

Smart Industry: The world of industry is turning into a trend that goes by various names including Industry 4.0, Industrial Internet of Things (IoT), and Smart Power Grid [10]. It is a safer, more experimental, more environmentally friendly design of smart industrial factories and functions. With factories accounting for 40% of the world's energy consumption, reducing their energy consumption will play a significant role in bringing the planet on a more sustainable path. Machines are evolving to be aware of the people around them and provide new interfaces such as smart interfaces, augmented reality, touchless interfaces for easy and secure communication. The devices are being integrated inside the factory and with the cloud, enabling optimal planning and flexibility for production and maintenance. Here Edge computing can help in a better way.

Autonomous Vehicles: The choice to stop or not for a pedestrian crossing in front of an autonomous vehicle [11] should be taken instantly. In that case, it is not appropriate to rely on a remote server to handle this decision. However, the vehicles that use edge computing can interconnect more systematically because they first communicate with each other to prevent accidents by sending data on the first trip to a remote server. Edge computing can be used here to overcome the said problem in autonomous vehicles applications.

Surveillance: Security systems can detect possible threats and then can notify users to abnormal activities in real-time. Responding to a threat within seconds, the security monitoring systems can also be benefited by incorporating edge computing mechanism.

Retail Advertising: Targeted advertisements for retailers and data fields are based on key parameters such as the population data set on the device. In this case, the edge computing can help to preserve user privacy. It can keep the source instead of encrypting the data and not sending secure information to the cloud.

Smart Speakers: Speakers with smart sensors can gain the potential to interpret voice commands locally. Adjust the thermostat settings on or off or even if the Internet connection fails. Edge technology is rapidly used in such an application.

Video Conferencing: Delay in audio, poor video quality, a slow link to the icy screen-cloud video conferencing can produce a lot of frustration. By keeping the server-side of the video conferencing software to the contributors, quality problems can be minimized. While edge computing is in many cases a wise alternative to cloud computing, there is always room for enhancement. But, according to [12], the existing IoE security protocols need to be enhanced so that it can be used in practical scenarios.

In the above-mentioned applications, the security in communication for edge technology is a primary concern. Besides, a possible solution to further secure IoE-generated data is an IoE management component known as a security agent. This new piece will use routers and other near-edge boxes that cannot accommodate IoE devices. As well as being more secure, it will also make it easier to manage the key. The security agent box can operate a large number of sensors that are difficult to use. The researchers said that IoE applications would fail if the required verification was not done quickly.

3 Architecture for MEC

In this section, the layered architecture of edge computing will be described. According to the communication, architecture can be divided into three layers, (a) layer for edge devices, (b) layer for computation, and (c) cloud layer. Figure 1 shows the layered architecture of mobile edge computing-based IoE applications.

a. *Layer for edge devices*: In this layer, edge devices like mobile, sensors, and laptop are connected to each other. These devices may use short communication interfaces like Bluetooth, ZigBee depending upon application and availability of the connection. For this purpose, a personal area network (PAN) can be used. The edge devices transmit data to the local edge server for processing (see Fig. 1).

b. *Layer for computation*: After collecting data from edge devices, in this layer, the edge server like fog server processes the data. The edge server periodically collects data from the edge devices. Sometimes, depending on the application, if any person wants to access fresh and real-time data, then after proper verification, he/she can get data from this layer. However, this is the local data as the edge server is connected to the edge devices locally. After processing data, the edge servers send the data to the cloud so that users can access data globally (see Fig. 1). For this purpose, the edge server uses the Internet for communication.

c. *Cloud layer*: After getting data from each edge server, in this layer, the cloud server stores the data in a secure way so that users can get data whenever they want via the Internet. However, the data in this layer may not be fresh because the edge servers do not send data periodically to the cloud.

All the communications are done in public channels like Bluetooth and the Internet; therefore, an attacker alters the messages and hampers the communications (see Fig. 1). Even the adversary may try to extract the secret information of edge devices, servers. Not only that, but the attacker may also try to access data from the cloud and edge server. Thus, the protection of unauthorized access is a key term in such critical communications. However, later, this chapter will discuss the security challenges and issues for mobile edge computing-based IoE applications.

3.1   Network Model

To design a secure communication protocol based on edge-cloud architecture, the network model plays an important role by which the flow of data and authentication can be achieved. For this purpose, researchers generally use two types of network model (a) single server environment, and (b) multi-server environment. The details are described as follows:

a. *Single server environment*: Edge devices are connected to the local edge server and each local edge server connected to a global cloud server. In this regard, the global cloud server controls all the communications and edge servers and edge devices. The global server serves all the requests and services to the users globally. Figure 2a shows the single server environment.

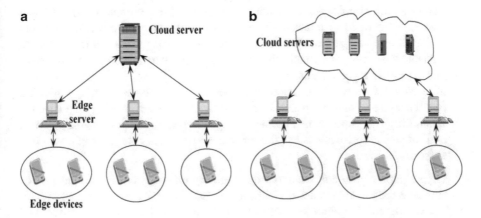

Fig. 2 Network model: (**a**) server environment, and (**b**) multi-server environment

b. *Multi-server environment*: Edge devices are connected to the local edge server and each local edge server connected to the corresponding global cloud server depending on the service provider. In this regard, the cloud servers distribute their tasks depending upon the availability of the resources. Figure 2b shows the single server environment.

c. *Hybrid*: In such an environment, edge servers and cloud servers are de-centralized. One registration center (maybe part of the governing body) controls the total networks. The networks are divided into several sub-networks as a company based and provides several services.

4 Possible Attacks and Cryptographic Solution

This section discusses the possible attacks on Mobile Edge Computing (MEC) during communication. Then a brief cryptographic solution is given on that direction. The possible attacks during communication in MEC listed below:

1. *DDoS attacks*: The goal of a DDOS attack is to connect all available resources and bandwidth to the target, and prevents malicious users from using the compromised system. The attacker constantly sends a large number of packets to the target (also known as 'flooding'), ensuring that all of the target's resources are exhausted to handle the corrupted packet, and therefore the actual requests cannot be processed. Such attacks are more important on edge computing paradigms because they are comparatively less powerful (compared to cloud servers), and therefore cannot run robust defenses.

2. *Malware attacks*: The inability to install a complete firewall on resource-limited edge devices makes them vulnerable to malware injection attacks, allowing an attacker to secretly install malicious programs on a target system.

3. *Authorization attacks*: Authentication processes in Edge computing systems can also be vulnerable to attacks. These types of attacks can be categorized into four different categories: dictionary attacks, attacks targeting vulnerabilities in authentication systems, attacks that exploit sensitivity to authorization protocols, and extra-privileged attacks.

4. *Side channel attacks*: Common examples of such attacks include capturing contact signals (such as packets or wave signals) to get user's personal data, monitoring the power consumption of edge devices to disclose usage patterns, and targeting end devices on file system and sensors like microphones, and cameras.

Cryptographic protocols used to protect privacy on secret information as well as to eliminate the possible attacks. The protocols used in MEC is categorized into (a) public key based, (b) secret key based, (c) only one-way hash function based, and (d) public plus secret key based (see Fig. 3). Depending on applications in MEC, public plus secret key based cryptosystem is used. For an example, an application where, wireless sensor devices are used in communication, in that case public key

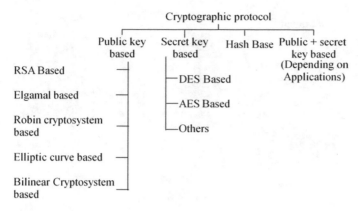

Fig. 3 Different cryptographic protocols used in MEC

cryptography cannot be used due to high computation cost. It results more energy consumption in sensor device during communication among IoE devices and edge server. In such case, secret key based protocol is used and in the higher level (i.e., edge to cloud communication), public key cryptography is used to provide more security during communication. This is because, edge and cloud servers have unlimited power as well can they can do the high computation operations.

In the next section, an Elliptic curve (ECC) based secure protocol [13] for communication in MEC environment has been discussed. This chapter picks ECC because; it can produce same security level with smaller key size. This work refers article [14] to know more about ECC. Moreover, in the protocol [13], sensor to edge server secure communication and vice versa has been done using secret key cryptography to reduce energy consumption of sensor devices. The remaining communication (edge to cloud and vice versa) has been done using ECC.

5 Secure Communication Protocol

This section discusses an edge-cloud based security protocol [13] which is applicable in the healthcare system. The protocol used in [13] is based on the elliptic curve cryptosystem [14].

5.1 Architecture

Before going to discuss the protocol [13] in detail, this section will discuss the architecture of the protocol (see Fig. 4). Sensors (the layer for edge devices) send messages periodically to the local edge server. The edge server forwards the message to the cloud server for authentication. After, correct verification, the cloud

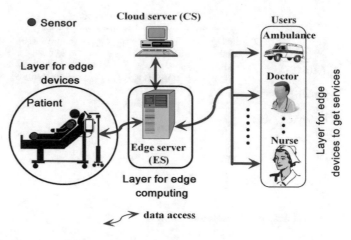

Fig. 4 Network structure of the existing secure protocol [13]

server replies back to the edge server. Upon getting a reply back from the cloud server, the edge server, checks the message and if the message is correct, then it forwards to the sensors. Finally, a secure session will be established between the edge server and the sensor (i.e., patient) for secure data transmission. However, in this protocol, how the other users like, doctors, nurses will get data from edge server is not demonstrated. But, they can get access to data from the edge server after proper authentication procedure.

5.2   Protocol in Details

The protocol [13] has four phases: (a) startup phase, (b) enrollment phase, (c) verification phase, and (d) data transmission phase.

a. **Startup phase**: A cloud server (CS) picks a long prime number y and makes an elliptic curve on a finite field of order m with a base point X. CS randomly selects a secret key $k \in_R [1, m - 1]$ and computes the corresponding public key $P = [k]X$. CS selects three cryptographic hash functions: $hf_1(.) : \{0, 1\}^* \to \{0, 1\}^n$ for a fixed n bits, $hf_2(.) : G_y \to \{0, 1\}^{n1}$ for a fixed $n1$ bits and $hf_3(.) : G_y \to \{0, 1\}^n$. Then CS announces $\langle X, m, p, hf_1(.), hf_2(.), hf_3(.) \rangle$ and k has been kept as a secret.
b. **Enrollment phase**: In this phase, CS supplies the information regarding registration to the edge servers as well as the healthcare sensors.

   Enrollment of edge servers: An edge server ES_i selects its unique identity EID_i and sends it to CS. After getting EID_i, CS selects a random number $a_i \in_R [1, m - 1]$ which is a secret key of ES_i and calculates a public key $EPK_i = [a_i]X$. CS then sends $\langle a_i \rangle$ to ES_i through secure channel and announces $\{EID_i, EPK_i\}$ publicly. Upon getting a_i, ES_i stores it securely.

Enrollment of sensors: Before going to place a healthcare sensor S_i on the patient's body, CS chooses an unique identity S_ID_i for S_i and calculates its key Key_i as $hf_2(e_i \| S\_ID_i)$, where e_i is a random number chosen by CS. CS again calculates a pseudo identity PS_ID_i as $hf_2(S\_ID_i \| k)$ for S_i and stores in its database as $Sensor\_DB = \{PS\_ID_i, ENC[S\_ID_i \| Key_i]_k\}$, where $ENC[.]_k$ means encrypted using a secret key k. Then CS burns $\langle PS\_ID_i, S\_ID_i, Key_i \rangle$ into the memory of S_i as temper resist.

c. **Verification phase**: If a healthcare sensor S_i has data to send, it sends a request to send message as $\langle EID_i, PS\_ID_i, V_i, W_i \rangle$ to ES_i after calculating $V_i = ENC[z_i \| SID_i \| EID_i]_{Key_i}$ and $W_i = hf_1(z_i \| S\_ID_i \| V_i)$ where, z_i is a random number chosen by S_i.

After receiving $\langle EID_i, PS\_ID_i, V_i, W_i \rangle$, ES_i forwards the message as $\langle EID_i, A_i, C_i, Q_i \rangle$ to CS through the Internet after calculating $A_i = [l_i]X$, $B_i = [l_i]P$, $C_i = (PS\_ID_i \| V_i \| W_i \| EID_i) \oplus hf_2(B_i)$ and $Q_i = [hf_1(C_i)]X + [a_i]P$, where l_i is a random number chosen by ES_i.

After receiving $\langle EID_i, A_i, C_i, Q_i \rangle$ from ES_i, CS calculates $B_i^\# = [k] A_i$, $\text{PSID}_i^\# \| V_i^\# \| W_i^\# \| \text{EID}_i^\# = C_i \oplus hf_2(B_i^\#)$ and extracts $S\_ID_i \| Key_i$ from its $Sensor\_DB$ by decrypting $ENC[S\_ID_i \| Key_i]_k$ using its secret key k corresponding to $\text{PSID}_i^\#$ if it exists into the database. CS then decrypts $V_i^\#$ using Key_i to extract $z_i^\# \| SID_i^\# \| EID_i^{\#\#}$ as $DEC[V_i^\#]_{Key_i}$ and, checks extracted $SID_i^\# \overset{?}{=} SID_i$ and $EID_i^{\#\#} \overset{?}{=} EID_i$. For the equality, CS calculates $W_i^{\#\#} = hf_1(z_i^\# \| SID_i \| V_i^\#)$ and $Q_i^\# = [hf_1(C_i)] X + [k] EPK_i$. CS then further checks $W_i^{\#\#} \overset{?}{=} W_i^\#$ and $Q_i^\# \overset{?}{=} Q_i$. For the equality, CS transmits a reply message $\langle CS_1, CS_2, CS_3 \rangle$ to ES_i via the Internet after calculating $CS_1 = [u_i]X$, $CS_2 = z_i^\# \oplus hf_3([u_i] EPK_i)$ and $CS_3 = [z_i^\#] X + [k] EPK_i$, where u_i is a random number chosen by CS.

After receiving $\langle CS_1, CS_2, CS_3 \rangle$, ES_i calculates $z_i^* = CS_2 \oplus hf_3([a_i]CS_1)$ and checks $CS_3 \overset{?}{=} [z_i^*] X + [a_i] P$. For the equality, ES_i transmits a clear to transmit message $\langle Y_i, H_i \rangle$ to S_i after computing $Session^k = hf_1(z_i^* \| t_i)$, $Y_i = t_i \oplus z_i^*$ and $H_i = hf_1(Session^k \| Y_i)$ where, t_i is a random number chosen by ES_i.

After receiving $\langle Y_i, H_i \rangle$, S_i calculates t_i as $Y_i \oplus z_i$, $Session^k = hf_1(z_i \| t_i)$ and verifies the received $H_i \overset{?}{=} hf_1(Session^k \| Y_i)$. For the equality, S_i agrees on the common secret session key $Session^k$ in data transmission phase.

d. **Data transmission phase**: After agreement on $Session^k$, S_i transmits its sensed data as a cipher $CIPHER\_DATA = ENC[DATA]_{Session k}$ to ES_i. After receiving $CIPHER\_DATA$, ES_i de-cipher it by using the same session key $Session^k$ as $DATA = DEC[CIPHER\_DATA]_{Session k}$ and analyzes the data. ES_i stores the data as cipher form using its secret key a_i corresponding to PS_ID_i as $\{PS\_ID_i, ENC[DATA]_{ai}\}$ for future reference to the users like doctors and nurses.

A flow chart of verification and data transmission phases of the proposed scheme in [13] is given in Fig. 5.

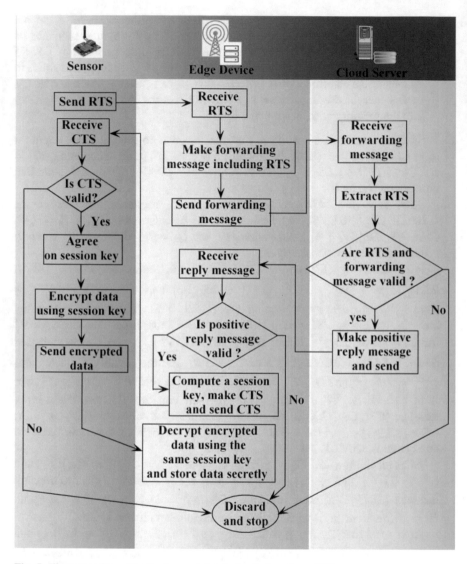

Fig. 5 Flow chart for authentication and data transmission phases [13]

6   Other Security Protocols: A Comparison

This section demonstrates the existing security protocols for a cloud-edge environment. This section also compares the related existing security schemes. By decreasing end-to-end delay and enhanced position perception with mobile facilities, *Mobile Edge Computing* (MEC) furnishes smooth services. Since MEC progressed from cloud computing, it has subsequently inherited many security and privacy issues. Besides, decentralized testing and diversified installation environments on MEC platforms exacerbate the problem; the research causes great concern for the community. So, in 2019, Kaur *et al.* [15] have proposed an efficient and lightweight mutual verification protocol for the environment of MEC; based on cryptography based on elliptic curves (ECC), cryptographic hash function and work with content. The designed protocol also presents the advantages of counteracting individual computational Diffie-Helman, logarithm problems, random numbers and time-stamps, multi-attack-resistant attacks, replay attacks, and man-in-the-middle attacks. The work in [15] claims that it is suitable for acquiring resource hindrance MEC environments. Omala et al. [16], Cheng et al. [17] and He et al. [18] introduced their security protocols that can enable a patient to securely transmit their data directly to application servers (mainly cloud servers) using their mobile application. However, such a situation is not always possible, as no patient may be able to manage his mobile application in his critical situation. So, an automated system is needed to handle this problem, where sensors can send their data securely from time to time. Recently, Maitra and Roy [19] suggested a secure communication scheme for patient monitoring system, known as *SecPMS*. In the approach [19], the end users such as doctors and nurses get patients' information securely from a local server (i.e., edge server) after performing authentication procedure.

On the other hand, IP-based communication is a serious security threat for MEC. Thus, secure information sharing between diverse communication agents has become an important concern in smart grid environments. In particular, to enable secure communication among smart meters and utilities, managing the key before authentication is the most important task. Mehmood *et al.* [20] proposed an identity-based signature to represent an anonymous key agreement protocol for smart grid infrastructure. The protocol [20] enables smart meters to be interconnected to anonymous utility controls for the services they provide. Smart meters recognize this purpose with a secret key in the absence of reliable authority, where the trusted officers are only intricate in the enrollment phase.

On the Internet of Thing (IoT) systems, large amounts of data are accumulated at any given time, which can capture human privacy, mostly when the system is used in medical or everyday environments. Privacy protection is an important issue and high privacy claims usually demand a weak identification. The earlier researches have stated that well built security demands strong identification, particularly in authentication processes. Therefore, defining a better business between privacy and security remains a challenging issue. Wang [21] introduced a security, accountability, privacy-protection, efficiency, and dynamic removal necessity for weakly identified IoT end-of-device authentication frameworks. For this purpose, the author in [21] used Shamir's secret sharing project [22] for a basic installation and distribution project for secure communication between the end device and the end device. A small-group signature scheme [22] has then been used to make a privacy-preserving and accountable verification protocol for weakly identified IoT end-devices.

Not only secure communication but secure database access also important in MEC. In this regard, Pang and Tan [23] have proposed an edge that creates a

Table 1 Existing security protocols for MEC: A comparison

Purpose	Protocols	Computational cost	Latency	Security	Network model
Secure Communication + Authentication	[15]	high	high	medium	single server
	[16]	high	medium	high	single server
	[20]	high	high	medium	multi server
	[21]	medium	medium	medium	single server
Authentication + Secure Data Store	[13]	medium	low	medium	single server
Secure database access	[23]	-	-	-	hybrid

validation object (VO) to verify the integrity of the result of each query generated by an edge server – the results of which do not tamper with the values; even though any attacker enthusiasts add fake tuples. The primary advantage of the proposed system [23] is that it is unique compared to the size of the VO database and those relevant activities can still be performed by the edge server. The said mechanism turns down the communication load and processing complexity at the client end.

Table 1 gives a summary of the aforementioned existing secure protocols, where, latency is considered with respect to the number of bits transmitted.

7   Issues and Challenges to Design Security Protocols

This section discusses the challenges to design a security protocol for the edge-cloud environment.

IoE Vulnerabilities at the Edge: Edge computing fixes a variety of IoE networking traffic issues; however, it often introduces new weaknesses that contribute to an overall wider attack surface, that is, the total number of access points for a network that can be used by an adversary. Networks become more vulnerable at ends and edges due to the condition of existing platforms. Some attacks may occur as end-users generally don't change their default passwords. This creates a path for malicious people to have access to the user's end devices, as they are now exposed to attack.

Internet resources that are not secure can be found easily and are accessible. In a 2017 "botnet barrage" bots were introduced to check for devices running default passwords at university campus. In the year 2013, an application was released that could scan for unsecured IoE devices around the world. Around 5,000 IoT devices have been hacked by 5,000 individual systems because these devices had default or weak passwords.

The above attacks have been carried out due to the weakness present at the end points, nonetheless edge computing complicates things by exposing new attack surfaces. IoE devices that link to the public Internet violate protection protocols at the edge of the network. This is partially attributed to the existing state of edge computing in which full-stack systems like sensors, applications and protected components are not common. Many of the approaches used to protect IoT networks at the edge can be ineffective. LPWAN protocols can become unstable if encryption keys are stolen. VPNs are vulnerable to man-in-the-medium attacks.

Physical Tampering: Edge computing being distributive in nature often leads to opening up of new, unexpected frontier of physical risks. Although servers and computers that drive conventional networks are typically located in large, sometimes extremely protected warehouses, the very tiny data centers that render edge computing such a massive leap forward may often be a security nightmare.

Instead of keeping in data centers, such micro-centers are mostly installed in an area that, as we think about IoE edge, may be a corporate office, a garden, and everything in between. An intruder who physically tampers with an edge system may bring down a network, or even damage one of its operators. Securing these systems is also far from straightforward – as they need to be protected against physical threats, it is often a tradeoff between reliability, expense, and ease of updating and maintaining edge data centers. Device manufacturers need to be aware of the threats to ensure the systems can be conveniently monitored to trigger remote and local alerts at any indication of interference.

Lacking Reflection of Secure Design: The primary aim of edge computing is to furnish a more powerful and lightweight computing environment for evolving technologies such as IoE and smart cities [3]. While building designs, device designers prefer to rely more on efficiency than on the security part, when building the application-specific edge computing architecture. Such a lackadaisical attitude towards security explicitly uncovers the edge computing infrastructures to larger attack sides.

Non-migratability of Security Frameworks: The security framework for general-purpose computer systems have been widely researched for a long time and are known to be capable of offering good security assurances in the defense against numerous threats [3]. Nonetheless, such security architectures cannot be explicitly transferred to edge computing platforms due to a variety of irresolvable differences, such as competing processing resources, diverse OSs and applications, specific network architectures, and incompatible protocols. Also, security frameworks outlined for an edge computing application may not be directly transferred to another scenario such as diversity of edge devices as well as diversity in intelligent transmission protocols.

Coarse-Grained and Fragmented Access Control: Current access management frameworks for edge computing are inconsistent and coarse-grained [3]. They are fragmented since various edge computing contexts can follow specific access management models that may be configured in a fully distinct way for segregating, granting, and obtaining permissions. This condition hinders the creation of a coherent and functional access control platform for different edge computing systems. Recent access control mechanisms for edge computing are also coarse-grained because, with compare to coarse-grained, permissions in fine-grained are largely complex and underexplored.

8 Conclusion and Future Direction

Based on the basic computing reasons, the status queues, and the magnificent challenges of achieving edge computing systems, this chapter can conclude that research on the security domain in edge computing technology is far from the delighted result. Future research focuses should lie in the grand challenges and should overcome the existing weaknesses. For such edge-based applications, more robust defense solutions are needed to reduce personal attacks, especially preventive measures; on the other hand, new architectures are needed that can integrate the entire system and can incorporate security measures to protect the secure information from an outsider when online communication will be done. Most significantly, the philosophy of safety by design should be widely adopted and always returned. Inspired from the article [3], below, this chapter outlines a basic concept that seeks to secure edge computing systems with integrated structure and current future directions along this line of research. The structure consists of three layers: (a) a fine-grained outer access control layer, (a) a medium-security function layer, and (c) an internal hardware-isolated OS layer.

The outer layer focuses on fine granular access control, which acts as a gate to prevent intruders from entering. If properly designed and strictly implemented, such fine access control systems can potentially reduce protocol-level design errors, implementation-level errors, and attacks generated by weak access control. It can carry flood-based DDoS, controllable side channels, malware injection attacks, and attacks in the verification process.

There are plans to implement medium level full security measures. This chapter proposes the adoption of software-defined networking (SDN) and network function virtualization (NFV) at the edge server level, where SDN is adopted to filter out malicious traffic on a per-packet basis. In contrast, NFV adopts more advanced algorithms such as intensive learning to detect malicious behaviors in autonomous and self-developed methods. SDN and NFV-enabled edge servers can prevent packet-based attacks such as DDoS, attacks arising from connected data (requiring learning-based detection), and poor access control (which can lead to attacks such as malware injection).

The inner layer notices unnecessary code-level vulnerabilities. Moreover, the IT and telecommunications worlds have experienced real ideological changes over the years. The concept of mobile edge computing has recently been published, applying fog computing (edge-on-cloud) to mobile network domains. However, edge technology will have a real impact on the way new services are installed as they will benefit from a combination of SDN plus NFV. Either way, IoT, which is highly connected with mobile networks, will benefit by expanding the concept of mobile edge agent computers to other areas such as VANET and WSN.

This chapter has first described some edge technology-based applications that are recently under consideration in the research domain. Then the system architectures have been discussed concerning the design of edge-based applications. Then one secure communication protocol has been highlighted for a cloud-edge based health-care system. After that brief overview of recent secure communication protocols for edge-based applications has been compared. The designing issues and challenges have been enlisted then. Lastly, future direction and probable solutions have been discussed in this section. After enlightening all the things, and then also this chapter can say that the developing research in edge computing security is still under construction and there have so many scopes to re-design the security protocols. Inspired by emerging applications and advances in modern cryptography, innovative design, and applications to secure edge computing systems will be enriched in the distant future.

References

1. Bradley, J., Barbier, J., Handler, D.: Embracing the Internet of Everything To Capture Your Share of $14.4 Trillion. published by cisco (2013). https://www.cisco.com/c/dam/en_us/about/ac79/docs/innov/IoE_Economy.pdf
2. Cisco IoT. http://www.cisco.com/web/solutions/trends/iot/overview.html
3. Xiao, Y., Jia, Y., Liu, C., Cheng, X., Yu, J., Lv, W.: Edge Computing Security: State of the Art and Challenges. in Proceedings of the IEEE. vol. 107. no. 8 (2019) 1608–1631.
4. Antonakakis et al.: Understanding the Mirai botnet. in Proc. of 26th USENIX Secur. Symp. Vancouver, BC, Canada: USENIX Association (2017) 1093–1110.
5. Dutta, J., Roy, S., C. Chowdhury, C.: Unified framework for IoT and smartphone based different smart city related applications. Microsyst Technol. Vol. 25. (2019) 83–96.
6. Maitra, T., Giri, D.,: An Efficient Biometric and Password-Based Remote User Authentication using Smart Card for Telecare Medical Information Systems in Multi-Server Environment. Journal of Medical Systems. Vol. 38. no. 12, article no. 142, (2014) 1–19.
7. Giri, D., Maitra, T., Amin, R., Srivastava, P. D.: An Efficient and Robust RSA-Based Remote User Authentication for Telecare Medical Information Systems. Journal of Medical Systems. Vol. 39. article no. 145, 2015.
8. Hu, L., Ni, Q.: IoT-Driven Automated Object Detection Algorithm for Urban Surveillance Systems in Smart Cities. IEEE Internet of Things Journal. Vol. 5, no. 2, (2018) 747–754.
9. Dutta, J., Wang, Y., Maitra, T., Islam, SK. H., Rawal, B. S., Giri, D.: ES3B: Enhanced Security System for Smart Building using IoT. in Proc. of The 3rd IEEE International Conference on Smart Cloud (SmartCloud 2018). New York, USA, (2018) 158–165.
10. Ou, Q., Zhen, Y., Li, X., Zhang, Y., Zeng, L.: Application of Internet of Things in Smart Grid Power Transmission. in the proc. of 2012 Third FTRA International Conference on Mobile, Ubiquitous, and Intelligent Computing. Vancouver, BC, (2012) 96–100.
11. Kong, L., Khan, M. K., Wu, F., Chen, G., Zeng, P.: Millimeter-Wave Wireless Communications for IoT-Cloud Supported Autonomous Vehicles: Overview, Design, and Challenges. IEEE Communications Magazine. Vol. 55. no. 1. (2017) 62–68.
12. Hsu, R., Lee, J., Quek, T. Q. S., Chen, J.: Reconfigurable Security: Edge-Computing-Based Framework for IoT, IEEE Network. Vol. 32. no. 5. (2018) 92–99.

13. Giri, D., Obaidat, M. S., Maitra, T.: SecHealth: An Efficient Fog based Sender Initiated Secure Data Transmission of Healthcare Sensors for e-Medical System. in Proc. of IEEE GLOBECOM 2017. Singapore, (2017) 1–6.
14. Maitra, T., Obaidat, M. S., Islam, SK, H., Giri, D., Amin, R.: Security analysis and design of an efficient ecc-based two-factor password authentication scheme. Security and Communication Networks. Vol. 9. no. 17. (2016) 4166–4181.
15. Kaur, K., Garg, S., Kaddoum, G., Guizani, M., Jayakody, D. N. K.: A Lightweight and Privacy-Preserving Authentication Protocol for Mobile Edge Computing. in Proc. of IEEE GLOBECOM 2019. Waikoloa, HI, USA, (2019) 1–6.
16. Omala, A.A, Kibiwott, K.P., Li, F.: An efficient remote authentication scheme for wireless body area network. Journal of Medical Systems. Vol. 41. no. 2. (2016) 1–9.
17. Cheng, Q., Zhang, X., and Ma, J.: Icasme: An improved cloud-based authentication scheme for medical environment. Journal of Medical Systems, Vol. 41. no. 3 (2017) 1–14.
18. He, D., Zeadally, S., Kumar, N., Lee, J.H.: Anonymous authentication for wireless body area networks with provable security. IEEE Systems Journal, Vol. 11. no. 4, (2016) 1–12.
19. Maitra, T., Roy, S.: Secpms: An efficient and secure communication protocol for continuous patient monitoring system using body sensors. in proc. of 9th International Conference on Communication Systems and Networks (COMSNETS 2017), Bangalore, India, (2017) 322–329.
20. Mahmood, K., Li, X., Chaudhry, S.A., Naqvi, H., Kumari, S., Sangaiah, A.K., Rodrigues, J.J.P.C.: Pairing based anonymous and secure key agreement protocol for smart grid edge computing infrastructure. Future Generation Computer Systems. Vol. 88. (2018) 491–500.
21. Wang, Z.: A privacy-preserving and accountable authentication protocol for IoT end-devices with weaker identity. Future Generation Computer Systems, Vol. 82. (2018) 342–348.
22. Shamir, A.: How to Share a Secret. Com. ACM, Vol. 22. no. 11. (1979) 612–613.
23. Pang, H.H., and K. Tan, K.: Authenticating query results in edge computing. in proc. of 20th International Conference on Data Engineering. Boston, MA, USA, (2004) 560–571.

Blockchain for Mobile Edge Computing: Consensus Mechanisms and Scalability

Jorge Peña Queralta and Tomi Westerlund

Abstract Mobile edge computing (MEC) and next-generation mobile networks are set to disrupt the way intelligent and autonomous systems are interconnected. This will have an effect on a wide range of domains, from the Internet of Things to autonomous mobile robots. The integration of such a variety of MEC services in an inherently distributed architecture requires a robust system for managing hardware resources, balancing the network load and securing the distributed applications. Blockchain technology has emerged a solution for managing MEC services, with consensus protocols and data integrity checks that enable transparent and efficient distributed decision-making. In addition to transparency, the benefits from a security point of view are evident. Nonetheless, blockchain technology faces significant challenges in terms of scalability. In this chapter, we review existing consensus protocols and scalability techniques in both well-established and next-generation blockchain architectures. From this, we evaluate the most suitable solutions for managing MEC services and discuss the benefits and drawbacks of the available alternatives.

Keywords Edge computing · Blockchain · Distributed ledger technology · Mobile edge computing · Multi-access edge computing · Scalability · Distributed consensus · Internet of things (IoT)

1 Introduction

The scope of the Internet of Things (IoT) has been growing over the past decade, encompassing an ever larger ecosystem that spans multiple domains. Some of the most prominent research directions are smart cities [1, 2], vehicular technology [3, 4], or smart healthcare systems [5–7]. In all these domains, a common

J. Peña Queralta (✉) · T. Westerlund
Turku Intelligent Embedded and Robotic Systems Lab, University of Turku, Turku, Finland
e-mail: jopequ@utu.fi; tovewe@utu.fi

© The Author(s), under exclusive license to Springer Nature Switzerland AG 2021   333
A. Mukherjee et al. (eds.), *Mobile Edge Computing*,
https://doi.org/10.1007/978-3-030-69893-5_14

factor is that IoT systems are evolving towards more distributed architectures [8]. This shift from more traditional cloud-centric architectures has crystallized in the edge computing paradigm [9–11]. At the same time, novel technologies are increasingly designed with decentralization in mind from their inception. Among these, blockchain technology is set to be one of the key drivers behind the disruption of the technological landscape in the near future [12, 13]. Decentralized technologies are also the cornerstone behind the Internet 3.0 and Industry 4.0 revolutions that are undergoing [14].

Blockchain technology is already a driver behind decentralized and distributed IoT systems, providing security [15], trust [16, 17], data management [18], peer-to-peer transactions [19], and fault-tolerand middlewares [20]. Blockchain platforms can be divided in two main types depending on how they manage user credentials, which have a direct impact on their applicability: (1) permissionless, or public, and (2) permissioned, private, or consortium, blockchains. They differentiate in that public blockchains are based on anonymous nodes with equivalent status, while consortium or private blockchains introduce different types of nodes and permissions, some of which require authentication in order perform certain actions. While trust in permissionless blockchains is shared and distributed, in permissioned blockchains there is a series of validator nodes that represented trusted authorities [21].

One of the main issues stopping a wider adoption of blockchain in IoT systems is scalability, an inherent problem to Bitcoin's architecture that multiple researchers have been addressing [22, 23]. While smart contracts have great potential in the IoT and distributed systems in general, their scalability and performance is closely tied to the overall performance of blockchain systems [24]. Nonetheless, multiple advances in recent years have demonstrated that novel technologies can bring significantly higher degrees of scalability and performance to next-generation blockchain systems. Among these, Elastico provided the first implementation of a sharding protocol in a permissionless blockchain [25]. Sharding is a technique that enables the distribution of nodes in a blockchain into subchains for performing parallel validation, thus increasing throughput and reducing latency. A more recent scalable blockchain is OmniLedger [26], which reports better scalability than Elastico and promises VISA-level latency and throughout if enough nodes form up the network.

Owing to the distributed nature of blockchain systems, and distributed ledger technology (DLT) in general, IoT systems integrating them must already have a distributed architecture by themselves. Therefore, it is only natural that blockchain is integrated at the edge layer in most occasions, which represents the most distributed and interconnected layer of a typical IoT system. While sensors and actuators could be considered more distributed, they are not necessarily capable of node-to-node communication. Through this chapter, we utilize the terms blockchain and distributed ledger equivalently. However, distributed ledger technology (DLT) is often utilized to include more general systems that do not implement blockchains per se, but instead rely on some other type of network or data management architecture. An example of this is IOTA, which utilizes acyclic directed graphs representing more general data structures. The rest of this introduction delves into more details behind the nature of mobile edge computing and its integration with blockchain/DLT technology.

1.1 MEC and Network Slicing

The European Telecommunications Standards Institute (ETSI) has promoted the standardization of Multi-Access Edge Computing (MEC) [27], which shares the acronym with Mobile Edge Computing (MEC). The "multi-access" term puts an emphasis on the multi-tenant infrastructure and better reflects non-cellular operators [27, 28]. In this chapter, we do not make distinctions between the two terms as our focus lays on the role of blockchain with edge computing. MEC standardization has been led by the MEC Industry Specification Group (ISG) since the end of 2014. One of the main objectives of the ETSI MEC ISG is to define the base technologies for distributed and multi-tenant clouds that are meant to be deployed at the edge of the radio access network (RAN) [9]. By deploying data aggregation and processing tasks directly at the edge of the network, MEC services can provide better reliability, lower latency and higher-throughput [7, 29, 30]. We will specifically discuss throughout this paper how blockchain technology can play a key role in terms of security and robustness for the resource management needed in a multi-tenant edge infrastructure, as well as enhance the services that MEC applications can provide [31–34].

One of the key architectural cornerstones enabling multi-tenancy and co-existing verticals at the MEC layer is network slicing [35]. Network slicing provides the base for interfacing blockchain with other MEC services for a wide array of application scenarios [36]. Network slicing refers to the co-existence of multiple software defined systems and networks (slices) sharing a common hardware infrastructure. Each of the slices can be thus designed independently and optimized for a particular application or business vertical [37]. In particular, slicing for vehicular communication and offloading, together with 5G-and-beyond connectivity, are set to define the mobility of the future [38].

1.2 Integration of Blockchain and MEC

The integration of blockchain within the MEC layer has been object of extensive research over the past few years. Systems integrating blockchain and edge computing can be roughly divided among those in which edge services are part of a larger blockchain system [39–41], and those in which blockchain is one of the services enhancing edge services [31, 33, 34, 42–44]. In this chapter, we are particularly interested in the latter type, as blockchain can provide a key piece in enabling truly distributed, secure and efficient edge computing. With monetization of MEC being a central topic of discussion since its early proposal [29], multiple works have focused towards either enhancing security or utilizing blockchain as a marketplace framework for users to access different applications at the edge [32, 34, 43]. More recently, other works have also delved into the potential of blockchain as a framework for managing edge resources [44–47], as well as supporting autonomy in distributed robotic systems [36].

From the security point of view, the integration of blockchain technology brings evident benefits to edge computing. Among the main threats identified in a recent report from the European Union Agency for Cybersecurity (ENISA) on 5G networks and edge infrastructure [48], blockchain and DLT technologies can help address multiple remaining challenges. For instance, permissioned DLTs with built-in identity management naturally provide an extra layer of resilience against malicious diversion of network traffic, manipulation of traffic, or authentication traffic spikes. When blockchain technology is applied to resource management, it can serve as a framework to mitigate risks in terms of abuse of third party hosted network functions, manipulation of the network resources orchestrator, or opportunistic and fraudulent usages of shared resources, among others. Moreover, safety-critical applications can benefit from the enhanced security that blockchains and other DLTs provide. These include the automotive sector with vehicle to everything communication routed at the edge [49, 50], and the healthcare sector [34, 51, 52].

1.3   Related Works

Multiple surveys and review papers have recently been published on the convergence of blockchain and mobile edge computing [53–56]. Other surveys in either the blockchain or edge computing domains also mention the potential for integrating one with another [57–60]. In these and other works, scalability is often identified as one of the key aspects limiting the adoption of blockchain in edge computing. Nonetheless, these works describe the scalability problem either as a systemic blockchain problem [53], or from a system point of view [55]. Most works also focus on a specific blockchain, Ethereum being the most widely researched blockchain for IoT [54]. In a blockchain, consensus algorithms are the main bottleneck in terms of scalability, i.e., the mechanisms enabling all nodes in the blockchain network to validate transaction and stay synced. Depending on the type of consensus algorithm, the scalability of the system might be limited by either the computational complexity of the algorithm, or its communication complexity. We believe there is a gap in the literature describing how the consensus algorithms affect the scalability from these two points of view. Our objective is to bring further insight in this area, providing a literature review and a discussion on the topic.

In this chapter, we introduce the main consensus algorithms that form the backbone of different blockchain solutions, including newer generation distributed ledgers that do not follow many of the paradigms defined within the Bitcoin and successive blockchains. We then describe what can be the role of edge computing when it integrates blockchain/DLT systems. In particular, we discuss the potential for the different solutions in the IoT, from the point of view of scalability but also discussing the different applications that are most suitable for different blockchain/DLT solutions. We do this from the point of view of consensus algorithms and their computational and communication complexity. Compared to previous works surveying the integration of blockchain and edge computing [53], we provide a novel classification of current research directions from an architectural point of view (Sect. 3), while giving more insight into how the different consensus algorithms affect the integration of blockchain/DLT and edge computing (Sect. 4).

1.4 Chapter Structure

The rest of this chapter is organized as follows. In Sect. 2, we introduce the main consensus algorithms in blockchain systems and other DLTs, together with the most prominent results in highly-scalable and low-latency blockchains. Section 3 then reviews specific applications of blockchain at the MEC layer, and discusses how the different consensus protocols integrate at the edge. In Sect. 4, we discuss on the best blockchain/DLT solutions for different applications in the IoT, and how next-generation systems that are currently under development might change the IoT and MEC landscape. Finally, Sect. 5 concludes this work.

2 Blockchain Technology: An Evolving Paradigm

In this section we start with the basics of blockchain technology and move into how the field is evolving towards lower-latency, higher-throughput, and new concepts aimed at increasing flexibility and scalability, such as sharding. We provide a historical point of view on the different consensus algorithms that have been proposed for blockchains and other distributed ledgers, and include an overview of the most prominent so-called third-generation blockchains. The main concepts, consensus protocols and applications are summarized in Fig. 1.

   Consensus mechanisms are one of the key aspects within the design of decentralized networked systems or distributed computing systems. Consensus mechanisms are those algorithms that enable multiple independent agents to reach an agreement on a certain value, operation, transaction, or other types of data. In a distributed and decentralized system, different agents, or nodes, need to be able to trust each other. Consensus mechanisms are the enablers of trust among agents. The most popular consensus mechanisms to date in blockchain systems, according to a survey from Li et al. [61], are proof of work (PoW), proof of stake (PoS) practical byzantine fault tolerance (PBFT) and delegated proof of stake (DPoS), with other significant approaches including proof of authority (PoA), proof of elapsed time (PoET) or proof of bandwidth (PoB). Apart from some of the more traditional consensus algorithms listed above (e.g. PoW utilized in Bitcoin or Ethereum, and PoS being

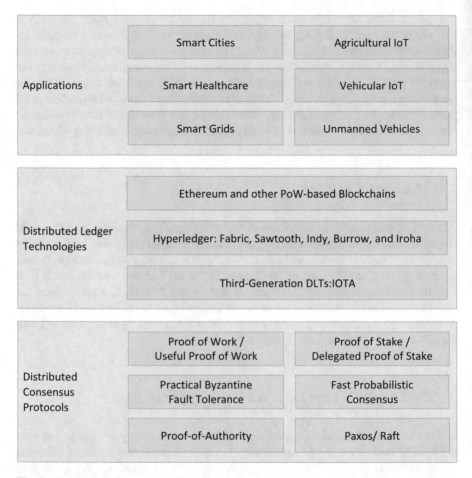

Fig. 1 Blockchain/DLT consensus protocols, systems, and applications in integration with the internet of things

part of Ethereum 2.0 plans), in this document we also review consensus protocols utilized in third- and fourth-generation distributed ledger systems such as the fast probabilistic consensus (FPC), and the cellular consensus (CC). We also put an emphasis on defining the key technologies behind IOTA, a DLT designed for the IoT and an ideal candidate for integrating DLTs with edge computing.

2.1 Proof of Work

Nakamoto's proof of work designed for Bitcoin [62] has heavily influenced the development of new solutions for newer-generation blockchain systems. The PoW implementation in Bitcoin was a new application for an old algorithm. Originally proposed by [63] as a solution to deter spam activity from email senders, the main idea behind PoW systems has remained unchanged: to request to all networked agents to solve computationally intensive cryptographic problems in order to validate their activity, their identity, or those of another agent. In general terms, a PoW algorithm is, at its most fundamental level, an algorithm that solves a cryptographic problem with a solution that is, in relative terms, hard to find and easy to validate. The computational complexity of the validation of a PoW solution is therefore considerably smaller than the complexity of finding such solution.

Ethereum, the second most popular blockchain system after Bitcoin, also relies on PoW-based consensus to validate new blocks in the blockchain. A block can be roughly defined as each of the entries in the distributed ledger that blockchains implement. A block does not include a single transaction, but often a set of transactions that are near in time. These transactions represent the block's body, where transactions are defined in a generic manner and do not represent only the exchange of cryptocurrencies. Transactions in PoW-based blockchains are not validated individually, but instead all the transactions in a block get validated when the block containing them is validated itself. A block is validated, or mined, by solving a PoW puzzle. The original and most widely used puzzle in blockchains can be summarized as follows: the PoW algorithm must find a block header, which is the result of applying a cryptographic hash function to the content of the block body, satisfying some predefined condition. However, for a fixed hash function and a fixed block body, the resulting hash will always be the same. In order to meet this condition (e.g., finding a hash smaller than a certain value), the algorithm must then find some other value, called a nonce, to be added to the current block body. Finding a nonce is the process often called mining. Once a block is mined, it is added to the blockchain and all other agents in the network can validate the solution. In Bitcoin and other blockchain systems, the miner of a block gets a reward in the form of new cryptocurrency, thus motivating nodes to participate in the transaction validation process.

One of the problems of PoW-based blockchains is that two agents could solve a PoW puzzle at virtually the same time, for the same or different nonces. This can create two branches, or forks, in the blockchain. Nodes are situated in the branch of the solution that they received first. In Bitcoin, a built-in policy establishes that if one fork is longer than the other (or it accumulates more cryptographic complexity), then all agents in the network judge it as the authentic one. This is a practical solution as it is highly improbable that two consecutive blocks will be solved simultaneously by two pairs of nodes. In any case, even if two or more blocks are solved at the same time, at some point one of the forks will become longer. This defines the so-called 51% or double spending attack, as malicious nodes would need to control at least 51% of the network's computing power in order to be able to introduce a faulty transaction in a block, validate it, and keep validating consecutive nodes in the corresponding fork so that it is accepted as the canonical fork by the network. When the size of the network and the number of miners increases, the probability of such attack is reduced, thus giving the blockchain its immutability and data integrity properties.

The benefit of having an expensive PoW solution in terms of hardware, energy consumption and time is that it is equally expensive for malicious nodes to attack the network. Part of the security of PoW thus comes from disincentivizing attackers because of the large a priori investment required in order to be able to attack and gain control of the network, which would not pay off even if the attack is successful [64].

2.2 Proof of Useful Work

Part of the research community has argued that taking into account the humongous amount of computational resources and electric energy put into mining to solve PoW puzzles, at least these could be defined in a way that the solutions found would help research in other fields. As an example, King et al. proposed the definition of PoW puzzles that would find long chains of primes [65]. Solving these PoW would be then dedicated to solve a mathematical problem which consists on finding the distribution of the Cunningham prime chain. In this case, the Fermat Primality Test would be used to validate the PoW solutions.

A different research approach is the definition of simpler PoW requiring less computational resources in order to reduce the entry barrier and provide a more uniform distribution of mined currency. Pagh et al. introduced the concept of Cuckoo hashing, in which the PoW difficulty would remain constant over time [66].

2.3 Proof of Stake

The basis for security and robustness in a PoW system comes from the amount of computational resources needed in order to gain control over the network. Nonetheless, this computational complexity also brings limitations. First, it limits the probability for news nodes to be able to mine new cryptocurrency by themselves if they join a large network. Second, it also limits the number of transactions that can be validated within a certain time interval. For instance, in Bitcoin, it takes an average time of 10 min to validate a block and all the transactions it includes [67]. A different consensus approach that does not rely on computational complexity and that has gained momentum in recent years is Proof of Stake (PoS). One of the main objective of PoS systems, which is being introduced, for instance, as part of Ethereum 2.0, is to reduce transaction validation latency. One of the first implementations of PoS in a blockchain system, which showed clear benefits in this direction, was demonstrated with Nxtcoin [68, 69]. The idea behind PoS is to value the cryptocurrency that validating nodes put *at stake*, instead of their computational power. PoS mechanisms elect validators with a probability proportional to the size of their stake, which is often closely related to the amount of cryptocurrency that the node, or miner, owns. Nodes can lose the total value of their stake if they incur in fraudulent validations. In [70], a similar PoS system was proposed where the probability of selection of the nodes validating transactions was calculated based on both the pure stake and the state of the block being validated in the blockchain.

The 51% attack discussed in the PoW consensus mechanism is still a potential attack vector in a PoS system. However, while in the PoW case attackers need to obtain control over 51% of the network's computing power, which becomes increasingly easy as larger pools monopolizing the mining process are created, in a PoS system an attacker needs control over 51% of the cryptocurrency's total supply. This is, in theory, a more difficult problem than gathering enough computing power.

Owing to the significant reduction of the computational complexity of the consensus algorithms with PoS when compared to PoW, the energy consumption footprint is also reduced. PoS thus provides a more energy-friendly alternative which in turn enables nodes with lower computational capabilities to participate in the blockchain as equals to all others. Multiple authors, such as [71] or [72], have studied the sustainability of Bitcoin's growth and its energy footprint, which researchers estimate to be the equivalent, on a yearly basis, to non-renewable energy resources consumed by entire nations of the size of Czech Republic or Jordan. Nevertheless, this also means that because miners do not need to dedicate large amounts of computational resources to mining, it is easier to perform Sybil attacks spawning multiple identities within a single malicious node.

In general terms, a PoS system relies on a validator or a set of validators which are eligible after depositing part of their stake. In other words, as described by Buterin et al. [73], nodes earn the right to propose a block only after locking part of the coins they own on the blockchain. This is an extended definition over the pure PoS system firstly implemented in [74] as part of PPCoin, in which the total miner's stake is directly considered.

2.4 Practical Byzantine Fault Tolerance

The Practical Byzantine Fault Tolerance (PBFT) consensus algorithm was first proposed by Castro et al. in 1999 [75]. PBFT was the first algorithm with the ability to operate in large asynchronous networks such as the Internet, while providing over one order of magnitude in processing power improvement over previous methods, allowing for high-performance Byzantine state machine replication, and demonstrating thousands of requests per second. Byzantine fault tolerance can be described as the capacity of a system to maintain proper operation when multiple errors or unexpected behaviour occur within part of the system, but not its totality [76]. In a distributed network and considering the consensus problem, this is equivalent to the ability of the network to provide a robust consensus even in an scenario where a subset of nodes act maliciously, failing to forward valid data or sending invalid information.

In a PBFT system, nodes are distinguished between validating and not-validating peers [77]. The validating nodes run the consensus algorithm, in which they replicate a state machine and evaluate its result. A client makes a request that is transmitted over the peer-to-peer network through the non-validating nodes, which act as proxies between clients and validators. Non-validating nodes do not participate in the consensus mechanism, but are able to confirm the results. The PBFT algorithm is able to provide consensus across the network when at most one third of the nodes behave arbitrarily or maliciously. Because the validator nodes need to arrive to the same results regarding the client request, the state machine that is replicated must be deterministic.

In comparison with PoW and PoS systems, in PBFT individual transactions can be confirmed without the need to wait for a block including several transactions to be added to the blockchain. In terms of energy efficiency, PBFT requires less computational resources than a PoW consensus, but increases the probability of a Sybil attack, where a malicious node would create multiple instances pretending to be a large number of parties. In practice, PBFT is often combined with a PoW that must be solved in order to join the network and within certain time intervals to ensure that every node in the network is dedicating some minimum computational resources to the collective validation effort. An important benefit of PBFT over PoW and PoS is the low reward variance, as every node can be incentivized. This lowers the reward variance across miners. Nonetheless, the scalability of PBFT is an issue due to the large number of peer-to-peer communication exchanges required.

2.5   Third-Generation DLTs: Beyond Blockchain

Excluding Bitcoin and Ethereum, which represent the majority of the cryptocurrency market capitalization, one of the most successful blockchains within the IoT and industrial domains has been Hyperledger [78]. Launched in 2016 by the Linux Foundation, the Hyperledger project is divided in five main subprojects where blockchain frameworks for different aims are being developed: Fabric, Sawtooth, Indy, Burrow, and Iroha [79]. Among these, Hyperledger Fabric is the most popular, an enterprise-level and production-ready permissioned distributed ledger framework that has already been applied across various industrial fields [80]. The aims behind the project include open-source and cross-industry development of an scalable framework for smart contracts. Through the rest of this chapter, we utilize Hyperledger to refer to Hyperledger Fabric unless otherwise specified.

The consensus mechanism utilized in Hyperledger vary depending on the subproject. For instance, Hyperledger Fabric relies on RAFT [81], while Hyperledger Indy utilizes Plenum, based on Redundant Byzantine Fault Tolerance (RBFT) [82]. Different blockchains following the hyperledger design ideas rely on PBFT or adapted BFT approaches.

In recent years, blockchain technology has evolved towards a wider range of network definitions that do not keep the original structure of a blockchain in terms of how to store data within a distributed ledger. Among these, one of the most prominent distributed open ledgers under development is IOTA [83]. IOTA's backbone is a directed acyclic graph that defines the *tangle*. The tangle is the underlying network upon which IOTA is built. While Bitcoin was born mainly as a distributed cryptocurrency, Ethereum evolved from it into a platform for smart contracts, and Hyperledger is intended for industrial use, IOTA was specifically designed with the IoT in mind [84]. In IOTA, there are no miner or validator nodes confirming transactions, but instead each user must participate in the validation of two transactions before being able to issue a new one on its own. This approach, together with the tangle's structure, makes IOTA highly scalable and free to use. IOTA's development is open-source and led by the IOTA foundation.

IOTA's consensus protocol is defined within the Concordice system [85]. The main differentiating aspect of IOTA's tangle is the fact that multiple disconnected subnetworks can coexist for certain periods of time. This means, for instance, that while a blockchain cannot contain two conflicting transactions in committed blocks, the tangle might temporarily contain two such transactions. IOTA deals with this, however, in a similar manner as Bitcoin does: the fact that a transaction is included in the blockchain does not automatically mean it is valid, as two forks of the chain might exist until one is deemed longer and this valid. Therefore, in both cases there is only information about the *probability* of a transaction being valid, which increases as the blockchain, or the tangle, grow after that given transaction. In order to make a decision on two conflicting transactions in IOTA and reach a consensus across the network, Concordice proposes two consensus protocols: the fast probabilistic consensus (FPC) and the cellular consensus (CC). FPC, introduced in [86], is a leaderless probabilistic binary consensus protocol. FPC has low complexity from the communication point pf view, and is robust in a Byzantine infrastructure. As with PBFT, the basic idea behind FPC is voting. In any case, IOTA is still under development and is not production-ready. More detailed information on IOTA's consensus and CC is available in [87] and [88].

Other DLT solutions claiming to be third-generation blockchain are Nano [89], with its underlying block lattice, and Skycoin [90], aimed at powering the Web 3.0. While Nano and IOTA are recent technologies, Skycoin has been under development for several years and was born out of a series of external audits into Bitcoin, which revealed the different flaws in the PoW consensus protocol.

2.6 Smart Contracts

Second-generation blockchain systems, largely represented by the Ethereum blockchain, were defined as those introducing the ability of executing distributed programs within the blockchain itself, therefore extending their applicability beyond cryptocurrency transactions and into the validation of more general types of transactions. These programs that can be executed within a blockchain are called *smart contracts*, with one of the most notorious implementations being part of the Ethereum Virtual Machine and its corresponding stack [91], which provides a Turing complete language as part of its framework [92]. Ethereum also introduced a new programming language to be dedicated to the development and implementation of smart contracts: Solidity [93]. Smart contracts as defined with Solidity code can be seen as a set of instructions defining transitions between states of the program, with both the data representing the different states and the code defining the transitions being stored at specific addresses within the Ethereum blockchain.

In Ethereum, smart contracts are part of the Ethereum Virtual Machine (EVM) [94]. The EVM is based on the existence of contract accounts in the blockchain, which extend the functionality of external accounts, those controlled by a human or network node through a public-private key pair. Contract accounts operate in an automated way as a function of the code stored within the account. While external accounts are defined based on their key pair, with an address determined based on the public key being assigned to each node joining the network, contract accounts have addresses that are determined when the contract is created. In Ethereum, the address space is shared among both types of accounts. Contract accounts are created through transactions that have a null or empty recipient. Those transactions must contain code that outputs the smart contract's code, which is then generated when the transaction's code is executed within the EVM. In general terms, transactions including a payload and Ether (Ethereum's cryptocurrency) between external accounts in Ethereum are extended so that when a transaction's target account is a contract account containing a set of code instructions, these are executed given the payload in the transaction. A key concept in Ethereum is gas. Upon creation, transactions are assigned a definite quantity of gas. The gas is a measure of the processing power that will be dedicated to that transaction. In other words, the gas is the transaction fee. The gas is initially charged into the transaction, and its reserve gradually decreases as a function of a set of predefined rules when the EVM executes the different transaction instructions. The gas that is left is refunded to the transaction creator. The gas price, which is paid upfront, is decided by the creator node. Miners, which obtain the gas price as a reward, decide which transactions to mine based on the amount of gas included. Therefore, the gas price is decided based on the market and the desired priority for a specific transaction.

2.7 Sharding and Scalability

While second-generation blockchains introduced new functionality and improvements over Bitcoin-based blockchains at different levels, one of the main challenges in blockchain systems remained: scalability [95]. This is mostly due to the large and increasing amount of computational resources required for mining. From the communication point of view, Bitcoin and other similar blockchains only require one broadcast per block, and therefore the main bottleneck comes from computation (which cannot be directly decreased while maintaining security). In PBFT-based systems, multicast messages are required for validation, and thus the main scalability problem is the communication cost [22] (which cannot be directly reduced either without compromising security and robustness of the consensus mechanism). Multiple research efforts have been directed towards the realization of more scalable systems, with new blockchains based on PoS and PBFT showing promising results. Elastico, introduced in [25], was one of the first scalable blockchains that introduced the concept of sharding: to divide the network in subnetworks, or *shards*, that would validate transactions in parallel. Elastico was the first blockchain system to provide a full implementation of a sharding scheme for a permisionless blockchain. A different early sharding proposal was presented in [96], where Merklix trees are utilized to merge the state of the different shards into the global blockchain state [97, 98].

Another blockchain system aimed at scalability that has had an important impact on subsequent research is OmniLedger [26]. Omniledger scales linearly with the number of nodes in the blockchain, and reports transaction times able to match credit card standards if the size of the network arrives to a certain threshold. The key difference with Elastico in terms of scalability is that in Elastico the network performance scales with the computational power in a linear fashion, while in Omniledger it does so with the number of validator nodes. In Hyperledger, the scalability of the network has seen significant improvements since the release of Fabric 1.1.0 [99]. Moreover, the number of channels can be scaled with little to no impact on performance according to the same report.

Perhaps the biggest effort that is currently being put into the development of a truly decentralized, permissionless and scalable yet secure blockchain is the design and development of Ethereum 2.0 [100], where huge amounts of computing resources will be no longer required for mining [101]. The Ethereum Foundation and other developers behind Ethereum 2.0 have embraced Proof of Stake as the main consensus mechanism, while still utilizing PoW to secure the network, and the concept of sharding towards scalability. The consensus is based on the Casper protocol [102], which incentives for mining have been described in [73]. The impact that shards have on transaction scalability is relatively clear, with a much larger throughput being possible in terms of transactions validated per second. Nonetheless, it is not straightforward to extend the implementation of smart contracts with sharding. As smart contracts have associated a series of data states corresponding to their code, each state change can be though of as a transaction. Contracts can be executed within a single shard, or a cross-shard synchronization mechanism must exist to allow for data to flow between shards. In [26], the authors introduced introduced Atomix, a client-driven lock/unlock protocol, to ensure that a single transaction can be committed across multiple shards, while enabling the possibility of unlocking rejected transaction proofs in specific shards. The original Atomix state machine can be extended to accommodate the execution of smart contracts across shards.

3 Blockchain Technology for Mobile Edge Computing

This section reviews and classifies the existing research in the integration of blockchain and MEC from an architectural point of view. We classify the different approaches on three main categories, illustrated in Fig. 2. The first category

UC1: Blockchain for Edge Resource Orchestration

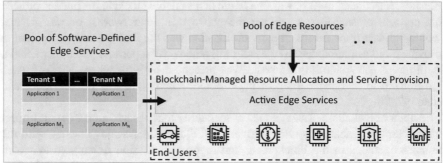

UC2: Blockchain Marketplace at the Edge

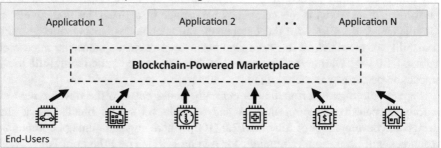

UC3: Blockchain-Enhanced Edge Services (Privacy, Security, Identity Management)

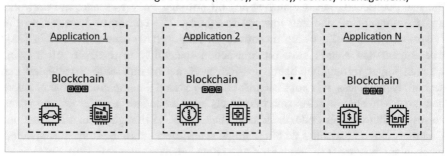

Fig. 2 Main use cases for blockchain within edge computing systems. (UC1) Blockchain-powered resource allocation and service provision; (UC2) Blockchain-powered marketplace for interfacing users and services; (UC3) Blockchain-enhanced individual edge services relying on blockchain technology for security, privacy, data management and audits or identity management, among others

encompasses works providing a system-level integration where a blockchain is one of the key pieces at the heart of the edge infrastructure, managing services and resources. The second category includes approaches that utilize blockchain as a middleware between the edge infrastructure (hardware and software) and the third-party services being provided through MEC. Finally, the last category comprises those works where the blockchain is part of individual applications, for aspects such as security or identity management.

In general terms, Ethereum is the most widely applied blockchain platform in the IoT, owing to the maturity of its smart contracts framework enabling complex interactions between data producers and consumers [103, 104]. In the same area, Hyperledger has potential to disrupt the IoT with more scalable solutions and the ability to run distributed programs as chaincode [105]. In all these cases, nonetheless, the blockchain runs in embedded edge gateways providing stable connectivity, and where enough power and computational resources is available. With the potential to reach embedded devices at the sensor layer, and being developed specifically for the IoT, IOTA is set to play an increasingly important role. Owing to its low inherent computational requirements and being highly scalable, IOTA is the ideal candidate for edge computing systems and hardware.

3.1 MEC Resource and Service Orchestration with Blockchain

One of the most critical points at the edge is resource orchestration [29]. In order to enable a wide variety of use cases, multi-tenant applications, and ad-hoc deployment of different modules, MEC infrastructure needs to be able to manage its resources in real time, while also orchestrating how the network is being utilized. This includes processes from allocating hardware resources for the different virtualized applications to managing the spectrum or the bandwidth that might be in use for computational offloading by different service providers.

Blockchain technology can provide multiple advantages to orchestration at the edge: enhanced security and identity management, together with distributed consensus algorithms to implement the resource allocation decision processes. In this area, EdgeChain was introduced by Zhu et al. as a middleware platform to deploy third-party applications across the MEC layer [31]. In [33], the authors introduce a blockchain framework that relies on smart contracts for managing network bandwidth and resource allocation in a distributed and collaborative computational offloading framework. In [36], a similar idea is extended towards managing network infrastructure and the available computational resources focused at enhancing autonomy of self-driving cars and other autonomous robots forming distributed robotic systems. In this paper, the blockchain MEC slice was the key slice managing the deployment of applications across other MEC slices supporting different verticals within the automotive sector. Further adoption of blockchain for computational offloading will require, however, higher-bandwidth and lower-latency blockchain frameworks enabling real-time sensor data to be streamed for applications such as autonomous mobile robots [30, 106].

Resource orchestration processes have underlying optimization algorithms that can be implemented either in a more traditional deterministic manner, or relying on machine learning models. Several authors have proposed the utilization of deep reinforcement learning for computational offloading in blockchain-powered edge computing. In [107], the authors demonstrate an approach that is able to improve long-term performance in a computational offloading scheme, with an adaptive genetic algorithm to improve the exploration processes while learning. In [43], the authors describe different situations in which blockchain can support resource management at the edge with deep reinforcement learning: spectrum sharing, vehicle-to-vehicle energy trading, computational offloading, or device-to-device content caching.

3.2 Blockchain for a MEC Services Marketplace

DLT can also provide a platform for building a marketplace between end-users and third-party edge application through either a transparent, secure and auditable monetization framework or as a middleware for sharing data securely between producers and consumers. In the former direction, Xiong et al. deployed a blockchain at the edge to enable resource-constrained devices producing data to sell it to third-party applications [32]. The pricing scheme introduced in the paper models the interactions within the IoT as market activities and the blockchain represented the framework for regulation of such activities. Distributed marketplaces based on blockchain for MEC services often utilize Ethereum as a base and the InterPlanetary File System (IPFS) for data storage. Examples are available in [108] or [109]. A study describing the different challenges and opportunities is available in [110].

3.3 Blockchain-Powered MEC Services

In [49], the authors describe how blockchain can play a key enabled role in interconnected vehicles from the security point of view. In particular, blockchain is exploited for data management, but also for energy management in electric vehicles, with the authors proposing blockchain inspired data coins and energy coins. An edge computing security scheme is proposed including these two interaction aspects. An approach more related to the nature of blockchain as a cryptocurrency framework was proposed by Liu et al. in [41], where the authors present an offloading framework not for data but for the blockchain itself and related mining operations. In general, blockchain can support edge services by providing enhanced privacy and security [40], decentralized data management [18], or identity management [111].

4 Performance and Scalability of DLTs at the Edge

In this section we describe the benefits and drawbacks of the different consensus protocols and DLT solutions for each of the three main use cases defined in

Table 1 Comparison of consensus protocols in terms of their applicability within resource-constrained devices in the IoT

	PoW	PoS/DPoS	PBFT	Concordice
Computationally-constrained devices	✗	✓	✗	✓
Communication-constrained devices	–	✗	✗	✓
Intermittent connectivity	✗	✗	✗	✓
Independent subnetworks	✗	✗[a]	✓[b]	✓[c]
Production-ready platform	✓	✓	✓	✗

[a] Recent proposals implementing sharding might be considered subnetworks, however here we refer to the ability of specifically creating a subnetwork from a given set of nodes
[b] Channels in Hyperledger enable data separation but need to remain connected to the main net
[c] The tangle in IOTA enables sets of nodes to be disconnected for certain periods of time and rejoin the network later on

the previous section and illustrated in Fig. 2, as well as for edge computing in the industrial internet of things. A basic classification of some of the protocols introduced in the previous section from the point of view of the capabilities of embedded IoT systems is given in Table 1.

4.1 Blockchain Technology in Resource-Constrained Devices

Consensus protocols in the different DLTs are the key performance indicators, and they are directly related to the minimum capabilities that nodes in the network must meet. In PoW-based blockchains, including Bitcoin and Ethereum, resource-constrained devices in the IoT that are potentially battery powered do not have the ability to participate as full nodes in the network. In Ethereum, nonetheless, the blockchain has adapted to some extent towards embedded IoT devices. For instance, the Zerynth Ethereum library provides basic capability to embedded microcontrollers running MicroPython [112]. It enables sensor nodes to create signed transactions and execute contract calls.

Hyperledger Fabric and IOTA, designed with scalability in mind, do not have such strong computational requirements. The consensus protocols at the hearth of Hyperledger, however, have high communication complexity and therefore require nodes to be able to communicate frequently and with low-latency. Hyperledger can therefore run in embedded IoT edge gateways with wired internet connection but its extendability to wireless and potentially battery-powered sensor nodes is limited. In this area, IOTA has a comparative advantage. In particular, STMicroelectronics has collaborated with the IOTA foundation in the development of X-CUBE-IOTA [113], a complete middleware that enables IoT sensor nodes based on STM32 microcontrollers to build IOTA applications and access the IOTA distributed ledger directly.

In terms of communication-constrained devices, low-power wide area networks (LPWANs) have emerged in recent years as a solution for extending the range of applications, with LoRa and LoRaWAN being the most prominent radio and network technologies [7, 114]. Edge computing is a natural paradigm to be integrated with LPWAN networks owing to the low-bandwidth available and thus the need to preprocess large amounts of raw data [115–117]. However, the integration of blockchain into LPWAN networks is not direct [118]. Current efforts deploy the blockchain either at the LPWAN gateways, which often have wired internet connection, or at the back-end servers [119, 120]. More interesting use cases will be possible when the blockchain nodes can be interconnected via low-bandwidth and high-latency LPWAN links, which might be soon possible with IOTA and STM.

4.2 Application Scenarios

From the point of view of edge computing as a system encompassing multiple independent applications, the simplest use case is such in which blockchains are managed by each application independently. This allows for the same orchestration algorithms to remain in place, as well as co-existence of blockchain-based and other applications running at the edge. Depending on the nature of each of the applications, all of the DLT solutions presented in this chapter might be applied. For general IoT systems where data is gathered from sensor nodes and transactions between either the user or the sensors and the application back-end (which may or may not be deployed entirely at the edge) are relatively simple, then IOTA stands out by providing free transactions. This can be a key differentiating point in applications where data is routinely gathered and does not have specific value. Because IOTA's consensus is built in a way that all nodes need to take the validator role before being able to commit transactions, nodes do no need an additional incentive to validate and therefore there is no need for a transaction fee as with other blockchain platforms. If more complex transactions are required, with either real-time interaction between users or a user and sensor data being processed, then smart contracts might be needed. Ethereum is by far the most extended and used blockchain platform for smart contracts, and therefore it would be natural to rely on it. This will be an even better solution when Ethereum 2.0 is available. Nonetheless, relying on Ethereum or similar solutions involves an extra transaction cost, due to the need for mining new cryptocurrency to compensate nodes participating in the validation process. Alternatively, private Ethereum networks can be deployed and infrastructure managed by the application developers. This is specially important in PoW-based systems, but also in PoS systems as otherwise nodes would have no incentives on putting their stakes at risk.

When blockchain is utilized to power a marketplace of services at the edge, the cryptocurrency that blockchains build upon might play a more important role with the introduction of monetization. In this sense, monetization does not necessarily refer only to paying for services, but can also encompass the edge resources that services rely on [29]. Similar to the previous case, the choice of DLT framework has a significant dependence on the type of data management and processing that needs to be done. For simple applications in which services and end-users are predefined and communicate independently, then IOTA can provide a fast and scalable framework, while Hyperledger could be an alternative if there is enough infrastructure set to sustain the blockchain and validate transactions. These applications can cover a wide variety of scenarios: paying a highway toll, exchange of information for coordination between autonomous cars, track-and-trace in the logistics sector, or providing digital identity to citizens in a smart city. In all these cases, a common denominator is that the transfers of value, or information, are small and frequent in time, and therefore there is not enough incentive to utilize other blockchain platforms such as Ethereum where transactions involve a fee. Hyperledger, nonetheless, is only a viable option if either public or private infrastructure supports its use without an impact on the end-user. For more complex applications, both Hyperledger and Ethereum provide extensive support for smart contracts and execution of distributed applications.

The last of the use cases presented in the previous section, and involving the most complex system-level integration of DLT technology at the edge layer is resource allocation and service provision. In this case, different optimization algorithms in which the resource orchestrator relies need to be implemented on top of the blockchain for transparent management of resources. The processes involved in dynamic resource allocation and service provision are complex and therefore require blockchains able of running smart contracts. Ethereum provides a suitable platform from the functionality point of view, but lacks the ability to scale and the low control over latency would significantly affect the real-time allocation of resources. Moreover, the computational power needed to validate transactions would reduce the availability of edge resources. Until Ethereum 2.0 or a more scalable solution is available, Hyperledger has multiple competitive advantages in this area.

A different application scenario that has not been directly covered in the previous section is the industrial IoT. Industrial scenarios often differentiate in that they operate on private networks. Moreover, safety-critical applications require more control over the network parameters as well as over the data management itself. In these directions, Hyperledger Fabric stands out, with design decisions targeting industrial use cases since its inception. Not only does a permissioned Hyperledger blockchain provide a secure framework for management of identities and network control, but it is the ability to separate data across channels that can provide wider adoption in privacy-critical and safety-critical use cases.

5 Conclusion and Future Work

We have reviewed the most important consensus protocols in traditional blockchains and novel distributed ledger technologies, together with the different applications and use cases resulting of the integration of blockchain and edge computing. In particular, we have described how the underlying consensus protocols affect the applicability of the different DLT systems for edge computing, with an emphasis on the current research trends in terms of scalability and performance. We have outlined the main benefits and drawbacks of Ethereum, Hyperledger and IOTA in four main use cases: (1) orchestration of edge resources and services, (2) implementation of a marketplace of edge services, (3) enhancing security, privacy or identity management of individual edge services, and (4) providing a framework for data management in the industrial Internet of Things.

Acknowledgments This work was supported by the Academy of Finland's AutoSOS project with grant number 328755.

References

1. Li Da Xu, Wu He, and Shancang Li. Internet of things in industries: A survey. *IEEE Transactions on industrial informatics*, 10(4):2233–2243, 2014.
2. Ola Salman, Imad Elhajj, Ali Chehab, and Ayman Kayssi. Iot survey: An sdn and fog computing perspective. *Computer Networks*, 143:221–246, 2018.
3. Celimuge Wu, Zhi Liu, Di Zhang, Tsutomu Yoshinaga, and Yusheng Ji. Spatial intelligence toward trustworthy vehicular iot. *IEEE Communications Magazine*, 56(10):22–27, 2018.
4. Jorge Peña Queralta, Tuan Nguyen Gia, Hannu Tenhunen, and Tomi Westerlund. Collaborative mapping with ioe-based heterogeneous vehicles for enhanced situational awareness. In *2019 IEEE Sensors Applications Symposium (SAS)*, pages 1–6. IEEE, 2019.
5. Charalampos Doukas and Ilias Maglogiannis. Bringing iot and cloud computing towards pervasive healthcare. In *2012 Sixth International Conference on Innovative Mobile and Internet Services in Ubiquitous Computing*, pages 922–926. IEEE, 2012.
6. Ammar Awad Mutlag, Mohd Khanapi Abd Ghani, Net al Arunkumar, Mazin Abed Mohammed, and Othman Mohd. Enabling technologies for fog computing in healthcare iot systems. *Future Generation Computer Systems*, 90:62–78, 2019.
7. Jorge Peña Queralta, Tuan Nguyen Gia, Hannu Tenhunen, and Tomi Westerlund. Edge-AI in LoRa based healthcare monitoring: A case study on fall detection system with LSTM Recurrent Neural Networks. In *2019 42nd International Conference on Telecommunications, Signal Processing (TSP)*, 2019.
8. Sam Edwards and Ioannis Profetis. Hajime: Analysis of a decentralized internet worm for iot devices. *Rapidity Networks*, 16, 2016.
9. Yun Chao Hu, Milan Patel, Dario Sabella, Nurit Sprecher, and Valerie Young. Mobile edge computing—a key technology towards 5g. *ETSI white paper*, 11(11):1–16, 2015.
10. Weisong Shi, Jie Cao, Quan Zhang, Youhuizi Li, and Lanyu Xu. Edge computing: Vision and challenges. *IEEE internet of things journal*, 3(5):637–646, 2016.
11. L. Qingqing, F. Yuhong, J. Peña Queralta, T. N. Gia, Z. Zou, H. Tenhunen, T. Westerlund. Edge Computing for Mobile Robots: Multi-Robot Feature-Based Lidar Odometry with FPGAs. In *12th ICMU*. IEEE, 2019.
12. Melanie Swan. *Blockchain: Blueprint for a new economy*. " O'Reilly Media, Inc.", 2015.
13. Sarah Underwood. Blockchain beyond bitcoin, 2016.
14. Yang Lu. Industry 4.0: A survey on technologies, applications and open research issues. *Journal of Industrial Information Integration*, 6:1–10, 2017.
15. Yongfeng Qian, Yingying Jiang, Jing Chen, Yu Zhang, Jeungeun Song, Ming Zhou, and Matevž Pustišek. Towards decentralized iot security enhancement: A blockchain approach. *Computers & Electrical Engineering*, 72:266–273, 2018.

16. Juah C Song, Mevlut A Demir, John J Prevost, and Paul Rad. Blockchain design for trusted decentralized iot networks. In *2018 13th Annual Conference on System of Systems Engineering (SoSE)*, pages 169–174. IEEE, 2018.
17. Mohamed Tahar Hammi, Badis Hammi, Patrick Bellot, and Ahmed Serhrouchni. Bubbles of trust: A decentralized blockchain-based authentication system for iot. *Computers & Security*, 78:126–142, 2018.
18. Gbadebo Ayoade, Vishal Karande, Latifur Khan, and Kevin Hamlen. Decentralized iot data management using blockchain and trusted execution environment. In *2018 IEEE International Conference on Information Reuse and Integration (IRI)*, pages 15–22. IEEE, 2018.
19. Jollen Chen. Devify: Decentralized internet of things software framework for a peer-to-peer and interoperable iot device. *ACM SIGBED Review*, 15(2):31–36, 2018.
20. Penn H Su, Chi-Sheng Shih, Jane Yung-Jen Hsu, Kwei-Jay Lin, and Yu-Chung Wang. Decentralized fault tolerance mechanism for intelligent iot/m2m middleware. In *2014 IEEE World Forum on Internet of Things (WF-IoT)*, pages 45–50. IEEE, 2014.
21. Zibin Zheng, Shaoan Xie, Hongning Dai, Xiangping Chen, and Huaimin Wang. An overview of blockchain technology: Architecture, consensus, and future trends. In *2017 IEEE international congress on big data (BigData congress)*, pages 557–564. IEEE, 2017.
22. Marko Vukolić. The quest for scalable blockchain fabric: Proof-of-work vs. bft replication. In *International workshop on open problems in network security*. Springer, 2015.
23. Ghassan Karame. On the security and scalability of bitcoin's blockchain. In *Proceedings of the 2016 ACM SIGSAC conference on computer and communications security*, pages 1861–1862, 2016.
24. Mattias Scherer. Performance and scalability of blockchain networks and smart contracts, 2017.
25. Loi Luu, Viswesh Narayanan, Chaodong Zheng, Kunal Baweja, Seth Gilbert, and Prateek Saxena. A secure sharding protocol for open blockchains. In *Proceedings of the 2016 ACM SIGSAC Conference on Computer and Communications Security*, pages 17–30, 2016.
26. Eleftherios Kokoris-Kogias, Philipp Jovanovic, Linus Gasser, Nicolas Gailly, Ewa Syta, and Bryan Ford. Omniledger: A secure, scale-out, decentralized ledger via sharding. In *2018 IEEE Symposium on Security and Privacy (SP)*, pages 583–598. IEEE, 2018.
27. Sami Kekki, Walter Featherstone, Yonggang Fang, Pekka Kuure, Alice Li, Anurag Ranjan, Debashish Purkayastha, Feng Jiangping, Danny Frydman, Gianluca Verin, et al. Mec in 5g networks. *ETSI white paper*, 28:1–28, 2018.
28. Sonia Shahzadi, Muddesar Iqbal, Tasos Dagiuklas, and Zia Ul Qayyum. Multi-access edge computing: open issues, challenges and future perspectives. *Journal of Cloud Computing*, 6(1):30, 2017.
29. Tarik Taleb, Konstantinos Samdanis, Badr Mada, Hannu Flinck, Sunny Dutta, and Dario Sabella. On multi-access edge computing: A survey of the emerging 5g network edge cloud architecture and orchestration. *IEEE Communications Surveys & Tutorials*, 19(3), 2017.
30. L. Qingqing, J. Peña Queralta, T. N. Gia, Z. Zou, H. Tenhunen, T. Westerlund. Visual Odometry Offloading in Internet of Vehicles with Compression at the Edge of the Network. In *12th International Conference on Mobile Computing and Ubiquitous Networking*, 2019.
31. He Zhu, Changcheng Huang, and Jiayu Zhou. Edgechain: Blockchain-based multi-vendor mobile edge application placement. In *2018 4th IEEE Conference on Network Softwarization and Workshops (NetSoft)*, pages 222–226. IEEE, 2018.
32. Zehui Xiong, Yang Zhang, Dusit Niyato, Ping Wang, and Zhu Han. When mobile blockchain meets edge computing. *IEEE Communications Magazine*, 56(8):33–39, 2018.
33. Jorge Peña Queralta and Tomi Westerlund. Blockchain-powered collaboration in heterogeneous swarms of robots. *Frontiers in Robotics and AI (to appear)*, 2020. Presented at the Symposium on Blockchain for Robotic and AI Systems, MIT Media Lab.
34. MD Abdur Rahman, M Shamim Hossain, George Loukas, Elham Hassanain, Syed Sadiqur Rahman, Mohammed F Alhamid, and Mohsen Guizani. Blockchain-based mobile edge computing framework for secure therapy applications. *IEEE Access*, 6:72469–72478, 2018.

35. 3GPP. Study on architecture for next-generation system rel. 14. *Technical Report*, 2016.
36. Jorge Peña Queralta, Li Qingqing, Zhuo Zou, and Tomi Westerlund. Enhancing autonomy with blockchain and multi-access edge computing in distributed robotic systems. In *The Fifth International Conference on Fog and Mobile Edge Computing (FMEC)*. IEEE, 2020.
37. N. Alliance. Description of network slicing concept. *NGMN 5G P*, 1:1, 2016.
38. Fabio Giust, Vincenzo Sciancalepore, Dario Sabella, Miltiades C Filippou, Simone Mangiante, Walter Featherstone, and Daniele Munaretto. Multi-access edge computing: The driver behind the wheel of 5g-connected cars. *IEEE Communications Standards Magazine*, 2(3):66–73, 2018.
39. Roberto Casado-Vara, Fernando de la Prieta, Javier Prieto, and Juan M Corchado. Blockchain framework for iot data quality via edge computing. In *Proceedings of the 1st Workshop on Blockchain-enabled Networked Sensor Systems*, pages 19–24, 2018.
40. A. Nawaz, J. Peña Queralta, T. N. Gia, H. Kan, T. Westerlund. Edge AI and Blockchain for Privacy-Critical and Data-Sensitive Applications. In *The 12th International Conference on Mobile Computing and Ubiquitous Networking (ICMU)*, 2019.
41. Mengting Liu, F Richard Yu, Yinglei Teng, Victor CM Leung, and Mei Song. Joint computation offloading and content caching for wireless blockchain networks. In *IEEE INFOCOM 2018-IEEE Conference on Computer Communications Workshops (INFOCOM WKSHPS)*, pages 517–522. IEEE, 2018.
42. Jorge Peña Queralta, Li Qingqing, Tuan Nguyen Gia, Hong-Linh Truong, and Tomi Westerlund. End-to-end design for self-reconfigurable heterogeneous robotic swarms. In *The 16th International Conference on Distributed Computing in Sensor Systems*. IEEE, 2020.
43. Yueyue Dai, Du Xu, Sabita Maharjan, Zhuang Chen, Qian He, and Yan Zhang. Blockchain and deep reinforcement learning empowered intelligent 5g beyond. *IEEE Network*, 33, 2019.
44. Nguyen Cong Luong, Zehui Xiong, Ping Wang, and Dusit Niyato. Optimal auction for edge computing resource management in mobile blockchain networks: A deep learning approach. In *2018 IEEE International Conference on Communications (ICC)*, pages 1–6. IEEE, 2018.
45. Mayra Samaniego and Ralph Deters. Hosting virtual iot resources on edge-hosts with blockchain. In *2016 IEEE International Conference on Computer and Information Technology (CIT)*, pages 116–119. IEEE, 2016.
46. Mayra Samaniego and Ralph Deters. Using blockchain to push software-defined iot components onto edge hosts. In *Proceedings of the International Conference on Big Data and Advanced Wireless Technologies*, pages 1–9, 2016.
47. Mayra Samaniego and Ralph Deters. Virtual resources & blockchain for configuration management in iot. *Journal of Ubiquitous Systems & Pervasive Networks*, 9(2):1–13, 2017.
48. The European Union Agency for Cybersecurity. Threat assessment for the fifth generation of mobile telecommunications networks (5g). *ENISA*, 2019.
49. Hong Liu, Yan Zhang, and Tao Yang. Blockchain-enabled security in electric vehicles cloud and edge computing. *IEEE Network*, 32(3):78–83, 2018.
50. Jiawen Kang, Rong Yu, Xumin Huang, Maoqiang Wu, Sabita Maharjan, Shengli Xie, and Yan Zhang. Blockchain for secure and efficient data sharing in vehicular edge computing and networks. *IEEE Internet of Things Journal*, 6(3):4660–4670, 2018.
51. T. N. Gia, A. Nawaz, J. Peña Queralta, T. Westerlund. Artificial Intelligence at the Edge in the Blockchain of Things. In *8th EAI International Conference on Wireless Mobile Communication and Healthcare*, 2019.
52. Eduardo Castelló Ferrer, Ognjen Rudovic, Thomas Hardjono, and Alex Pentland. Robochain: A secure data-sharing framework for human-robot interaction. *arXiv preprint arXiv:1802.04480*, 2018.
53. Ruizhe Yang, F Richard Yu, Pengbo Si, Zhaoxin Yang, and Yanhua Zhang. Integrated blockchain and edge computing systems: A survey, some research issues and challenges. *IEEE Communications Surveys & Tutorials*, 21(2):1508–1532, 2019.
54. Pietro Danzi, Anders E Kalør, Čedomir Stefanović, and Petar Popovski. Delay and communication tradeoffs for blockchain systems with lightweight iot clients. *IEEE Internet of Things Journal*, 6(2):2354–2365, 2019.

55. Seyednima Khezr, Md Moniruzzaman, Abdulsalam Yassine, and Rachid Benlamri. Blockchain technology in healthcare: A comprehensive review and directions for future research. *Applied Sciences*, 9(9):1736, 2019.
56. Dinh C Nguyen, Pubudu N Pathirana, Ming Ding, and Aruna Seneviratne. Blockchain for 5g and beyond networks: A state of the art survey. *Journal of Network and Computer Applications*, page 102693, 2020.
57. Weichao Gao, William G Hatcher, and Wei Yu. A survey of blockchain: techniques, applications, and challenges. In *2018 27th International Conference on Computer Communication and Networks (ICCCN)*, pages 1–11. IEEE, 2018.
58. Archana Prashanth Joshi, Meng Han, and Yan Wang. A survey on security and privacy issues of blockchain technology. *Mathematical Foundations of Computing*, 1(2):121–147, 2018.
59. Wazir Zada Khan, Ejaz Ahmed, Saqib Hakak, Ibrar Yaqoob, and Arif Ahmed. Edge computing: A survey. *Future Generation Computer Systems*, 97:219–235, 2019.
60. Jose Moura and David Hutchison. Fog computing systems: State of the art, research issues and future trends. *arXiv preprint arXiv:1908.05077 [v2]*, pages 1–32, 2020.
61. Xiaoqi Li, Peng Jiang, Ting Chen, Xiapu Luo, and Qiaoyan Wen. A survey on the security of blockchain systems. *Future Generation Computer Systems*, 2017.
62. Satoshi Nakamoto et al. *Bitcoin: A peer-to-peer electronic cash system*. 2008.
63. Cynthia Dwork and Moni Naor. Pricing via processing or combatting junk mail. In *Annual International Cryptology Conference*, pages 139–147. Springer, 1992.
64. Giang-Truong Nguyen and Kyungbaek Kim. A survey about consensus algorithms used in blockchain. *Journal of Information processing systems*, 14(1), 2018.
65. Sunny King. Primecoin: Cryptocurrency with prime number proof-of-work. 1:6, 2013.
66. Rasmus Pagh and Flemming Friche Rodler. Cuckoo hashing. *Journal of Algorithms*, 51(2):122–144, 2004.
67. Simon Barber, Xavier Boyen, Elaine Shi, and Ersin Uzun. Bitter to better—how to make bitcoin a better currency. In *Financial Cryptography and Data Security*. Springer, 2012.
68. Serguei Popov. A probabilistic analysis of the nxt forging algorithm. *Ledger*, 1:69–83, 2016.
69. Nxt Wiki. *Whitepaper: Nxt*. Nxtwiki. org [online] https://nxtwiki.org, 2018.
70. Iddo Bentov, Ariel Gabizon, and Alex Mizrahi. Cryptocurrencies without proof of work. In *International Conference on Financial Cryptography and Data Security*. Springer, 2016.
71. Karl J O'Dwyer and David Malone. *Bitcoin mining and its energy footprint*. IET, 2014.
72. Alex De Vries. Bitcoin's growing energy problem. *Joule*, 2(5):801–805, 2018.
73. Vitalik Buterin, Daniel Reijsbergen, Stefanos Leonardos, and Georgios Piliouras. Incentives in ethereum's hybrid casper protocol. *arXiv preprint arXiv:1903.04205*, 2019.
74. Sunny King and Scott Nadal. Ppcoin: Peer-to-peer crypto-currency with proof-of-stake. *self-published paper, August*, 19, 2012.
75. Miguel Castro, Barbara Liskov, et al. Practical byzantine fault tolerance. In *OSDI*, volume 99, pages 173–186, 1999.
76. RM Keichafer, Chris J. Walter, Alan M. Finn, and Philip M. Thambidurai. The maft architecture for distributed fault tolerance. *IEEE Transactions on Computers*, 37(4), 1988.
77. Joao Sousa, Alysson Bessani, and Marko Vukolic. A byzantine fault-tolerant ordering service for the hyperledger fabric blockchain platform. In *48th DSN*, pages 51–58. IEEE, 2018.
78. C. Cachin. Architecture of the hyperledger blockchain fabric. In *Workshop on distributed cryptocurrencies and consensus ledgers*, volume 310, page 4, 2016.
79. Chinmay Saraf and Siddharth Sabadra. Blockchain platforms: A compendium. In *2018 IEEE International Conference on Innovative Research and Development (ICIRD)*, pages 1–6. IEEE, 2018.
80. Elli Androulaki, Artem Barger, Vita Bortnikov, Christian Cachin, Konstantinos Christidis, Angelo De Caro, David Enyeart, Christopher Ferris, Gennady Laventman, Yacov Manevich, et al. Hyperledger fabric: a distributed operating system for permissioned blockchains. In *Proceedings of the Thirteenth EuroSys Conference*, pages 1–15, 2018.
81. Diego Ongaro and John Ousterhout. In search of an understandable consensus algorithm. In *2014 {USENIX} Annual Technical Conference ({USENIX}{ATC} 14)*, pages 305–319, 2014.

82. Pierre-Louis Aublin, Sonia Ben Mokhtar, and Vivien Quéma. Rbft: Redundant byzantine fault tolerance. In *2013 IEEE 33rd International Conference on Distributed Computing Systems*, pages 297–306. IEEE, 2013.
83. S Popov. The tangle, iota whitepaper. Technical report, IOTA, Tech. Rep.[Online]. Available: https://iota.org/IOTA_Whitepaper.pdf, 2018.
84. M Divya and Nagaveni B Biradar. Iota-next generation block chain. *International Journal Of Engineering And Computer Science*, 7(04):23823–23826, 2018.
85. Serguei Popov, Hans Moog, Darcy Camargo, Angelo Capossele, Vassil Dimitrov, Alon Gal, Andrew Greve, Bartosz Kusmierz, Sebastian Mueller, Andreas Penzkofer, et al. The coordicide, 2020.
86. Serguei Popov and William J Buchanan. Fpc-bi: Fast probabilistic consensus within byzantine infrastructures. *arXiv preprint arXiv:1905.10895*, 2019.
87. Daniel Ramos and Gabriel Zanko. Review of iota foundation as a moving force for massive blockchain adoption in different industry sectors.
88. KENRIC NELSON and ANDRÉ VILELA. Majority vote dynamics for iota transaction consensus. 2020.
89. Colin LeMahieu. Nano: A feeless distributed cryptocurrency network. *Nano [Online resource]. URL: https://nano.org/en/whitepaper (date of access: 24.03. 2018)*, 2018.
90. Skycoin.com. Skycoin whitepaper v1.2. Technical report, [Online]. Available: https://downloads.skycoin.com/whitepapers/Skycoin-Whitepaper-v1.2.pdf, 2020.
91. Gavin Wood et al. Ethereum: A secure decentralised generalised transaction ledger. *Ethereum project yellow paper*, 151(2014):1–32, 2014.
92. Everett Hildenbrandt, Manasvi Saxena, Nishant Rodrigues, Xiaoran Zhu, Philip Daian, Dwight Guth, Brandon Moore, Daejun Park, Yi Zhang, Andrei Stefanescu, et al. Kevm: A complete formal semantics of the ethereum virtual machine. In *2018 IEEE 31st Computer Security Foundations Symposium (CSF)*, pages 204–217. IEEE, 2018.
93. Ethereum Revision 7709ece9. *Solidity Documentation*. Solidity Read The Docs [online] https://solidity.readthedocs.io/en/v0.5.12/., 2016–2019.
94. Chris Dannen. *Introducing Ethereum and Solidity*. Springer, 2017.
95. Dejan Vujičić, Dijana Jagodić, and Siniša Randić. Blockchain technology, bitcoin, and ethereum: A brief overview. In *17th INFOTEH-JAHORINA*, pages 1–6. IEEE, 2018.
96. Deadalnix's den. *Using Merklix tree to shard block validation*. [online] https://deadalnix.me/2016/11/06/, 2016.
97. Deadalnix's den. *Introducing Merklix tree as an unordered Merkle tree on steroid*. Accessed October 2019 [online] https://www.deadalnix.me/2016/09/24/introducing-merklix-tree-as-an-unordered-merkle-tree-on-steroid/, 2016.
98. Bo Qin, Jikun Huang, Qin Wang, Xizhao Luo, Bin Liang, and Wenchang Shi. Cecoin: A decentralized pki mitigating mitm attacks. *Future Generation Computer Systems*, 2017.
99. C. Ferris. "does hyperledger fabric perform at scale? *Blockchain Pulse: IBM Blockchain Blog*, 2, 2019.
100. Vitalik Buterin et al. A next-generation smart contract and decentralized application platform. *white paper*, 3:37, 2014.
101. Serenity Ethereum Foundation et al. *Ethereum 2.0 Specifications*. [online] https://github.com/ethereum/eth2.0-specs, 2018.
102. Vitalik Buterin and Virgil Griffith. Casper the friendly finality gadget. *arXiv preprint arXiv:1710.09437*, 2017.
103. Seyoung Huh, Sangrae Cho, and Soohyung Kim. Managing iot devices using blockchain platform. In *19th ICACT*, pages 464–467. IEEE, 2017.
104. Matevž Pustišek and Andrej Kos. Approaches to front-end iot application development for the ethereum blockchain. *Procedia Computer Science*, 129:410–419, 2018.
105. Martin Valenta and Philipp Sandner. Comparison of ethereum, hyperledger fabric and corda. *no. June*, pages 1–8, 2017.

106. Li Qingqing, Jorge Peña Queralta, Tuan Nguyen Gia, and Tomi Westerlund. Offloading Monocular Visual Odometry with Edge Computing: Optimizing Image Compression Ratios in Multi-Robot Systems. In *The 5th International Conference on Systems, Control and Communications (ICSCC)*, 2019.

107. Xiaoyu Qiu, Luobin Liu, Wuhui Chen, Zicong Hong, and Zibin Zheng. Online deep reinforcement learning for computation offloading in blockchain-empowered mobile edge computing. *IEEE Transactions on Vehicular Technology*, 68(8):8050–8062, 2019.

108. Kazim Rifat Özyilmaz, Mehmet Doğan, and Arda Yurdakul. Idmob: Iot data marketplace on blockchain. In *Crypto Valley Conference on Blockchain Technology (CVCBT)*. IEEE, 2018.

109. Vishnu Prasad Ranganthan, Ram Dantu, Aditya Paul, Paula Mears, and Kirill Morozov. A decentralized marketplace application on the ethereum blockchain. In *4th International Conference on Collaboration and Internet Computing (CIC)*. IEEE, 2018.

110. Blesson Varghese, Massimo Villari, Omer Rana, Philip James, Tejal Shah, Maria Fazio, and Rajiv Ranjan. Realizing edge marketplaces: challenges and opportunities. *IEEE Cloud Computing*, 5(6):9–20, 2018.

111. Yongjun Ren, Fujian Zhu, Jian Qi, Jin Wang, and Arun Kumar Sangaiah. Identity management and access control based on blockchain under edge computing for the industrial internet of things. *Applied Sciences*, 9(10):2058, 2019.

112. Zerynth Docs r2.5.2. Ethereum modules. Technical report, [Online]. Available: https://docs.zerynth.com/latest/official/lib.blockchain.ethereum/docs/index.html, 2020.

113. IOTA Distributed Ledger Technology software expansion for STM32Cube. X-cube-iota1. Technical report, [Online]. Available: https://www.st.com/en/embedded-software/x-cube-iota1.html, 2020.

114. Jorge Peña Queralta, Tuan Nguyen Gia, Hannu Tenhunen, and Tomi Westerlund. Comparative study of LPWAN technologies on unlicensed bands for M2M communication in the IoT: beyond LoRa and LoRaWAN. *Procedia Computer Science*, 2019.

115. V. K. Sarker, J. Peña Queralta, T. N. Gia, H. Tenhunen, T. Westerlund. A survey on lora for iot: Integrating edge computing. In *SLICE- FMEC*, 2019.

116. T. N. Gia, L. Qingqing, J. Peña Queralta, H. Tenhunen, T. Westerlund. Edge AI in Smart Farming IoT: CNNs at the Edge and Fog Computing with LoRa. In *IEEE AFRICON*, 2019.

117. T. N. Gia, J. Peña Queralta, T. Westerlund. Exploiting LoRa, Edge and Fog Computing for Traffic Monitoring in Smart Cities. In *Book Chapter: LPWAN Technologies for IoT and M2M Applications*. Elsevier, 2020.

118. Kazim Rıfat Özyılmaz and Arda Yurdakul. Work-in-progress: integrating low-power iot devices to a blockchain-based infrastructure. In *2017 International Conference on Embedded Software (EMSOFT)*, pages 1–2. IEEE, 2017.

119. Jun Lin, Zhiqi Shen, Chunyan Miao, and Siyuan Liu. Using blockchain to build trusted lorawan sharing server. *International Journal of Crowd Science*, 2017.

120. Arnaud Durand, Pascal Gremaud, and Jacques Pasquier. Resilient, crowd-sourced lpwan infrastructure using blockchain. In *CryBlock*, pages 25–29, 2018.

Evaluation of Collaborative Intrusion Detection System Architectures in Mobile Edge Computing

Rahul Sharma, Chien Aun Chan, and Christopher Leckie

Abstract With the advent of 5th Generation (5G) of mobile networks, a diverse range of new computer networking technologies are being devised to meet the stringent demands of applications that require ultra-low latency, high bandwidth and geolocation-based services. Mobile Edge Computing (MEC) is a prominent example of such an emerging technology, which provides cloud computing services at the edge of the network using mobile base stations. This architectural shift of services from centralised cloud data centers to the network edge, helps reduce bandwidth usage and improve response time, meeting the ultra-low latency requirements laid out for 5G. However, MEC also inherits some of the vulnerabilities affecting traditional networks and cloud computing, such as coordinated attacks. Previous works have proposed the use of Intrusion Detection Systems (IDS), specifically Collaborative Intrusion Detection Systems (CIDS), which have proven to be effective in identifying distributed attacks. However, identifying the right CIDS model is not straightforward due to the tradeoff between different factors such as detection accuracy, network overhead, computation and memory overhead. In this chapter, we outline some of the characteristics relevant for evaluating CIDS deployment models and survey existing CIDS architectures in the context of MEC, while presenting novel strategies and architectures of our own.

Keywords Mobile edge computing · Intrusion detection · Cybersecurity · 5G

R. Sharma (✉) · C. Leckie
School of Computing and Information Systems, The University of Melbourne, Melbourne, Australia
e-mail: sharma1@student.unimelb.edu.au

C. A. Chan
Department of Electrical and Electronic Engineering, The University of Melbourne, Melbourne, Australia

1 Introduction

The rapid adoption of the Internet of Things (IoT) and mobile devices has prompted the need for additional compute and storage resources to handle the resulting influx of generated data. Cloud computing, which provides a seamlessly scalable infrastructure seems like an ideal candidate to manage these needs, but is not suitable for latency sensitive applications that require geographical proximity for fast response time. These use-cases have driven the need for evolutionary architecture patterns and technologies to meet these ultra-low latency requirements, motivating the introduction of Mobile Edge Computing (MEC). MEC provides computational and storage services at the edge of the network, closer to end users/devices where the data is being generated.

Edge computing classifies a broad range of techniques, designed to move compute and storage capabilities from centralized data centers (public and/or private) to the edge of the mobile network [1, 2]. This architecture facilitates data processing closer to end users, which significantly improves the response time by leveraging a heterogeneous set of resource constrained servers at the network edge. However, edge computing also inherits the underlying vulnerabilities of cloud data centers to cyber-attacks such as Denial of Service (DoS) and Distributed Denial of Service (DDoS) [3–12]. This is reflected in the dramatic increase of attacks on these edge computing infrastructures in recent years. For instance, the Mirai botnet attack gained control of more than 65,000 IoT devices within the first 20 h of its release in August 2016 [3]. These compromised devices were used to form a botnet to launch DDoS attacks on edge servers, affecting more than 178,000 domains [4]. Following this incident, variations of Mirai such as IoTReaper and Hajime were identified, which reportedly affected more than 378 million devices in 2017 [3].

To safeguard MEC nodes against such attacks, we require mechanisms capable of identifying these attacks in near-real time. Hence, [5–7] have recommended the use of Intrusion Detection Systems (IDS). However, the majority of existing IDS solutions are deployed on individual hosts and/or the core backbone network, with edge-focused solutions still being new [13]. These early IDSs act as isolated instances monitoring traffic across a single host/network, with no interaction taking place between peers. This works well if one is trying to protect a single system or network against known attacks. However, it performs poorly in detecting sophisticated coordinated attacks due to the limited context shared between nodes. Hence, looking at the complex attack surface present in MEC, some solutions [6, 7] have proposed the use of an IDS capable of identifying trends between malicious activities occurring at multiple locations at scale, like a Collaborative Intrusion Detection System (CIDS). Even then, there are different classifications of CIDS architectures, so finding the right fit is not straightforward. For instance, some of the edge-based CIDS solutions proposed [14, 15] use a Centralised CIDS approach with a cloud-based backend for processing compute intensive workloads. While this approach works well for workload optimisation, it fares poorly in response latency and network overhead due to the dependency on centralised data centers. Similarly,

Sharma et al. [16] evaluated the use of a Distributed CIDS architecture in MEC and outlined the trade-off in detection accuracy for fault tolerance and lower network overhead.

In this chapter, we survey some of the proposed CIDS architectures in an MEC context and discuss their performance using parameters such as detection accuracy as well as computational and network overhead. We also present possible improvements and new research avenues in some of these solutions to detect attacks at scale in near-real time. Our chapter is organised as follows: Sect. 2 discusses the different parameters to consider when choosing CIDS architectures and presents a literature review of the current state of the art CIDS solutions in traditional networking and its progression towards MEC. Section 3 presents a discussion on different types of CIDS architectures and their operation. Section 4 summarises the advantages and disadvantages of the solutions proposed previously, and we conclude in Sect. 5 with a discussion on possible future research avenues.

2 Related Work

In this section, we review some of the different classifications of CIDS and the various measures used to evaluate their performance.

2.1 CIDS Classification and Requirements

While traditional IDSs are limited to the scope of their own network, CIDS leverage a global view across networks by scaling and sharing context between peers. Thus, they can extend their detection range, enabling them to make better decisions. There are different classifications of CIDS based on their communication architecture [16–18], as follows:

- **Centralised CIDS:** These comprise multiple monitoring nodes analysing traffic flowing through their underlying host/network and sharing their findings with a central analysis unit. This central analysis unit applies alert correlation and anomaly detection algorithms on the incoming data to identify attacks. This architecture gains a better perspective of the underlying hosts/networks by scaling the number of monitoring nodes to obtain more information. However, despite the scalability of the monitoring nodes, the processing capability of the central analysis node remains the same, acting as a potential processing bottleneck. Also, if the central analysis unit goes offline, then the system is rendered useless, presenting a single point of failure.
- **Hierarchical CIDS:** These comprise a multi-layered architecture of monitoring nodes, filtering alerts based on specific rulesets and transmitting relevant data only to the layer above. The filtered data keeps moving up the hierarchy until it

reaches a central processing unit for aggregation. This works well for reducing the volume of data being forwarded to the central node, thus reducing the processing bottleneck. However, it still presents a single point of failure as the central processing unit needs to remain online.

- **Distributed CIDS:** The data filtering, detection and processing tasks are shared between all peers in a decentralised manner using Peer to Peer (P2P) communication. This enables each node to analyze their local networks while retaining a global view of all networks through data sharing and computational offloading. It addresses the issue of a single point of failure present in Centralised and Hierarchical CIDS as whenever a node malfunctions, it can be removed/replaced from the communication channel without breaking the entire system. However, the data maintained and processed by the faulty node may be lost if not replicated. Also, the data shared between peers may increase the data transmission overhead depending on the type or volume of data being shared.

Each of these architectures presents their own strengths and weaknesses based on the risk-sensitivity of the underlying use-case. While some would prefer having high detection accuracy over fault tolerance and reliability, others would focus on ensuring the system is reliable with failover properties at the cost of lower detection accuracy. To evaluate the performance of these architectures further, Vasilomanolakis et al. [17] outlined the following requirements needed for CIDS to protect large networks/IT systems.

- **Accuracy:** For a CIDS to be accurate, it needs to increase the percentage of successfully identified attacks and reduce the percentage of attacks that are undetected. In addition to these metrics, the number of falsely detected alerts needs to be decreased for measuring accuracy of a CIDS.
- **Minimal Overhead:** The overhead associated with computational and communication tasks in the CIDS system need to be as low as possible for the system to use the underlying resources efficiently. Given that MEC uses a set of heterogenous resources with varying degrees of compute and storage capabilities, having a low resource footprint is beneficial for it to function properly.
- **Scalability:** This property states that the performance of the CIDS increases linearly with increases in resources introduced into the network. This helps in coping with varying network sizes and needs.
- **Resilience:** Failures in hardware and software components of the system during attacks from both external and internal entities/systems should not affect the availability of the CIDS. This also focuses on addressing single points of failure to avoid bringing down the entire system abruptly.
- **Privacy:** In a CIDS, data shared between peers may contain sensitive information that needs to be protected from some/all components of the CIDS system. This aspect becomes crucial when data is shared between peers across different domains/namespaces that are governed by privacy principles and security regulations posed by users, organizations and network providers.
- **Self-Configuration:** The ability to adjust the settings of the CIDS automatically based on different factors without manual intervention is important to reduce

errors in the system. Most attackers use a variety of attack patterns so the CIDS needs to be able to dynamically fine-tune itself to detect these varying attacks.

- **Interoperability:** This property states that the CIDS systems need to be able to collaborate with a variety of networks and other CIDS implementations. Hence, establishing a common interface and data communication format for heterogenous CIDS systems to collaborate is important.

Using these requirements as a base, we focus on Accuracy and Minimal Overheads in terms of the computation and network as our evaluation measures to assess different CIDS architectures. These help in ensuring strong security patterns without degrading networking performance in MEC to fulfil the stringent requirements laid out for 5G.

2.2 Traditional CIDS Solutions

CIDS have been an active area of research for identifying coordinated attacks across multiple hosts/networks. The earliest known CIDS solution was the Distributed Intrusion Detection System (DIDS) introduced by [19], which followed a Distributed monitoring approach while analysing data centrally. They used host and network monitoring nodes that recorded the underlying network activities and aggregated data before forwarding them to a central analysis unit. This central analysis unit used a rule-based expert system to aggregate and analyse the data to identify attacks. DIDS only applied simplistic detection techniques so it can be evaded easily by sophisticated adversaries, resulting in poor accuracy. Similarly, as the amount of data being captured and forwarded by the monitoring nodes to the central analysis unit increases, the communication and computation overhead increases, degrading response latency. Also, the central analysis unit is a single point of failure as the system becomes unusable if this unit ever goes offline.

In 2007, [20] proposed Large Scale Intrusion Detection (LarSID), a Distributed CIDS using a P2P publish-subscribe model. They used a modified Pastry Distributed Hash Table (DHT) called Bamboo [21, 22] to share alerts in a single dimensional <Key, Value> format with peers, with the source IP address as the Key. Here, each node maintains a watch list corresponding to its local subnetwork, analysing traffic and inserting data that is suspected to be malicious, into a global DHT network. Peers who identify the same data to be suspicious, subscribe to those source IP addresses and update their watchlist accordingly. When more than a set number of nodes flag the same source IP address as suspicious, a notification is generated to every node using a callback functionality of the DHT, thus, communicating the validation of the malicious source IP address. The distributed nature of LarSID allows it to scale well and monitor independently, but certain nodes can be overloaded when a large number of attacks originate from the same source IP address, thus storing the metadata on the same node. One of the main disadvantages of LarSID is that it can only detect attacks involving a common source or destination

IP address. Focused attacks on one node may be flagged in the local watchlist of one/few node(s) but the Source IP address might not receive a consensus from peers regarding its suspicious behaviour since it is not visible to a majority of the nodes.

Blaise et al. [18] proposed an anomaly detection method called Split-and-Merge, using a Centralised CIDS deployment method. It uses multiple local detection modules across different subnetworks, detecting anomalies based on variations in port centric traffic. These changes are tracked using multiple features such as percentage of unique source addresses, unique destination addresses, unique source ports, mean packet size, standard deviation of packet sizes, percentage of SYN packets, and number of packets. They evaluate changes in these parameters using a modified Z-score, which uses the median and the median of the standard deviation of the individual field being analysed, creating a baseline that is outlier resistant [23]. Any traffic deviating from this baseline is forwarded to a central correlation module, which aggregates and analyses changes on ports using multiple local modules. An anomaly score is allocated for each feature deviating from the baseline, where the higher the score, the higher the concern for this type of traffic affecting the network. Evaluation of its performance with a real-world dataset displayed high accuracy with a smaller number of false positives. However, it needs to train on datasets representing normal traffic prior to analyzing live traffic. Hence, it is not suitable for real-time anomaly detection [18]. Also, it uses a characterisation of attacks based on the aforementioned features, meaning any attack deviating from these norms may not be easy to identify, thus decreasing accuracy.

2.3 Edge-Based CIDS Solutions

The majority of the research in this space was focused on Mobile Cloud Computing [6], where centralised data centers are leveraged for their storage and compute capabilities. However, Intrusion Detection in MEC has started to attract attention in recent years, with a majority of the work focusing on an algorithmic and process perspective with less focus on the design decisions for architecture deployments. These solutions leverage a hybrid layered architecture with cloud data centers to offload computationally heavy workloads, which works well due to the elastic nature of the cloud. However, this approach introduces response latency and communication overhead, which might not be suitable for real-time intrusion detection.

Lin et al. [5] proposed a six-layered edge computing Intrusion Detection model, where each layer performs a specific role in the overall architecture. One of the layers in their solution uses detection modules in the edge network, which are responsible for monitoring the underlying state of their host and identify attacks. The logs and metrics generated by these detection modules are forwarded to servers in the cloud layer to analyse and generate reports. The cloud layer derives insights and orchestrates the edge nodes to perform intrusion forensic investigation. This setup works well in coordinating data sharing and segregating functionalities between the two layers but introduces latency in coordinating between the edge nodes and the cloud data center.

In 2018, [15] proposed a framework to evaluate intrusion detection accuracy using edge nodes. They leveraged a three-layered model containing an additional component called the Edge manager working as the core of the solution. This component is responsible for picking different machine learning models dynamically based on the data being processed, thus improving detection accuracy. It also manages the pre-filtering of data locally at different IDS while coordinating data sharing between them. The global sharing of data outlined improvement in detection accuracy by enabling different models to gain a complete view of the network. The authors highlighted that pre-processing the data and coordinating data sharing between peers in the edge layer, limited data transmission to the centralised data center. This displayed significant improvement in data transmission overhead and the latency involved. The authors did not delve into the percentage of improvement in detection accuracy gained from this deployment. However, their experiment did identify that coordinating data sharing between edge servers could assist in reducing the overall overhead (network and computation) involved as outlined in similar works looking at resource utilization in MEC [5, 24, 25].

Observing these different security architecture patterns in use for MEC currently, most IDS solutions leverage the vast compute and storage capabilities of cloud data centers for compute intensive/coordination tasks. However, there is a gradual shift towards managing the data processing tasks across multiple edge nodes to remove the dependency on cloud data centers [16], thus, reducing the response latency and overhead (compute and network). As part of this chapter, we explore some of these proposed solutions across the different classifications of CIDS as outlined previously.

3 CIDS Architectures in MEC

In this section, we discuss the working of some representative CIDS architectures and how they function in an MEC environment.

3.1 Centralised CIDS

This architecture has multiple monitoring nodes scattered across networks, analysing data flowing through the underlying hosts/networks and forwarding them to a central analysis unit. This central analysis unit applies alert detection/correlation algorithms on the overall data to identify attacks. These systems seemingly improve the detection accuracy as all the data is analysed centrally in one place but they do not scale well and present a single point of failure as the absence of the central analysis unit will bring the system to a halt.

Sharma et al. [16] evaluated the performance of a Centralised CIDS architecture in an MEC environment by using multiple MEC nodes as Local Filtering (LF_i) nodes, scattered across different subnets as seen in Fig. 1. These LF_i nodes analyse incoming traffic and filter packets (pkt_i) containing TCP traffic with the SYN flag set, i.e., traffic to initiate a connection using the TCP 3-way handshake. These filtered packets are forwarded to an MEC node working as a Central Processing Node (CP) for aggregation and analysis using different threshold values to detect malicious traffic. The CP maintains a local watch list to track analyzed source IP addresses (src_ip_i) and maintain a count of its occurrence. After a set time frame of 10 mins, this watch list is refreshed, reducing the overall memory requirements of this architecture. They performed their experiment using a real-world worm dataset called "Three Days of Conficker" [26] made available by the Center for Applied Internet Data Analysis (CAIDA). Their architecture's performance was evaluated based on the Data Transmission Overhead, Accuracy Model, and the CPU and Memory Requirements needed to perform Intrusion Detection.

Their results demonstrated that a Centralised CIDS displayed higher detection accuracy as all the alerts identified by the multiple LF_i nodes were aggregated and analysed at a single location. This meant that the CP node had a comprehensive view of the complete traffic context across all monitored subnets. However, this

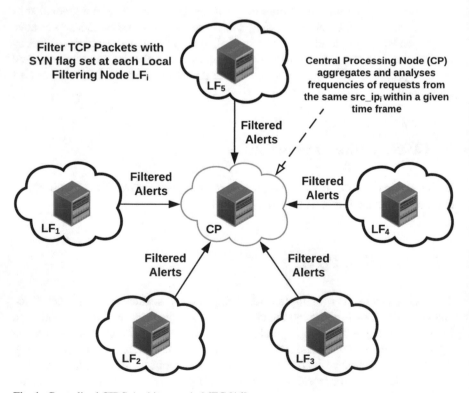

Fig. 1 Centralised CIDS Architecture in MEC [16]

also presented a bottleneck in terms of scalability, as the number of LF_i nodes could be increased but the computation, memory and storage capabilities of the CP node remained the same. Although the amount of data being processed in their experiment was not enough to overwhelm the CP node, they discussed that increasing the amount of data being forwarded centrally could cause delays in processing. This would not be ideal for achieving near-real time detection of attacks. The CPU and memory requirements outlined in their experiment displayed low CPU utilisation, and a stable memory utilisation, but they noted that increases in data could impact these metrics.

Algorithm 1: Centralised CIDS Processing

1:   // **Local Filtering Module**
2:   **while** Incoming Network Traffic **do**
3:       $pkt_i \leftarrow$ next packet from incoming network traffic
4:       **if** pkt_i.hasTCP && pkt_i.flags == "SYN" **then**
5:           filtered_data $\leftarrow pkt_i$
6:           send_data(filtered_data)
7:       **end**
8:   **end**
9:
10: // **Central Processing Module**
11: **while** Incoming Filtered Data **do**
12:     Queue $\leftarrow$ filtered_data
13: **end**
14:
15: // **Aggregation Logic Running In Separate Thread**
16: **Function** data_aggregator():
17:     pkt $\leftarrow$ Poll(Queue)
18:     **if** pkt_i.src_ip != watch_list {src_ip$_i$} **then**
19:         watch_list {src_ip} = 1
20:     **else if** pkt_i.src_ip == watch_list {src_ip$_i$} **then**
21:         watch_list {src_ip} += 1
22:     **end**
23:     **if** watch_list {src_ip} % threshold == 0 **then**
24:         Log $\leftarrow pkt_i$.src_ip
25:     **end**
26: **End Function**

Since all the filtered data from the LF_i nodes are being forwarded to the CP node, the Centralised CIDS has a high network transmission overhead. However, this data sharing segment of the architecture helped increase the detection accuracy, presenting a tradeoff between bandwidth usage and detection accuracy. Some organisations would place detection accuracy as a priority over network overhead, making this architecture more suitable to such use-cases. However, in a public shared network context like MEC, where third party organisations can deploy their applications to an Internet Service Provider's (ISP) infrastructure, there is a strong need for a balance between network overhead and detection accuracy.

3.2   Hierarchical CIDS

A Hierarchical CIDS architecture uses multiple monitoring nodes arranged in a hierarchical tree-like structure with a central analysis unit at the root of the hierarchy. Each layer of the hierarchy filters, aggregates and correlates data, forwarding only the results of this processing to the layer above. This process continues until it reaches the central processing unit at the top of the hierarchy to aggregate and apply alert correlation algorithms/mechanisms for detecting attacks. This architecture works well in terms of scaling and covering multiple subnets to identify the underlying trends. However, the filtering at each layer can cause loss of valuable network context. This may result in being unable to detect coordinated and/or sophisticated distributed attacks across multiple networks.

To the best of our knowledge, there has been little research in evaluating the performance of a Hierarchical CIDS in an MEC environment. However, there has been research to evaluate the resource consumption and orchestration of workloads across multiple MEC nodes in a hierarchical manner [24, 27–29]. In this chapter, we propose a novel Hierarchical CIDS architecture for MEC using the same principle of data processing and workload orchestration as these works. Here, we discuss the working of this architecture and the potential strengths and weaknesses.

In this architecture, we arrange our MEC nodes in a hierarchical tree-like manner with each hierarchy composed of multiple Hierarchical Nodes (HN) filtering traffic present at that layer, and a central analysis unit at the root of the hierarchy. As seen in Fig. 2, starting at the bottom most layer we have multiple MEC nodes monitoring traffic flowing through the underlying network at different geo-locations. Each of these edge devices filter traffic based on certain parameters and protocols. For instance, if we follow the same process as [16] we will filter TCP traffic containing the SYN flag, indicating the start of the TCP 3-way handshake. These packets will be aggregated based on the source IP address, using a watch list over fixed timeframes and compared against a threshold value indicating the number of connection requests allowed within a given timeframe. This threshold is based on the resource being accessed, as a rate limiting policy introduced for monitoring and controlling access across our edge devices.

Packets originating from the same source IP address matching a multiple of the defined threshold will be forwarded to the layer above this hierarchy. The same process will be followed across all MEC nodes at the bottom most layer, forwarding data to the layer above. The second layer will receive this aggregated data from multiple subnetworks and combine it to provide better coverage. Traffic incoming at this layer is further aggregated based on the source IP address over fixed timeframes against a set threshold. Packets originating from the same source IP address exceeding this threshold are forwarded to the layer above, with each layer performing similar aggregations over fixed time frames based on a set threshold. This process continues until the data reaches the central analysis unit at the root of this architecture, where we apply alert correlation algorithms to aggregate and detect malicious traffic.

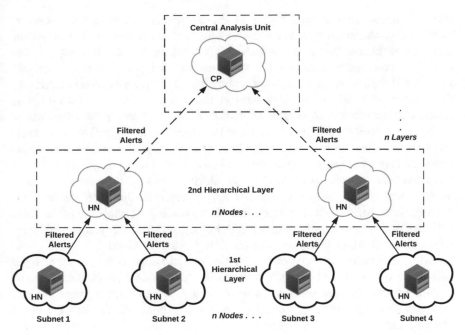

Fig. 2 Hierarchical CIDS in MEC

Algorithm 2: Hierarchical CIDS Processing

1: // **Local Filtering Module At Bottom-most Layer**
2: **while** Incoming Network Traffic **do**
3: pkt_i ← next packet from incoming network traffic
4:   **if** pkt_i.hasTCP && pkt_i.flags == "SYN" **then**
5:   Queue ← pkt_i
6:   end
7: **end**
8:
9: // **Aggregation Logic Running In Separate Thread**
10: Function data_aggregator():
11: pkt_i ← Poll(Queue)
12:   **if** pkt_i.src_ip != watch_list {src_ip_i} **then**
13:   watch_list {src_ip} = 1
14:   **else if** pkt_i.src_ip == watch_list {src_ip_i} **then**
15:   watch_list {src_ip} += 1
16:   **end**
17:   **if** watch_list {src_ip} % threshold == 0 **then**
18:   send_data(pkt.src_ip)
19:   **end**
20: End Function

This architecture can span multiple subnets and trust domains managed by different ISPs, filtering and aggregating data, and forwarding network context to the layer above. Through this process, it enables us to gather network context across different subnets for analysis of the underlying trends, making it easier to scale the solution further. Since this architecture can reduce the computational and network load across our edge nodes by forwarding focused data only, we can leverage a heterogenous set of MEC nodes across our layers to perform analysis. However, if the architecture continues scaling horizontally, for example - increasing the number of MEC nodes being used at the bottom most layer for analysing network traffic across our subnets, without increasing the number of nodes across the layers vertically can cause a processing bottleneck in the higher layers. To avoid this potential issue, scaling needs to be balanced not just within one layer alone but across all layers to evenly balance the increase in load. Cloud computing addresses this issue well through load balancing and elasticity by deploying more resources as and when needed. However, it is not easy to replicate this aspect in an MEC context. Since MEC nodes are dependent on the underlying hardware of the ISPs, their availability across multiple geo-locations may not always be guaranteed due to potential resource constraints and geo-proximity of the workload.

Also, this architecture is prone to a single point of failure as the central analysis unit at the root of the hierarchy is responsible for the final attack detection and reporting. Hence, scaling of MEC nodes horizontally and vertically might increase detection coverage but if this central analysis unit goes offline, then the entire system loses its main processing node for attack detection. This results in network correlation being locked down to localized hierarchies, increasing the risk profile of our security measures.

3.3 Distributed CIDS

This architecture deploys multiple self-contained nodes across different subnets where each node processes and analyses data flowing through their subnets locally. They aggregate and use alert correlation algorithms on their local data and share the results of their network context between peers using P2P communication. This setup enables nodes to gain a global view of the network while being decoupled such that failures are isolated without bringing down the entire system.

Sharma et al. [16] proposed a Distributed CIDS architecture for MEC using a Kademlia [30] based Distributed Hash Table (DHT) called OpenDHT [31]. The authors deployed their DHT instances across multiple MEC nodes in different subnets, communicating with one another using P2P communication as seen in Fig. 3. Each node monitors the traffic flowing through their local subnet and filters TCP traffic having the SYN flag set. The local DHT nodes aggregate and analyse the filtered traffic locally using set thresholds as their baseline to identify suspicious traffic. The packets flagged as suspicious are added to a local watch list and inserted (*PUT*) into the global DHT network in a single dimensional <Key, Value> format, with the Key represented as the source IP address indicated in the packet.

These single dimensional queries are stored in one of the DHT nodes across the network based on the hash computation of the data to be inserted. The data insertion invocation is followed by a callback (*LISTEN*) being set on the query Key, such that

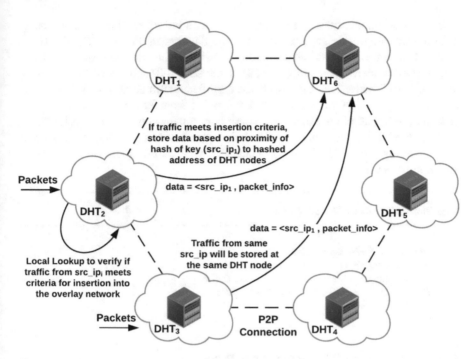

Fig. 3 Distributed CIDS Architecture in MEC [16]

any and all updates to the value of this key are notified to the subscriber, similar to a publish-subscribe model. If multiple nodes above a threshold detect a particular/set of source IP address(es) as suspicious, then the source IP address is considered to be malicious and a notification is shared with all subscribed peers. This model works well from a consensus-based approach to validate and detect malicious behavior through a decentralised analysis of network traffic.

The authors experiment used Data Transmission Overhead, Accuracy Model, and the CPU and Memory Requirements as their performance metrics for intrusion detection using a real-world worm dataset called – "Three Days of Conficker" [26]. Their results outlined that a Distributed CIDS requires far less data transfer, as data is only transmitted when it is inserted into the DHT network or upon a callback invocation. Since it follows a publish-subscribe model, only subscribed nodes would receive a callback notification, which reduces the need for transferring large volumes of data through the network. The authors also outlined that this architecture works well in scenarios where the attacks are spread out across multiple nodes, enabling a consensus to be reached. However, when attacks are focused on one or a few nodes only, this architecture will be unable to detect these attacks since the DHT nodes will not reach a consensus, resulting in reduced detection accuracy.

The DHT nodes also present an initial steep increase in CPU and Memory utilization across all nodes before reaching a saturation point. Since each DHT node is responsible for filtering, aggregating and publishing network data into the DHT network, the computational requirements fluctuate before reaching a stable usage pattern. For memory usage however, since the data inserted into the DHT network is stored on the DHT node whose address hash matches the hash of the inserted data, incoming alerts originating from the same source IP address will be stored on the same DHT node. This can also cause significant storage issues for the chosen DHT node if there is a heavy influx of data arriving from the same source IP address or if there are multiple packets whose hash computation matches the hash address of the same DHT node. This is particularly important in MEC, where nodes may have a heterogeneous set of resources allocated where some nodes may have fewer available resources.

Algorithm 3: Distributed CIDS Processing

1: **// Local DHT Node Entry Point**
2: **while** Incoming Network Traffic **do**
3:     $pkt_i \leftarrow$ next packet from incoming network traffic
4:     **if** pkt_i.hasTCP && pkt_i.flags == "SYN" **then**
5:         Queue $\leftarrow pkt_i$
6:     **end**
7: **end**
8:
9: **// Aggregation Logic Running In Separate Thread**
10: **Function** data_aggregator():
11:     **while** true **do**
12:         $pkt_i \leftarrow$ Poll(Queue)
13:         **if** pkt_i.src_ip != watch_list {src_ip_i} **then**
14:             watch_list {src_ip} = 1
15:             DHT $\leftarrow$ PUT(pkt_i.src_ip, {Msg})
16:             LISTEN(src_ip)
17:         **else if** pkt_i.src_ip == watch_list {src_ip_i} **then**
18:             watch_list {src_ip} += 1
19:         **end**
20:         **if** watch_list {src_ip} % threshold == 0 **then**
21:             DHT $\leftarrow$ PUT(pkt_i.src_ip, {Msg})
22:         **end**
23:     **end**
24: **End Function**
25:
26: **// Track Consensus Using Callback**
27: **Function** listen_callback():
28:     **while** true **do**:
29:         $p_i \leftarrow$ callback_response
30:         **if** "expired" != p_i.status **then**
31:             **if** node != p_i.current_node **then**
32:                 **if** p_i.src_ip != peers[src_ip] **then**
33:                     **if** len(peers) >= threshold **then**
34:                         Notify(peers[src_ip])
35:                     **end**
36:                 **end**
47:             **end**
48:         **end**
49:     **end**
50: **End Function**

This Distributed CIDS architecture displays a promising approach to create a fault tolerant system, which can overcome the single point of failure present in the Centralised CIDS architecture. However, this fault tolerance is only from an infrastructure perspective rather than the detection process. This means that whenever a node goes offline due to faults, all the data stored on that node will be lost. Although the DHT network will re-arrange itself to restore the current state of the network, the network context in the offline node will not be recovered.

3.4   Load Balancing Distributed CIDS

This architecture is proposed as a novel variation of the Distributed CIDS [16] seen previously, with an additional capability of performing load balancing of data to avoid overwhelming the storage capacity of the DHT nodes. As seen in Fig. 4, we have a cluster of DHT instances running on MEC nodes spread across multiple subnets and/or trust domains, connected with each other using P2P communication. All of these instances are connected to a central node acting as an orchestrator referred to as the Global Notification Node (GNN) using P2P communication.

The GNN periodically retrieves node status metadata, such as CPU and Memory utilization statistics from each of the DHT nodes and compiles a list of nodes that are reaching their resource threshold for computation and/or storage. For nodes that

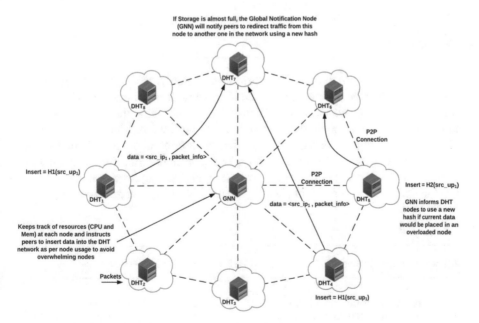

Fig. 4 Load Balancing Distributed CIDS Architecture in MEC

cross their resource capacity threshold, the GNN creates a blacklist of hash ranges to avoid storing data at those nodes and shares this blacklist with every DHT node in its trusted network.

Algorithm 4: Load Balancing Distributed CIDS Processing GNN

```
 1:  // GNN Health Check
 2:  while true do
 3:      for node in DHT_nodes:
 4:          health_status ← GET(node(CPU, Mem))
 5:      end
 6:      if health_status[node(CPU, Mem)] < threshold(CPU, Mem)
             && node != blacklisted_nodes then
 7:          Notify(DHT_nodes[blacklist_hashrange])
 8:      else if node == blacklisted_nodes && health_status
                 [node(CPU, Mem)] > threshold(CPU, Mem) then
 9:          Notify(DHT_nodes[remove_blacklistrange])
10:      end
11:  end
12:
13:  // Track New Hash Functions Used
14:  Function new_hash_mappings():
15:      while true do
16:          hash_mappings {hash, src_ip} ← receive_new_mapping
                            (hash_function, src_ip)
17:          Notify(original_DHT) ← new_mapping(hash, src_ip)
18:      end
19:  End Function
```

The DHT nodes use the blacklist notification shared by the GNN to verify that the hash of the data to be inserted into the DHT network does not fall in that blacklisted range. If the computed hash of the data falls in that range, the DHT uses a new hash function to recompute the hash of the data until the resulting hash is outside the blacklisted range. Consequently, the data is inserted into the DHT network on a new node to avoid overwhelming the resource capability of a single or few DHT nodes. This blacklist is computed by the GNN periodically to check the health of the DHT network and re-enable healthy nodes whose hash ranges were previously blacklisted.

Algorithm 5: Load Balancing Distributed CIDS Processing DHT Nodes

---

```
 1:  // Local DHT Node Entry Point
 2:  while Incoming Network Traffic do
 3:      if pkt_i.hasTCP && pkt_i.flags == "SYN" then
 4:          pkt_i ← next packet from incoming network traffic
```

```
5:        Queue ← pkt_i
6:      end
7:   end
8:
9:   // Aggregation Logic Running In Separate Thread
10:   Function data_filter():
11:     while true do
12:        pkt_i ← Poll(Queue)
13:        if pkt_i.src_ip != watch_list {src_ip_i} then
14:          watch_list {src_ip} = 1
15:          DHT ← PUT(pkt_i.src_ip, {Msg})
16:          LISTEN(src_ip)
17:        else if pkt_i.src_ip == watch_list {src_ip_i} then
18:          watch_list {src_ip} += 1
19:        end
20:        if watch_list {src_ip} % threshold == 0 then
21:          if hash(src_ip) == blacklist_hashrange
22:             while recomputed_hash == blacklist_hashrange
                    && new_hash[src_ip].isEmpty() do
23:               new_hash(src_ip)
24:             end
25:          end
26:          DHT(new_hash) ← PUT(pkt_i.src_ip, {Msg})
27:          Notify(GNN(new_hash, src_ip))
28:        end
29:     end
30:   End Function
31:
32:   // Track Consensus Using Callback
33:   Function listen_callback():
34:     while true do:
35:        p_i ← callback_response
36:        if "expired" != p_i.status then
37:          if node != p_i.current_node then
38:            if p_i.src_ip != peers[src_ip] then
39:               if len(peers) >= threshold then
40:                 Notify(peers[src_ip])
41:               end
42:            end
43:          end
44:        end
45:     end
46:   End Function
```

This process will initiate re-balancing of the data generated from the same source IP address as the Key, since the new function stores the data on a different node, which may cause drifts in the lookup. To reconcile the different hash computations of the same Key stored on different nodes, the GNN will retain a mapping of new functions used against Keys as a lookup and share that mapping with the DHT node storing the original <Key, Value> pairs. This enables callback invocations on a particular Key to register the new location of that Key based on the updated hash function used, hence, ensuring that data is being load balanced without affecting the publish-subscribe mechanism of the DHT. However, this also means that different DHT nodes inserting data related to the same source IP address into the DHT network can have different hash functions for recomputing their hash. This would result in the GNN retaining all of those mappings in-memory till the black listed DHT node recovers and is usable again. At which point, the DHT node will retain the mappings to alternate sources of the same Key for a set period of time for expiry of the data and will refresh its list of Key mappings to alternate nodes. Similarly, the GNN will also refresh its list of mappings after a set period of time to remove stale mappings.

This setup works well in ensuring that the resource utilization of all DHT nodes are balanced without affecting their availability in the global network, especially since MEC nodes can have a heterogeneous set of resources. However, it also increases data transmission overhead due to the periodic health checks and notifications sent to all MEC nodes in the DHT network. Also, the load balancing aspect of the solution can introduce delays associated with reconciling the lookup mapping of source IP addresses. For instance, when a DHT node subscribes to a source IP address which may be load balanced across multiple nodes, the callback invoked on the original storage location will push the notification for data stored on itself immediately. However, there might be delays associated with the GNN able to map the new location on the original storage node, to link the load balanced alternate storage node for the same Key, leading to loss of context and/or delays in pushing all notifications associated with that Key.

The GNN could potentially act as a bottleneck as new DHT nodes are added and the network size increases, which can potentially introduce processing delays in the network. To avoid turning it into a single point of failure, it would require replication to facilitate a failover strategy in case the original node starts to display issues, which may introduce the additional complexity of process migration between multiple GNNs. Also, given the distributed nature of the CIDS following the same processing and detection pattern, some of the disadvantages associated with Distributed CIDS, such as the inability to detect focused attacks, would be prevalent in this architecture as well. The process to re-compute the hash for data to be inserted into the DHT network and then validate it against the blacklist hash ranges will require additional computation and may potentially introduce delays, which will affect the response latency and resource utilization at MEC nodes.

Looking at some of the tradeoffs associated with the above architecture, it becomes evident that applying fault tolerance strategies to infrastructure and data can increase latency and network overhead. These factors could significantly affect the Quality of Service (QoS) associated with 5G as the network scales and more MEC nodes and applications are deployed. To prevent some of these issues, researchers can use a hybrid model [14, 15] leveraging a cloud-based backend to offload heavy processing. However, that architecture leads to an increase in response latency as well.

4 Comparison of CIDS Approaches

In this section we give an overall summary of the different CIDS architectures discussed in this chapter. Table 1 provides an overview of the performance as well as the pros and cons of these architectures based on requirements such as the Detection Accuracy, CPU and Memory utilisation, and Data Transmission Overhead.

We can observe that a Centralised CIDS, albeit having a single point of failure, maintains the highest Detection Accuracy due to the centralized processing capability of this architecture. However, this feature becomes overshadowed by the potential increase in response latency due to all the network data flowing to the same location, which can become a processing bottleneck. A Distributed CIDS alleviates this drawback by distributing the computational tasks across multiple nodes but at the cost of Detection Accuracy, CPU and Memory utilization. Since each node in the Distributed architecture filters, aggregates, and performs attack detection on its own local subnet, using shared findings from its peers - the overall detection process is spread across the network avoiding a single point of failure. However, whenever a DHT node goes offline, all the data stored on that node is lost. Although the DHT network will recover from an infrastructure service perspective by removing the offline node from the routing table of all the DHT nodes, it will be unable to recover the lost network context.

Since the Distributed CIDS architecture discussed in this chapter relies on consensus from a set number of DHT nodes to validate attacks, focused attacks on one or a few nodes may be missed, leading to lower Detection Accuracy. Also, if all nodes keep observing alerts originating from the same source IP address, they will compute the same hash based on the source IP address as the single dimensional correlation query. This will result in all of those alerts being stored on the same DHT node. Since MEC nodes have a heterogenous set of compute and storage resources, if the DHT node where all of those incoming alerts are stored has less available storage, the insertion process will eventually overwhelm that node bringing it offline if not addressed promptly.

The Hierarchical CIDS combines aspects of both Centralised and Distributed CIDS by having multiple layers of monitoring nodes feeding focused data to a central analysis unit. This setup allows it to monitor multiple subnets across different trust domains, while maintaining a central processing unit for attack detection and reporting. There are multiple issues present in this architecture, like low Detection Accuracy due to the filtering undertaken across layers. Although the filtering process is efficient in reducing noise across layers it can also reduce the amount of valuable network context shared across layers, thus reducing Detection Accuracy. Also, scaling horizontally is viable but it can cause strain in processing at the higher layers if scaling is not carried out across all the layers. For instance, scaling in one layer only, like the bottom-most layer, can help increase the geographical view of the CIDS system. However, it also adds additional processing strain on the layers above to manage and analyze the incoming data rapidly to meet the stringent needs of applications requiring real-time detection.

Table 1 Summary of the different CIDS solutions discussed in this chapter

Properties	Centralised CIDS	Hierarchical CIDS	Distributed CIDS	Load Balancing Distributed CIDS
Detection Accuracy	**High** **Pros:** • High detection accuracy due to centralised aggregation. • Captures global network context. • Good for identifying concentrated attacks. **Cons:** • Single point of failure.	**High - medium** **Pros:** • Data sharing between layers. • Captures global network context. **Cons:** • Possible loss of valuable information across layers. • Horizontal scalability at lower layers alone can cause bottlenecks at higher layers. • Single point of failure.	**High - medium** **Pros:** • High accuracy for distributed attacks. • Captures global network context. **Cons:** • Low accuracy for concentrated attacks. • Data replication/recovery in case of failures not yet supported.	**High-medium** **Pros:** • High accuracy for distributed attacks. • Captures global network context. • Ensures individual nodes are not overwhelmed by load balancing data storage and route requests. **Cons:** • Significantly low accuracy for concentrated attacks. • Data replication to counter node failures is not supported.
CPU and Memory Usage	**Stable** **Pros:** • Consistent usage of CPU and Memory. **Cons:** • Increased delay in reaction time. • Resource utilisation can increase if number of monitoring nodes increase.	**Fluctuates** **Pros:** • Usage at lower layers may be high but lesser utilisation at higher layers. • Allows different layers to manage using heterogenous set of resources. **Cons:** • Horizontal scaling at lower layers alone may add additional stress on usage.	**Fluctuates then stabilise** **Pros:** • Improved reaction time due to offloading processing across peers. **Cons:** • CPU and Memory utilisation fluctuate based on DHT requirements for data storage and processing.	**Stable and controlled** **Pros:** • CPU and Memory Utilisation will be actively monitored and controlled through load balancing. **Cons:** • Validating computed hash of data against blacklisted ranges and re-hashing can increase computational overhead.

(continued)

Data Transmission Overhead	High	High	Less	Medium
	Pros: • Pre-filtering ensures focused data only is forwarded to central node. **Cons:** • Needs more data transmission overhead to transfer data to the central node.	**Pros:** • Pre-filtering ensures that only focused data is forwarded to the layer above. **Cons:** • Multiple layers equate to more transmissions and hence increase in bandwidth usage and potentially response time delay.	**Pros:** • Requires less data transmission overhead due to publish-subscribe model. **Cons:** • DHT operations also require network transfer overhead, which introduces response time delay.	**Pros:** • Detection process would require less network context shared with peers due to publish-subscribe model. **Cons:** • Use of GNN will require periodic health checks and notifications to DHTs, increasing transfer overhead and potentially affecting response time delay.

The Load Balanced Distributed CIDS addresses most of the fault tolerance issues outlined in the proposed Distributed CIDS by using a central GNN to track resource utilization across the DHT network. It performs health checks and helps re-direct traffic from nodes that are reaching their maximum capacity in terms of CPU and Memory utilisation, thus, alleviating the load on those nodes. However, this increases the processing needs across the network as nodes need to validate the output of hash computations of the data prior to inserting into the DHT. If the hash output of the data is within blacklisted ranges as shared by the GNN, those data need to be recomputed using a new hash function and the output re-verified against the blacklisted range. This could potentially increase the response latency of the solution significantly, which is not ideal for real-time detection. Also, the periodic health checks and event-based notifications of black list ranges across all nodes in the DHT network increases the Data Transmission Overhead of this architecture. This overhead can potentially be equal to or higher than the Data Transmission Overhead observed for the Centralised CIDS architecture as the GNN needs to perform health checks periodically on all DHT nodes in the network.

Similar to the Centralised CIDS, both Hierarchical and Load Balanced Distributed CIDS have a single point of failure in respect to their central analysis unit and the GNN, which could significantly affect the functioning of these architectures, especially the GNN, as it manages mappings of source IP addresses to new hash functions used by different DHT nodes across the network. If this context is lost or inaccessible, the DHT nodes could still store data for the same source IP address across different nodes in the network. However, they will be unable to receive a callback on updates made on that source IP address as the original storage node will not have access to the mappings for that Key due to loss of connectivity with the GNN. This will break the publish-subscribe model followed by the Distributed CIDS, leading to a significant loss of Detection Accuracy and rendering the system unusable.

Based on the observations outlined in Table 1, it becomes evident that there is no one ideal solution available for CIDS in MEC. Each approach comes with its own caveats which need to be considered during deployment to understand the impact it will have in the overall application use-case.

5   Future Research Directions

Reviewing the working of the different CIDS architectures discussed in this chapter, we outline some of the potential research directions to explore in this domain as follows.

- **Use of multi-dimensional queries:** The authors of [16] used a DHT for their Distributed CIDS architecture, which leveraged a single dimensional query Key for storage in their DHT network. It would be interesting to explore the effects on Detection Accuracy if we increase the scope of network context shared amongst peers [16]. For instance, including an additional Key such as port information or trend based information to form a multi-dimensional query. The current state of the Distributed CIDS is unable to detect attacks that affect fewer nodes than the number required to form a consensus. Adding another dimension could potentially address this issue by using additional network context for peers to look up and validate attack patterns on their local nodes.

- **Hybrid architectures:** As observed in Table 1, each CIDS architecture discussed in this chapter has its own strengths and weaknesses. Using a combination of some of these architectures could help alleviate the bottlenecks present in individual architecture deployment models, enabling further improvement of their combined performance [16]. Most hybrid architectures use a MEC hosted CIDS with a cloud based backend to offload compute intensive processing tasks [14, 15]. However, it would be useful to understand the performance metrics and capabilities of a purely edge-deployed hybrid architecture, collaborating and offloading tasks between peers at the edge of the network.
- **Enforce trust between peers across untrusted domains:** In modern times, trust is becoming an increasingly important trait to have for any data processing system. For CIDS, which is a core security system used in most complex network setups (perimeter-oriented or otherwise) across organizations, it is vital to ensure that the interactions between its different components can be trusted. This factor is especially significant to explore for understanding the complexities involved in an MEC context [32, 33], with some researchers proposing the use of technologies like Blockchain [34, 35] for this. Since edge devices are usually deployed in locations without strict controls and protection capabilities [36], being able to establish trust domains with authentication and authorisation solutions at scale is a challenging problem to address.
- **Coordinating cross-network mitigation strategies:** One of the main benefits outlined for adopting MEC is support for location aware services and applications [1]. In Intrusion Detection, we might observe attacks originating from one or multiple sources across different networks. Some of these sources might be different but the underlying attack patterns used can be quite consistent based on the vulnerabilities targeted. To mitigate these attacks, a combination of firewall rules and request throttling can be used. However, given the wide attack surface that MEC presents, coordinating the same mitigation strategies across affected nodes and networks is an interesting problem to tackle.
- **Enabling security at scale:** With the increasing global community shifting to an online medium to consume and produce information, work, study, and perform other day to day activities, providing a more active approach to intrusion detection is highly important. The use of MEC will enable us to deliver such solutions at an ultra-low latency response time but will require elasticity and scalability to manage the vast volumes of incoming data at any point in time [37–39]. Being able to coordinate and auto-scale our security solutions to manage these variable volumes of high velocity streaming data will be key in defining the resilience of our setup. Hence, it is important to understand the different

metrics usable for auto-scaling the Intrusion detection system and its impact on the performance of the security solution.

- **Self-healing mechanisms:** Faults are a natural occurrence in any software and hardware system. Recovering from faults is key to maximising the uptime of our system components, especially when these elements are our security mechanisms [1, 37, 39–41]. Given the diverse nature of MEC nodes, it is important to have fault tolerant architectures which are capable of self-healing to ensure a consistent level of security coverage at any point in time. Identifying these faults and triggering self-healing without overloading the other components of our security architecture are important properties to explore in an MEC context.

6 Conclusion

This chapter gives an overview of some of the current state-of-the-art CIDS solutions in MEC and proposes two novel solutions. We survey key requirements for evaluating the performance of CIDS, and out of these use Detection Accuracy, CPU and Memory Utilisation, and Data Transmission Overhead as our base measures for comparison. Based on our evaluations, we identify that there is no one CIDS architecture that covers all the requirements needed for near-real time detection while providing fault tolerance and an optimised use of bandwidth. Each of these architectures require a tradeoff between one of these parameters and fault tolerance to function properly. Hence, it is crucial to understand the underlying needs of the application use-case carefully prior to deciding on an architecture as there is no "one size fits all" CIDS architecture that meets all the requirements of the Mobile Edge Computing paradigm.

References

1. European Telecommunications Standards Institute (2014). *Mobile-Edge Computing – Introductory Technical White Paper*. Retrieved from https://portal.etsi.org/Portals/0/TBpages/MEC/Docs/Mobile-edge_Computing_-_Introductory_Technical_White_Paper_V1%2018-09-14.pdf.
2. O. Mäkinen, "Streaming at the Edge: Local Service Concepts Utilizing Mobile Edge Computing," in *2015 9th International Conference on Next Generation Mobile Applications, Services, and Technologies*, 1–6, 2015.
3. M. Antonakakis, T. April, M. Bailey, M. Bernhard, E. Bursztein, J. Cochran, Z. Durumeric, J. A. Halderman, L. Invernizzi, M. Kallitsis, D. Kumar, C. Lever, Z. Ma, J. Mason, D. Menscher, C. Seaman, N. Sullivan, K. Thomas, and Y. Zhou, "Understanding the Mirai botnet," in *26th USENIX Conference on Security Symposium*, 1093–1110, 2017.
4. S. Weagle, *"Financial Impact of Mirai DDoS Attack on Dyn Revealed in New Data"*. Retrieved from https://www.corero.com/blog/797-financial-impact-of-mirai-ddos-attack-on-dyn-revealed-in-new-data.html.

5. F. Lin, Y. Zhou, X. An, I. You, and K. R. Choo, "Fair Resource Allocation in an Intrusion-Detection System for Edge Computing: Ensuring the Security of Internet of Things Devices," in *IEEE Consumer Electronics Magazine*, 45–50, 2018.
6. R. Roman, J. Lopez, and M. Mambo, "Mobile edge computing, Fog et al.: A survey and analysis of security threats and challenges," in *Future Generation Computer Systems*, 680–698, 2018.
7. K. Sha, A. Yang, W. Wei, and S. Davari, "A survey of edge computing based designs for IoT security," in *Digital Communications and Networks*, 2019.
8. A. Mtibaa, K. Harras, H. Alnuweiri, "Friend or Foe? Detecting and Isolating Malicious Nodes in Mobile Edge Computing Platforms," in *2015 IEEE 7th International Conference on Cloud Computing Technology and Science*, 42–49, 2015.
9. S. N. Shirazi, A. Gouglidis, A. Farshad, and D. Hutchison, "The Extended Cloud: Review and Analysis of Mobile Edge Computing and Fog From a Security and Resilience Perspective," in *IEEE Journal on Selected Areas in Communications*, 35(11), 2586–2595, 2017.
10. S. Raponi, M. Caprolu, and R. D. Pietro, "Intrusion Detection at the Network Edge: Solutions, Limitations, and Future Directions," in *Zhang, T., Wei., J., Zhang, L. J. (eds) Edge Computing – EDGE 2019*. 59–75, 2019.
11. R. Roman, R. Rios, J. A. Onieva, J. Lopez., "Immune System for the Internet of Things Using Edge Technologies," in *IEEE Internet of Things Journal*, 6(3), 4774–4781, 2019.
12. R. Liao, H. Wen, J. Wu, F. Pan, A. Xu, H. Song, F. Xie, and Y. Jiang, "Security Enhancement for Mobile Edge Computing Through Physical Layer Authentication," in *IEEE Access*, 116390–116401, 2019.
13. N. Abbas, Y. Zhang, A. Taherkordi, and T. Skeie, "Mobile Edge Computing: A Survey," in *IEEE Internet of Things Journal*, 5(1), 450–465, 2018.
14. Y. Wang, L. Xie, W. Li, W. Meng, and J. Li, A Privacy-Preserving Framework for Collaborative Intrusion Detection Networks Through Fog Computing," in S. Wen, W. Wu, & A. Castiglione (Eds.), *International Symposium on Cyberspace Safety and Security* (pp. 267–279). Springer, Cham, 2017.
15. W. Meng, Y. Wang, W. Li., Z. Liu, J. Li., and C. W. Probst, "Enhancing Intelligent Alarm Reduction for Distributed Intrusion Detection Systems via Edge Computing," in W. Susilo, G. Yang (Eds.), *Australasian Conference on Information Security and Privacy* (pp. 759–767). Springer, Cham, 2018.
16. R. Sharma, C. A. Chan, C. Leckie, "Evaluation of Centralised vs Distributed Collaborative Intrusion Detection Systems in Multi-Access Edge Computing," in *IFIP Networking 2020*, 2020.
17. E. Vasilomanolakis, S. Karuppayah, M. Mühlhäuser, M. Fischer, "Taxonomy and Survey of Collaborative Intrusion Detection" in *ACM Computing Surveys (CSUR)*, 47(4), 55, 2015.
18. A. Blaise, M. Bouet, S. Secci, V. Conan, "Split-and-Merge: Detection Unknown Botnets," in *2019 IFIP/IEEE Symposium on Integrated Network and Service Management (IM)*, 153–161, 2019.
19. S. R. Snapp, J. Brentano, G. V. Dias, T. L. Goan, L. T. Heberlain, C. Ho, K. N. Levitt, B. Mukherjee, S. E. Smaha, T. Grance, D. M. Teal, and D. Mansur, "DIDS (Distributed Intrusion Detection System) – motivation, architecture, and an early prototype," in *14th National Computer Security Conference*, 167–176, 1997.
20. C. V. Zhou, S. Karunasekara, and C. Leckie, "Evaluation of a Decentralised Architecture for Large Scale Collaborative Intrusion Detection," in *10th IFIP/IEEE International Symposium on Integrated Network Management*, 80–89, 2007.
21. S. Rhea, D. Geels, T. Roscoe, and J. Kubiatowicz, "Handling churn in a DHT," in *USENIX Annual Technical Conference*, 10–10, 2004.
22. S. Rhea, B. Godfrey, B. Karp, J. Kubiatowicz, S. Ratnasamy, S. Shenker, I. Stoica, and H. Yu, "OpenDHT: a public DHT service and its uses," in *Conference on Applications, Technologies, Architectures, and Protocols for Computer Communications (SIGCOMM '05)*, 73–84, 2005.
23. B. Iglewicz, and D. Hoaglin (1993). How to detect and handle outliers *The ASQC Basic References in Quality Control: Statistical Techniques*. [Online] Available at: https://hwbdocuments.env.nm.gov/Los%20Alamos%20National%20Labs/TA%2054/11587.pdf

24. M. M. Shurman, and M. K. Aljarah, "Collaborative execution of distributed mobile and IoT applications running at the edge," in *2017 International Conference on Electrical and Computing Technologies and Applications (ICECTA)*, 1–5, 2017.
25. A. Reiter, B. Prünster, and T. Zefferer, "Hybrid Mobile Edge Computing: Unleashing the Full Potential of Edge Computing in Mobile Device Use Cases," in *2017 17th IEEE/ACM International Symposium on Cluster, Cloud and Grid Computing (CCGRID)*, 935–944, 2017.
26. The CAIDA UCSD "Three Days of Conficker Traffic from the UCSD Network Telescope" Dataset: http://www.caida.org/data/passive/telescope-3days-conficker_dataset.xml
27. L. Tong, Y. Li, and W. Gao, "A hierarchical edge cloud architecture for mobile computing," in *IEEE INFOCOM 2016 – The 35th Annual IEEE International Conference on Computer Communications*, 1–9, 2016.
28. A. Kiani, and N. Ansari, "Toward Hierarchical Mobile Edge Computing: An Auction-Based Profit Maximization Approach," in *IEEE Internet of Things Journal*, 2082–2091, 2017.
29. C. Song, M. Zhang, Y. Zhan, D. Wang, L. Guan, W. Liu, L. Zhang, and S. Xu, "Hierarchical edge cloud enabling network slicing for 5G optical fronthaul," in *IEEE/OSA Journal of Optical Communications and Networking*, B60–B70, 2019.
30. P. Maymounkov, and D. Mazieres, "Kademlia: A peer-to-peer information system based on the xor metric," in *International Workshop on Peer-to-Peer Systems*, 53–65, 2002.
31. Savoirfairelinux (2014). savoirfairelinux/opendht. [Online] Available at: https://github.com/savoirfairelinux/opendht.
32. J. P. Martin, A. Kandasamy, K. Chandrasekaran, and C. T. Joseph, "Elucidating the challenges for the praxis of fog computing: An aspect-based study," in *International Journal of Communication Systems*, 32(7), p.e3926, 2019.
33. B. Varghese, N. Wang, S. Barbhuiya, P. Kilpatrick, and D. S. Nikolopoulas, "Challenges and opportunities in edge computing," in *2016 IEEE International Conference on Smart Cloud (SmartCloud)*, 20–26, 2016.
34. H. Yang, Y. Liang, J. Yuan, Q. Yao, A. Yu, and J. Zhang, "Distributed Blockchain-Based Trusted Multidomain Collaboration for Mobile Edge Computing in 5G and Beyond," in *IEEE Transactions on Industrial Informatics*, 2020.
35. D. C. Nguyen, P. N. Pathirana, M. Ding, and A. Seneviratne, "Blockchain for 5G and beyond networks: A state of the art survey," in *Journal of Network and Computer Applications*, 102693, 2020.
36. P. Hu, S. Dhelim, H. Ning, and T. Qiu, "Survey on fog computing: architecture, key technologies, applications, and open issues," in *Journal of Network and Computer Applications*, 27–42, 2017.
37. A. Samir, and C. Pahl, "Self-Adaptive Healing for Containerized Cluster Architectures with Hidden Markov Models," in *2019 Fourth International Conference on Fog and Mobile Edge Computing (FMEC)*, 68–73, 2019.
38. B. Magableh, and M. Almiani, "A Self Healing Microservices Architecture: A Case Study in Docker Swarm Cluster," in *International Conference on Advanced Information Networking and Applications*, 846–858, 2019.
39. A. Samir, N. E. Ioini, I. Fronza, H. R. Barzegar, V. T. Le, and C. Pahl, "Anomaly Detection and Analysis for Reliability Management in Clustered Container Architectures," in *International Journal on Advances in Systems and Measurements*, 247–264, 2020.
40. V. K. Singh, E. Vaughan, and J. Rivera, "SHARP-Net: Platform for Self-Healing and Attack Resilient PMU Networks," in *IEEE Power and Energy Society Innovative Smart Grid Technologies Conference (ISGT)*, 1–5, 2020.
41. S. Al-Rubaye, J. Rodriguez, A. Al-Dulaimi, S. Mumtaz, and J. J. P. C. Rodrigues, "Enabling Digital Grid for Industrial Revolution: Self-Healing Cyber Resilient Platform," in *IEEE Network*, 219–225, 2020.

Part III
Applications

Edge Computing Based Conceptual Framework for Smart Health Care Applications Using Z-Wave and Homebased Wireless Sensor Network

Shouvik Chakraborty, Kalyani Mali, and Sankhadeep Chatterjee

Abstract Rapid advancement of the technology makes the system more reliable and the outcome from the system produces in a timely fashion. In this work, a conceptual framework for biomedical image analysis is considered which is based on wireless sensor networks. Here, Z-Wave based wireless biomedical image analysis system is analyzed that can be implemented to provide a concrete WSN based health care system. This work can serve as a foundation to the real-life remote health care system based on Z-Wave. Periodic study of different patients is possible from their own home which can help the physicians to take appropriate decisions in stipulated time that will certainly accelerate the physical and mental improvement. This paper studies the concepts of wireless biomedical image monitoring systems along with their features. In this context mobile edge computing can play a vital role because biomedical image monitoring systems needs to deal with huge amount of data. In general, image data consists of large volume of information. Storage and processing of such a huge amount of data is really a headache. Technologies based on mobile edge computing allows us to save valuable resources in the processing nodes and suitable to handle the resource-hungry applications. Various aspects of the WSN healthcare systems are analyzed and future directions are reported and analyzed in a comprehensive way so that this work will be beneficial for the society and can be extended towards real life implementation.

Keywords Health information management · Wireless sensor networks · Public healthcare · Biomedical imaging · Biomedical communication

S. Chakraborty · K. Mali
University of Kalyani, Nadia, West Bengal, India

S. Chatterjee (✉)
University of Engineering & Management, Kolkata, West Bengal, India

© The Author(s), under exclusive license to Springer Nature Switzerland AG 2021
A. Mukherjee et al. (eds.), *Mobile Edge Computing*,
https://doi.org/10.1007/978-3-030-69893-5_16

1 Introduction

Biomedical image analysis is one of the most popular and necessary non-invasive tool for monitoring health and inevitable to make appropriate diagnosis for many diseases [1–3]. Recent development in the field of medical imaging makes this domain highly useful and most of the diagnostic systems have high dependency on the biomedical image processing tools [2, 4–6]. Modern healthcare industry achieves high reliability based on the advanced medical image diagnostic methods that can be employed to study various diseases and can be helpful to find a pathway towards solutions. Several components of the health care industry use image analysis [7–11] technologies directly or indirectly to enhance the efficiency of various fields like neuro-medicines, orthopedics, gynecology etc. [12].

Lots of research has been carried out in this domain addressing several issues. Section 2 describes some of the related works. Different works are focused on various section of the biomedical image analysis process [13–20]. It includes image acquisition, enhancement and noise removal [6], segmentation [21] and feature extraction [22], decision making process etc. [5, 23, 24]. The main target of these systems is to make the life of the common people easier by bringing the advantages of the sophisticated technologies in affordable price [25].

Wearable technologies have changed the face of the healthcare automation. It can help physicians to observe a human body continuously that was not possible before some decades. It can reveal some precious information about the living body that can help in further diagnosis [26–28]. Sometimes it is unavoidable and can save the life of different patients by continuously recording different parameters. It is a revolution in the field of medical imaging that is changing the life and improves the impact of the automation. The combined effort of Internet of things (IoT), Wireless technologies, wearable technologies, artificial intelligence, machine learning, big data and some other technologies is changing and forwarding the biomedical imaging industry towards a new direction [29]. Major advancements of the modern technologies can be observed in various sectors like spacecraft, vehicles, software and hardware industry. But it is true that biomedical imaging is no lagging behind. Besides the fact that many thing cannot be explored from the biomedical imaging but the advantages that can be obtained from it cannot be ignored. In recent days, researchers are interested about various virtual environments that can make the task of a physician easier.

Wearable technologies are not very widely used for biomedical imaging and needs to be improved in different ways. This technology and trend is still in its inception phase for the domain of biomedical imaging and analysis. There is a lot of scope in this filed in near future and it can be applied to predict various diseases in advance and has the power to transform the radiology by boosting the analysis tools that can enhance conventional treatment [30]. Moreover, high quality of the acquired data and a platform for its efficient automated analysis is required to precisely analyze the condition of the patient in real-time [31]. Various tools [32, 33] have been invented and available in market and for consumers which are may not be directly adapted for health care applications but can be useful in health care applications. Some of the research works can be found in literature that uses these tools directly or indirectly for healthcare applications. For example, these products are used in neuro-navigation [34], surgical and non-surgical fields [35, 36], neurology [37] etc. These kinds of wearable devices can be used with association with the radiological diagnostic tools. In general, most of the available wearable devices are not directly useful for medical applications. European union uses a definition for "medical" devices that can be found in [38].

Wearable devices can help physicians to study various conditions with the help of the augmented reality [39]. In general, biomedical images can be used as an alternative and effective tool for virtual interventional study where holographic projection is made by capturing important interest points. Good quality images can ensure the personalized care and virtual reality can explore several perspectives that may not be visible by the human eye. Design of remote monitoring systems for biomedical images is one of the growing research topics and has various prospects. It is not always possible to move a large clinical device to a remote location and therefore home-based healthcare and monitoring with the help of conventional appliances is also a troublesome and sometimes not possible at all. So, some devices are invented to give the facility and comfort to the user to wear and transmit the images with the application of wireless sensor networks. It can also be incorporated with the smart home concept [40] with some modifications that can help in further advancement. The collected signals are sent to the local hub and then transmitted to the central server which is generally located in hospital or monitoring station. The signals can be analyzed centrally or in a distributive environment but the results can be monitored centrally and more importantly patients can sit in their own home. Due to the rapid advancement in the field of sensors and medical imaging, it is possible to build such wireless technologies. Moreover, with the growth in artificial intelligence and development of various machine learning based tools, it is possible to generate automated alerts by analyzing real-time data and give some prediction based on previous history of the patient that can reduce the task of the physicians and can save some precious life. Personalized care with less cost is one of the major advantages of these systems.

In this work, Z-Wave is considered for the wireless communication purpose. In general, zigbee, Z-Wave, Bluetooth etc. are more or less similar. However, in case of interoperability, Z-Wave outperforms the Zigbee or Bluetooth and proven to be run smooth [41]. It is because Z-Wave is standardized by private organization and it is guaranteed that every device can communicate with one another. Some recent developments made the Bluetooth and zigbee interoperable to some extent. Z-Wave does not interfere with the other devices and works very fast [42]. Moreover the signal strength of Z-Wave is higher than Bluetooth [43]. Near about 1.5 k products are running currently using Z-Wave [42]. Z-Wave is widely used because unlike zigbee or Bluetooth, Z-Wave alliance [44] makes it certain that all devices follow some standard set of rules and definitions which makes it interoperable which is highly desirable in remote health care systems and these property makes Z-Wave more suitable than zigbee or bluetooth. Z-wave uses very low energy radio waves for communication that in turn reduces the power consumption [45]. This work is focused to develop remote biomedical image analysis system using wireless sensor networks with the help of Z-Wave and smart home concept to make the biomedical image analysis process simpler. Properties and other advantages of using Z-Wave is illustrated in Sect. 3. Comparison of Z-Wave with some other standard technologies are given in Table 1. However, Z-wave plus can also be adopted in place of traditional Z-wave.

Typically, every industry requires sophisticated methods for real-time data analysis. The availability of important and critical information in real-time is one of prime importance for almost every industry. It certainly helps in their productivity. But, when we are talking about the healthcare industry, the availability of critical information at an appropriate time is highly essential and it can make a difference between life and death. Typically cloud-based infrastructures process the data at some particular distance from the location from where data are being collected. It has some obvious drawbacks like communication de-lay due to congestion in bandwidth, poor reliability, etc. Although, we are living in an era of 5G still, these issues persist and can be well understood when every second count. Moreover, some security and s are also involved. Mobile edge computing can address this issue by bringing the data processing approaches closer to the data collection points by reducing the communication-related overheads. It is helpful to take immediate actions depending on the processing results without depending on the updation delays.

The rest of the article is organized as follows: Sect. 2 illuminates the concepts about Z-Wave and its applications in smart home-based health care monitoring. Section 3 discusses about the wireless biomedical image analysis system using Z-Wave. Section 4 gives an overview of the various challenges and future direction of this work. Section 5 concludes the article.

2   Literature Review

The development of remote healthcare systems is very prominent and gained the attention of many researchers and scientists. A residential health care monitoring system is developed in [26] to process ECG signals using existing ECG sensors. This article reports the concepts and future directions to acquire and process ECG signals using Zigbee communication network. The study reveals the possibility of developing a real-world system by using residential wireless sensor network. A distributed system for remote healthcare is developed by the media laboratory of Massachusetts Institute of Technology (MIT). The system is based on mobile communication and known as LiveNet [46]. This system has the capability to process real-time data using a Linux based personal digital assistant and a sensor hub. To handle data, a three-layered software architecture is developed which is capable to efficiently process and transmit real-time data. Another wearable sensor for remote health monitoring is developed and reported in [47]. It is a wrist-worn

Table 1 Comparison of different standard wireless technologies

Attributes	Zigbee	Bluetooth	Wi-Fi	Z-Wave
Design focus	Home automation, smart grid, and remote control	Exchanging data over short distances	Connection to WLAN for devices	Wireless communication for home automation and security
IEEE Standard	802.15.4	802.15.1	802.11 standards	802.15.4
Network Type	Mesh	Mesh	Star	Mesh
Network	ZigBee	Bluetooth	Wi-Fi	Z-Wave
Distance	Approximately 10–20 meters	Approximately 10–100 meters	20 meters	100 meters with no obstructions
Max Nodes Connected	65,536	7	Router-dependent	232
Operating Band	2.4 Ghz, 915 MHz and 868 MHz (license-free ISM band)	ISM band, 2.4–2.485 GHz	2.4 gHz UHF and 5 gHz SHF ISM radio bands	915 MHz ISM band and 868 MHz RFID band
Spread Spectrum	Direct Sequence Spread Spectrum (DSSS)	Adaptive Frequency-hopping spread spectrum (AFH)	Direct-sequence spread spectrum (DSSS)	Direct sequence spread spectrum (DSSS)
Throughput	110 kbps maximum	24 Mbit/s	900 Mbps	40 kbit/s
Data	Monitoring and control data	Exchanging data	Transporting data	Monitoring and control data
Voice Capable	Yes	Yes	Yes	Yes
Security	AES encryption, cipher block chaining message authentication code	Confidentiality, authentication and key derivation	Wi-Fi Protected Access encryption (WPA2)	AES-encrypted
Power Consumption	Low	Low	High	Low
Modulation	Quadrature phase-shift keying (OQPSK)	Gaussian Frequency Shift Keying (GFSK)	Quadrature Phase Shift Keying (QPSK)	Gaussian frequency shift keying (GFSK)

device can measure body temperature, blood pressure, ECG etc. This project is named as AMON and is sponsored by EU FP5 IST program. A physiological parameter screening device is proposed in [48] which is based on a wireless telephone, a GPS device and a biomedical examination device. This device can monitor several parameters like blood pressure, temperature etc. This device uses radio frequency which is obsolete and the device is too bulky.

Another remote health care and monitoring system is proposed in [49]. This system is known as LifeGuard and it is mainly used for space related applications. This device can measure heart rate, oxygen level etc. and can record different parameters in data card. It can store data up to 9 h. The collected data are transmitted via satellites. A cell phone based ECG monitoring system is proposed in [50]. A mobile based physiological data monitoring system is proposed in [51]. This device uses Bluetooth sensors to collect data and transmits it using GPRS system. This wearable system is can detect abnormal patterns from the ECG signal by using machine learning methods. A new approach is proposed in to track the status of the brain. It can collect and record various parameters like oxygen level, rate of respiration etc. and store it on a storage card. The data is transmitted using a Bluetooth to a home personal computer and then the data is transmitted to a local medical hub. This device is not very suitable to be worn because of its wired connectivity between different modules. An another approach for ECH monitoring is proposed in [52]. In this work ECG signals are processed by a personal digital assistant. Signals are continuously transmitted by the ECG sensors. This system can detect arrhythmia symptoms with more than 99% accuracy. A medical hub can be informed with some significant parameters which are processed and transmitted by the hand-held device using GPRS so that doctors can take necessary actions.

Several other wearable devices and technologies are available using which remote health care systems can be established. Smart textiles based frameworks are proposed in some articles [53–58] where bio-sensors are incorporated with the garments. A remote health care system can also comprise of some small nodes with wireless transmission capability (known as motes). Various researches [59–63] reports the efficiency and application of the mote based wireless sensor networks in remote healthcare. Motes creates a body area network (BAN) [64] that collects data about one or more than parameter and transmits it to a central hub. Some other real-time patient monitoring systems are discussed in [65]. In this work, a comprehensive collection of IoT based healthcare system is presented. Apart from this article also discusses about the fog computing based remote healthcare systems. A mobile and handheld devices based remote health monitoring system is designed in [66]. Four different parameters i.e. ECG, pulse rate, oxygen saturation, and the temperature of the body is monitored using a mobile application in IoT environment. In this work, the Arduino microcontroller is used. A comprehensive study on IoT based smart health care system is presented in [67, 68]. Different applications of the IoT based infrastructures in smart healthcare monitoring systems is presented in this work that is beneficial to understand the recent advancements in this field. A solution for smart and remote healthcare systems based on mobile edge computing is presented in [69]. In this work, internet of medical things environment is used to provide a smart healthcare solution. A multiclass edge computing solution is presented in [70]. This approach is a solution for the energy efficient smart healthcare systems. This approach is named as s-health and this approach is efficient enough to adopt according to specific applications or data. A comprehensive overview of the Z-wave based smart healthcare infrastructure is presented in [71–74].

In this work, a concept is presented to process biomedical image as a part of remote healthcare system using Z-Wave. Magnetoencephalography is used as a tool for demonstrating the concept of the biomedical image analysis framework coupled with home based wireless sensor network that can be implemented in reality. This work shows a new dimension to the remote health care industry by providing a concept of real-time biomedical image processing system.

3   Z-Wave Based Smart Homes and Their Application in Health Care

Smart home-based health care system is one of the emerging trends and has huge prospect in future. These types of systems are based on wireless networks and wearable devices that can take some input from the body. In case of biomedical imaging devices, it can continuously take images of different organs and sends it to the central hub or node. It can be beneficial in several situations like, wearable head-mounted devices can continuously scan the head and send some scanned images that can be useful to monitor head injuries and can predict different diseases like strokes and can provide quick response and treatment. Various applications of the smart home-based systems are found in the literature. In includes energy control and monitoring [75, 76], home control and automation [77], controlling and monitoring environmental issues [78], home area networks [40, 79], wireless device control [80, 81], integration and collaboration of different devices [82–86]. Smart home based frameworks also support some types of robots to perform different jobs [21, 87, 88].

3.1   Architecture and Illustration of the Monitoring System

Wearable biomedical imaging devices can scan different parts of the body but the most popular type of wearable scanning device is used for cognitive neuroscience. Several types of applications include MRI, functional neuro-imaging like magnetoencephalography etc. To illustrate the system, the magnetoencephalography based wearable system is considered. It helps in the understanding of the functional behavior of certain parts of the brain and the relationship with different segments [89].

3.2 Basics of Magnetoencephalography

Magnetoencephalography (abbreviated as MEG) is based on the magnetic fields those are generated in the brain due to the natural electrical activity of the brain. There are several applications of the MEG process starting from simple experiments to detect several abnormalities. It is based on the magneto meter that can sense the magnetic activity which is occurring in the brain [90].

To understand the MEG signals, we have to start from the basics of magnetism. Let the electric field E that has been generated due to the charge density ρ and the magnetic field B is generated by the movement of the charge. The current density is denoted by J. Now based on these parameters we have four Eqs. (1) to (4) namely Faraday's equation, the Ampere's circuital law including Maxwell's correction, Gauss's general law and Gauss's law for magnetism respectively.

$$\nabla X E = -\frac{\partial B}{\partial t} \tag{1}$$

$$\nabla X B = \mu_0 J + \mu_0 \varepsilon_0 \frac{\partial E}{\partial t} \tag{2}$$

$$\nabla \bullet E = \frac{\rho}{\varepsilon_0} \tag{3}$$

$$\nabla \bullet B = 0 \tag{4}$$

In the above equations, ε_0 denotes the permittivity of the free space and μ_0 denotes the magnetic permeability. These four equations are considered as the fundamental equations that describes functionality and the generation process of the electric and the magnetic fields from the charge and current density. The presence of the time derivatives in the above equations describes the fact that the magnetic field is generated from the varying electric field and electric field is generated from the varying magnetic field. These four basic equations can be used to form the equation that describes the propagation of electric and magnetic fields [91]. The propagation speed of these waves is similar to light. The electromagnetic wave equation is given in (5) and (6).

$$\left(v_{phase}^2 \nabla^2 - \frac{\partial^2}{\partial t^2} \right) E = 0 \tag{5}$$

$$\left(v_{phase}^2 \nabla^2 - \frac{\partial^2}{\partial t^2} \right) B = 0 \tag{6}$$

Here the term v_{phase} is the phase velocity which is given (7). It similar to the speed of light. The symbol ∇^2 denotes the Laplace operator.

$$v_{phase} = \frac{1}{\sqrt{\mu\varepsilon}} \tag{7}$$

This is the basic concept behind the MEG signals generated due to the electromagnetic activity in the brain which can be measured from outside of the brain. These waves are generated from the neuronal sources and propagates with the speed of light [89]. The wearable devices are helpful in detecting these changes (i.e. change in magnetic and electric fields) instantly because these devices are placed close to the head and the speed of these signals are very fast. It is beneficial over other methods like PET, MRI etc. because these methods depend on the change of the body fluids or other substances and give indirect response of the neuro-functions. Hence MEG signals are more prominent and give better results [92].

3.3 Basic Architecture of the Z-Wave

Z-Wave is one of the popular protocols which is generally used for wireless communication. It is widely applied in home automation systems. Z-Wave architecture is based on the mesh topology that uses radio waves to communicate among different appliances inside the home. It uses low energy radio waves and consumes very less power. It provides wireless control over various devices i.e. different mobile devices like smart phones, keyfobs (a kind of wireless keypad) and can be used to control several other devices remotely. It uses a Z-Wave gateway which acts as the central device that manages the data collected from the internal network and communicate with the outside world. Different systems support Z-Wave protocol that makes it suitable for various applications. This technology was developed by Zensys in 2001. The range of the operational frequency is 800–900 MHz and it uses part 15 ISM band for communication. It has near about 100 meters operational range.

One of the important features of the Z-Wave protocol is that it uses mesh topology. One device can communicate to another device directly if the second device is within the range. If the second device is out of the operational range then the first device can use one or more than one intermediate node to communicate with the desired device. Moreover, when a particular device is communicating with another device, it can send some control signal to other devices because one particular device is connected directly to all other devices. In 2016, a public version of the interoperability layer has been published that makes several things easier for the developers. Z-Wave uses Z/IP technology to transmit Z-Wave signals over IP network.

The Z-Wave protocol has been modified and a new upgraded protocol called Z-Wave Plus [93] is published in 2013. Z-Wave provides reliable communication and functional behavior that makes it suitable for used in several wireless devices and sensor-based communications. The Z-Wave provides a low-latency architecture that is helpful in wireless data transmission. It can transmit small data packets with the rate of transmission up to 100 kilo bits/second. IEEE 802.11 architecture (i.e. WiFi) is used to handle higher data rate. In contrast to that, Z-Wave can effectively control the communication among sensor-based devices with a throughput of 9.6 kilobits/second. The throughput is improved in new chips and it can be up to 40 kilobits/second. It uses Manchester channel encoding modulation technique and it has the capability to take four hops between any two nodes. The distance between two nodes must be within 30 meters. The underlying band (i.e. Part 15 ISM band) does not interfere with other standard technologies like Bluetooth, WiFi etc. The physical and media access control layers have been included in the G.9959 standard [94] by the international telecommunication union. Data rate can be 9600 bits per second and 40 kilobits per second. The output power can be 1 mW or 0 dBm.

Z-Wave uses source routing i.e. the sending station can partially or completely specify the route that should be followed by the packet. It is helpful for a certain node to explore all paths using which it can reach the host. So it uses a mesh network topology with source routing. It is based on the wireless ad-hoc network architecture i.e. it does not depend on the predefined network resources like switches or routers in a wired network. So, here the decision about selecting the node that forwards the data is made dynamically. It depends on the connectivity and the selection of the routing method. The advantage of these kind of systems is the robustness and less cost. There is no need to install huge infrastructure and single point failure can be recovered. The Z-Wave can transmit a data packet to a distance much greater than the range of the radio wave using the intermediate hops. But it can introduce some delay in the overall transmission.

For every Z-Wave network, one network id is assigned. Similarly, for every node, one node id is assigned. Network id consist of 32 bits and it is same for all nodes in a logical Z-Wave network. One node is assigned with a node id of length 8 bits and it must be unique inside a network.

Z-Wave technology tries to optimize the battery power by remaining in the power saving state. It only consumes the power from the battery when it needs to perform some function. Nodes in the mesh network exploits the walls of the house to reflect the signal so that less power is consumed to transmit a signal. The hardware chip that is used for Z-Wave is based on a microcontroller. The clock frequency of the internal system is 32 MHz. It uses a GisFSk transceiver for communication purposes that consumes 23 mA power and requires a power supply of 2.2–3.6 volts. It also provides AES-128 encryption mechanism and supports simultaneous listening. Nodes in the Z-Wave network provides efficient power management technologies that helps to increase the battery life. Z-wave can provide large battery life that can greatly enhance the performance of the overall system [95].

3.4 Evaluation of Z-Wave Based Biomedical Image Analysis Framework

Biomedical image analysis is considered as the necessary and sometimes inevitable step for various medical applications. Wearable devices can send continuous signals that can help to monitor several parameters. Conventional analog systems are very difficult to use in some situations where continuous monitoring is necessary. The major problem related with the conventional analog systems is the sensors are connected via wires to the analog monitoring devices. These systems are definitely not suitable for continuous monitoring at home. Analog equipment is not flexible due to the movement constraint. Moreover, sometimes it is necessary to communicate the images to the expert immediately so that physicians can take proper action. Analog systems are not suitable for data communication and storage. So, wireless networks can open a new dimension in the field of biomedical image analysis. It removes the barrier of the wires that restricts the home-based continuous monitoring.

Wireless sensor network provides a flexible solution to this problem. Remote health care and monitoring is possible by using some processing nodes that monitors and analyze the data transmitted by the sensor nodes. Wireless biomedical sensor network can be carried by the patient which facilitates the personalized health care and provides a scalable solution for the smart home-based biomedical image analysis. In addition to that, local signal processing methods are used to reduce the amount of data to be transmitted to the main processing node by selecting some important features from the captured data. It reduces the overhead of transmitting a huge amount of data to the central hub. Obviously, there is a tradeoff between the amount of data to be processed and the power consumed by the sensor node. Transmission of large amount of data consumes more power. Moreover, processing at sensor nodes also consumes more power. Hence, the decision is dependent on the designer and completely subjective.

To construct a wireless health care monitoring system, a network of the sensor nodes must be created. This type of network is called Wireless Body Area Network (WBAN) [96]. It is based on the Information and Communication Technologies that can sense and transmit some early stage data that can be helpful in preventing several diseases [97, 98]. Each node is used to sense different physiological data continuously. The major advantage of it is that it reduces the frequent visits to the doctors and save some precious time. It does not restrict the patient from performing their daily activities [99]. Intelligent systems can be developed to process and display accurate results [100] by analysis the collected information. This kind of monitoring systems have some promising scope in near future to construct efficient biomedical image analysis frameworks. These types of networks are completely based on the battery and hence the energy efficient network is desirable.

Z-Wave based wireless systems are emerging as one of the latest wireless standards that provides low power consumption, installation support for many nodes in a single network, longest open-air operational range that makes the Z-Wave technology suitable for home based smart health care monitoring systems.

3.5   Function of Sensor Nodes in Z-Wave

Sensor nodes play a vital role in acquiring data from different body parts in WBAN. Sensor nodes are responsible for capturing and processing different signals and images of different organs. Sensor nodes can perform some initial processing to reduce the amount of data by selecting important information and features from the collected data. Sensor nodes can transmit the reduced data to the central hub by any four transmission methods. Anycast, broadcast, multicast and unicast are the four modes of transmission that can be used to perform data transmission from sensor nodes. In case of unicasting method, data are transmitted to one node from another. It involves less traffic overhead and faster communication. But sometimes, unicasting may not be suitable. Then the multicasting or broadcasting methods can be selected. Broadcasting refers to the one to many communication methods. Multicasting can be one to many or many to many communications. In case of anycast communication, data are transmitted from a group of nodes to one of the nearest nodes.

In Z-Wave based transmission of MEG signals, MEG sensors sense the change in the magnetic field in the brain and forms the image. The sensors are called magnetometers and it can measure the very small change in the magnetic field (in the order of femotesla i.e. 10^{-15} tesla). The sensors are Superconducting Quantum Interference Devices. Therefore, it is also known as SQUID Magnetometers. These sensors are placed within the wearable helmet of the patient. It can continuously sense and form the images from the changing magnetic field. It is one of the non-invasive biomedical imaging method and Z-Wave based wireless network can make it more useful for the patients. Not only for MEGs, other wearable imaging methods can also take the advantages of smart Z-Wave based wireless sensor networks. One thing should be noted that in case of MEG, the experiment is performed in the magnetically shielded room. MEG is considered just for the sake of example and the assumption is that the experiment is performed in the magnetically shielded rooms only. Z-Wave based module transmits the signal to the nearest hub by finding the appropriate route. To find the appropriate route, various routing protocols are used [101]. Some of the popular methods are flat routing, hierarchical routing, location-based routing, negotiation-based routing, multipath based routing, query-based routing, QoS based routing, Coherent based routing etc. Here the first three methods i.e. flat routing, hierarchical routing and location-based routing depends on the structure of the network. Rest of the methods depends on the underlying protocol [101]. Periodic data are collected from the sensor unit and useful data are transmitted by the Z-Wave enabled node.

Z-Wave based nodes uses Radio Frequency (RF) technology for the communication purpose. RF technology helps to minimize the cost of installation and increase

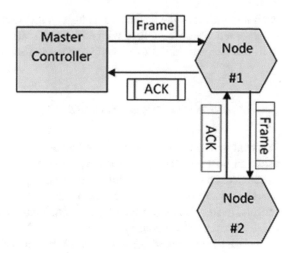

Fig. 1 Routed singlecast frame pattern

the communication flexibility [102]. Z-Wave can efficiently cover the whole room or area using the mesh topology that can use the walls, floors, and ceiling of the room to transmit and receive the control commands. Optimal route to the destination can be determined with the help of intermediate nodes in the mesh network. It can reach some node which is out of the radio range by using intermediate hops. Z-Wave uses an internet gateway that can be used to personalize the network and user can control and get the data from anywhere in the world. The general gateway that is used for this purpose is known as VERA.

There are two types of frames available in the routing layer. These frames types are applied when the data transmission is performed [102]. These two frame patterns are illustrated as follows:

Routed singlecast frame pattern: Here, single destination frame is used. It incorporates the acknowledgement packet that contains refined information. It is illustrated in Fig. 1.

Routed acknowledges frame pattern: In this method, no acknowledgement is transmitted back to the sending station. Here also, single destination frame is used.

4   Wireless Biomedical Image Analysis System Using Z-Wave

Modern diagnostic and health care industry is highly dependent on the non-invasive biomedical image analysis systems. Wireless sensors and constituting network is very much useful for acquiring data from different body parts. This process is highly dependent on the sensors that can acquire and effectively perform some initial processing and transmits it to the nearest hub. Several hospitals and medical research institutes can use these data to analyze and take useful decisions. Biomedical imaging sensors are equipped with embedded software, processing and transmission units that helps in initial processing and transmission of the collected information.

4.1 Biomedical Image Sensors

In recent years, wearable sensors gained popularity because these sensors are very useful in different scenarios and frequently used in many biomedical applications. Wireless sensors are very useful in constructing portable diagnostic tools. Biomedical images are can be collected from various body parts continuously using these sensors. In this discussion the MEG i.e. Magnetoencephalography is considered for the explanation of the concept.

In case of portable MEG sensors, patients can wear it in a helmet like device and allowed for free or natural movement of the head. For portable MEG image sensing purpose, quantum sensors are used that captures the magnetic activity of the brain and records the information. This technology allows imaging of the human brain by detecting the neural electromagnetic activity. These sensors can sense the signals and construct the 3-dimensional image of the human brain. Some superconducting sensors are used to place around the head to capture the weak magnetic fields which are in the range of femotesla. Optically pumped magneto meters are used as the magnetic field sensors. Now, the earth's magnetic field have a major impact on these sensors. The room is basically magnetically shielded but the residual magnetic field of the earth has significant impact on the optically pumped sensors. These sensors are consisting of 3 on-board coils. These coils are used to eliminate the static magnetic field in the cell. The change in the magnetic field can be detected using the change in the intensity of the transmitted light. Figure 2 is used to demonstrate the effect of the external magnetic field on the sensors [103].

The external magnetic field is quite large than the neuro-magnetic fields generated by the electrical activity in the human brain. To overcome this problem, field nullifying coils are used. Figure 3 demonstrates the placement of the field nullifying coils [103]. These coils are helpful in reducing the residual magnetic field of the earth so that the MEG sensors can accurately records the data. Coils are placed in both the sides of the object. The MEG contour map pattern is shown in Fig. 4 [104].

4.2 Biomedical Image Communication Using Z-Wave

Z-Wave based protocols can consist of two types of devices, one is controller and other one is slave. Controller devices send some command to the slaves for execution. Slave nodes generally does not equip with the routing table. It may contain a snapshot of the network which is nothing but the information about the network which serves like a map that helps to transmit the data in the network.

Fig. 2 Effect of the external magnetic field on the Optically Pumped Magnetometers sensors

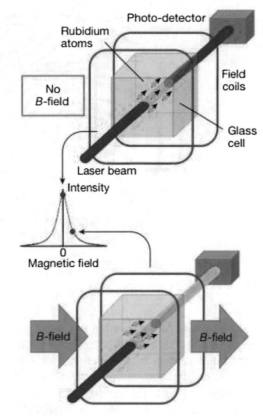

Fig. 3 Placement of the field nullifying coils

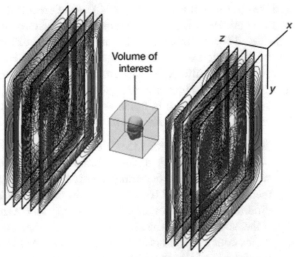

More than one controller can be used for better security and reliability but only one central controller takes care about the network topology [105]. So, the

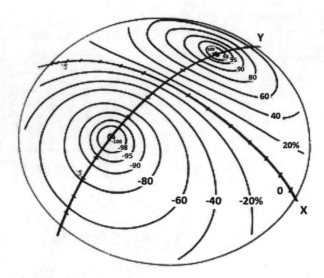

Fig. 4 The MEG contour map pattern

controllers can be classified in two ways such as primary and secondary. Primary controllers act as the administrator of the devices whereas secondary controllers decide the routing table based on the information obtained from the primary controllers. These controllers can determine the optimal path from the source to the destination by using the routing table. It also determines the hops required by a data packet to reach the destination. In standard Z-Wave network, the hop threshold is 5 and the optimal value of the hop is 2 [106]. Direct transmission is always preferable by the controllers. If the direct transmission is not possible, then the optimal path is considered for the transmission. The position of different devices must be optimal so that the efficiency of the system will be maximum. Optimization can be done with the help of different metaheuristic [1, 107–114] algorithms. Moreover, the load distribution should be done using efficient algorithms [115] for optimal results.

Z-Wave architecture is based on four broad layers as shown in Fig. 5 and the layers are described below in brief.

A. *Media Access Control (MAC) Layer:* The MAC layer is responsible for the radio frequency (RF) based communication. RF medium is controlled by the wireless equipment. Generally, controllers are completely independent of the RF medium. Figure 6 [116] gives an overview of the Z-Wave data transmission in different layers. In general, the encoding scheme that is used for the data stream is the Manchester encoding. Generally, the data stream is consisting of encoded digits, coherent signals and preamble. In the MAC layer, the data are fragmented into frames of length 8 bits each. These frames are forwarded in the network by the MAC layer. These data are coded and transmitted like a unidirectional flow of the electric charges

Fig. 5 Layered architecture of Z-Wave

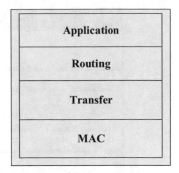

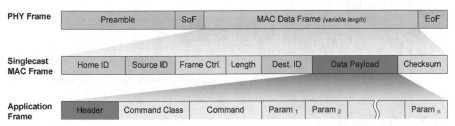

Fig. 6 Data in Z-Wave layers

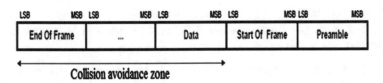

Fig. 7 Collision avoidance mechanism in Z-Wave

The MAC layer provides a collision avoidance mechanism. It increases the reliability of the total system by reducing the data loss. Transmission of the data is initiated only when the channel is vacant and there is no other competing nodes. It there is any other node(s) which is attempting to send data then, the data transmission is restrained and delayed for the random amount of time. It also provides data retransmission mechanism which is optional in nature. Retransmission method is based on the acknowledgements send by the receiver. One particular node can be in the receiving mode or in the sending mode. If a particular node is currently receiving data then there must be some delay before the data transmission by the same node [36]. The collision avoidance technique is somewhat complex for the wireless networks. Figure 7 [36] demonstrates the collision avoidance technique.

B. *Transfer Layer:* This layer acts like an administrator of two sequential nodes. It monitors retransmission, error detection, connection related issues, acknowledgement services and the error free transmission of the data. This layer contains four basic formats of the frames. These formats are used to transmit different commands of the Z-Wave in a wireless network. The four types of frames are: (i)

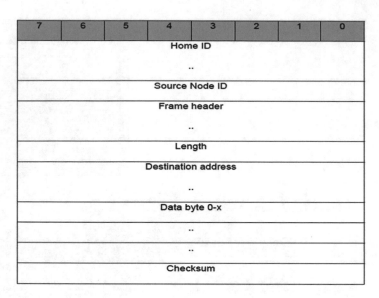

7	6	5	4	3	2	1	0
Home ID							
..							
Source Node ID							
Frame header							
..							
Length							
Destination address							
..							
Data byte 0-x							
..							
..							
Checksum							

Fig. 8 Z-Wave frame format

Singlecast frame pattern, (ii) Transfer acknowledge frame pattern, (iii) Multicast frame pattern, (iv) Broadcast frame pattern. Figure 8 [102] shows the basic frame pattern in this layer.

(i) Singlecast frame pattern: In this case, the frames are transmitted to the single host only. After receiving a frame, the recipient sends an acknowledgement to the sender. If the acknowledgement is not received by the sender then the sender retransmit the frame. To avoid the collision, sender waits for some time and then retransmit the frame again.

(ii) Transfer acknowledge frame pattern: It is one of the singlecast frame pattern where the frame may not be transmitted with the acknowledgement service.

(iii) Multicast frame pattern: It is one kind of one-to-many communication. One device can send a frame to many devices. No acknowledgement is returned to the sender. Hence it cannot be used for reliable communication. To achieve reliability, one singlecast frame is transmitted.

(iv) Broadcast frame pattern: In this type of frame pattern, the broadcasted frame is received by the devices in the home area network (HAN). No acknowledgement is used in this case and hence, to achieve reliability, we need to transmit single cast frames following the broadcast frames

C. *Routing Layer:* The main job of this layer is to forward the frames. It helps in the communication throughout the Z-Wave based network. It helps to forward frames from one node to another. Forwarding procedure involves the controller and slave nodes where these nodes are placed at certain positions.

    Routing layer is also responsible for accumulating various information from different nodes which are used to construct and maintain the routing table at the primary controller. This information is helpful in determining the optimal path from source to destination. It is not a very easy task because of the movement of the nodes. Primary controller takes all the responsibility and route the packet using the best possible path.

D. *Application Layer:* This layer provides a mechanism using which the users and other devices can communicate with the Z-Wave network. It receives and distributes the payload, decodes and executes different commands using the received parameters and performs some other tasks. The frame pattern of the application layer can be visualized from the Fig. 6. Application commands helps to interact other devices and perform different functions.

4.3 Personalized Healthcare Systems Using Z-Wave Based WSN

Personalized home-based health monitoring systems are very effective to prevent different diseases. Personalized health care systems includes ECG monitoring, blood pressure monitoring, continuous image analysis etc. [117]. Wireless sensor networks can be very helpful in this context. WSN can communicate data from one node to another without the help of any wires. Hence, the patients can be monitored from their homes and need not to be admitted in the hospitals because of the early signals. Various researches are going on to improve the home based health monitoring systems [118, 119]. Different technologies are available that can be used to transmit data in WSN. Some of the popular technologies are Bluetooth, Z-Wave, Zigbee, Radio-frequency identification (RFID), WiFi etc. Comparison of Z-Wave with some other standard technologies are given in Table 1.

    Z-Wave is one of the major competitors of Zigbee protocol. Z-Wave based wireless networks have several advantages. Z-Wave based systems are inexpensive, scalable and battery efficient. It can cover up to 100 meters without any obstruction. None of the standard wireless methods can reach more than 100 meters. It possesses low latency which reduces the bottleneck. One of the major drawbacks of using Z-wave is the number of nodes that can be connected is lower than the zigbee network which limits the large-scale implementation.

    One of the foremost advantages of Z-Wave technology is its backward compatibility. This feature is not there in Zigbee. All of the older versions are compatible to the newer ones which is a great advantage from the users' point of view. Z-Wave is equipped with AES encryption method which provides a secure and reliable connectivity [120]. Security can also be imposed and evaluated on the image explicitly [121–128]. Although the Bluetooth technology is energy efficient and gives better performance in terms of interference than Zigbee, WiFi and Z-Wave. But it cannot be used in congested areas. Hence it is not applicable in clinical applications. The data rate of the Z-Wave protocol is lesser than the Zigbee. It is another issue associated with the Z-Wave protocol. But, due to several advantages (as discussed earlier), Z-Wave is adapted in this work as one of the reliable protocols for smart wireless image analysis systems.

4.4 Biomedical Image Processing Method

The image processing algorithm is one of the most important part and should be designed carefully. The image processing algorithm should be optimized in such a way so that it can take optimum power and provide accurate results in a timely manner. Some of the recently developed biomedical image analysis algorithms are [129–131]. Stipulated resources make the scenario harder because complex image analysis algorithms may not be suitable in these kinds of framework. Moreover, the image preprocessing, feature extraction, classification and other required modules of the image analysis framework should be optimized and tested to get better performance. Medical image analysis algorithm should take care about the modality, noise present in the image, scale, zoom and other features, otherwise the model can deliver erroneous results. Therefore, careful investigation is required before deploying any method for real life implementation otherwise it can produce some drastic side effects to the health of the patient such as, wrong treatment can lead to many issues including death. Moreover, it can reduce the faith on the automated healthcare systems.

5 Challenges and Future Works

There is several healthcare equipment which are available and frequently used with both wired and wireless technologies. One of the major problems associated with these devices is the compatibility related issues. Moreover, those devices that uses cables or some guided media for communication are generally not easily portable. So, the systems based on the wired connections are not useful in most of the situations specifically when the home-based smart health care systems are to be implemented.

Z-Wave provides the advantage of using wireless sensor networks and provides a feasible way to communicate with different devices that makes the system portable and helps in establishing a low-power, home based healthcare monitoring system. It is reliable and can be used for continuous monitoring of different parameters associated with patients where patients can pursue their regular jobs or can stay in their comfort zone. Z-Wave based networks can be simply installed and the devices or nodes can be easily added and removed. Remote control over the network makes the data collection and analysis easier. This technology provides affordable solutions for various other healthcare systems. Interoperability is one of the major advantage of the Z-Wave based systems. Different devices can be connected in IoT domain using Z-Wave and their computational power can be exploited. Z-Wave uses AES-128 bits encryption for its security. It requires previous knowledge to prevent unauthorized access. It works on radio frequency and can be accessed by anyone from anywhere. Moreover, the number of nodes (i.e. 232) that can be connected are much lesser than the Zigbee networks. The data transmission speed is also lesser than the Zigbee network.

The operational band (i.e. 915 MHz ISM band and 868 MHz RFID band) of the Z-Wave provides a wider range of communication than other competitive protocols. The use of sub-GHz band improves the reliability and suffers with less interference. The data rate is not very satisfactory for Z-Wave protocol. Moreover, the spectrum efficiency is also not up to the mark. It is due to the GFSK modulation technique. But the latest version of the Z-Wave technology provides a data rate of 100 kbps. Although the maximum number of nodes that can be connected to the Z-Wave network is 232 but the different manufacturers recommend to restrict this number up to 40–50 nodes. This is quite a small number but it can be applied for wireless home-based biomedical image processing network.

6 Conclusion

This article is illustrating and investigating the huge potential associated with the home-based health care systems which can provide the affordable health care solutions to many people at the comfort of their homes. Lots of possibility can be observed and there is a good scope of research and development in this field. This field is a part of the smart home-based health care which needs to be investigated more deeply so that reliable infrastructure can be developed which will help the whole mankind. Moreover, this concept can be extended to the home-based signal processing which can be used to process different signal like ECG, EEG etc. Deployment of different processing nodes and the load distribution is crucial and should done using efficient algorithms. Cloud based architectures can be used for faster data storage and processing. Development of the faster, reliable and secure home-based health care infrastructure is the prime objective of this work. Since this article is not intended for proposing a new image analysis algorithm, authors give only the conceptual overview of the system. The proposed Z-Wave based framework can bring a new paradigm in IoT based health care and will be highly beneficial for remote biomedical image analysis.

References

1. Roy M, Chakraborty S, Mali K, et al (2017) Biomedical image enhancement based on modified Cuckoo Search and morphology. In: 2017 8th Annual Industrial Automation and

Electromechanical Engineering Conference (IEMECON). IEEE, pp 230–235

2. Hore S, Chakroborty S, Ashour AS, et al (2015) Finding Contours of Hippocampus Brain Cell Using Microscopic Image Analysis. J Adv Microsc Res 10:93–103. https://doi.org/10.1166/jamr.2015.1245

3. Chakraborty S, Chatterjee S, Dey N, et al (2017) Modified cuckoo search algorithm in microscopic image segmentation of hippocampus. Microsc Res Tech 80:. https://doi.org/10.1002/jemt.22900

4. Chakraborty S, Chatterjee S, Dey N, et al (2017) Gradient approximation in retinal blood vessel segmentation. In: 2017 4th IEEE Uttar Pradesh Section International Conference on Electrical, Computer and Electronics (UPCON). IEEE, pp 618–623

5. Chakraborty S, Mali K, Chatterjee S, et al (2017) An integrated method for automated biomedical image segmentation. In: 2017 4th International Conference on Opto-Electronics and Applied Optics (Optronix). IEEE, pp 1–5

6. Chakraborty S, Chatterjee S, Ashour AS, et al (2017) Intelligent Computing in Medical Imaging: A Study. In: Dey N (ed) Advancements in Applied Metaheuristic Computing. IGI Global, pp 143–163

7. Chakraborty S, Roy M, Hore S (2016) A Study on Different Edge Detection Techniques in Digital Image Processing. In: Feature Detectors and Motion Detection in Video Processing. IGI Global, pp 100–122

8. Hore S, Chakraborty S, Chatterjee S, et al (2016) An Integrated Interactive Technique for Image Segmentation using Stack based Seeded Region Growing and Thresholding. Int J Electr Comput Eng 6:2773–2780. https://doi.org/10.11591/ijece.v6i6.11801

9. Chakraborty S, Mali K, Banerjee S, et al (2017) Bag-of-features based classification of dermoscopic images. In: 2017 4th International Conference on Opto-Electronics and Applied Optics (Optronix). IEEE, pp 1–6

10. Chakraborty S, Raman A, Sen S, et al (2019) Contrast Optimization using Elitist Metaheuristic Optimization and Gradient Approximation for Biomedical Image Enhancement. In: 2019 Amity International Conference on Artificial Intelligence (AICAI). IEEE, pp 712–717

11. Chakraborty S, Chatterjee S, Chatterjee A, et al (2018) Automated Breast Cancer Identification by analyzing Histology Slides using Metaheuristic Supported Supervised Classification coupled with Bag-of-Features. In: 2018 Fourth International Conference on Research in Computational Intelligence and Communication Networks (ICRCICN). IEEE, pp 81–86

12. Wiemer J, Schubert F, Granzow M, et al (2003) Informatics united: Exemplary studies combining medical informatics, neuroinformatics and bioinformatics. In: Methods of Information in Medicine. pp 126–133

13. Hore S, Chakraborty S, Chatterjee S, et al (2016) An integrated interactive technique for image segmentation using stack based seeded region growing and thresholding. Int J Electr Comput Eng 6:. https://doi.org/10.11591/ijece.v6i6.11801

14. Chakraborty S, Chatterjee S, Dey N, et al (2018) Gradient approximation in retinal blood vessel segmentation. In: 2017 4th IEEE Uttar Pradesh Section International Conference on Electrical, Computer and Electronics, UPCON 2017

15. Roy M, Chakraborty S, Mali K, et al (2017) Biomedical image enhancement based on modified Cuckoo Search and morphology. In: 2017 8th Annual Industrial Automation and Electromechanical Engineering Conference (IEMECON). IEEE, pp 230–235

16. Chakraborty S, Mali K, Chatterjee S, et al (2017) Detection of skin disease using metaheuristic supported artificial neural networks. In: 2017 8th Annual Industrial Automation and Electromechanical Engineering Conference (IEMECON). IEEE, pp 224–229

17. Chakraborty S, Mali K, Chatterjee S, et al (2017) Image based skin disease detection using hybrid neural network coupled bag-of-features. In: 2017 IEEE 8th Annual Ubiquitous Computing, Electronics and Mobile Communication Conference (UEMCON). IEEE, pp 242–246

18. Roy M, Chakraborty S, Mali K, et al (2017) Cellular image processing using morphological analysis. In: 2017 IEEE 8th Annual Ubiquitous Computing, Electronics and Mobile Communication Conference (UEMCON). IEEE, pp 237–241
19. Roy M, Chakraborty S, Mali K, et al (2017) Biomedical image enhancement based on modified Cuckoo Search and morphology. In: 2017 8th Industrial Automation and Electromechanical Engineering Conference, IEMECON 2017
20. Chakraborty S, Mali K, Chatterjee S, et al (2018) Bio-medical image enhancement using hybrid metaheuristic coupled soft computing tools. In: 2017 IEEE 8th Annual Ubiquitous Computing, Electronics and Mobile Communication Conference, UEMCON 2017
21. Chakraborty S, Mali K (2018) Application of Multiobjective Optimization Techniques in Biomedical Image Segmentation – A Study. In: Multi-Objective Optimization. Springer Singapore, Singapore, pp. 181–194
22. Hore S, Chatterjee S, Chakraborty S, Shaw RK Analysis of Different Feature Description Algorithm in object Recognition. pp 66–99
23. Chakraborty S, Roy M, Hore S (2018) A study on different edge detection techniques in digital image processing
24. Chakraborty S, Roy M, Hore S (2016) A study on different edge detection techniques in digital image processing
25. Ritter F, Boskamp T, Homeyer A, et al (2011) Medical image analysis. IEEE Pulse 2:60–70. https://doi.org/10.1109/MPUL.2011.942929
26. Dey N, Ashour AS, Shi F, et al (2017) Developing residential wireless sensor networks for ECG healthcare monitoring. IEEE Trans Consum Electron 63:442–449. https://doi.org/10.1109/TCE.2017.015063
27. Chakraborty S, Mali K, Chatterjee S, et al (2018) Dermatological effect of UV rays owing to ozone layer depletion. In: 2017 4th International Conference on Opto-Electronics and Applied Optics, Optronix 2017
28. Chakraborty S, Mali K, Banerjee S, et al (2018) Bag-of-features based classification of dermoscopic images. In: 2017 4th International Conference on Opto-Electronics and Applied Optics, Optronix 2017
29. How Wearable Devices Are Changing the Paradigm of Medical Imaging? – QuEST Global. https://www.quest-global.com/how-wearable-devices-are-changing-the-paradigm-of-medical-imaging/. Accessed 27 Apr 2018
30. Rodgers MM, Pai VM, Conroy RS (2015) Recent Advances in Wearable Sensors for Health Monitoring. IEEE Sens J 15:3119–3126. https://doi.org/10.1109/JSEN.2014.2357257
31. Datta S, Chakraborty S, Mali K, et al (2017) Optimal usage of pessimistic association rules in cost effective decision making. In: 2017 4th International Conference on Opto-Electronics and Applied Optics (Optronix). IEEE, pp 1–5
32. Microsoft HoloLens | The leader in mixed reality technology. https://www.microsoft.com/en-us/hololens. Accessed 27 Apr 2018
33. Glass. https://x.company/glass/. Accessed 27 Apr 2018
34. Frantz T, Jansen B, Duerinck J, Vandemeulebroucke J (2018) Augmenting Microsoft's HoloLens with vuforia tracking for neuronavigation. Healthc Technol Lett 5:221–225. https://doi.org/10.1049/htl.2018.5079
35. Wei NJ, Dougherty B, Myers A, Badawy SM (2018) Using Google Glass in Surgical Settings: Systematic Review. JMIR mHealth uHealth 6:e54. https://doi.org/10.2196/mhealth.9409
36. Dougherty B, Badawy SM (2017) Using Google Glass in Nonsurgical Medical Settings: Systematic Review. JMIR mHealth uHealth 5:e159. https://doi.org/10.2196/MHEALTH.8671
37. Sahyouni R, Moshtaghi O, Tran D, et al (2017) Assessment of google glass as an adjunct in neurological surgery. Surg Neurol Int 8:68. https://doi.org/10.4103/sni.sni_277_16
38. REGULATION (EU) 2017/745 OF THE EUROPEAN PARLIAMENT AND OF THE COUNCIL of 5 April 2017 on medical devices, amending Directive 2001/83/EC, Regulation (EC) No 178/2002 and Regulation (EC) No 1223/2009 and repealing Council Directives 90/385/EEC and 93/42/EEC

39. Ghamari M, Janko B, Sherratt R, et al (2016) A Survey on Wireless Body Area Networks for eHealthcare Systems in Residential Environments. Sensors 16:831. https://doi.org/10.3390/s16060831
40. Hui TKL, Sherratt RS, Sánchez DD (2017) Major requirements for building Smart Homes in Smart Cities based on Internet of Things technologies. Futur Gener Comput Syst 76:358–369. https://doi.org/10.1016/j.future.2016.10.026
41. Understanding Zigbee and Z-Wave Standards. https://www.reviews.com/blog/zigbee-vs-z-wave-guide/. Accessed 14 Jun 2019
42. Z-Wave vs Zigbee vs Bluetooth vs WiFi 2016 | Inovelli. https://inovelli.com/z-wave-vs-zigbee-vs-bluetooth-vs-wifi-smart-home-technology/. Accessed 3 May 2018
43. What is Z-Wave and How Does it Work? | Safety.com. https://www.safety.com/z-wave/. Accessed 4 May 2019
44. Z-Wave Alliance. https://z-wavealliance.org/. Accessed 4 May 2019
45. Gomez C, Oller J, Paradells J, et al (2012) Overview and Evaluation of Bluetooth Low Energy: An Emerging Low-Power Wireless Technology. Sensors 12:11734–11753. https://doi.org/10.3390/s120911734
46. Sung M, Marci C, Pentland A (2005) Wearable feedback systems for rehabilitation. J Neuroeng Rehabil 2:17. https://doi.org/10.1186/1743-0003-2-17
47. Anliker U, Ward JA, Lukowicz P, et al (2004) AMON: A Wearable Multiparameter Medical Monitoring and Alert System. IEEE Trans Inf Technol Biomed 8:415–427. https://doi.org/10.1109/TITB.2004.837888
48. Lin B-S, Lin B-S, Chou N-K, et al (2006) RTWPMS: A Real-Time Wireless Physiological Monitoring System. IEEE Trans Inf Technol Biomed 10:647–656. https://doi.org/10.1109/TITB.2006.874194
49. Mundt CW, Montgomery KN, Udoh UE, et al (2005) A Multiparameter Wearable Physiologic Monitoring System for Space and Terrestrial Applications. IEEE Trans Inf Technol Biomed 9:382–391. https://doi.org/10.1109/TITB.2005.854509
50. Zhanpeng Jin, Oresko J, Shimeng Huang, Cheng AC (2009) HeartToGo: A Personalized medicine technology for cardiovascular disease prevention and detection. In: 2009 IEEE/NIH Life Science Systems and Applications Workshop. IEEE, pp 80–83
51. Moron MJ, Luque JR, Botella AA, et al (2007) J2ME and smart phones as platform for a Bluetooth Body Area Network for Patient-telemonitoring. In: 2007 29th Annual International Conference of the IEEE Engineering in Medicine and Biology Society. IEEE, pp 2791–2794
52. Guo L, Chen Z, Zhang D, et al (2020) Age-of-information-constrained Transmission Optimization for ECG-based Body Sensor Networks. IEEE Internet Things J 1–1. https://doi.org/10.1109/jiot.2020.3025543
53. Habetha J (2006) The myheart project – Fighting cardiovascular diseases by prevention and early diagnosis. In: 2006 International Conference of the IEEE Engineering in Medicine and Biology Society. IEEE, pp 6746–6749
54. Luprano J, Sola J, Dasen S, et al (2006) Combination of Body Sensor Networks and On-Body Signal Processing Algorithms: the practical case of MyHeart project
55. Pacelli M, Loriga G, Taccini N, Paradiso R (2006) Sensing Fabrics for Monitoring Physiological and Biomechanical Variables: E-textile solutions. In: 2006 3rd IEEE/EMBS International Summer School on Medical Devices and Biosensors. IEEE, pp 1–4
56. Lymberis A, Paradiso R (2008) Smart fabrics and interactive textile enabling wearable personal applications: R&D state of the art and future challenges. In: 2008 30th Annual International Conference of the IEEE Engineering in Medicine and Biology Society. IEEE, pp 5270–5273

57. Scilingo EP, Gemignani A, Paradiso R, et al (2005) Performance Evaluation of Sensing Fabrics for Monitoring Physiological and Biomechanical Variables. IEEE Trans Inf Technol Biomed 9:. https://doi.org/10.1109/TITB.2005.854506
58. Pandian PS, Mohanavelu K, Safeer KP, et al (2008) Smart Vest: Wearable multi-parameter remote physiological monitoring system. Med Eng Phys 30:466–477. https://doi.org/10.1016/J.MEDENGPHY.2007.05.014
59. Milenković A, Otto C, Jovanov E (2006) Wireless sensor networks for personal health monitoring: Issues and an implementation. Comput Commun 29:2521–2533. https://doi.org/10.1016/J.COMCOM.2006.02.011
60. Montón E, Hernandez JF, Blasco JM, et al (2008) Body area network for wireless patient monitoring. IET Commun 2:215. https://doi.org/10.1049/iet-com:20070046
61. Wan-Young Chung, Young-Dong Lee, Sang-Joong Jung (2008) A wireless sensor network compatible wearable u-healthcare monitoring system using integrated ECG, accelerometer and SpO2. In: 2008 30th Annual International Conference of the IEEE Engineering in Medicine and Biology Society. IEEE, pp 1529–1532
62. Farella E, Pieracci A, Benini L, et al (2008) Interfacing human and computer with wireless body area sensor networks: the WiMoCA solution. Multimed Tools Appl 38:337–363. https://doi.org/10.1007/s11042-007-0189-5
63. Loew N, Winzer K-J, Becher G, et al (2007) Medical Sensors of the BASUMA Body Sensor Network. In: 4th International Workshop on Wearable and Implantable Body Sensor Networks (BSN 2007). Springer Berlin Heidelberg, Berlin, Heidelberg, pp 171–176
64. Hao Y, Foster R (2008) Wireless body sensor networks for health-monitoring applications. Physiol Meas 29:R27–R56. https://doi.org/10.1088/0967-3334/29/11/R01
65. Chaudhury S, Roy S, Agarwal I, Ray N (2020) Real-time processing and monitoring in health care. In: EAI/Springer Innovations in Communication and Computing. Springer Science and Business Media Deutschland GmbH, pp 99–116
66. Al-Sheikh MA, Ameen IA (2020) Design of Mobile Healthcare Monitoring System Using IoT Technology and Cloud Computing. In: IOP Conference Series: Materials Science and Engineering. Institute of Physics Publishing, p 012113
67. Neranjan Thilakarathne N, Krishna Kagita M, Reddy Gadekallu T The Role of the Internet of Things in Health Care: A Systematic and Comprehensive Study. Int J Eng Manag Res. https://doi.org/10.31033/ijemr.10.4.22
68. Kadhim KT, Alsahlany AM, Wadi SM, Kadhum HT (2020) An Overview of Patient's Health Status Monitoring System Based on Internet of Things (IoT). Wirel. Pers. Commun. 114:2235–2262
69. Dong P, Ning Z, Obaidat MS, et al (2020) Edge Computing Based Healthcare Systems: Enabling Decentralized Health Monitoring in Internet of Medical Things. IEEE Netw 34:254–261. https://doi.org/10.1109/MNET.011.1900636
70. Abdellatif AA, Mohamed A, Chiasserini CF, et al (2020) Edge computing for energy-efficient smart health systems. In: Energy Efficiency of Medical Devices and Healthcare Applications. Elsevier, pp 53–67
71. Pateraki M, Fysarakis K, Sakkalis V, et al (2020) Biosensors and Internet of Things in smart healthcare applications: challenges and opportunities. In: Wearable and Implantable Medical Devices. Elsevier, pp 25–53
72. Alhussein M, Muhammad G, Hossain MS, Amin SU (2018) Cognitive IoT-Cloud Integration for Smart Healthcare: Case Study for Epileptic Seizure Detection and Monitoring. Mob Networks Appl 23:1624–1635. https://doi.org/10.1007/s11036-018-1113-0
73. Saha HN, Mandal A, Sinha A (2017) Recent trends in the Internet of Things. In: 2017 IEEE 7th Annual Computing and Communication Workshop and Conference, CCWC 2017. Institute of Electrical and Electronics Engineers Inc.
74. Gardašević G, Katzis K, Bajić D, Berbakov L (2020) Emerging Wireless Sensor Networks and Internet of Things Technologies – Foundations of Smart Healthcare. Sensors 20:3619. https://doi.org/10.3390/s20133619

75. Han J, Choi C, Park W, et al (2014) Smart home energy management system including renewable energy based on ZigBee and PLC. IEEE Trans Consum Electron 60:198–202. https://doi.org/10.1109/TCE.2014.6851994

76. Han D-M, Lim J-H (2010) Design and implementation of smart home energy management systems based on zigbee. IEEE Trans Consum Electron 56:1417–1425. https://doi.org/10.1109/TCE.2010.5606278

77. Kushiro N, Higuma T, Nakata M, et al (2007) Practical solution for constructing ubiquitous network in building and home control system. IEEE Trans Consum Electron 53:1387–1392. https://doi.org/10.1109/TCE.2007.4429228

78. Byun J, Jeon B, Noh J, et al (2012) An intelligent self-adjusting sensor for smart home services based on ZigBee communications. IEEE Trans Consum Electron 58:794–802. https://doi.org/10.1109/TCE.2012.6311320

79. Costa LCP, Almeida NS, Correa AGD, et al (2013) Accessible display design to control home area networks. IEEE Trans. Consum. Electron. 59:422–427

80. Zualkernan IA, Al-Ali AR, Jabbar MA, et al (2009) InfoPods: Zigbee-based remote information monitoring devices for smart-homes. IEEE Trans Consum Electron 55:1221–1226. https://doi.org/10.1109/TCE.2009.5277979

81. Sleman A, Moeller R (2011) SOA distributed operating system for managing embedded devices in home and building automation. IEEE Trans Consum Electron 57:945–952. https://doi.org/10.1109/TCE.2011.5955244

82. Ramli AR, Leong CY, Perumal T (2011) Interoperability framework for smart home systems. IEEE Trans Consum Electron 57:1607–1611. https://doi.org/10.1109/TCE.2011.6131132

83. Park H, Lee I, Hwang T, Kim N (2008) Architecture of home gateway for device collaboration in extended home space. IEEE Trans Consum Electron 54:1692–1697. https://doi.org/10.1109/TCE.2008.4711222

84. Chakraborty S, Chatterjee S, Mali K (2020) An optimized intelligent dermatologic disease classification framework based on IoT. In: Advances in Intelligent Systems and Computing. Springer, pp 131–151

85. Chakraborty S, Mali K (2020) An Overview of Biomedical Image Analysis From the Deep Learning Perspective. In: Chakraborty S, Mali K (eds) Applications of Advanced Machine Intelligence in Computer Vision and Object Recognition: Emerging Research and Opportunities. IGI Global

86. Chakraborty S (2020) An Advanced Approach to Detect Edges of Digital Images for Image Segmentation. In: Chakraborty S, Mali K (eds) Applications of Advanced Machine Intelligence in Computer Vision and Object Recognition: Emerging Research and Opportunities. IGI GLobal

87. Kim K, Cha YS, Park JM, et al (2011) Providing services using network-based humanoids in a home environment. IEEE Trans Consum Electron 57:1628–1636. https://doi.org/10.1109/TCE.2011.6131135

88. Roy M, Chakraborty S, Mali K (2020) A Robust Image Encryption Method Using Chaotic Skew-Tent Map. In: Chakraborty S, Mali K (eds) Applications of Advanced Machine Intelligence in Computer Vision and Object Recognition: Emerging Research and Opportunities

89. Hämäläinen M, Hari R, Ilmoniemi RJ, et al (1993) Magnetoencephalography – theory, instrumentation, and applications to noninvasive studies of the working human brain. Rev Mod Phys 65:413–497. https://doi.org/10.1103/RevModPhys.65.413

90. Ioannides AA (2009) Magnetoencephalography (MEG). Methods Mol Biol 489:167–188. https://doi.org/10.1007/978-1-59745-543-5_8

91. Mellinger J, Schalk G, Braun C, et al (2007) An MEG-based brain-computer interface (BCI). Neuroimage 36:581–593. https://doi.org/10.1016/j.neuroimage.2007.03.019

92. Cichocki A, Sanei S (2007) EEG/MEG signal processing. Comput. Intell. Neurosci. 2007

93. Z-Wave Plus™ Certification – Z-Wave Alliance. https://z-wavealliance.org/z-wave_plus_certification/. Accessed 5 May 2019

94. G.9959: Short range narrow-band digital radiocommunication transceivers – PHY, MAC, SAR and LLC layer specifications. https://www.itu.int/rec/T-REC-G.9959. Accessed 5 May 2019

95. Wei C-C, Chen Y-M, Chang C-C, Yu C-H (2015) The Implementation of Smart Electronic Locking System Based on Z-Wave and Internet. In: 2015 IEEE International Conference on Systems, Man, and Cybernetics. IEEE, pp 2015–2017

96. Ghamari M, Janko B, Sherratt R, et al (2016) A Survey on Wireless Body Area Networks for eHealthcare Systems in Residential Environments. Sensors 16:831. https://doi.org/10.3390/s16060831

97. Fouad H (2014) Continuous Health-monitoring for early Detection of Patient by Web Telemedicine System. https://doi.org/10.13140/2.1.3495.1041

98. Jara AJ, Zamora-Izquierdo MA, Gomez-Skarmeta AF (2009) An Ambient Assisted Living System for Telemedicine with Detection of Symptoms. Springer, Berlin, Heidelberg, pp. 75–84

99. Bradai N, Chaari L, and LK-IJ of E-H, 2011 undefined A comprehensive overview of wireless body area networks (WBAn). igi-global.com

100. GK R, Engineering KB-P, 2012 undefined A survey on futuristic health care system: WBANs. Elsevier

101. Al-Karaki J, communications AK-I wireless, 2004 undefined Routing techniques in wireless sensor networks: a survey. ieeexplore.ieee.org

102. Yassein M, Mardini W, (ICEMIS) AK-E& M, 2016 undefined Smart homes automation using Z-wave protocol. ieeexplore.ieee.org

103. Boto E, Holmes N, Leggett J, et al (2018) Moving magnetoencephalography towards real-world applications with a wearable system. Nature 555:657–661. https://doi.org/10.1038/nature26147

104. Cohen D, Halgren E (2003) Magnetoencephalography (Neuromagnetism). Encycl Neurosci 3rd:1–7

105. Khamayseh Y, Mardini W, ... SA-IJ of, 2015 undefined Integration of wireless technologies in Smart University Campus environment: framework architecture. igi-global.com

106. Paetz C (2015) Z-Wave Basics

107. Chakraborty S, Bhowmik S (2013) Job Shop Scheduling using Simulated Annealing. In: First International Conference on Computation and Communication Advancement. McGrawHill Publication, pp 69–73

108. Chakraborty S, Bhowmik S (2015) Blending roulette wheel selection with simulated annealing for job shop scheduling problem. In: Michael Faraday IET International Summit 2015. Institution of Engineering and Technology, pp 100 (7 .)-100 (7.)

109. Chakraborty S, Mali K, Chatterjee S, et al (2017) Detection of skin disease using meta-heuristic supported artificial neural networks. In: 2017 8th Industrial Automation and Electromechanical Engineering Conference, IEMECON 2017. pp. 224–229

110. Chakraborty S, Mali K, Chatterjee S, et al (2017) Image based skin disease detection using hybrid neural network coupled bag-of-features. In: 2017 IEEE 8th Annual Ubiquitous Computing, Electronics and Mobile Communication Conference (UEMCON). IEEE, pp 242–246

111. Chakraborty S, Mali K, Chatterjee S, et al (2017) Bio-medical image enhancement using hybrid metaheuristic coupled soft computing tools. In: 2017 IEEE 8th Annual Ubiquitous Computing, Electronics and Mobile Communication Conference (UEMCON). IEEE, pp 231–236

112. Chakraborty S, Seal A, Roy M (2015) An Elitist Model for Obtaining Alignment of Multiple Sequences using Genetic Algorithm. In: 2nd National Conference NCETAS 2015. International Journal of Innovative Research in Science, Engineering and Technology, pp 61–67

113. Chakraborty S, Chatterjee S, Dey N, et al (2017) Modified cuckoo search algorithm in microscopic image segmentation of hippocampus. Microsc Res Tech 1–22. https://doi.org/10.1002/jemt.22900

114. Chakraborty S, Bhowmik S (2015) An Efficient Approach to Job Shop Scheduling Problem using Simulated Annealing. Int J Hybrid Inf Technol 8:273–284. https://doi.org/10.14257/ijhit.2015.8.11.23

115. Sarddar D, Chakraborty S, Roy M (2015) An Efficient Approach to Calculate Dynamic Time Quantum in Round Robin Algorithm for Efficient Load Balancing. Int J Comput Appl 123:48–52. https://doi.org/10.5120/ijca2015905701

116. Fouladi B, Ghanoun S (2013) Security Evaluation of the Z-Wave Wireless Protocol. Black hat 6

117. Hung C, Bai Y, Consumer RT-IT on, 2012 undefined Design of blood pressure measurement with a health management system for the aged. ieeexplore.ieee.org

118. Kim K, Shin S, Suh J, et al Home healthcare self-monitoring system for chronic diseases. ieeexplore.ieee.org

119. Tung H, Tsang K, ... HT-IT on, 2013 undefined The design of dual radio ZigBee homecare gateway for remote patient monitoring. ieeexplore.ieee.org

120. Knight M (2006) How safe is Z-Wave? [Wireless standards]. Comput Control Eng 17:18–23. https://doi.org/10.1049/cce:20060601

121. Seal A, Chakraborty S, Mali K (2017) A New and Resilient Image Encryption Technique Based on Pixel Manipulation, Value Transformation and Visual Transformation Utilizing Single–Level Haar Wavelet Transform. In: Proceedings of the First International Conference on Intelligent Computing and Communication. Springer, Singapore, pp. 603–611

122. Mali K, Chakraborty S, Seal A, Roy M (2015) An Efficient Image Cryptographic Algorithm based on Frequency Domain using Haar Wavelet Transform. Int J Secur Its Appl 9:279–288. https://doi.org/10.14257/ijsia.2015.9.12.26

123. Chakraborty S, Seal A, Roy M, Mali K (2016) A novel lossless image encryption method using DNA substitution and chaotic logistic map. Int J Secur its Appl 10:205–216. https://doi.org/10.14257/ijsia.2016.10.2.19

124. Mali K, Chakraborty S, Roy M (2015) A Study on Statistical Analysis and Security Evaluation Parameters in Image Encryption. IJSRD-International J Sci Res Dev 3:2321–0613

125. Roy M, Mali K, Chatterjee S, et al (2019) A Study on the Applications of the Biomedical Image Encryption Methods for Secured Computer Aided Diagnostics. In: 2019 Amity International Conference on Artificial Intelligence (AICAI). IEEE, pp 881–886

126. Roy M, Chakraborty S, Mali K, et al (2020) Data Security Techniques Based on DNA Encryption. In: Advances in Intelligent Systems and Computing. Springer, pp 239–249

127. Roy M, Chakraborty S, Mali K, et al (2020) Biomedical Image Security Using Matrix Manipulation and DNA Encryption. In: Advances in Intelligent Systems and Computing. Springer, pp 49–60

128. Roy M, Chakraborty S, Mali K, et al (2019) A dual layer image encryption using polymerase chain reaction amplification and dna encryption. In: 2019 International Conference on Opto-Electronics and Applied Optics, Optronix 2019. Institute of Electrical and Electronics Engineers Inc.

129. Chakraborty S, Mali K (2020) SuFMoFPA: A superpixel and meta-heuristic based fuzzy image segmentation approach to explicate COVID-19 radiological images. Expert Syst Appl 114142. https://doi.org/10.1016/j.eswa.2020.114142

130. Chakraborty S, Mali K (2020) Fuzzy Electromagnetism Optimization (FEMO) and its application in biomedical image segmentation. Appl Soft Comput 97:106800. https://doi.org/10.1016/j.asoc.2020.106800

131. Xie Y, Xing F, Kong X, et al (2015) Beyond classification: Structured regression for robust cell detection using convolutional neural network. In: Lecture Notes in Computer Science (including subseries Lecture Notes in Artificial Intelligence and Lecture Notes in Bioinformatics). Springer Verlag, pp 358–365

Mobile Edge Computing Based Internet of Agricultural Things: A Systematic Review and Future Directions

Anirbit Sengupta, Sukhpal Singh Gill, Abhijit Das, and Debashis De

Abstract In the modern era of Information Technology, a combined solution framework integrating Wireless Sensor Network (WSN), Internet of Things (IoT), cloud and edge computing, data analytics, and other related technologies are explored and the newest proposals for its probable implementation in the arena of farming is stated in this chapter. Briefing Mobile edge computing (MEC) is an up-coming framework in which the cloud computing services are stretched to the boundary of mobile end-nodes. Further, to boost up the productivity of the crops and working efficacy in the agriculture area, the practice of IoT, edge computing data analytics, etc., are introduced. In this chapter, we surveyed the crucial propositions, the contemporary research efforts, the recent innovations in technologies and research topics, and those explicit edge-cloud integrated IoT solutions that have direct application to agriculture. We aim to design a complete image of both enduring research efforts and upcoming research possibilities through comprehensive and elaborated deliberations. The chapter presents a study of more than a hundred papers, which constitute the most significant work in the relevant field along with research challenges and future open issues and which arc also identified and discussed thoroughly.

A. Sengupta
Electronics and Communication Engineering, Dr Sudhir Chandra Sur Institute of Technology and Sports Complex, Kolkata, West Bengal, India

S. S. Gill
School of Electronic Engineering and Computer Science, Queen Mary University of London, London, UK
e-mail: s.s.gill@qmul.ac.uk

A. Das (✉)
Information Technology, RCC Institute of Information Technology, Kolkata, West Bengal, India

D. De
Centre of Mobile Cloud Computing, Department of Computer Science and Engineering, Maulana Abul Kalam Azad University of Technology, Kolkata, West Bengal, India

© The Author(s), under exclusive license to Springer Nature Switzerland AG 2021
A. Mukherjee et al. (eds.), *Mobile Edge Computing*,
https://doi.org/10.1007/978-3-030-69893-5_17

415

Keywords Precision agriculture · Cloud computing · Mobile edge computing · Smart farming · Internet of things · Survey

1 Introduction

Applying Information Technology (IT) into agriculture techniques has been proven beneficial for more than a decade. Through Precision Agriculture (PA) [1–5], we get better production and quality of crops, with minimal energy and water resources, overlooking the environmental influence. Though the widespread of precision agriculture has been restricted, due to some bottlenecks such as expensive equipment, troublesome operations, maintenance hazards, and the standardization problems for sensor networks.

Recently, new technological progress in different segments, especially in embedded systems, Internet technologies like, Internet of Things (IoT), communication protocols and pervasive computing like Ubiquitous Sensor Networks, facilitate the development of low power and cost-effective solutions, user-friendly devices, hassle-free installation and maintenance of the same. Today, technological growth in Wireless Sensor Networks (WSN) has made the monitoring and control of greenhouse factors much more effortless and accurate while applying [1, 4, 6–12] in the precision agriculture domain.

The different crop has different requirement of water [1]. Hence, to have a uniformity of water distribution on the field, the farmers have to be very alert, as the regular rainfall is very uneven and unpredictable as well. Every greenhouse parameter like, weather condition, soil structure, variety of crop cultures, etc., requires a detailed analysis to choose an appropriate irrigation method [13]. Improper selection of irrigation methods and incorrect weather predictions often leads to massive financial damage to the farmers.

Now, the evolution in WSN technologies and IoT devices, makes the farmers able to monitor the environment and control the parameters of the greenhouse [4] easily.

This survey work says about precision agriculture (Fig. 1) in general, cloud and edge computing methods in brief, sensor/actuator network platforms, and the Internet of Things, integrating machine-to-machine (M2M) and Human-Machine-Interface (HMI) protocols [14, 15]. A clear picture has been shown with proper control and monitoring by WSN and mobile edge computing integrated with IoT archetype. Finally, this study projects a possible combination of mobile edge computing and IoT to encourage the advancement of Precision Agriculture.

We have prepared this book-chapter in the following way.

Review works on precision agriculture is presented in Sect. 2. The impact of IT on precision agriculture is also given here. In Sect. 3, general cloud computing platforms along with different cloud computing circumstances applied to PA are analyzed. Details of edge computing are also given in this section. Sensor architecture and IoT technologies for the development of agricultural services are discussed

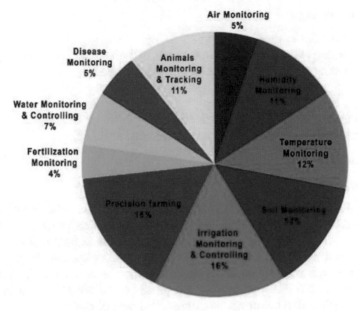

Fig. 1 Tasks related to precision agriculture

in Sect. 4. Section 5 says about mobile edge computing-based IoT applications in agriculture scenario. Overall smart farming and various future possibilities are being discussed in Sects. 6 and 7 respectively. Finally, Sect. 8 concludes the chapter.

2 Precision Agriculture

2.1 General Overview

Generally, we term Precision Agriculture as the combination of information and control technologies in agriculture procedures [2, 5]. In other words, Precision Agriculture is giving the right input such as fertilizer, water, pesticides, etc. at the right location i.e., agricultural farm and at the right time to get the right output in the form of enhanced quality and production of the crops, by utilizing various sensors and computing methods [16–28]. To achieve full optimization and maximum profit, PA engages usual farming techniques to the specific conditions of each point of the crop. The right application of different technologies like WSNs, micro-electro-mechanical Systems, computing techniques, and enhanced machinery, guarantees acceptable results. These technologies can be applied in indoor, outdoor, and hydroponics crops [16–22]. The management of the above can be divided into three stages:

Determination stage:

- Identification of crop category.
- Clustering of areas are done on the basis of their similarity.
- Analyzing characteristics of each area using sensors.

Analysis stage:

- Computer processing of collected data.
- Launches processes to put on respective area.

Implementation:

- Use of cutting-edge technology and machines.

Several approaches [23–42] based on diverse and scalable platforms have been developed.All of these approaches are now able to acquire, process, accumulate, and monitor data from different crop farming structures using a mobile pervasive approach in a much less costly way [7, 16, 20]. Following the abovementioned three stages, the majority of these approaches are developed with WSNs and IoT paradigms [26–30]. The agricultural processes treated are based in various subsystems (Fig. 2): monitoring, assessment, and control models.

2.2 Challenges in PA Work

Precision Agriculture is reactive to inter-field and intra-field unevenness in crops. In this case, the paybacks are mainly incremented in crop production which in turn increases profitability. Other than the sustainability of agricultural production, the improvements can also be visible in proper farming controlling actions such as cultivation, sowing, fertilization, herbicide application, and reaping [16–20].

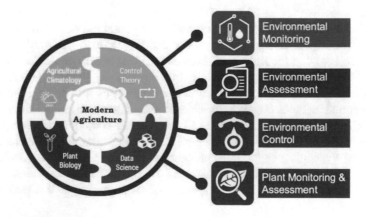

Fig. 2 Tasks in precision farming/agriculture

Devices do exist to measure the grade of soils, such as gamma radiometric soil sensors, apparent EC sensors, and soil moisture devices, etc. [2, 4]. Thermometer, hygrometer, etc. are available to record weather information or micro-climate data. Connectivity between various sensors is made utilizing networks – either wired or wireless [3]. Despite the paybacks provided by precision agriculture, there may exist several negative issues to decelerate its assimilation:

- Preliminary potentials and benefits guaranteed remain unsatisfied
- Lack of support from the PA technicians during maintenance/fault
- Lack of confidence of farmers in how to deal with changeability using technology
- Lack of rapport and effort in collaboration of farmers with PA experts
- A complication in technological theories and inconsistency in apparatuses
- Constraints to adapt the technical issues with equipment and software
- Lack of products that bring together industry and agronomics
- Poor integration among these three – data collection, it's handling, and actuators
- Huge investment cost and also much high maintenance hazards, in turn, draws a big threat of unsatisfactory RoI

Earlier interview data show that farmers dithered to be acquainted with precision agriculture technology, mostly due to the enormous costs of the installation and maintenance of the same.

3 Cloud and Edge Computing

Cloud facilitates a huge amount of storage space through large virtual servers thatare interconnected [43–45]. Clouds arc not only to store data but also to produce information for decision making where huge amount of data from different applications are supplied to analyze and manage [120].

Several platforms have been suggested based on four layers mainly, that are cloud storage layer, network gateway, computing layer, and a physical layer or the hardware modules. Cloud services can also access several analytical resources along with web services that are already pre-installed on the cloud or internet. Physical layer devices or hardware may not be designed in an Internet-friendly way for data sharing purposes. Hence, local gateways are introduced to act as a bridge between all sensors and hardware devices and providing added features like security and controllability [45, 46].

Implementing gateway in the agricultural field or farms actually increases the capacity of automation control. Now, fog computing [46] is introduced to integrate the distributed and heterogeneous resources to the distributed cloud services. Fog computing also minimizes the computational load of cloud and hence guarantees real-time processing of data. The preliminary aim of fog computing is to control the urging expandability of resources of cloud which takes into account the benefits of the combined infrastructure of both edge and cloud modules. Physical layer hardware segments can be dispersed in global or local networks [46] and can be utilized to create services or processes.

As discussed before, cloud computing now plays a vital role for numerous agricultural needs, encountered upon demand over the network and various execution processes. The application of cloud and edge computing in agriculture [41, 42] also offers ubiquitous access to remote cloud and edge resources to perform communications and computations.. Literature have proposed various cloud-based software solutions that develop information retrieval and other agricultural tasks in a more efficient manner. In the agricultural arena, the total physical level data handling is now being solved enabling edge computing methods [47–51]. Edge, dew, and fog computing are now measured as the backbone of cloud computing to reach the source of data generation point comprise of sensors, actuators, and many other embedded systems.

Very rapid evolution in the IoT is growing day by day connecting billions or sometimes trillions of edge devices. This could potentially produce a massive amount of high-speed data. Some of the applications may even need very low latency and response time as well. Because of the centralized network, the small number of data centers, the distance gap among the edge devices, and remote data centers – the traditional cloud infrastructure may face numerous problems [52–55]. Edge computing seems to be a promising possibility to handle this challenge. Edge cloud may offer the resource position closer to the starving edge IoT devices and substantially can build up a novel IoT environment. In this way, edge computing signifies the actions of IoT devices at the boundary of the network associated with the remote Cloud. The most recent literatures [56–58] have revealed that Edge systems are the ideal answer to the above mentioned challenges like latency, privacy, and bandwidth costs.

For the practical implementation of cloud structure in agriculture [38, 44], two more things are very important – fast response time and capability to exchange information. Several protocols like Representational State Transfer (REST) and Message Queuing Telemetry Transport (MQTT) supports this.

4   WSN and IoT

Recent technological advances have stimulated the development of autonomous, wireless communication devices with a smaller size, more power, energy-efficient, and having the capacity to dispose of themselves at any given location [59]. All these devices communicate for a common purpose and send the collected data to a central processing unit. This gives benefits to those network applications, who entail hundreds or even thousands of wireless sensor nodes, to be deployed in inaccessible and remote locations. Consequently, apart from a sensing module, a wireless sensor node has an on-board processing unit, communication features, and also storage facilities. The new generation sensor nodes [60–62] are now so enhanced that along with data collection they are also capable of doing Intranet analysis, correlation, and routing its sensor data through other sensor nodes. This is how a WSN is formed when multiple sensors coordinate with each other to monitor significantly large physical environments. There also exists a centralized control station or base station, where the sensor nodes connect to broadcast their data and do further processing for visualization, analysis, and data storing.

4.1 IoT in Precision Agriculture

Several WSN applications have been developed and applied in PA to increase crop productivity, farm efficiency, and profitability in many agronomic production systems [63–65], at the same time minimalizing unintentional impacts on domestic farm animals, wildlife, and the overall nature. The WSN solutions provide the farmers with information in real-time so that they can change and adjust new strategies from time to time. As the precision farming approaches are more practical than only remaining mere theoretical propositions, farmers can recognize the transformations and controls actions accordingly. The amalgamation of WSN along with intelligent embedded systems becomes much cheaper than its wired counterpart. Hence, this combination gives rise to the technology of ubiquitous systems and leads to the design and development of low-cost solutions for agricultural environment monitoring. Because of their low cost, these solutions are well fitted for developing countries and to places where physical intervention or access is quite difficult. Various state of the art solutions [66–69] has been proposed that address different problem areas. All these solutions are needed to be put together that will combine IT with other recent technologies to design standard procedures for farming activities (Fig. 3).

Different literature proposes [70–73] IoT models to be used in PA with three layers: control, communication, and application cloud layer. Few IoT based solutions are also available on smartphones which help control crops in farm areas.

Various literature proposes [70–73, 119] some novel services and platforms where the traditional Internet paradigms like web services are blended with WSN protocols such as ZigBee, Bluetooth, Z-Wave, etc. to build agricultural applications.

4.2 IoT Limitations in PA

Few early challenges in implementing IoT in agriculture are:

- Use of traditional automated systems on web services
- The application models have yet to be put into execution and tested with a real-world scenario
- Lack of coordination between agricultural agronomist and solution developer
- Unavailability of low-cost prototypes

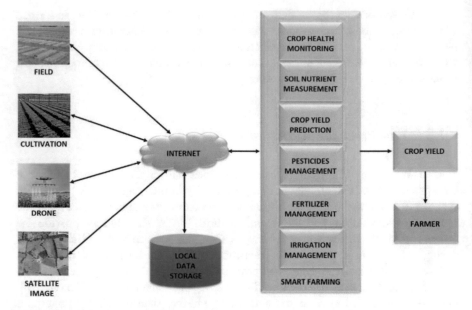

Fig. 3 Modern farming activities in general

- Poor control of turn-around time on an amalgamation of multiple protocols
- Very expensive business and commercial applications do exist, those which are very costly and incurs high expertise to control and maintain the characteristics after applying into the agricultural scenario

Keeping in mind the above bottlenecks, cost-effective prototypes could be designed, developed, simply tested, and adapted by agronomists in practical agriculture scenarios. Human to machine interface (HMI) and machine to machine (M2M) solutions [59] might be assimilated and reformed towards the requirements of the end-users and agro-manufacture, making all IoT devices interoperable controlling the response time of the applications.

5 MEC Based Internet of Agricultural Things (IoAT) Framework

Previously we have discussed various new technologies, which are intended to perform within the network boundary, for example, fogs, cloudlet, dew, edge, micro data-hubs, etc., all of which have developed in the recent past to combat with delay sensitivity and instant response.

MEC or Mobile Edge Computing [73–75] is a promising architectural design in which cloud computing functionalities remain stretched out towards the boundary or edge of the cloud network, empowering mobile base terminals. We can apply this technology to any situation stationary or mobile, wired or wireless, placing the software modules and hardware infrastructures at the boundary of the network and within the neighborhood or proximity of the users' end. MEC delivers a continuous amalgamation of various application service providers and sellers concerning mobile end users, enterprises, and other stakeholders [76].

Edge computing targets to bring down all the resources and services of cloud to the network boundary, to offer quick service response with the least delay because of its "close to you" nature. Two most important objectives [77–80] of edge computing can be represented as:

(i) Delay in servicing users' request at distant located cloud data centers is minimized by servicing the response at the network edge level.
(ii) Minimalize top-down and bottom-up data traffic in the network core.

Reduction of data traffic in the network core naturally boosts up energy efficiency and in turn reductions in data costs. Our major concern is IoT and sensors monitored data, which is first filtered and processed in the edge layer and then uploaded to the cloud, thus minimizing the bottom-up data traffic significantly [80–85].

Pervasive computing permits an N–to–M sensor nodes communication model. Any sensor node here in the network can query and vice-versa. Besides, the sinknode or the node acting as the base station is capable of conveying all its information to the remote cloud data center through a gateway device [78].

5.1 Platform Design

As we have discussed already in Sect. 2, agriculture is an intricate system. Dealing with several issues become extremely complicated because of the wide range of environmental parameters. In the maximum of the agricultural systems, there exist hierarchical levels. If we take an example of a crop irrigation scenario, the previous level of hierarchy becomes crop, harvesting arrangements, farming, and water draining schemes. Therefore, all the submodule in any agriculture is built with IoT edge devices, which can be linked and managed by IoT archetypes and WSN [74, 76]. The basic IoT platform necessities recognized for precision agriculture situations are as follows:

- Less costly components for all devices installed
- Power-efficient solutions to improve the establishment and development
- Standard communication protocols to develop open-source applications
- Reusability of the solutions
- User-friendliness to improve its acceptability among nontechnical farming people
- Easy and cheap maintenance and proper after-sales support
- Modularity and scalability to support the amalgamation of new control modules

- Interoperability should be ensured when new devices are added
- Nonproprietary hardware and software to minimize dependencies and legal issues

If we add the platform communication which follows a sequence like, device-to-gateway, edge computing layer can be introduced. The newly formed platform is now based on three foundations [76, 80]:

- Internet of Things:
  Nowadays trillions of Internet-enabled sensors, devices or things are there in various agricultural applications, commercial sectors, and industrial scenarios in a wireless manner. Typically, the solutions in IoT have filtered things and organized in the locally used data in the edge layer, or connected to gateways that provide comprehensive functionality. Individual IoT has its sharable data which is usually shared on the Internet.
- Gateway:
  The majority of the present IoT could not share data with the cloud data centers as they are not intended to have a connection to the Internet. Gateways act as mediators in between things and the cloud platform, resolves the aforesaid difficulty, and provides the required connectivity, data privacy, and data management operations.
- Cloud Network:
  Cloud arrangement comprises multiple numbers of gigantic sized effective data storage and data servers which are again connected. To produce service facilities, IoT solutions run specific agricultural applications to organize and analyze data taken from various sensors and devices. This in turn generates information to facilitate result-driven decision-making processes to help farming (Fig. 4).

The communication arrangement from agricultural IoT devices to the local gateway often can be seen with distributions of smart entities that involve distant configuration capacities and interfaces of real-time. The local gateway is in that way presumed to be always linked to the Internet. Nevertheless, this gateway can be a mobile smart-phone. It is worth mentioning from an interoperability point of view, that smart-phones, with their refined software update procedures, allow new features to be updated frequently and sometimes this happens even at the IoAT device as well [78].

Following platform design model [86–88] in the general IoT-edge-cloud scenario, exclusive PA processes can be established ensuing various phases mentioned below:

- Analysis: IT specialists and agronomists fix the elementary objectives for any agricultural project work. Scenario study, requirement analysis are done in this phase.
- Design requirements: In this phase, requirements related to set up the agronomic work beinginvestigated. An IoT based strategy is projected by IT specialists and agronomists along with investigation towards computational and commu-

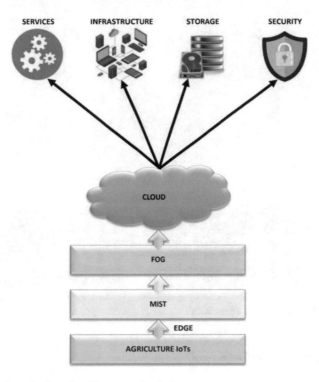

Fig. 4 IoAT-edge-mist-fog-cloud-(agro-application)

nicational necessities. All the processes related to things and agriculture are identified.

- Wireless Sensor Network: IoT sensors and/or actuators and their processing capacities should be clearly defined in this phase. The communication layer architecture is also proposed at this time.
- Control Processes: In this phase, agronomists identify agricultural activities between things with preliminary and most innovative rules. ICT engineers also come up with middleware to facilitate the effective use of a WSN in any particular application. The relation between IoT and control regulation is exhibited here.
- Edge services: Generates analytical and logical information base structures at the data foundation. In this phase, edge computing pushes applications, data and processes away from embedded nodes integrating M2M protocol, control, data processing and web services. Edge is the logical extreme of a cloud network system.
- Cloud services: Using Internet technologies, we store, monitor, handle, and analyze several services that need to be planned in this stage. The design of queries and analytical layers are also done here.
- Testing: All the physical devices – things, their control methods, WSN, Internet communication, and Edge and Cloud services are verified and validated in actual agricultural field before mass implementation (Fig. 5).

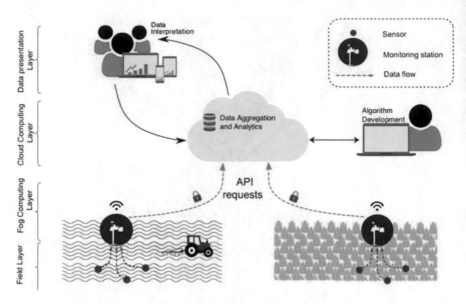

Fig. 5 Layered view of MEC based IoAT

5.2   Platform Structure

Actions and facilities can be constructed and dispersed in components localized in different storages – be it mobile or a cloud. Furthermore, IoTs can be implemented locally in various devices like sensors, actuators or any control device, or can be installed in mobile systems like smartphones or any embedded devices, etc. Because of the aforesaid, the projected system architecture is a collection of dispersed components – where a group of sensor devices, associated procedures, virtual facilities, storage, analytical power, etc., primarily resides on a four-layered structure [89–92]: IoT, Edge Computing, Gateway and Cloud Network.

Agronomists along with experts in ICT must resolve the applications for cloud and procedures for an edge. When cloud services offer data storage, web, and analytical services, Edge service offers interoperability and real-time answer. Software platform comprises data collection, control-communication methods, cloud facilities, and agronomists' tools [76, 81].

In the following Fig. 6 shows the rate of growth of IoT and Edge devices in agriculture, the volume of generated data, and gain in latency in due course of time [80, 90, 92]. The IoAT device number is in trillions and data volume from farms is in Tera Bytes. Figure 6 clearly shows the result that we have achieved through maximizing the use of more IoT devices in agriculture and significant control over latency is also visible after increasing the use of fog, dew and edge technologies in between.

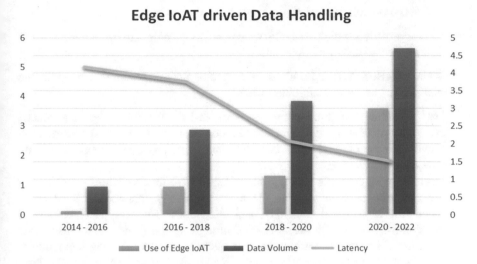

Fig. 6 Growth of IoAT and latency curve by the time

6   Towards Smart Farming

Till now we have discussed various IoT based solutions that have been developed to maintain and monitor agricultural farms automatically. The current section presents the key components of IoT based smart farming.

6.1   *Smart Farming Components*

There are four key components in IoT based smart farming [93, 94]. They are the physical component, data procurement, data handling component, and data analytics.

The physical component is the utmost significant element in the case of PA to evade any unseen, undesirable incident. This component comprises of all the sensors and devices or things controlled under the system design. A device executes several agro jobs like sensing the soil, temperature, weather, light, and moisture. Similarly, hardware devices execute numerous control functions like, node discovery, device identification, and naming services etc. There is a microcontroller to control all these devices and sensors. This regulatory operation can be performed by any remote device or a computer with an Internet connection.

- Data Procurement component can further be categorized into two sub-components:

IoT data procurement and *regular data procurement*.

- Several protocols which are being used in smart farming, are the elements of *IoT data procurement* sub-component.

While, ZigBee, WIFI, LoraWan, etc., protocols can be implemented in the *regular data procurement* sub-component.

- Data Handling component comprises of various functionalities like, image and video processing, data storing, decision support system, and data mining. Simultaneously other services can be served by adding extra functionalities by the system necessities.
- Data Analytics component comprises of mainly two functionalities – *monitoring* and *controlling*. In *monitoring* the main three tasks that are involved are – Stock Checking, Field Checking, and Greenhouse Checking. IoT empowers agronomists to check for the stock data through various devices and sensors that are utilized to monitor various animals' sicknesses such as body temperature, heart-beat anomaly, indigestion, etc. While applications for field checking anticipate different conditions of the field like richness of a soil, pH value, temperature, humidity, gas, air pressure and water pressure, turbidity, and crop disease monitoring.

Below a picture (Fig. 7) of a smart greenhouse design [95–97] that removes human intervention and is capable of measuring various climate parameters by smart IoT devices and sensors according to plants' necessities.

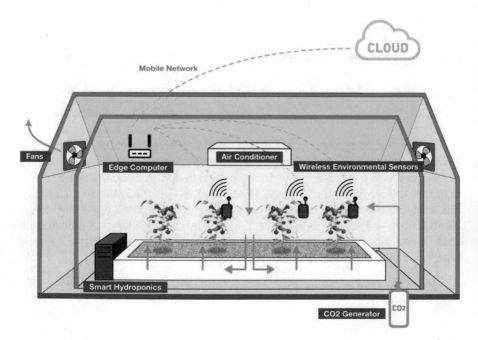

Fig. 7 Case study – sample greenhouse

Smart agriculture solutions need to be implemented in a dispersed cloud environment, rather than putting it within a single, large data-center. Doing this will necessitate dividing hefty and difficult calculations into minor agro-jobs – irrigation, weather, images, crop, energy, water, nutrients all of these can be dispersed. These minor agro-jobs now build interoperable diverse data origins and algorithms to control processes being part of the edge computing layer [93, 94, 97–99].

Requirements of the tentative platform arealso conveyed to the explicit WSN/IoT scheme:

- Cost-effective deployment: All devices should be inexpensive. Low-cost technology to be used to build sensors like temperature, moisture, pH, electrical conductivity (EC), luminosity, electro-valves, pumps, lamps, etc. Extensive use devices like controllers, routers should be implanted devices with proper hardware compatibility.
- Regular network protocols with open source software: To build up data/message communication services, WSN networks should practice various protocols like WiFi, Bluetooth, serial bus protocols, etc.
- Ease of access and low maintenance: All IoT devices should be easy to detect, easy to connect, easy to debug, and also easy to sustain.
- Physical edge computing layer development: Elementary control procedures function in the native system. Analytical, data stores, and GUIs should be dispersed in the separate cloud and associated Internet services.
- Support for amalgamation of smart control modules: To program new modules and for easy integration, support of various web services protocols like REST, HTTP, MQTT, etc. and open-source hardware-software models is required. IoT applications should allow interoperability between devices or things.
- Should offer timely support for agronomist use, initial installation, routine maintenance, and elementary add–on.
- Should analyze agronomist's feedback (Fig. 8).

7 Future Directions

Use of Data Analytics/Big Data/Blockchain
There is a huge change over from usage of the WSN as a key catalyst of smart farming to the practice of IoT and Data Analytics [119]. While IoT incorporates numerous technologies thatare currently available, such as WSN, Radio Frequency Identification (RFID), cloud computing, middleware methods, and end-user applications. Several challenges and limitations are also identified and they have been solved with a joint approach of IoT and *Data Analytics*, enabling smart agriculture [100].

Since its inception, IoT has always been influenced by very recent technologies such as *Big Data* and cloud computing to overcome its shortcomings [98]. Few

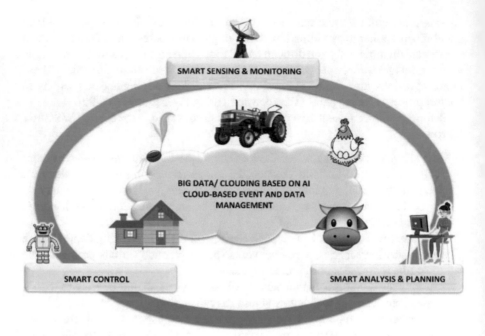

Fig. 8 Smart farming

researchers propose *Blockchain* as one of the next ultimate solutions [69, 101–104]. Few works examine limitations in applying blockchain to IoT applications. Further studies have revealed the most significant works to improve the application of IoT in precision agriculture using blockchain technology.

Use of AI/ML

The incapability of communicating and computing of the remote cloud gives rise to edge computing, where the IoT data handling begins at the boundary of the same network and converts the associated devices from normal to intelligent one. *Machine Learning*(ML) here can play the key role to transfer the information flow smoothly from cloud to things [105].

Fog computing-based solutions generate a huge amount of data. Several researchers are working on the research of deploying ML to unravel fog computing glitches. Modern times witnessing a popular trend in implementing *Artificial Intelligence* (AI) and ML to improve different applications of fog computing and provide various fog services, like effective resource management, privacy, regulating latency and consumption of energy, and traffic modeling while applying into Smart Agriculture [105–108].

Use of DB

Data generated from the IoAT are categorized by its huge amount, continuity, and random presentation. Due to the limited handling speed and the substantial

Fig. 9 UAV based advanced agriculture

storage cost, the current relational database management systems are insufficient to handle such unstructured data. Therefore several propositions [109–111] of big data processing technologies, *Distributed Database Management systems*, distributed file systems, and parallel processing techniques, have risen as fundamental know-how to apply PA IoT produced data storehouses. Researchers have also proposed sensor-integrated RFID data repository-implementation model using *MongoDB* to handle the gigantic volume of unstructured data.

Researchers from China have suggested that a combined solution framework integrating the IoT, cloud computing, *data mining*, and other information technology tools can meet up the elementary tasks of the IoT based agricultural monitoring system [110]. They also have proposed one experimental framework and simulation design to realize the same. Researchers have enhanced the efficiency and safety of production and management of agricultural products and also have minimalized the pollution of the environment from agricultural activities.

Use of Drone/UAV

Modern day's farmers especially in USA and European countries, are keener to use Unmanned Aerial Vehicles (UAV) or drones [112–116] to assess their farm lands as part of an agricultural control system. This type of safer, faster, and cost effective vehicles surely assist them in precision control over pesticides and fertilizer application rates and hence can significantly improve the overall profitability.

There is a need of IoT based unmanned aircraft systems to gather the topological and meteorological data. Further, UAS based agriculture systems can increase the automation gathering and analyzing of data collected from different sources. The multi-UAV sub-systems (Fig. 9) can solve the data collection and management problems together, which can further reduce its cost.

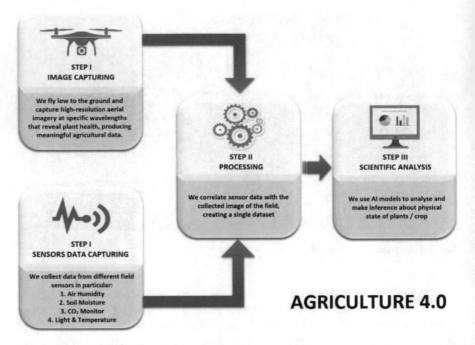

Fig. 10 Future agricultural standards

The complete prospect of these above-mentioned technologies can integrate innovative functionalities and enhancements which are yet emergent in real-life agricultural situations.

Agriculture 4.0
An integration of new technologies such as IoT, 5G and AI into agriculture system is occurring, which fulfills the demand of modern agriculture. The implementation of Agriculture 4.0 (Fig. 10) can increase the revenue of agriculture industry. Software-Defined Industrial Internet of Things in the Context of Industry 4.0 has been proposed [117] to standardize the IoT devices and protocols all over the world. On a similar note Agriculture 4.0 [118] has also been designed and the following picture can give an idea about how it may standardize the agricultural processes with the help of recent technologies.

Agriculture Intelligence
With the recent developments of new computing paradigms such as Internet of Agriculture Things (IoAT), the automation in agriculture sector is growing by using the concept of Artificial Intelligence (AI), which manages the big data efficiently. AI increases the system's ability to gather, process and analyze data in an efficient manner, considered as Agriculture Intelligence. Further, deep learning-based image processing can be used to solve the problems such as fruit gradingand weed detection to maximize the production.

Smart Farming and Climate

Smart farming(land management and precision agriculture) improves the production of agriculture substantially by utilizing the concept of IoAT but the impact of smart farming on environment is increasing day by day. There is need to explore and reduce the impact of agriculture advancements on climate change.

Prediction Models

The prediction models in future agriculture systems can improve using new deep learning techniques, which approximate the yield improving the production chain downstream in an efficient manner.

8   Conclusions

The massive flow in the global population is compelling a transferal toward smart agriculture practices. As a result, the use of technology is in high demand to enhance operational efficiency and productivity in the agriculture area.

In this chapter, a detailed study on various aspects of using IoT in agriculture has been stated, which comprises steps of implementation, solution platform design, architecture and layers, solution framework, etc. Moreover, the association of some relevant technologies likes, cloud computing, edge computing, and its encouraging effect on IoT based agricultural systems have also been shown. Furthermore, the latest technologies in precision agriculture have been emphasized. A framework of smart farm management with IoT and Mobile Edge Computing has also been presented. Some open research issues and challenges in IoT agriculture and the cloud agriculture field have been given as well.

In the end, some very recent technologies and its probable application on agriculture have been discussed to exploit the advantages of these technologies in PA installations.

Feedback from the stakeholders – farmer, agronomist, and technologist is an important issue for a continuous improvement process. We also have tried to analyze various gaps residing in the theoretical propositions and practical implementations in brief.

State of the art literature from every corner of recent technologies is incorporated in this survey work. This elaborated study is to make the new researchers aware of the current developments and imminent prospects in the domain of Mobile Edge Computing based Internet of Agricultural Things.

We hope new crops will soon be grown-up with the help of the integration of fresh ideas and services using the newly invented tools and techniques.

References

1. KshitijShinghal, Dr. Arti Noor, Dr. Neelam Srivastava, Dr. Raghuvir Singh, "Intelligent Humidity Sensor for – Wireless Sensor Network Agricultural Application", International Journal of Wireless & Mobile Networks (IJWMN), Vol. 3, No. 1, pp. 118–128, February 2011, DOI : https://doi.org/10.5121/ijwmn.2011.3111
2. Kiruthika M, ShwetaTripathi, MritunjayOjha, Kavita S, "Parameter Monitoring for Precision Agriculture", IJRSI, Volume II, Issue X, October 2015, ISSN 2321 – 2705
3. Tim Wark, Peter Corke, PavanSikka, Lasse Klingbeil, Ying Guo, Chris Crossman, Phil Valencia, Dave Swain, and Greg Bishop-Hurley, "Transforming Agriculture through Pervasive Wireless Sensor Networks", IEEE Pervasive Computing Magazine, April-June 2007, pp. 50–57
4. Awati J.S., Patil V.S. and Awati S.B., "Application of Wireless Sensor Networks for Agriculture Parameters", International Journal of Agriculture Sciences, ISSN: 0975-3710 & E-ISSN: 0975-9107, Volume 4, Issue 3, 2012, pp-213–215
5. AnjumAwasthi and S.R.N Reddy, "Monitoring for Precision Agriculture using Wireless Sensor Network-A Review", Global Journal of Computer Science and Technology Network, Web & Security, Publisher: Global Journals Inc. (USA) Online ISSN: 0975-4172 & Print ISSN: 0975-4350, Volume 13, Issue 7, Version 1.0, Year 2013
6. Jenna Burrell, Tim Brooke, and Richard Beckwith, "Vineyard Computing: Sensor Networks in Agricultural Production", IEEE Pervasive Computing Magazine, Jan-March 2004, pp. 38–45
7. Herman Sahota, Ratnesh Kumar, Ahmed Kamal and Jing Huang, "An Energy-efficient Wireless Sensor Network for Precision Agriculture", White Paper – under the grants supported in part by the National Science Foundation CNS-0626822, NSF-ECS-0601570, NSF-ECCS-0801763, NSFCCF-081141, and NSF-ECCS-0926029
8. D.D. Chaudhary, S.P. Nayse, L.M. Waghmare, "Application of Wireless Sensor Networks for Greenhouse Parameter Control in Precision Agriculture", International Journal of Wireless & Mobile Networks (IJWMN) Vol. 3, No. 1, February 2011, pp. 140–149, DOI : https://doi.org/10.5121/ijwmn.2011.3113
9. Lianjie Zhou, Nengcheng Chen, Zeqiang Chen, and Chenjie Xing "ROSCC: An Efficient Remote Sensing Observation-Sharing Method Based on Cloud Computing for Soil Moisture Mapping" in Precision Agriculture IEEE Journal of Selected Topics in Applied Earth Observations and Remote Sensing, Vol. 9, No. 12, December 2016
10. Spyridon NektariosDaskalakis, George Goussetis, Stylianos D. Assimonis, Manos M. Tentzeris and ApostolosGeorgiadis "A uW Backscatter-Morse-Leaf Sensor for Low-Power Agricultural Wireless Sensor Networks", IEEE Sensors Journal, Vol. 18, No. 19, October 1, 2018
11. Wen-Liang Chen, Yi-Bing Lin , Yun-Wei Lin, Robert Chen, Jyun-Kai Liao, Fung-Ling Ng, Yuan-Yao Chan, You-Cheng Liu, Chin-Cheng Wang, Cheng-Hsun Chiu, and Tai-Hsiang Yen "AgriTalk: IoT for Precision Soil Farming of Turmeric Cultivation" IEEE Internet of Things Journal, Vol. 6, No. 3, June 2019
12. Johan J. Estrada-López , Alejandro A. Castillo-Atoche, Javier Vázquez-Castillo , and Edgar Sánchez-Sinencio, "Smart Soil Parameters Estimation System Using an Autonomous Wireless Sensor Network With Dynamic Power Management Strategy" IEEE Sensors Journal, Vol. 18, No. 21, November 1, 2018
13. Joaquín Gutiérrez, Juan Francisco Villa-Medina, Alejandra Nieto-Garibay, and Miguel Ángel Porta-Gándara, "Automated Irrigation System Using a Wireless Sensor Network and GPRS Module", IEEE Transactions on Instrumentation and Measurement, DOI: https://doi.org/10.1109/TIM.2013.2276487
14. William A. Jury and Henry J. Vaux, Jr., "The Emerging Global Water Crisis: Management Scarcity and Conflict between Water Users", Advances in Agronomy, Elsevier, Vol. 95, 2007, DOI: https://doi.org/10.1016/S0065-2113(07)95001-4

15. Guofu Yuan, Yi Luo, Xiaomin Sun, Dengyin Tang, "Evaluation of a crop water stress index for detecting water stress in winter wheat in the North China Plain", Agricultural Water Management, Elsevier, Vol. 64, 2004, pp. 29–40, DOI:https://doi.org/10.1016/S0378-3774(03)00193-8

16. BrunellaMorandi, Luigi Manfrini, Marco Zibordi, Massimo Noferini, Giovanni Fiori, and Luca Corelli Grappadelli1 "A Low-cost Device for Accurate and Continuous Measurements of Fruit Diameter" HORTSCIENCE 42(6):1380–1382. 2007.

17. S.O. Link, M.E. Thiede and M.G. van Bavel "An improved strain-gauge device for continuous field measurement of stem and fruit diameter" Journal of Experimental Botany, Vol. 49, No. 326, pp. 1583–1587, September 1998

18. Subir Das, ShikhaNayak, Badal Chakraborty, SabyasachiMitra, "Continuous radial growth rate monitoring of horticultural crops using an optical mouse" Sensors and Actuators A 297 (2019) 111526

19. Martin Thalheimer" A new optoelectronic sensor for monitoring fruit or stem radial growth", Computers and Electronics in Agriculture 123 (2016) 149–153

20. P. Dangare, T. Mhizha, E. Mashonjowa "Design, fabrication and testing of a low cost Trunk Diameter Variation (TDV) measurement system based on an ATmega 328/P microcontroller" Computers and Electronics in Agriculture 148 (2018) 197–206

21. David M. Drewa, Geoffrey M. Downes "The use of precision dendrometers in research on daily stem size and wood property variation: A review", Dendrochronologia 27 (2009) 159–172

22. Robert G. Evans and E. John Sadler "Methods and technologies to improve efficiency of water use" WATER RESOURCES RESEARCH, VOL. 44, W00E04, DOI: https://doi.org/10.1029/2007WR006200, 2008

23. K. H. Higgs and H. G. Jones, "A Microcomputer-Based System for Continuous Measurement and Recording Fruit Diameter in Relation to Environmental Factors" Journal of Experimental Botany, Vol. 35, No. 160, pp. 1646–1655, November 1984

24. ALEXANDER LANG "Xylem, Phloem and Transpiration Flows in Developing Apple Fruits", Journal of Experimental Botany, Vol. 41, No. 227, pp. 645–651, June 1990

25. Subhanshu Gupta, Ajay Mudgil, AmitaSoni Plant Growth Monitoring System International Journal of Engineering Research & Technology (IJERT)Vol. 1 Issue 4, June – 2012 ISSN: 2278-0181

26. Slamet W, M Irham N and Sutan M S an "IoT based Growth Monitoring System of Guava (PsidiumGuajava L.) Fruits" IOP Conf. Series: Earth and Environmental Science 147 (2018) 012048 DOI: https://doi.org/10.1088/1755-1315/147/1/012048

27. Tingzhu Wu, Yue Lin, Lili Zheng, ZiquanGuo, Jianxing Xu, Shijie Liang, Zhuguagn Liu, Yijun Lu, Tien-Mo Shih, And Zhong Chen, "Analyses of multi-color plant-growth light sources in achieving maximum photosynthesis efficiencies with enhanced color qualities" Vol. 26, No. 4 | 19 Feb 2018 | OPTICS EXPRESS 4135

28. MohdFauzi Othman, KhairunnisaShazali "Wireless Sensor Network Applications: A Study in Environment Monitoring System" International Symposium on Robotics and Intelligent Sensors 2012 (IR IS 2012)

29. AlessioBotta, Walter de Donato, Valerio Persico, Antonio Pescape "Integration of Cloud Computing and Internet of Things: a Survey" IEEE Pervasive Computing Magazine

30. Cesar Encinas, Erica Ruiz, Joaquin Cortez and Adolfo Espinoza "Design and implementation of a distributed IoT system for the monitoring of water quality in Aquaculture" 978-1-5090-3599-1/17/$31.00 2017 IEEE

31. Jing Hu, Lianfeng Shen, Yang Yang, RuichaoLv "Design and Implementation of Wireless Sensor and Actor Network for Precision Agriculture", 978-1-4244-5849-3/10/$26.00 ©20 1 0 IEEE

32. Jeonghwan Hwang, Changsun Shin and Hyun Yoe "Study on an Agricultural Environment Monitoring Server System using Wireless Sensor Networks", Sensors 2010, 10, 11189–11211; DOI: https://doi.org/10.3390/s101211189

33. Jerrin James, Manu Maheshwar P, "Plant growth monitoring system, with dynamic user interface", IEEE Magazine
34. Ji-chun Zhao, Jun-feng Zhang, Yu Feng, Jian-xinGuo "The Study and Application of the IOT Technology in Agriculture" 978-1-4244-5540-9/10/$26.00 ©2010 IEEE
35. NattapolKaewmard, SaiyanSaiyod, "Sensor Data Collection and Irrigation Control on Vegetable Crop Using Smart Phone and Wireless sensor Networks for Smart Farm" 2014 IEEE Conference on Wireless Sensors (ICWISE), October, 26–28 2014, Subang, Malaysia
36. Meonghun Lee, Jeonghwan Hwang, and Hyun Yoe, "Agricultural Production System based on IoT", 2013 IEEE 16th International Conference on Computational Science and Engineering
37. Sang Gyu Lee, Sung Kyeom Kim, HeeJu Lee, Hee Su Lee, JinHyoung Lee "Impact of moderate and extreme climate change scenarios on growth, morphological features, photosynthesis, and fruit production of hot pepper", October 2017, DOI: https://doi.org/10.1002/ece3.3647
38. Shubo Liu Internet of "Things Monitoring System of Modern Eco-agriculture Based on Cloud Computing", DOI https://doi.org/10.1109/ACCESS.2019.2903720, IEEE
39. MahtaMoghaddam, Dara Entekhabi, YuriyGoykhman, Ke Li, Mingyan Liu, Aditya Mahajan, AshutoshNayyar, David Shuman, and DemosthenisTeneketzis "Wireless Soil Moisture Smart Sensor Web Using Physics-Based Optimal Control: Concept and Initial Demonstrations" IEEE Journal of Selected Topics in Applied Earth Observations and Remote Sensing, Vol. 3, No. 4, December 2010
40. David J. Mulla, "Twenty five years of remote sensing in precision agriculture: Key advances and remaining knowledge gaps",Biosystem engineering 114 (2013) 358E371
41. ArathiReghukumar, VaidehiVijayakumar "Plant Watering System with Cloud Analysis and Plant Health Prediction" Procedia Computer Science 165 (2019) 126–135
42. P. Subashini, Abhishek Pandey, Sourav Jaiswal, Anurag Sharma "Real Time Plant Health Monitoring System using Sensors and Clouds" International Research Journal of Computer Science (IRJCS) ISSN: 2393–9842 Issue 04, Volume 6 (April 2019)
43. Kashif Bilal, Marc Manzano, Samee U. Khan, EusebiCalle, Keqin Li and Albert Y. Zomaya, "On the Characterization of the Structural Robustness of Data Center Networks", IEEE Transactions On Cloud Computing, Vol. 1, No. 1, January-June 2013
44. Xicheng Tan, Liping Di, Meixia Deng, Aijun Chen, Fang Huang, Chao Peng, Meng Gao, Yayu Yao, and Zongyao Sha, "Cloud and Agent-Based Geospatial Service Chain: A Case Study of Submerged Crops Analysis During Flooding of the Yangtze River Basin", IEEE Journal of Selected Topics in Applied Earth Observations and Remote Sensing, Vol. 8, No. 3, March 2015
45. Wes J. Lloyd, ShrideepPallickara, Olaf David, MazdakArabi, Tyler Wible, Jeffrey Ditty and Ken Rojas "Demystifying the Clouds: Harnessing Resource Utilization Models for Cost Effective Infrastructure Alternatives", IEEE Transactions on Cloud Computing, Vol. 5, No. 4, October-December 2017
46. Rodrigo N. Calheiros, Rajiv Ranjan, Anton Beloglazov, C'esar A. F. De Rose and Rajkumar-Buyya, "CloudSim: a toolkit for modeling and simulation of cloud computing environments and evaluation of resource provisioning algorithms", Softw. Pract. Exper. Journal, John Wiley & Sons, Ltd. 2011; 41:23–50 DOI: https://doi.org/10.1002/spe
47. Pablo Chamoso, Alfonso González-Briones, Sara Rodríguez, and Juan M. Corchado, "Tendencies of Technologies and Platforms in Smart Cities: A State-of-the-Art Review", Wireless Communications and Mobile Computing, Wiley Hindawi, Article ID 3086854, 17 pages https://doi.org/10.1155/2018/3086854
48. Kiryong Ha, Zhuo Chen, Wenlu Hu, Wolfgang Richter, PadmanabhanPillaiy, and MahadevSatyanarayanan, "Towards Wearable Cognitive Assistance", MobiSys'14, June 16–19, 2014, Bretton Woods, New Hampshire, USA. Copyright 2014 ACM 978-1-4503-2793-0/14/06 ...$15.00. https://doi.org/10.1145/2594368.2594383

49. Biljana L. RisteskaStojkoska, Kire V. Trivodaliev, "A review of Internet of Things for smart home: challenges and solutions", Journal of Cleaner Production, October 2016, DOI: https://doi.org/10.1016/j.jclepro.2016.10.006

50. Xuezhi Zeng, Saurabh Kumar Garg, Peter Strazdins, Prem Prakash Jayaraman, Dimitrios Georgakopoulos and Rajiv Ranjan, "IOTSim: a Simulator for Analysing IoT Applications", Journal of Systems Architecture, (2016), DOI: https://doi.org/10.1016/j.sysarc.2016.06.008

51. Michael Armbrust, Armando Fox, Rean Griffith, Anthony D. Joseph, Randy Katz, Andy Konwinski, Gunho Lee, Dav id Patterson, Ariel Rabkin, Ion Stoica, and MateiZaharia, "A View of Cloud Computing", Communications of the ACM, April 2010, Vol. 53, No. 4, DOI:https://doi.org/10.1145/1721654.1721672

52. Cisco and/or its affiliates, "Fog Computing and the Internet of Things: Extend the Cloud to Where the Things Are", Cisco Public White Paper

53. Nasir Abbas, Yan Zhang, Amir Taherkordi, and Tor Skeie "Mobile Edge Computing: A Survey" IEEE Internet of Things Journal, Vol. 5, No. 1, February 2018

54. Kashif Bilal, Osman Khalid, AimanErbad, Samee U. Khan "Potentials, Trends, and Prospects in Edge Technologies: Fog, Cloudlet, Mobile Edge, and Micro Data Centers" IEEE Journal of Computer Networks, PII: S1389-1286(17)30377-8, DOI: https://doi.org/10.1016/j.comnet.2017.10.002

55. Byung-Gon Chun, SunghwanIhm, PetrosManiatis, MayurNaik, Ashwin Patti "Clone Cloud: Elastic Execution between Mobile Device and Cloud" EuroSys'11, April 10–13, 2011, Salzburg, Austria. Copyright © 2011 ACM 978-1-4503-0634-8/11/04... $10.00

56. Weisong Shi, SchahramDustdar, "The Promise of Edge Computing", Computer Published by the IEEE Computer Society 0018-9162 / 16 /$33.00 © 2016 IEEE

57. Weisong Shi, Jie Cao, QuanZhang,Youhuizi Li, and Lanyu Xu "Edge Computing: Vision and Challenges" IEEE Internet of Things Journal, Vol. 3, No. 5, October 2016

58. Massimo Villari, Maria Fazio, SchahramDustdar, Omer Rana, Rajiv Ranjan "A New Paradigm for Edge/Cloud Integration" IEEE Cloud Computing Published By the IEEE Computer Society 2325-6095/16/$33.00 © 2016 IEEE

59. PallaviSethi and Smruti R. Sarangi "Internet of Things: Architectures, Protocols, and Applications" Hindawi Journal of Electrical and Computer Engineering Volume 2017, Article ID 9324035, 25 pageshttps://https://doi.org/10.1155/2017/9324035

60. John A. Stankovic "Research Directions for the Internet of Things" IEEE Internet of Things Journal, Vol. 1, No. 1, February 2014

61. Jianli Pan, Raj Jain, Subharthi Paul, TamVu, AbusayeedSaifullah and Mo Sha an "Internet of Things Framework for Smart Energy in Buildings: Designs, Prototype and Experiments" IEEE Internet of Things Journal, Vol. 2, No. 6, December 2015

62. Mohammad AbdurRazzaque, MarijaMilojevic-Jevric, Andrei Palade, and Siobhán Clarke "Middleware for Internet of Things: A Survey" IEEE Internet of Things Journal, Vol. 3, No. 1, February 2016

63. Jun Huang, Yu Meng, Xuehong Gong, Yanbing Liu, and QiangDuan, "A Novel Deployment Scheme for Green Internet of Things", IEEE Internet of Things Journal, Vol. 1, No. 2, April 2014

64. XiangpingZhai, Xiaoxiao Guan, Chunsheng Zhu, Lei Shu and Jiabin Yuan, "Optimization Algorithms for Multi access Green Communications in Internet of Things" IEEE Internet of Things Journal, Vol. 5, No. 3, June 2018

65. Anandarup Mukherjee, SudipMisra, Narendra Singh Raghuwanshi, and SushmitaMitra "Blind Entity Identification for Agricultural IoT Deployments" IEEE Internet of Things Journal, Vol. 6, No. 2, April 2019

66. Debasmit Banerjee, Bo Dong, Mahmoud Taghizadeh, and Subir Biswas "Privacy-Preserving Channel Access for Internet of Things" IEEE Internet of Things Journal, Vol. 1, No. 5, October 2014

67. Chao Li and BalajiPalanisamy "Privacy in Internet of Things: From Principles to Technologies" IEEE Internet of Things Journal, Vol. 6, No. 1, February 2019

68. Qi Jing, Athanasios V, Vasilakos, Jiafu Wan, JingweiLu ,DechaoQiu "Security of the Internet of Things: perspectives and challenges", Wireless Network (2014) 20:2481–2501DOI https://doi.org/10.1007/s11276-014-0761-7

69. Minhaj Ahmad Khan, Khaled Salah "IoT security: Review, blockchain solutions, and open challenges" Future Generation Computer Systems 82 (2018) 395–411

70. Jie Lin, Wei Yuy, Nan Zhangz, Xinyu Yang, Hanlin Zhang, and Wei Zhao Xi'an Jiaotong, "A Survey on Internet of Things: Architecture, Enabling Technologies, Security and Privacy, and Applications", IEEE Internet of Things Journal, DOI: https://doi.org/10.1109/JIOT.2017.2683200

71. Mohammad AbdurRazzaque, MarijaMilojevic-Jevric, Andrei Palade, and Siobhán Clarke "Middleware for Internet of Things: A Survey" IEEE Internet of Things Journal, Vol. 3, No. 1, February 2016

72. C. Stergiou, K.E. Psannis, B.-G. Kim, B. Gupta Secure "Integration of IoT and Cloud Computing" Future Generation Computer Systems (2016), DOI: https://doi.org/10.1016/j.future.2016. 11.031

73. Jiale Zhang, Bing Chen, Yanchao Zhao, Xiang Cheng and Feng Hu "Data Security and Privacy-Preserving in Edge Computing Paradigm: Survey and Open Issues" DOI https://doi.org/10.1109/ACCESS.2018.2820162, IEEE Access

74. Andreas Kamilaris and Andreas Pitsillides "Mobile Phone Computing and the Internet of Things: A Survey" IEEE Internet of Things Journal, Vol. 3, No. 6, December 2016

75. WeigangHou, Wenxiao Li, Lei Guo, Yiwei Sun, and XintongCai "Recycling Edge Devices in Sustainable Internet of Things Networks" IEEE Internet of Things Journal, Vol. 4, No. 5, October 2017

76. Jianli Pan and James McElhannon "Future Edge Cloud and Edge Computing for Internet of Things Applications", IEEE INTERNET OF THINGS JOURNAL, VOL. 5, NO. 1, FEBRUARY 2018

77. Xiaomin Li, Di Li, Jiafu Wan, Chengliang Liu and Muhammad Imran Adaptive "Transmission Optimization in SDN-Based Industrial Internet of Things with Edge Computing" IEEE Internet of Things Journal, Vol. 5, No. 3, June 2018

78. Xiaomin Li, Jiafu Wan, Hong-Ning Dai, Muhammad Imran, Min Xia, and Antonio Celesti, "A Hybrid Computing Solution and Resource Scheduling Strategy for Edge Computing in Smart Manufacturing" IEEE Transactions on Industrial Informatics, Vol. 15, No. 7, July 2019 4225

79. Alexander Nelson, Greg Toth, Dennis Linders, Cuong Nguyen, and Sokwoo Rhee "Replication of Smart-City Internet of Things Assets in a Municipal Deployment" IEEE Internet of Things Journal, Vol. 6, No. 4, August 2019

80. Inés Sittón-Candanedo, Ricardo S. Alonso, Juan M. Corchado, Sara Rodríguez-González, Roberto Casado-Vara "A review of edge computing reference architectures and a new global edge proposal" Future Generation Computer Systems 99 (2019) 278–294

81. Inés Sittón-Candanedo, Ricardo S. Alonso, ÓscarGarcía, Ana B. Gil and Sara Rodríguez-González" A Review on Edge Computing in Smart Energy by means of a Systematic Mapping Study", December 2019

82. ÓscarGarcía, Ricardo S. Alonso, Javier Prieto and Juan M. Corchado Energy "Efficiency in Public Buildings through Context-Aware Social Computing", April 2017

83. Antonio Brogi, Stefano Forti "QoS-aware Deployment of IoT Applications through the Fog" Internet of Things Journal, DOI: https://doi.org/10.1109/JIOT.2017.2701408, IEEE

84. Fernando De la Prieta and Juan Manuel Corchado "Cloud Computing and Multi agent Systems, a Promising Relationship", Springer International Publishing Switzerland 2016J. Kołodziej et al. (eds.), Intelligent Agents in Data-intensive Computing, Studies in Big Data 14, DOI https://doi.org/10.1007/978-3-319-23742-8_7

85. Yun Chao Hu, Milan Patel, Dario Sabella, NuritSprecher and Valerie Young "Mobile Edge computing a key technology towards 5G" First edition – September 2015 ISBN No. 979-10-92620-08-5

86. Frieder Ganz, Daniel Puschmann, PayamBarnaghi, and Francois Carrez A "Practical Evaluation of Information Processing and Abstraction Techniques for the Internet of Things", IEEE Internet of Things Journal, DOI: https://doi.org/10.1109/JIOT.2015.2411227

87. Pedro Garcia Lopez, Alberto Montresor, Dick Epema, AnwitamanDatta, TeruoHigashino, Adriana Iamnitchi, MarinhoBarcellos, Pascal Felber, Etienne Riviere "Edge-centric Computing: Vision and Challenges" ACM SIGCOMM Computer Communication Review Volume 45, Number 5, October 2015

88. Harshit Gupta, Amir VahidDastjerdi, Soumya K. Ghosh, RajkumarBuyya "iFogSim: A toolkit for modelling and simulation of resource management techniques in the Internet of Things, Edge and Fog computing environments", May 2017, DOI: https://doi.org/10.1002/spe.2509

89. Najmul Hassan, SairaGillani, Ejaz Ahmed, IbrarYaqoob, and Muhammad Imran "The Role of Edge Computing in Internet of Things" Digital Object Identifier: https://doi.org/10.1109/MCOM.2018.1700906

90. Gopika Premsankar, Mario Di Francesco, and Tarik Taleb "Edge Computing for the Internet of Things: A Case Study", IEEE Internet of Things Journal, DOI: https://doi.org/10.1109/JIOT.2018.2805263

91. Tarik Taleb, Konstantinos Samdanis, BadrMada], HannuFlinck, Sunny Dutta, and Dario Sabella "On Multi-Access Edge Computing: A Survey of the Emerging 5G Network Edge Cloud Architecture & Orchestration" IEEE Communications Surveys & Tutorials

92. Wei Yu, Fan Liang, Xiaofei He, William G. Hatcher, Chao Lu, Jie Lin, and Xinyu Yang "A Survey on the Edge Computing for the Internet of Things" This article has been accepted for publication in a future issue of this journal, but has not been fully edited. Content may change prior to final publication. Citation information: DOI https://doi.org/10.1109/ACCESS.2017.2778504, IEEE Access

93. Muhammad Shoaib Farooq, ShamylaRiaz, Adnan Abid, Kamran Abid, and Muhammad AzharNaeem "A Survey on the Role of IoT in Agriculture for the Implementation of Smart Farming" Received October 3, 2019, accepted October 18, 2019, date of publication October 25, 2019, date of current version November 6, 2019.

94. Nurzaman Ahmed, Debashis De and Md. Iftekhar Hussain "Internet of Things (IoT) for Smart Precision Agriculture and Farming in Rural Areas" IEEE Internet of Things Journal, Vol. 5, No. 6, December 2018

95. TanmayBaranwal, Nitika, Pushpendra Kumar Pateriya "Development of IoT based Smart Security and Monitoring Devices for Agriculture" 978-1-4673-8203-8/16/$31.00_c 2016 IEEE

96. Mahammad ShareefMekala, P Viswanathan "CLAY-MIST: IoT-Cloud Enabled CMM index for Smart Agriculture Monitoring System", Measurement (2018), DOI: https://doi.org/10.1016/j.measurement.2018.10.072

97. Mahammad ShareefMekala, Dr P. Viswanathan, "A Survey: Smart Agriculture IoT with Cloud Computing" 978-1-5386-1716-8/17/$31.00 ©2017 IEEE

98. HemlataChanne, Sukhesh Kothari, Dipali Kadam, "Multidisciplinary Model for Smart Agriculture using Internet-of-Things (IoT), Sensors, Cloud Computing, Mobile Computing & Big-Data Analysis" HemlataChanne et al, Int. J. Computer Technology & Applications, Vol 6 (3),374–382

99. Prathibha S R, AnupamaHongal, Jyothi M P, "IOT based Monitoring System in Smart Agriculture", 2017 International Conference on Recent Advances in Electronics and Communication Technology, 978-1-5090-6701-5/17 $31.00 © 2017 IEEE, DOI https://doi.org/10.1109/ICRAECT.2017.5281

100. Olakunle Elijah, Tharek Abdul Rahman, IgbafeOrikumhi, Chee Yen Leow and MHD NourHindia "An Overview of Internet of Things (IoT) and Data Analytics in Agriculture: Benefits and Challenges", IEEE Internet of Things Journal, Vol. 5, No. 5, October 2018

101. Mandrita Banerjee, Junghee Lee, Kim-Kwang Raymond Choo "A Blockchain Future to Internet of Things Security: A Position Paper" PII: S2352-8648(17)30290-0DOI: https://doi.org/10.1016/j.dcan.2017.10.006Reference: DCAN 118

102. Xiaoqi Li, Peng Jiang, Ting Chen, Xiapu Luo, Qiaoyan Wen, "A survey on the security of blockchain systems", Future Generation Computer Systems Journal
103. Ana Reyna, Cristian Mart'ın, Jaime Chen, Enrique Soler, Manuel D'ıaz, "On blockchain and its integration with IoT. Challenges and opportunities", Future Generation Computer Systems, May 2018 PII: S0167-739X (17) j.future.2018.05.046
104. Mauro Isaja, John K. Soldatos, Volkan Gezer, "Combining Edge Computing and Blockchains for Flexibility and Performance in Industrial Automation", UBICOMM 2017: The Eleventh International Conference on Mobile Ubiquitous Computing, Systems, Services and Technologies
105. FarzadSamie, Lars Bauer, and Jörg Henkel, "From Cloud Down to Things: An Overview of Machine Learning in Internet of Things", IEEE Internet of Things Journal, Vol. 6, No. 3, June 2019
106. Yi-Fan Zhang, Peter J. Thorburn, Wei Xiang and Peter Fitch, "SSIM – A Deep Learning Approach for Recovering Missing Time Series Sensor Data", IEEE Internet of Things Journal, Vol. 6, No. 4, August 2019
107. Karrar Hameed Abdulkareem, Mazin Abed Mohammed, SaraswathyShaminiGunasekaran, Mohammed Nasser Al-Mhiqani, Ammar AwadMutlag, Salama A. Mostafa, NabeelSalih Ali, And Dheyaa Ahmed Ibrahim, "A Review of Fog Computing and Machine Learning: Concepts, Applications, Challenges, and Open Issues", October 2019, Digital Object Identifier https://doi.org/10.1109/ACCESS.2019.2947542
108. A. Rakotoasimbahoaka, I. Randria, N. R. Razafindrakoto "Malicious URL Detection by Combining Machine Learning and Deep Learning Models EDMI", University, BP 1264 – Campus Universitaired'Andrainjato, Fianarantsoa, 301, Madagascar
109. Yong-Shin Kang, I-Ha Park, Jongtae Rhee, and Yong-Han Lee, "Mongo DB-Based Repository Design for IoT-Generated RFID/Sensor Big Data", IEEE Sensors Journal, Vol. 16, No. 2, January 15, 2016
110. Shubo Liu, LiqingGuo, Heather Webb, Xiao Ya and Xiao Chang, "Internet of Things Monitoring System of Modern Eco-Agriculture Based on Cloud Computing", IEEE Magazine, March 2019
111. Fadi Al-Turjman, Enver Ever, Yousaf Bin Zikria, Sung Won Kim and AbdulmalekElmahgoubiSahci, "Scheduling Approach for Heterogeneous Content-Centric IoT Applications", IEEE Access Journal, June 14, 2019, DOI: https://doi.org/10.1109/ACCESS.2019.2923203
112. Charles Malveaux, Steve Hall, Randy R. Price, "Using Drones in Agriculture: Unmanned Aerial Systems for Agricultural Remote Sensing Applications", 2014 ASABE – CSBE/SC-GAB Annual International Meeting Paper, Paper Number: 141911016, Montreal, Quebec Canada, July 13–16, 2014
113. Rutten et al., "Assessing Agricultural Damage by Wild Boar Using Drones", Wildlife Society Bulletin; DOI: https://doi.org/10.1002/wsb.916
114. Frank Veroustraete, "The Rise of the Drones in Agriculture", EC Agriculture 2.2 (2015): 325–327
115. Per Frankelius, Charlotte Norrman, Knut Johansen, "Agricultural Innovation and the Role of Institutions: Lessons from the Game of Drones", Journal of Agriculture Environment Ethics, Springer, https://doi.org/10.1007/s10806-017-9703-6
116. Marek Kulbacki et al., "Survey of Drones for Agriculture Automation from Planting to Harvest", INES 2018, 22nd IEEE International Conference on Intelligent Engineering Systems, June 21–23, 2018, Las Palmas de Gran Canaria, Spain, 978-1-5386-1122-7/18/$31.00 ©2018 IEEE
117. Jiafu Wan, Shenglong Tang, Zhaogang Shu, Di Li, ShiyongWang,Muhammad Imran, and Athanasios V. Vasilakos, "Software-Defined Industrial Internet of Things in the Context of Industry 4.0", IEEE Sensors Journal, Vol. 16, No. 20, October 15, 2016
118. Sayan Kumar Roy, and Debashis De, "Genetic Algorithm based Internet of Precision Agricultural Things (IopaT) for Agriculture 4.0." Internet of Things (2020): 100201.

119. Sukhpal Singh Gill, Inderveer Chana, and Rajkumar Buyya. "IoT based agriculture as a cloud and big data service: the beginning of digital India." Journal of Organizational and End User Computing (JOEUC), Vol. 29, No. 4: 1–23, 2017.
120. Sukhpal Singh, Inderveer Chana, and Rajkumar Buyya, "Agri-Info: Cloud Based Autonomic System for Delivering Agriculture as a Service." Internet of Things, Vol. 9 (2020): 100131.

Deep Learning in Computer Vision through Mobile Edge Computing for IoT

Abu Sufian, Ekram Alam, Anirudha Ghosh, Farhana Sultana, Debashis De, and Mianxiong Dong

Abstract The success of Artificial Intelligence (AI) through Deep Learning (DL) and Computer Vision has inspired many researchers to work on many real-life and human-centered tasks. These current AI systems are in use to augment the intelligence of IoT. IoT devices are equipped with very low computing and fewer storage resources. In the case of visual computing, a massive number of images or video data are needed to be processed, which seems to be not feasible for an IoT device. Therefore, those data are needed to transfer to a cloud machine for computation. However, in this case, bandwidth scarcity is a huge problem. Real-time computation and security and privacy of data are also very challenging issues. To handle this problem, Mobile Edge Computing (MEC) is used in IoT to perform the real-time computation locally. Combining state-of-the-art computer vision algorithms such as DL, especially Deep Convolutional Neural Network (CNN) based algorithms and MEC, can be a smart solution for onsite visual computing. This chapter scholarly discussed how deep CNN through MEC could be a potential technique for IoT based solutions. It also discuss how a deep transfer learning procedure can be applied in this method. This chapter proposes how different layers of deep CNN can be split up among Edge devices, Fog gateway, and Cloud servers to do visual computing at IoTs. Relevant technical backgrounds, current state-of-the-art, and future scopes are also emphasized in this chapter.

A. Sufian (✉) · A. Ghosh · F. Sultana
Department of Computer Science, University of Gour Banga, Malda, West Bengal, India
e-mail: sufian@ieee.org

E. Alam
Department of Computer Science, Gour Mahavidyalaya, Malda, West Bengal, India

D. De
Centre of Mobile Cloud Computing, Department of Computer Science and Engineering, Maulana Abul Kalam Azad University of Technology, Kolkata, West Bengal, India
e-mail: dr.debashis.de@ieee.org

M. Dong
Department of Sciences and Informatics, Muroran Institute of Technology, Hokkaido, Japan
e-mail: mx.dong@csse.muroran-it.ac.jp

© The Author(s), under exclusive license to Springer Nature Switzerland AG 2021
A. Mukherjee et al. (eds.), *Mobile Edge Computing*,
https://doi.org/10.1007/978-3-030-69893-5_18

443

Keywords AI in edge · Computer vision · Convolutional neural network · Deep learning · Embedded systems · IoT · Mobile edge computing

1 Introduction

In the year 2011, the number of interconnected devices had overtaken the number of people in the world, and it is estimated that this figure has been reached 24 billion by the end of the year 2020 [1]. The GSMA estimates that there have been 26 smart connected devices for each person by 2020 [2]. The GSMA also mentioned that in the year 2018, mobile technologies and its services had added 3.9 trillion dollars of market value (4.6% of GDP) globally, and that shall reach 4.8 trillion dollars (4.8% of GDP) by the year 2023. On the other hand, applications of 5G networks are also gaining momentum [3]. This growing demand for interconnected devices and 5G networks pushes the revolution of the Internet of Things (IoT) upwards. Researchers of these areas suggest that the future IoT will be smarter, more automated, fast, and capable of making an inference based on data at site [4, 5]. To make these feasible, Artificial Intelligence (AI), especially Machine Learning (ML), as well as Deep Learning (DL), will play crucial roles. However, the real problem is that IoT mostly depends on server (cloud) computing. IoT device senses the data and sends it to a server for processing and making inferences. Therefore, latency, data security and privacy become challenging issues [6]. Mobile Edge Computing (MEC) can be exploited to counter these challenges, where most of the computing is done near to IoT Device. IoT device is sometimes referred to as an edge device, so these two terms are interchangeably used in this chapter. A hierarchical relationship among edge devices, fog gateway, and the cloud server has depicted in Fig. 1. Most of the IoT or edge devices have minimal computing and storage resources. So, to benefit from deep learning in edge devices, some alternate implementing strategies

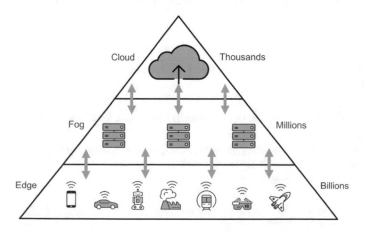

Fig. 1 Hierarchy of cloud, fog and edge computing

are required. Obviously, many works have been proposed so far by researchers from all over the world [7–9]. However, most of the works suggest some hardware accelerators, which is not cost-effective and not suited for very lightweight edge devices. Some works also are suggested to trade-off the accuracy with pruning the networks, which is also one kind of performance compromising.

This chapter, 'Deep Learning in Computer Vision through Mobile Edge Computing for IoT (DCMIoT)', scholarly discusses these issues. It has been proposed some of the software accelerated MEC approaches: one is deep transfer learning-based. Another one is splitting the deep learning model or algorithm among Edge, Fog, and Cloud servers. It has also suggested a distributed computing among edge devices. These are explained in the perspective of Computer Vision and Convolutional Neural Networks (CNN). This chapter also discussed background details for a better understanding of the topic. A brief chronological survey on recent existing state-of-the-art is also done in this chapter. Some highlights of the chapter are:

- A study of onsite visual computing through MEC using CNN.
- A survey of the recent state-of-the-art and brief technical background details.
- Proposed three MEC approaches that could exploit Deep Learning at Edge.
- An analysis of proposed models for onsite visual computing.

The rest of the chapter is organized as follows: background details are discussed in Sect. 2. In Sect. 3, literature review of notable state-of-the-arts. Three software accelerated MEC approaches are proposed in Sect. 4, whereas Sect. 5 analyses our proposed technique. Finally, conclusion, and future scope in Sect. 6.

2   Background

The main focus of this chapter is mobile edge computing (MEC) for IoT or Edge Devices. Here, computing algorithms are based on deep learning, and the target applied domain is computer vision. Therefore, some technical terms that are related to this area are briefly discussed in the following subsections.

2.1   IoT or Edge Device

IoT is comprised by the US National Intelligence Council (NIC) in the record of six "Disruptive Civil Technologies" with significant influence on US national power.[1] According to NIC, IoT nodes may use in everyday things: from food packages to healthcare equipment [6]. Empowered by the latest progress in Communication and Information Technology, Data Analytics, and Artificial Intelligence, the IoT

---

[1] https://fas.org/irp/nic/disruptive.pdf accessed on 11/02/2020.

has been revolutionized the world. It is opening new opportunities and presenting unimaginable solutions a few years before [2].

As mentioned in study [1], Kevin Ashton first raised the term Internet of Things (IoT) in the late 1990s in the context of the supply chain management [2]. Many definitions of IoT are available in various literature based on their approaches, backgrounds, and needs. So, it is not easy to have a universal definition of it. The reason for today's apparent fuzziness around this term 'Internet of Things' itself, which is consists of two terms; the first one focuses on a network-oriented approach, whereas the second one drifts the focus on generic 'objects' that to be combined into a common framework [6].

The IoT is highly multidisciplinary because it presents a wide variety of protocols, technologies, disciplines, and applications concurrently [1, 6]. The International Telecommunication Union (ITU) defines it as a global infrastructure that enables advanced services by the interconnection of physical and virtual things based on existing and evolving compatible technologies [2]. Xia and others define IoT as a networked interconnection of intelligent objects [10]. In simple words, IoT is anything that can be a part of a network and can be communicated by driving different types of sensors [11, 12]. As IoTs are the lowest level equipment, so it may be called edge devices too.

Functional Architecture of IoT

A typical functional architecture of the IoT has been shown in Fig. 2. There are five layers in this architecture, namely Perception Layer, Transmission Layer, Middleware Layer, Application Layer, and Business Layers. Similar architectures are shown in other proposed works [13, 14]. A brief explanation of the layers of this architecture is mentioned below.

L1: Perception Layer It can also be called 'Object Layer' or 'Device Layer'. These objects can be fitted in Mobile Phones, Cars, Drones, Security Cameras, Trains, Aeroplanes, etc. This is the lowest-level layer where, according to the requirements, actual data are collected through different types of sensor devices, actuators, RFID tags, etc. Collected data, which can be about location, vibration, proximity, humidity, motion, illuminance temperature, etc., are converted to digital form. This digital data is transferred to the Transmission Layer through secure channels for further processing.

L2: Transmission Layer It is also called the Network Layer. This layer securely transfers the data from sensor-enabled devices to the middleware layer. The transmission medium can be guided or unguided with different technologies [13]. The main communication technologies used here shall be classified as Home Area Networks (HAN), Field Area Network (FAN), and Wide Area Networks (WAN). In HAN, available technologies that can be used are RFID, NFC, ZigBee, Wi-Fi, Bluetooth, Dash7, etc. For FAN, PLC (Power Line Communication) can be used. Similarly, for WAN, WiMAX and Cellular Technologies (GSM, GPRS, EDGE, 3G, 4G, LTE, 5G) can be used. These technologies can be used depending on the data

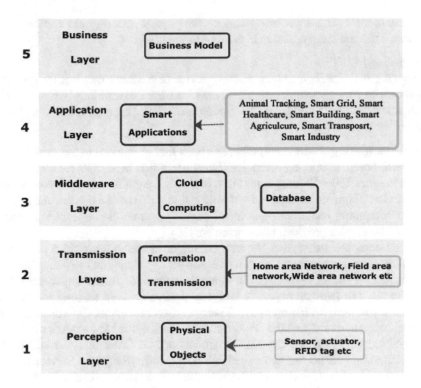

Fig. 2 Typical functional architecture of IoT

rate, coverage range, location, etc. [15]. Some literature also mentioned this layer as 'The Transport Layer' [16].

L3: Middle-Ware Layer In some literature, this layer has been mentioned as 'The Processing Layer' [16]. The IoT components implement different types of services, where each component connects and communicates with a peer component that enforces the same type of service. This layer is liable for service management, and it has a link to the database. It takes input from the network layer and stores it in the database. It also executes processing, ubiquitous computation, cloud computing and takes decisions based on the results.

L4: Application Layer The application layer presents applications to users based on the computed data in the middleware layer. Some examples of this layer's smart applications are smart houses, smart farming, smart city, smart transport, smart healthcare, etc. This layer can also act as the interface for users interacting with a physical device to access the required data.

L5: Business Layer This is the higher-level layer that manages the overall IoT as a product. Based on the imputed data from the application layer, it can make several business models. This layer also manages the privacy, security, and authorization, which are the challenging issues in the development of IoT.

Computing in IoT

Computing is the main backbone for any device or machine, and it is also for IoT. As shown in Fig. 1, computing in IoT may be Cloud Computing (CC) [17], Fog Computing (FC) [18], and Edge Computing (EC) [19]. These are briefly mentioned below.

Cloud Computing Cloud computing has been first introduced in the year 1996 as a network-based computing archetype. However, it first used in its modern context was in the year 2006. Cloud computing is basically a parallel and distributed system that consists of interconnected and virtualized nodes that can be used as one or more unified computing resources on-demand based on some service-level agreements between the service provides and consumers [20].

Cloud computing describes the new paradigm in which it provides processing capabilities and storage in an on-demand manner by relying on high-capacity data centers that are available through the Internet connection. This arrangement allows users to retrieve their applications and data from anywhere as long as they are connected through the Internet [21]. There are two Models of Cloud Computing: The deployment model and the Service model. Further, the Deployment model can be classified as (1) Private cloud, (2) Public cloud, (3) Community cloud, and (4) Hybrid cloud. Whereas Service model can be: (1) Everything as a Service (EaaS), (2) Infrastructure as a Service (IaaS), (3) Platform as a Service (PaaS), (4) Software as a Service (SaaS), (5) Hardware as a Service (HaaS), (6) Workspace as a Service (WaaS), (7) Data as a Service (DaaS) [22].

Fog Computing Fog computing was first mentioned by Bonomi et al. [23] as a highly virtualized system that gives computing, storage, and networking services between end devices and traditional cloud computing data centers generally located at the edge of the network. Fog computing sometimes referred to as 'cloudlet', lies in between two extremes: Cloud Computing and Edge Computing (at Edge or IoT devices). It places near the edge to make a bridge in computing between cloud and edge computing [24].

Edge Computing In many pieces of study, the terms 'Fog computing' and 'Edge computing' have been used interchangeably. Though both FC and EC try to bring the cloud resource and services near the edge, the FC edge is the edge of the Internet, and the EC edge is the edge of edge devices or IoT. The term 'Edge computing' was first presented around the year 2002 [25] but it became popular recently because of IoT revolutions [2]. EC is motivated by bandwidth scarcities between the edge device and cloud server, and the need for data security and privacy, improved performance in computing at edge devices. EC's main feature is that data can be computed locally in edge devices rather than being sent as raw to a cloud server for computing.

2.2 Mobile Edge Computing

The Mobile Edge Computing (MEC) is an extended Edge Computing technique where edge devices are mobile [24]. The formal ideas of MEC were first presented by the "European Telecommunications Standard Institute (ETSI)" in 2014. According to ETSI, MEC has the potential of cloud computing within the Radio Access Network (RAN) near to mobile subscribers [26]. MEC aims are low latency, reduce bandwidth scarcity, security, and privacy, implementing 5G, etc. [27]. The MEC brings computation and storage into the edge of mobile network-enabling devices virtually and sometimes physically [28] for computing nearby IoT devices. The MEC may work with the association of FC and CC [29] as they have a hierarchical relationship as shown in Fig. 1.

Since IoT is the main driver of 5G and other smart Edge-based solutions [30], so, MEC in IoT becomes an important issue to address. Many works have been proposed about implementing MEC in IoT [31–33]. Artificial Intelligence (AI), especially machine learning and deep learning, are used in MEC to make IoT smarter [8, 34–36]. Therefore, the discussion of MEC using deep learning is one of the main points of this chapter. To successfully apply deep learning in IoT through MEC, many approaches could be adopted, as mentioned in Sect. 3. Some of them are Computational offloading in Cloud-Fog Scenario, Transfer Learning-based MEC, Splitting layers of deep neural networks into Edge, Fog, and Cloud for load balancing, and distributed computing among edges. This chapter discussed three approaches in detail in Sects. 4 and 5 in the perspective of computer vision in IoT.

2.3 Computer Vision

Humans can easily see and understand the things around us using our eyes and brains. For example, consider an image, as shown in Fig. 3. In the first image of this figure, we can easily identify the object inside the image. Here basically, we are classifying the image, so this is the classification problem. In the second image of the same figure, the task is to classify the image and locate that particular object in the image. Here, the task is to draw a bounding box around the object. So, this is the Classification as well as the Localization task of Computer Vision. There is only one object in the figure in the first and second images, but in the third image, there is more than one object in one figure. So, here the task is to classify and localize all the objects of the image. In computer vision, this task is called Object Detection. The last image of Fig. 3 split all the object pixels from the background. Here a different instance of the same class is identified individually. This is called Instance Segmentation. The Computer vision aims to give the computer the capabilities of vision like humans [37]. Lots of work has been done in this direction, but still, this is a challenge to beat or at least have the same Computer Vision cognition as the

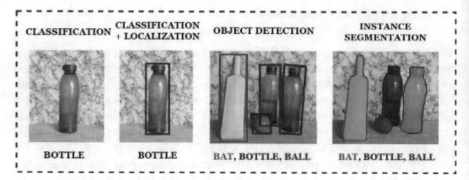

Fig. 3 Typical computer vision tasks

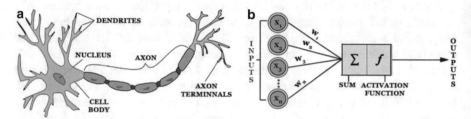

Fig. 4 Biological neural network versus artificial neural network

human visual system [38]. Recently deep learning, especially CNN for computer vision, has achieved huge success [39, 40]. A lot of visual automation can be done using IoT and Computer Vision [35, 41]. This chapter emphasizes these issues.

2.4 Deep Learning

Deep Learning (DL) is a kind of machine learning algorithm that extracts features directly from data. Therefore, unlike traditional machine learning, handcrafted features are not required here. DL is based on Artificial Neural Networks (ANN), and the main driving force is the backpropagation algorithm [42, 43]. The biological Neural Network inspires ANN, and the relationship between these two is shown in Fig. 4. The basic components of a biological neural network are dendrites, cell body (soma), and axon, as shown in part (a) of Fig. 4. Dendrites receive the inputs and pass them to the cell body; the cell body process the inputs. Axon receives the processed signals and transfers them to other neurons through axon terminals. ANN corresponding to a biological neuron is shown in part (b) of this figure.

Let us consider a single layer perceptron of ANN which is shown in part (b) of Fig. 4. Here $x_1, x_2, x_3, \ldots, x_n$ are the inputs (sensors) and $w_1, w_2, w_3, \ldots, w_n$ are

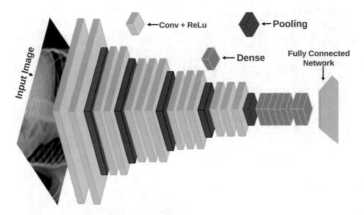

Fig. 5 A typical convolutional neural networks

the weights of each inputs. Output (y) is calculated as below where b is the bias term.

$$y = \begin{cases} 1 & \text{if } \sum_{i=1}^{n}(w_i * x_i) + b > 0 \\ 0 & \text{otherwise} \end{cases}$$

The activation function used here is a step function which is useful for linearly separable problems. For linearly non-separable problems, we use multi-layer perceptron (MLP) with non-linear activation functions like Sigmoid, Tanh, ReLU, etc. In the case of visual computing, CNN [44] based architectures are very useful for the data's spatial nature. Besides, CNN has a weight sharing feature, which makes it useful for image or video data. A typical CNN for classification is shown in Fig. 5, which consists of the following components.

- Convolution Layer
- Activation Layer
- Pooling Layer
- Fully Connected or Dense Layer
- Classification Layer

Convolution Layer An image is represented as a collection of pixel values. For a binary or gray image, an image is as a 2D array, as shown in Fig. 6. To perform the convolution operation, we need a filter matrix of the size $k \times k$. The convolution operation is done by summarizing the element-wise multiplication of the kernel matrix and input matrix (image) from the first position and shifting by a specific stride depth. We can notice that the size of the input and output matrix is not the same. We can add some padding value to the input matrix before the convolution operation to get the same size. We can also shift the matrix by more than one, i.e., we can use stride value as more than one.

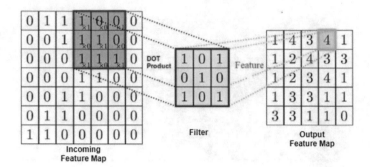

Fig. 6 Convolutional layer

Fig. 7 A Max-Pooling operation

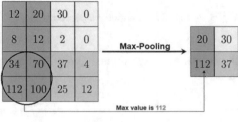

Fig. 8 A typical fully-connected layer

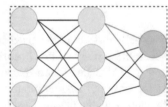

Activation Layer Activation functions determine the output of a particular neuron. It decides whether a neuron will fire or not. In CNN, typically ReLU activation function is used; it changes negative values to zeros as the following calculation:

$$ReLU(x) = \max(0, x)$$

Pooling Layer Pooling is basically the downsampling or subsampling operation which reduces the number of parameters of the input layer but retains the important features. There are different types of pooling operations like Max Pooling, Average Pooling, Sum Pooling, etc. For example, in Fig. 7, 2×2 maxpooling layer is shown.

Fully-Connected Layer (FC or Dense Layer) In this layer, we flatten the matrix into a column vector and feed it to a feed-forward fully connected (FC) neural network. Backpropagation is applied to every iteration of training. A fully connected layer has full connections to all activation functions in the previous layer. It looks like a classical ANN as shown in Fig. 8.

Softmax Softmax function transforms a set of values to its corresponding probability values. It is very useful for a classifier. Mathematically Softmax classifier can be defined as the following expression. Here $x_1, x_2, \ldots, x_3(x_i)$ are the values (scores) of the individual classes.

$$softmax(x_i) = \frac{exp(x_i)}{\sum_j exp(x_j))}$$

Many deep learning models have come after the success of AlexNet [45]. Some of these are Recurrent Neural Network (LSTM), Generative Adversarial Networks (GAN), Endocder-decoder, etc. [43]. In the case of image segmentation or object detection, some modifications are required such as up-sampling, RoI detection, etc. [46, 47].

3 Literature Survey

As mentioned before, this chapter focuses on MEC with deep learning algorithms for IoT or edge devices with special attention to computer vision. Therefore, this section points out some notable state-of-the-art works on deep learning-based MEC for IoT (Edge) devices. Although this chapter focuses on applications of visual data, the idea of similar works on other types of data may be worthy, so this literature survey is not restricted to works of visual data only. Since MEC became popular in the last 5 years [24], this brief survey is restricted to the works of the last 5 years in chronological order.

In study [48], N. D. Lane et al. explain that making inference from raw data by the classical algorithm is difficult for IoT, smartphones, and wearable devices. They have investigated how deep learning could be used in such devices. In another study, F. Alam et al. experimented with eight data mining algorithms, including deep learning for IoT [49]. They have found that deep learning gives the highest accuracy on their used datasets, but it was computationally expensive for IoT. DeepX [50], a deep learning model for low power devices proposed by N. D. Lane et al. They broke the deep neural networks into unit-blocks and did resource scaling to run on heterogeneous small devices. In study [51], D. Ravi et al. proposed a deep learning methodology for wearable devices and smartphones. Here, they used inertial sensor data along with a set of shallow features. In another study, S. Bhattacharya et al. proposed SparseSep [52]. In their work, sparsification and separation are done for FC layers and convolutional kernels to minimize the resource requirements to run on mobile devices.

MobileNets [53], a low resource deep learning model for embedded vision applications proposed by A. G. Howard et al. They used depth-wise separable convolutions, two global hyper-parameters, to the trade-off between latency, resources, and accuracy. In a study, J. Tang et al. suggested two methodologies to enable deep learning for IoT devices in their article [54]. They have suggested an offloading workload to a cloud server where the model will run. They also have suggested bringing deep learning frameworks into embedded devices. In another study [55], H.Y. Kim and J.M. Kim proposed a load balancing strategy. They used deep learning-based protocol to balance the computing load of IoT. On the other hand, S. Teerapittayanon et al. proposed deep learning among End device, Edge, and Cloud [56]. In their object recognition task, they trained the model jointly by the End device, Edge, and Cloud. They have claimed that it reduces communication cost, minimizing resource uses at the end device, and maximizes feature extraction for inference.

DeepThings [57], a framework of CNN for resource-constrained IoT edge proposed by Z Zhao et al. They have used the Fused Tile Partitioning of convolutional layers to minimize memory uses during parallel processing. They also use a new scheduling approach to balance workloads to reduce execution latency and inference time. M. Song et al. proposed 'In-Situ AI' [58], an incremental framework of deep learning for IoT. Here, the author used IoT data diagnosis, incremental and unsupervised training to tackle big raw sensor data with minimum movement. They used a two-level weight share to deploy this framework in IoT easily. In [8], He Li et al. suggested an approach of DL in IoT with edge computing. They mentioned that edge computing could easily be adopted as deep learning with a multi-layer structure. They proposed a new offloading strategy to optimized their works. M. Ali et al. proposed a distributed deep learning-based pipeline between the edge and cloudlet (fog) [59] for edge computing. They suggested that initial processing should be done in edge devices with cloudlets before sending it to the cloud. eSGD [60], a distributed deep learning for edge device, proposed by Z. Tao and Q. Li. That eSGD first finds an important gradient coordinate and then sends it to the cloud, which reduces communications cost. It also designs momentum residual accumulation for tracing idle residual gradient coordinates to turn aside a low convergence rate.

NoNN [61], a compressed distributed deep learning paradigm for IoT proposed by K. Bhardwaj et al. Here, they proposed 'teacher' and 'student' model, where a large pre-trained neural network at teacher are distributed among students, then distributed inference are made at edge device. Filter pruning strategy is also applied to implement deep learning in IoT in works [62]. In a study, J. Zhou et al. proposed AAIoT [63], where a distributed computing is proposed. Here, each layer of a large neural network is distributed to several IoT devices, and dynamic programming is used to reduce computational redundancy. In another study [64], M. Min et al. presented a deep learning-based MEC model for IoT. They have applied a reinforcement learning-based offloading technique with energy harvesting in IoT. Their scheme reduces energy consumption and latency along with increasing learning speed. Similar kinds of work are also proposed by J. Kang et al. in [65]. S. Tuli et al. proposed deep learning-based object detection frameworks, called EdgeLens [66]. Here IoT works with Fog and Cloud server for computing. The authors were used the 'Aneka platform service' to deploy and experiment with the effectiveness of the model in terms of accuracy, response time, power consumption, etc. Another distributed deep learning model through edge computing is proposed by J. Chen et al. [67] for Distributed Intelligent Video Surveillance. They have used parallel training, model synchronization, and dynamic data migration for balancing workload. In-Edge AI [68], an integrated Deep Reinforcement Learning as well as Federated Learning model for mobile edge proposed by X. Wang et al. This work has tried to utilize the collaboration among devices for the low overhead of learning.

In a study [69], F. Liang et al. mentioned an edge-based deep learning model for Industrial IoT. They applied a test-bed in Google cloud and deployed it in Industrial IoT. iSEC [70], a deep learning model on edge computing for image classification proposed by E. Kristiani et al. For faster training, the authors used hyper-parameter tuning at the CPU level. They used a model optimizer to train some state-of-the-art CNN at the edge. In another study, [71], J. Azar et al. proposed data compression and deep learning for IoT time-series data classification. They mainly have focused on data compression and used some compression techniques such as 'Squeeze (SZ).' They did a trade-off between data quality and compression.

Through the above survey and other literature surveys [72, 73], it could be concluded that many related works have been proposed for many different tasks. Some techniques are suggested to trade-off the accuracy with pruning the networks or model. Some techniques have suggested some hardware accelerators, which is not cost-effective and not suited for very lightweight edge devices. However, very few works are dedicated to onsite visual computing using onsite computing techniques, viz. the edge or fog computing. Therefore, this chapter is proposing three deep learning-based MEC approaches.

4   Three Deep Learning-Based MEC Approaches

As mentioned in Sect. 2.3, computer vision may be used in many application areas. Deep learning can be used in computer vision, as mentioned in Sect. 2.4. On the other hand, IoT has become prime components of many networking based automation systems, as discussed in Sect. 2.1. IoT or edge device has limited computing resources and small storage capacity, but deep learning is resource hungry algorithms. Therefore, deep learning in computer vision is a challenging task for IoT based applications [41, 74]. Through Mobile Edge Computing (MEC) for IoT (DCMIoT), Deep Learning in Computer Vision tries to bring AI into vision-based IoTs such as smartphones, drones, web cameras, etc. Here, MEC concepts are discussed for IoTs with special attention to visual sensor data (images, videos, etc.). Although many MEC techniques have been proposed, this chapter is theoretically proposing three deep learning-based approaches. The first one is the Transfer Learning Approach, and the other two include Split layers of deep neural networks among edges, fog gateway, and cloud server. These are described in subsequent subsections below:

4.1 Transfer Learning Approach in MEC

Transfer Learning or domain adaption is a methodology where an algorithm or model is trained in one task and applied on another task with required fine-tuning [75]. Several machine learning-based transfer learning techniques have been proposed, including instance-based, inductive based, transductive, etc. [76, 77]. Some of them are under the umbrella of classical machine learning-based, and some of them are under deep learning-based. In deep transfer learning (a deep learning-based), most of the pre-trained layers of a model can be used in a different task where dataset scarcity is there [78, 79].

Deep learning became successful because of three main factors: Innovative Algorithms, Computation Power of Modern Machine, and Availability of Large Scale Datasets. Nowadays huge size of the dataset are available such as ImageNet [80], Openimages [81] and many more. However, the dataset from IoTs, especially IoT based camera sensors, are very rare. So, if we want to get the success of deep learning in IoT based computer vision, then we have to create many large size datasets captured by IoT or edge devices-based cameras such as drone, mobile camera, web camera, etc. Hopefully, such a dataset will be available in near future. However, for IoT-based device dataset is the problems, but another big problem is limited computing power. These two problems can be tackled using transfer learning into IoT or edge devices. Here edge devices will work with cloud computing through a communication medium. A deep learning model shall be trained using a benchmark dataset at a cloud server. After that trained model (except for a few high-level layers (s)) shall be pushed into IoT or edge devices. Required fine-tuning could be done at edge devices using MEC computing to orient the target task model. Similarly, CNN, a deep learning approach for computer vision, could use in edge devices using transfer learning. Here we have discussed a CNN-based transfer Learning for mobile edge devices for possible onsite visual computing. This subsection tried to explain how a CNN model can be used in edge devices using transfer learning.

In this approach, a CNN model has to be trained using some benchmark dataset at a cloud. Since the lower layer extracts only low-level features like edges, corners, etc., these layers can be frozen after training and can be used in any other task. So, after training at a cloud server, lower layers are frozen and transferred to edge devices. In the edge device, only a few last layers are trained or fine-tuned using task-oriented data. In this technique, the powerful computing resources such as the GPU of the cloud is utilized in training and then transferred to the edge. Edge devices generally have low computing power, so this technique improves the response time, and real-time application could be feasible.

Figure 9 shows a typical procedure of deep transfer learning in the edge device. Here, part A: a Cloud Server consisting of GPU enabled large computing devices, where a CNN can be trained using a large benchmark dataset such as ImageNet or Open images. After training, the trained model shall be pushed down to part B: an Edge Device (IoT). In the edge device, pre-trained layers will be frozen except for

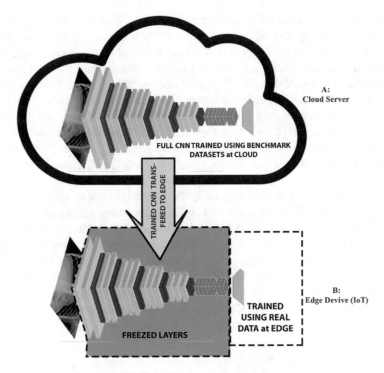

Fig. 9 Transfer learning approach for MEC

the last few layers. The last few layers can be fine-tuned or trained using real images captured by the edge device to orient the model towards the target task. Therefore, a small number of total parameters of a deep learning model will be trained at the edge that has been analyzed in Sect. 5.1. The number of freezing layers will depend on the trade-off between the accuracy and power of edge devices. It will also depend on the nature of the target task, dataset availability, and limitation of edge devices' computing power.

4.2 Splitting Layers of Deep Neural Networks into Edge, Fog and Cloud

Deep neural networks consist of several layers, which makes it suitable to be distributed through splitting. An edge device (IoT) has limited computing resources, so it will be beneficial if it works with Fog and Cloud, and if it uses deep learning, it becomes more relevant [8, 56, 59, 66]. The lower layers of the deep network extract low-level features such as edges, dots, color, etc. Middle layers extract high-level features, whereas higher layers that are few end layers are works for inference or decision making. On the other hand, the edge or IoT device works with fog and cloud servers. In general, edge devices sense the data and send it to a could for processing and making an inference, but latency, bandwidth, security, and privacy become challenging issues. Therefore, instead of sending whole raw data to a cloud, if the edge device uses the first few layers of deep neural networks to the nearest Fog Gateway, then the above-mentioned issues can be reduced. Similarly, Fog Gateway also shall process those data forwarded by Edge Devices before sending it to its cloud server. Therefore, the cloud server shall receive almost processed data. So, it would be easier to process the remaining processing and making an inference. Here, communications and synchronization among edge, fog, and cloud would be very crucial.

Consider Fig. 10 where a typical CNN is shown before splitting and after splitting. Here, this CNN consists of 22 layers, including pooling and FC networks. Then it is split into three parts A, B, and C, where A for Edge, B for Fog, and C for Cloud. Part A consists of the first 6 layers, including four convolutions shown by the color blue and two pooling layers, shown by green color. These layers of part A are allotted to the edge (IoT) device. After feeding an image into this part, it will collect some low-level features and reduce features maps before sending it to the nearest fog server. Part B of CNN consists of 7 layers among 4 convolutions and

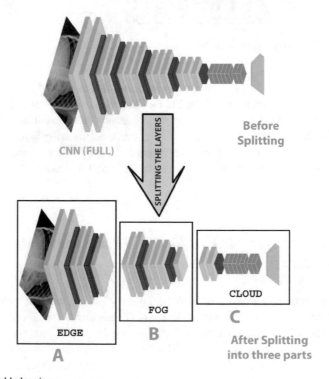

Fig. 10 Load balancing

two pooling; it will extract high-level features and reduce feature maps' size. Finally, Part C of the CNN, which are remaining parts, are allotted in the cloud server to do the remaining processing, including required inference. This distribution describes a typical scenario of these ideas, and it will vary depending on tasks and systems. An analysis is of this approach are mentioned in Sect. 5.2.

4.3   Splitting Layers of a Deep Neural Network into Different Edge Devices

A Deep Neural Network can be executed and trained in a distributed fashion. The whole network may be split into many small pieces, and those pieces may be assigned into different small devices to work collectively for a single task [57]. However, unlike in the last Sect. 4.2, here distribution is done among nearby edge devices [60, 61]. A task scheduling algorithm can be used here for distributing, balancing loads, and synchronizing. These task scheduling algorithms can be run at the edge device at ground zero or run a nearby fog server. Therefore, this kind of MEC computing can use a deep learning model to do a task in an edge or IoT device.

Consider Fig. 11, where some middle layers of a full CNN are split into four pieces and assigned into four nearby edge devices. Now processing could be initiated at the edge device at ground zero where few starting layers are in use. Then by task scheduling, forwards the rest of the processing to edge device 1. After

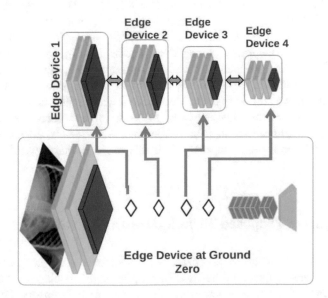

Fig. 11 A typical distribution of CNN among edge devices

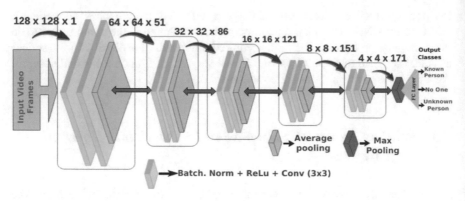

Fig. 12 Architecture of our CNN

processing at edge device 1, processed data will go to edge device 2, then from edge device 2 to edge device 3 to edge device 4. Finally, the flow goes back to the edge at ground zero, where the last few layers are also in use. Therefore, an inference can be made at this edge device where the task was started. This is a forward pass description, but the backward pass also follows the same procedure during training. However, in the reverse analysis of the advantage of proposed MEC approaches, we have considered a CNN model that may use in mobile edges for classifying the object in input images or video frames senses by edge devices or IoT sensors. The architecture of the used CNN model is shown in Fig. 12, and the structure are divided into 6 blocks, where each of first 5 blocks consist of $\ldots \rightarrow BatchNorm \rightarrow ReLU \rightarrow ConV2d(3 \times 3) \rightarrow BatchNorm \rightarrow ReLU \rightarrow ConV2d(3 \times 3) \rightarrow Avg.Polling \rightarrow \ldots$ and the last block consist of $\ldots \rightarrow BatchNorm \rightarrow ReLU \rightarrow Max.Polling \rightarrow Softmax$. The number of block-wise trainable parameters in this CNN is shown in Fig. 13. We have used this CNN model to explain and analyze the advantages of the proposed MEC approaches direction in the following subsections. Here other neighboring edge devices help the computing in an ad-hoc manner. Here edge devices could be connected using ad-hoc networks or any other networks to work jointly. Therefore, a big deep learning model could be used in an ad-hoc manner where nearby edge devices share a model's total parameters. An analysis of this proposed strategy is discussed in Sect. 5.4.

5 Analysis of Proposed Technique with Case Studies

To analyze the advantage of proposed MEC approaches, we have considered a typical CNN model that may be used in mobile edges to classify the object in input images or video frames senses by edge device or IoT sensors. The structure of the used CNN model is mentioned in Fig. 12, and the structure are divided

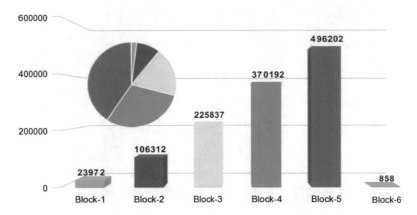

Fig. 13 Block-wise parameters of our CNN

into 6 blocks, where each of first 5 blocks consist of $\ldots \rightarrow BatchNorm \rightarrow ReLU \rightarrow ConV2d(3 \times 3) \rightarrow BatchNorm \rightarrow ReLU \rightarrow ConV2d(3 \times 3) \rightarrow Avg.Polling \rightarrow \ldots$ and the last block consist of $\ldots \rightarrow BatchNorm \rightarrow ReLU \rightarrow Max.Polling \rightarrow Softmax$. The number of block-wise trainable parameters in this CNN is mentioned in Fig. 13. We have used this CNN model to explain and analyze the advantages of proposed MEC approaches in the following subsections.

5.1 An Analysis of Transfer Learning Approach in MEC

In this transfer learning-based MEC approach mentioned in Sect. 4.1, we have been proposing to reuse a pre-trained model to solve another task with required fine-tuning. As mentioned, this methodology is instrumental when a task has a shortage of training data and limited computing power in devices like mobile edge or IoT. Here, only a few parameters of a deep learning model are needed to train for fine-tuning.

For case studies, we can train the above mentioned CNN model with ImageNet [80] dataset at a cloud server with high computing resources and then push the trained model into an edge device. In the edge device, re-train the last few layers of the model with actual training data using transfer learning procedures with required fine-tuning. This training process in edge devices includes reducing output classes from 1000 (output classes of ImageNet) to 3 (our output classes for a study). It makes a few first layers to be frozen except the last few layers. The number of freezing layers will depend on the trade-off between edge devices' accuracy and computing power. Figure 14 shows the total number of parameters trained in cloud server as well as in edge device in two different cases:

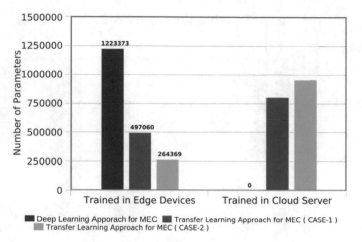

Fig. 14 Impact of transfer learning in parameter's training

- **Case 1:** Block-1 to block-4 of the CNN shown in Fig. 12 are frozen.
- **Case 2:** Block-1 to block-4 and the first $BatchNorm \rightarrow ReLU \rightarrow ConV2d(3 \times 3)$ layers of block-5 are frozen.

Although the graph is self-explanatory, for more explanation, we can say that only very few parameters are needed to train in edge for case-1 and case-2 compare to normal deep learning at the mobile edge. Therefore, the benefit of deep learning could be used to exploit it in MEC.

5.2 An Analysis of Splitting Layers of Deep Neural Networks into Edge, Fog, and Cloud

In this MEC approach described in Sect. 4.2, we split the CNN model's several layers. We distributed them between the edge, fog, and cloud to reduce the latency, bandwidth, security, and privacy. Here, we have analyzed bandwidth reductions with two possible parameter sharing strategies.

Reducing Bandwidth Requirements In the traditional MEC computing approach, all the sensed data must be processed locally to make an inference or send whole data to a cloud server for cloud computing. However, the first one seems to be infeasible, and for the second-case, latency, bandwidth, security, and privacy issues will arise. Since we use the computational load distribution approach instead of the traditional MEC approach, the bandwidth requirement is less. In this MEC approach, the edge device contains a part of the CNN model, which processes the sensed data locally and reduces the size of sending data by extracting high-level features. Only these high-level features are needed to be sent in fog. In fog, there is also some processing on received data, and therefore, it again reduces the size of sending data to the cloud. For example, let's take two cases:

- **Case 1:** We placed block-1 in edge device, block-2, and block-3 in fog, and block-4, block-5, and block-6 of the CNN shown in Fig. 12 in a cloud server.
- **Case 2:** We placed block-1, block-2 in edge device, block-3, and block-4 in fog, and block-5 and block-6 of the CNN in a cloud server.

The reduction of bandwidth requirement in case 1 is shown in Table 1 and case 2 is shown in Table 2 with different video frame rates.

5.3   Distribution of Parameters

The CNN model's parameter distribution includes the computation or resource distribution among the system, which reduces the dependency on the cloud and reduces the system's latency. Figure 15 shows the distribution of the parameters on CNN in the traditional MEC approach and two different scenarios of load balancing MEC approach. The formula to find the number of parameters required by a convolution operation as $(n \times m \times p + 1) \times k$, where n denotes the width of the filter, m denotes the height of the filter, p denotes the shape of input feature maps, k denotes the number of filters and $(+1)$ is for the bias of each feature map. Similarly, only the 1 parameter is required for each feature map in both $BatchNorm$ and $ReLU$ operation.

Therefore, in case-1, if we only use 23972 and 332149 number of parameters of total 1223373 parameters of the CNN, as shown in Fig. 12 at edge and fog respectively, then almost 8.50% bandwidth could be reduced before sending to a cloud server as calculated in Table 1. Similarly, in case-2, if we use 130284 and 596029 at edge and fog of that CNN, then almost 62.71% bandwidth uses could be reduced as calculated in Table 2.

5.4   An Analysis of Splitting Layers of a Deep Neural Network into Different Edge Devices

Here instead of assigning the split blocks of CNN among edge, fog, and cloud, we assign them into different neighbor edge devices in an ad-hoc manner as described in Sect. 4.3. It substantially reduces the system's latency because the whole job of sense and making an inference is done locally with the assistance of nearby edge devices. So the distribution of split jobs between edge devices is very much needed and challenging because each edge device has limited resources with meager computational power. If we are assigning the whole CNN into a single Edge device, that device will not run the assigned job. For case studies, we calculate the possible

Table 1 Bandwidth utilization through splitting MEC approach in case 1

Video frame per second	Traditional edge–cloud computing approach	Splitting CNN in MEC approach	Bandwidth reduction
4 frames	Sensed image size: 128×128 of grayscale image. So the bandwidth required for send it from edge to fog is: $128 \times 128 \times 8 \times 0.125 = 16384$ bytes and for fog to cloud is 16384 bytes. So in total, minimum bandwidth requirement is: $2 \times 16384 = 32768$ bytes $= 32$ KB for each frame. So, overall 128 KB bandwidth is required per second for each edge devices.	Here since the edge contains block-1 of CNN, the edge processed the sensed image and reduced it to 64×64 with 51 depth. The bandwidth required for sending sensed image from edge to fog is: $64 \times 64 \times 51 \times 0.125 = 26112$ bytes and again in the fog, receiving data is further reduced to $16 \times 16 \times 121 \times 0.125 = 3872$ bytes due to the processing of block-2 and block-3, and this 3872 bytes data need to send into the cloud. So in total, the minimum bandwidth requirement is: $26112 + 3872 = 29984$ bytes $= 29.282$ KB for each frame. So, overall ≈ 117.125 KB bandwidth is required per second for each edge device.	$\approx 8.50\%$
8 frames	Overall, 256 KB bandwidth is required per second for each edge device.	≈ 234.26 KB bandwidth is required per second for each edge device.	$\approx 8.51\%$
16 frames	Overall, 512 KB bandwidth is required per second for each edge device.	≈ 468.512 KB bandwidth is required per second for each edge device.	$\approx 8.50\%$

Table 2 Bandwidth utilization through load balancing MEC approach in case 2

Video frame per second	Traditional edge–cloud computing approach	Load balancing MEC approach	Bandwidth reduction
4 frames	Sensed image size: 128 × 128 of grayscale image. So the bandwidth required for send it from edge to fog is: 128 × 128 × 8 × 0.125 = 16384 bytes and for fog to cloud is 16384 bytes. So in total, minimum bandwidth requirement is: 2 × 16384 = 32768 bytes = 32 KB for each frame. So, overall 128 KB bandwidth is required per second for each edge devices.	Here since the edge contains block-1 and block-2 of CNN, so the edge processed the sensed image and reduced it to 32 × 32 with 86 depth, and the bandwidth required for sending sensed image from edge to fog is: 32 × 32 × 86 × 0.125 = 11008 bytes and again in the fog, receiving data is further reduced to 8 × 8 × 151 × 0.125 = 1208 bytes due to the processing of block-3 and 4 and this 1208 bytes data need to send into the cloud. So in total, the minimum bandwidth requirement is: 11008 + 1208 = 12216 bytes = 11.93 KB for each frame. So, overall ≈47.72 KB bandwidth is required per second for each edge device.	≈62.71 %
8 frames	Overall 256 KB bandwidth is required per second for each edge device.	≈95.44 KB bandwidth is required per second for each edge devices.	≈62.70 %
16 frames	Overall 512 KB bandwidth is required per second for each edge device.	≈190.9 KB bandwidth is required per second for each edge device.	≈62.71 %

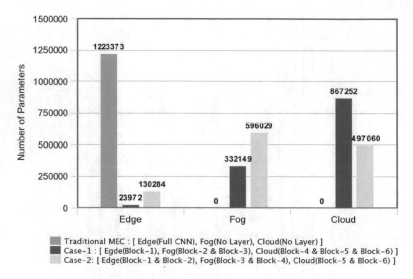

Fig. 15 Parameters in load balancing MEC approach

parameter distribution of the above mentioned CNN for a task in two different ways to see the computational load reduction.

– **Case 1:** We placed block-1, block-2, and block-6 of CNN in edge-1 (ground zero) and then splitting all the block-3, block-4, and block-5 of CNN into two equal parts and assigned them into separate edge devices. Each of those splitter parts contains $BatchNorm \rightarrow ReLU \rightarrow ConV2d(3 \times 3)$ layers.
– **Case 2:** Like case-1, here we also splitting all the block-3, block-4, and block-5 of CNN into two equal parts, and then except the first split part of block-3, we assigned other split parts into separate edge devices. Finally, blocks-1, blocks-2, the first split part of block-3, and block-6 of CNN are placed together in edge-1 (ground zero).

The parameter distribution in both cases with the traditional MEC approach (full CNN is processed in a single edge device) is shown in Fig. 16. From this figure, it is clear how a load of processing a CNN in a single edge could be reduced to use a CNN in MEC possibly.

6 Conclusion and Future Scopes

This chapter has been discussed onsite visual computing and proposed deep learning-based mobile edge computing method. Here, an explanation has been made from the perspective of a convolutional neural network for computer vision in IoT or Edge devices. To understand the issues and challenges, the chapter has described

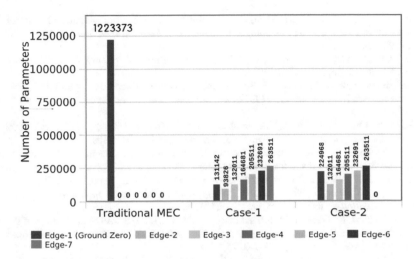

Fig. 16 Parameters in both cases due to assigning split layers to different edge devices

relevant background details and a survey of state-of-the-arts. Three deep learning-based mobile edge computing approaches have been theoretically described as possible solutions to such challenges. Some methodologies have already been proposed by the other researchers, as mentioned in the literature survey. However, the approaches discussed in this chapter are slightly different concepts for IoT based onsite visual computing as a MEC.

A combined model of these three approached could also be designed and experimented with. The back-propagation algorithms also are needed to be oriented carefully to train for such models. Cloud and distributed simulation techniques may be adopted for experimenting. Training and testing with a visual dataset are the one immediate future scope of the proposed techniques. These are a few of the many open future scopes and challenges to address.

References

1. J. Gubbi, R. Buyya, S. Marusic, and M. Palaniswami, "Internet of things (iot): A vision, architectural elements, and future directions," *Future generation computer systems*, vol. 29, no. 7, pp. 1645–1660, 2013.
2. C. Granell, A. Kamilaris, A. Kotsev, F. O. Ostermann, and S. Trilles, "Internet of things," in *Manual of Digital Earth.* Springer, 2020, pp. 387–423.
3. P. Schulz, M. Matthe, H. Klessig, M. Simsek, G. Fettweis, J. Ansari, S. A. Ashraf, B. Almeroth, J. Voigt, I. Riedel *et al.*, "Latency critical iot applications in 5g: Perspective on the design of radio interface and network architecture," *IEEE Communications Magazine*, vol. 55, no. 2, pp. 70–78, 2017.
4. M. Youssef and M. Hassan, "Next generation iot: Toward ubiquitous autonomous cost-efficient iot devices," *IEEE Pervasive Computing*, vol. 18, no. 4, pp. 8–11, 2019.

5. B. Afzal, M. Umair, G. A. Shah, and E. Ahmed, "Enabling iot platforms for social iot applications: vision, feature mapping, and challenges," *Future Generation Computer Systems*, vol. 92, pp. 718–731, 2019.
6. L. Atzori, A. Iera, and G. Morabito, "The internet of things: A survey," *Computer networks*, vol. 54, no. 15, pp. 2787–2805, 2010.
7. M. Mohammadi, A. Al-Fuqaha, S. Sorour, and M. Guizani, "Deep learning for iot big data and streaming analytics: A survey," *IEEE Communications Surveys & Tutorials*, vol. 20, no. 4, pp. 2923–2960, 2018.
8. H. Li, K. Ota, and M. Dong, "Learning iot in edge: Deep learning for the internet of things with edge computing," *IEEE Network*, vol. 32, no. 1, pp. 96–101, 2018.
9. R. F. Molanes, K. Amarasinghe, J. Rodriguez-Andina, and M. Manic, "Deep learning and reconfigurable platforms in the internet of things: Challenges and opportunities in algorithms and hardware," *IEEE industrial electronics magazine*, vol. 12, no. 2, pp. 36–49, 2018.
10. F. Xia, L. T. Yang, L. Wang, and A. Vinel, "Internet of things," *International Journal of Communication Systems*, vol. 25, no. 9, p. 1101, 2012.
11. A. Al-Fuqaha, M. Guizani, M. Mohammadi, M. Aledhari, and M. Ayyash, "Internet of things: A survey on enabling technologies, protocols, and applications," *IEEE communications surveys & tutorials*, vol. 17, no. 4, pp. 2347–2376, 2015.
12. L. Atzori, A. Iera, and G. Morabito, "Understanding the internet of things: definition, potentials, and societal role of a fast evolving paradigm," *Ad Hoc Networks*, vol. 56, pp. 122–140, 2017.
13. R. Khan, S. U. Khan, R. Zaheer, and S. Khan, "Future internet: the internet of things architecture, possible applications and key challenges," in *2012 10th international conference on frontiers of information technology*. IEEE, 2012, pp. 257–260.
14. J. Lin, W. Yu, N. Zhang, X. Yang, H. Zhang, and W. Zhao, "A survey on internet of things: Architecture, enabling technologies, security and privacy, and applications," *IEEE Internet of Things Journal*, vol. 4, no. 5, pp. 1125–1142, 2017.
15. X. Liu, K. Lam, K. Zhu, C. Zheng, X. Li, Y. Du, C. Liu, and P. W. Pong, "Overview of spintronic sensors, internet of things, and smart living," *arXiv preprint arXiv:1611.00317*, 2016.
16. M. Wu, T.-J. Lu, F.-Y. Ling, J. Sun, and H.-Y. Du, "Research on the architecture of internet of things," in *2010 3rd International Conference on Advanced Computer Theory and Engineering (ICACTE)*, vol. 5. IEEE, 2010, pp. V5–484.
17. A. Botta, W. De Donato, V. Persico, and A. Pescapé, "Integration of cloud computing and internet of things: a survey," *Future generation computer systems*, vol. 56, pp. 684–700, 2016.
18. P. Bellavista, J. Berrocal, A. Corradi, S. K. Das, L. Foschini, and A. Zanni, "A survey on fog computing for the internet of things," *Pervasive and mobile computing*, vol. 52, pp. 71–99, 2019.
19. W. Yu, F. Liang, X. He, W. G. Hatcher, C. Lu, J. Lin, and X. Yang, "A survey on the edge computing for the internet of things," *IEEE access*, vol. 6, pp. 6900–6919, 2017.
20. R. Buyya, C. S. Yeo, S. Venugopal, J. Broberg, and I. Brandic, "Cloud computing and emerging it platforms: Vision, hype, and reality for delivering computing as the 5th utility," *Future Generation computer systems*, vol. 25, no. 6, pp. 599–616, 2009.
21. Y. Zhao, W. Wang, Y. Li, C. C. Meixner, M. Tornatore, and J. Zhang, "Edge computing and networking: A survey on infrastructures and applications," *IEEE Access*, vol. 7, pp. 101 213–101 230, 2019.
22. K. Jain and S. Mohapatra, "Taxonomy of edge computing: Challenges, opportunities, and data reduction methods," in *Edge Computing*. Springer, 2019, pp. 51–69.
23. F. Bonomi, R. Milito, J. Zhu, and S. Addepalli, "Fog computing and its role in the internet of things," in *Proceedings of the first edition of the MCC workshop on Mobile cloud computing*, 2012, pp. 13–16.
24. P. Escamilla-Ambrosio, A. Rodríguez-Mota, E. Aguirre-Anaya, R. Acosta-Bermejo, and M. Salinas-Rosales, "Distributing computing in the internet of things: cloud, fog and edge computing overview," in *NEO 2016*. Springer, 2018, pp. 87–115.

25. P. Garcia Lopez, A. Montresor, D. Epema, A. Datta, T. Higashino, A. Iamnitchi, M. Barcellos, P. Felber, and E. Riviere, "Edge-centric computing: Vision and challenges," 2015.
26. Y. C. Hu, M. Patel, D. Sabella, N. Sprecher, and V. Young, "Mobile edge computing-a key technology towards 5g," *ETSI white paper*, vol. 11, no. 11, pp. 1–16, 2015.
27. E. Ahmed and M. H. Rehmani, "Mobile edge computing: opportunities, solutions, and challenges," 2017.
28. Y. Mao, C. You, J. Zhang, K. Huang, and K. B. Letaief, "A survey on mobile edge computing: The communication perspective," *IEEE Communications Surveys & Tutorials*, vol. 19, no. 4, pp. 2322–2358, 2017.
29. H. Elazhary, "Internet of things (iot), mobile cloud, cloudlet, mobile iot, iot cloud, fog, mobile edge, and edge emerging computing paradigms: Disambiguation and research directions," *Journal of Network and Computer Applications*, vol. 128, pp. 105–140, 2019.
30. S. Li, L. Da Xu, and S. Zhao, "The internet of things: a survey," *Information Systems Frontiers*, vol. 17, no. 2, pp. 243–259, 2015.
31. X. Sun and N. Ansari, "Edgeiot: Mobile edge computing for the internet of things," *IEEE Communications Magazine*, vol. 54, no. 12, pp. 22–29, 2016.
32. D. Sabella, A. Vaillant, P. Kuure, U. Rauschenbach, and F. Giust, "Mobile-edge computing architecture: The role of mec in the internet of things," *IEEE Consumer Electronics Magazine*, vol. 5, no. 4, pp. 84–91, 2016.
33. N. Ansari and X. Sun, "Mobile edge computing empowers internet of things," *IEICE Transactions on Communications*, vol. 101, no. 3, pp. 604–619, 2018.
34. H. Khelifi, S. Luo, B. Nour, A. Sellami, H. Moungla, S. H. Ahmed, and M. Guizani, "Bringing deep learning at the edge of information-centric internet of things," *IEEE Communications Letters*, vol. 23, no. 1, pp. 52–55, 2018.
35. B. Blanco-Filgueira, D. García-Lesta, M. Fernández-Sanjurjo, V. M. Brea, and P. López, "Deep learning-based multiple object visual tracking on embedded system for iot and mobile edge computing applications," *IEEE Internet of Things Journal*, vol. 6, no. 3, pp. 5423–5431, 2019.
36. A. Sufian, A. Ghosh, A. S. Sadiq, and F. Smarandache, "A survey on deep transfer learning to edge computing for mitigating the covid-19 pandemic," *Journal of Systems Architecture*, vol. 108, p. 101830, 2020.
37. R. Szeliski, *Computer vision: algorithms and applications.*   Springer Science & Business Media, 2010.
38. M. Nixon and A. Aguado, *Feature extraction and image processing for computer vision.* Academic Press, 2019.
39. Y. Guo, Y. Liu, A. Oerlemans, S. Lao, S. Wu, and M. S. Lew, "Deep learning for visual understanding: A review," *Neurocomputing*, vol. 187, pp. 27–48, 2016.
40. A. Voulodimos, N. Doulamis, A. Doulamis, and E. Protopapadakis, "Deep learning for computer vision: A brief review," *Computational intelligence and neuroscience*, vol. 2018, 2018.
41. Y. Shen, T. Han, Q. Yang, X. Yang, Y. Wang, F. Li, and H. Wen, "Cs-cnn: Enabling robust and efficient convolutional neural networks inference for internet-of-things applications," *IEEE Access*, vol. 6, pp. 13 439–13 448, 2018.
42. Y. LeCun, Y. Bengio, and G. Hinton, "Deep learning," *nature*, vol. 521, no. 7553, pp. 436–444, 2015.
43. I. Goodfellow, Y. Bengio, and A. Courville, *Deep learning.*   MIT press, 2016.
44. A. Ghosh, A. Sufian, F. Sultana, A. Chakrabarti, and D. De, "Fundamental concepts of convolutional neural network," in *Recent Trends and Advances in Artificial Intelligence and Internet of Things.*   Springer, 2020, pp. 519–567.
45. A. Krizhevsky, I. Sutskever, and G. E. Hinton, "Imagenet classification with deep convolutional neural networks," in *Advances in neural information processing systems*, 2012.
46. F. Sultana, A. Sufian, and P. Dutta, "A review of object detection models based on convolutional neural network," in *Intelligent Computing: Image Processing Based Applications.*   Springer, 2020, pp. 1–16.

47. F. Sultana, A. Sufian, and P. Dutta, "Evolution of image segmentation using deep convolutional neural network: A survey," *Knowledge-Based Systems*, vol. 201–202, p. 106062, 2020.

48. N. D. Lane, S. Bhattacharya, P. Georgiev, C. Forlivesi, and F. Kawsar, "An early resource characterization of deep learning on wearables, smartphones and internet-of-things devices," in *Proceedings of the 2015 international workshop on internet of things towards applications*, 2015, pp. 7–12.

49. F. Alam, R. Mehmood, I. Katib, and A. Albeshri, "Analysis of eight data mining algorithms for smarter internet of things (iot)," *Procedia Computer Science*, vol. 98, pp. 437–442, 2016.

50. N. D. Lane, S. Bhattacharya, P. Georgiev, C. Forlivesi, L. Jiao, L. Qendro, and F. Kawsar, "Deepx: A software accelerator for low-power deep learning inference on mobile devices," in *2016 15th ACM/IEEE International Conference on Information Processing in Sensor Networks (IPSN)*. IEEE, 2016, pp. 1–12.

51. D. Ravi, C. Wong, B. Lo, and G.-Z. Yang, "A deep learning approach to on-node sensor data analytics for mobile or wearable devices," *IEEE journal of biomedical and health informatics*, vol. 21, no. 1, pp. 56–64, 2016.

52. S. Bhattacharya and N. D. Lane, "Sparsification and separation of deep learning layers for constrained resource inference on wearables," in *Proceedings of the 14th ACM Conference on Embedded Network Sensor Systems CD-ROM*, 2016, pp. 176–189.

53. A. G. Howard, M. Zhu, B. Chen, D. Kalenichenko, W. Wang, T. Weyand, M. Andreetto, and H. Adam, "Mobilenets: Efficient convolutional neural networks for mobile vision applications," *arXiv preprint arXiv:1704.04861*, 2017.

54. J. Tang, D. Sun, S. Liu, and J.-L. Gaudiot, "Enabling deep learning on iot devices," *Computer*, vol. 50, no. 10, pp. 92–96, 2017.

55. H.-Y. Kim and J.-M. Kim, "A load balancing scheme based on deep-learning in iot," *Cluster Computing*, vol. 20, no. 1, pp. 873–878, 2017.

56. S. Teerapittayanon, B. McDanel, and H.-T. Kung, "Distributed deep neural networks over the cloud, the edge and end devices," in *2017 IEEE 37th International Conference on Distributed Computing Systems (ICDCS)*. IEEE, 2017, pp. 328–339.

57. Z. Zhao, K. M. Barijough, and A. Gerstlauer, "Deepthings: Distributed adaptive deep learning inference on resource-constrained iot edge clusters," *IEEE Transactions on Computer-Aided Design of Integrated Circuits and Systems*, vol. 37, no. 11, pp. 2348–2359, 2018.

58. M. Song, K. Zhong, J. Zhang, Y. Hu, D. Liu, W. Zhang, J. Wang, and T. Li, "In-situ ai: Towards autonomous and incremental deep learning for iot systems," in *2018 IEEE International Symposium on High Performance Computer Architecture (HPCA)*. IEEE, 2018, pp. 92–103.

59. M. Ali, A. Anjum, M. U. Yaseen, A. R. Zamani, D. Balouek-Thomert, O. Rana, and M. Parashar, "Edge enhanced deep learning system for large-scale video stream analytics," in *2018 IEEE 2nd International Conference on Fog and Edge Computing (ICFEC)*. IEEE, 2018, pp. 1–10.

60. Z. Tao and Q. Li, "esgd: Communication efficient distributed deep learning on the edge," in {USENIX} *Workshop on Hot Topics in Edge Computing (HotEdge 18)*, 2018.

61. K. Bhardwaj, C.-Y. Lin, A. Sartor, and R. Marculescu, "Memory-and communication-aware model compression for distributed deep learning inference on iot," *ACM Transactions on Embedded Computing Systems (TECS)*, vol. 18, no. 5s, pp. 1–22, 2019.

62. A. Ashiquzzaman, L. Van Ma, S. Kim, D. Lee, T.-W. Um, and J. Kim, "Compacting deep neural networks for light weight iot & scada based applications with node pruning," in *2019 International Conference on Artificial Intelligence in Information and Communication (ICAIIC)*. IEEE, 2019, pp. 082–085.

63. J. Zhou, Y. Wang, K. Ota, and M. Dong, "Aaiot: Accelerating artificial intelligence in iot systems," *IEEE Wireless Communications Letters*, vol. 8, no. 3, pp. 825–828, 2019.

64. M. Min, L. Xiao, Y. Chen, P. Cheng, D. Wu, and W. Zhuang, "Learning-based computation offloading for iot devices with energy harvesting," *IEEE Transactions on Vehicular Technology*, vol. 68, no. 2, pp. 1930–1941, 2019.

65. J. Kang and D.-S. Eom, "Offloading and transmission strategies for iot edge devices and networks," *Sensors*, vol. 19, no. 4, p. 835, 2019.

66. S. Tuli, N. Basumatary, and R. Buyya, "Edgelens: Deep learning based object detection in integrated iot, fog and cloud computing environments," *arXiv preprint arXiv:1906.11056*, 2019.
67. J. Chen, K. Li, Q. Deng, K. Li, and S. Y. Philip, "Distributed deep learning model for intelligent video surveillance systems with edge computing," *IEEE Transactions on Industrial Informatics*, 2019.
68. X. Wang, Y. Han, C. Wang, Q. Zhao, X. Chen, and M. Chen, "In-edge ai: Intelligentizing mobile edge computing, caching and communication by federated learning," *IEEE Network*, vol. 33, no. 5, pp. 156–165, 2019.
69. F. Liang, W. Yu, X. Liu, D. Griffith, and N. Golmie, "Towards edge-based deep learning in industrial internet of things," *IEEE Internet of Things Journal*, 2020.
70. E. Kristiani, C.-T. Yang, and C.-Y. Huang, "isec: An optimized deep learning model for image classification on edge computing," *IEEE Access*, vol. 8, pp. 27 267–27 276, 2020.
71. J. Azar, A. Makhoul, R. Couturier, and J. Demerjian, "Robust iot time series classification with data compression and deep learning," *Neurocomputing*, 2020.
72. X. Wang, Y. Han, V. C. Leung, D. Niyato, X. Yan, and X. Chen, "Convergence of edge computing and deep learning: A comprehensive survey," *IEEE Communications Surveys & Tutorials*, vol. 22, no. 2, pp. 869–904, 2020.
73. M. Aazam, S. Zeadally, and K. A. Harras, "Offloading in fog computing for iot: Review, enabling technologies, and research opportunities," *Future Generation Computer Systems*, vol. 87, pp. 278–289, 2018.
74. M. Verhelst and B. Moons, "Embedded deep neural network processing: Algorithmic and processor techniques bring deep learning to iot and edge devices," *IEEE Solid-State Circuits Magazine*, vol. 9, no. 4, pp. 55–65, 2017.
75. S. J. Pan and Q. Yang, "A survey on transfer learning," *IEEE Transactions on knowledge and data engineering*, vol. 22, no. 10, pp. 1345–1359, 2009.
76. K. Weiss, T. M. Khoshgoftaar, and D. Wang, "A survey of transfer learning," *Journal of Big data*, vol. 3, no. 1, p. 9, 2016.
77. F. Zhuang, Z. Qi, K. Duan, D. Xi, Y. Zhu, H. Zhu, H. Xiong, and Q. He, "A comprehensive survey on transfer learning," *Proceedings of the IEEE*, 2020.
78. C. Tan, F. Sun, T. Kong, W. Zhang, C. Yang, and C. Liu, "A survey on deep transfer learning," in *International conference on artificial neural networks*. Springer, 2018, pp. 270–279.
79. M. Wang and W. Deng, "Deep visual domain adaptation: A survey," *Neurocomputing*, vol. 312, pp. 135–153, 2018.
80. J. Deng, W. Dong, R. Socher, L.-J. Li, K. Li, and L. Fei-Fei, "Imagenet: A large-scale hierarchical image database," in *2009 IEEE conference on computer vision and pattern recognition*. Ieee, 2009, pp. 248–255.
81. I. Krasin, T. Duerig, N. Alldrin, V. Ferrari, S. Abu-El-Haija, A. Kuznetsova, H. Rom, J. Uijlings, S. Popov, A. Veit *et al.*, "Openimages: A public dataset for large-scale multi-label and multi-class image classification," *Dataset available from https://github.com/openimages*, vol. 2, no. 3, p. 18, 2017.

Mobile Edge Computing for Content Distribution and Mobility Support in Smart Cities

Pedro F. do Prado, Maycon L. M. Peixoto, Marcelo C. Araújo,
Eduardo S. Gama, Diogo M. Gonçalves, Matteus V. S. Silva, Roger Immich,
Edmundo R. M. Madeira, and Luiz F. Bittencourt

Abstract The pervasiveness of mobile devices is a common phenomenon nowadays, and with the emergence of the Internet of Things (IoT), an increasing number of connected devices are being deployed. In Smart Cities, data collection, processing, and distribution play critical roles in everyday quality of life and city planning and development. The use of Cloud computing to support massive amounts of data generated and consumed in Smart Cities has some limitations, such as increased latency and substantial network traffic, hampering support for a variety of applications that need low response times. In this chapter, we introduce and discuss aspects of distributed multi-tiered Mobile Edge Computing (MEC) architectures, which offer data storage and processing capabilities closer to data sources and data consumers, taking into account how mobility impacts the management of such infrastructure. The main goal is to address topics on how such infrastructure can be used to support content distribution *from and to* mobile users, how to optimize the resource allocation in such infrastructure, as well as how an intelligent layer can be added to the MEC/Fog infrastructure. Furthermore, a multifaceted literature review is given, as well as the open issues and challenging aspects of resource and application management will also be discussed in this chapter.

P. F. do Prado · M. C. Araújo · E. S. Gama · D. M. Gonçalves · M. V. S. Silva · E. R. M. Madeira
L. F. Bittencourt (✉)
Institute of Computing (IC), University of Campinas (UNICAMP), Campinas, Brazil
e-mail: pfprado@unicamp.br; marcelo.araujo@ic.unicamp.br; eduardogama@lrc.ic.unicamp.br;
diogomg@lrc.ic.unicamp.br; edmundo@ic.unicamp.br; bit@ic.unicamp.br

M. L. M. Peixoto
Departamento de Ciência da Computação, Federal University of Bahia (UFBA), Salvador, Brazil
e-mail: maycon.leone@ufba.br

R. Immich
Metropolis Digital Institute (IMD), Federal University of Rio Grande do Norte (UFRN), Natal,
Brazil
e-mail: roger@imd.ufrn.br

© The Author(s), under exclusive license to Springer Nature Switzerland AG 2021   473
A. Mukherjee et al. (eds.), *Mobile Edge Computing*,
https://doi.org/10.1007/978-3-030-69893-5_19

Keywords Mobile edge computing · Multi-access edge computing · Fog computing · Mobility · Content distribution · Resource allocation · Smart cities

1 Introduction

The evolution of wireless communication networks has changed our interaction as a ubiquitously connected society. This was driven by the number of mobile devices, their ever-increasing hardware capabilities, and systematic cost reductions. To put this into perspective, mobile devices are nowadays prevalent and present an annual growth rate of around 25%. Literature reports such an increase to reach the expected amount of 80 billion mobile devices by 2030 [13]. On top of that, the number of bandwidth-hungry applications is also gaining apace, with the estimated global monthly mobile data traffic expected to raise 3.7 exabytes per month in 2015 to 30.6 exabytes in 2020 [15]. Moreover, these new devices are also expanding their ability to produce data. This leads to a broad collection of information ranging from weather-related data to social behavior, which can be stored, transferred, processed, and analyzed in several distinct ways. This new dynamic reflects on how the devices use the available networks, putting forward stringent resource demands.

At the same time, it is important to notice that the network transformations are continually evolving. In a related manner, the diffusion of the Internet of Things (IoT) will have a central role in this renewal [38]. This technology envisaged that, in essence, all objects would have some type of communications capabilities. This will lead to an unprecedented amount of data that will flood the access networks daily. The integration of both mobile and IoT devices with the Cloud allows alleviating some of these stringent requirements as it provides resource elasticity on-demand, reduces compatibility issues, and provides high availability [16]. However, in doing that, it also introduces new entanglements such as higher latency and core network surcharge as well as security and privacy concerns.

To improve on the aforementioned challenges while increasing the location awareness, Fog and Edge computing can be used. The main idea of both is to provide Cloud-like features (e.g., resource elasticity and virtualization) closer to the end-user. To put in another way, they aim to bring a snippet of the processing power from the Cloud to where the data source and/or devices are [42]. It is worth noticing that this does not mean relinquishing Cloud structures but instead putting it together with Fog and Edge technologies to enable a multi-tier computing hierarchy [7]. This arrangement yields a number of advantages, for example, reduced delays and network traffic as the data can be stored and processed closely [6], which is imperative for delay-sensitive applications. Security and privacy may also be impacted as, in this case, only summarized can be transferred to the Cloud.

The convergence of Cloud, Fog, and Edge computing provides several benefits; on the other hand, it also imposes brand-new constraints and challenges [7]. For example, this architecture needs to be able to handle heterogeneous devices with distinct communication capabilities, uneven processing power, and limited energy-capabilities. Incidentally, the advent of the fifth and sixth generation of wireless systems (5G and 6G) will help furnish this resource-demanding upsurge and better accommodate both network and device heterogeneity. This builds an ecosystem of technologies and value chains aiming to cater to the swift and flexible deployment of innovative services and applications. The 5G systems are designed to provide high bandwidth capacity, low latency, support for dense networks, and improved seamless mobility. In order to enable these highly-desired features, 5G will heavily depend on Mobile (or Multi-access) Edge Computing (MEC), which is standardized by the European Telecommunications Standards Institute (ETSI) and was formally known as Mobile Edge Computing. This adjustment is an attempt to adopt a broader posture regarding which network access technologies will be sanctioned under the proposed framework [7, 29]. This paved a new direction on accepting a comprehensive set of wired and wireless communication technologies and not only carrier-grade cellular equipment.

It is expected that MEC will play a pivotal role in 5G systems by addressing a range of use cases. In order to do that, it aims to bring together the telecommunication-capabilities and the Cloud service environment within the radio access networks (RAN), in the close vicinity to the end-users, and being able to attend applications on a localized basis [50]. Moreover, it can cost-effectively enable high-performance computing on-demand to support a growing number of services and applications at the network's edge. To do that, it will be able to host compute-intensive applications/services and process large chunks of data before sending it to the Cloud. This leads to low latency connectivity and also the possibility to deploy localized content caching.

This chapter brings an overview of problems that have to be addressed to achieve efficient content distribution when mobility is expected to play an important role in the resource management of distributed infrastructures. In Sect. 2, a general view of a multi-tiered Edge computing infrastructure is presented, and the ETSI reference architecture is briefly presented to match requirements. A literature review is presented in Sect. 3. Additionally, Sect. 4 provides details about content distribution and mobility in a MEC scenario. After that, the open challenges are described in Sect. 5, while Sect. 6 brings remarks and concludes the chapter.

2 Multi-Tiered Architecture: Concepts and Definitions

This section introduces the concepts and definitions of MEC and its variations. First, a general view of multi-tiered computing infrastructure for Edge computing and IoT in Smart Cities is presented. Then, it is discussed how this infrastructure can be managed using current standardization efforts.

2.1 Edge and Fog Computing in Smart Cities

Nowadays, Cloud computing has been established as the computing infrastructure to provide computing services to many applications. More recently, Edge and Fog computing [7] are being developed to, in conjunction with the Cloud, improve computing capabilities to fulfill application demands with stricter delay requirements as well as to reduce network traffic by distributing computing capacity closer to the users.

Figure 1 illustrates a scenario where users connect to their access points while traveling in smart cities. Those access points provide cloudlets (fog nodes, or microdata centers) as a first-mile distributed computing capacity, providing lower response times and reducing network traffic to the Cloud by aggregating data and/or fulfilling application computing needs at the Edge. These fog nodes can be arranged in a hierarchy, forming a multi-tiered distributed computing infrastructure from the edge to the cloud.

As users move, for example, in a smart city, their computation should, ideally, be kept as close as possible, i.e., at the cloudlet available in the access point the user is currently connected. Therefore, to manage applications and data from mobile users, management entities distributed in this hierarchy must act to optimize the overall system performance (e.g., response times, utilization, cost, energy consumption).

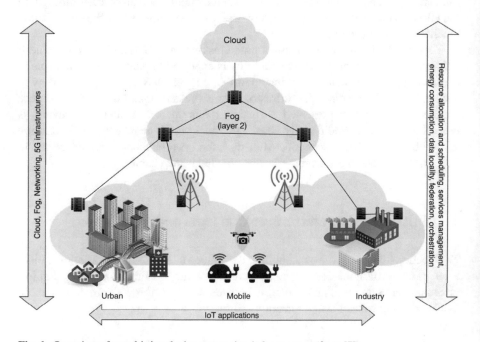

Fig. 1 Overview of a multi-tiered edge computing infrastructure (from [7])

Management and resource allocation in the Edge computing distributed infrastructure brings many challenges, and standardization and specification efforts are under development. One of these efforts is discussed in the next section.

2.2 Mobile Edge Computing Specification

The ETSI Mobile Edge Computing Industry Specification Group (MEC ISG) published a reference architecture for Mobile Edge Computing [18]. The reference architecture is divided into three layers: System Layer, Host Layer, and Network Layer, as illustrated in Fig. 2.

The groups of reference points are divided into (Mp), related to MEC platform functions, (Mm), linked to management; and (Mx), working as external elements connections. The (Mp) group includes $(Mp1, Mp2, Mp3)$ reference points. The Mp1 reference point connects the MEC platform to Applications, providing registration and discovery services. The Mp2 reference point manages applications routing between the MEC platform and the Virtualization Infrastructure's Data Plane. The Mp3 controls the communication between MEC platforms. The (Mm) group includes $(Mm1, Mm2, \ldots, Mm9)$ reference points. Mm1 is used to instantiate

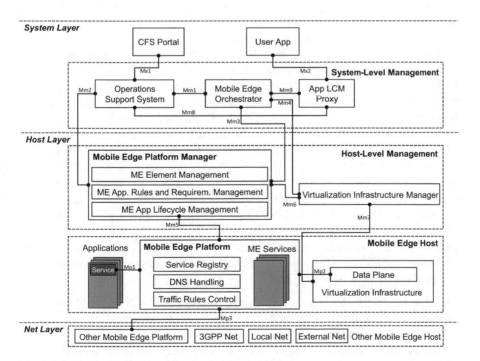

Fig. 2 Mobile edge computing reference architecture [18]

and terminate MEC applications between Operations Support System (OSS) and Orchestrator in the System Layer. Mm2 is responsible for the configuration and performance management between OSS and MEC Platform Manager in the Host Layer. Mm3 manages the lifecycle, application rules, and requirements service between Orchestrator and MEC Platform Manager. Mm4 connects Orchestrator to the Virtualization Infrastructure Manager, and it is used to manage the virtualized resources. Mm5 is for the configuration of applications and services between MEC Platform Manager and MEC Platform in the Host Layer. Mm6 manages the virtualized resources related to the application lifecycle, which is linking the MEC Platform Manager and Virtualization Infrastructure Manager. Mm7 is used to manage the virtualization infrastructure between Virtualization Infrastructure Manager from Host-Level Management and Virtualization Infrastructure from MEC Host. Mm8 connects Orchestrator to App LCM Proxy, and it handles the requests for running applications in the System Layer. Mm9 links Orchestrator to App LCM Proxy, and it is used for MEC application management. The (Mx) group includes $(Mx1, Mx2)$ reference points. Mx1 connects OSS to CFS Portal and deals with third-parties' requests for running applications in the System Layer. Mx2 connects APP LCM Proxy to User App and is used by a device application to request and run an application in the System Layer.

System Layer The upmost layer is the System Layer, composed of Customer-Facing Service (CFS)/Applications and the System-Level Management, which is necessary to run mobile edge applications within an operator network, thus providing system-wide management functions.

The User Application is a mobile edge application running an application requested by a user in the mobile edge system, and the User Application Lifecycle Management Proxy (App LCM Proxy) is the component that deals with the instantiation and termination of the applications. The Customer-Facing Service Portal (CFS) is the first step for providing applications. CFS handles the operations with third-party customers, providing information for instantiation of a set of mobile edge applications that meet specific needs and the termination of these MEC applications. An Mx1 reference point is used to connect CFS to the OSS. OSS manages the operators' network services, which receives and decides on granting requests from the CFS portal and ME Applications. The granted requests are forwarded to the Mobile Edge Orchestrator (MEO) for further processing. MEO has the System Layer's primary function due to wide visibility over the entire mobile network's resources and functionalities. MEO is responsible for maintaining information of all available applications and following their requirements to perform the deploying into mobile edge host [11, 18, 48].

Host Layer At the Host Layer, the Mobile Edge Platform Manager, Mobile Edge Platform, Mobile Edge Host, and the Virtualization Infrastructure are used to execute the user applications.

Mobile Edge Platform Manager (MEPM) is an entity that is further divided into Mobile Edge Element Management, Mobile Edge Application Rules, Requirements Management functions, and Mobile Edge Application Lifecycle Management. Mm3 reference point connecting the MEPM to MEO provides support for the application and services in the System Layer. Mm2 reference point linking MEPM and OSS is used for fault reports, configuration, and performance measurements received from the Virtual Infrastructure Manager via Mm6 reference point. Meanwhile, VIM is responsible for allocating, managing, and releasing the virtualized resources, such as compute, storage, and network, to the mobile edge applications [18, 48].

The Mobile Edge Platform (MEP) is responsible for offering services such as discovering and advertising to the mobile edge applications. MEP is also used to manage the networking environment by handling the service registry, DNS configuration, and the traffic rules control accordingly [18].

The Virtualization Infrastructure is located in or close to the network edge, e.g., the Network Functions Virtualization Infrastructure (NFVI), which offers virtualized resources to mobile edge applications. Moreover, the virtualization infrastructure brings a Data Plane that runs traffic rules from MEP and manages the traffic among services, applications, DNS, 3GPP, and other local and external networks [18].

Network Layer The Network Layer is further related to the connectivity to cellular networks (3GPP), Local and External networks such as the Internet. The Host Layer consists of Mobile Edge Host and the Host-Level Management. However, to include the benefits of heterogeneous access technologies to the MEC, e.g., 4G, 5G, and WiFi, ETSI ISG changed the name of Mobile Edge Computing (MEC) to Multi-access Edge Computing in 2017 [29], maintaining the acronym MEC. In this chapter, we use the general term MEC to refer to this architecture's latest developments. From this expansion, Fig. 3, the intelligence is moved to the, bringing communication functionalities as well as computation, caching, and additional control services. The overall layering organization remains similar to the previous one, but the network layer has been modified to consider multiple different access technologies.

The integration of MEC and 5G is shown in Fig. 3. In addition to Radio Access Network (RAN) and User Equipment (UE), the main 3GPP 5G network functions are briefly summarized below.

- User Plane Function (UPF): controls the plane operations and may even be part of the MEC Layer in some specific deployments.
- Authentication Server Function (AUSF): acts as an authentication server.
- Session Management Function (SMF): performs the session management functions.
- Access and Mobility Management Function (AMF): handle the procedures related to mobility and deals with the RAN control plane.
- Network Slice Selection Function (NSSF): selects the network slice resources and AMF for users.
- Network Repository Function (NRF): maintains the network functions and their supported services.
- Unified Data Management (UDM): deals with users and subscription services.

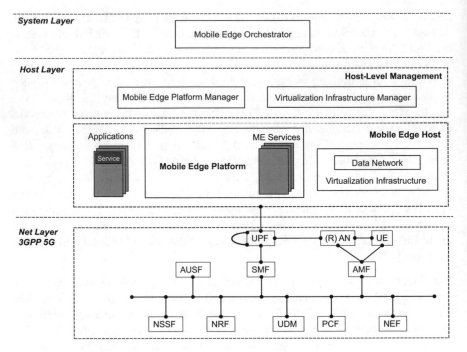

Fig. 3 MEC and 5G architecture [29]

- Policy Control Function (PCF): handles network policies and rules in the 5G control plane.
- Network Exposure Function (NEF): acts as a service that manages all access requests outside the system.

The ETSI reference architecture brings an overview of the management needs to support application mobility at the network's edge. Several algorithms and mechanisms need to be incorporated into the architecture to provide reduced delays and improved Quality of Service (QoS). The remainder of this chapter discusses a few problems that, when addressed, can provide better support for mobile applications in smart city scenarios.

3 Literature Review

MEC's main idea is to offer processing and storage services at the Edge of the network, increasing computing services proximity to users. Recently, MEC architecture is a topic that has been gaining attention from industry and academic researchers: several surveys analyze the state of the art, discuss definitions, and identify the main challenges to be overcome. In [59], Wang et al. surveyed caching, communication, and computing issues at the Edge of the network. Mach et al. [36] surveyed existing MEC concepts, functionalities, mobility awareness, and computing offloading. In [21], Habibi et al. surveyed architectural distinctions between existing Edge computing models and analyzes the different aspects of the practical implementation of Fog computing, such as security, computing resource management, networks, and systems design. Furthermore, Abbas et al. [2] surveyed architectures, application areas, and highlights futures directions related to MEC.

Although Edge and Cloud infrastructure composition is a topic that has been extensively investigated, mobility management is one of the biggest challenges to be yet overcome in MEC. For example, in [27] the authors analyze the impact of mobility on the caching process at the Edge of the network. In specific scenarios, the characteristics and properties of users' mobility are unknown. Some research [35, 39] proposed strategies to predict user's mobility. The information obtained through prediction allows the content management process's actions to offer a higher Quality of Experience (QoE) for users.

Due to the importance of ensuring continuity of access to content and services during users' movement, migration also emerges as one of the core research issues in the context of MEC. In [32], a decision policy is proposed to determine when the VM migration process should start—after each handoff performed by the user, a decision is made based on the trade-off between the gain and cost of migration. The authors modeled the decision policy using the Continuous-Time Markov Decision Process (CTMDP). Moreover, the Follow-me Cloud [51] concept proposes that users' content should be migrated, on-demand, to the cloudlet closest to the user, reducing latency and improving the QoS offered.

Mobility management in MEC can impact several types of applications, among which video delivery is a trendy one. MEC architectures for video delivery offers an environment characterized by high bandwidth and low latency. In [25, 47, 54, 62], the authors focus on decreasing the traffic overload in the network core and improving the QoE aided by MEC. Yang et al. [62] explore machine learning models to incorporate into the MEC node for decision-making on storing popular videos. Experimental results suggest good performance for mobile video streaming services. Furthermore, Petrangeli et al. [41] proposed an advanced architecture in which additional intelligent components are placed to support video delivery. Instead of considering low-level network performance parameters, the designed network components focus on optimizing the QoE parameters that directly affect users' experience.

Rectal and Benkacem et al. [5, 46] propose a content delivery network as a service (CDNaaS), where content providers can create a CDN slice that includes cache, transcoder, and streamers for several videos for their users. The objective is to find an efficient cost for creating a slicing following requirements of the network administrator in terms of QoE and the cost of setting up the Cloud infrastructure.

MEC enables data collected at the Edge to be processed at the Edge. Associating the high amount of data from IoT with the MEC architecture [66], it is possible to explore new applications and services at the Edge when data collection is allied with Artificial Intelligence (AI). Large data sets generated at the Edge of the network along with benefits brought by MEC urges for distributed intelligence to be supported close to the end-users.

In [60, 66], the authors explore the feasibility of Deep Learning (DL) in terms of applications and how to improve networking aspects to make it possible to deploy DL at the Edge. From this perspective, the work of [33] refers to the use of Federated Learning (FL), a method that executes DL at the Edge of the network using distributed local user data, requiring the transmission of only the learning model in the aggregation period.

Valério et al. [55] focuses on energy usage by choosing to go a layer upwards and do more work in Fog, distributing the learning through the cloudlets. This way, it is possible to have energy gains using short-range technologies with little loss of precision. Their work discusses that the type of wireless technology cannot directly impact intelligence, but how energy and traffic must be well aligned with the chosen wireless technology.

Park et al. [40] also considers wireless networks, but with a focus on modeling methods for both learning and its algorithms to fit the principle of providing the most learning at the most extreme point possible. Zhang et al. [65] follow this line of learning to model but explores MEC in vehicles. Offloading and edge caching is essential for good management of aspects of the network, with the use of storage resources and extra resources.

This book chapter aims to congregate the discussion on how mobility management in MEC can impact the applications and the Edge-Cloud infrastructure.

4 Content Distribution and Mobility

Significative growth in mobile connectivity is expected in the next few years. The addition of mobile users will undeniably change the dynamics of MEC environments. Introducing mobility support in a multi-tier MEC translates some traditional resource management problems, such as service placement and routing path calculation, into a more complex and dynamic case. Aiming to deal with such a scenario, the MEC infrastructure requires new approaches to orchestrate this environment. For example, the adoption of static or dynamic service allocation and content migration can result in distinct levels of QoE delivered to the users and different resource usage in the MEC infrastructure.

Figure 4 illustrates this situation where the user's latency is affected when the application is static or dynamically allocated. It is important to notice that if the offloaded data/processing is migrated along with the user in his/her path, the application delays can be kept at lower levels. In a scenario where there is no migration (illustrated by the blue line), as the user moves away from the cloudlet where his/her content is allocated, the delay increases, degrading the QoS. On the other hand, the red line represents the scenario where content is constantly migrated to the cloudlet that is closest to the user at a given time, keeping latencies as low as

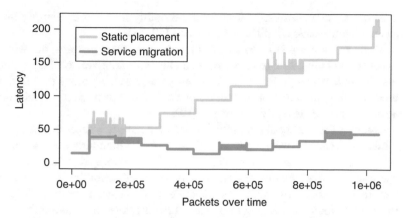

Fig. 4 Latency provided by the Fog in scenarios with and without VM migrations

possibly supported by the Fog architecture. The interested reader can find detailed results and different mobility scenarios in [44].

In such a dynamic environment, the MEC architecture needs to deal with user mobility to deliver the required content. In this scenario, the content distribution needs to take advantage of MEC architecture not only for caching data but also using MEC's processing capacities to, for instance, perform real-time video transcoding in a faster way, also to avoid data transfer into the core network towards the Cloud. Such dynamism in the density of the network increases the complexity of the content distribution problems.

This section discusses the impact of mobility support in the orchestration of MEC infrastructures and the role of content distribution and processing in such an environment. Additionally, it is shown several typical management and optimization problems related to data collection, distribution, and processing in scenarios with user mobility. Several uses cases are going to be addressed, such as the migration of mobile users data/applications throughout the multi-tiered infrastructure, the support for high-definition video streaming for mobile users, and the use of machine learning in an intelligent edge layer for vehicular traffic and safety.

4.1 Mobility and Content Migration

Similar to the Cloud paradigm, MEC can provide its resources in the form of virtualized environments, such as containers or virtual machines (VMs), providing an isolated environment that contains all the resources required by the user.

The constant movement of devices is one of the biggest challenges for MEC architecture as it needs to be able to reduce the latency between the user and his/her content. According to Yan et al. [61], the study of human mobility shows that people tend to visit specific places at constant time intervals, setting standards.

In the literature, it is possible to find several mobility models that identify human movement characteristics in different scenarios [17, 58].

The study of mobility is important to identify movement patterns, allowing the process of content migration (e.g., VM or container migration) to occur according to each user's movement's particularities. Mobility models also provide the possibility of a proactive migration approach; that is, the content can be migrated in advance to locations that the user is likely to move to [19].

To guarantee the quality of the mobile user experience, it is necessary to decrease the physical distance between content and users. In the literature, there are several strategies [31, 51, 64] for content management at the network's edge. In general, they propose user's content should be dynamically allocated according to their current position. In such scenarios, whenever a mobile user changes him/her position, the relevant application/contents should be moved from a host server to another one in closer proximity to the current user position.

Recently, proactive content management strategies have been gaining attention from the scientific community. Proactive strategies [4, 19] aim to predict when and where users will need their content/applications in order to perform management decisions efficiently, ensuring the quality of the users' experience and highly improving the QoS for delay-sensitive applications.

In this context, maintaining the application (geographically or logically) as close as possible to the user is a great challenge [43], mainly due to a trade-off in the migration process. Frequent migrations will allow greater proximity between user and content, resulting in lower latency. However, migrating too often between cloudlets may enlarge the application downtime, which is not desirable. Furthermore, in scenarios with a large number of users, frequent migrations will congest the network, compromising its stability and reducing the QoS offered by the infrastructure. On the other hand, insufficient migrations may keep applications away from their users, resulting in increased latency. Both scenarios can impair mobile users' QoS. Therefore, MEC architecture's content management strategies must offer solutions to improve user experience quality without compromising the network operation.

The problem of content migration at the Edge of the network with mobile users has been a focus of researchers' attention, with several different approaches being proposed at this time. Several metrics and criteria can be used to define when and whether the user's content should be migrated, such as latency and throughput requirements, load balancing, user speed, or application priority [44]. Further discussion on this can be found in the following section. Once the mobile users change their locations, the MEC node serving them may not fulfill their application requirements (e.g., latency) anymore. Other objectives, such as load balancing or energy-saving, can also lead to migrations in the architecture.

Figure 5 depicts a hierarchical MEC architecture. A number of different combinations of origin and destination nodes can be found in the migration process. The user content can be moved in both horizontal and vertical directions in terms of the MEC nodes' hierarchical organizations. Horizontal migrations occur between MEC nodes at the same hierarchical level, as illustrated as the type 1 migration. Once the

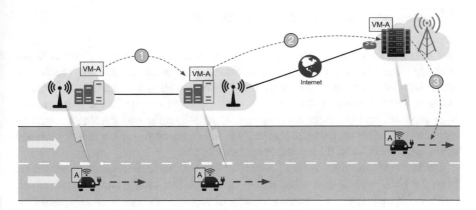

Fig. 5 VM migration scenarios in a fog computing architecture

MEC nodes, at the same level, usually have similar computing power, that kind of migration tends to keep, in a stable range, the levels of QoS offered to the users. Furthermore, vertical migrations may also be needed if, for example, the users' requirements or the MEC's resources availability change dynamically over time. If the user increases their requests for computing power, for instance, the resources demand on the current MEC node may surpass its capability. A resource richer MEC node, used to be closer to the network's core, should fulfill the new user's requirement (illustrated as the type 2 migration). Similarly, if the user decreases him/her computing and storage requirements or the required latency should be improved, the user content can be migrated to a MEC node closer to the Edge of the network (type 3 migration). Moreover, fog nodes at higher levels can be used to reduce the number of migrations (and, consequently, downtime) when, for example, high-speed users are moving at the Edge.

User access to content can also be performed in different ways based on the user's location and his/her content. Access can be direct if the content is one hop away from the user, which provides the lowest possible latency. However, if necessary, multiple hops may be traversed when user contents are not placed in the closest fog node.

Therefore, one main concern of models like MEC is the proximity between mobile users and their contents, as well as reducing network congestion while maintaining QoS for mobile users [14]. However, the development of strategies to realize this management is far from trivial. In the light of that, it is necessary to develop solutions that orchestrate content migration considering several aspects, such as user mobility patterns, characteristics of applications, migration costs, networking utilization and congestion, and so on.

4.2 Resource Allocation and Optimization

One of the main questions that arise in the MEC architecture is how to distribute heterogeneous services and their data throughout the MEC hierarchy such that application requirements are obeyed, even in a constrained infrastructure. For example, latency is one of the utmost importance requirements for many interactive edge applications. Scheduler decision making heavily relies on such requirements to model an optimization problem that outputs the resource allocation that determines where applications and their components should run.

Furthermore, the possibility of mobile users continuously requesting resources from the MEC infrastructure has a considerable effect on the environment which needs to be managed. In a static scenario, once the resources were allocated to a user, it will be reserved until the tasks are finished. In this case, changes in the resources demand will only occur when the number of active users increases or decreases. On the other hand, in the mobility scenario, this change of resource demand in the infrastructure also happens when a relevant number of users move to a specific area. Figure 6 illustrates a scenario where a large number of mobile users can be temporally concentrated in a reduced part of the map. The red circle

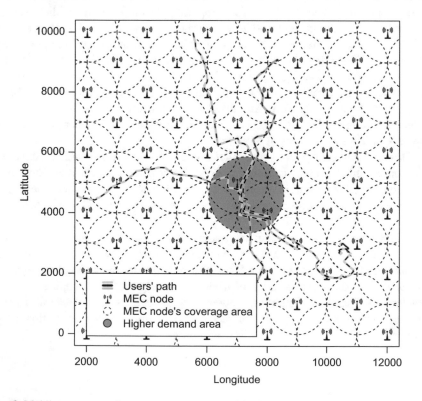

Fig. 6 Mobile user converging to a common area resulting in a resource concurrency

illustrates such an area. In this case, MEC allocation approaches need to deal with such a dynamic environment. Circles represent base-stations/access points antenna range, where each of these access points has a cloudlet offered to the mobile users. Illustrative routes from these users are illustrated in blue, purple, orange, and green. When mobile users reach a certain position, which can be pre-defined or calculated in real-time, a decision-making algorithm should run to choose the best new location (cloudlet) for his/her VM, based on current mobility (e.g., prediction of next position) and also on current load of cloudlets in the user's path. Based on that, good resource management approaches are a goal for both users, which then experience a better QoE, and MEC resource providers, which can improve profit metrics as energy or network usage by better allocating resources.

The resource allocation imposes challenging problems in distributed systems. In other to alleviate these issues, one prominent component of the MEC infrastructure is the scheduler. This component is responsible for allocating resources from the distributed infrastructure to users' applications. The decision-making on which applications should run where is taken by following an optimization model. In general, it takes information about the application requirements and infrastructure characteristics as input. The scheduler defines one or more objective functions, whose output maximizes or minimizes single or multiple objectives.

Considering that, one important aspect of MEC architectures is related to users' mobility along the infrastructure edge. In MEC, optimization modeling should consider user mobility as a determining factor of future allocation needs. How to model this problem in a hierarchical infrastructure will impact which optimization technique is more appropriate: when a larger scope is considered, faster optimization is needed. When mobility is added, the environment's dynamics brings the need for faster optimization techniques to be developed for this computing model. The scheduler should then run an optimization algorithm to find the best allocation possible for applications considering requirements and resources capacity.

In general, the scheduling problem, which involves finding the optimal solution among a universe of exponential possibilities, is considered a hard problem to solve among computer problems. Most of these problems are classified into classes of problems named as NP-Complete and NP-Hard [28]. One of the most classical problems is known as Knapsack Problem (KP) [30]. This problem consists of, based on a set of items with different sizes and a knapsack with a defined capacity, finding the optimal set of items that maximize the use of the knapsack capacity.

To exemplify the KP in the MEC architecture context, consider a system with five cloudlets and 100 VMs. The basic version of the scheduler just needs to find a valid solution for the allocation of the VMs in the cloudlets, considering the needs of each VM (e.g., processing power, memory) and the capacities of each cloudlet. This can be expanded to consider multiple cloudlets at the same level, multiple levels, and also include the Cloud. As users move, the problem becomes dynamic in nature, and the modeling should be adapted to be able to find solutions in a reasonable time. Different optimization algorithms and techniques can be applied to behave according to the current dynamicity observed in the system.

Many different types of algorithms can be used to solve optimization problems, such as the classic KP problem and its variations. The most basic is an exhaustive search (or Brute force) that will test for each possible valid solution and find the best one. In practice, this algorithm can be used only in very small search space sizes because it has an exponential execution time. However, if the search space size is small enough, it always guarantees the global optima (best solution). In the VM placement problem for MEC, the search space can vary in size: from a single cloudlet to the whole hierarchy. Brute force may be a choice for local optimization in a single cloudlet when a few users are currently at that location.

Another class of algorithms used to solve optimization problems, including the KP problem, is Dynamic Programming. The Branch and Bound algorithm focus on solving combinatorial optimization problems. Basically, in combinatorial optimization, the choices to be made are discrete (i.e., where to allocate each VM), and in continuous optimization, the choices to be made are based on continuous values (i.e., real numbers). Dynamic programming can speedup the scheduler solution to be applicable in larger scenarios, e.g., considering multiple fog nodes and hierarchical levels.

Other optimization techniques include heuristics and meta-heuristics, where solution quality is not guaranteed, but the algorithms running times are reduced. For example, artificial intelligence has also been used to solve KP problems. Some examples are Genetic Algorithms (GA), Ant Colony Optimization (ACO), as well as hybridizations combining two or more techniques. Heuristics and meta-heuristics are suitable for larger and more dynamic scenarios, where multiple runs of the optimization are needed to keep the objective functions optimized. This is clearly the case in MEC, for example, in rush hours when a great percentage of users move around and need to have their VMs/containers properly placed to improve QoS and obey requirements.

4.3 Streaming Services

Combining Edge and Cloud computing environments bring to streaming services attractive improvements in terms of bandwidth usage and reduced latency. End-users can expect high-quality video applications to work anywhere and on a variety of heterogeneous devices, including mobile ones. In Video-on-Demand (VoD) services, the edge resources of Internet Service Providers can be utilized to host video contents in the proximity of end-users, thereby reducing latency and mitigating load on core networks and data centers. This is especially helpful for live streaming scenarios that require low latency [24, 47]. Moreover, pre-processing can be done in multiple streaming flows deployed at the Edge. Consequently, reducing the download traffic needed from the Cloud. An edge architecture for video streaming delivery has the following purposes: (1) Improving the users QoE, serving the requested edge content as close as possible to the user; (2) Reduce congestion at

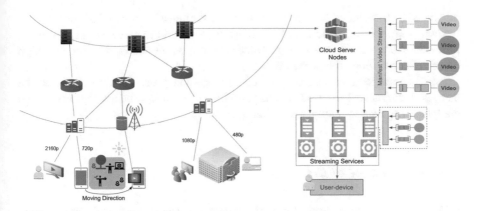

Fig. 7 Illustration of collaborative video delivery on a MEC network

the core of the network; (3) Efficiently deal with the amount of data that needs to be processed and extract meaningful data to create more intelligence.

Figure 7 depicts a network service scenario that uses intelligent video streaming in a MEC architecture. A MEC server (i.e., an fog node) is connected to base stations to perform data storage and processing. A MEC client can access video streaming services being run in the infrastructure [62]. This video service can cache videos and run analytics to extract knowledge about video content and video service performance, such as estimating QoE from throughput for different users. This can assist network-level decisions to adjust the data rate accordingly to the available downlink bandwidth, presenting real-time network information and context in addition to reduced latency.

To provide cache services in a MEC architecture, it is important to effectively deliver the video content through smart caching mechanisms. Such mechanisms can be based, for example, on content popularity and geographical location/distribution of mobile devices. With this strategy, it is possible to efficiently use VoD and live broadcast services to a wide range of heterogeneous devices. In order to improve this, a good idea is to distribute the service closer to the region with more bandwidth consumption. This approach is similar to the existing overlay cache that is applied to services with lower latency indexes due to edge utilization. This can lead to the improvement of the QoE for the majority of users. In other words, smart caching available on the fog nodes enable popular videos to be available closer to the user, thus reducing traffic load and delay [54].

Besides promoting caching, a MEC architecture can also perform data processing at the Edge. Figure 7 gives another example, the deployment of a transcoding service closer to the end-users can improve the QoE in dense networks with heterogeneous resolutions being requested. For instance, transcoding of cached videos can be run in a MEC server when a user requests a different version. This task can be run in the MEC server that stores the original video (data provider node) or the MEC node serving the video (delivery node). For example, a video with a 5 Mbps (720p) bit rate could be transcoded from a cached copy presenting a bit rate of 8 Mbps (1080p). In doing that, the fog node uses the bandwidth available to serve as many users as possible. Moreover, the content provider does not waste bandwidth, sending high bit rate video through the core network.

MEC infrastructures can be utilized to store and process video closer to the user, performing real-time transcoding, caching for reduced bandwidth use, video analytics, augmented reality, and so on.

4.4 Intelligence at the Edge

Edge devices produce large amounts of data nowadays, enabling the so-called Smart Environments, also as a consequence of the current pervasiveness of personal mobile and IoT devices [56]. The massive data source has considerably changed in this scenario, moving from Cloud data centers to end devices. Bringing Artificial Intelligence (AI) and Machine Learning (ML) to be run at the Edge of the network is seen as a possibility to enable the full potential of Big Data processing in MEC infrastructures.

In the standard Big Data scenario, data is generated at the Edge of the network and must be transported to data centers, which contains a very high processing and storage capacity. Then, AI is applied to generate knowledge about those data and keep it in a central location. Data centers are often geographically far from end-users, which implies in transferring a large volume of data across links, resulting in increased latency and congestion. In MEC, AI can be applied at the Edge as well, processing local data to generate knowledge about specific regions, but can also aggregate and send data to the Cloud for additional processing to generalize the knowledge with a wider view from the data gathered at the Edge.

Machine Learning provides the most prominent set of tools currently to achieve the mentioned AI objectives, to gain insights, perform classifications and predictions through training with data obtained at the Edge in a process with feed-forward and backpropagation [49]. Among ML methods, Deep Learning (DL) stands out for its unique performance in many tasks. DL is a variation of Neural Networks (NN), which can then be called Deep Neural Networks (DNN). DNNs can learn high-level resources by providing highly accurate inferences on tasks. As shown in Fig. 8, DL works with several neurons in the entrance, called Input Layer, which receives raw data. It is connected to middle layers, known as the hidden layer, that they are going to perform complex operations of learning, sending their results to the output layer. The hidden layer gives more complexity than a Simple Neural Network, which requires more computational power; however, it gives better work results in learning tasks.

Run the DNN models on edge devices requires large computing capacity for DNN algorithms. Therefore, actual intelligence at the Edge depends on architectures and mechanisms able to maintain accuracy by running learning algorithms collaboratively at the Edge in a distributed way, and, complementary, using the synergy

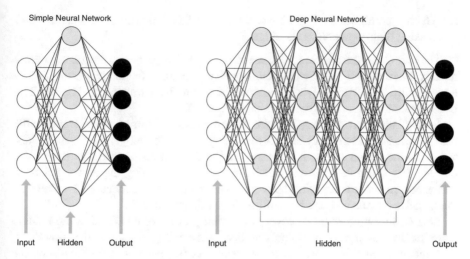

Fig. 8 Deep learning structure

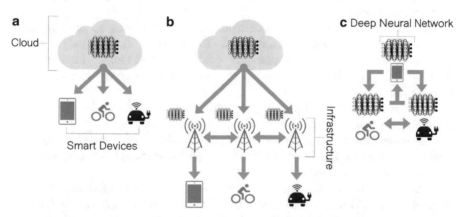

Fig. 9 Three architectures for DNN training: (**a**) Cloud to devices (**b**) Devices keep training DNN models and (**c**) Cloud to Edge Infrastructure, then, to devices

between the Cloud and the Edge in the considered MEC computing hierarchy. In this scenario, the AI model's training can be carried out in the Cloud data centers, which then makes the trained model available to the edge devices at synchronization rounds. Also, Edge computing can use data center resources when necessary to optimize DNN training since transmitting DNN models through the network is less expensive than transferring all raw data to the Cloud.

According to Zhou et al. [66], there are three ways to architect DNN training: centralized, decentralized, and hybrid (Fig. 9):

(a) Centralized: the most common, carried out in data centers;
(b) Decentralized: aims to train models directly on the edge devices, updating the models from time to time;

(c) Hybrid: combines the two above, training of DNN models in data centers and making them available at the Edge.

The first (a) is the classic one, carried out in data centers. The second (b) aims to train the models directly on the edge devices, updating the models from time to time. Finally, the hybrid (c) that combines the two with the training of DNN models in data centers and making them available at the Edge.

Items *b* and *c* involve edge mobile devices running learning models, but *c* still uses the Cloud infrastructure as a form of support. The learning model is massively trained in the Cloud and then forwarded to the Edge infrastructure and then to the devices. Here, end devices will not have the task of training the model but only applying it in accordance with the current application. Adjustments and updates to the model are made with the help of the Edge infrastructure.

Item *b*, on the other hand, covers the entire process of constituting the model, from training the model to its applicability, going through model updates, without the support of other infrastructures. The details of this process are at the discretion of the chosen harvesting method. What matters in this context is that it is all done on mobile devices.

Computationally, learning methods require a lot of resources, so applying them to mobile devices is not straightforward. To avoid significant changes in the architecture of mobile devices (memory, processing, and storage capacity), the way forward would be to optimize the models in order to make them as light as possible [10].

An interesting method is compressing the models [45]. This method generalizes a learning structure by removing weights or operations that are less useful for predictions and divides a large model into smaller models, each focused on a specific application scenario. This improves processing performance as fewer operations are done to achieve similar results.

Some care with the use of computational resources must be taken into account. Bonawitz et al. [8] makes some recommendations in this regard. A new function when learning on the mobile device is the use of a local data repository for training and model evaluation. It is recommended to use simple and small databases like SQLite, and its available storage size is small and non-negotiable, in addition to establishing an expiration date for the data.

As for the user experience and battery life, it is preferred to invoke the learning method only when the device is idle and with a sufficient battery is remaining or when it is connected to the charger. Finally, a cleaning of temporary resources must be scheduled as soon as their execution is complete.

Technologies dedicated to working with distributed DNN at the edge are currently under development, such as Federated Learning [12], Aggregation Frequency Control [22], Gradient Compression [34], DNN Splitting [37], Knowledge Transfer Learning [57], and Gossip Training [9]. Many of these methods work with local data on the device, which increases data privacy.

The availability of high-quality intelligent services is a combination of the chosen AI method with computing performance and network data transfer. Some metrics are adopted to describe the QoS of the Edge computing model inference, such as latency, precision (DNN model), energy efficiency, data privacy, and communication overhead. Introducing mobility with MEC gives rise to new challenges in intelligence at the Edge, where now, more dynamic evaluation of distributed learning models is necessary. For example, in smart cities, traffic management can be performed mostly at the Edge with data from users/vehicles. A more precise estimate of traffic can be performed in real-time with low latency at the Edge, while relevant data are still sent to the Cloud for model training and to produce a wider view of the current traffic landscape. Therefore, in this scenario, the MEC architecture acts to reduce data transmission to the Cloud as well as to produce faster and more precise results in this mobility scenario.

5 Challenges

Since the MEC paradigm is an architecture that extends the Cloud computing concept, it can share some common solutions of other distributed systems. However, the MEC architecture's unique characteristics make it seek new approaches to manage its environment properly. Many approaches have been proposed over the last years, however, many problems still have no definitive solutions. This section introduces some of the open problems present in MEC's development that still are challenging the area.

5.1 Resource Management

In order for users to take advantage of the new possibilities offered by the MEC architecture, storage and computing resources are distributed across the edge of the network, ensuring access to infrastructure for any users who wish to use MEC services. Identifying strategies to define where physical servers with computational resources should be allocated is a significant challenge. To allow resources to be used efficiently, physical servers must be allocated based on users' expected demand, ensuring that users' QoE and QoS requirements are met.

The development of routines capable of managing computational resources is another challenge to ensure MEC's proper functioning. For the resources contained in the MEC infrastructure to be orchestrated efficiently, it is necessary to define signaling messages capable of transmitting information about the status of the resources, such as capacity, availability, and workload. However, signaling messages must not occur so frequently as not to compromise the performance of the MEC infrastructure, and at the same time, they cannot be rare enough so that resource information becomes outdated. The multi-tiered layout in a MEC architecture can help resource management to be performed more efficiently, but proper mechanisms should be designed to work in this computing hierarchy.

5.2   Mobility Management

Besides the requirements of MEC users in terms of computing, storage, and network resources, the MEC infrastructure also needs to manage their different mobility patterns. For example, when moving by foot, bicycle, car, bus, or train, each one of them presenting a specific route and speed. That characteristic of mobile users introduces several challenges for the MEC infrastructure in terms of service availability. Such a dynamic scenario affects different MEC's resource management processes such as load balance, service placement and migration, packet routing, and handoff.

Different researches have been made to increase the capability of MEC infrastructures to support mobile users. However, the impact of user mobility is not completely understood in these infrastructures. More accurate algorithms for predictive mobility patterns can help some processes to plan their future demand in a specific area. Based on such information, the infrastructure can prepare the required resources to serve that increasing demand. This process can prepare MEC to scale up or scale down or even triggers a load balance, service migration, or caching data.

Furthermore, in this context, technologies like Software Defined Networks (SDN), Network Function Virtualization (NFV) [63], and network slicing [3] have been introduced to increase the flexibility of these infrastructures. Besides the capability of network slicing to dynamically reallocate MEC resources to serve these mobile users [20], further studies on that context need to be made to evaluate the computing overhead of that resource reallocation.

5.3   Data Transmission

Although the allocation of computing and storage resources is a key point in the impact of QoE guarantees, the management of network resources can either perform several improvements or impair the user experience. Due to the close relationship between IoT, MEC, and big data, a colossal amount of data is transferred between different architecture points. To properly serve delay-sensitive applications, placing data and computing close to the users is not enough if the MEC architecture cannot deliver the users' requests within the required deadline. Based on that, transmission techniques need to be optimized enough to provide a good connection among the MEC nodes and their users. Moreover, in MEC, it is expected that different wireless and wired technologies work together and seamlessly. Inter-operation and seamless connection maintenance among a variety of protocols is a challenge yet to be overcome.

In this scenario, both wireless technologies and routing protocols must be optimized to provide a faster and more stable connection to the users. One of the main challenges of developing these protocols is dealing with the trade-off between energy efficiency, latency, reliability, and throughput. Predictive offloading [1] and transmission protocols that avoid wireless package collision and improve latency and throughput are some candidate solutions. End-to-end network slicing has also been rising as a promising solution.

5.4   QoS and QoE Guarantees

MEC servers can help guarantee QoS for latency-sensitive applications from mobile users using a resource reservation method. Whereas for static latency-tolerant users, the MEC management system can perform on-demand provisioning to allocate computational resources and provide reliable computing services. However, provisioning schemes that have to take into account high-mobility users is a complex task. Therefore, novel hybrid MEC server schemes must be developed to enable increased MEC providers' revenue through serving a maximum number of users with guarantees on their QoS requirements.

Research studies in QoE show that the changing conditions of best-effort networks introduce numerous problems. In traditional video streaming, each client typically streams a video that is available in a single bitrate on the server-side [23, 26]. A MEC architecture should exploit users' context information to optimize content management and video delivery, which may result in better utilization of network resources and QoE.

5.5   Intelligence at the Edge

Introducing intelligence techniques at the Edge comes with new challenges that must be faced. When considering a MEC learning network, the data can be distributed to be processed on more than one node. In this situation, the development of a tool that offers an automatic and efficient partitioning is both a challenge and an opportunity in this scenario. It is also interesting to note that offloading a training model from the Cloud to the edge nodes can incur high communication costs, especially when considering applications that require persistent training models.

Studying the trade-offs between transferring data to the Cloud and implementing adaptive learning models at the edge, as well as designing adaptation mechanisms for model distribution, is a current challenge. It is important to note that distributed learning also comes with the challenge of privacy-preserving mechanisms, which should also be developed for sensitive data (e.g., medical applications).

Mobility within MEC gives rise to additional challenges for proper implementation of intelligence at the Edge, where a more dynamic evaluation of distributed learning models is necessary. For example, in smart cities, traffic management can be performed mostly at the Edge with real-time data from users/vehicles. A more precise estimate of traffic can be performed in real-time with low latency at the Edge, while relevant data are still uploaded to the Cloud for model training and to produce a wider view of the current traffic landscape. Other mobile application scenarios can present the same characteristics, where a dynamic composition of data from edge devices is crucial for the learning model to provide relevant results.

5.6 Green MEC

Energy consumption has gained attraction from researchers in different areas of computing, such as embedded systems and resource management in Cloud computing and networking. For example, to manage the increase in energy consumption, the InterSCity project[1] has different approaches to this challenge. In a CF-RAN architecture proposed in [52, 53], they introduce local nodes closer to the users where they perform part of the processing tasks. The cloud-level nodes manage the workloads sent to the fog on demand to process the surplus traffic from the front-haul.

The computation on fog nodes is performed through virtualized network functions, where they are activated or deactivated in real-time depending on the network demand. In [55], IoT data are collected at the Edge by nodes called gateways. Communication between The IoT devices and gateways is done using wireless cellular technology. Then, they are used to train a distributed machine learning solution model. Both energy consumption and training performance are evaluated with different configurations and compared to the centralized cloud model. Such a distributed solution significantly mitigates the traffic sent to the Cloud. On the other hand, a reduction in distributed learning precision training has to be made. With the network's edge addition, the energy consumption shows savings of over 90% in data transmission and 2% in precision loss when compared to the centralized cloud-level. Further studies in energy management with mobility and Edge computing are still needed to tackle heterogeneous devices' complexities in a Smart City and mobility.

Each MEC node can use considerably less power than a conventional large Cloud data centers. At the same time, it has lower processing power, requiring a higher number of active locations. Because of that, the increase of new small-scale MEC servers being created becomes a big concern for energy consumption. This way, it is unquestionable to develop innovative techniques for achieving power energy saving. At the same time, computational resources need to be manageable to guarantee satisfactory computational performance.

The small area serviced by each MEC server impacts resource allocation and service management, especially when considering user mobility. The consequence of this architecture is a highly dynamic workload, with a fast change in load patterns. More advanced prediction techniques could be developed to enable optimized resource utilization, focusing on load distribution and reduced power consumption. Moreover, management services for dynamic scaling workloads that require significant computational resources need to be developed. Also, note that

---

[1] www.interscity.org.

as MEC systems grow over a region, a green load balancing solution needs to be optimized in the best way using further available renewable energy.

6 Conclusion

We have presented in this chapter a distributed, multi-tiered Mobile Edge Computing (MEC) architecture. MEC was introduced by the ETSI Mobile Edge Computing Industry Specification Group (MEC ISG) as a means of offering data storage and processing closer to data sources and data consumers, taking into account the mobility aspects impact on infrastructure management.

We have covered topics on the benefits of using the MEC architecture, such as support for content distribution to mobile users, optimization of resource allocation, video delivery, and intelligence at the Edge. Besides, we have pointed out that MEC was designed to offer low latency connectivity for delay-sensitive applications due to users' proximity at the network's edge.

It becomes clear that many research challenges are still essential to be carried out to properly manage data and resources in MEC architectures, especially with the high heterogeneity in application requirements and into the future. We discussed some directions, providing insights on interesting potential problems for further research.

References

1. Aazam, M., Zeadally, S., Harras, K.A.: Offloading in fog computing for iot: Review, enabling technologies, and research opportunities. Future Generation Computer Systems **87**, 278–289 (2018)
2. Abbas, N., Zhang, Y., Taherkordi, A., Skeie, T.: Mobile edge computing: A survey. IEEE Internet of Things Journal **5**(1), 450–465 (2017)
3. Afolabi, I., Taleb, T., Samdanis, K., Ksentini, A., Flinck, H.: Network Slicing and Softwarization: A Survey on Principles, Enabling Technologies, and Solutions. IEEE Communications Surveys Tutorials **20**(3), 2429–2453 (thirdquarter 2018). https://doi.org/10.1109/COMST. 2018.2815638
4. Araújo, M.C., Curado, M., Sousa, B.M., Bittencourt, L.F.: Cmfog: Proactive content migration using Markov chain and madm in fog computing. In: Proceedings of the 13th IEEE/ACM International Conference on Utility and Cloud Computing (2020)
5. Benkacem, I., Taleb, T., Bagaa, M., Flinck, H.: Optimal vnfs placement in cdn slicing over multi-cloud environment. IEEE Journal on Selected Areas in Communications **36**(3), 616–627 (March 2018). https://doi.org/10.1109/JSAC.2018.2815441
6. Bittencourt, L., Diaz-Montes, J., Buyya, R., Rana, O., Parashar, M.: Mobility-aware application scheduling in fog computing. IEEE Cloud Computing **4**(2), 26–35 (March 2017). https://doi. org/10.1109/MCC.2017.27
7. Bittencourt, L., Immich, R., Sakellariou, R., Fonseca, N., Madeira, E., Curado, M., Villas, L., DaSilva, L., Lee, C., Rana, O.: The internet of things, fog and cloud continuum: Integration and challenges. Internet of Things **3–4**, 134 – 155 (2018)

8. Bonawitz, K.A., Eichner, H., Grieskamp, W., Huba, D., Ingerman, A., Ivanov, V., Kiddon, C.M., Konečný, J., Mazzocchi, S., McMahan, B., Overveldt, T.V., Petrou, D., Ramage, D., Roselander, J.: Towards federated learning at scale: System design. In: SysML 2019 (2019), https://arxiv.org/abs/1902.01046, to appear
9. Boyd, S., Ghosh, A., Prabhakar, B., Shah, D.: Randomized gossip algorithms. IEEE transactions on information theory **52**(6), 2508–2530 (2006)
10. Caldas, S., Konečný, J., McMahan, B., Talwalkar, A.: Expanding the reach of federated learning by reducing client resource requirements (2018), https://arxiv.org/abs/1812.07210
11. Carrega, A., Repetto, M., Gouvas, P., Zafeiropoulos, A.: A middleware for mobile edge computing. IEEE Cloud Computing **4**(4), 26–37 (2017)
12. Chen, Q., Zheng, Z., Hu, C., Wang, D., Liu, F.: Data-driven task allocation for multi-task transfer learning on the edge. In: 2019 IEEE 39th International Conference on Distributed Computing Systems (ICDCS). pp. 1040–1050. IEEE (2019)
13. Chettri, L., Bera, R.: A comprehensive survey on internet of things (iot) toward 5g wireless systems. IEEE Internet of Things Journal **7**(1), 16–32 (2020)
14. Chiang, M., Shi, W.: Nsf workshop report on grand challenges in edge computing. In: Tech. Rep. (2016)
15. Cisco: Cisco visual networking index: Global mobile data traffic forecast update, 2015–2020. Tech. Rep. 1 (2016)
16. Curado, M., Madeira, H., da Cunha, P.R., Cabral, B., Abreu, D.P., Barata, J., Roque, L., Immich, R.: Internet of Things - Next Generation Cyber-Physical Systems, pp. 381–401. Springer (2019)
17. Cuttone, A., Lehmann, S., González, M.C.: Understanding predictability and exploration in human mobility. EPJ Data Science **7**(1), 2 (2018)
18. ETSI, M.: Mobile edge computing (mec); framework and reference architecture. ETSI, DGS MEC **3** (2016)
19. Gonçalves, D., Velasquez, K., Curado, M., Bittencourt, L., Madeira, E.: Proactive virtual machine migration in fog environments. In: 2018 IEEE Symposium on Computers and Communications (ISCC). pp. 00742–00745. IEEE (2018)
20. Gonçalves, D., Puliafito, C., Mingozzi, E., Rana, O., Bittencourt, L., Madeira, E.: Dynamic network slicing in fog computing for mobile users in mobfogsim. In: Proceedings of the 13th IEEE/ACM International Conference on Utility and Cloud Computing (2020)
21. Habibi, P., Farhoudi, M., Kazemian, S., Khorsandi, S., Leon-Garcia, A.: Fog computing: A comprehensive architectural survey. IEEE Access (2020)
22. Hsieh, K., Harlap, A., Vijaykumar, N., Konomis, D., Ganger, G.R., Gibbons, P.B., Mutlu, O.: Gaia: Geo-distributed machine learning approaching {LAN} speeds. In: 14th {USENIX} Symposium on Networked Systems Design and Implementation ({NSDI} 17). pp. 629–647 (2017)
23. Immich, R., Cerqueira, E., Curado, M.: Adaptive qoe-driven video transmission over vehicular ad-hoc networks. In: IEEE Conference on Computer Communications Workshops (INFOCOM WKSHPS). pp. 227–232 (April 2015). https://doi.org/10.1109/INFCOMW.2015.7179389
24. Immich, R., Cerqueira, E., Curado, M.: Towards a qoe-driven mechanism for improved h.265 video delivery. In: Mediterranean Ad Hoc Networking Workshop (Med-Hoc-Net). pp. 1–8 (June 2016). https://doi.org/10.1109/MedHocNet.2016.7528427
25. Immich, R., Villas, L., Bittencourt, L., Madeira, E.: Multi-tier edge-to-cloud architecture for adaptive video delivery. In: 2019 7th International Conference on Future Internet of Things and Cloud (FiCloud). pp. 23–30 (Aug 2019). https://doi.org/10.1109/FiCloud.2019.00012
26. Immich, R., Borges, P., Cerqueira, E., Curado, M.: Adaptive motion-aware fec-based mechanism to ensure video transmission. In: IEEE Symposium on Computers and Communication (ISCC). pp. 1–6 (June 2014). https://doi.org/10.1109/ISCC.2014.6912571
27. Jarray, C., Giovanidis, A.: The effects of mobility on the hit performance of cached d2d networks. In: 2016 14th international symposium on modeling and optimization in mobile, ad hoc, and wireless networks (WiOpt). pp. 1–8. IEEE (2016)

28. Karp, R.M.: Reducibility among combinatorial problems. In: Complexity of computer compu-
    tations, pp. 85–103. Springer (1972)
29. Kekki, S., Featherstone, W., Fang, Y., Kuure, P., Li, A., Ranjan, A., Purkayastha, D., Jiangping,
    F., Frydman, D., Verin, G., et al.: Mec in 5g networks. ETSI white paper **28**, 1–28 (2018)
30. Kellerer, H., Pferschy, U., Pisinger, D.: Multidimensional knapsack problems. In: Knapsack
    problems, pp. 235–283. Springer (2004)
31. Kikuchi, J., Wu, C., Ji, Y., Murase, T.: Mobile edge computing based vm migration for qos
    improvement. In: 2017 IEEE 6th Global Conference on Consumer Electronics (GCCE). pp. 1–
    5. IEEE (2017)
32. Ksentini, A., Taleb, T., Chen, M.: A Markov decision process-based service migration
    procedure for follow me cloud. In: 2014 IEEE International Conference on Communications
    (ICC). pp. 1350–1354. IEEE (2014)
33. Lim, W.Y.B., Luong, N.C., Hoang, D.T., Jiao, Y., Liang, Y.C., Yang, Q., Niyato, D., Miao,
    C.: Federated learning in mobile edge networks: A comprehensive survey. arXiv preprint
    arXiv:1909.11875 (2019)
34. Lin, Y., Han, S., Mao, H., Wang, Y., Dally, W.J.: Deep gradient compression: Reducing the
    communication bandwidth for distributed training. arXiv preprint arXiv:1712.01887 (2017)
35. Liu, L., Guo, J., Zhang, S., Zhu, J.: Similar user assisted mobility prediction. In: 2019 11th
    International Conference on Wireless Communications and Signal Processing (WCSP). pp. 1–
    6. IEEE (2019)
36. Mach, P., Becvar, Z.: Mobile edge computing: A survey on architecture and computation
    offloading. IEEE Communications Surveys & Tutorials **19**(3), 1628–1656 (2017)
37. Mao, Y., Yi, S., Li, Q., Feng, J., Xu, F., Zhong, S.: A privacy-preserving deep learning approach
    for face recognition with edge computing. In: Proc. USENIX Workshop Hot Topics Edge
    Comput.(HotEdge). pp. 1–6 (2018)
38. Mckinsey, Company: Mapping the value beyond the hype. Executive Summary pp. 1 – 144
    (2015)
39. Nadembega, A., Hafid, A.S., Brisebois, R.: Mobility prediction model-based service migration
    procedure for follow me cloud to support qos and qoe. In: 2016 IEEE International Conference
    on Communications (ICC). pp. 1–6. IEEE (2016)
40. Park, J., Samarakoon, S., Bennis, M., Debbah, M.: Wireless network intelligence at the edge.
    Proceedings of the IEEE **107**(11), 2204–2239 (2019)
41. Petrangeli, S., Wauters, T., Turck, F.D.: Qoe-centric network-assisted delivery of adaptive
    video streaming services. In: 2019 IFIP/IEEE Symposium on Integrated Network and Service
    Management (IM). pp. 683–688 (April 2019)
42. Pisani, F., de Oliveira, F., Gama, E.S., Immich, R., Bittencourt, L.F., Borin, E.: Fog computing
    on constrained devices: Paving the way for the future iot. Advances in Edge Computing: Mas-
    sive Parallel Processing and Applications **35**, 22 (2020). https://doi.org/10.3233/APC200003
43. Puliafito, C., Mingozzi, E., Anastasi, G.: Fog computing for the internet of mobile things:
    Issues and challenges. In: 2017 IEEE International Conference on Smart Computing (SMART-
    COMP). pp. 1–6 (2017)
44. Puliafito, C., Gonçalves, D.M., Lopes, M.M., Martins, L.L., Madeira, E., Mingozzi, E., Rana,
    O., Bittencourt, L.F.: Mobfogsim: Simulation of mobility and migration for fog computing.
    Simulation Modelling Practice and Theory **101**, 102062 (2020)
45. Ravi, S.: Custom on-device ml models with learn2compress (05 2018), https://ai.googleblog.
    com/2018/05/custom-on-device-ml-models.html
46. Retal, S., Bagaa, M., Taleb, T., Flinck, H.: Content delivery network slicing: Qoe and cost
    awareness. In: 2017 IEEE International Conference on Communications (ICC). pp. 1–6 (May
    2017)
47. S. Gama, E., Immich, R., F. Bittencourt, L.: Towards a multi-tier fog/cloud architecture
    for video streaming. In: 2018 IEEE/ACM International Conference on Utility and Cloud
    Computing Companion (UCC Companion). pp. 13–14 (2018)

48. Sabella, D., Vaillant, A., Kuure, P., Rauschenbach, U., Giust, F.: Mobile-edge computing architecture: The role of mec in the internet of things. IEEE Consumer Electronics Magazine 5(4), 84–91 (2016)
49. Svozil, D., Kvasnicka, V., Pospichal, J.: Introduction to multi-layer feed-forward neural networks. Chemometrics and intelligent laboratory systems 39(1), 43–62 (1997)
50. Taleb, T., Samdanis, K., Mada, B., Flinck, H., Dutta, S., Sabella, D.: On multi-access edge computing: A survey of the emerging 5g network edge cloud architecture and orchestration. IEEE Communications Surveys Tutorials 19(3), 1657–1681 (thirdquarter 2017). https://doi.org/10.1109/COMST.2017.2705720
51. Taleb, T., Ksentini, A.: Follow me cloud: interworking federated clouds and distributed mobile networks. IEEE Network 27(5), 12–19 (2013)
52. Tinini, R.I., Batista, D.M., Figueiredo, G.B.: Energy-efficient vpon formation and wavelength dimensioning in cloud-fog ran over twdm-pon. In: 2018 IEEE Symposium on Computers and Communications (ISCC). pp. 521–526. IEEE (2018)
53. Tinini, R.I., Batista, D.M., Figueiredo, G.B., Tornatore, M., Mukherjee, B.: Low-latency and energy-efficient bbu placement and vpon formation in virtualized cloud-fog ran. IEEE/OSA Journal of Optical Communications and Networking 11(4), B37–B48 (2019)
54. Tran, T.X., Hajisami, A., Pandey, P., Pompili, D.: Collaborative mobile edge computing in 5g networks: New paradigms, scenarios, and challenges. IEEE Communications Magazine 55(4), 54–61 (2017)
55. Valerio, L., Conti, M., Passarella, A.: Energy efficient distributed analytics at the edge of the network for iot environments. Pervasive and Mobile Computing 51, 27–42 (2018)
56. Valerio, L., Passarella, A., Conti, M.: A communication efficient distributed learning framework for smart environments. Pervasive and Mobile Computing 41, 46–68 (2017)
57. Wang, J., Zhang, J., Bao, W., Zhu, X., Cao, B., Yu, P.S.: Not just privacy: Improving performance of private deep learning in mobile cloud. In: Proceedings of the 24th ACM SIGKDD International Conference on Knowledge Discovery & Data Mining. pp. 2407–2416 (2018)
58. Wang, M., Yang, S., Sun, Y., Gao, J.: Human mobility prediction from region functions with taxi trajectories. PloS one 12(11), e0188735 (2017)
59. Wang, S., Zhang, X., Zhang, Y., Wang, L., Yang, J., Wang, W.: A survey on mobile edge networks: Convergence of computing, caching and communications. IEEE Access 5, 6757–6779 (2017)
60. Wang, X., Han, Y., Leung, V.C., Niyato, D., Yan, X., Chen, X.: Convergence of edge computing and deep learning: A comprehensive survey. IEEE Communications Surveys & Tutorials (2020)
61. Yan, X.Y., Wang, W.X., Gao, Z.Y., Lai, Y.C.: Universal model of individual and population mobility on diverse spatial scales. Nature communications 8(1), 1639 (2017)
62. Yang, S., Tseng, Y., Huang, C., Lin, W.: Multi-access edge computing enhanced video streaming: Proof-of-concept implementation and prediction/qoe models. IEEE Transactions on Vehicular Technology 68(2), 1888–1902 (2019)
63. Zaidi, Z., Friderikos, V., Yousaf, Z., Fletcher, S., Dohler, M., Aghvami, H.: Will SDN Be Part of 5G? IEEE Communications Surveys Tutorials 20(4), 3220–3258 (Fourthquarter 2018). 10.1109/COMST.2018.2836315
64. Zhang, C., Zheng, Z.: Task migration for mobile edge computing using deep reinforcement learning. Future Generation Computer Systems 96, 111–118 (2019)
65. Zhang, J., Letaief, K.B.: Mobile edge intelligence and computing for the internet of vehicles. Proceedings of the IEEE (2019)
66. Zhou, Z., Chen, X., Li, E., Zeng, L., Luo, K., Zhang, J.: Edge intelligence: Paving the last mile of artificial intelligence with edge computing. Proceedings of the IEEE 107(8), 1738–1762 (2019)

Complex Event Processing in Sensor-Based Environments: Edge Computing Frameworks and Techniques

A. Dhillon, S. Majumdar, M. St-Hilaire, and A. El-Haraki

Abstract By performing latency-sensitive computations at the edge and the remaining computations on a backend server, edge computing systems can effectively handle the processing of data in a timely manner. This chapter focuses on an edge computing framework that partitions the processing of sensor data at a mobile node placed at the edge and backend computations at a powerful server. The primary application of the framework is in the area of processing of complex events each of which may correspond to the simultaneous occurrence of multiple raw events generated by sensors that are monitoring the phenomena of interest. Application of such complex event processing techniques spans smart buildings, smart machinery as well as smart healthcare systems. This chapter focuses on using the proposed framework and techniques to a smart phone based remote patient monitoring system and by using prototyping and measurement presents a rigorous performance analysis of the system.

Keywords Mobile complex event processing · Remote patient monitoring system · Internet of things · Smart healthcare

1 Introduction

Data acquisition and the processing of the acquired data are two components of various computing applications. Traditionally, they have been performed by two separate system components. The data handling components that perform inputting/outputting of data send the data to another processing node that runs the data processing component and sends the results back to the data handling

A. Dhillon · S. Majumdar · M. St-Hilaire (✉)
Carleton University, Ottawa, ON, Canada
e-mail: amarjitdhillon@sce.carleton.ca; majumdar@sce.carleton.ca; marc_st_hilaire@carleton.ca

A. El-Haraki
TELUS, Ottawa, ON, Canada
e-mail: ali.el-haraki@telus.com

© The Author(s), under exclusive license to Springer Nature Switzerland AG 2021
A. Mukherjee et al. (eds.), *Mobile Edge Computing*,
https://doi.org/10.1007/978-3-030-69893-5_20

components. Examples include systems that use sensors (actuators) for data handling and a backend server for analyzing the sensor data. The intercommunication with the backend server is often achieved with the help of an inter-communication network which can introduce significant inter-communication delays. This model in which data handling and data processing are done by two separate components is adequate for delay tolerant systems for which the latency of data processing is not a concern. It fails, however, for delay sensitive systems where the results of processing sensor data must become available within a short period of time. Examples include sensor-based remote patient monitoring systems, various types of industrial controllers and aerospace systems that must quickly react to the sensor data crossing a particular threshold. Using a multi-tiered edge computing system in which a part of the data processing is performed at the edge near the data handling device and the remaining processing on the backend server is crucial for producing the results in a timely manner and achieving the latency goals of the system. The availability of inexpensive sensing devices as well as small computing systems is fuelling the rapidly increasing deployment of such edge computing systems.

This book chapter focuses on a mobile edge computing framework that is applicable to various smart systems that are described in the next paragraph. The application of the framework and associated techniques for a real-time remote patient monitoring system that includes a mobile edge computing device connected to sensors and a backend server is described. The system uses mobile edge computing and Internet of Things (IoT) technologies to perform complex event processing for detecting an oncoming health problem for the patient being monitored.

Complex Event Processing (CEP) is the technique used to find the patterns in real time data streams. This chapter compares two CEP architectural frameworks: Server CEP (SCEP) and Mobile CEP (MCEP). The SCEP framework uses the mobile device as a gateway to forward data streams from sensors to a remote IoT server where complex events are detected. A drawback of this existing methodology is that the mobile phone always needs to remain connected to the back-end server. Also, the mobile device's network consumption is increased while transferring large volumes of sensor data streams leading to an increase in the user cost. Additionally, it leads to an increase in the workload at the back-end server that serves multiple users. In the MCEP framework, as briefly introduced in [10], the detection of complex events is performed on an edge device (such as a smart phone) that receives data from sensors. Only the detected complex events are sent to a back-end IoT server for further processing. The edge-based technique can be used in various cases such as smart home, smart building and Remote Patient Monitoring (RPM). In this chapter, a RPM use case is considered to validate and compare the two frameworks. A thorough performance analysis is performed using a synthetic workload which provides insights into system scalability and the relationship between system/workload parameters and performance. This technique can be adapted to handle various different use cases as well.

1.1 Overview of the Chapter

This section provides a short overview of the material presented in this chapter. Section 2 describes a representative set of related work and Sect. 3 discusses the system architecture for the server CEP system. Then, the architecture of the mobile CEP system is discussed in Sect. 4. Implementation details for the proof of concept prototype are discussed in Sect. 5. Section 6 presents a performance analysis of the system followed by experimental results in Sect. 7. Finally, Sect. 8 provides our conclusions and Sect. 9 outlines possible directions for future work.

2 Related Work

A representative set of works on CEP and smart healthcare systems is presented. A more detailed literature survey is available from [9].

In 2016, Higashino proposed the idea of CEP-as-a-Service (CEPaaS) in his Ph.D. dissertation [18]. The goal is to leverage the advantages of Software-as-a-Service (SaaS) to provide Complex Event Processing as-a-Service (CEPaaS) so that there is no upfront charges and maintenance cost is low. He proposed Attributed Graph Rewriting for Complex Event Processing (AGeCEP) as a language agnostic technique to model the Continuous Query Language (CQL) queries. To support his proposition for CEPaaS, Higashino designed a simulator called CEPSim that runs on top of the CloudSim simulator [5, 6]. CloudSim is a popular cloud simulator written in Java which can effectively model a public, private or hybrid cloud. It allows the users to create a data-center, cloudlet, and broker in addition to defining different policies. The CEPSim module creates a query model and supports the operator placement and the operator scheduling for performing the CEP simulation. It also provides the mechanism to compute various CEP specific metrics for performance evaluation. A major limitation of CEPSim is that it does not have single and multiple query optimization mechanisms and assumes that a submitted query is already optimized. Another limitation is that it only supports the scenarios in which the query does not fail at runtime. It is important to mention that our work compares the performance of the edge-based mobile CEP with state-of-the-art CEPaaS system considered as a baseline system.

Another work reported in [25] describes a pulse monitoring system which also used the Android application as an edge gateway and sends data to a web portal for analysis and visualization. A similar approach is described in [31] which uses an Android device as a gateway agent. Another research in [11] and [26] employed an IoT-based approach to process the health sensor data streams on the cloud. The authors have used an *Intel Galileo Gen 2* IoT agent to collect the sensor data streams from the mobile device and forward these to an IoT server deployed on the cloud. However, the authors have not used any real-time analytics system as the computation is done by a batch processing-based Hadoop system. Further, no performance analysis is done in any of these two papers to demonstrate the effectiveness of the technique.

Woodbridge et al. have proposed an RPM system for congestive heart failure named as *WANDA* [30]. *WANDA* has a three-tier architecture in which the first tier consists of various health sensors that transmit the health sensor data streams to the second tier consisting of a web server. The third tier uses database servers to persist the health sensor data streams and perform the analysis using linear regression. Further, this system is not a real-time system and does not involve any CEP engine. However, as the authors are predicting a heart stroke, performing batch analysis seems to be appropriate. In 2017, Naddeo et al. [22] have proposed a real-time m-health monitoring system. Their system consists of an Android application which receives various physiological sensor data using the *Zephyr Bioharness BH3* sensors and performs noise filtering using various high-pass and low-pass filters. This filtered data is sent by an Android application to a remote Personal Health Record (PHR) server for analysis and visualization. A major shortcoming of this paper is that it does not describe the real-time analysis technique required for this system. Another similar work is reported in [23] where the authors proposed to integrate the CEP engine and the IoT server for smart healthcare. This paper is primarily focused on the key benefits of using CEP on the cloud. However, no actual system is designed and no performance analysis is done.

More recently, several survey papers such as [17], are bridging the concepts of edge computing and healthcare. The paper by Abdellatif et al. [1] is of particular interest as it reviews the opportunities and challenges for enabling smart healthcare (s-health). They mention that edge-computing capabilities and next-generation wireless networking technologies will be the enablers to achieve this goal. One of the interesting functionalities that their architecture provides is called "edge-based feature extraction for event detection". Our work is one step in this direction. By performing latency sensitive computations at the edge and the remaining computations on a backend server, we can ensure fast response time for critical applications such as remote patient monitoring.

Table 1 shows a summary of the various techniques presented in this section along with the two proposed techniques (SCEP/MCEP) described in this chapter. The comparison is based on the following parameters:

1. Simulation/Prototype/Concept/Review: This parameter indicates the methodology that was used in the papers. Four options are possible: 'Simulation' means that the performance of the model was evaluated through simulation. Similarly, 'prototype' means that a proof of concept was implemented and evaluated. 'Concept' denotes a paper where only a high-level description of the concept is presented and 'review' designates a review paper where multiple techniques are reviewed.
2. Edge/back-end: This parameter shows whether the complex event processing is done on the edge mobile device or on a back-end server.
3. Gateway/Filter: This parameter shows the technique used to forward the health data to the back-end server. 'Gateway' signifies that the mobile device is used as

Table 1 Comparison of various techniques based on different parameters

Technique/paper	Simulation/ prototype/ concept/ review	Edge/ back-end	Gateway/ filter	Security	Cost	Performance analysis
SCEP	Prototype	Back-end	Filtering	Yes	Yes	Yes
MCEP	Prototype	Edge	Filtering	Yes	Yes	Yes
ARM7 [25]	Prototype	Back-end	Gateway	Yes	No	No
eHealthNet [22]	Prototype	Back-end	Gateway	No	No	Yes
WANDA [30]	Prototype	Back-end	Gateway	Yes	No	Yes
[31]	Prototype	Back-end	Gateway	No	No	No
[11]	Prototype	Back-end	Gateway	Yes	No	No
[26]	Prototype	Back-end	Gateway	Yes	No	Yes
[1]	Prototype	Back-end	Filtering	Yes	No	Yes
AGeCEP [18]	Simulation	Back-end	Gateway	No	No	Yes
[23]	Concept	Back-end	Gateway	Yes	No	No
[17]	Review	n/a	n/a	n/a	n/a	n/a

a gateway to forward all the sensor data whereas 'Filter' signifies that data has been reduced (filtered) by the mobile device to reduce user cost and data transfer latency.

4. Security: This parameter is 'yes' if various security related issues have been considered in the paper.
5. Cost: This parameter is 'yes' if a cost related analysis is provided in the paper.
6. Performance analysis: This parameter shows whether a rigorous performance analysis is provided.

From the comparison provided in Table 1, we can see that unlike other methodologies which perform the CEP analysis on the back-end IoT server, our proposed techniques (MCEP and SCEP) can process data on the edge and on the back-end server respectively. It is worth mentioning that authors in [1] have done data compression and edge-based feature extraction on the edge device. However, in our work, we have done complete complex event detection on the device itself. Also, various security features have been implemented in our proof of concept prototype to help insure integrity and safety of patient health data. As compared to most of the other papers, some of which are missing performance analysis, cost analysis and security features, the proposed techniques consider these factors into account.

3 Server CEP System

In this chapter, we have considered the remote patient monitoring use case. As shown in Fig. 1, the Server Complex Event Processing (SCEP) system architecture

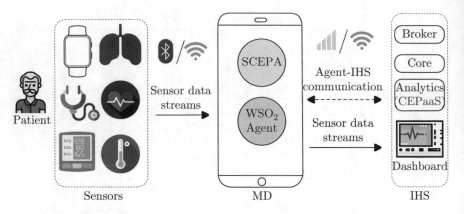

Fig. 1 Server CEP system architecture

is three-tiered consisting of multiple sensors, a Mobile Device (MD), and an IoT Hospital Server (IHS).

The mobile device along with the sensors comprise the edge system that communicates with the centralized back-end server. Multiple bluetooth and WiFi enabled wireless sensors can be used by the sensor-based system which can forward the sensor data to an Android or iOS device. For example, in a remote patient monitoring system, the sensors can be wearable health sensors worn by the patient. Such cheap and efficient sensors are provided by Cooking Hacks for example [7]. Some other commercial health monitoring sensors that can be used include the *Zeo Sleep Monitor* [13], which monitors sleep disorders, and *ViSiMobile* [29] which can measure Electrocardiogram (ECG), Heart Rate (HR), Arterial Oxygen Saturation (SpO2), skin temperature, etc. As shown in Fig. 1, the multiple sensors send the sensor data streams to a mobile device which consists of a Server Complex Event Processing Application (SCEPA) and a WSO_2 agent gateway application. The WSO_2 agent is used to register the mobile device with the IoTs server. The server complex event processing application forwards the health sensor data streams to the IHS. Communication between the sensors and the mobile device is done using bluetooth or WiFi whereas data transmission between the mobile device and the IHS is performed using either a cellular or a WiFi connection. The architecture shown in Fig. 1 can be used in other use cases such as smart buildings and smart homes as well. In the smart building use case, the wearable health sensors can be replaced by wired/wireless sensors deployed in a smart building such as room temperature sensors and light intensity sensors. In such a case, the mobile device can be replaced by a local server or a Raspberry-Pi board depending upon the workload.

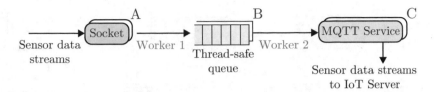

Fig. 2 Various components of the SCEP application

3.1 Components of the SCEP Application

Figure 2 shows the components of SCEPA which is used to forward the raw sensor data streams from the mobile device to the IoT server.

The various components that are stacked over one another represent multiple parallel instances of that component and a solid line represents multiple parallel sensor data streams. The various data streams are received by the Transmission Control Protocol (TCP) socket objects (one socket for each sensor) and appended to a thread-safe linked-blocking queue by a producer thread (Worker 1). A dedicated thread-safe queue is used for each sensor data stream. Further, the dequeue worker (Worker 2) retrieves the sensor data stream from a queue and sends it to the IHS using the Message Queuing Telemetry Transport (MQTT) service running on the mobile device. The MQTT protocol is used here as it is made specifically for low power devices such as sensors and mobile devices [20]. This MQTT service forwards the sensor data streams to the back-end IoT server as per the selected Quality of Service (QoS). Please note that the MQTT service also has its own queues for enabling the persistent session, and if the QoS ≥ 1 is selected, the sensor data stream tuples are temporarily persisted in case the back-end server goes offline.

3.2 Components of CEP-as-a-Service

This section discusses the various components of the CEPaaS module which is running on the IoT server.

As indicated earlier, a solid line represents multiple parallel sensor data streams whereas a dashed line represents a single sensor data stream. Each component which is shown as a box in Fig. 3 receives an input data stream and emits an output data stream as a result of the operation performed by that component. Thus, various output streams must be defined before starting the service such that an output stream contains all the attributes which have been emitted by its predecessor component. When an attribute is added or removed from an input data stream (RE.v.1 for example) as a result of an operation done by a component (MQTT receiver in this case), then the output stream can be referred to as a stream having a different version (RE.v.2 in this case). As shown in Fig. 3, a raw stream has 9 versions (RE.v.1

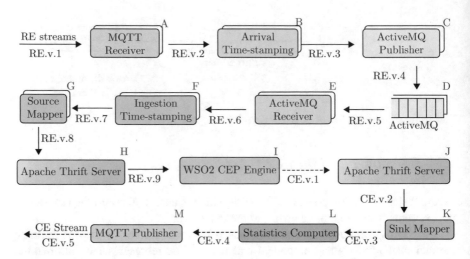

Fig. 3 Components of the CEPaaS module

to RE.v.9) whereas a complex event stream has 5 versions (CE.v.1 to CE.v.5). A brief discussion of each component is provided next in the order of the processing performed.

(A) MQTT Receiver: It receives a raw sensor stream on a particular topic after validating the content using the default/custom content validator. Multiple instances of the MQTT receivers (one for each sensor stream) receive raw sensor data streams in parallel.

(B) Arrival time-stamping: Multiple arrival time-stamping components run in parallel. Each component receives a particular stream and appends a system generated nanosecond precision time-stamps to indicate the arrival time.

(C) ActiveMQ publisher: An ActiveMQ [28] is used as a Java Message Service (JMS) queue [16]. The ActiveMQ publisher is responsible for sending the messages to a particular brokered-queue managed by an ActiveMQ broker. ActiveMQ supports both topics and brokered-queues to transfer messages, but we are using the brokered-queue in this case. For setting a JMS publisher, the various adapter properties such as JMS destination type, JMS destination name, JMS factory name, JMS provider Uniform Resource Locator (URL), JMS Connection Factory name, Java Naming and Directory Interface (JNDI) name, a username and a password need to be defined as per ActiveMQ server configurations which is running on the IoT server.

(D) ActiveMQ: ApacheMQ provides support for Advanced Message Queuing Protocol (AMQP), Streaming Text Oriented Message Protocol (STOMP), MQTT, OpenWire [2] and other protocols. The size of each ActiveMQ queue size is set to a maximum of 2 GB (restrained by the maximum value of an integer). A web-based Graphical User Interface (GUI) can be used to view the list of all ActiveMQ queues, topics and the number of messages enqueued/dequeued in each of the queue/topic.

(E) ActiveMQ subscriber: It is used to receive the sensor data stream events from a particular ActiveMQ queue. A subscriber subscribes to a particular queue using a unique queue name identifier and then forwards the received sensor tuples as an output sensor data stream (RE.v.6 in this case).

(F) Ingestion time-stamping: This module is used to append the CEP engine ingestion time-stamps using a nanosecond precision system clock, before sending the sensor data streams to the CEP engine. Multiple ingestion time components work in parallel to time-stamp each sensor stream.

(G) Source mapper: A CEP system supports various event formats such as eXtensible Markup Language (XML), JavaScript Object Notation (JSON), key-value pairs and Health Level-7 (HL7). The role of the source mapper is to convert the type of the sensor data stream event to the format required by the CEP engine.

(H) Apache thrift server: It is the binary communication protocol originally developed by Facebook [27]. It provides a Remote Procedure Call (RPC) framework to build the cross-platform services written in different frameworks and languages [12]. WSO$_2$ Data Analytics Server (DAS) running inside the analytics tier provides real-time, batch and predictive analytics by using the other services such as the CEP engine and Apache Spark. Thus, the Apache thrift acts as a mediator to perform RPC on the CEP engine using the data bridge agent.

(I) CEP engine: It receives multiple sensor data streams and finds the complex events according to the CQL query which has been deployed. A single complex event stream, as shown by a dashed line, is sent to the sink mapper. The complex event detection time-stamping is done in the CEP engine.

(J) Apache thrift server: The detected complex events are sent back to the thrift server which sends them back to the data analytics server for further processing.

(K) Sink mapper: The sink mapper converts the data type of the events in CEP stream to the type required by the event publisher.

(L) Statistics computer: It computes various CEP specific metrics such as the average CEP latency by using the time-stamps taken by the IoT server.

(M) MQTT publisher: The MQTT broker component publishes the various streams to the event listener such as a dashboard, email, or a database.

4 Mobile CEP System

The mobile CEP system prototype has been designed to perform complex event detection on the edge device using an embedded CEP engine that forwards the complex events to an IHS. Although the following discussion refers to the RPM use case, the MCEP architecture can be used in the context of other use cases as well. As shown in Fig. 4, similar to the SCEP architecture, the MCEP architecture also consists of three components.

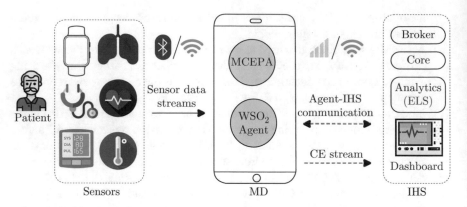

Fig. 4 Mobile CEP system architecture

1. Sensors: For the RPM use case, various wearable health sensors such as an Apple watch, Glucometer sensor, and Pulse-oximeter are used.
2. Mobile device: The mobile device uses Apache Siddhi CEP engine embedded with the mobile CEP application to perform complex event detection and sends the detected complex events to the back-end hospital server.
3. IHS: An Event Listening Service (ELS) running on the analytics tier receives the complex event alerts which are then sent to a DataDog dashboard [8] to notify the hospital staff.

The main difference between the Mobile Complex Event Processing (MCEP) system and the SCEP system is that in the mobile CEP system all the complex events are detected on the mobile device instead of processing them on a centralized IoT server. Unlike the SCEP system, which has a CEP running on the IHS, the MCEP system has an event listening service (ELS) running on the hospital server which is subscribed to listen to the complex events sent by the Mobile Complex Event Processing Application (MCEPA) running inside the mobile device.

5 Experimental Setup

The experimental setup used for analyzing the performance of both the MCEP and SCEP systems is discussed in this section. As shown in Fig. 5, the setup for both the server CEP and mobile CEP systems consist of five components: a timekeeper, a Sensor Simulator (SS), an IoT hospital server, a mobile device, and a wireless router.

Note that the timekeeper used in the experimental setup for performance measurement is not needed in a production system in which sensor simulator is replaced by the actual senor devices. The timekeeper is used to perform global time-

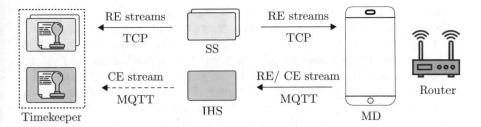

Fig. 5 System prototype setup

stamping to compute the end-to-end latency. This module is required as various components (with different un-synchronized clocks) contribute to the computing of the end-to-end latency. Therefore, a timekeeper is required to provide a global time-stamping for raw event streams (coming from the sensor simulator) and the complex event stream (from IHS) using a single clock. The various components which are stacked over one another inside the sensor simulator and the timekeeper represent multiple instances of the respective component running in parallel. The solid line represents multiple parallel data streams while a dashed line represents a single sensor data stream. As shown in Fig. 5, the data streams generated by the sensor simulator are sent in parallel to both the mobile device and the timekeeper (for global generation of time-stamping). In the SCEP system, raw event streams are sent from the mobile device to the IoT server whereas only a complex event stream is sent from the mobile device to the IoT server for the MCEP system. For both architectures, a single complex event stream is sent from the IHS to the timekeeper for global notification time-stamping. The system configuration for the aforementioned components is provided next.

1. Timekeeper: The timekeeper module is written in Java and deployed on a computer workstation having 16 GigaByte (GB) of RAM, a 2.8 GHz Intel Core i7 processor and a 1 TB Hard Drive (HD) running on Ubuntu 14.04 Long Term Support (LTS).
2. Sensor Simulator: The Java-based sensor simulator program is running on a workstation equipped with 8 GB of RAM, a 2.8 GHz Intel Core i7 processor and a 1 TB HD using Ubuntu 14.04 LTS. A multi-threaded sensor simulator program is used to simulate multiple sensors generating data at a given input rate. A nanosecond sleep time is used to generate a constant inter-arrival time for each sensor. As shown in Fig. 5, the data streams generated by the sensor simulator are sent simultaneously to the mobile device and the timekeeper using TCP sockets. All the sensor simulator daemons send data streams concurrently on separate threads, where each thread generates a stream of JSON tuples. A JSON tuple consists of both metadata and payload data. The metadata includes information such as patient id, sensor id and tuple id whereas the payload data includes the respective sensor value(s) and an event generation time-stamp (Tg). In certain

cases, the sensor data stream tuple may consist of an array of data values instead of a single value, but in our experimentation, a single value is used. $Patient_{id}$ is required at the IHS in order to uniquely identify a patient when multiple patients are enrolled with the RPM service. Also, a combination of $Patient_{id}$, $Sensor_{id}$, and $Tuple_{id}$ can be used to uniquely identify an event received at the IHS when multiple patients are enrolled. The sensor simulator can generate both synthetic and real data using synthetic and real datasets respectively. For simulating the real data, the sensor simulator uses sensor data available at the *slp01a/slpdb* dataset from the MIT-BIH polysomnographic database [14]. This dataset consists of 2-h duration data of 4 health signals recorded at 250 Hz. In a synthetic dataset, the tuple values are uniformly distributed integers ranging from 1 to 100. The real dataset was used to test the functional correctness of the proof of concept prototype, whereas all the other experiments were performed using a synthetic dataset. For performance analysis, a synthetic dataset is preferred over a real dataset because of the ability to control the various workload parameters including tuple values and tuple inter-arrival times.

3. IHS: An IoT server is deployed on a workstation having 16 GB of RAM, a 3.5 GHz Intel Core i7 Processor and a 1 TeraByte (TB) Solid State Drive (SSD) running under High Sierra MacOS. The MQTT broker and the MQTT subscriber are deployed on the broker and the analytics tiers of the IoT server respectively. The Java Virtual Machine (JVM) configurations for the broker, core, and analytics components of IHS used in the prototype are given in Table 2. Setting the configurations helps to dedicate the CPU resources to each component such as broker, core and analytics. Here, $-Xmx$ represents the maximum size of the JVM heap (4 GB in this case) which can be allocated to the respective tier.

4. Mobile Device: A Google Pixel smart-phone [32] having 4 GB of RAM, 32 GB of storage, and an AArch64 quad-core processor (1.6 GHz) running Android Nougat is used as the mobile device. WSO_2 IoT server version 3.0 is deployed on IHS along with its compatible Android agent version 3.1.27 running on the mobile device. Both the mobile CEP and server CEP applications that are written using Java are built on Android Studio 3.0.1 IDE using Gradle build tools version 26.0.2 [21]. For the mobile CEP application, due to the large size of the Siddhi CEP libraries, the multidex feature has to be enabled to overcome the 64K limit of the Android Dalvik compiler. Relevant Internet, WiFi, and network permissions must be enabled for the MCEP and the SCEP applications. The MQTT publisher is deployed on the mobile device.

5. Router: A 5 GHz AC1750 Tp-Link dual-band wireless router with a maximum bandwidth of 1350 Mbps is used to transfer data between the various components.

Table 2 Java memory configurations

Parameter	Broker	Core	Analytics
$-Xmx$	4096 MB	4096 MB	4096 MB

6 Performance Analysis

6.1 The Complex Event Use Case Modeling

A survey conducted by World Health Organization (WHO) reported that the occurrence of fall is common among elderly people and seems to increase with age and frailty level. In accordance to this survey, each year approximately 28–35% people more than 65 years of age fall whereas this number reaches to 32–42% for 70 years old [24]. Falls lead to 20–30% of mild to severe injuries and are the underlying cause of 10–15% of all emergency department visits [24]. However, if a fall is notified to hospital staff as soon as possible, further loss can be circumvented. Fall detection can be monitored remotely using a combination of mobile sensors and physiological sensors. Mobile sensors used for fall detection include a mobile camera, accelerometer sensor, gyroscope sensor and Global Positioning System (GPS) sensor. The various physiological sensors include heart rate and respiration rate sensors [15]. In a simpler case, a fall can be identified with more certainty, if events happen in certain order for example, a fall event followed by an increase in heart rate event followed by a reduction in body movement event. Detecting the occurrence of the fall event can be done using the gyroscopic sensor as well as phone camera whereas patient's reduction in body movement can be detected by a combination of an accelerometer sensor and a Global Positioning System (GPS) sensor. Another event that indicates that the person has not responded to a call from the hospital staff within specific time can confirm the fall event.

6.2 Workload and System Parameters

The various workload and system parameters used in analyzing the performance of the SCEP and MCEP prototypes are described next.

- Average raw event arrival rate (λ_{RE}): It is the average rate of the raw events generated by the sensor simulator.
- Threshold for sensor stream x (Th_x): The value of the threshold parameter is used by the selection predicate (π) to filter the sensor data streams tuples which are greater than Th_x.
- $Count_x$: Count is used to specify the number of times a particular event has to occur. An exact number of occurrences can also be specified through the count parameter. We have used the $\langle min{:}max \rangle$ specifier for $Count_x$ where $\langle min{:} \rangle$ means that an event has to happen at-least min times while no upper bound is specified. In other words, the notation $\langle min{:}max \rangle$ means that the event should happen at least min times but less than max times.
- Time window (T_{win}): The time window specifies the maximum time for which event A will wait for event B to occur. Please note that this time will be different for each instance of the state machine. The time window starts as soon as event

Table 3 Workload and
system parameters

Parameter	Description	Units
λ_{RE}	200, 300, **500**, 1000, 2000	Events/second
Th_x	10, 30, **50**, 70, 90, 99	–
$Count_x$	1, 5, **10**	–
T_{win}	0.005, 0.035, 0.06, 0.1, 0.2, **10**	Seconds
T_{run}	**5**, 60	Minutes

A arrives at the CEP system. Then a separate instance of the state machine is
started and it waits for event B for a time less than T_{win}.

- Simulation runtime in minutes (T_{run}): It is the length of the simulation runtime
in minutes.

The various values for the workload and system parameters used in the experiments are presented in Table 3. Factor-at-a-time experiments were performed on
the system in which one parameter was varied in a given experiment while others
were held at their default values. The value in bold for each parameter presented in
Table 3 corresponds to the default value of the parameter.

6.3   Performance Metrics

The CEP specific performance metrics used in the analysis are the average
CEP latency (L) and the average complex event End-to-End (E2E) latency (E).
Application specific metrics are average CPU utilization and average network usage.
An application profiler such as Trepn, PowerTutor or Intel Performance Viewer [3]
can be used to perform system level and application level performance profiling.
However, the accuracy of these applications is a concern, thus various application
metrics have been calculated using a bash script which reads *dumpsys* information
using Android Debug Bridge (ADB) shell. This script reads various application and
system specific metrics and parses this information using a combination of various
grep commands, regular expressions, awk scripts and *sed* expressions.

Let T_a^x and T_i^x be the arrival time and ingestion time respectively for the earliest
arriving event, among all the events from the different sensor data streams that led to
the complex event. Let T_g^x and T_{gg}^x be the generation time and global generation time
respectively for the earliest arriving events that corresponded to the complex event.
Also, let T_d^x, T_n^x and T_{gn}^x represent the complex event detection time, complex event
notification time and complex event global notification time respectively. Below, we
discuss how the various metrics are computed.

- Average CEP latency (L): A complex event is generated when a CQL pattern
  match occurs by ingesting data from multiple sensor data streams. The latency
  of a complex event processing is measured from the time of ingestion (T_i) for
  the first event (from any sensor data stream) that leads to the complex event
  to the time at which the complex event gets detected (T_d). If the total number

of complex events detected during an experiment is N, then the average CEP latency is given by Eq. (1).

$$L = \frac{\sum_{x=1}^{N} T_d^x - T_i^x}{N} \tag{1}$$

The average CEP latencies for the MCEP and SCEP systems are represented by L_{MCEP}, and L_{SCEP} respectively.

- Average complex event E2E latency (E): It is the average time taken by an event (which corresponds to the earliest raw event leading to a complex event) from the time it is generated by the sensor simulator (T_g) to the time it is notified at the IoT server (T_n). However, as discussed earlier, T_g and T_n are time-stamped in the sensor simulator and the IoT server respectively using clocks that are not synchronized with one another. Thus, E is computed using T_{gg} and T_{gn} (instead of T_g and T_n) both of which are time-stamped on the timekeeper module. E is computed using Eq. (2), where T_{gg}^x and T_{gn}^x represent the global generation time for the xth raw event that corresponds to a complex event and the global notification time for the xth complex event, both time-stamped at the timekeeper.

$$E = \frac{\sum_{x=1}^{N} T_{gn}^x - T_{gg}^x}{N} \tag{2}$$

The average E2E latency for the MCEP and SCEP systems is represented by E_{MCEP} and E_{SCEP} respectively. A diagram showing the relationship among CEP specific metrics L, Q (complex event queuing delay), and E is presented in Fig. 6. In this figure, the multiple instances of input sensor data streams (one for each sensor) are shown in parallel such that tuples in the nth sensor data stream (where $n \in 1 \dots y$) are denoted by T_a^n and T_i^n as arrival time and ingestion time respectively. However, as the complex event is generated from a pattern which ingests multiple sensor data events, only one complex event is shown on the right-hand side of Fig. 6.

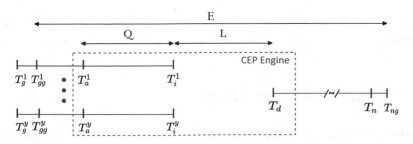

Fig. 6 CEP specific metrics

- Average CPU utilization (CU): It is the average CPU utilization by the mobile application during an experiment. CU_{SCEPA} and CU_{MCEPA} represent the average CPU utilization for the SCEP application and MCEP application respectively. The application is un-installed and installed again for each experiment.
- Average CPU utilization by IHS (CU_{IHS}): CU_{IHS} represents the average CPU utilization of the IoT server. $CU_{IHS-SCEP}$ and $CU_{IHS-MCEP}$ represent the average CPU utilization by the IHS for the SCEP system and MCEP system respectively.
- User cost (UC): The UC is the average cost (in \$/hour) by the user for using the CEP service. UC_{SCEP} and UC_{MCEP} represent the UC for using SCEP service and MCEP service respectively. Assuming that a user (patient) is using bluetooth or WiFi for connecting the sensors with the mobile device, TX can be used to compute the user cost. Here, we assume that a patient is using the mobile network for the transfer of data between the mobile device and the back-end IoT server. The user cost can be computed by as:

$$\text{User Cost } (\$/hour) = TX * \text{cost per MB} * 3600 \tag{3}$$

- Remaining Battery Life (RBL): It is the amount of remaining battery power (in %) by the application running on the mobile device during an experiment. It is an important metric representing the power consumption of an application. The different types of RBL used in the experimentation are provided next.

  - The $RBL_{SCEPA-FG}$ and $RBL_{MCEPA-FG}$ represent the battery usage for the server CEP and mobile CEP applications respectively when these applications are running in the foreground fn the mobile device and no other service is running on the background.
  - The $RBL_{SCEPA-BG}$ and $RBL_{MCEPA-BG}$ represent the battery usage for the server CEP and mobile CEP applications respectively when these applications are running in the background of the mobile device and no other application is running on the foreground.

7   Experimental Results

In this section, the performance comparison between the MCEP and SCEP systems is presented.

7.1   Comparison of Battery Usage

The impact of T_{run} on the power consumption of the MCEP and SCEP applications is presented in Fig. 7.

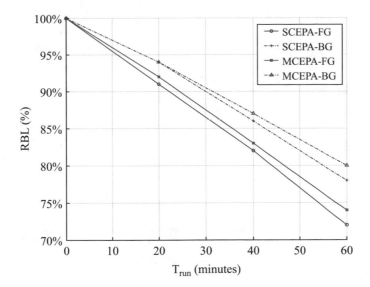

Fig. 7 Impact of runtime on battery usage

The experiment was performed for 60 min with an initial battery level of 100%. During the experiment, the values of the battery level on the mobile device were noted every 20-min interval, as shown by T_{run} in Fig. 7. Recall that scenario 1 corresponds to SCEP/MCEP application running in the Foreground (FG) and no other application running in the background. In scenario 2, the SCEP/MCEP application is running in the Background (BG) with no other application running in FG on the mobile device. It is found that the battery usage of an application for a scenario 1 is always lower in comparison to scenario 2. Also, for a given scenario the battery usage for the MCEP application is lower than that for the SCEP application. This is due to the fact that only complex events are transferred to the IoT server when the MCEP application is used. On the other hand, all the raw events (from multiple sensors) are forwarded to IoT server when the SCEP application is used, causing an increase in the battery consumption. The energy consumption due to data transfer is higher in comparison to the energy consumption due to running the CEP engine on the mobile device. This experiment shows that the proposed MCEP system provides approximately 2% power savings (both in background and foreground), in comparison to the SCEP system.

7.2 Comparison of Average CEP Latency

As shown in Fig. 8, for a particular λ_{RE}, the average CEP latency for the SCEP system is much higher than the average CEP latency for the MCEP system. For

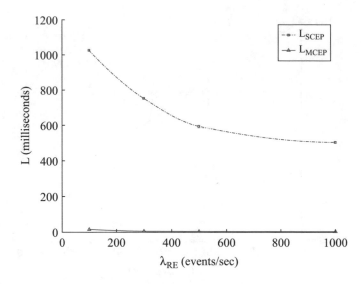

Fig. 8 Impact of the arrival rate of raw events on average CEP latency

both MCEP and SCEP systems, the average CEP latency decreases with an increase in the average raw event arrival rate. This is because, with an increase in λ_{RE}, the inter-arrival time of the event B is reduced. This led to a decrease in the waiting time of the A events in the CEP engine, resulting in the lower values of L_{SCEP}. In the case of server CEP, the data analytics server uses Apache thrift as a middle-ware to send the requests to the CEP engine using remote method invocations, causing the additional delays. This results in a higher CEP latency for SCEP in comparison to the MCEP system which does not use a middleware system. This leads to the important conclusion that there is a trade-off between security and latency for the SCEP system. Although enabling additional features in the IoT server provides more security, it also leads to a significant increase in CEP processing latency.

7.3 Comparison of Average End-to-End Latency

The end-to-end latency depends upon various factors such as the sum of various transmission times, queuing delays and event processing latencies. As shown in Fig. 9, as λ_{RE} is increased, more complex events are detected per unit time for both MCEP and SCEP systems.

This seems to increase the resource contention resulting in an increase in the transmission delay (as more complex events will be sent to the timekeeper) and the queuing delay (see [9] for an analysis on the queuing latency) leading to an increase in the average end-to-end delay. For a given λ_{RE}, the end-to-end delay for the SCEP system is higher than that for the MCEP system. Forwarding all the raw

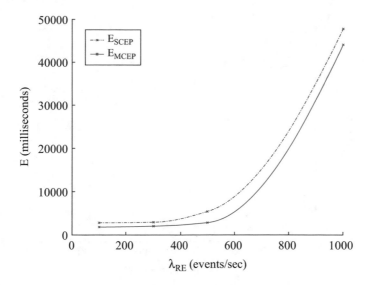

Fig. 9 Impact of the arrival rate of raw events on average end-to-end latency

sensors streams to the IoT server results in larger transmission delays that seem to lead to a higher E for the SCEP system. From Fig. 9, we can conclude that, in spite of using the large time window of 10 s (default time window) that leads to additional queuing delays on the memory constrained mobile device, E_{MCEP} achieved on the MCEP system with a given λ_{RE} is less than E_{SCEP} achieved on the SCEP system.

7.4 Comparison of IoT Server CPU Utilization

Figure 10 shows the impact of λ_{RE} on the CPU utilization of the IoT server in for the MCEP system ($CU_{IHS-MCEP}$) and SCEP system ($CU_{IHS-SCEP}$). For a given λ_{RE}, $CU_{IHS-MCEP}$ is lower than $CU_{IHS-SCEP}$. This is because of the difference in the amount of computation performed by the CPUs. In case of the SCEP system, all the raw sensor data streams are received, parsed, type converted, enqueued, dequeued and processed in the IoT server and then complex events are forwarded to the timekeeper by using the MQTT broker and metrics are sent to the DataDog dashboard by the Java Management eXtensions (JMX) agent. However, in case of the MCEP system, only CEP alerts are received by the IoT server and no further processing has to be done. The lower processing performed in case of the MCEP system leads to a lower CPU utilization. From this graph, we can conclude that the MCEP system leads to a smaller load on the IoT server, which is one of the advantages of the MCEP system.

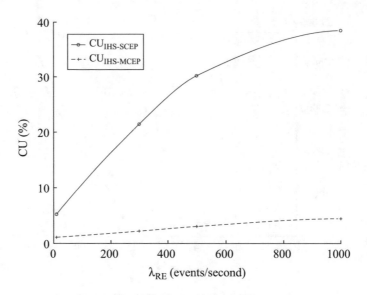

Fig. 10 Impact of the arrival rate of raw events on the IHS CPU utilization

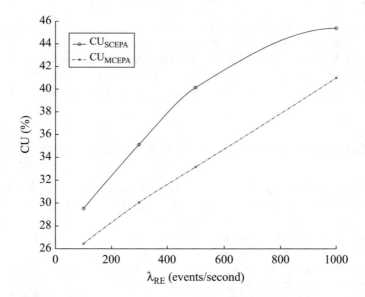

Fig. 11 Impact of the arrival rate of raw events on mobile device CPU utilization

7.5 *Comparison of Mobile Device CPU Utilization*

Figure 11 shows the CPU utilization observed for the MCEP application and the SCEP gateway application.

For the MCEP application, CU_{MCEPA} seems to increase steadily with the increase of λ_{RE} as more processing is done inside the CEP engine for the higher raw event arrival rates. Also, it is interesting to note that for any given value of λ_{RE}, the CPU utilization of the MCEP application is lower than the one for the server CEP application. For example, the CU_{MCEPA} is 41.01% when 2 sensors are sending data streams at 1000 Hz, which is lower in comparison to the 45.40% CPU utilization reported in the case of the SCEP application.

7.6 Comparison of User Cost

As shown in Fig. 12, for any value of raw event arrival rate, the amount of data transferred per second (TX) is more for the server CEP in comparison to the mobile CEP. This is because the SCEP application forwards all the raw events to IoT server. Equation (3) (discussed in Sect. 6.3) is used to compute the data transfer cost incurred by the user for using the MCEP and SCEP systems. The rate of $0.05/MB offered by Bell (a major telecommunication company in Canada) is used [4]. For any given λ_{RE}, a significantly lower data transfer cost is observed for the MCEP system in comparison to the SCEP system as in case of MCEP system only the complex events are sent while in case of the SCEP application the entire raw event streams are forwarded. It is interesting to note that at an arrival rate of 1000 events/second, the MCEP system provides a significant savings of $12.74/h ($13.32/h–$0.58/h).

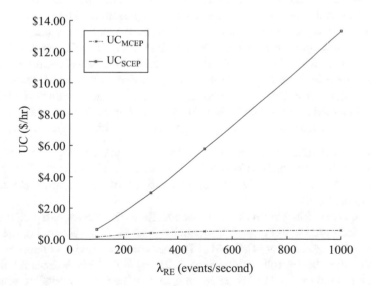

Fig. 12 Impact of the arrival rate of raw events on user cost

8   Conclusions

The availability of mobile devices and sensors at a reasonable price is rapidly increasing the use of mobile edge computing systems that are deployed in various applications that include smart homes, smart industrial machinery and smart healthcare systems. This chapter presents an edge computing framework and complex event processing technique for such systems. It includes a description of an application of these to real-time remote health monitoring that leverages both mobile system technology and edge computing techniques for the detection of complex events which typically indicate the potential occurrence of a health problem for the person being monitored.

One of the goals of this chapter was to compare two different architectural frameworks for performing complex event processing in sensor-based systems: SCEP (centralized server-based approach) and MCEP (edge device-based approach). Unlike the high-level simulation-based SCEP approach provided in [19], we have described an SCEP architecture and implementation of its prototype (in Sect. 3) that also has more features. However, such an SCEP system has some disadvantages including the necessity of a persistent network connectivity, high data transfer cost for the user, and a larger mobile device power consumption as shown in Sect. 7.1. On the other hand, the MCEP system can effectively handle the network unavailability problem by performing CEP on the edge device instead of processing the sensor data streams on a remote cloud. This system has been realized by successfully embedding a CEP engine on the mobile device to perform the complete complex event detection on the edge device and send various complex events (alerts) to a remote back-end server to notify the concerned personnel. The proof of concept prototype for the proposed technique has been built successfully and tested using a synthetic workload on a Google Pixel mobile device running *Android Nougat*. As discussed in Sect. 7.6, the MCEP system leads to a reduction in the user cost and the mobile device energy consumption and improves the overall latency of the system. A thorough experimental investigation based on measurements made on the prototype has led to a number of insights into the impact of system and workload parameters on performance. The key insights are summarized.

- Network connectivity requirement: The MCEP system does not mandate a persistent Internet connection with the back-end IoT server. Thus, if the network is not available temporarily, the user can still receive local alarms generated by the mobile device.
- User cost: As shown in Fig. 12, the user cost for the MCEP system is significantly lower compared to the cost of the centralized server CEP system. For the typical pricing data available at [4], the MCEP system provides savings of approximately $13/h, over the central server-based SCEP system. This is because the data transfer is reduced in the MCEP system, as only complex events are sent to the IoT server.
- Security and data privacy: As the mobile CEP system processes the sensor data streams locally, the user has better data privacy in comparison to the SCEP

system. In order to ensure the data privacy and security for the SCEP system, various authentication and authorization methods have to be employed on the IoT server which can lead to additional delays. Ensuring data privacy and security of a centralized server comes at the expense of processing latency. Thus, the MCEP system has an advantage over the SCEP system as it requires relatively lesser security mechanisms to be imposed on the system for ensuring data privacy.

- Out-of-order message delivery: As the SCEP gateway application forwards all the sensor data streams, this can lead to synchronization issues among various sensor streams at the back-end server. This issue is less evident in the MCEP system as the sensor devices are locally connected to the edge device using Wi-Fi or bluetooth connections.

These characteristics lead to the conclusion that the MCEP system has a significant number of benefits over the SCEP system. However, the SCEP system also has a few benefits over the MCEP system as described next.

1. Predictive analytics: In the MCEP system, only the complex events are sent to the IoT server. This means that the historical data of the patient is not retained. However, in the case of the SCEP system, the historical data can be further used by various predictive analytics algorithms using machine learning to predict future alerts.
2. Easier to deploy security mechanisms: The IoT server comes with off-the-shelf authentication and authorization features which are easily configured. However, in the case of mobile CEP, such features have to be manually added and customized.

9 Future Work

Directions for further research include the following:

- The MCEP system can be extended to form a hybrid CEP system such that real-time analytics is performed on the mobile device and the predictive analytics is being performed on the IoT server using the stored historical data. Investigation of such a system forms an important direction for future research.
- The performance of the current system can be analyzed when multiple devices (one device per user) are enrolled with the IoT server. This would test the scalability of the system as the number of users using sensor-based systems is expected to grow.
- MCEP leads to a lower battery usage in comparison to SCEP. Irrespective of the system type, a mobile device based remote health monitoring can be performed only for a number of hours after which the device needs to be recharged. This is acceptable for a number of different situations. Using multiple mobile devices with one serving as the primary device and the other(s) serving as backups may be helpful when the system is continuously used without an opportunity for recharging the battery of the mobile device. The secondary device can replace

the primary device when it runs out of battery power for a duration during which the primary device can get charged. The investigation of such a system focusing on how to perform an effective hand-off from one device to the other devices forms an interesting direction for future research.

Acknowledgments We are grateful to TELUS and Natural Sciences and Engineering Research Council of Canada (NSERC) for providing financial support for this research.

References

1. Abdellatif, A.A., Mohamed, A., Chiasserini, C.F., Tlili, M., Erbad, A.: Edge computing for smart health: Context-aware approaches, opportunities, and challenges. IEEE Network **33**(3), 196–203 (2019)
2. Apache Software Foundation: OpenWire Protocol. [Online available at]: http://activemq. apache.org/apollo/documentation/openwire-manual.html, [Accessed: 13-Jan-2019]
3. Bakker, A.: Comparing energy profilers for android. In: 21st Twente Student Conference on IT, vol. 21 (2014)
4. Bell Canada: Bell pay per use rates. [Online available at]: https://support.bell.ca/Mobility/ Rate_plans_features/What-are-Bell-Mobilitys-current-pay-per-use-rates, [Accessed: 12-Jan-2019]
5. Buyya, R., Ranjan, R., Calheiros, R.N.: Modeling and simulation of scalable Cloud computing environments and the CloudSim toolkit: Challenges and opportunities. In: International Conference on High Performance Computing Simulation, pp. 1–11 (2009). https://doi.org/ 10.1109/HPCSIM.2009.5192685
6. Calheiros, R.N., Ranjan, R., Beloglazov, A., De Rose, C.A.F., Buyya, R.: CloudSim: A Toolkit for Modeling and Simulation of Cloud Computing Environments and Evaluation of Resource Provisioning Algorithms. Journal of Software—Practice & Experience **41**(1), 23–50 (2011). https://doi.org/10.1002/spe.995
7. Cooking Hacks: MySignals changes the future of medical and eHealth applications. [Online available at]: http://www.my-signals.com/, [Accessed: 13-Jan-2019]
8. DataDog: Modern monitoring and analytics. [Online available at]: https://www.datadoghq. com/, [Accessed: 13-Jan-2019]
9. Dhillon, A.: An Edge Computing-based Complex Event Processing Technique for Sensor-based Systems. Master's thesis, Carleton University, Ottawa, ON, Canada (2018)
10. Dhillon, A., Majumdar, S., St-Hilaire, M., Haraki, A.E.: MCEP: a Mobile device based Complex Event Processing System for Remote Healthcare. In: the International Conference on Internet of Things (iThings), pp. 203–210 (2018)
11. Dineshkumar, P., SenthilKumar, R., Sujatha, K., Ponmagal, R.S., Rajavarman, V.N.: Big data analytics of IoT based Healthcare Monitoring System. In: 2016 IEEE Uttar Pradesh Section International Conference on Electrical, Computer and Electronics Engineering (UPCON), pp. 55–60 (2016). https://doi.org/10.1109/UPCON.2016.7894624
12. Foundation, A.S.: Apache thrift™. [Online available at]: https://thrift.apache.org/. [Accessed: 13-Jan-2019]
13. Gibson Research Corporation: Zeo Sleep Manager Pro. [Online available at]: https://www.grc. com/zeo.htm, [Accessed: 14-Jan-2019]
14. Goldberger, A.L., Amaral, L.A., Glass, L., Hausdorff, J.M., Ivanov, P.C., Mark, R.G., Mietus, J.E., Moody, G.B., Peng, C.K., Stanley, H.E.: PhysioBank, PhysioToolkit, and PhysioNet: components of a new research resource for complex physiologic signals. Circulation Journal **101**(23), e215–e220 (2000)

15. Habib, M.A., Mohktar, M.S., Kamaruzzaman, S.B., Lim, K.S., Pin, T.M., Ibrahim, F.: Smartphone-based solutions for fall detection and prevention: challenges and open issues. Sensors Journal **14**(4), 7181–7208 (2014)
16. Hapner, M., Burridge, R., Sharma, R., Fialli, J., Stout, K.: Java™ Message Service API Tutorial and Reference: Messaging for the J2EE™ Platform. Addison-Wesley Professional (2002)
17. Hartmann, M., Hashmi, U.S., Imran, A.: Edge computing in smart health care systems: Review, challenges, and research directions. Transactions on Emerging Telecommunications Technologies **n/a**(n/a), e3710. https://doi.org/10.1002/ett.3710
18. Higashino, W.A.: Complex Event Processing as a Service in Multi-Cloud Environments. Ph.D. thesis, Department of Electrical and Computer Engineering at University of Western Ontario (UWO) (2016). URL [Online available at]: https://ir.lib.uwo.ca/etd/4016
19. Higashino, W.A., Capretz, M.A.M., Bittencourt, L.F.: CEPaaS: Complex Event Processing as a Service. In: IEEE International Congress on Big Data (BigData Congress), pp. 169–176 (2017). https://doi.org/10.1109/BigDataCongress.2017.31
20. Hunkeler, U., Truong, H.L., Stanford-Clark, A.: MQTT-S – A publish/subscribe protocol for Wireless Sensor Networks. In: 3rd International Conference on Communication Systems Software and Middleware and Workshops (COMSWARE '08), pp. 791–798 (2008). https://doi.org/10.1109/COMSWA.2008.4554519
21. Kousen, K.: Gradle Recipes for Android: Master the New Build System for Android. "O'Reilly Media, Inc." (2016)
22. Naddeo, S., Verde, L., Forastiere, M., De Pietro, G., Sannino, G.: A Real-time m-Health Monitoring System: An Integrated Solution Combining the Use of Several Wearable Sensors and Mobile Devices. In: International Conference on Health Informatics (HEALTHINF), pp. 545–552 (2017)
23. Naqishbandi, T., Imthyaz Sheriff, C., Qazi, S.: Big data, CEP and IoT: redefining holistic healthcare information systems and analytics. International Conference on Advances Research in Engineering and Technology **4**(1), 1–6 (2015)
24. Organization, W.H.: WHO Global Report on Falls Prevention in Older Age. [Online available at]: http://www.who.int/ageing/publications/Falls_prevention7March.pdf, [Accessed: 8-March-2018]
25. Reza, T., Shoilee, S.B.A., Akhand, S.M., Khan, M.M.: Development of Android based Pulse Monitoring System. In: Second International Conference on Electrical, Computer and Communication Technologies (ICECCT), pp. 1–7 (2017). https://doi.org/10.1109/ICECCT.2017.8118045
26. Senthilkumar, R., Ponmagal, R., Sujatha, K.: Efficient Health Care Monitoring and Emergency Management System using IoT. International Journal of Control Theory and Applications **9**(4), 137–145 (2016)
27. Slee, M., Agarwal, A., Kwiatkowski, M.: Thrift: Scalable cross-language services implementation. Facebook White Paper Journal **5**(8) (2007)
28. Snyder, B., Bosnanac, D., Davies, R.: ActiveMQ in Action. Manning Publications (2011)
29. Sotera Wireless: About Visi Mobile. [Online available at]: https://www.soterawireless.com/visi-mobile/, [Accessed: 13-Jan-2019]
30. Suh, M., Chen, C., Woodbridge, J., Tu, M.K., Kim, J.I., Nahapetian, A., Evangelista, L.S., Sarrafzadeh, M.: A Remote Patient Monitoring System for Congestive Heart Failure. Journal of medical systems **35**(5), 1165–1179 (2011)
31. Wahane, V., Ingole, P.: An Android based wireless ECG Monitoring System for Cardiac Arrhythmia. In: Healthcare Innovation Point-Of-Care Technologies Conference (HI-POCT), pp. 183–187 (2016)
32. Wikipedia: Google Pixel. [Online available at]: https://en.wikipedia.org/wiki/Google_Pixel, [Accessed: 13-Jan-2019]

Application Design and Service Provisioning for Multi-access Edge Cloud (MEC)

Muhammad Jaseemuddin, Hager Ghouma, Maysam Fazeli, Ameera Al-Karkhi, Mohamad Eldakroury, and Uvaiz Ahmed

Abstract The edge cloud is attractive to provide low latency services to mobile users. It overcomes computation, storage, and energy limitations of mobile devices through computation offloading. It also avoids long delays in migration of big data from the point of their generation by IoT devices to the centralized data centers. Context-aware edge cloud design provides mobile users with more personalized and customized services that improve their over-all experience. It manages the cloud infrastructure for resource provisioning, scheduling, and load balancing. The latency constraints of MEC applications need light-weight container service in the edge cloud. Kubernetes container orchestration is popular in the industry that is supported by all major edge cloud platforms. Container migration is important for ensuring low latency to new mobile applications of connected vehicles and drones. In this chapter we present the current state of research and development in the application design and service provisioning for edge cloud.

Keywords Edge cloud · Computation offloading · Context · Container · Container migration · Container orchestration · Task graph · Kubernetes · Docker · Video-analytics

1 Introduction

The original design goal of edge computing was to meet the stringent low latency requirements of some mobile applications [1]. Recently, commercial applications emerge in Business Intelligence (BI), Smart Cities, Intelligent Transportation, and

M. Jaseemuddin (✉) · H. Ghouma · M. Fazeli · A. Al-Karkhi
Department of Electrical, Computer & Biomedical Engineering, Ryerson University, Toronto, ON, Canada
e-mail: jaseem@ryerson.ca; maysam.fazeli@ryerson.ca

M. Eldakroury · U. Ahmed
Telus, Toronto, ON, Canada
e-mail: mohamed.eldakroury@telus.com; uvaiz.ahmed@telus.com

A. Mukherjee et al. (eds.), *Mobile Edge Computing*,
https://doi.org/10.1007/978-3-030-69893-5_21

Industry 4.0 that drive the use of edge computing to deal with scarce bandwidth and unreliable connections to cloud data centers [2]. The 5G wireless networks will deploy edge cloud to provide multi-access edge computing for mobile user applications [3] and to implement common network services as Virtual Network Functions (VNFs) and Cloud-RAN [4]. The Multi-Access Edge Cloud (MEC) overcomes computation, storage, and energy limitations of mobile devices through computation offloading. It allows machine learning computation on big data closer to IoT devices, thus avoids long delays associated with the migration of big data to the centralized cloud data centers. The MEC architecture deals with the following design issues:

- *Distributed Architecture:* In contrast to central cloud (e.g. public cloud) datacenters, the MEC datacenters are smaller datacenters located at network edges that are inter-connected to offer edge cloud services.
- *Multi-cloud:* Distributed edge clouds of diverse administrative domains are inter-connected.
- *Distributed Computing:* Highly distributed computing structure for the application design.
- *Distributed Data:* Data is distributed and co-located with computing.
- *Lowe latency:* Real-time cloud native applications need low latency.
- *Reliable Connectivity:* Edge clouds are connected through short routing paths making it easy to deal with bandwidth and reliability constraints.

The MEC is exposed to the challenges arise from the intrinsic and dynamic characteristics of mobile devices such as mobility and device constraints (computation, storage, and energy). Mobile context information is used to provide the mobile users with more personalized and customized services that improve their overall experience. It can also be used by the MEC infrastructure for resource provisioning, scheduling, and load balancing. Context-aware edge cloud design provides a unified approach of managing and offering cloud services to mobile users at the edge. The latency constraints of applications require light-weight virtualization in the edge cloud that is achieved through container technology. Kubernetes container orchestration is popular in the industry that is supported by all major edge cloud platforms. Emerging mobility scenarios for connected vehicles and drones need support for real-time context transfer and container migration from one edge to another spanning over a single cloud or multi-cloud systems.

Figure 1 shows the main building blocks of edge cloud and their functional decomposition. The architecture of edge cloud varies with the business focus of its providers. Some reference architectures are published such as ETSI's MEC [3] and Open Stack's StarlingX [5].

The applications on edge devices need support of local edge-specific components to optimize their execution as edge native applications. All such edge supportive functions are provided by the *Edge Enabler* building block in the device [6]. For example, many applications perform computation offloading decisions [7] such as Augmented Reality (AR) and Wearable Cognitive Assistance (WCA) applications that run some image processing functions in the edge cloud [8]. The

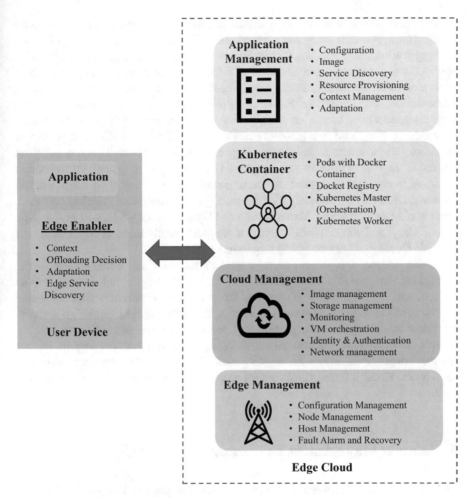

Fig. 1 Functional decomposition of edge cloud infrastructure

WCA applications go through active and passive phases with high to low resource requirements during those phases, respectively. The passive phase involves human intervention which requires less sampled video frames; hence sampling rate can be adapted to reduce resource allocation [8]. Some applications are flexible in adapting their functionalities with the availability of resources in the edge cloud, such as a camera manager in a video analytics application can adjust the frame rate, resolution, and video quality [9]. In this case, the edge enabler coordinates with the resource management in the edge cloud to perform adaptation of functions. The offloading and adaptation decisions also need monitoring of user and device context to optimize their objective functions. For example, device power and locations are used to optimize energy saving function through offloading and adaptation. All edge native applications need to discover services in the edge cloud.

The functions related to edge cloud infrastructure management is broadly grouped in application, container, cloud, and edge management building blocks. The application management provides support for optimal execution of edge native applications, container is the basic virtualization unit for running an application in edge cloud that needs container management functions such as containerization, orchestration, and clustering. For some applications, such as connected vehicles, their containers need migration from one edge cloud to another to meet the latency requirement. The cloud management deals with orchestration of VMs and allocation of computation, storage, and networking resources to them. The orchestration requires image and identity management functions. The physical infrastructure of the edge requires configuration, management and monitoring of hardware and software, which are provided by the edge management functions. Wireless operators employ Network Function Virtualization (NFV) to deploy VNFs and in the edge cloud. They perform network slicing to support multi-tenant orchestration and multiple Quality of Service (QoS) requirements [6].

In this chapter we present current state of research and development in the application design and service provisioning for mobile edge cloud. It first presents a framework of integrating the role of the context in different components and functions of the edge cloud system in Sect. 2. Then, the application design presents workflow model, application partitioning and computation offloading techniques in Sect. 3. In Sect. 4, the service provisioning presents container and its benefit for providing low latency, container orchestration and lastly container migration techniques. Finally, future directions of research in this new and growing area is discussed.

2 Context Management Framework for Edge Cloud

The most comprehensive and utilizable definition of context is given by Dey and Abowd [10] as "any information that can be used to characterize the situation of an entity". From a mobile user's perspective, context means things such as activity, ambient condition (e.g. temperature, lighting etc.), computing and communication resources (e.g. network connectivity, communications costs, communications bandwidth, computing power, battery power etc.) and the social situation. The context in mobile edge cloud computing is mainly divided into four categories: user context, device context, mobile service context and physical context. The user context consists of the user's profile, people nearby, current activity (meeting, driving), location (GPS or IP address if wifi is connected), time and emotional state. The device context includes battery level, network connectivity, communication bandwidth, data rate, and connection type (cellular 3G/wifi). The Radio Network Information Service (RNIS) in 5G network provides user-specific detailed network-level information that helps in detecting and making mobility related decisions such as for service migration (as discussed in Sect. 4.5) and Location Based Services (LBS) [3]. The service context is information related to services including

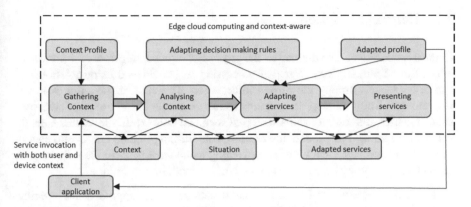

Fig. 2 Context framework for service management in a mobile edge cloud

social network connections, likings etc. The physical context comprises of the environmental states like the temperature, traffic conditions and noise level.

In edge cloud, service infrastructure resides in the cloud that includes service provisioning, invocation, runtime, and data subsystems. When context is used in managing the cloud service, then in addition to context gathering components at the client side, it introduces service selection and adaptation processes to service invocation and runtime subsystems in the cloud. Figure 2 shows a context framework for service management in a mobile edge cloud. The context gathering and analyzing stages include components in the cloud related to interacting with the client in collecting and storing the context information, which is later used for context analysis, reasoning and decision making for service selection and adaptation. The object of service adaptation varies including service personalization, location-aware adjustments to QoS and new service discovery, QoS adaptation, and fault recovery. Some applications can adapt its configuration based on resource availability such as camera manager in a video analytics application can adjust the frame rate, resolution, and video quality [8]. The framework also provides support for *context transfer* when a user moves from one edge cloud to another.

A typical context-aware mobile edge cloud computing framework performs service adaptation, service provisioning, and cloud resource management. It implements four stages: data acquisition, context storage, context management and intelligent decision making. The data acquisition stage represents the context collection unit and could include number of heterogeneous and distributed sensors types such as, sensed context (physical or software sensors), interaction or control sensors. It offers monitoring, collecting, and processing of user's context and environmental data. The context storage comprises of user's knowledge base component which includes the user's context profile and context history. The context management system performs following key functions: context modelling, context classification, context aggregation, and context reasoning. Finally, machine intelligence and optimization techniques are employed for making service and resource provisioning decisions.

2.1   Context Modeling

Context modeling can be defined as the process of representing context information into a format suitable to automated processing. It is achieved using relationships and dependencies among the sensed information. The context modeling is a two-step process. The first step defines new context information in terms of attributes, characteristics, and relationships with past specified context. In the second step, the context is organized to validate the results of the first step. There are several context modeling techniques, each with its own strength and weakness. In the following we present an overview of the most popular context modeling techniques.

1. **Key-Value Modeling:** It is the simplest data modeling approach that specifies (model) the context as a list of attributes and their values (key-value pairs) in text or binary files format. It does not support hierarchal structures and relationships, making it hard to retrieve modeled data efficiently. It is suitable for less complex application configurations and user preferences [11].
2. **Markup Scheme Modeling (Tagged Encoding):** This is an improvement of the key-value technique. It uses tags to store context within markup tags that allows efficient data retrieval. It is commonly used in modeling profiles using XML.
3. **Graphical Modeling:** This technique is better than markup language and key-value because it allows relationships to be captured into the context model. An example is unified modelling language (UML) [12].
4. **Object based modeling:** It is a comprehensive model supports encapsulation and re-usability in addition to capturing hierarchal relationships [12].
5. **Logic based modelling:** The context information is represented as facts, expressions, and rules. It provides more expressive richness and allows extracting new high-level context information using low level context data.
6. **Ontology based modelling:** It represents the contextual information concepts, relations, entities, and functions between them. The ontology-based technique enables sharing and reusing of context knowledge in computational entities (services and agents) to form a common set of concepts about context and help context reasoning and interoperability while interacting with one another. The context is represented by ontology using semantic language.

2.2   Context Reasoning

Context reasoning is an essential component of a context management system. It defines methods of inferring new knowledge and better understanding of the current context. It deduces high–level context from a set of low-level context data. Reasoning models are required to deal with imprecision, erroneity and uncertainty of raw context data. Context reasoning model has three phases [13]:

- Context pre-processing involves cleaning, filtering, and removing error from the collected sensor data that is affected by sensor malfunction.
- Sensor data infusion combines the data from multiple sensors to obtain more accurate and complete information which could not be achieved by one sensor.
- Context inference involves inferring high-level context from low level context information.

The reasoning techniques can reduce the complexity of context-aware applications and improve their maintainability. In addition, as collecting and maintaining context information is expensive, sharing and re-using this information should be considered from the beginning in any context –aware application [14]. Important reasoning techniques are summarized as follows:

- **Supervised learning techniques can** be applied when the data set is clear and easy to identify, while the potential outcome is known. Artificial neural network, Bayesian networks, case-based reasoning, decision tree and support vector machine are the examples of supervised learning.
- **Unsupervised learning techniques** are used when the potential outcome is unknown for example abnormal user behaviour. Examples of these techniques are clustering and, and K-nearest neighbour.
- **Rule-based techniques** defined a set of rules that is applied on raw data for conversion to high-level context, for example using if-then rules or other AI techniques.
- **Logic Programming techniques** provide an approximate reasoning instead of a fixed reasoning. For example, in fuzzy logic, the data values have a range between 0 and 1 that is used to specify partial the truth when the truth is in between true and false. It is used to handle the uncertainty, but it must be used in combination with other technique such as the rule-based technique to represent context.
- **Probabilistic logic techniques** allow the reasoning to be made according to the probability approach based on the facts associated with the problem. For example, Hidden Markov Model is used in activity inference.

2.3   Context Monitoring and Storage

A mobile device can acquire context information from many different sensors, such as accelerometer, microphone, environmental sensors (e.g. light, temperature, humidity), location information from GPS or indoor positioning system, etc. Some of these sensors are located outside the device that are used to collect environmental data, while others are located inside the device that are used to collect device specific context. The sensors are activated at the behest of an application, which identifies a set of context information to be monitored and collected by the mobile device. Figure 3 shows a general context-monitoring framework of the mobile device, which is largely based on [15]. The sensor manger represents a stage for creating filtering and aggregation processes to any piece of context information.

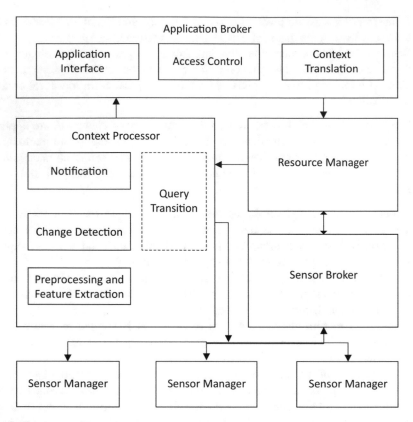

Fig. 3 Context monitoring framework of a mobile device

Context processor represents the part of the mobile edge cloud where all the processes of preprocessing, updating and context extraction are taking place. The resource manager is responsible on creating various alternative resource schedules for processing a high-level context from an application. Finally, the application broker where the adaptation process is occurred, it continuously changes running the resource schedules to adapt its performance to the dynamic resource system where the resources and applications needs are changing constantly. Whenever a change of application request or device (sensor) availability, the system reconfigures and updates the resources schedules that outcome resource use under the change of the system conditions. Such system would offer a flexibility of many applications if possible, in dynamic environment. The framework monitors and senses the mobile context information from devices, sensors, applications and human interaction with the surrounding smart and dynamic environments, to make intelligent edge cloud resource allocation and tasks scheduling decisions. The objective of resource allocation and scheduling is to reduce the execution cost of a job while meeting the job deadline of a mobile user and save cost for a user.

2.4   Privacy Challenges of Context

It is vital to develop and create privacy sensitive context framework for MEC systems to mitigate the privacy breach and relevant risks. Thus, it is important to provide a mechanism that ensures privacy is always maintained. There are five characteristics that make such systems very different from the current data collection systems [16], which are:

1. New coverage of smart environments and objects are presented everywhere in our life.
2. Data collection are invisible and unnoticeable.
3. The collected data are more intimate than ever before; for example, how do people feel while doing something.
4. The underlying motivation behind the data collection.
5. The increasing interconnection of smart devices to cooperate for providing a service to users, which results in new level of data sharing making unwanted information flows much more possible.

Developing privacy policies for the exchange of personal information based on interpreting and abstracting users' contextual information. Contextual information may be used to provide insight to the system for deciding which parts of the user information is needed (for a specific functionality) and hence retrieve the relevant information without exchanging the irrelevant parts. Research would be needed to define dynamic policies for this purpose.

Extensions of the anonymity and pseudonymity concepts could be applied to prevent the leakage of personal information in MEC environments. Such extensions will protect the users' privacy and provide them with flexibility by giving the rights to users to choose whether to distribute and exchange their personal data or not. One possible extension is to provide multiple levels of anonymity, in which the users could make informed choice as a trade-off between privacy and functionality. Also, implementing approaches for investigating and developing new privacy architectures which can measure how much of user personal information should be given and determine which bit of the user personal information needs to be collected by the environment for a particular purpose. These architectures will provide users in MEC environments with greater control over the way in which their information is being exchanged. A well-designed pervasive system can eliminate the need for giving out some items of personal information. For example, schemes based on "digital pseudonyms" could eliminate the need to give out items of personal information that are routinely entrusted to the networks today. To build context aware MEC systems, a consideration to the privacy of individual users must be highlighted because it is necessary to recognize when people feel their privacy has been invaded. Current Big Data mining techniques for minimizing privacy risks such as k-anonymity model that guarantees that a record is indistinguishable from at least k-1 other records can be utilized for context processing [17].

3 Application Design

Mobile devices access the edge cloud by using a mobile-cloud application framework. The framework offloads the mobile application to the MEC such that a part or the whole application is stored and processed in the cloud. Application offloading could be done by either migrating the whole application, partitioning the application, and migrating the computation-intensive and/or data-intensive partitions, or uploading the VM or container image of the application to the MEC. The offloading decision optimizes one or more of the user's goal of achieving application latency or device power efficiency. The decision considers the values of the parameters gleaned through the context framework.

A computation offloading process first partitions the application to separate the functionality of mobile applications into different partitions that are independent of each other. Then, it makes the decision of offloading the partitions using specific criteria depending on the application and user requirements. Finally, the partitions that are designated for computational offloading are distributed on edge containers and/or the cloud to be executed. Different computation offloading frameworks have been proposed.

The mobile user sends a request in the form of a job (computational activity) consisting of a set of tasks to be executed in the cloud; a task is an indivisible minimum computation unit to be run on the resource. The user request also describes the tasks dependencies, the job processing requirements, the input data, and job priority. In addition, the job description might also include some constraints such as application deadline and budget of the user. The user location information and mobility pattern provide user context in which the task scheduling performs scheduling decisions. In the next section a workflow of a mobile application is described as well as the application partitioning process. Section 3.2 describes a latency-aware offloading mechanism, finally in Sect. 3.3 computation offloading using machine learning techniques is outlined.

3.1 Location-Aware Workflow and TIG

Mobile application workflow $W = (T, E)$ is modeled as Directed Acyclic Graph (DAG), where $T = \{t_1, t_2, t_3, \ldots t_n\}$ is the set of tasks and E is the set of directed edges. The tasks are a combination of sequential and concurrent tasks [18]. An Example of DAG of a sub workflow is shown in Fig. 4, which is based on [45]. If a data dependency exists between t_i and t_j, then an edge $e_{ij} \in E$, exists between these two tasks and t_i is said to be a parent of the child t_j. Each task t_i is associated with a data output size DS_{out}^{ti} and duration of the intended task execution in the cloud is defined by ST_{ti} and ET_{ti}. In addition, each workflow is associated with a deadline called W_d based on the user's desired QoS [45]. The workflow execution time is

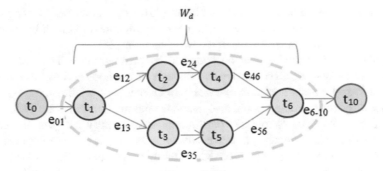

Fig. 4 Example of a task directed graph of a sub workflow

constrained by W_d. The notation T represents one job to be offloaded and executed in the edge cloud and the tasks are indexed as $i = \{1, 2, \ldots . n\}$.

Mobility of users is also integrated in modeling mobile application workflows. Rahimi et al. [21, 22] developed a framework to model the mobile application as a workflow of tasks. The mobile usage patterns are directly translated from user mobility patterns. Each pattern captures the trajectory of the mobile user and is donated by a set tuple of location of the user and duration of time the user is residing in the location. The workflow is represented as a location time workflow, LTW; which consists of a sequence of sub-workflows indexed by the user trajectory tuple (location and duration). In addition, the mobile application workflow consists of a sequence of logical and precise steps known as functions. Services that can implement a function are associated with that function. The user location information and mobility pattern provide user context in which the task scheduling performs scheduling decisions.

For tasks to be offloaded, the application needs to be partitioned into a set of tasks. Application partitioning splits the computation structure into a set of tasks that are either executed locally on the mobile device or remotely on the edge containers. Full application offloading is achieved when the mobile device is only used for data input and display without executing any other computation, for example mobile web browsers [25]. However, some latency sensitive edge native applications that have high computation demand require partial offloading, which can be achieved through different partitioning strategies. In this case, some of the application tasks are offloaded for execution in the edge containers. For example, Augmented Reality (AR) is composed of four major tasks: video feed from the camera, object tracking, scene rendering, and display. The object tracking is a compute intensive task that needs to be offloaded. In another strategy, both object tracking and scene rendering can be offloaded [25].

The applications are partitioned at many different granularity levels. Partitioning algorithms model workflows at method or class level [20], functional level [19], object level, or thread level [26]. In edge computing it is more cost effective to partition at a task/component level as partitioning at coarser levels is expensive due to data and context dependency at those levels [25]. Application design using micro-service architecture facilitates the migration of applications to cloud by deploying each service and its dependencies in its own container [28].

Application partitioning can be specified by programmers. The code is analyzed to identify compute-intensive components or methods and assign them with bandwidth and compute criteria that needs to be met for the offloading to happen. Alternatively, programmers could also annotate computation-intensive methods that need to be offloaded. Automated partitioning subsequently analyzes the code at runtime using this annotation to make offloading decisions [20]. Program analysis is usually done by using a graph-based model that represents interactions between different levels of partition granularities – methods, objects, or tasks [25].

Static partitioning by programmers may not be the optimal solution to use when offloading the latency-sensitive application components to the edge cloud. The wireless network parameters such as bandwidth and latency change with time, and the dynamic partitioning of the application are more effective in meeting these time dependent constraints.

3.2 Latency-Aware Offloading

The partitions offloaded to the edge cloud are intrinsically latency-sensitive for edge native applications. This latency can be represented as the turnaround time of a service request launched from the mobile device [23]. The *turnaround time* is defined as the duration from the submission time of the request to the time when the results are back to the device from the edge cloud. This duration TAT_R is represented as:

Turnaround time of Request R:

$$TAT_R = \sum_{i=1}^{n} PT_{ti} + TT_{Mob}^{C} + TT_{C}^{Mob}$$

Where:

$\sum_{i=1}^{n} PT_{ti}$ is the total execution time of all the tasks in the container
TT_{Mob}^{C} is the input data transmission time from the mobile to the container
TT_{C}^{Mob} is the transmission time of the results back to the mobile device
$TT_{Mob}^{C} = \frac{DS_{ij}^{out}}{DR}$ is the transmission time of the result to the mobile device, DR is the data rate allocated to the mobile device at the submission of the job to the container, and t_j is the last task executed in the container.

The data rate of a mobile device varies due to mobility and wireless channel conditions. For example, a mobile device may move from one network type (e.g.

cellular) to another (e.g. WiFi), or it may move from one cell to another within the same network. When the mobile device is connected through a high data rate link, the task's execution could be slowed down without causing major noticeable change in user experience. This can offer edge cloud providers an opportunity to reduce its cost by exploiting the elongated deadline. Alternatively, when the data rate is low, the execution times in the cloud shrinks to make up for the lost time due the communication delay. This concept is facilitated by introducing the slack time [24].

3.2.1 Slack Time (Float Time)

The workflow has a deadline W_d that needs to be met when executing the workflow tasks in the cloud container. The turnaround time of the workflow TAT should be equal to or less than W_d, $TAT \leq W_d$. The difference between W_d and TAT is called slack time T_{slack}.

$$T_{slack} = W_d - TAT$$

If the slack time is small, then the workflow needs to be executed closer to the deadline. Alternatively, if the slack time is large, then the cloud can slow down the execution to reduce computing and resource usage cost.

Adapting the system to the new slack time: If the slack time increases by a margin Δ, then the start time of the task could be delayed. This may release a resource that can be given to a long-awaited task belonging to another workflow. However, this arrangement can only work for the workflows that are executed in the same cloud container.

3.3 Computation Offloading (Machine Learning-Based Algorithms)

In [27] the computation offloading is modeled as a job shop scheduling problem. Offloading from a mobile user perspective can be viewed as a Directed Acyclic Graph as shown in Fig. 5. The user is presented as the root node and the vertex weights represent costs of energy or latency that are associated with the vertex. Moreover, the partition/aggregate application structure is adopted where the aggregate node A_i represents the independent job shop to which a user sends a set of jobs J that are to be scheduled on the available servers (worker machines) on the worker nodes $W_{(n,m)}$.

An intelligent computation framework using the concepts of knowledge-Defined Networking (KDN) is designed in [27]. The KDN uses Network Analytics (NA) and Software-Defined Network (SDN) to build a Knowledge Plane (KP) and a control

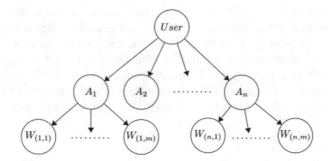

Fig. 5 Job scheduling problem represented as a multi-tier partition/aggregate application structure [27]

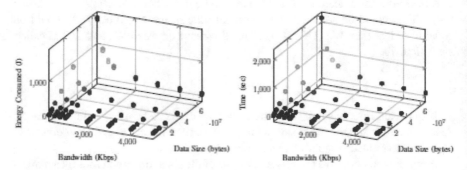

Fig. 6 Energy and time vs data size relationship for varying bandwidth based on the training data collected through simulation [27]

plane, respectively. The KP is a high-level model of the network system that builds a Machine Learning (ML) model using historical data as the training data for the model and uses ML techniques to perform the offloading decision.

The framework consists of a pre-trained prediction model for estimating network features, namely energy consumption and transmission time, by varying bandwidth and transmitted data size. The prediction model was built by first collecting network data for training. The plots of sample training data in Fig. 6 shows that both features, energy consumption and transmission time, have a linear relationship with the data size. The slopes of the energy-data and time-data lines are exponential functions of bandwidth. Hence, the predicted feature values can be computed using the following function:

$$f_b(d_s) = m(b)\,d_s + c(b)$$

where $m(b)$ and $c(b)$ are slope and y-intercept respectively that are functions of the bandwidth b, and the predicted feature, energy and time, is a function of data size d_s. A multi-step regression approach was used to estimate the slope function $m(b)$ from the historical data set as training data.

The predicted network feature values are laid out in a multi-dimensional space (e.g. a two-dimensional energy-time space) called a *hyper-profile* to make offloading decisions. The hyper-profile is a feature space that consists of points and dimensions. A single point represents a unique server instance, and each dimension of the point represents a predicted metric. These metrics are qualitative measures that indicate how fit each server is with respect to the user device (aggregator), which is placed in the hyper-profile feature space. The position of the user device is considered as the origin so that the distance between the user device and the server can be used as a measure for server selection. The smaller the distance between the origin and the node (server), the more desirable the node is as a target for offloading. For this purpose, *kNN* (k-nearest neighbor) algorithm is used and a kNN query is performed at the origin to select the optimal destination nodes for computation offloading for the placement of k jobs (application partitions). The kNN (q) returns a set of points for a query point q such that $p \in kNN(q)$ iff $|\{j \in P: d(j, q) < d(p, q)\}| < k$ where d is a predefined distance metric.

kNN often uses Euclidean as a distance metric. Using Euclidean distance means that $x_i^2 + y_i^2$ values are minimal for the points $p_i = (x_i, y_i)$ returned by kNN ($\vec{0}$), where in this case x is the energy consumption, y is the transmission time, and points represented by kNN ($\vec{0}$) are the servers that minimize energy consumption and latency.

The application for edge cloud designed for offloading utilizes platforms for their deployment in the edge cloud. Container is generally used for their low startup time and small memory footprint as discussed in the next section.

4 Service Provisioning in Edge Cloud

In contrast to central cloud datacenters, edge clouds need a mechanism to provision resources for backend services of mission critical applications with stringent low latency (~10 ms) requirements such as IoT, augmented reality (AR) and autonomous vehicles etc. The resource provisioning needs an abstraction with the ability to migrate these services between the heterogeneous computing servers located in geographically distributed edge clouds. Virtualization technologies including virtual machines (VMs) and containers provide the abstraction of the execution environment to run applications inside and allow them to utilize emulated hardware resources through hypervisors. This supports hardware heterogeneity and facilitates VM or container migration between physical servers without impacting execution results. Another important benefit of virtualization is the isolation of an instance of a VM from other instances of VMs meaning that every single instance gets a unique environment on the same physical hardware; therefore, any fault or security breach experienced by one instance does not affect all other VM instances. However, complete isolation cannot be achieved for containers since they share the same operating system (OS); hence, they need to be designed in a way that minimizes such incidents. Below we will review some of the important advantages and disadvantages of using VMs and containers and why containers are a better choice in edge computing environments. We will then review some container orchestration technologies available and how the edge applications and resources can be managed with some insights to locality-aware container scheduling methods and state-of-the-art container migration algorithms to move containers between nodes quickly.

4.1   Container and VM Provisioning

The design consideration for edge clouds is to provide latency, bandwidth constraints and reliability to applications, whereas the focus of central cloud (such as public cloud) design is to meet the scalability requirements. Hence, the edge clouds are generally smaller in size with a lower pool of resources available as compared to central clouds. Enterprise edge clouds may have large pool of resources, but they are fewer than other edge clouds. The virtual machines (VMs) normally have a large footprint of resources allocated to them mainly the disk storage space managed by their own dedicated operating systems (OS). Provisioning VMs with large amount of resources in edge clouds where available resources are limited become unattractive. Further, the VMs host a limited number of containers. Slow migration of VMs is another reason why VMs are unattractive virtualization technology for edge clouds. The migration of VMs (or containers) between edge nodes without noticeable downtime is a requirement especially for some applications such as connected vehicles that move between edge clouds. Since a VM runs dedicated OS, its migration involves transfer of large disk space and memory footprint between edge clouds that are connected through limited bandwidth over the WAN. Containers on the other hand are small in size and take a small footprint of resources such as disk space compared to VMs as they share the underlying OS. The sensitive data is stored locally at the edge and the passive data is pushed back to the central cloud networks via NFS or other secure protocols. The containers may have similar read-only base image layers that may already exist on most of the edge nodes, which are normally bootstrapped with the large part of the preinstalled daemons and software templates. The container migration involves dumping and transferring only the modified part of the memory and writeable image layer(s) that are required to bring up the container in the destination edge node. Another factor that impacts migration latency is the VM or container boot time. In the case of a VM, the boot time of an instance is equal to the time to accomplish boot process of a full-fledged computer system. In contrast, the container boot time is much lower as it uses the host OS kernel which is already loaded into the memory of the host. The availability of shared OS for containers is a major benefit to edge clouds where fast service provisioning is critical to reduce latency. Management, maintenance, and patching of a single OS for containers is relatively easy compared to updating isolated VM OS upgrades and patching. Figure 7 depicts a high-level overview of the VM and container management systems [29]. The study of an I/O intensive application over

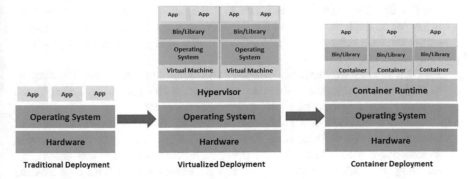

Fig. 7 Traditional, VM, and container deployment system [29]

VM (using KVM hypervisor) and container shows that the container gives either equal or better transactions/sec performance as compared to KVM [30]. This shows that the I/O overhead of hypervisor (KVM) is higher for the VM I/O especially for short I/Os than the container's I/O overhead. Overall, containers allow real-time service provisioning, reduce migration time, and require less resources as compared to VMs, which make them a preferable virtualization technology for edge clouds.

4.2 Container Orchestration

Containers are generally used as the virtualization technology in edge clouds. The edge-aware service provisioning utilizes the process and tools developed for container orchestration on heterogenous hardware resources to achieve application level quality of service (QoS) management policies, fault tolerance, energy and cost efficiency and resource utilization. There have been several efforts in academia and industry to develop service provisioning systems for cloud. The following are more mature container orchestration and edge cloud technology designed specifically for edge workloads, some of which are used in practice: Kubernetes [31] KubeEdge [32], Baidu OpenEdge [33] and StarlingX [34].

4.2.1 Kubernetes

Kubernetes [31] is developed by Google for large-scale container cluster orchestration and management that employs Docker as underlying container management system. It is now an opensource container cluster orchestration and management tool hosted by Cloud Native Computing Foundation (CNCF). Some features of the Kubernetes include:

- **Service discovery and load balancing:** Kubernetes provides access to containers either through the DNS name or IP addresses. It also distributes the network traffic for load balancing if the container traffic is high so that the deployment remains stable.
- **Storage orchestration:** Kubernetes allows automatic mount of a variety of storage systems selected by the user suitable for their deployment strategy, such as local storage, storage with public cloud providers etc.
- **Automated rollouts and rollbacks:** A desired state for the deployment of containers can be defined using Kubernetes that it attains through a transition process at a controlled rate. For example, the process of creating new containers, adapting the resource allocation to the new container, and removing existing containers can be automated through Kubernetes.
- **Automatic bin packing:** Kubernetes automate the deployment of containers on a cluster of nodes by selecting best node through bin packing based on container's CPU and memory (RAM) needs.
- **Self-healing:** Kubernetes performs container health check and restarts a failed container and replaces or shuts down a non-responsive container. It only advertises a ready container to the clients.
- **Secret and configuration management:** Kubernetes allows storing and managing sensitive information, such as passwords, OAuth tokens, and SSH keys.

Kubernetes Cluster is a set of compute nodes or machines for running containerized applications, which is managed through at least one Master. It works on a variety of underlying infrastructure such as bare metal servers, virtual machines, public cloud providers, private clouds, and hybrid cloud environments. Figure 8 shows components of the Kubernetes cluster. In general, it consists of a few key components that form the complete cluster solution:

- **Control Plane or Master:** One or more Master nodes that control all aspects of the cluster like node provisioning, scheduling, decommissioning, and scaling of the cluster.
- **Worker Node(s):** These are hosts or servers that can be physical or virtual where container pods are deployed. They are managed by the master node.
- **Kubelet:** It is an agent that runs on worker nodes and interact with the control plane for container management and reporting.
- **Pods:** It represents a single instance of an application. Each pod is a container, such as a Docker container, or a series of tightly coupled containers, along with options that govern how the containers are run.
- **Container runtime engine:** Each compute node has a container runtime engine to run the containers. For example, Docker or an Open Container Initiative-compliant runtime such as containerd, rkt and CRI-O.
- **Kube-API-Server:** It exposes Kubernetes API as a frontend for interacting, commanding, and managing a cluster.
- **ETCD:** It is a key-value repository of cluster data information.

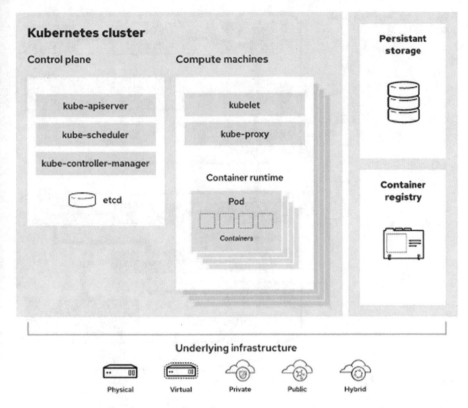

Fig. 8 Kubernetes cluster components [31]

- **Kube-Scheduler:** It selects a compute node and assigns that to a newly created Pods to run on. It makes the scheduling decision based on parameters, such as resource requirement, policy constraints, data locality, deadlines etc.
- **Kube-Controller-manager:** It manages the operation of a cluster and includes following functions: The Replication controller consults the scheduler to ensure correct number of pods are running. The Endpoints controller populates the endpoints object, such as it joins services and pods. The Service Account controller creates default accounts and a Token controller provides API access tokens for new namespaces. There is also a Node controller that detects when a node goes down and responds to it.
- **Kube-proxy:** Each compute node also contains a kube-proxy, which is a network proxy to manage network communication inside or outside of the cluster.
- **Persistent storage:** Kubernetes also manages the application data attached to a cluster. It allows users to request a persistent storage in a cluster independent of a pod, which can outlive the life of a pod.
- **Container registry:** Kubernetes provides its own container registry to store container images. It also allows using a third-party registry.

Fig. 9 High level design of
KubeEdge [32]

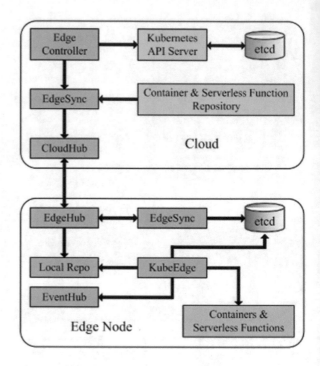

4.2.2 KubeEdge

KubeEdge [32] is an opensource project based on Kubernetes that offers edge-cloud
infrastructure to connect resource-constrained devices at the edge with the central
cloud. Figure 9 shows architecture of KubeEdge. In the edge platform, KubeEdge
downloads containers and serverless functions from remote repository in the cloud
via EdgeHub and saves them locally. It retrieves the data from EventHub, which
collects data and events from end device. It then launches containers and serverless
functions to serve the requests and start computations. EdgeSync synchronizes the
information about the containers and serverless functions among the edge nodes by
using ETCD distributed key-value store of Kubernetes.

4.2.3 StarlingX

StarlingX [34] is a fully integrated edge cloud software stack based on Open Stack
cloud suite [36]. It is an open source project supported by major industry leaders.
It offers Kubernetes powered containerized clusters with the ability to deploy up
to a hundred of edge server nodes in a single cluster. Some of the key features of
StarlingX are as follows:

1. All-In-One (AIO) solution to create a fully functional multipurpose edge cloud
   optimized for the ultra-low latency and performance goals of edge applications.

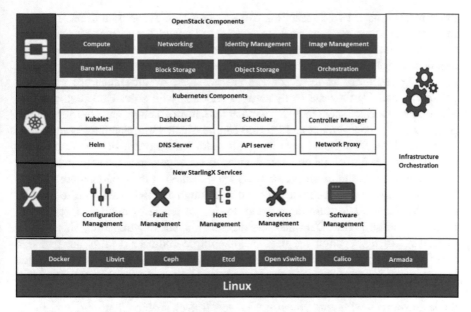

Fig. 10 shows building blocks of the StarlingX edge cloud platform [34]

2. Ease of deployment: Predefined configurations to support different edge cloud deployment models. Tested and released as a complete full-stack solution with compatibility between its opensource components.
3. Features to offer service management, high security, fault tolerant, high service uptime, high availability, fast response to events and fast recovery.

It integrates Open Stack and Kubernetes with the following additional building blocks for the deployment of distributed edge sites controlled through a centralized edge cloud as shown in Fig. 10: Configuration Management, Fault Management, Host Management, Service Management, and Software Management. The StarlingX edge cloud infrastructure is similar to Kubernetes with some additional components that includes controller node(s) to control the edge stack; worker nodes to run the containers; optional storage nodes with CEPH software to store file and objects; management network between the controller, worker, storage and other nodes for management of nodes; optional storage network for data transfer; data network for internal and external communication of containers; optional IPMI and PXE-boot networks for booting and configuration management of servers; and external OAM network for StarlingX API calls.

4.3   Cloud Resource Management

The edge cloud brings compute and data resources closer to the end-user devices to process these data. This decreases the amount of data transferred to and from the central cloud networks resulting in faster communication with users. The non-real-time data can be sent back to the central cloud for further processing as needed. Unlike central cloud resources, the resources that are available in the edge cloud have following features: (1) limited computing power, (2) heterogeneous computing resources as the resources are provided by different third party and end-users, and (3) they are to dynamic workloads with strict QoS requirements. The resource management includes architecture, infrastructure, and algorithms [35]. Edge resource management architecture can be divided into dataflow, control, and tenancy architectures. Dataflow architecture defines the movement of workloads and data from the central cloud and user devices to the edge cloud. Control architecture defines how the available edge resources are managed in the cloud network, either through a single centralized management or through a **distributed** multi-controller setup. Tenancy architecture defines the hosting of single or multiple instances or entities on edge nodes. Data-flow architecture includes aggregation, sharing and offloading. In aggregation the data from multiple end-user devices are gathered and filtered to remove and filter excess data, which reduces the communication overhead and decreases the data transfer between edge and central clouds. Resource sharing helps satisfy the computing requirements of the workload by using peer device resources with enough battery power. It avoids offloading workload to the cloud. Finally, offloading techniques are used when sharing of the workload is not feasible. It allows the application to be offloaded to the edge cloud for processing to take advantage of more powerful and resourcefulness of the edge. For example the database of an application can be replicated at the edge from the central cloud to be used and shared by different applications or for the purpose of seamless query execution at the edge only if the edge nodes are not resource constrained.

Infrastructure management is the second component of resource management that includes hardware, software, and middleware to manage the computing, network, and storage resources. Hardware component of infrastructure management includes low-power mobile devices, routers, and gateways. Another aspect is the design and implementation of algorithms for proper management of the cloud resources. These algorithms include: (1) Discovery algorithms to identify the edge cloud resources for distributed computation; (2) Benchmarking algorithms to capture the performance of the edge cloud resource for better decision-making in service deployments; (3) Load balancing algorithms to distribute the cloud workload based on defined criteria such as fairness and priorities; and (4) Placement algorithms to find a suitable location for containers and services to reduce IO and network contention [35].

4.4   Locality-Aware Container Scheduling

Classical hypervisors provide an isolated environment and dedicate exact amount of resource to every virtual machine it hosts without the need for resolving resource contention among those VMs. Unlike virtual machines, containers share the operating system kernel and boot up as applications running on a server. The container takes a part of or the whole system IO, disks, and network bandwidth. When multiple containers and their dependent services run on a system and compete for resources, the ensuing resource contention increases the application response time [36].

The design objective of edge clouds is to minimize the response time of applications to meet the latency requirement of users. Container scheduler is responsible for assuring contention-free resource assignment, but most of the existing schedulers employ simple load balancing schemes such as round-robin without making application-specific dependency checks between containers for their IO, computing and network contentions. The round robin placement of applications without collocating their dependent services on the same node can cause inter-node traffic surge [36]. Hence, bundling the application with its dependent services in a single container reduce this traffic overhead. Even containerized deployment of data intensive applications can cause disk IO contention that can increase the execution time of an application [36]. The disk IO contention happens due to contention for using a single disk head. However, compute intensive and data intensive applications do not intervene and exhibit sufficient isolation among resource usage [36].

Based on above observations Zhao et al. proposed a locality-aware container scheduling algorithm that considers both IO contention and network traffic in making container placement decisions [36]. The algorithm, as shown in Table 1, schedules applications $A_1 \ldots A_i$ on $C_1 \ldots C_j$ containers locating all IO access within the container. These containers are deployed on nodes that are organized in Zones such that inter-zone traffic is several orders of magnitude slower than intra-zone traffic. The zone represents a geographical area. The dependencies among applications are captured in a Dependency matrix D, where $D_{ij} = 1$ indicates that A_i has IO dependency on A_j. The traffic exchange among containers are captured in a Traffic matrix T, where $T_{ij} = 1$ indicates the cost of traffic exchange between containers C_i and C_j, which is significantly different when the containers are located within the same zone as compared to when they are located in different zones. The problem of locality-aware scheduling is to minimize the IO contention of a container, which occurs when the total application IO bandwidth of all the applications scheduled on the container exceeds the container's IO bandwidth. Since the solution of this problem is exponential, instead of minimizing IO contention the algorithm maximizes the number of applications scheduled on a container such that the total IO bandwidth of the applications does not exceed the container's IO bandwidth. It sorts both applications in the increasing order of their IO requirements and containers in the increasing order of their available IO bandwidth. It assigns an application to the first container in the sorted container list that has available IO resource close to or higher than the application's IO needs while satisfying the application's CPU, Memory, and disk space requirements. It iterates over all applications and within each iteration the position of a container in the sorted list is adjusted after assigning an application to that container [36].

The above algorithm assigns applications to a container without factoring in its network traffic load. Considering network traffic, the problem becomes finding

Table 1 Heuristic container deployment algorithm [36]

Input: Application to be scheduled: $A_1 .... A_i$; Available cells C_j $where$ $1 \leq j \leq |C|$

Output: The mapping between A and C: $M[k] := j$

    1. Sort A_k $(1 \leq k \leq i)$ in the increasing order of $A_k.io$
    2. Sort C in the increasing order of:

$$C_j.io\_avail := C_j.io - \sum \{A_m.io | cell\,(A_m) == C_j\}$$

    3. for $k := 1 .. i$ **do**
    4.   Binary search for C_j such that:
            $C_j.io\_avail \geq A_k.io$ && $C_{j-1}.io\_avail < A_k.io$ if $j > 1$
    5.   **if** C_j does not exist **then**
    6.   return M
    7.   **else**
    8.   **for** $(t := j; t \leq |C|; t := t + 1)$ **do**
    9.   **if** $(C_t.cpu \geq A_k.cpu$ && $C_t.ram \geq A_k.ram$ && $C_t.disk \geq A_k.disk)$
        then
   10. $M[k] := t$
   11.   break
   12.   **end if**
   13.   **end for**
   14. **end if**
   15. **if** $(t \leq |C|)$ **then**
   16. $C_t.io\_avail := C_t.io\_avail - A_k.io$
   17.   Adjust the position of C_t in C (binary search)
   18. **end if**
   19. **end for**

---

out placement of applications in zones while upholding following condition in addition to satisfying their CPU, memory, and disk constraints: The total traffic cost between an application and the services it depends on is minimized while keeping the covariance of the load in a zone within a user defined threshold. Therefore, the problem for an application to achieve the minimal network traffic is defined in the following formula. Given A_i we find Z_j $(1 \leq j \leq |Z|)$ such that [36]:

$$\arg_j \min \sum_k D_{i,k} \times T_{j,zone(A_k)}$$

subject to

$$CV(Z) \leq UDT$$

$$Z_{j.cpu} > A_{i.cpu}.$$

$$Z_{j.ram} > A_{i.ram}$$

$$Z_{j.disk} > A_{i.disk}$$

Where CV(Z) is the covariance of a zone's load and UDT is a user defined threshold. The load and traffic can be combined for the joint optimization of the locality-aware scheduling. The scheduler output is a mapping function F(M) that finds the best zone to deploy the container based on the weighted combination of the normalized network traffic (tr) and its weight α with the normalized coefficient of variance (cv) and its weight β, as shown in the following equation [36].

$$\arg_M \min\ (FM)$$

where

$$F(M) = \frac{\propto .tr(M) + \beta.cv(M)}{\alpha + \beta}$$

subject to

$$Z_{j.cpu} > A_{j.cpu}$$

$$Z_{j.ram} > A_{j.ram}$$

$$Z_{j.disk} > A_{j.disk}$$

$$Z_{j.io} > A_{j.io}$$

In above equation the normalized traffic is computed as the ratio of the application's actual traffic to the aggregate bandwidth, and the normalized load is computed as the coefficient of variance of all the loads on a zone [36]. The Diego scheduler [37] of Cloud Foundry was modified to simulate and analyze the algorithm. In one test case eight random containers were deployed on two nodes (REP1 and REP2) in two zones (Z0 and Z1). The application dependency matrix includes two independent applications and six applications that are dependent on each other. The traffic matrix includes the cost of inter-node traffic, which is ten times higher than the cost of intra-node traffic. The result shows that the unmodified Diego scheduler performed simple load balancing and placed 4 containers on different nodes generating significant inter-node traffic. The locality-aware Diego scheduler placed 6 containers on one node and 2 containers on another node to achieve tenfold reduction of the inter-node traffic.

4.5 Container Migration

Container migration is a method of migrating lightweight containers between one server to another within the same edge or between two different edge clouds. The migration schemes are available for both Linux containers (LXC) and Docker. As we mentioned earlier initialization and start-up of containers is quite fast, which helps expedite the migration process. Migration of live containers is desirable for several reasons, for instance: (1) to maintain low latency access in case of mobile users such as connected vehicles, (2) to distribute load across servers, and (3) to optimize energy consumption by consolidating loads on few servers and shutting down the remaining servers. Reasons 2 and 3 provide the rationale for Virtual Machine (VM) migration too. Even though VM migration exists in datacenters and its technology has matured over the years, container migration is a relatively new area with potential for improvement in developing its algorithm. VM migration works well but its process is slow due to the big size of VMs and long VM boot time, which is another reason that VM is not suitable for edge computing, where low latency applications need fast migration during service hand-over between edge servers.

The container migration involves a migration decision that triggers the migration process. The migration decision could be a simple trigger detecting the mobility of the user device, e.g. the Radio Network Information Service (RNIS) in 5G network can provide an early indicator of user experiencing cell change [3]. Alternatively, it could be a complex algorithm that may use context framework as discussed in Sect. 2 and consider multiple factors such as mobility, resource availability, QoS assurance etc. The container migration process includes three basic steps:

1. Freeze the operation of the container and checkpoint its state.
2. Transfer the container image along with saved state to the target server.
3. Restart container operation from the point of migration at the target server by restoring the saved state.

In the following subsections we only focus on the container migration process and discuss two important container migration systems – LXC migration and Docker migration.

4.5.1 Linux Container (LXC) Container Migration

LXC container is a container hypervisor solution that provides full virtualization, and it is a viable choice for containers in edge clouds environments. It offers near bare-metal virtualization and has advanced storage and network support.

The LXC container migration follows a three step migration process. In steps 1 and 3 it needs a checkpoint and recovery tool to save and restore the container state. CRIU is a software tool to perform checkpoint and restore in user space. It is used to freeze a live container and checkpoint its state in a set of files. After transferring

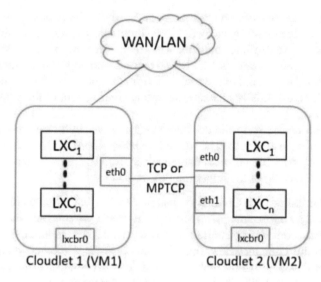

Fig. 11 LXC container migration with MPTCP [38]

the files, CRIU is called at the destination to restore the state from the files. CRIU assumes that both checkpoint and restore happens under the same file structure, which can be achieved either by using the shared file system at both source and destination or copy the file structure at the source and transfer that to the destination. The files corresponding to the container image are transferred using either RSYNC or SCP. RSYNC is Linux's de-facto differential file transfer tool with the ability to ignore duplicates. SCP copies files from the source to the destination servers and overwrites existing files. It is good for first stage copying. To accelerate and improve file transfer speed and stability, failover Multiprotocol TCP (MPTCP) can be employed instead of normal TCP to create parallel connection links.

In [38], a container migration algorithm is presented. The algorithm is tested by migrating a LXC container from one VM on the source server to another VM on the destination server. The containers on edge servers are installed inside virtual machines to create an extra layer of security. The CRIU works on privileged containers that may have full root access. In this installation, if the containers are compromised, the hackers cannot access the host server but only the VM that significantly reduces the risk of compromising the server due to security breach. Figure 11 shows the above implementation of the LXC based container system with MPTCP [38]. The end-users and mobile applications access the edge services and containers through the WAN. Lxcbr0 is a bridge that connects all the containers to the host system which in this case is an edge Virtual Machine.

The migration steps are as follows [38]:

1. Checkpoint the running container *LXC* to a directory specified by */tmp/check-point* in the *lxc-checkpoint -s -D /tmp/checkpoint -n LXC* command to freeze and dump the container files. The files will be saved as. MG and dump.log.

2. Copy the files from */tmp/checkpoint* and */var/lib/lxc/container-name* to the destination edge server by using RSYNC command. The files in the first directory contains saved state of the container. The second directory is the default directory of the privileged containers. The RSYNC command copies both the frozen state and the entire filesystem of the container from the source server to the destination server, which essentially recreates the whole environment of the container at the destination.
3. Restore the container in the destination edge server by using *lxc-checkpoint -r* command that restores the files from the */tmp/checkpoint* and */var/lib/lxc/container-name* directories. It then starts the container from the point its state was frozen. This is the last step of the migration process.

One of the issues with CRIU is its inability to live migrate the container that is it needs to suspend the container operation and freeze its state and then restore the container state from the transferred files and resume its operation. This approach leads to a small container downtime for the end-user. However, there are some projects like P.haul [39] that makes it possible to live-migrate the container, but the current implementation is based on freeze/restore approach.

4.5.2 Docker Container Migration

Docker is a container management system for creating and managing containers and it is widely used in practice. Docker images are available via DockerHub central repository which makes it easy to maintain and distribute custom-made images. It has a large community of developers that provides a strong support base for adding new features. The Docker release has no mechanism to manage the migration of containers. A migration algorithm is proposed in [40] that utilizes the benefit of layered structure of Docker to achieve low downtime. The Docker's storage driver supports multi layered image system of a running container with one top writable (R/W) layer, called *container layer*, and several bottom Read-Only (RO) base image layers. This makes it ideal for the migration algorithm to select and migrate the modified data only during migration. Docker supports copy-on-write (COW) which means all the writeable layers of the container are put into a thin layer of image file and we just need to transfer this layer to migrate the container. The Base images that are RO can be fetched from the DockerHub to the destination server before even migration begins provided destination server is known in advance. Prefetching of RO layers reduces the transfer time for base images significantly which leads to fast migration process between the servers. Thus, Docker containers become viable service provisioning abstraction for edge clouds serving mobile nodes such as connected vehicles.

The storage management driver of Docker's file system, AUFS, creates the layered images upon container creation and stacks them in a way that each layer references the other image layers as a hierarchy. The topmost layer is a writeable (R/W) layer that refers to the next RO layer underneath and the reference goes down

Fig. 12 Memory layout of a
Docker container [40]

R/W	febfb1642ebeb25857bf2a9c558bf695
RO	fac86d61dfe33f821e8d0e7660473381
RO	984034c1bb9c62ac63fff949a70d1c06
RO	2de00a5b0fb59d8eb7301b7523d96d3e
RO	0cff6d24b7f45835d42401ec28408b34
RO	....
RO	87b1dd26596e8e78e294a47b6b3fc3e9
RO	80db20d8e37dc3795b17e0e59930a408

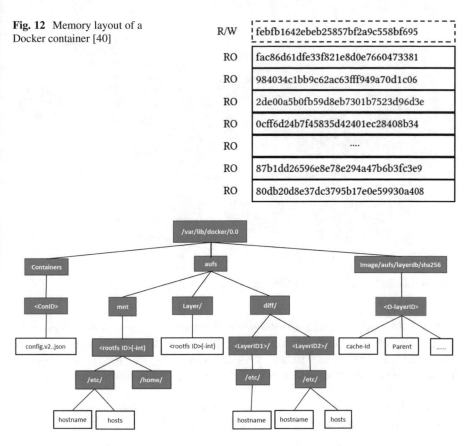

Fig. 13 Docker AUFS layered file system structure [40]

the chain of layers to the bottom most. Figures 12 and 13 depicts the layered file
system approach [40].

During the migration of Docker images, only the run-time memory states, and the
thin top writeable (R/W) image layer are transferred to the destination. Furthermore,
the size of the memory states and writeable layer can be decreased by using
compression methods. This leads to a fast hand over operation which is suitable
for migration of Docker containers over low-capacity WAN networks.

When a Docker container resumes its operation at the destination server, it
mounts all read-only and writeable image layers on a union mount point under
/mnt/<rootfs ID>/ so the filesystem appears unified with the file system before it
was powered off. The migration tools such as CRIU employs RSYNC to move
the files between the servers when the container is still running. It slows down
the migration process as it needs to transfer the whole file system. Another issue
that may arise is the filesystem contention error between the OS and RSYNC tool
since both need to access the files at the same time which may lead to migration

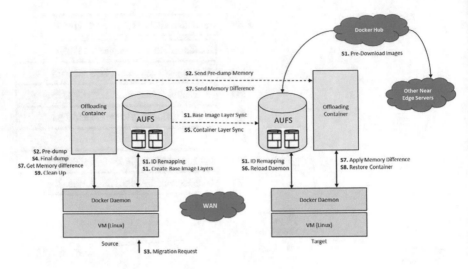

Fig. 14 Handoff service system architecture [40]

failure. Lastly, RSYNC transfers the whole file system into a single directory on the destination server and corrupt the layered filesystem of Docker container and the containers loses its layered storage system. To avoid moving the whole filesystem an algorithm is designed as shown in Fig. 14 to accomplish this task and speed up the process [40].

The migration algorithm for a running container from a source server to a target destination server is described in the following steps [40]:

1. **Synchronize Base Image Layers:** Find the target server through a separate mechanism, and then contact the target server to synchronize the base image layers of the container.
2. **Pre-dump Container:** While the container is still running and before shutting it down for migration, create a snapshot of the container runtime memory and dump it to the target server.
3. **Migration Request:** The migration request received at the source server triggers the migration process.
4. **Stop and Checkpoint the Container:** The migration process stops the container and checkpoints its runtime states.
5. **Synchronize Container Layer:** The file system does not change after container checkpoint. The container layer along with the checkpointed runtime states and configuration files are transferred to the target server.
6. **Reload Docker Daemon:** The Docker daemon is reloaded at the target server to reload the runtime state and configuration files and build the container.
7. **Apply Memory Difference**: After checkpointing the final memory dump is compared to the pre-dumped memory in step 2. The memory differences are generated and sent to the target server.

8. **Restore Container:** After receiving the memory difference, the container is restored at the target server.
9. **Clean Up Source Node:** Finally, the container footprint at the source server is removed by simply removing the container.

The data transfer time from the source to the target server is the dominant component of the migration time [40]. The migration time can be reduced by (1) reducing the amount of data transfer, and (2) parallelizing and pipelining some migration steps. The writable container layer can only be transferred after shutting down the container. However, base image layers are RO layers that can be transferred earlier. There are two different types of base image layers – the common base image layers are from the DockerHub that can be transferred as soon as the target server is known, while the other type includes base image layers that created locally by a running container from its container layer. As soon as the container creates its base image layer, it can be transferred to the target server. The container memory dump can also be transferred in two steps to reduce the exposure of transfer time to the container shutdown time. The initial memory dump is created before starting the container that can be transferred as soon as the target server is known. After checkpointing container, a memory difference is created and only the difference is transferred while the container is shut down for migration. The memory and disk dumps are compressed by bzip2 compression method to further speedup the transfer process. The compression and transfer can happen in parallel using Linux pipes over secure SSH channels to speed up the process. The layered architecture of Docker AUFS makes the migration process more efficient that results in reduced migration time. However, the drawback of AUFS is that it has high I/O overhead that reduces the performance of I/O intensive applications [30].

4.6   Case Study: Rocket Video Analytics

Real-time video analytics involve recognition and tracking of objects in video streams collected from multiple video cameras each generates 30 frames per second that require high compute power. The applications that use analytics to interact with human (augmented reality) or activate an actuator (traffic light control) require low latency. A team in Microsoft research has developed software stack of video analytics, called *Rocket*, which was deployed in Bellevue, Washington, to track volumes of cars, bikes, and pedestrians and raise alerts when anomalous traffic pattern is detected [9]. Figure 15 shows the Rocket software stack that is used by applications for traffic planning, surveillance, etc. The applications involve processing of high-level video queries, for instance tracking a suspicious person for a surveillance application. The video cameras are deployed with local computation serving as fog nodes where frames can be pre-processed. The frames and associated data are dispatched to the edge cloud for further processing. The *video pipeline optimizer* of the stack converts a raw video query into a pipeline process of

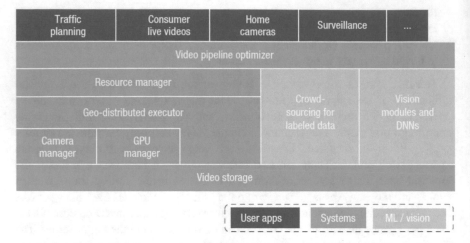

Fig. 15 Software stack of Rocket video analytics [9]

vision modules such as a pipeline of video decoding, object recognition and object tracking modules. It develops a resource-accuracy profile of the query based on the relationship between the resource configuration of modules and the desired level of accuracy of their execution. Generating resource-accuracy profile is a challenging task because it involves processing a large number of configuration parameters and their combinations. The profile is processed by the *resource manager* to allocate CPU, GPU, network, and other resources that are geo-distributed over fog nodes, private clusters, and edge clouds. The manager schedules resources to thousands of query profiles for accuracy instead of fairness, which gives profiles that require high accuracy preferential access to resources for the same level of allocated resources. Video-analytics of live streams from traffic monitoring cameras at intersections and surveillance cameras showed that accuracy-based scheduler achieves 80% more average accuracy than a fairness-based scheduler.

The modules of the pipeline are deployed at the camera or offloaded to the edge cloud server. The placement and offloading decisions are application dependent that utilize intelligent frame processing and application level optimization. The processing of every frame is prohibitive. An object tracking application detects a moving object and follows it from one frame to the next in a stream of video frames. It is a compute intensive task that processes a single frame on a 8-core processor in 1 s [9]. It can be performed in two stages – object recognition followed by object tracking [44]. The object tracking is a less compute intensive task; hence, it can be performed in the fog node. The object recognition pipeline includes three modules that are offloaded to the edge cloud as shown in Fig. 16. The detection module detects an object through high level features such as contours of a car and locate it using bounding boxes. The feature extraction module extracts features from within the bounding boxes. Finally, the recognition module labels the object. The object recognition incurs significant delay during that the camera view moves 20

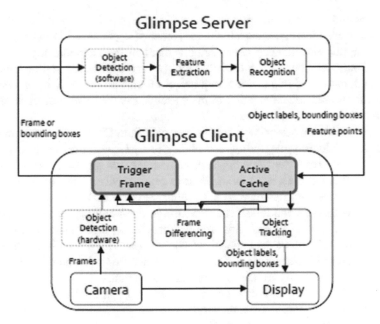

Fig. 16 Glimpse processing [44]

frames forward finding the location of the object stale in the new frame [44]. For example, the object moves away from its location in frame 0, which is selected for object recognition, in a future frame 20 representing the current view. Rocket stack incorporates a technique developed in Glimpse [44], which selects a frame, called *trigger frame*, and uploads it for deep vision processing to the object recognition pipeline in the edge cloud server. The fog node (camera) stores subsequent frames in its *active cache* as shown in Fig. 16. The server performs object detection, feature extraction, and object recognition by labeling the object through the Deep Neural Network (DNN) machine learning process. It returns bounding boxes, object features, and the object label to the fog node for object tracking. The fog node tracks the object in the sequence of frames stored in the active cache by estimating the displacement of object features from one frame to another. It cannot process every frame from the trigger frame up to the current frame because the processing delay will cause user view to move forward many frames. The Glimpse employs an adaptive subsampling strategy to select a subset of frames compromising accuracy of tracking for low processing delay.

5 Future Work

The application design and service provisioning for edge cloud is a growing area. The new paradigm of microservice architecture for cloud applications provides natural boundaries for the partitioning of applications to optimize offloading decisions. It also facilitates scalable deployment of applications in the edge cloud. The low application latency needs improvement in the container registry design for fast container image download that reduces the application startup time. The distributed nature of edge cloud requires a cloud service broker for container placement and resource allocation to meet user SLAs. We discussed each of these new areas below for future work.

Cloud application design based on the new paradigm of microservice architecture utilizes its modularity, flexibility, and ability to scale with user demands. Unlike monolithic code base, the cloud application, with the new approach, is composed of modules that are implemented as stand-alone microservices. The service interfaces of these modules are implemented using either event-based or asynchronous calls to interact with other modules. The new design approach facilitates migration of applications to clouds as each microservice can be deployed independently in its own container with all its dependencies [28]. Microservice design is also amenable for computation offloading since the placement decision of a microservice can be optimized independently for the local objective function.

The low-latency operation of containers requires fast bootstrapping. The container framework incorporates a registry where users upload their container images for sharing. Dockerhub is one popular registry that stores terabytes of data and adds 1500 repositories of images daily. The Docker daemon gets an image from the registry when it is needed by the container it runs. The startup time of containers grows with the size of the images and the number of concurrent requests at the registry. A trace-based analysis of IBM Docker cloud registry shows that more than 80% requests that most of the registry sites receive are pull requests for layers [41]. The distribution of layers shows that 80% of the layers were of the size less than 10 MB. The concurrent request load experienced by some registry sites was as high as 100 requests per minute for 80% of the requests. The response time distribution shows that up to 60% response times were within 1 s while top 25% response times were 10 s or higher. This study shows that there is a need to improve the registry design for faster container startup time [41].

The diversity of edge clouds administered by different service providers and mobile network operators (MNO) form federated cloud structure. The deployment of edge cloud applications and their dependencies in federated cloud requires cloud brokering service [42], which negotiates SLAs with the service providers for resource allocation and service availability. The broker performs service discovery, service ranking, service selection, service allocation and monitoring of SLAs [42]. Containerization of microservice based cloud applications provides a common virtualization platform for resource allocation across diverse clouds through cloud service broker, which decides deployment and migration of containers to meet latency requirements [43]. Some emerging use cases require application federation across operators that are local and across borders. For example, public safety applications (V2X use cases) where users/vehicles need to communicate to the same backend.

References

1. M. Satyanarayanan and N. Davies, Augmenting Cognition Through Edge Computing, IEEE Computer, pp. 37–46, July 2019.
2. S. Noghabi, L. Cox, S. Agarwal and G. Ananthanarayanan, The Emerging Landscape of Edge Computing, ACM GetMobile, Vol. 23, No. 4, pp. 11–20, Dec. 2019.
3. MEC in 5G networks, ETSI White Paper No. 28, June 2018 (www.etsi.org)
4. Cloud RAN and MEC: A Perfect Pairing, ETSI White Paper No. 23, Feb 2018 (www.etsi.org)
5. StarlingX Project Overview, https://www.starlingx.io/collateral/StarlingX_Onboarding_Deck_for_Web.pdf
6. Harmonizing standards for edge computing, ETSI White Paper No. 36, July 2020 (www.etsi.org)
7. L. Lin, X. Liao, H. Jin and P. Li, Computation Offloading Toward Edge Computing, Proc. Of The IEEE, Vol. 107, No. 8, pp. 1584–1607, Aug. 2019.
8. J. Wang, Z. Feng, S. George, R. Iyengar, P. Pillai, and M. Satyanarayanan, "Towards Scalable Edge-native Applications," in Proceedings of the 4th ACM/IEEE Symposium on Edge Computing (SEC'19), pp. 152–165, Nov. 2019.
9. G. Ananthanarayanan, et al, Real-Time Video Analytics: The Killer App for Edge Computing, IEEE Computer, pp. 58–66, Oct. 2017.
10. Dey and G. Abowd, "Towards a better understanding of context and context-awareness", Proceedings of Workshop on the What, Who, Where, When and How of Context-Awareness, The Hague, Netherlands, April 2000.
11. T. Gu, et al., An ontology-based context model in intelligent environments, Proceedings of Communication Networks and Distributed Systems Modeling and Simulation Conference. San Diego, California, USA, 2004.
12. T. Strang, C. Linnhoff-Popien, A Context Modeling Survey. In: Workshop on Advanced Context Modeling, Reasoning, and Management as part of UbiComp 2004, Nottingham 2004.
13. P. Nurmi, M. Martin, and J. A. Flanagan, Enabling proactiveness through Context Prediction, in Proceedings of the Workshop on Context Awareness for Proactive Systems (CAPS, Helsinki, Finland, June 2005), Helsinki University Press, pp 159–168, 2005.
14. Claudio Bettini, Oliver Brdiczka , Karen Henricksen, Jadwiga Indulska, Daniela Nicklas, Anand Ranganathan, Daniele Riboni, A survey of context modeling and reasoning techniques, Pervasive and Mobile Computing, v.6 n.2, p.161–180, April 2010.
15. Y. Lee, Y. Ju, C. Min, J. Yu and J. Song, "MobiCon: Mobile context monitoring platform: Incorporating context-awareness to smartphone-centric personal sensor networks," 2012 9th Annual IEEE Communications Society Conference on Sensor, Mesh and Ad Hoc Communications and Networks (SECON), Seoul, 2012, pp. 109–111, doi: https://doi.org/10.1109/SECON.2012.6275765.
16. Lahlou, S., Langheinrich, M. and Rocker, C. (2005), "Privacy and Trust Issues with Invisible Computers". Communications of the ACM, 48.
17. Liang, Y., and Samavi, R. (2020), "Optimization-Based k-Anonymity Algorithms", Computers & Security, 93:101753, 2020.
18. M. Jia, J. Cao and L. Yang, "Heuristic offloading of concurrent tasks for computation-intensive applications in mobile cloud computing," 2014 IEEE Conference on Computer Communications Workshops (INFOCOM WKSHPS), Toronto, ON, 2014, pp. 352–357.
19. I. Giurgiu, O. Riva, D. Juric, I. Krivulev, and G. Alonso, "Calling the cloud: Enabling mobile phones as interfaces to cloud applications," in Lecture Notes in Computer Science (including subseries Lecture Notes in Artificial Intelligence and Lecture Notes in Bioinformatics), 2009, vol. 5896 LNCS, pp. 83–102.
20. E. Cuervo and A. Balasubramanian, "MAUI: making smartphones last longer with code offload," Proc. 8th . . . , vol. 17, pp. 49–62, 2010.
21. M. R. Rahimi, N. Venkatasubramanian, S. Mehrotra, and A. V. Vasilakos, "MAPCloud: Mobile applications on an elastic and scalable 2-tier cloud architecture," in Proceedings – 2012

IEEE/ACM 5th International Conference on Utility and Cloud Computing, UCC 2012, 2012, pp. 83–90.

22. M. R. Rahimi, N. Venkatasubramanian, and A. V. Vasilakos, "MuSIC: Mobility-aware optimal service allocation in mobile cloud computing," in IEEE International Conference on Cloud Computing, CLOUD, 2013, pp. 75–82.

23. A. U. R. Khan, M. Othman, S. A. Madani, and S. U. Khan, "A survey of mobile cloud computing application models," IEEE Commun. Surv. Tutorials, vol. 16, pp. 393–413, 2014.

24. P. Balakrishnan and C. K. Tham, "Energy-efficient mapping and scheduling of task interaction graphs for code offloading in mobile cloud computing," in Proceedings – 2013 IEEE/ACM 6th International Conference on Utility and Cloud Computing, UCC 2013, 2013, pp. 34–41.

25. L. Lin, X. Liao, H. Jin and P. Li, "Computation Offloading Toward Edge Computing," in Proceedings of the IEEE, vol. 107, no. 8, pp. 1584–1607, Aug. 2019, doi: https://doi.org/10.1109/JPROC.2019.2922285.

26. B. Chun, S. Ihm, P. Maniatis, M. Naik, and A. Patti, "CloneCloud: Elastic execution between mobile devices and cloud," in Proc. 6th Conf Comput. Syst., Apr. 2011, pp. 301–314.

27. A. Crutcher, C. Koch, K. Coleman, J. Patman, F. Esposito and P. Calyam, "Hyper Profile-Based Computation Offloading for Mobile Edge Networks," 2017 IEEE 14th International Conference on Mobile Ad Hoc and Sensor Systems (MASS), Orlando, FL, 2017, pp. 525–529, doi: https://doi.org/10.1109/MASS.2017.91.

28. V. Singh, and S. K. Peddoju, Container-based microservice architecture for cloud applications. In IEEE International Conference on Computing, Communication and Automation (ICCCA), pp. 847–85, 2017.

29. Doug Chamberlain. Containers vs. Virtual Machines. [Online]. Available: https://blog.netapp.com/blogs/containers-vs-vms

30. W. Felter, A. Ferreira, R. Rajamony, and J. Rubio, An Updated Performance Comparison of Virtual Machines and Linux Containers, In IEEE ISPASS (2015).

31. Kubernetes overview. [Online]. Available: https://kubernetes.io/docs/concepts/overview/what-is-kubernetes/

32. KubeEdge, a Kubernetes Native Edge Computing Framework. [Online]. Available: https://kubernetes.io/blog/2019/03/19/kubeedge-k8s-based-edge-intro/

33. Zeyi Tao, Qi Xia, Zijiang Hao, Cheng Li, Lele Ma, Shanhe Yi, and Qun La. A Survey of Virtual Machine Management in Edge Computing. Proceedings of the IEEE | vol. 107, no. 8, pp. 1–16, August 2019.

34. StarlingX Project Overview. https://www.starlingx.io/collateral/StarlingX_Onboarding_Deck_for_Web.pdf

35. Cheol-Ho Hong and Blesson Varghese. A Survey on Resource Management in Fog/Edge Computing, ACM Computing Surveys, vol. 52, no. 1, pp. 1–37, 2019.

36. Dongfang Zhao, Mohamed Mohamed and Heiko Ludwig. Locality-Aware Scheduling for Containers in Cloud Computing, IEEE Transactions on cloud computing, vol. 8, no. 2, pp. 1–12, 2020.

37. Diego Project. (2015). [Online]. Available: https://github.com/cloudfoundry-incubator/diego-release

38. Yuqing Qiu, Evaluating and Improving LXC Container Migration between Cloudlets Using Multipath TCP, pp. 38–60, 2016

39. P. Haul, https://criu.org/P.Haul. Last accessed on Jul 20, 2016.

40. Lele Ma, Shanhe Yi, Qun Li, Efficient Service Handoff Across Edge Servers via Docker Container Migration, pp.1–11, 2017

41. A. Anwar, et al, Improving Docker Registry Design based on Production Workload Analysis, 16th USENIX Conference on File and Storage Technologies, Feb. 2018. https://www.usenix.org/conference/fast18/presentation/anwar

42. S. S. Chauhan, E. S. Pilli, R. Joshi, G. Singh, and M. Govil, Brokering in interconnected cloud computing environments: A survey, Elsevier Journal of Parallel and Distributed Computing, Vol. 133, pp. 193–209, Nov. 2019.

43. N. D. Keni and A. Kak, Adaptive Containerization for Microservices in Distributed Cloud Systems, IEEE 17th Annual Consumer Communications and Networking Conference (CCNC), 2020.
44. T. Chen et al., "Glimpse: Continuous, Real-Time Object Recognition on Mobile Devices," Proc. ACM Conf. Embedded Networked Sensor Systems (SenSys 15), 2015, pp. 26–29. DOI: https://doi.org/10.1145/2809695.2809711.
45. M. Rodriguez and R. Buyya, Deadline Based Resource Provisioning and Scheduling Algorithm for Scientific Workflows on Clouds, IEEE Transactions on Cloud Computing, vol. 2, no. 2, pp. 222–235, April-June 2014.

Simulating Fog Computing Applications Using iFogSim Toolkit

Kamran Sattar Awaisi, Assad Abbas, Samee U. Khan, Redowan Mahmud, and Rajkumar Buyya

Abstract Fog computing is a novel distributed computing paradigm that provides cloud-like services at the edge of the network. It emerges as an efficient paradigm to process the enormous amount of Internet of Things (IoT) data and can address the limitations of cloud-centric IoT models in terms of large end-to-end delays, and huge network bandwidth consumption. Recently, fog computing and IoT have been employed in several domains, including transportation, education, healthcare, and manufacturing industry. To imitate different complex application scenarios for these domains, a notable number of fog computing-based simulators has already been developed. Among them, iFogSim has attained significant attention because of its simplified interface and low complexity. In this article, we present a tutorial on how to use iFogSim toolkit to simulate four real-time case studies for (1) smart car parking, (2) smart waste management system, (3) smart coal mining industry, and (4) sensing as a service. This article is expected to assist the researchers in understanding and implementing various aspects of fog computing using the iFogSim toolkit.

Keywords Fog computing · iFogSim · Smart car parking · Smart waste management system · Smart mining industry

K. S. Awaisi · A. Abbas (✉)
COMSATS University Islamabad, Islamabad, Pakistan
e-mail: assadabbas@comsats.edu.pk

S. U. Khan
Mississippi State University, Mississippi, MS, USA
e-mail: skhan@msstate.edu

R. Mahmud · R. Buyya
Cloud Computing and Distributed Systems (CLOUDS) Laboratory, School of Computing and Information Systems, The University of Melbourne, Melbourne, VIC, Australia
e-mail: mahmudm@student.unimelb.edu.au; rbuyya@unimelb.edu.au

1 Introduction

Internet of Things (IoT) has connected billions of devices across the world and is consistently promoting the realization of smart cyber-physical environments including smart factories, smart homes, smart transport, and smart healthcare. However, due to limited processing and storage capabilities of IoT devices, cloud computing is often used as the backbone platform to provide computational capacity and storage services to the IoT-enabled environments [1]. Nevertheless, cloud data-centers have some potential challenges, such as large end-to-end delays and huge network bandwidth consumption. These challenges pertinent to cloud computing impact the response time of latency-sensitive real-time applications, for example healthcare systems, traffic management, and fire control systems. Additionally, IoT devices can generate an enormous amount of data within a very short period. When every IoT device initiates sending these data to cloud servers, the performance of cloud services is more likely to degrade.

Fog computing extends the cloud services near the edges of the network and overcomes the challenges of cloud computing [2]. This new distributed computing paradigm has exhibited tremendous potential to effectively process the data generated by millions of IoT devices [3]. Since fog computing brings computations closer to the data generating devices, consequently the latency and network bandwidth utilization are significantly minimized [4]. Compared to the cloud data centers, fog nodes have less computational power and storage capacity. Therefore, fog and cloud computing paradigms work in an integrated manner to provide resources for large-scale IoT systems.

Since the fog computing systems involve fog nodes, cloud data centers, and IoT devices; therefore, the real-world implementation of fog scenarios for research purposes is very expensive [5]. In such situations, simulation and validation of fog scenarios with the help of toolkits are very beneficial. Currently, there are several simulation toolkits available, such as FogNetSim++ [6], Edgecloudsim [7], and iFogSim [8] for modeling and simulating the fog computing environments. Among these toolkits, iFogSim has significantly attracted the attention of the researchers and is being used to model a variety of fog computing cases. In this article, we aim at providing a tutorial on iFogSim to help the researchers quickly understand the fundamental concepts and the advanced implementation steps. To make the study more intriguing, we implement four real-time fog-based scenarios namely, (1) smart car parking system, (2) smart waste management system, (3) smart mining industry, and (4) sensing as a service in the iFogSim. The tutorial not only provides step by step installation guidelines but also contains instructions to simulate the scenarios and create devices, classes, and objects in the iFogSim. Moreover, the tutorial also presents the corresponding code snippets of all the case studies simulated in iFogSim. The remainder of the article is organized as follows: Sect. 2 briefly discusses the installation and setup of iFogSim. Section 3 presents case studies and code snippets whereas Sect. 4 concludes the paper.

2 Installation and Setup of iFogSim

iFogSim is a Java based open-source simulation tool for simulating fog computing scenarios. It is developed by Harshit Gupta and the team at the Cloud Computing and Distributed Systems (CLOUDS) Lab University of Melbourne Australia [8]. The following are the steps to download, install, and setup the iFogSim.

1. Download the iFogSim source code in the zip file from the GitHub https://github.com/Cloudslab/iFogSim.
2. Extract the iFogSim zip file and there will be a folder named *iFogSim-master*.
3. Make sure that you have installed Java Runtime Environment (JRE) or Java Development Kit (JDK) 1.7 or more.
4. Install Eclipse Mars or any latest release on the computer.
5. Define the workspace for the Eclipse Integrated Development Environment (IDE).
6. Create a new folder for the iFogSim in the Eclipse workspace and paste all the files and content of the *iFogSim-master* in this folder or you can simply copy the *iFogSim-master* folder and paste it into the workspace folder
7. Open the Eclipse IDE and create the new Java project.
8. Make sure that the name of the Java project is the same as the name of the folder as you have created in the workspace for iFogSim.
9. Now open the *src* of the project and explore the package *org.fog.test.perfeval*. In this package, you will find three example scenarios of iFogSim.
10. Open any example scenario, explore it, and run it. You will get the results on the console.

3 Case Studies

This section presents the four case studies that are implemented using the iFogSim toolkit. Section 3.1 presents the case study of a smart car parking system, Sect. 3.2 explains the smart waste management system, Sect. 3.3 describes the smart mining industry case study and Sect. 3.4 discusses the sensing as a service case study.

3.1 Smart Car Parking System

Most of the people are moving towards the cities due to better facilities and resources. Owing to the increasing population to the cities, the number of vehicles on the roads have increased enormously as the personal vehicles have become a significant transportation resource nowadays. Consequently, finding the vacant car parking space has become a potential issue in the populated areas. People spend a lot of time finding the vacant car parking space which essentially results in CO_2

emission, time wastage, and fuel wastage. Parking problems have attracted more consideration in the past few years and many researches have proposed IoT based car parking solutions. We presented a fog based smart car parking architecture in [9] to solve the car parking issues by using fog computing. The fog-based car parking architecture consists of the following:

- Smart cameras
- Fog nodes
- Light Emitting Diode (LED) display screens
- A cloud server

The smart cameras are deployed in the parking lanes which take the image of the parking lanes and transmit the images to the fog node. On the fog node, we have implemented an image processing algorithm to identify those parking slots which are vacant. After detecting the vacant parking slots, the parking slots information is updated on the LED. The data is stored in the fog node for a limited amount of time, and then it is moved to the cloud server for permanent storage. When the vehicle arrives at the parking gate, the driver finds the vacant car parking space immediately and parks the vehicle on the desired location. The information on the LED is updated after every 5 s interval. The communication between the fog node and the cloud server is enabled through a proxy server. The fog-based car parking system is displayed in Fig. 1.

Building Scenario with iFogSim for Smart Parking System To simulate the smart car parking scenario, we need to create two modules in iFogSim i.e.

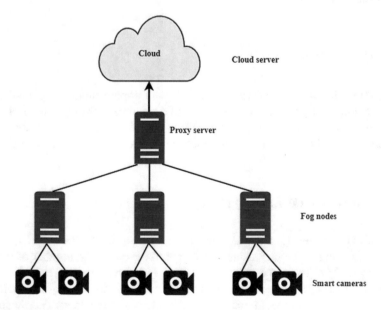

Fig. 1 Fog based smart car parking system

Fig. 2 Fog based smart car parking system application model of iFogSim

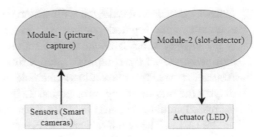

picture-capture and *slot-detector*. The *picture-capture* module is embedded in smart cameras. The smart cameras are programmed in such a way that it takes the pictures after a specific time interval of 5 s and transmits the images to the fog node. We can attach the micro-controller device with the smart cameras to establish a connection with the fog node.

Moreover, we create a proxy server and a cloud server. The proxy server enables the communication between the fog node and the cloud server. The cameras here act as the sensor as well. In iFogSim, when we create any device which takes the input to the system for processing, we call it a sensor and any device which receives the output after processing is termed as the Actuator. The sensors, actuators, and fog devices are created in iFogSim using their respective classes. In the smart parking system scenario, the cameras are created and attached to the fog node. Figure 2 depicts the data flow of the smart parking application model. The *picture-capture* module is created in smart cameras. It is programmed to capture the pictures of parking lane after every 5 s.

The pictures are handed over to the second module which is a *slot-detector* and it detects the vacant parking slots. In iFogSim, any computation elements are called modules.

Building Simulation with iFogSim for Smart Car Parking System The iFogSim provides built-in classes to create fog nodes, sensors, and actuators. It also takes care of resource allocation and management policies. The following classes will be used to create a smart car parking scenario in iFogSim.

1. **FogDevice:** This class provides a constructor to create the fog devices and to define the hardware properties of the fog devices i.e. node name (name of the device to be used in simulation), MIPS (Million Instructions Per Second), RAM (main memory of the fog node), uplink bandwidth, downlink bandwidth, level (hierarchy level of the device), ratePerMips (cost rate per MIPS used), busyPower (the amount of power consumed when the fog node is in busy state), and idlePower (the amount of power used when the fog node is in the idle state). When we create the fog device, all these parameters are assigned values. In our implementation of the case studies, all the computational devices are created using the FogDevice class.
2. **Sensor:** By using the sensor class, we create IoT devices in iFogSim. While creating the sensors, we define the gateway device id and setup link latency.

Gateway device is the device with whom the sensor is attached and any devices, such as a router, fog node, or a proxy can serve as the Gateway. Setup link latency is the latency time to create a connection between the sensor and fog device. Normally, we set the setup link latency time between 1 to 3 ms.

3. **Actuator:** Actuator class allows to create the objects in iFogSim that are used to display the output or any information. In the smart car parking scenario, the LED is created actuator because the vacant car parking slot position will be displayed on the LEDs. The actuator needs to be connected with any gateway device. The gateway device sends the data to actuator. Therefore, when we create actuator in iFogSim, we define the gateway device id and setup link latency.

A new class in *org.fog.test.perfeval* package is required to create for simulating this scenario in iFogSim. The *FogDevice* class lets you to create fog nodes with different configurations by providing a constructor. A code snippet to create heterogeneous fog devices is given below:

Code Snippet-1 This code snippet is to be placed in the **main** class.

```
//Here we are creating a list for fog devices.
static List<FogDevice> fogDevices = new ArrayList<FogDevice>();
static List<Sensor> sensors = new ArrayList<Sensor>();
static List<Actuator> actuators = new ArrayList<Actuator>();
static int numOfAreas = 7; //the   number   of   fog   nodes
static int numOfCamerasPerArea1=10;
// the   number   of   cameras per fog node.
static double CAM_TRANSMISSION_TIME = 5; //time interval
private static boolean CLOUD = false;
private static void createFogDevices(int userId, String appId) {
FogDevice cloud = createFogDevice("cloud", 44800, 40000,
100, 10000, 0, 0.01, 16*103, 16*83.25);
cloud.setParentId(-1);
fogDevices.add(cloud);
FogDevice proxy = createFogDevice("proxy-server", 2800, 4000,
10000, 10000, 1, 0.0, 107.339, 83.4333);
proxy.setParentId(cloud.getId());

double costPerStorage
proxy.setUplinkLatency(100);
fogDevices.add(proxy);
for(int i=0;i<numOfAreas;i++){
addArea(i+"", userId, appId, proxy.getId());
}
}

private static FogDevice addArea(String id, int userId,
String appId, int parentId){
FogDevice router = createFogDevice("a-"+id, 2800, 4000,
1000, 10000, 2, 0.0, 107.339,83.4333);
fogDevices.add(router);
router.setUplinkLatency(2);
for(int i=0;i<numOfCamerasPerArea1;i++){
String mobileId = id+"-"+i;
```

```
FogDevice camera = addCamera(mobileId, userId,
appId, router.getId());
camera.setUplinkLatency(2);
fogDevices.add(camera);
}
router.setParentId(parentId);
return router;
}

private static FogDevice addCamera(String id, int userId,
String appId, int parentId){
FogDevice camera = createFogDevice("c-"+id, 500, 1000, 10000,
10000, 3, 0, 87.53, 82.44);
camera.setParentId(parentId);
Sensor sensor = new Sensor("s-"+id, "CAMERA", userId, appId, new
DeterministicDistribution(CAM_TRANSMISSION_TIME));
sensors.add(sensor);
Actuator ptz = new Actuator("ptz-"+id, userId,
appId, "PTZ_CONTROL");
actuators.add(ptz);
sensor.setGatewayDeviceId(camera.getId());
sensor.setLatency(40.0);
ptz.setGatewayDeviceId(parentId);
ptz.setLatency(1.0);
return camera;
}
```

Code Snippet-2 This code snippet is to be placed in the newly created **main** class. In this code snippet we are creating the modules on fog devices and assigning these modules to fog nodes. Figure 3 illustrates the physical topology of the car parking system in iFogSim that we have created in the code-snippet 1 and code-snippet 2.

```
private static Application createApplication
(String appId, int userId){
Application application =
Application.createApplication(appId, userId);
application.addAppModule("picture-capture", 10);
application.addAppModule("slot-detector", 10);
// adding edge from CAMERA (sensor) to picture-capture module
carrying tuples of type CAMERA
application.addAppEdge("CAMERA", "picture-capture", 1000, 500,
"CAMERA", Tuple.UP,
AppEdge.SENSOR);
application.addAppEdge("picture-capture", "slot-detector",
1000, 500, "slots",Tuple.UP, AppEdge.MODULE);
// adding edge from Slot Detector to PTZ CONTROL (actuator)
application.addAppEdge("slot-detector", "PTZ_CONTROL", 100,
28, 100, "PTZ_PARAMS",
Tuple.UP, AppEdge.ACTUATOR);
application.addTupleMapping("picture-capture", "CAMERA", "slots",
new FractionalSelectivity(1.0));
application.addTupleMapping("slot-detector", "slots",
"PTZ_PARAMS", new FractionalSelectivity(1.0));
```

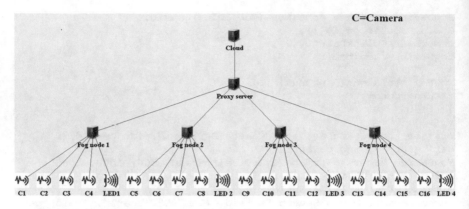

Fig. 3 iFogSim topology of smart car parking system

```
final AppLoop loop1 = new AppLoop(new ArrayList<String>()
{{add("CAMERA");
add("picture-capture");add("slot-detector");
add("PTZ_CONTROL");}});
List<AppLoop> loops = new ArrayList<AppLoop>(){{add(loop1);}};
application.setLoops(loops);
return application;
}
```

3.2 Smart Waste Management System

With the rapid increase in population and urbanization, the waste generation level in the cities is increasing day by day. Waste is generated by humans and by every living thing. Wherever life and human beings are, the waste will be generated there. According to the World Bank Report published in 2012 [10], the solid waste management generation level was about 1.3 billion tons per year and it will reach 2.2 billion tons per year in 2025. Nonetheless, the generation of waste cannot be prevented; however, introducing smart measures to collect and manage the generated waste can help in providing health environments [11]. The timely collection of waste not only prevents the spread of several diseases but also plays its part in keeping the environment green, clean, and healthy. A cloud-based waste management system is presented in [12] where authors used the cloud server to automate the waste management system. The smart waste bins are connected to the cloud server. The waste level information is transmitted to the cloud server after a specific time interval. If the waste level has reached the threshold value, then the waste is collected otherwise no action is taken unless the waste bin generates an alert indicating that the threshold level is reached.

Cloud computing is suffering from many problems like a large end to end delay and huge network bandwidth consumption [13]. In case, if we increase the number of smart waste bins connected with the cloud server, then there will be network congestion and it will not be easy to handle and manage the waste data from all the areas. In a certain community belonging to developing countries, there is a need to place smart waste bins at different points in streets that people can use to throw the waste. In this case, if all the waste bins are connected to the cloud server, it will cause latency and network usage problems. The best possible solution for this is to geographically partitions different areas and subsequently connect the waste bins of a particular area to a specific data management server. Consequently, deployment of fog nodes in the waste management system will make it more efficient and easily manageable for all the concerned stakeholders.

Building Scenario with iFogSim for Smart Waste Management System In the proposed fog-based waste management system, there are different waste bins. Each waste bin is allocated to a different kind of waste, such as kitchen waste, plastic, paper and cardboard, and metal. Smart waste bins will be placed in rural areas to manage and collect waste properly and efficiently. Each waste bin is equipped with the sensor (Ultrasonic sensor HC-SR04) to notify the waste level. Ultrasonic sensors emit the waves at a specific frequency and then wait for the wave to be reflected back. Based on the distance and the time taken back after reflection, we measure the percentage or level of waste in the bin. Figure 4 depicts the fog-based waste management system. The smart waste bins are connected to the fog server via a router device.

Figure 5 shows the data flow application model of the fog-based smart waste management system. In this scenario, five modules will be created. *Waste-info-module* collects the waste level information of the waste bins. The module passes the data to the *master-module* which is basically responsible for managing the waste information on the fog node. We create the separate modules for all the stakeholders, such as healthcare department, recycling unit, and head of the municipal authority to disseminate the waste collection information among the relevant collection staff. These modules represent the logical placement and creation of connection for each stakeholder at the fog node. The location tracking feature of waste collectors can be implemented in real time implementation of smart waste management system.

Building Simulation with iFogSim for Smart Waste Management System To simulate the smart waste management scenario, first make a new class in *org.fog.test.perfeval package.*

Code Snippet-3 This code snippet is to be placed in **main** class. In this code snippet we are adding the modules to the fog devices. Cloud mode is set to FALSE, and all the computational operations will be performed at fog nodes. In case if cloud mode is set to TRUE, then all the modules will be placed on cloud server, and all the computations will be performed on cloud server. There is no need to change the module placement. The code is commented so that you can develop the understanding of code. This code snippet should be added in the main method after initializing the module mapping.

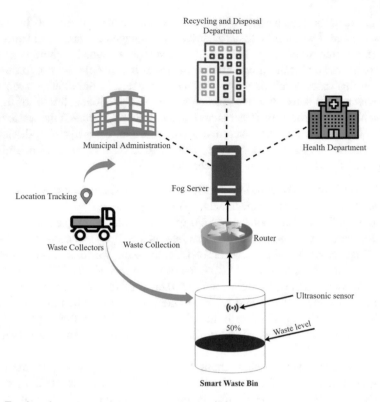

Fig. 4 Fog-based smart waste management system architecture

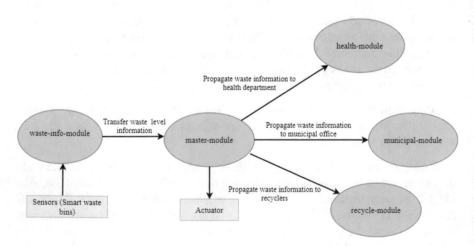

Fig. 5 Fog based smart waste management system application model of iFogSim

```
    //Create the list of fog devices
static List<FogDevice> fogDevices = new ArrayList<FogDevice>();
//Create the list of sensors
static List<Sensor> sensors = new ArrayList<Sensor>();
//Create the list of actuators
static List<Actuator> actuators = new ArrayList<Actuator>();
//Define the number of areas
static int numOfTotalAreas = 10;
//Define the number of waste bins with each fog nodes
static int numOfBinsPerArea=1;
//We are using the fog nodes to perform the operations.
//cloud is set to false
private static boolean CLOUD = false;
public static void main(String[] args) {
Log.printLine("Waste Management system...");
try {
Log.disable();
int num_user = 1; // number of cloud users
Calendar calendar = Calendar.getInstance();
boolean trace_flag = false; // mean trace events
CloudSim.init(num_user, calendar, trace_flag);
String appId = "swms"; // identifier of the application
FogBroker broker = new FogBroker("broker");
Application application = createApplication(appId,
broker.getId());
application.setUserId(broker.getId());
createFogDevices(broker.getId(), appId);
Controller controller = null;
ModuleMapping moduleMapping = ModuleMapping.createModuleMapping();
for(FogDevice device : fogDevices){
if(device.getName().startsWith("b")){
// names of all Smart Bins start with 'b'
moduleMapping.addModuleToDevice("waste-info-module",
device.getName());
// mapping
waste information module on waste bins
}
}
for(FogDevice device : fogDevices){
if(device.getName().startsWith("a")){
// names of all fog devices start with 'a'
// mapping master-module on area devices.
moduleMapping.addModuleToDevice("master-module",
device.getName());
// mapping health-module on area devices
moduleMapping.addModuleToDevice("health-module",
device.getName());
// mapping recycle-module on area devices.
moduleMapping.addModuleToDevice("recycle-module",
device.getName());
// mapping municipal-module on area devices.
moduleMapping.addModuleToDevice("municipal-module",
device.getName());
}
```

```
}
if(CLOUD){ // if the mode of deployment is cloud-based
// placing all instances of master-module in the Cloud
moduleMapping.addModuleToDevice("master-module", "cloud");
// placing all instances of health-module in the Cloud
moduleMapping.addModuleToDevice("health-module", "cloud");
//placing all instances of recycle-module in the Cloud
moduleMapping.addModuleToDevice("recycle-module", "cloud");
// placing all instances of municipal-module in the Cloud
moduleMapping.addModuleToDevice("municipal-module", "cloud");
}

controller = new Controller("master-controller",
fogDevices, sensors, actuators);
controller.submitApplication(application,
(CLOUD)?(new ModulePlacementMapping(fogDevices,
application, moduleMapping))
:(new ModulePlacementEdgewards(fogDevices, sensors,
actuators, application, moduleMapping)));
TimeKeeper.getInstance().setSimulationStartTime(
Calendar.getInstance().
getTimeInMillis());

CloudSim.startSimulation();

CloudSim.stopSimulation();

Log.printLine("waste management simulation finished!");
}
 catch (Exception e) {
e.printStackTrace();
Log.printLine("Unwanted errors happen");
}
}
```

After adding this code snippet initialize the controller object.

Code Snippet-4 This code snippet is to be placed in **main** class. In this code snippet we are creating the heterogeneous fog devices. The fog nodes will be placed in geographical distributed location and we will also need the location of the smart bin therefore, while creating the fog nodes and smart bins, we are setting the x-coordinate and y-coordinate value of the fog nodes and smart bin. In case of smart bin, the location awareness will help us to know that in which area or street, a particular waste bin is placed. Moreover, the fog node location will help us to be aware of the location of the particular fog node. In code snippet-6, we have created a method which generates the random values and these random value are then assigned as x and y coordinate to the waste bins and fog nodes.

```
private static void createFogDevices(int userId, String appId) {
FogDevice cloud = createFogDevice("cloud", 44800, 40000, 100,
10000, 0, 0.01, 16*103, 16*83.25);
cloud.setParentId(-1);
fogDevices.add(cloud);
```

```
FogDevice router = createFogDevice("proxy-server", 7000, 4000,
10000, 10000, 1, 0.0,
107.339, 83.4333);
router.setParentId(cloud.getId());
// latency of connection between proxy server and cloud is 100 ms
router.setUplinkLatency(100.0);
fogDevices.add(router);
for(int i=0;i<numOfTotalAreas;i++){
addArea(i+"", userId, appId, router.getId());
}
}
//creating the fog nodes for each area
private static FogDevice addArea(String id, int userId,
String appId, int parentId){
FogDevice area_fognode = createFogDevice("a-"+id, 5000, 4000,
10000, 10000, 3, 0.0, 107.339, 83.4333);
fogDevices.add( area_fognode);
area_fognode.setUplinkLatency(1.0);
for(int i=0;i<numOfBinsPerArea;i++){
String mobileId = id+"-"+i;
FogDevice bin = addBin(mobileId, userId,
appId, area_fognode.getId());
bin.setUplinkLatency(2.0);
fogDevices.add(bin);
}
//assigning x coordinate value to the fog node
area_fognode.setxCoordinate(getCoordinatevalue(10));
//assigning y coordinate value to the fog node
area_fognode.setyCoordinate(getCoordinatevalue(10));
area_fognode.setParentId(parentId);
return area_fognode;
}
//creating  the smart waste bins
private static FogDevice addBin(String id, int userId,
String appId, int parentId){
FogDevice bin = createFogDevice("b-"+id, 5000, 1000, 10000,
10000, 4, 0, 87.53, 82.44);
bin.setParentId(parentId);
Sensor sensor = new Sensor("s-"+id, "BIN", userId, appId,
new DeterministicDistribution(getCoordinatevalue(5)));
sensors.add(sensor);
Actuator ptz = new Actuator("act-"+id, userId,
appId, "ACT_CONTROL");
actuators.add(ptz);
sensor.setGatewayDeviceId(bin.getId());
sensor.setLatency(1.0);
ptz.setGatewayDeviceId(parentId);
ptz.setLatency(1.0);
//assigning x coordinate value to the smart bin
bin.setxCoordinate(getCoordinatevalue(10));
//assigning y coordinate value to the smart bin
bin.setyCoordinate(getCoordinatevalue(10));
return bin;
}
```

Code Snippet-5 This code snippet is to be placed in **main** class.

```
private static Application createApplication
(String appId, int userId){

Application application =
Application.createApplication(appId, userId);
application.addAppModule("waste-info-module", 10);
application.addAppModule("master-module", 10);
application.addAppModule("recycle-module", 10);
application.addAppModule("health-module", 10);
application.addAppModule("municipal-module", 10);

application.addAppEdge("BIN", "waste-info-module",1000, 2000,
"BIN", Tuple.UP,
AppEdge.SENSOR);
application.addAppEdge("waste-info-module", "master-module",
1000, 2000, "Task1",
Tuple.UP, AppEdge.MODULE);
application.addAppEdge("master-module", "municipal-module",
1000, 2000, "Task2",
Tuple.UP, AppEdge.MODULE);
application.addAppEdge("master-module", "recycle-module",
1000, 2000, "Task3",
Tuple.UP, AppEdge.MODULE);
application.addAppEdge("master-module", "health-module",
1000, 2000, "Task4",
Tuple.UP, AppEdge.MODULE);
application.addAppEdge("master-module", "ACT_CONTROL",
100, 28, 100, "ACT_PARAMS",
Tuple.UP, AppEdge.ACTUATOR);
application.addTupleMapping("waste-info-module",
"BIN", "Task1",
new FractionalSelectivity(1.0));
application.addTupleMapping("master-module", "BIN", "Task2",
new FractionalSelectivity(1.0));
application.addTupleMapping("master-module", "BIN", "Task3",
new FractionalSelectivity(1.0));
application.addTupleMapping("master-module", "BIN", "Task4",
new FractionalSelectivity(1.0));
application.addTupleMapping("master-module", "BIN", "ACT_CONTROL",
new FractionalSelectivity(1.0));

final AppLoop loop1 = new AppLoop(new ArrayList<String>()
{{add("BIN");
add("waste-info-module");add("master-module");
add("municipal-module");
add("recycle-module");add("health-module");
add("ACT_CONTROL");}});
List<AppLoop> loops = new ArrayList<AppLoop>(){{add(loop1);}};

application.setLoops(loops);
return application;
}
```

Code Snippet-6 This code snippet is to be placed in **main** class. In this code snippet, we have created a method will generate the random number.

```
private static double getCoordinatevalue(double min)
{
Random rn=new Random();
return rn.nextDouble()+min;
}
```

Code Snippet-7 This code snippet is to be placed in FogDevice class. This code snippet is taken from [5]. We have declared two variables xCoordinate, and yCoordinate to store the value of x and y coordinate respectively.

```
public double xCoordinate;
//specifying the xCoordinate of the fog device
public double yCoordinate;
//specifying the yCoordinate of the fog device
//method to set the value of xCoordinate
public void setxCoordinate(double xCoordinate)
{
this.xCoordinate=xCoordinate;
}
//method to get the value of xCoordinate
public double getxCoordinate()
{
return xCoordinate;
}
//method to set the value of yCoordinate
public void setyCoordinate(double yCoordinate)
{
this.yCoordinate=yCoordinate;
}
//method to get the value of yCoordinate
public double getyCoordinate()
{
return yCoordinate;
}
```

3.3 Smart Mining Industry System

Mining is one of the most important and prominent industries that requires a lot of data analysis. With every passing day, the enormity of mining industry is increasing day by day. According to the IBM research [14], the requirement of mines increasing day by day and every individual requires approximately 3.11 million pounds of fuel, minerals, and metals in his/her life. Despite its significance, mining industry entails multiple risks. During the mineral and coal mining, chemical reactions, hazardous gas emission, suffocation, and rock sliding are among the probable risks that are hazardous for the lives of mining personnel [16]. Therefore, it is important to employ the IoT devices, such as heterogeneous sensors to pick up the

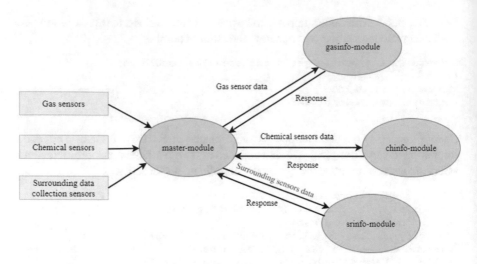

Fig. 6 Fog based smart mining industry application model of iFogSim

gases, chemicals, and the surrounding data and to inform the concerned personnel regarding the undesired and dangerous situations. The surrounding sensors will collect the data before the digging process. This can also reduce cost and save the energy by predicting the probability of finding coal and minerals at certain places before the actual digging process. Gas sensors can be deployed everywhere in the mines that cannot only help in measuring the biological gases value in the mines and tunnels but also control the emission of gases. Moreover, numerous chemical reactions occur in the mines which can be very dangerous for human labors working in the mine. Therefore, collecting and analyzing the surrounding, biological gases and chemical reactions' data is very useful in the mining industry in making predictions about the digging process and hazardous events.

Building Scenario with iFogSim for Smart Mining Industry System To simulate this case study, first make a new class in *org.fog.test.perfeval* package. In the fog based smart mining industry, there would be heterogeneous sensors i.e. surrounding sensors, biological sensors, and chemical sensors that are connected to the fog nodes through a router device. In the fog nodes, we create four modules that include: (1) *master module,* (2) *gasinfo-module,* (3) *chinfo-module,* and (4) *srinfo-module.* The *master-module* will collect the sensors data from all type of sensors. It will categorize the data and send the specific data to the respective modules. For example, the gas sensors data will be sent to the *gasinfo-moudule.* The *gasinfo-module* will process the gas sensors data, analyze the gas values, and it will send the response back to the master-module. The response is basically the action, which will be taken in account of gas sensors values. Figure 6 depicts the data flow of the smart mining industry application model.

Building Simulation with iFogSim for Mining Industry System To simulate this scenario, first make a new class in *org.fog.test.perfeval* package.

Code Snippet-8 This code snippet is to be placed in the **main** class. In this code snippet we created the variables for fog devices and sensors. Three type of sensors variables are created for biological, chemical and surrounding sensors. Moreover, the modules are placed on the fog nodes. This code snippet should be added in the main method after initializing the module mapping.

```
//Create the list of fog devices
static List<FogDevice> fogDevices = new ArrayList<FogDevice>();
//Create the list of sensors
static List<Sensor> sensors = new ArrayList<Sensor>();
//Create the list of actuators
static List<Actuator> actuators = new ArrayList<Actuator>();
//Define the number of fog nodes will be deployed
static int numOfFogDevices = 10;
//Define the number of gas sensors with each fog nodes
static int numOfGasSensorsPerArea=1;
//Define the number of chemical sensors with each fog nodes
static int numOfChSensorsPerArea=1;
//Define the number of surrounding sensors with each fog nodes
static int numOfSrSensorsPerArea=1;
//We are using the fog nodes to perform the operations.
//cloud is set to false
private static boolean CLOUD = false;
public static void main(String[] args) {
Log.printLine("Waste Management system...");
try {
Log.disable();
int num_user = 1; // number of cloud users
Calendar calendar = Calendar.getInstance();
boolean trace_flag = false; // mean trace events
CloudSim.init(num_user, calendar, trace_flag);
String appId = "mins"; // identifier of the application
FogBroker broker = new FogBroker("broker");
Application application =
createApplication(appId, broker.getId());
application.setUserId(broker.getId());
createFogDevices(broker.getId(), appId);
Controller controller = null;
// initializing a module mapping
ModuleMapping moduleMapping =
ModuleMapping.createModuleMapping();
for(FogDevice device : fogDevices){
if(device.getName().startsWith("a")){
moduleMapping.addModuleToDevice("master-module",
device.getName());
if(device.getName().startsWith("g")){
moduleMapping.addModuleToDevice("gasinfo-module",
device.getName());     }
if(device.getName().startsWith("c")){
moduleMapping.addModuleToDevice
```

```
("chemicalinfo-module", device.getName());    }
if(device.getName().startsWith("s")){
moduleMapping.addModuleToDevice
("srinfo-module", device.getName());
}}}
// if the mode of deployment is cloud-based
if(CLOUD){
// placing all instances of master-module in Cloud
addModuleToDevice("mastermodule", "cloud");
moduleMapping.addModuleToDevice("gasinfo-module", "cloud");
moduleMapping.addModuleToDevice("chinfo-module", "cloud");
moduleMapping.addModuleToDevice("srinfo-module", "cloud");}

controller = new Controller("master-controller", fogDevices,
sensors, actuators);
controller.submitApplication(application,
(CLOUD)?(new ModulePlacementMapping(fogDevices, application,
moduleMapping))
:(new ModulePlacementEdgewards(fogDevices, sensors, actuators,
application, moduleMapping)));

 TimeKeeper.getInstance().setSimulationStartTime(
   Calendar.getInstance().
getTimeInMillis());

CloudSim.startSimulation();

CloudSim.stopSimulation();

Log.printLine("mining industry simulation finished!");
} catch (Exception e) {
e.printStackTrace();
Log.printLine("Unwanted errors happen");
}
}
```

Code Snippet-9 It is to be placed in the **main** class. In this code snippet we are creating cloud server, proxy server, fog nodes, gas sensors, chemical sensors, and surrounding sensors.

```
private static void createFogDevices(int userId, String appId) {
FogDevice cloud = createFogDevice("cloud", 44800, 40000, 100,
10000, 0, 0.01, 16*103,
16*83.25);
cloud.setParentId(-1);
fogDevices.add(cloud);
FogDevice router = createFogDevice("proxy-server", 7000, 4000,
10000, 10000, 1, 0.0, 107.339, 83.4333);
router.setParentId(cloud.getId());
router.setUplinkLatency(100.0);
fogDevices.add(router);
for(int i=0;i<numOfFogDevices;i++){
addFogNode(i+"", userId, appId, router.getId());
}
```

```
}
private static FogDevice addFogNode(String id,
int userId, String appId, int parentId)
{
FogDevice fognode = createFogDevice("a-"+id, 5000, 4000, 10000,
10000, 3, 0.0, 107.339, 83.4333);
fogDevices.add( fognode);
fognode.setUplinkLatency(1.0);
for(int i=0;i<numOfGasSensorsPerArea;i++){
addGasSensors(i+"", userId, appId, fognode.getId());
}
for(int i=0;i<numOfChSensorsPerArea;i++){
addChSensors(i+"", userId, appId, fognode.getId());
}
for(int i=0;i<numOfSrSensorsPerArea;i++){
addSrSensors(i+"", userId, appId, fognode.getId());
}
return fognode;
}
private static FogDevice addGasSensors(String id, int userId,
String appId, int parentId){
FogDevice gasSensor = createFogDevice("g-"+id, 5000, 1000, 10000,
10000, 4, 0, 87.53, 82.44);
gasSensor.setParentId(parentId);
Sensor sensor = new Sensor("s-"+id, "GAS", userId, appId, new
DeterministicDistribution(5));
sensors.add(sensor);
Actuator ptz = new Actuator("act-"+id, userId,
appId, "ACT_CONTROL");
actuators.add(ptz);
sensor.setGatewayDeviceId(gasSensor.getId());
sensor.setLatency(1.0);
ptz.setGatewayDeviceId(parentId);
ptz.setLatency(1.0);
return gasSensor;
}
private static FogDevice addChSensors(String id, int userId,
String appId, int parentId){
FogDevice chSensor = createFogDevice("c-"+id, 5000, 1000, 10000,
10000, 4, 0, 87.53, 82.44);
chSensor.setParentId(parentId);
Sensor sensor = new Sensor("sch-"+id, "CH", userId, appId,
new DeterministicDistribution(5));
sensors.add(sensor);
Actuator ptzch = new Actuator("actch-"+id, userId,
appId, "ACT_CONTROLCH");
actuators.add(ptzch);
sensor.setGatewayDeviceId(chSensor.getId());
sensor.setLatency(1.0);
ptzch.setGatewayDeviceId(parentId);
ptzch.setLatency(1.0);
return chSensor;
}
private static FogDevice addSrSensors(String id, int userId,
```

```
String appId, int parentId){
FogDevice srSensor = createFogDevice("s-"+id, 5000, 1000, 10000,
10000, 4, 0, 87.53, 82.44);
srSensor.setParentId(parentId);
Sensor sensor = new Sensor("ssr-"+id, "SR", userId, appId,
new DeterministicDistribution(5));
sensors.add(sensor);
Actuator ptzch = new Actuator("actsr-"+id, userId,
appId, "ACT_CONTROLSR");
actuators.add(ptzch);
sensor.setGatewayDeviceId(srSensor.getId());
sensor.setLatency(1.0);
ptzch.setGatewayDeviceId(parentId);
ptzch.setLatency(1.0);
return srSensor;
}
```

Code Snippet-10 It is to be placed in the **main** class. In this code snippet we are creating the modules and mapping it to the fog devices.

```
private static Application createApplication(String appId,
int userId){
Application application = Application.createApplication(appId,
userId);
application.addAppModule("gasinfo-module", 10);
application.addAppModule("master-module", 10);
application.addAppModule("chinfo-module", 10);
application.addAppModule("srinfo-module", 10);
application.addAppEdge("GAS", "master-module",1000,
2000, "GAS", Tuple.UP, AppEdge.SENSOR);
application.addAppEdge("CH", "chinfo-module", 1000,
2000, "CH", Tuple.UP, AppEdge.SENSOR);
application.addAppEdge("SR", "srinfo-module", 1000, 2000,
"SR",
Tuple.UP, AppEdge.SENSOR);
application.addAppEdge("master-module", "gasinfo-module",
1000, 2000,
"gasTask", Tuple.UP, AppEdge.MODULE);
application.addAppEdge("master-module", "chinfo-module", 1000,
2000, "chTask", Tuple.UP, AppEdge.MODULE);
application.addAppEdge("master-module", "srinfo-module", 1000,
2000, "srTask", Tuple.UP, AppEdge.MODULE);
//Response
application.addAppEdge("gasinfo-module", "master-module",
1000, 2000, "gasResponse", Tuple.UP, AppEdge.MODULE);
application.addAppEdge("chinfo-module", "master-module",
1000, 2000, "chResponse", Tuple.UP, AppEdge.MODULE);
application.addAppEdge("srinfo-module", "master-module",
1000, 2000,"srResponse", Tuple.UP, AppEdge.MODULE);
application.addTupleMapping("master-module", "GAS", "gasTask",
new FractionalSelectivity(1.0));
application.addTupleMapping("master-module", "CH", "chTask",
new FractionalSelectivity(1.0));
application.addTupleMapping("master-module", "SR", "srTas",
```

```
new FractionalSelectivity(1.0));
application.addTupleMapping("gasinfo-module",
"gasTask", "gasResponse",
new FractionalSelectivity(1.0));
application.addTupleMapping("chinfo-module",
"chTask", "chResponse",
new FractionalSelectivity(1.0));
application.addTupleMapping("srinfo-module",
"srTask", "srResponse",
new FractionalSelectivity(1.0));

final AppLoop loop1 = new AppLoop(new ArrayList<String>()
{{add("GAS");
add("master-module");add("gasinfo-module");add("gasTask");
add("gasResponse");}});
final AppLoop loop2 = new AppLoop(new
ArrayList<String>(){{add("CH");
add("master-module");add("chinfo-module");
add("chTask")
;add("chResponse");}});
final AppLoop loop3 = new AppLoop(new
ArrayList<String>(){{add("SR");
add("master-module");add("srinfo-module")
;add("srTask");add("srResponse");}});
List<AppLoop> loops = new
ArrayList<AppLoop>(){{add(loop1);add(loop2)
;add(loop3);}};

application.setLoops(loops);
return application;
}
```

3.4 Sensing as a Service

Nowadays Unmanned Aerial Vehicles (UAVs) are widely used to support on-demand IoT services [15]. The sensors and actuators associated with an UAV helps in perceiving the external environments and triggering physical actions respectively where the structured deployment of IoT devices is infeasible and costly. However, UAVs are mobile in nature and most of them are energy constrained and are equipped with limited processing capabilities [17]. Therefore, the data generated by the UAVs requires assistance from Fog or Cloud computing paradigms to be processed. It also demands faster networking support for real-time interactions [18]. Considering these requirements, we model an application case scenario and build a simulation setup to illustrate the UAV-based sensing as a service in integrated Fog-Cloud environments.

Building Scenario with iFogSim for UAV-Based Sensing as a Service Figure 7 depicts the conceptual integration of UAVs with gateways, Fog nodes and Cloud

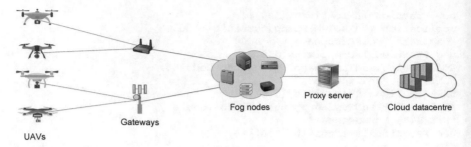

Fig. 7 Prospective computing environments for UAV-based sensing as a service

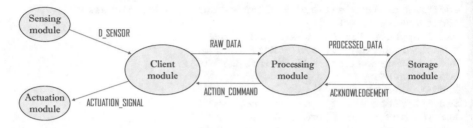

Fig. 8 Application model for UAV-based sensing as a service

data centers. Additionally, the data-driven interactions among these heterogeneous components can be realized through a distributed application as shown in Fig. 8 where the Sensing and Actuation module operate on the UAV-based sensor and actuator, respectively. The Sensing module forwards *D_SENSOR* to the Client module which is more likely to be placed in the UAV. Later, the Client module performs pre-processing of the sensor generated data and dispatches to the Processing module. This module incorporates data analytic that help in transforming the *RAW_DATA* to a meaningful information suitable for evaluation, comparison and making actuation decisions. After performing such operations, the Processing module generates two types of data namely *PROCESSED_DATA* and *ACTION_COMMAND* that are directed to Storage and Client module respectively. The Storage module preserves the outcome of Processing module for location-independent and scalable distribution whereas the Client module digest the outcome for generating the *ACTUATION_SIGNAL* for the Actuation module.

Building Simulation with iFogSim for UAV-Based Sensing as a Service To simulate the prospective UAV-based sensing as a service scenario, a new class in *org.fog.test.perfeval* package is required to be created.

Code Snippet-11 This code snippet helps in creating the computing environments for UAV-based sensing as a service and it should be placed in the main class.

```
private static void createFogDevices(int userId, String appId) {

FogDevice cloud = createFogDevice("cloud", 44800, 40000, 100,
```

```
10000,0.01, 16*103, 16*83.25);
cloud.setParentId(-1);
locator.setLevel(cloud, 0);
FogDevice proxy = createFogDevice("proxy-server", 2800, 4000,
10000, 10000, 0.0, 107.339, 83.4333);
proxy.setParentId(cloud.getId());
proxy.setUplinkLatency(100);
locator.setLevel(proxy, 1);

fogDevices.add(cloud);
fogDevices.add(proxy);

for(int i=0;i<numOfGatewayDevices;i++){
FogDevice gateway = addGw("gateway_"+i,
userId, appId, proxy.getId());
gateway.setUplinkLatency(4);
locator.setLevel(gateway, 2);
fogDevices.add(gateway);
}

for(int i=0;i<numOfIoTDrones;i++){
FogDevice drone = addDrone("drone_"+i, userId, appId, -1);
drone.setUplinkLatency(2);
locator.setLevel(drone, 3);
fogDevices.add(drone);
}
}

private static FogDevice addGw(String name, int userId,
String appId, int parentId){
FogDevice gateway = createFogDevice(name, 2800, 4000, 10000,
10000, 0.0, 107.339, 83.4333);
//locator.setInitialLocation(name,gateway.getId());
gateway.setParentId(parentId);
return gateway;
}

private static FogDevice addDrone(String name, int userId,
String appId, int parentId){
FogDevice drone = createFogDevice(name, 500, 20,
1000, 270, 0, 87.53, 82.44);
drone.setParentId(parentId);
//locator.setInitialLocation(name,drone.getId());
Sensor droneSensor = new Sensor("sensor-"+name, "D-SENSOR",
userId, appId,
new DeterministicDistribution(SENSOR_TRANSMISSION_TIME));
sensors.add(droneSensor );
Actuator dronedisplay = new Actuator("actuator-"+name, userId,
appId, "D-DISPLAY");
actuators.add(dronedisplay);
droneSensor.setGatewayDeviceId(drone.getId());
droneSensor.setLatency(6.0);
dronedisplay.setGatewayDeviceId(drone.getId());
dronedisplay.setLatency(1.0);
```

```
return drone;
}
```

Code Snippet-12 This code snippet creates the application model for UAV-based sensing as a service and it is also required to be placed in the **main** class.

```
private static Application createApplication(String appId,
int userId){

Application application =
Application.createApplication(appId, userId);

application.addAppModule("clientModule", 10);
application.addAppModule("processingModule", 10);
application.addAppModule("storageModule", 10);


if(SENSOR_TRANSMISSION_TIME==5.1)
application.addAppEdge("D-SENSOR", "clientModule",
2000, 500, "D-SENSOR", Tuple.UP, AppEdge.SENSOR);
else
application.addAppEdge("D-SENSOR", "clientModule",
3000, 500, "D-SENSOR", Tuple.UP, AppEdge.SENSOR);
application.addAppEdge("clientModule",
"processingModule", 3500, 500, "RAW_DATA",
Tuple.UP, AppEdge.MODULE);
application.addAppEdge("processingModule",
"storageModule", 1000, 1000, "PROCESSED_DATA",
Tuple.UP, AppEdge.MODULE);
application.addAppEdge("processingModule",
"clientModule", 14, 500, "ACTION_COMMAND",
Tuple.DOWN, AppEdge.MODULE);
application.addAppEdge("clientModule", "D-DISPLAY",
1000, 500, "ACTUATION_SIGNAL", Tuple.DOWN,
AppEdge.ACTUATOR);

application.addTupleMapping("clientModule",
"D-SENSOR", "RAW_DATA",
new FractionalSelectivity(1.0));
application.addTupleMapping("processingModule",
"RAW_DATA", "PROCESSED_DATA",
new FractionalSelectivity(1.0));
application.addTupleMapping("processingModule",
"RAW_DATA", "ACTION_COMMAND",
new FractionalSelectivity(1.0));
application.addTupleMapping("clientModule",
"ACTION_COMMAND", "ACTUATION_SIGNAL",
new FractionalSelectivity(1.0));


final AppLoop loop1 = new AppLoop(new ArrayList<String>()
{{add("D-SENSOR");
add("clientModule");add("processingModule");
add("clientModule");
```

```
add("D-DISPLAY");}});
List<AppLoop> loops = new ArrayList<AppLoop>(){{add(loop1);}};
application.setLoops(loops);

return application;
}
```

4 Conclusions

In this article, we described the key features of iFogSim along with a step by step installation and simulation guide to help researchers model and simulate difference IoT and fog-based scenarios. To help readers gain a better understanding of the iFogSim toolkit, we modeled four real-time case studies related to smart car parking, smart waste management system, the smart mining industry and UAV-based sensing as a service. Moreover, we provided the corresponding code snippets of every case study. The simulation source codes of the case studies can be accessed from the link: https://sites.google.com/site/assadabbasciit/.

References

1. R. Mahmud, K. Ramamohanarao, and R. Buyya, "Edge Affinity-based Management of Applications in Fog Computing Environments," in Proceedings - 12th IEEE/ACM International Conference on Utility and Cloud Computing, UCC 2019, 2019, pp. 61–70.
2. S. Yi, Z. Hao, Z. Qin, and Q. Li, "Fog computing: Platform and applications," in Proceedings - 3rd Workshop on Hot Topics in Web Systems and Technologies, HotWeb 2015, 2016, pp. 73–78.
3. I. Stojmenovic and S. Wen, "The Fog computing paradigm: Scenarios and security issues," in 2014 Federated Conference on Computer Science and Information Systems, FedCSIS 2014, 2014, pp. 1–8.
4. M. Afrin, M. R. Mahmud, and M. A. Razzaque, "Real time detection of speed breakers and warning system for on-road drivers," in Proceedings - IEEE International WIE Conference on Electrical and Computer Engineering, WIECON-ECE 2015, 2015, pp. 495–498.
5. R. Mahmud and R. Buyya, "Modeling and Simulation of Fog and Edge Computing Environments Using iFogSim Toolkit," in Fog and Edge Computing, 2019, pp. 433–465.
6. T. Qayyum, A. W. Malik, M. A. K. Khattak, O. Khalid, and S. U. Khan, "FogNetSim++: A Toolkit for Modeling and Simulation of Distributed Fog Environment," IEEE Access, vol. 6, pp. 63570–63583, 2018.
7. C. Sonmez, A. Ozgovde, and C. Ersoy, "EdgeCloudSim: An environment for performance evaluation of edge computing systems," Trans. Emerg. Telecommun. Technol., vol. 29, no. 11, Nov. 2018.
8. H. Gupta and R. Buyya, "iFogSim: A toolkit for modeling and simulation of resource management techniques in the Internet of Things , Edge," no. October 2016, pp. 1275–1296, 2017.
9. K. S. Awaisi et al., "Towards a Fog Enabled Efficient Car Parking Architecture," IEEE Access, vol. 7, no. 1, pp. 159100–159111, 2019.

10. D. Hoornweg and P. Bhada-Tata, "What a waste: a global review of solid waste management," 2012.

11. M. Aazam, S. Zeadally, and K. A. Harras, "Deploying Fog Computing in Industrial Internet of Things and Industry 4.0," IEEE Trans. Ind. Informatics, vol. 14, no. 10, pp. 4674–4682, 2018.

12. M. Aazam, M. St-Hilaire, C. H. Lung, and I. Lambadaris, "Cloud-based smart waste management for smart cities," in IEEE International Workshop on Computer Aided Modeling and Design of Communication Links and Networks, CAMAD, 2016, pp. 188–193.

13. R. Mahmud, A. N. Toosi, K. Ramamohanarao, and R. Buyya, "Context-aware Placement of Industry 4.0 Applications in Fog Computing Environments," IEEE Transactions on Industrial Informatics, vol. 16, no. 11, pp. 7004–7013, 2020.

14. "IBM",https://www.ibm.com/blogs/internet-of-things/mining-industry-benefits/, Accessed on August 14, 2020 .

15. M. Afrin, J. Jin, and A. Rahman, "Energy-delay co-optimization of resource allocation for robotic services in cloudlet infrastructure," in International Conference on Service-Oriented Computing, 2018, pp. 295–303.

16. M. Afrin, J. Jin, A. Rahman, Y. Tian, and A. Kulkarni, "Multi-objective resource allocation for Edge Cloud based robotic workflow in smart factory," Future Generation Computer Systems, vol. 97, pp. 119–130, 2019.

17. R. Mahmud, S. N. Srirama, K. Ramamohanarao, and R. Buyya, "Quality of Experience (QoE)-aware placement of applications in Fog computing environments," Journal of Parallel and Distributed Computing, vol. 132, pp. 190–203, 2019.

18. A. N. Toosi, R. Mahmud, Q. Chi, and R. Buyya, "Management and Orchestration of Network Slices in 5G, Fog, Edge and Clouds," in Fog and Edge Computing, 2019, pp. 79–102.

Index

© The Author(s), under exclusive license to Springer Nature Switzerland AG 2021   591
A. Mukherjee et al. (eds.), *Mobile Edge Computing*,
https://doi.org/10.1007/978-3-030-69893-5

Printed in the United States
by Baker & Taylor Publisher Services